P9-CBR-983

THE INSIDERS' GUIDE® TO LAS VEGAS

by
David Stratton
and
Ken Ward

Insiders' Publishing Inc.

Co-published and marketed by:
Las Vegas Review-Journal
1111 West Bonanza Rd. (89106)
P.O. Box 70 (89125-0070)
Las Vegas, NV
(702) 383-4698
www.lasvegas.com

Co-published and distributed by:
Insiders' Publishing Inc.
105 Budleigh St.
P.O. Box 2057
Manteo, NC 27954
(919) 473-6100
www.insiders.com

•

FIRST EDITION
1st printing

•

•

Printed in the United States
of America

•

Publications from The Insiders' Guide® series are available at special discounts for bulk purchases for sales promotions, premiums or fundraisings. Special editions, including personalized covers, can be created in large quantities for special needs. For more information, please write to Insiders' Publishing Inc., P.O. Box 2057, Manteo, NC 27954 or call (919) 473-6100 x 233.

ISBN 1-57380-032-5

Las Vegas Review-Journal

Publisher
Sherman Frederick

Project Coordinator
Dale C. Wetenkamp

Sales Assistants
Dave Schoolcraft
Staci Fike

Graphics Supervisor
Naysan Gray

Staff Photographer
James Decker

Insiders' Publishing Inc.

Publisher/Editor-in-Chief
Beth P. Storie

President/General Manager
Michael McOwen

Director of Advertising
Rosanne Cheeseman

Creative Services Director
Giles MacMillan

Sales and Marketing Director
Jennifer Risko

Director of New Product Development
David Haynes

Managing Editor
Dave McCarter

Fulfillment Director
Gina Twiford

Project Editor
Molly Harrison

Project Artist
Stephanie Wills

Preface

Viva Las Vegas . . . this book's for you.

Whether you're new in town or just here for a weekend of sun and fun, Las Vegas can be a virtual pleasure dome. As America's premier gambling mecca, its adult diversions are legendary. At the same time, stoked by a superheated job market, southern Nevada is also fast evolving into a well-rounded, family-oriented community with parks, churches, museums and schools popping up everywhere.

To say that Las Vegas is growing quickly is a bit like observing that Secretariat was a pretty good horse. More than 30 million tourists visit the city each year, and 6,000 new residents call this place home every month. Yet no one publication has pulled together a comprehensive guide for both of these groups — until now.

The Insiders' Guide® to Las Vegas is your entree to southern Nevada. Written for vacationers and locals alike, its 26 chapters have something for everybody. We offer detailed and descriptive sections on casinos, accommodations, nightlife and restaurants. We also have compiled extensive listings of the things that make the Las Vegas Valley home — from shopping and spectator sports to real estate and the arts.

What's more, *The Insiders' Guide® to Las Vegas* goes beyond the city limits. We take you to quaint Boulder City, the river town of Laughlin and golf-crazy Mesquite. Our Daycations chapter ventures out to Death Valley and the Grand Canyon.

Each of our chapters contains the latest and best information available, including phone numbers, hours and prices. That's to be expected. But a good book is more than a collection of facts and figures. As such, we have strived to entertain as well as enlighten.

We, David Stratton and Ken Ward, both Las Vegas residents, spent 10 months researching and writing this guide. We drew upon seven years of day-to-day experience in southern Nevada, sharing our perspective on this vibrant valley, its people, its attractions and its customs.

We think you'll find Las Vegas is a special place, with a ravenous appetite for fun and work, pleasure and profit. Thanks to hungry gamblers, this desert oasis consumes more shrimp than any U.S. city. As its building boom continues, Las Vegas developers are devouring land at the rate of 2 acres every hour of every day. And, hey, where else could you place a bet at a drive-through sports book, get married at a drive-through wedding chapel and walk from the Statue of Liberty to an Egyptian pyramid? Where else indeed.

So enjoy this weird and wonderful town with us. Whether you're taking a trip to the buffet or enrolling your child in school, take this book along as your personal companion — and be a Las Vegas Insider too!

While we have made every effort to ensure accuracy and to include all the best of Las Vegas, we're only human. Las Vegas is a city that constantly reinvents itself, and changes occur, often from month to month. If you find mistakes in our book, if you disagree with something we've said or if you'd like to see additions or changes in future editions, we would appreciate your taking the time to write us in care of Insiders' Publishing Inc., P.O. Box 2057, Manteo, North Carolina 27954. Or you can visit our book online at www.insiders.com and make your comments there.

About the Authors

Preparing for his first trip to Las Vegas, **David Stratton** packed hardback novels, swim trunks, sun screen and a tennis racket. His friends and veteran co-travelers brought the clothes on their backs and bail money. The world of contrast he found in Las Vegas during the 1970s justified everything they brought and much more.

From the sublime to the exotic, from outrageous to bewildering, Las Vegas has remained a fascinating anomaly for David, who has lived here since 1989, when he relocated from California to accept the job of features editor at the *Las Vegas Sun*.

Although born and raised in the Hawaiian Islands, David spent most of his adult life in California. Before moving to Las Vegas, he worked as a writer and editor for a magazine in San Bernardino and later a beat reporter and features editor for a newspaper in California's High Desert.

In addition to magazine and newspaper work, David has served as a staff writer, editor and graphic designer for the publisher of gaming books and a graphic designer for the Las Vegas-Clark County Library District. He's also had a stint as the publicity director for a Las Vegas gaming resort, where he received an Insiders' look at the workings of a major Strip resort hotel and casino.

Most recently, David's written two books about Las Vegas and contributed to a third, a Frommer's guidebook to California and Nevada. He also wrote a guidebook to Arizona and currently writes a weekly column for a national gaming magazine.

Over his 13 years as a journalist David has written hundreds of articles and columns covering subjects as diverse as crooked lawyers, armed insurrection, police brutality and maneating plants. His interviews have been with characters ranging from Bianca Jagger and G. Gordon Liddy to Troy Aikman and Pauly Shore. Still he finds in Las Vegas a never-ending supply of fresh stories that keep the city a fascinating and exciting world apart.

Ken Ward has lived in Las Vegas for more than seven years. Like many Southern Nevadans, the native Californian came to Nevada in search of career opportunities. But in his case, he did it twice.

After graduating from the University of California at Los Angeles in 1975, Ken worked as a copy editor at the *Las Vegas Review-Journal*. Missing the Golden State, he soon returned to California to take jobs at the *Pasadena Star-News* and *San Jose Mercury News*. From there, he accepted a management position at an Indiana newspaper, the *Fort Wayne News-Sentinel*. In 1986 he was named editor-in-chief of the *Columbus* (Ind.) *Republic*.

But Nevada beckoned again. And after eight Midwestern winters the desert looked like heaven. In 1990 Ken was hired as assistant managing editor of the *Las Vegas Sun*. During that period Ken earned a master's degree in business administration and was honored nationally for his investigative reporting and commentary on education issues.

After 22 years in daily newspapers, Ken launched a freelance writing career. He contributes regularly to alternative weeklies, business publications and trade journals. He is a fanatical swimmer and frustrated golfer. And, for the record, he doesn't gamble.

His wife, Margaret, is a registered dietitian. They live with their daughter and son in northwest Las Vegas.

Acknowledgments

Putting together the most comprehensive guidebook ever written about Las Vegas was a group effort; I'm grateful for having contributed to the process. There were many talented people who either worked on the project or provided valued support.

My heartfelt thanks to the professional staff at Insiders' Publishing Inc.: publisher Beth Storie who saw the possibilities; managing editor Theresa Chavez who brought the project into focus; and editor Molly Perkins, whose insights, tough questions and occasional swift kicks in the pants kept the project on target.

I also want to extend special thanks to project manager Dale Wetenkamp at the *Las Vegas Review-Journal*. In addition to providing the support of the city's largest newspaper, Dale's advice, guidance and enthusiasm were essential to uncovering information that residents as well as tourists are likely to appreciate.

Special thanks and recognition to my co-author, Ken Ward, a top-notch editor in his own right, whose dialogue, suggestions and humorous anecdotes helped keep the monumental task at hand. It had been several years since our paths last crossed at the *Las Vegas Sun*, and I'm happy they did again. I look forward to working with Ken in the future.

I would also like to thank the Las Vegas News Bureau's Mike Donahue, another refugee from the *Las Vegas Sun*, for his special help in generating material for the Daycations chapter. But next time, Mike, when you hire a tour bus, make sure it's outfitted with a parachute. There are literally hundreds of people throughout the city — publicists, marketing directors, restaurant owners, bartenders, showgirls, librarians, secretaries, limo drivers, dealers, ticket sellers, etc. — who helped the process by answering questions, opening doors and sometimes turning the other way. I thank them all for allowing me to unearth the jewels from the city's landscape that became part of this book.

Closer to home, I want to thank Linda for her unwavering support and encouragement and boundless patience. How she slept through the countless nights of keyboard pounding is beyond reason. How she rewarded us with a baby boy three weeks after the book's publication is beyond belief. It was the perfect epilogue.

— David Stratton

The task of cataloguing Las Vegas is a bit like trying to describe an amoeba. Its constantly changing scope and shape defy easy description. The rapidity of those changes makes the undertaking even more daunting.

But, hey, that's what has made this venture so exciting.

The people who have made this work possible are too numerous to list here. Countless sources have contributed information and insights that I hope are faithfully reflected in the chapters of this book. I know that the gas stations appreciated my patronage in the past year as I crisscrossed this valley in pursuit of the best (fill in the blank) Las Vegas has to offer.

A few folks merit special mention, however.

David Stratton, my co-author, has been a knowledgeable resource, a solid sounding board and a true friend. His experience in the guidebook business has been invaluable to this novice. And his extensive background in the local entertainment, nightlife and casino scene broadened my vision of Las Vegas. Above all, David's good humor, even in the crucible of deadline, kept me focused with a smile.

Dale Wetenkamp, our project coordinator at the *Las Vegas Review-Journal*, has been a supportive task master. He has backstopped my work at every step, offering helpful perspectives and suggestions along the way.

Thanks, too, to *R-J* photographer Jim

Decker, whose work graces this volume from front to back. Jim's keen visual eye has provided important images that words cannot always convey. (I just wish he could have found a way to put some more hair on my head!)

Among the hundreds of contacts I have made, Myram Borders of the Las Vegas News Bureau stands well above the crowd. A veteran newswoman who knows this town inside out, Myram has endeavored to keep me apprised of the ever-changing Las Vegas landscape. That's no mean feat, but her years with United Press International trained her well in the art of frenetic activity.

And then there are our publishing partners at the Insiders' Publishing Inc. Writers usually like a little distance from their editors — and we certainly got that. Corresponding via e-mail and express delivery with the Insiders' Publishing offices in Manteo, North Carolina, we have bridged 2,500 miles to pull this project together. Publisher Beth Storie and editors Molly Perkins and Theresa Chavez have been a joy to work with. Thanks to each of you for the timely encouragement and constant patience. I think I've got that IG stylebook emblazoned in my brain!

Last and certainly not least, a word about my family. Through all the ups and downs of this project, my wife, Margaret, was there for me. As a supportive (and hard-working) spouse of a freelance writer, she indulged my moods and tended to my needs. She and our children, Kristina and Ryan, were ever-present reminders that writers must have a life too.

— Ken Ward

Table of Contents

Directory of Maps

Greater Las Vegas

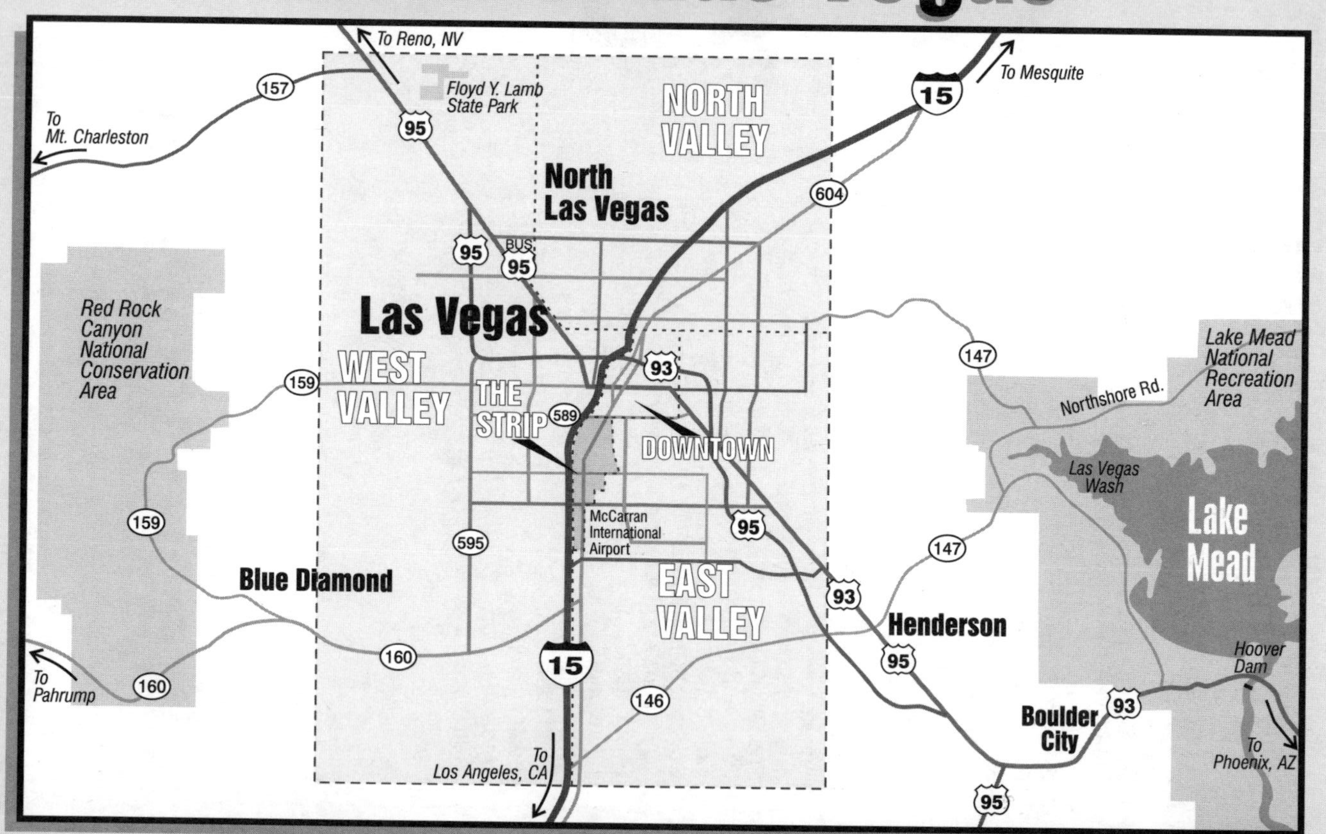

Las Vegas

and Surrounding Areas

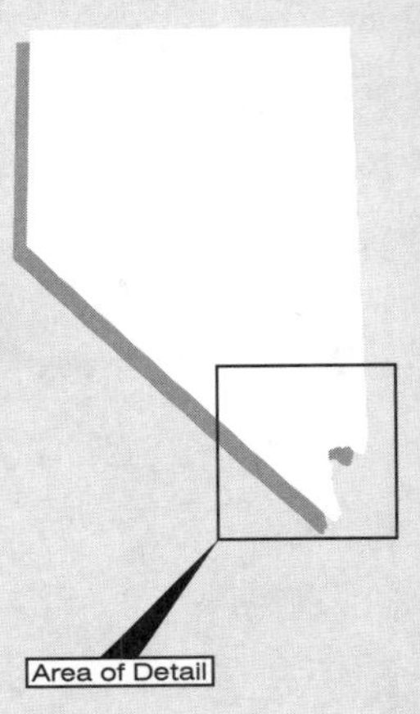

UTAH
UTAH
ARIZONA
93
168
Mesquite
Glendale
Bunkerville
Moapa
Amargosa Valley
Mercury
Indian Springs
95
15
Logandale
Overton
160
Mt. Charleston
156
158
157
Lake Mead
Pahrump
Las Vegas
N. Las Vegas
127
178
160
Blue Diamond
Henderson
Hoover Dam
Boulder City
Goodsprings
Sandy Valley
161
Jean
165
ARIZONA
Nelson
93
Primm
Cottonwood Cove
Dolan Springs
164
Searchlight
Cottonwood Cove
127
Chloride
CALIFORNIA
Laughlin
68
Kingman
15
Bullhead City

Downtown Las Vegas

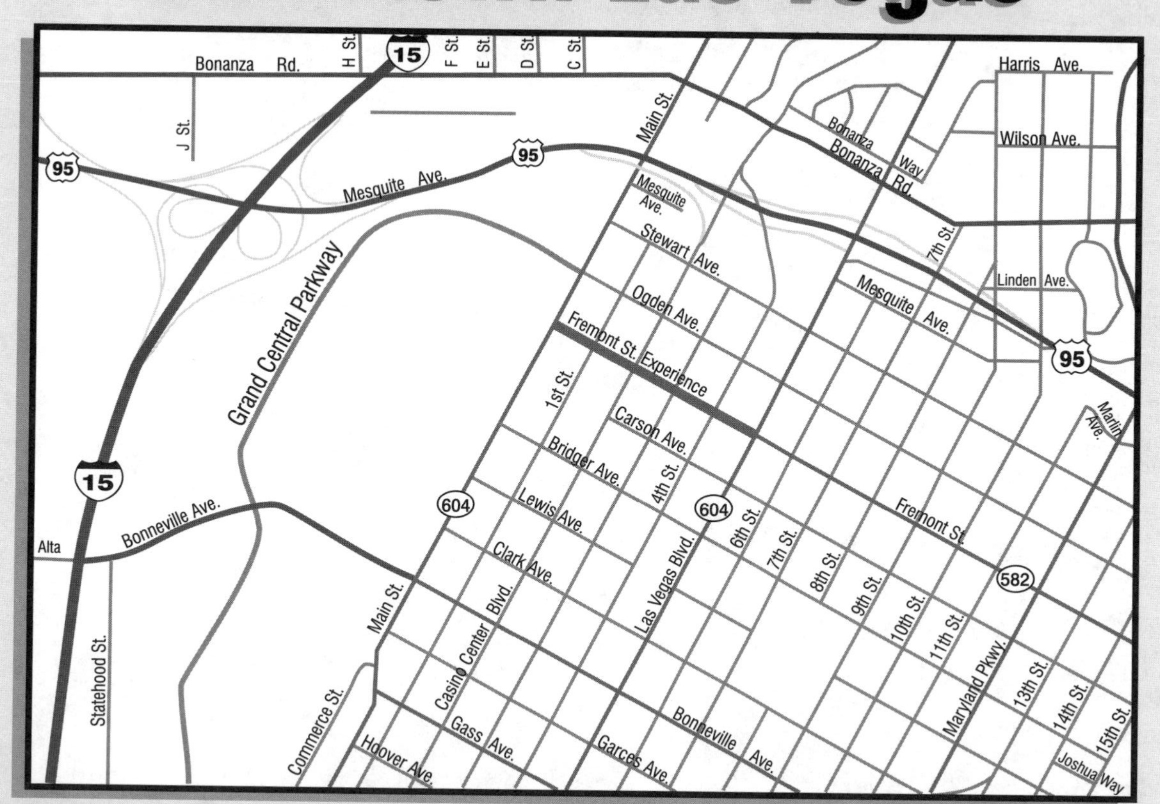

The Strip Area

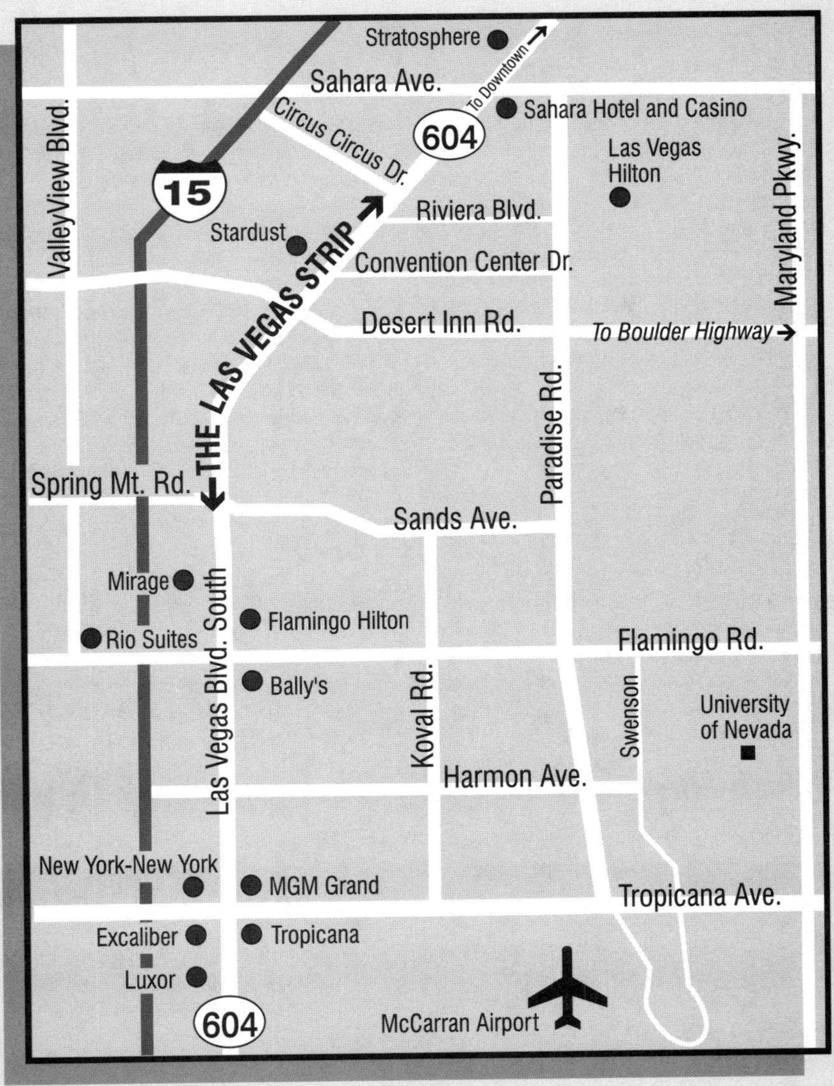

How to use this book

No other American city has the flashcard recognition of Las Vegas. Mention its name and you evoke images of luxurious resort hotels, high-stakes gambling, fast-paced production shows and a sort of frantic pursuit of adult entertainment that lasts 24 hours a day, 365 days a year. Visitors come to experience Las Vegas, to have their senses stimulated and bombarded and perhaps to break a few rules along the way. In addition to a run for their money, Las Vegas visitors get a sabbatical from their ordinary lives back home.

In this book we cover all of the extravagance that has made Las Vegas the nation's No. 1 tourist destination. But we cover much more than that. Beyond the flamboyance of this adult amusement park is a neo-Southwestern city sprawling across the desert, begging to be explored. And this book is your travel guide.

For seekers of the neon transgressions, we'll escort you through the brightly lit fantasy world of the casinos, resort hotels, celebrity showrooms, production extravaganzas, all-you-can-eat buffets and the other attractions and establishments that have made Las Vegas "The Entertainment Capital of the World." But we'll also take you beyond the neon, where you'll discover the city's best and most unusual local haunts —restaurants, piano bars, sports taverns, nightclubs and shopping opportunities—oftentimes hidden in the jumbled cityscape.

Our book tells you how you can water ski in the morning and snow ski in the afternoon; where to buy a slot machine or blackjack table; where the local dealers and keno runners gather after work; where to take the kids when they've run out of video-game quarters; how to see a concert or play; and many more things that tourists seldom discover, even if they have the time to search for them. This book is about the vast wilderness that surrounds the city, harsh and cruel in some places, but always fascinating and beautiful. In the serenity of the nearby desert, you can experience the tranquillity that preceded Kit Carson and the other pioneers who passed this way before.

The Insider's Guide® to Las Vegas escorts you through the entire Las Vegas experience with a focus on quality and value, the exemplary and the unique. Take the time to delve below the surface, rather than skim along from one casino to another, nourished by 99¢ shrimp cocktails. Discover the various layers of the Las Vegas valley, and you will be alternately charmed and perplexed, or enchanted and horrified, but never bored. You might go home empty handed, but you won't go home empty.

Besides tourists and visitors, newcomers and residents alike will find valuable and pertinent information to help them either relocate to Las Vegas, or better enjoy their quality of life in the valley. Even long-term locals, who may believe they've experienced all that Vegas has to offer, will be surprised to discover some of the hidden gems that *The Insiders' Guide® to Las Vegas* uncovers.

Glimpse our Table of Contents and notice how easy we've made it for you to explore areas that interest you and to bypass those that don't. If you're looking for the best seafood in town, turn to our Restaurants chapter. If you're a new resident to Las Vegas and want to learn about the local school districts, flip ahead to our Education chapter. If you're thinking of moving to Las Vegas, see our Real Estate chapter, which gives detailed descriptions

www.insiders.com
See this and many other Insiders' Guide® destinations online — in their entirety.
Visit us today!

of local neighborhoods and real estate agents. All chapters are independent and can be read in any order, from start to finish or inside out.

Because Las Vegas has been built on commercial gambling, we've included three gambling-related chapters. In the Gaming Resorts chapter you'll find everything you need to know about the hotel-casinos that have made Las Vegas famous; in the Independent Casinos chapter you'll find listings and information about stand-alone casinos that are not part of a resort hotel; and in the Gaming Guide chapter you'll learn all about the uniquely Las Vegas phenomenon called a casino, the games people play here and how to best enjoy them.

The Greater Las Vegas Metropolitan Area is the size of San Francisco but spread across an area 20 times larger. Included within the valley are the cities of Las Vegas, Henderson and North Las Vegas, unincorporated communities such as Paradise and Spring Valley as well as unincorporated sections of Clark County. In order to simplify the organization of the vast amount of information in our book, we've divided the Las Vegas valley into geographic areas — The Strip Area, Downtown, East Valley, West Valley and North Valley. These areas are then used to arrange the contents of the chapters. Most visitors to Las Vegas are acquainted with The Strip Area, which includes the megaresorts and other tourist destinations along Las Vegas Boulevard from Sahara Avenue south to Vacation Village. For our purposes it also includes the corridor formed between The Strip and Paradise Road, from Sahara Avenue to the airport as well as venues within a block or two of Las Vegas Boulevard.

The downtown area includes the 20 blocks surrounding the Fremont Street Experience and generally bounded by I-15 on the west, Eastern Avenue on the east, Sahara Avenue on the south and Lake Mead Boulevard on the north. The East Valley includes locations east of The Strip Area, and the West Valley encompasses the area west of The Strip. The North Valley takes in the area north of downtown and not included in either the East or West valleys. (See our maps in the front of the book.) While most visitors to Las Vegas never venture beyond the two major tourist destinations, The Strip and downtown, we recommend you take the time to explore the "other side" of Las Vegas. You may be surprised at what you discover.

You'll notice throughout the book that Nevada listings include only a seven-digit telephone number. This is because the 702 area code serves the entire state. This doesn't mean all calls within 702 are local. You will incur long distance charges when dialing numbers outside the Las Vegas Local Calling Area, which includes Las Vegas, North Las Vegas, Henderson, Boulder City, Blue Diamond, Mt. Charleston, Nelson, Searchlight, Cottonwood Cove and Cal-Nev-Ari. When placing calls to communities outside the Local Calling Area, such as Reno, Laughlin or Mesquite, you must dial 1 + 702 + the seven-digit number.

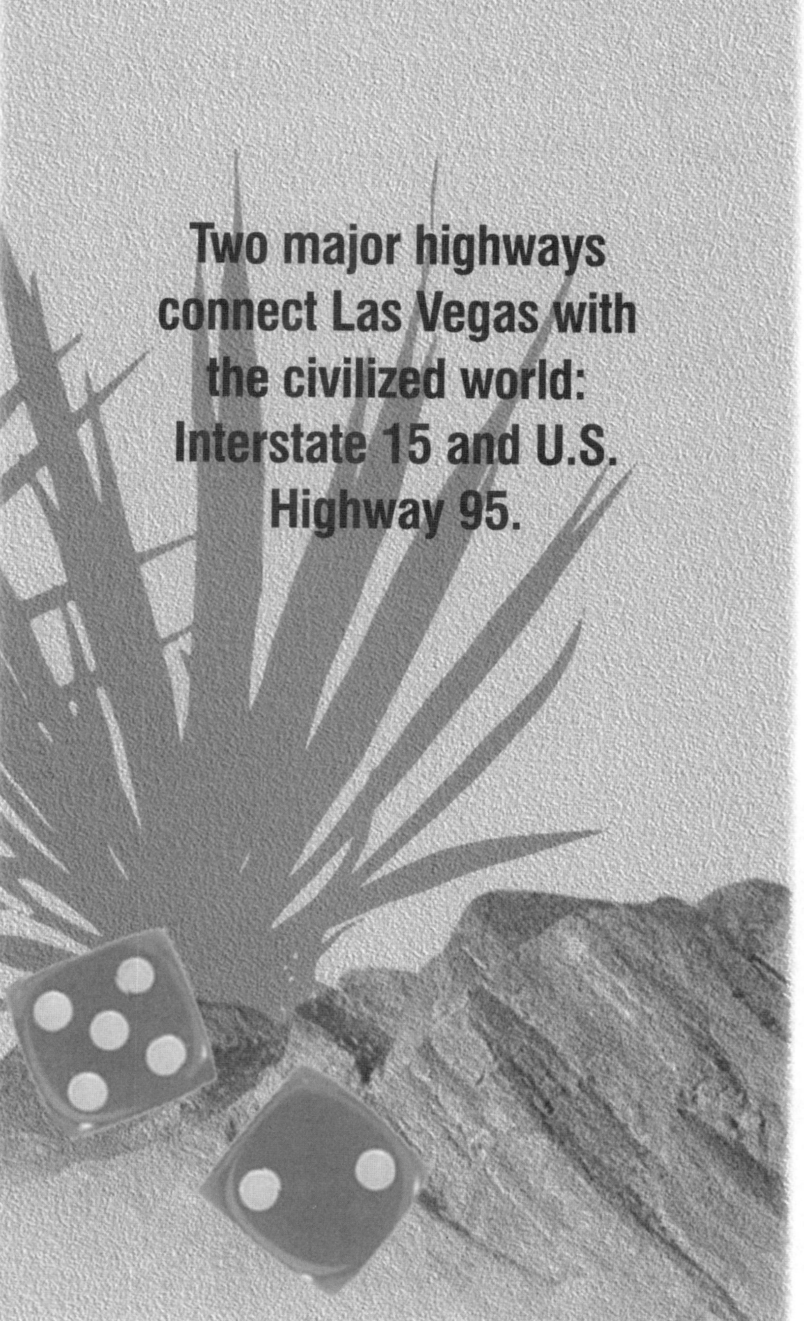

Two major highways connect Las Vegas with the civilized world: Interstate 15 and U.S. Highway 95.

Getting Around

Despite its remote Mojave Desert location, Las Vegas is easily accessed by two major highways, dozens of commercial and charter airlines and Greyhound. Moreover, the city's southern Nevada location puts it at the hub of "puddle jumper" commuter flights from Los Angeles, San Francisco, Phoenix, Denver, Kansas City and other destinations in the western half of the United States.

While getting here is easy, traveling around town is a challenge. Because of Las Vegas' unprecedented growth, which started in the late 1980s and continues with no end in sight, the city's streets have become a maze of traffic, gridlock and road construction. Throw in a fleet of frenetic cab drivers, an erupting volcano and a pirate battle, and it's like bumper cars gone wild.

The worst traffic is on The Strip — the stretch of Las Vegas Boulevard from Sahara to Tropicana avenues — and on Paradise Road from the Convention Center to McCarran Airport. And the congestion worsens every time a new hotel dumps 3,000 guest rooms and 6,000 employees into the mix.

But traffic congestion is not confined to the resort corridor. The influx of 6,000 new residents a month has pushed the Greater Las Vegas population to more than 1 million, while the existing infrastructure was designed to handle less than half that amount.

To help unclog city streets, Clark County's Regional Transportation Commission (RTC) has earmarked more than $800 million for new construction and road improvements through the end of 1998. It's also likely the Commission will invest double that over the next decade to keep up with the anticipated growth.

In 1996 several key road improvement projects were completed. They include the Interstate 15 to E. Sahara Avenue flyover ramp; the second section of the Southern Nevada Beltway, which eventually will encircle the entire city; and the Desert Inn Road Super Arterial. The most effective of the improvements has been the Super Arterial, which connects the east and west sides of Las Vegas with a nonstop, high-speed route under the congested Strip.

To better handle traffic into and out of McCarran Airport, a stretch of highway called the Airport Connector (Interstate 215) was completed, providing a direct connection from McCarran to I-15, including a half-mile-long tunnel beneath two of the airport's runways. Future plans call for I-215 to tie into the Southern Nevada Beltway.

The local bus system is also doing its part to ease the traffic crunch. In 1996, Citizens Area Transit (CAT) increased its hours of service by 16 percent, which resulted in an increase in bus riders of 10 percent; the result is a monthly bus ridership of about 2.5 million.

Long-range plans for solving our traffic problems include an underground subway system or elevated monorail. The RTC is evaluating a high-tech, fixed guideway system. If approved and built, such a rail or monorail would link downtown with the resort corridor and would be operating shortly after the turn of the century.

Highways

Two major highways connect Las Vegas with the civilized world: **Interstate 15** and **U.S. Highway 95**. Heading southwest, I-15 is the major connector to Southern California and the city of Los Angeles, which is about 280 miles from Las Vegas. The major hotels, McCarran International Airport and the Convention Center all have exits along I-15, which also connects The Strip with the downtown area.

Another way to reach Las Vegas from Southern California is to take **Interstate 40** across the desert to Needles, California, then north on U.S. 95 to the Colorado River resort town of Laughlin, about 100 miles south of Las Vegas.

Driving I-15 northeast from Las Vegas leads to the Valley of Fire State Park, the border town of Mesquite and St. George, Utah, about 95 miles from Las Vegas.

Traveling south on U.S. 95 takes you to Lake Mead, Hoover Dam and Boulder City, about 30 miles from Las Vegas, and into Arizona. Motorists from points east usually drive I-40 to Kingman, Arizona, then take U.S. 95 north to Las Vegas, about 100 miles.

Driving north on U.S. 95 leads to Tonopah, Reno and Lake Tahoe, about 450 miles from Las Vegas, and the Northern California cities of Sacramento, Stockton and San Francisco.

Surface Streets

Las Vegas streets are laid out in a north-south, east-west grid pattern, so finding your way around town is relatively simple. The city's most prominent street, **Las Vegas Boulevard**, is home to most of the major resort hotels. It also divides the valley into east and west hemispheres, and serves as starting point for the streets' east-west numbering system.

FYI

Unless otherwise noted, the area code for all phone numbers listed in this chapter is 702.

Another major connector is **Paradise Road**, which runs roughly parallel to Las Vegas Boulevard from Sahara Avenue to McCarran Airport. Along the way, Paradise is home to many nongaming hotels and inns, which serve the massive Convention Center complex at Paradise and Desert Inn roads.

In the downtown area, **Fremont Street** is the main drag, even though its Glitter Gulch frontage has been converted to a pedestrian mall. Most downtown casinos are in Glitter Gulch, where you'll also find clusters of souvenir shops and restaurants. Fremont Street also marks the starting point for addresses with north-south numbers.

Many of the major streets identify their more famous residents — **Sahara**, **Desert Inn**, **Flamingo**, **Tropicana** and the **Convention Center**. However, it's undecided what will happen to Sands Avenue, since the Sands Hotel was leveled in 1996. Hopefully, it won't be renamed for a resort yet to be built. The street is already the city's most confusing: it is Sands Avenue from The Strip to Paradise Road, where it turns into Twain Avenue, and from The Strip west it is called Spring Mountain Road. New residents who drive the street must feel like they're riding with Siegfried & Roy.

Commuters have a variety of options when driving downtown or to The Strip resorts. Residents of the east side find **Boulder Highway**, **U.S. 95**, **Maryland Parkway** and **Eastern Avenue** as quick connectors to downtown Las Vegas. The major routes to The Strip are **Tropicana Avenue**, **Flamingo Road**, **Desert Inn Road** and **Sahara Avenue**. During rush hour, traffic on these streets slows to a crawl, so use less-traveled **Harmon**, **Twain** and **Karen** avenues.

From the southwest side of town, residents are locked into taking I-15 downtown, unless they opt for a stop-and-go ride on **Valley View Boulevard**, **Industrial Road** or **Rancho Drive**. There are more choices to reach The Strip, such as **Tropicana Avenue**, **Spring Mountain Road**, **Flamingo Road**, **Desert Inn Road**, **Sahara Avenue** and **Oakey Boulevard**.

The sprawling northwest side is experiencing a population explosion, resulting in major traffic congestion along U.S. 95 during peak rush hours. Smart commuters use alternatives such as **Lake Mead Boulevard**, **Smoke Ranch Road** and **Cheyenne Avenue** as connectors to downtown, and **Rainbow Boulevard**, **Jones Boulevard**, **Rancho Drive** and **Decatur Boulevard** to access the southwest Strip connectors.

Even though Las Vegas is a 24-hour, three-shift town, rush hour is at its peak during the morning and afternoon commutes. During these times it's best to avoid the downtown interchange, appropriately called the Spaghetti Bowl, where I-15 and U.S. 95 entangle.

On holiday weekends, traffic in and near the resort corridor — formed by The Strip, Paradise Road and the streets connecting them — can be especially brutal. Driving near the convention center can also be a nightmare during the larger expositions such as Comdex in November, the Consumer Electronic Show (CES) in January, MAGIC in August and the National Association of Broadcasters in April.

INSIDERS' TIP

About 41 percent of visitors to Las Vegas arrive by car, 44 percent by air, 7 percent by bus and 8 percent by RV.

Even though the east and west sides of town are only a few miles apart, residents have always treated The Strip boundary as if it were the Mason-Dixon line. But the new Desert Inn Super Arterial, which spans The Strip with an underpass, has made east-west travel much quicker and easier.

Observing the rules of the road in Las Vegas is relatively straightforward, with a few exceptions. The large number of pedestrian tourists presents more of a driving hazard than in most communities. Especially when many of them ignore crosswalks, stop signs and red lights, often with tragic results. Drivers must also be on the lookout for school speed zones, which control traffic near schools, often reducing it to 15 and 20 miles per hour. These are usually marked with signs and flashing yellow lights, but not always. Exceeding the posted limits in these zones carries hefty traffic fines.

If you're a new resident to Las Vegas, you have 30 days to get a Nevada driver's license and register your vehicles with the Nevada Department of Motor Vehicles and Public Safety. Foreign drivers should get an international license before driving here, and most likely will need one to rent a car.

Airports

McCarran International Airport

5757 Wayne Newton Blvd. • 261-5743

McCarran International Airport handles more passengers per capita than any other airport in the world. And with 30 million passengers a year passing through its gates, the airport is ranked among the 10 busiest, even ahead of Boston, Orlando and New York's La Guardia.

Because of the rapid growth in Las Vegas air traffic — passenger volume doubled between 1987 and 1996 — the ultramodern facility, complete with slot and video poker machines, seems to be in a perpetual state of expansion.

Currently in Phase 4 of a master plan that will carry the airport into the 21st century, McCarran will spend a half-billion dollars meeting the needs of the 90,000 passengers who travel through the airport each day.

New development at McCarran includes expanded facilities in Terminal 1, specifically at the ticketing and baggage claim areas, and a new D gate scheduled for completion in 1998. The D gates will open with 26 gates, eventually building out to 60, and will have an automated tram to shuttle passengers to and from the main terminal.

In order to better handle the nearly 800 flights a day, one runway is being extended, and another is being upgraded from a small general aviation runway to a full-size air carrier runway.

The first major improvement for Phase 4, a nine-story, 6,000-space parking garage, was completed in late 1996. The new facility, just east of the existing garage, gives airport customers more options: metered, daily and short-term, frequent-flyer and valet parking. See the Airport Parking section for details. Airline traffic at McCarran includes more than 780 flights a day, with direct flights to 71 U.S. and two European cities. In 1996, about 30.5 million passengers passed through McCarran, nearly double 15.5 million passengers who traveled in 1987.

The airport is served by 23 domestic and foreign airlines, two commuter lines, one helicopter service and, depending on the season, up to 20 charters.

Arriving passengers find a well-designed facility and have no problem locating the baggage claim area, even though it is often a long walk from the gate. Just outside the baggage claim, you may be picked up in the Ground Transportation area, where you'll also find taxi stands, hotel shuttles, city buses and courtesy shuttles for the many car rental companies just a few blocks away.

Airport Access

Driving into the airport via Paradise Road to drop off or pick up passengers is easy if you follow the signs: "Departing Flights" takes you directly to the terminals' drop off or to the parking garage; "Arriving Flights" directs you to the curb-side pickup area (no waiting is allowed) and the parking garage. If you get confused, miss your turn or make the wrong one, don't panic. Just stay on the airport loop and it will take you around for another shot at redemption.

Las Vegas is one of the few major cities in which the main airport is close and accessible to the city's business and tourist destinations. Visitors find that trips from McCarran to The Strip and downtown resorts take just a matter of minutes. Conversely, the airport is easily accessible from a number of sources.

The simplest route to the airport is Paradise Road, which connects with practically all The Strip resorts beginning at Sahara Avenue and working south. Paradise also connects with the downtown area via either Las Vegas Boulevard or Main Street.

From the Henderson and Green Valley areas, take Russell Road west to the airport and follow the signs to the appropriate terminal. Or you can take Warm Springs Road west and the Airport Connector tunnel to the terminals. You can also reach the Airport Connector from I-15 south of The Strip resorts. If you're driving north on I-15, take Exit 34 to I-215 (Airport Connector) and follow the signs to Exit 8, then proceed through the tunnel.

Parking

In late 1996, McCarran opened its new Parking Plaza designed to handle a variety of parking needs in two main garages: the Gold Garage and Silver Garage. At the same time the airport installed a valet parking service and a new Park-a-Lot area for monthly parking spaces.

Both garages offer metered, short-term parking for up to three hours, with rates of 25¢ per 15-minute period. Each garage also has longer-term parking for $1 an hour up to a maximum of $6 a day. In addition, the Silver Garage has reserved spaces for $90 a month. The area is accessed through a personal card swiped for entry and exit, and tenants needn't depart through the Parking Plaza toll booth.

Valet parking is available 24 hours a day, seven days a week in the Silver Garage. Rates are $9 for the first day and $7 for each additional day.

If you have an oversized vehicle or don't mind parking outside, there's a surface lot next to the Gold Garage and one adjacent to Terminal 2. Rates are $1 an hour up to a maximum of $4 a day. There's also a 4,200-space, remote parking lot at Kelly Lane on the north side of Russell Road between Paradise Road and Maryland Parkway. The lot is paved and lighted with 24-hour security and free shuttle buses running every 15 minutes, 24 hours a day.

INSIDERS' TIP

For current road conditions in southern Nevada, call the Nevada Highway Patrol at 486-3116. You will need a touch-tone phone to access information for Interstate 15, U.S. Highway 95, etc.

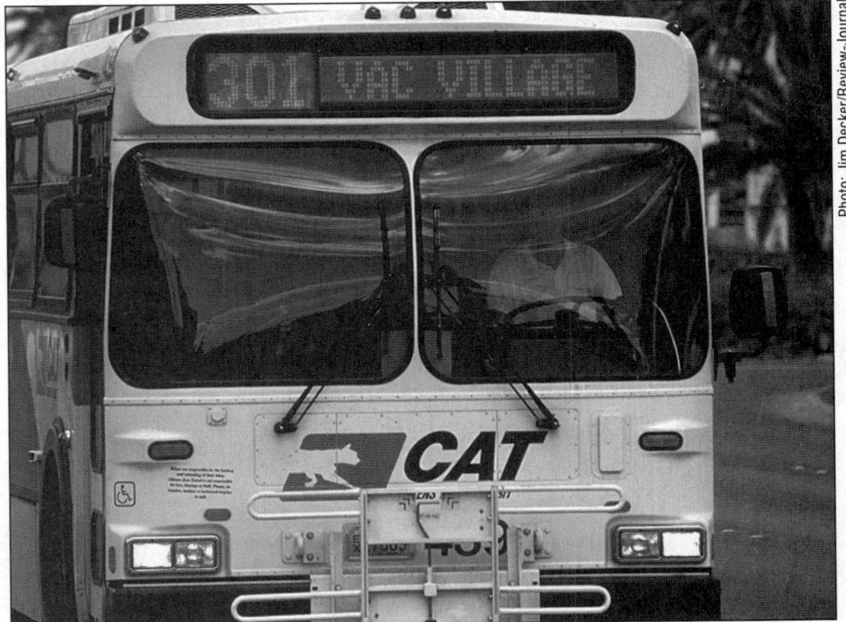

Photo: Jim Decker/Review-Journal

The city's CAT buses run 24 hours a day between Strip and downtown resorts.

See our Rental Car section in this chapter for information on renting a car at the airport.

North Las Vegas Airport
2730 Airport Dr., North Las Vegas
• 261-3800

Known as the North Las Vegas Air Terminal until 1996, the airport is owned by Clark County and serves mostly private fixed-wing aircraft, flight services and tour operators. A recent $15 million face-lift included resurfacing the runways and a 15,600-square-foot terminal. Among the major tenants are Aerleon Flight Services, 647-6100 (flight training, tours and rentals); Civil Air Patrol USAF Auxiliary, 642-6288; Las Vegas Airlines, 647-3056 (training, charters, tours and sales); Scenic Airlines, 638-3200 (tours and charters); and a very good coffee shop.

Buses

Greyhound Bus Line
200 S. Main St. • 384-9561, (800) 231-2222

It may not be the quickest way to travel, but taking the bus is usually the lest expensive mode for getting here. Buses leave for Los Angeles and Southern California throughout the morning and afternoon, with one-way fares ranging from $37 to $74, depending on the time of year. There is also service to Phoenix ($32 to $64), Denver ($85 to $170) and San Francisco ($52 to $104), to name a few destination cities. Buses arrive daily from Los Angeles, Phoenix, Salt Lake City, Denver, Reno and San Diego. Buses arriving from Los Angeles stop at Harrah's and the Tropicana hotels before reaching the downtown depot, which is adjacent to Jackie Gaughan's Plaza Hotel. Tickets can be purchased at time of departure, and discounts are available for advance purchases (three to 21 days in advance).

Mass Transit

Citizens Area Transit (CAT)
301 Clark Ave. • 228-7433

CAT, The countywide bus system, replaced Las Vegas Transit in 1992 and has vastly improved the quality and range of service for bus riders. While the bus service can hardly be called "rapid" transit, CAT has expanded residential routes and other services, such as equipping buses with bicycle racks and hydraulic lifts for wheelchair-bound passengers.

The buses run seven days a week between 5:30 AM and 1:30 AM for residential routes and 24 hours a day on The Strip. Residential buses are scheduled every 15 to 30 minutes, depending on the route, while Strip buses (No. 301) run in 10-minute intervals, starting downtown and traveling south to Vacation Village (south of Sunset Road).

The Strip Express (No. 302) runs from 6 PM to 12:30 AM but only makes selected stops between Fremont Street (downtown) and Vacation Village.

Unlike the old bus system, CAT buses now service the airport with routes along Paradise Road (No. 108) and Maryland Parkway (No. 109), between the hours of 5 AM and 1 AM.

Bus fare is $1 each way on all residential routes and $1.50 on The Strip buses. Seniors older than 62 and children between 5 and 17 ride for half-fare, while children younger than 5 ride free. Transfers are free, and frequent riders can purchase a monthly pass for $20, which is good for unlimited riding.

Taxis

Taxis are plentiful in Las Vegas — the city has about 1,100 of them — but they're clustered mainly around the hotels, convention center and airport. It's often difficult to flag one, so if you're away from your hotel, it's best to call ahead.

The basic rate is $2.20 for the first mile plus $1.50 for each additional mile. There is no charge for extra riders, but the maximum per cab is five. On average, a taxi ride from the airport to The Strip costs about $6 to $9, and from the airport to downtown the ride costs from $12 to $17. **Desert Cab**, 386-9102, **Whittlesea Blue Cab**, 384-6111, and **Yellow and Checker Cab**, 873-2000, are the principal operators in the city.

Limousines

There's something poetic about Sin City having more limousines per capita than any other city in the world. If you want to arrive in unabashed style, there are a dozen limousine services to accommodate you.

Most "stretch" limos feature a wet bar, stereo, TV, telephone, moon roof, intercom and chauffeur, of course. The average cost for a limo and driver starts at about $25 an hour. A stretch limo will cost between $40 and $50. A super stretch is available for about $65 an hour.

Operators include **Bell Transportation**, 385-5466, **Presidential Limousine**, 731-5577, **Las Vegas Limo**, 739-8414, **On Demand Sedan**, 876-2222, **CLS Las Vegas**, 740-4545, and **Lucky 7 Limousine**, 739-6177.

In addition, many of the wedding chapels offer limousine service to their blissful clients, and all the major resorts have in-house limos for their guests.

Rental Cars

If you're a visitor, perhaps the best way to see Las Vegas is to drive. The city is laid out in a north-south and east-west grid, with The Strip serving as the main north-south artery, so finding your destination in town is not difficult. Plus a car will allow you to visit some of the nearby sights, such as Lake Mead, Hoover Dam, Boulder City and Red Rock Canyon, which are all less than a half-hour's drive from the city. Rates vary but the average price for an economy car starts in the mid-$20 range. There is an 8 percent airport surcharge, 7 percent sales tax and 6 percent license tag fee added to the rental rate. For an extra $8 to $10 you can purchase the collision damage waiver. If you'd like something sexier than a Ford Fiesta, you can rent just about anything in Las Vegas — for a price. Choose from a Corvette, Mustang or Porsche Cabriolet. If you prefer something slightly more exotic, opt for a BMW, Mercedes, Jaguar, Ferrari or even a Rolls Royce. But be prepared to pay handsomely — these cars rent from $75 to $500 a day. There are even firms that rent cars by the hour. Most agencies require a major credit card, a driver's license and a second form of I.D.; some require the driver to be at least 25 years old. If you don't have a credit card, a few companies accept a cash deposit (from $100 to $250) and often require proof of employment and a round-trip ticket as well.

Nearly every resort hotel has a car rental booth in or near the lobby. Or you can call any of the rental car companies, and they will gladly pick you up.

Photo: Jim Decker/Review-Journal

The Strip Trolley provides inexpensive transportation up and down The Strip.

There are a few agencies that maintain rental desks in the airport terminal next to the baggage claim. They include:

Allstate, 736-6147
Avis, 265-5595, (800) 331-1212
Dollar, 739-8408, (800) 800-4000
Hertz, 736,4900, (800) 654-3131
National, 261-5391, (800) 227-7368
Sav-Mor, 736-1234, (800) 634-6779

Most of the car rental firms have their outlets on Paradise Road, between Flamingo Road and McCarran Airport. You can check the phone book for car rental agencies or try one of these:

Airport Rent-a-Car, 795-0800, (800) 785-8578
Alamo Rent-a-Car, 263-8411, (800) 327-9633
Budget Car Rental, 736-1212, (800) 527-0700
Enterprise, 735-2124, (800) 325-8007
Ladki Rent-A-Car, 597-1501, (800) 245-2354
Preferred Car Rental, 894-9936
Rebel Rent-A-Car, 597-0427, (800) 346-4222
Thrifty Car Rental, 896-7600, (800) 367-2277
U.S. Rent A Car, 798-6100, (800) 777-9377
Value Rent A Car, 733-8886, (800) 468-2583

For nearly half the year
daily temperatures
approach 100 F. In July
and August, the
highs routinely hover
near 105 F.

Area Overview

While other metropolises measure time in centuries, it seems Las Vegas counts its accomplishments in weeks and months. Things happen quickly here, and if you blink, you're likely to miss them.

Indeed, if you haven't been to Las Vegas for a few years, you may not recognize the urban landscape. Since 1990, the city and surrounding Clark County have grown by 400,000 people. A half-dozen megaresorts with more than 18,000 rooms have opened along The Strip. Fremont Street has become a downtown pedestrian mall covered by a high-tech, laser-lighted canopy. Never lacking for hubris, local promoters call Las Vegas "the last great American city."

If you've never been here, the spectacle can be overwhelming. Flying in at night, you see the valley's lights extend as far as the eye can see. The Strip, formally known as Las Vegas Boulevard, showcases architecture that ranges from Roman forums to Egyptian pyramids to New York City Gothic. In all, the city is home to 10 of the world's 12 biggest hotels. The four hotels at Tropicana Avenue and The Strip — the Tropicana, Excalibur, MGM Grand and New York New York — have more rooms than all of San Francisco.

Las Vegas is, first and foremost, a tourist town. Each year more than 30 million visitors fly or drive here. If they're typical, they leave slightly larger around the waist, having consumed their share of bargain buffets. And, with a few lucky exceptions, their wallets are appreciably lighter. Tourists spend more than $22 billion annually, including $6 billion in wagers of all sizes and odds.

Nowadays, Las Vegas fashions itself as a "resort destination" where families can indulge in an ever-widening variety of restaurants, jump on thrill rides and enjoy cosmopolitan surroundings. Liberace has given way to U2. And while Wayne Newton still performs periodically, he's not "Mr. Las Vegas" anymore. This city has grown up — it's not a one-horse (or one-singer) town anymore.

Population

Many visitors are surprised to learn that regular folks actually live in Las Vegas. As of 1996, Clark County was home to 1.1 million people. Las Vegas, the county seat, accounted for nearly half that population, with 405,000 residents. Two neighboring cities — North Las Vegas and Henderson — are among the fastest growing cities in the nation. If it continues to expand at its current pace, Clark County is projected to top 2 million people by as early as 2006.

The state of Nevada, in fact, has grown 32 percent in the last decade, with nearly three-quarters of the newcomers landing in southern Nevada and a larger share of the rest settling in the Reno area 450 miles to the north. Though the state's total population is just 1.6 million, these migration trends, combined with the federal government's control of vast tracts of uninhabited land throughout the state, make Nevada the most "urban" state in the nation, according to the U.S. Census Bureau.

The new arrivals to Las Vegas are young and old, rich and poor. In short, this is an all-American melting pot. Yet some interesting trends are evident. Senior citizens represent a growing percentage of the region's population. Many are affluent retirees residing in two rapidly expanding Sun City communities in the northwest and southeast sections of the valley. These neighborhoods, restricted to homeowners 55 and older, are among the most popular in the Del Webb-owned household chain. (See our Retirement chapter.)

Hispanics represent the fastest-growing segment of the workforce. Now the second-largest racial group in Las Vegas after Caucasians, Hispanics have moved into gaming, construction and a variety of service-sector positions. Many of these people came here from California, which has been plagued by a soft economy and high unemployment since the 1980s. In fact, 42 percent of Las Vegas' newcomers hail from California.

To put the local growth in perspective, consider this: Half of Clark County's residents weren't even here 10 years ago. Just 6 percent are natives. All of which helps explain why this is the biggest United States city founded in this century.

Economy on a Roll

Newcomers are attracted by a robust economy that seems to have an almost insatiable appetite for employment. The biggest job-creating engine is the gaming industry (casino executives think that sounds better than gambling). Nearly 200,000 people are in casino jobs, which account for 30 percent of the region's total workforce.

The casinos calculate that at least two workers are needed for each new hotel room that is constructed. This giant army of service employees includes direct hires, such as maids, bellhops and dealers. But there's a dynamic ripple effect too. More rooms require more restaurant servers, more cab drivers, more theme-park attendants, more store clerks, more police officers . . . the list goes on and on.

In 1996 alone, the metropolitan area added 46,700 new jobs. Some of the biggest gains were in hotel, gaming and recreation positions. But, in percentage terms, the No.1 growth category was construction. While some of that building work is performed on The Strip, the larger share is done in the residential tracts and commercial centers sprawling in every direction of the valley.

Each year more than 30,000 residential-unit permits are issued in Clark County. Neighborhoods of stucco homes with tile roofs spring up seemingly overnight. Master-planned communities, which feature strictly conformist building codes and lush landscaping, are particularly popular. Summerlin, in the northwest foothills, has been the nation's fastest-growing master-planned community since 1995. (See our Real Estate chapter for more about neighborhoods.)

The residential boom feeds a commercial and retail economy. Taxable sales annually exceed $14 billion — nearly double the 1992 figure. The county is in the top 50 in the nation for retail sales.

Though driven by the growth in gaming, newcomers have other sound economic reasons to come to southern Nevada. The state levies no personal income tax. There is no corporate income tax. Property taxes are relatively low. This all is possible because casinos pay a 6.25 percent gaming tax, which generates nearly half the state's tax revenue.

Just a five-hour drive (or one-hour flight) from Los Angeles, San Diego and Phoenix, Las Vegas is attracting more industry and warehousing operations. Each year more than 30 companies open up shop here. Recent arrivals included the Bank of America, G.E. Capital credit company and Medco-Merck medical supplies. Meantime, Levi Strauss, Good Humor-Breyers ice cream and Berry Plastics have expanded their presence.

In the last three years, Nevada led the nation in the percentage of manufacturing employment, with Las Vegas' manufacturing employment growing by 34 percent. That was second only to Reno's 37 percent gain. New employers include international companies that have formed U.S. divisions. And while such subsidiaries account for just 3 percent of Nevada's total workforce, the number of Nevadans working in these operations has increased more than 400 percent since 1980. In

INSIDERS' TIP

Crowds on The Strip can be pushy, so if you're walking, keep your wallet and purse close. Also, be prepared to have an advertising flier (or two) thrust in your face by nightclub barkers. And the traffic on the street isn't much better. On weekends and evenings it can take 30 minutes to drive a mile along the six-lane thoroughfare that more closely resembles a parking lot.

addition, these companies pay, on average, 17 percent higher wages than other Nevada businesses.

In its lust for new business, the city even agreed to rename a section of town to host Citibank's Western credit card billing center. It seems that the company didn't think its cardholders would want to send their payments to a place that has a similar ring to Lost Wages. So Citicorp's address is simply "The Lakes."

New nongaming projects in 1995 were valued at $115 million, with a combined payroll of $88 million. The diversification has helped keep the unemployment rate below 5 percent.

But that doesn't mean prosperity is omnipresent. While the median household income of $36,700 is roughly average among Western cities, Las Vegas' spiraling growth has pushed prices up at a rapid clip. In the '90s, the city's cost-of-living index has climbed at roughly double the U.S. rate. Costs for groceries and housing are now above the national average. Factoring in overall household expenses and income, the composite cost-of-living index ranks the area less affordable than such Western cities as Albuquerque, New Mexico; Bakersfield, California; Boise, Idaho; Denver, Colorado; Phoenix and Tucson, Arizona. Among the cities surveyed, only Reno and the California cities of Los Angeles, San Diego and Riverside are pricier.

While Las Vegas flashes its glittery facade, and millions of dollars wash over casino floors every night, a substantial segment of the local population struggles with its family pocketbook. More than a quarter of the local households earn less than $20,000 a year. Meantime, the median price for a single-family home has risen to more than $120,000.

The result is a good news-bad news scenario: There are lots of jobs, but they tend to be in the lower-paying service sector, so most households must have two wage earners just to make ends meet. It's not unusual for full-time casino workers, especially those at non-union hotels, to qualify for food stamps and welfare programs.

Some salient statistics about Las Vegas and Clark County:

Median age — 34.7
Percent white— 81.3%
Percent Hispanic —11.2%
Percent African American — 9.5%
Percent Asian — 3.2%
Percent male — 49%
Percent female — 51%
Marriage licenses — 100,562 per year
Divorce decrees — 7,941 per year
Hotel occupancy rate —91.4%
Average apartment rent — $615 a month
Retail space — 27.5 million square feet
Industrial space — 36.2 million square feet

Growing Pains

With 5,000 to 6,000 newcomers arriving every month, and births more than doubling deaths, local governments are straining to provide services. Increased air pollution and traffic are two of the most acute growing pains. Crosstown trips that once took 15 minutes can now take triple that time. As a solution, a public transit system was funded through a sales tax increase in 1991. Ridership has been building steadily, especially along the downtown-to-Strip corridor, but Las Vegas is still primarily an auto-driven town, with as many cars per-capita as Los Angeles.

With urban sprawl, road construction and fender benders are a way of life. Car insurance rates reflect that reality. Frazzled motorists hitting the freeways during peak commute times — which seem to run from 6 to 10 AM and 4 to 7 PM — are well-advised to tune in to news radio stations that give traffic reports every 10 minutes and to drive defensively at all times. Until re-engineering work is completed some-

INSIDERS' TIP

The brightest man-made light is illuminated every night at sunset atop the Luxor Hotel. It shines the equivalent of 40 billion candle power and provides enough light to read a newspaper 10 miles into space.

time in 1999, it's always sound advice to avoid the interchange of Interstate 15 and U.S. Highway 95 during rush hour. Likewise, motorists should eschew The Strip from Sahara to Tropicana avenues after dark — it's a virtual parking lot. (See our Getting Around chapter.)

If you look past the car in front of you and gaze at the horizon, you'll note that the once-crystal-clear mountain vistas are more hazy now. Winter months are particularly smoggy as a dirty brown inversion layer settles over the valley.

The county health district has ordered the use of cleaner-burning oxygenated fuel from November to May in an effort to clear the air. But Mother Nature's contribution, the frequent desert winds, don't tend to clarify things much because they stir up the dust from the many construction sites around the valley. "Vegas nose," congestion from the airborne grit, is a common malady here. So, too, are spring and fall allergies when desert blooms are most prolific. Flowering mulberry trees, a particularly hearty plant, are a prime culprit for pollen, and nurseries are now prohibited from selling them.

Water continues to be a source of concern. While the nearby Colorado River is a bounteous and primary spigot, Nevada gets only 10 percent of the allowed annual allocation (Arizona and California soak up the rest). Ongoing efforts are being made to boost the percentage that was established back in the 1930s, and conservation programs also are cracking down on usage. From May to October, lawn watering is prohibited between noon and 7 PM, peak hours for evaporation.

In the meantime, environmentalists express increasing concern that Lake Mead, created by the damming of the Colorado, is experiencing rising levels of pollution. The lake, which supplies fresh water to the valley, also receives treated effluent pumped back by Las Vegas' sewage plants. Water district officials maintain that the size of the lake and the efficiency of the system ensure safe drinking water for the foreseeable future. After all, we're talking about the largest man-made lake in the Western Hemisphere, with 28.5 million acre-feet of water.

Nevertheless, the need for new facilities and finite resources are steadily boosting water rates. A quarter-percent boost in the 7 percent local sales tax also is being sought to fund expansion of the water-delivery system.

Longtime residents see these problems and their attendant costs as the dark side of growth. They remember when the sales tax was just 3 percent in the 1960s and recall when the Clark County School District could afford to build campuses and keep pace with the population. Today, lively debate revolves around who should pay for the bricks, mortar and services — and how the costs should be borne. In virtually every election, voters are asked to approve bond issues to finance parks, schools, police and other social services. Some of these revenue-raisers pass, and some fail. But, on balance, the result is that property taxes, while still relatively low by national standards, are creeping higher.

Hot Enough For You?

Las Vegas is in what's called the High Desert. Actually, it's situated on the tip of three deserts — the Mojave, the Sonoran and the Great Basin. That makes for only about 4 inches of rainfall a year and an average of 294 sunny days. Such atmospheric conditions prompted the U.S. government to place a military flying school here at what is now called Nellis Air Force Base. The sunny weather also continues to act as a magnet for sun-starved retirees and others looking for a refuge from blizzards, floods and other natural cataclysms.

But if you think the weather doesn't pose a challenge here, you've probably been out in the sun too long. The heat can be oppressive from May through September. For nearly half the year, daily temperatures approach 100 F. In July and August, the highs will routinely hover near 105 F.

While Easterners hibernate in the winter, Las Vegans try to seal themselves during the torrid days of summer. That means running air conditioning at home and in your car. When temperatures hit 110 F, as they do a few days

Photo: Jim Decker/Review-Journal

As megaresorts expand, The Strip is becoming a man-made canyon of high-rises.

each year, the heat can test even the most grizzled desert rat. At that point, shade doesn't even help and any breeze feels like a blast furnace.

Civic boosters are quick to note that it's "a dry heat." And, true enough, relative humidity rarely exceeds 20 percent. Unlike Phoenix and Palm Springs in the Low Desert, the Las Vegas Valley gets very few afternoon showers, so mugginess is not usually a factor. But the dry heat will dehydrate your body quickly. It's advisable to carry a water bottle (or two) and to wear a hat anytime you venture outdoors. Sunscreen is also in order, as the ultraviolet index is usually stuck on high.

So how about the low temperatures? Doesn't it cool off at night? Yes, the mercury might dip to 90 degrees F by 10 PM. Many sun-stunned newcomers are surprised to learn it's hotter at 5 PM than it is at noon. That's because of the "heat island" effect of urban Las Vegas. As the city pours more concrete and asphalt, the ground retains and radiates heat well into the evening hours. As a result, the average minimum temperature has been steadily rising over the last 20 years. This means summer-evening readings may not dip below 75 degrees. And by 10 AM, the mercury is pushing past 90 again.

Outlying regions can get even hotter. Lake Mead and Laughlin to the south will flirt with 115-degree days, though they may cool off a bit more in the nighttime. One popular respite from the heat is Mt. Charleston, 40 miles north of the city. It features scenic outlooks on winding trails and highs that rarely exceed 80 degrees. Evening temperatures dip sharply at dusk.

As befitting a land of extremes, the entire southern Nevada desert can get downright frigid in the winter. Low temperatures from December through February will dip below freezing on many nights. Highs may not hit 50. This temperature variation, spanning 80 degrees from winter to summer, necessitates a good heating system too. The rainy season,

Wedding Chapels

If you've got a few minutes, a willing partner and $70, you can get married in Clark County.

The County Courthouse at 200 S. Third Street is open 24 hours on Fridays and Saturdays to the would-be betrothed (8 AM to midnight on the other days). Pay $35 for a license and walk over to the marriage commissioner (same hours), put down another $35 for a four-minute civil ceremony and, voilà, you're hitched! No blood test. No waiting period.

The only requirements are that you must be at least 18 (though 16-year-olds can be married with parental consent). Divorcés must know the month, year, city and state on their final decree, but no papers are necessary.

Of course, the majority of lovebirds want to make their moment of a lifetime a little more special, and there are more than 100 local wedding chapels ready to serve them. Some offer full, albeit short, affairs, complete with flowers, music, photos, albums and limousines. A few offer balloon rides over town or trips over the Grand Canyon. One enterprising couple repeated vows on a 171-foot-high bungee-jumping platform in front of Circus Circus — and then dove off. Talking about taking the plunge!

In true Las Vegas fashion, a number of chapels have Elvis on staff to croon a few tunes to the newlyweds. For a sense of tradition, the Little Church of the West, 3960 Las Vegas Boulevard S., 739-7971, opened in 1942, is the area's oldest wedding chapel. About 120 couples a week marry in this tidy redwood-sided chapel bordered by a colorful flower garden. And, yes, there's even 24-hour drive-through service at one of Las Vegas' longest standing hitchin' posts, the Little White Chapel.

It's so easy, no wonder more than 100,000 couples wed here each year. While many chapels used to keep their doors open 24 hours, that's a rarity these days. It seems that most couples are pre-arranging their vows. You'll definitely want to make a reservation on Valentine's Day —or make another date. Each year, thousands line up to tie the knot.

Costs for basic chapel ceremonies run around $100. Selected hotels have chapels that charge up to $300 for special themes. The Excalibur, for example, will outfit you in medieval consumes for a ceremony reminiscent of merry old England.

Quick or elaborate, you'll be in good company. Celebrities who have said "I do" in Las Vegas include: Paul

— continued on next page

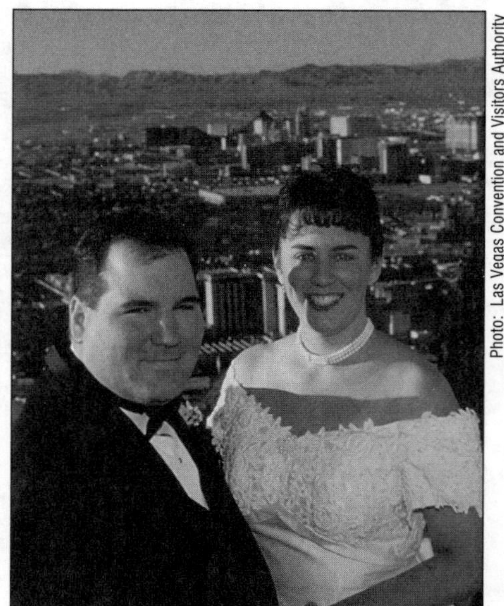

Photo: Las Vegas Convention and Visitors Authority

More than 100,000 couples are married in Las Vegas each year.

Newman and Joanne Woodward, Richard Gere and Cindy Crawford, Bruce Willis and Demi Moore, Steve Lawrence and Edyie Gorme, Michael Jordan, Jon Bon Jovi, Clint Eastwood, Mary Tyler Moore and Mickey Rooney (many times). And, hey, some of them are even still married! Here's wishing you good luck!

For information, call the Clark County Marriage Bureau, 455-4416, which handles the paperwork and makes the official communication to the state offices in Carson City.

The Wedding Network, 256-0908 or (800) 451-9703, maintains a helpful referral list of area chapels and services.

and we're using that term loosely, tends to fall mainly in January and February, when nearly half of the 4-inch annual total is registered.

City vs. County

Las Vegas is the term that generically applies to southern Nevada. It is, after all, the largest city in the state. But, to be politically and factually correct, the majority of residents and the biggest casinos are in Clark County.

While the city has its own mayor and council, the county has its county commission. Like the city, the county is divided into five districts, with a commissioner elected from each area. But the county zones are much larger and overlap the city's districts, so city residents are represented on both governmental bodies.

It's been said that a seat on the county commission holds more power and prestige than a seat in the state legislature. In fact, over the years, many ambitious members of the state assembly and state senate have run for the commission. Few have run the other way. Certainly, commissioners represent far more constituents. And by holding the property-tax pursestrings on all the high-priced real estate along The Strip, the commission wields much financial clout.

Las Vegas and Clark County have a generally workable coexistence, but the bureaucratic intricacies can be confusing. Though the city and county have their own fire departments, the Metropolitan Police Department is headed by a popularly elected sheriff whose force serves both jurisdictions. The city and county have separate parks departments, but residents are encouraged to cross city-county boundaries to use the facilities. The Las Vegas-Clark County Library District is similar to the police model and spans the areas as its name implies.

Indeed, not many Las Vegans could show you the borders of their city — the lines are that indistinguishable. Generally, the city limits are north of Sahara Avenue and west of Eastern Avenue. But within that region are pockets of unincorporated county territory. The day may come when those lines are erased altogether, as wished for by the proponents of a truly consolidated regional government. With City Hall and the County Government Center a mere 2 miles from each other downtown, a merger is always possible. But that's a subject for another day.

City Areas

The downtown area, covering a roughly 2-mile radius emanating from Fremont Street and Las Vegas Boulevard, has long been a center for courts, banks, government and, of course, casinos. While the legal eagles and public workers still tend to congregate here, businesses and residents are moving ever-outward. The migration began to the south and east in the 1950s. Boulder Highway, the main southeastern road running out of down-

INSIDERS' TIP

By 1998 Nevada will get its second telephone area code. The 702 area code already has 5.1 million phone numbers and has been adding 90,000 new numbers each year. It is likely that Las Vegas will retain the 702 designation while the remainder of the state gets a new number.

town, became a bustling thoroughfare in those days. It has not aged well, however. Today, Boulder Highway is, for the most part, a 24-mile stretch of faded and ramshackle buildings, many of them vacant. South of Charleston Boulevard is a particularly scruffy area descriptively known as "Hell Town."

Similarly, the near-west and south-central sections of the city have the look of mean streets. These are low-income, high-crime areas notorious for drug dealing and violence. The pocket between downtown and The Strip is locally known as the "Naked City" for its proclivity to prostitution and other vices. While legal in the rural counties of Nevada, prostitution is prohibited in Clark County.

Despite ongoing redevelopment efforts, newcomers have steered clear of these areas. Many commercial enterprises have set up shop north of the city and south near McCarran International Airport. Light industrial companies stretch south along the frontage roads and railroad tracks paralleling I-15.

The fastest-growing residential section of the city is the northwest, where suburbia now stretches 20 miles toward the foothills past U.S. 95. This has made for ever-worsening rush-hour traffic jams, as legions of workers commute 20 or 30 miles south to The Strip. The crush has spurred robust new neighborhoods in more accessible areas beyond the city limits, such as the southeast and the southwest valley. In general, the valley is split along an east-west line, with The Strip serving as the divider. A patchwork of incorporated and unincorporated areas, the East and West valleys are similar in many ways. U.S. 95 bisects each of them. Increasingly, these regions share the same types of shopping, dining and residential offerings. Chain-operated stores tend to place equal numbers of outlets on each side of the valley. Yet as the region's population sprawls — and travel times lengthen — residents increasingly identify themselves as west siders or east siders. Leisure and entertainment activities tend to coalesce accordingly. It may not say much about a distinguishable lifestyle, but it puts people on the map.

And casinos? Well, they're spreading in virtually every direction. Despite efforts to confine their presence to the existing "resort corridors," the city and county have allowed exceptions. This has yielded a proliferation of gaming establishments throughout the valley, ranging from corner bars with a handful of slot machines to full-service casinos with sports books, keno lounges and hotel rooms. Indeed, things have come a long way since 1906, when the Hotel Nevada opened at Main and Fremont streets.

Beyond the City Limits

In addition to Las Vegas, there are three other incorporated cities in the valley. Each has its own police, fire and parks departments, and each has its own identity. Here are thumbnail sketches of the three.

Henderson

The third-biggest city in Nevada after Las Vegas and Reno, this fast-growing suburb lies 15 miles southeast of Las Vegas. Once known primarily as an industrial and manufacturing town, Henderson, incorporated in 1944, has historically had a blue-collar feel. Uppity denizens of Las Vegas derisively refer to it as "Hooterville."

The city still maintains some of that down-home ambiance, especially in the old downtown area along Water Street. Many of the small clapboard shops look as if they haven't changed in 30 years. But the newer, growing section, popularly called Green Valley, is the picture of modern, upscale suburbia. Tree-lined streets, fancy shopping centers and a large regional mall characterize this master-planned community. Henderson's population has surpassed 120,000, and it's the fastest-growing city of its size in the nation.

INSIDERS' TIP

McCarran International Airport is named after Senator Pat McCarran. The Democratic senator of the 1950s directed federal aviation funds to Nevada.

North Las Vegas

Bordering Las Vegas' to the north, this city, established in 1946, has traditionally attracted low- and moderate-income residents. It also has suffered from a high per-capita crime rate and less than favorable reputation.

However, with a population of 85,000, North Las Vegas has become Nevada's fastest-growing city in percentage terms. Homeowners are enticed by the lower land costs, and scores of housing developments are springing up along the northern tier of the city. Houses tend to be less expensive than elsewhere in the valley, and big families can get more square footage for their dollar. Businesses, too, are flooding into town. The city leads all others in attracting new companies, especially warehousing and manufacturing firms. Like Henderson, it also has become home to major new casinos.

Boulder City

Twenty-five miles southeast of Las Vegas, this quaint and quiet community is a Nevada jewel. It is the only city in the state that does not have legalized gambling. It is also unique for its strict, slow-growth zoning, which has kept the population less than 20,000.

The city began as a housing area for the 4,000 workers on the Boulder Dam in the early 1930s. The government-run town became an independent municipality in 1960. It boasts of many lush green parks and an active arts scene.

Nearby Communities

Outside the Las Vegas Valley but still within Clark County are a smattering of small but growing communities. Notable among them are Laughlin and Mesquite. (See our Daycations chapter for more information on these areas.)

Laughlin lies 90 miles south of Las Vegas via Nev. Highway 163. Located across the Colorado River from Arizona, the town was once called South Point. It was little more than a restaurant, bar and eight-room motel on a dead-end dirt road. In 1966, casino operator Don Laughlin purchased the 6-acre site for $235,000 and has built it into a small city with 10 resorts. The town's 11,014 hotel rooms outnumber its 8,000 residents.

Mesquite is 80 miles northeast of Las Vegas on I-15. The town was originally settled by Mormon farmers. Since the '80s, it has become home to four hotel-casinos and has grown to more than 7,000 residents. The town's golf courses enjoy a brisk business from Las Vegas and from southeastern Utah, whose state line is just 30 miles up I-15.

The newest dot on the Clark County map is **Primm**, which is on the border with California, 60 miles south of Las Vegas on I-15. Three hotel-casinos are the only substantial structures in the yet-to-be-incorporated burg. With only a few trailers and mobile homes in the vicinity, casino workers commute in from Las Vegas and other cities. Immediately across the border is a California lottery outlet inside a mini mart. It is the highest volume lottery dispenser in the entire state. Since there is no lottery in Nevada, there would appear to be more than a few action-crazed Nevadans looking for additional places to bet.

Outside of Clark County, the closest Nevada town is **Pahrump**, 60 miles west of Las Vegas on Nev. Highway 160. A fertile agricultural area, the town produces cotton, alfalfa and grapes and is even home to a winery. And since it's in Nye County, prostitution is legal in Pahrump. There's a bordello on the main street just south of town.

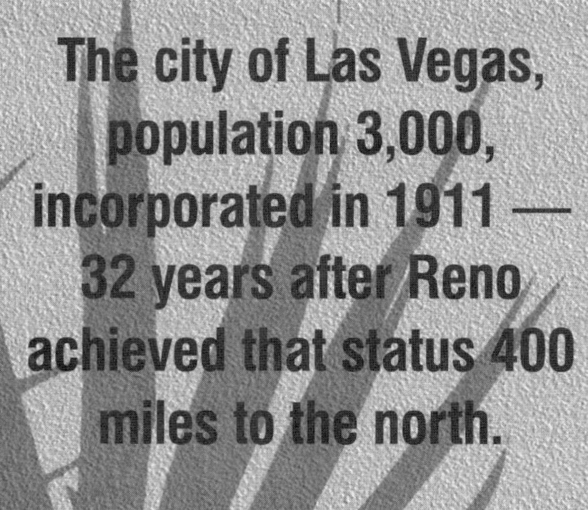

The city of Las Vegas, population 3,000, incorporated in 1911 — 32 years after Reno achieved that status 400 miles to the north.

History

Most cities treasure history. Las Vegas blows it up.

Thirty-year-old buildings like the Dunes hotel-casino are imploded for movie footage and to make way for even grander resorts. In Las Vegas, the question is not just "What have you done?" it's "What have you done lately?"

It's not surprising that Las Vegas is a city with so little institutional memory. A melting pot of newcomers looking for a new life and a new start, Las Vegas inspires people to look forward, not backward. A little more than four decades ago, there were only 5,600 inhabitants here. That's doesn't make for much of an old guard to preserve and protect history. The 1 million people who have arrived here since have been intent on making their own mark in a once-barren desert.

With lots of wide-open spaces, and a gambling industry that encourages risk and entrepreneurship, the Las Vegas Valley isn't into dwelling on the past. Its people are writing modern American history today. This quintessentially 20th-century city wasn't incorporated until 1911, and half of its current residents weren't here 10 years ago. But that's not to say this desert community, whose name means "the meadows" in Spanish, doesn't have some old stories to tell.

Ancient Roots

Ancient signs of human activity date back 11,000 years, but archeologists believe that the region wasn't truly inhabited until about 2500 B.C. A hunting-and-gathering Indian society took root, and around 300 B.C. a group called the Basket Makers appeared on the scene. Pit houses were dug into the earth, and a semblance of a village lifestyle had begun.

Anasazi Indians settled around the washes and valleys to the north and east of what is now Las Vegas around A.D. 800. They grew mainly corn, beans and squash, hunted with bows and arrows, and made baskets and pottery. Adobes began to dot the landscape. But by A.D. 1050 the area was abandoned. Scientists suggest that a prolonged drought, or flooding, may have destroyed the Anasazis' agricultural base. Others cite malaria, and still others see a connection with the collapse of Mexico's Toltec empire.

For the next seven centuries, the Paiute tribe occupied the region. These peaceful people greeted their first European in 1776 when Father Francisco Garces, a Franciscan friar, was blazing the Old Spanish Trail. That encounter, a fleeting one, was followed 50 years later when trader and explorer Jedediah Smith ambled through. Then, John C. Fremont led a party through town. Fremont — an expedition leader, Army general and future presidential candidate — described in detail the gushing springs in the valley in 1844. Though he discovered little that hadn't already been seen by previous explorers, his ventures had lasting significance for painstakingly and accurately mapping the Nevada landscape. He was the first to identify the stark region as "the Great Basin." Fremont's name today adorns downtown's most famous street.

The Old West

As the story goes in the West, so it went here. Exploration eventually ended in exploitation. The Paiutes lost control of their land. By the mid-1850s, the Las Vegas Valley was a stop on what had become a well-traveled stretch now dubbed the Mormon Trail. Mail service and freight trains began to ply the route between Salt Lake City and Los Angeles — and the spring waters of the valley provided a bit of refreshment along the way.

The Mormons, now established in Salt Lake City, aggressively moved into northern and southern Nevada to proselytize and establish settlements. The settlement of the Las Vegas Valley began in earnest in 1855 when Mormon Prophet Brigham Young sent a group led by William Bringhurst to begin a Las Vegas Mission. The mission was to serve a dual purpose: establish supply stations along the Old Spanish Trail and convert the Native Americans.

The missionaries truly felt exiled in the wilderness. Despite the natural springs, the desert heat tortured them, and the Southern Paiutes were not receptive to their message. Though some Indians were converted, they also indulged in the pastime of carrying off crops and stealing livestock. For the Mormons, sustenance consisted mainly of dry bread. A year later, in 1856, Young sent another group to mine lead ore in the area.

The discouraged missionaries pulled out by 1858, but small-scale mining continued until 1861, when small traces of silver were found and a sizable gold strike was made near the current site of Hoover Dam.

A permanent settlement took root in 1865, when Octavius Decatur Gass took ownership of the Old Mormon Fort and established a station to supply Las Vegas Valley miners and settlers.

Meantime, Civil War brought "Battle Born" Nevada into the Union in 1864, and dusty Las Vegas had its first post office by 1892. But this windblown corner of the Mojave Desert, which actually remained part of the Arizona Territory until 1867, wasn't going to be easily tamed.

Water was, and is, the key to Las Vegas' evolution. A few hearty homesteaders tapped into the valley's aquifers to build a rudimentary trading economy.

A ranch was established on the site of an abandoned infantry station known as Fort Baker. In 1903, the ranch was purchased by the San Pedro, Los Angeles and Salt Lake Railroad as a division point on its freight line. By now, freighting had become big business, stimulated by gold and silver strikes at Tonopah and Goldfield, 150 miles to the north. The commerce began to transform Las Vegas from a tent town to a community with house and stores.

Then, in 1910, Mother Nature struck. Flash floods washed out more than 100 miles of track on the Nevada route to Salt Lake. It took five months to fix the track. Coupled with the boom-and-bust cycle of mining operations, the calamity nearly wiped out Las Vegas.

The town clung to life as a ramshackle railroad town. Hardscrabble residents were mainly railroad employees, miners and merchants doing most of their business with Mormon ranchers and farmers scattered around southern Nevada. It wasn't much more than a subsistence economy.

Gradually, the economy revived. The railroad and its Las Vegas Land and Water subsidiary opened more tracts for development. Then the Union Pacific Railroad bought the San Pedro, Los Angeles and Salt Lake line, opening up a transcontinental connection. Land speculation wasn't far behind.

The City's Beginnings

The city of Las Vegas, population 3,000, incorporated in 1911 — 32 years after Reno achieved that status 400 miles to the north.

Las Vegas was a wide-open town. It got through Prohibition and the Depression with bootlegging, bawdy houses, quickie divorces and, of course, gambling. While other states were outlawing prize fights, Nevada saw pugilism as a profit center too. Gov. Reinhold Sadler signed into law the nation's first formal prize-fighting legislation, saying, "I believe it will bring not only a great deal of money, but it will bring monied men." Nevadans didn't worry much about their "rotton burrough" reputation as long as the dollars kept flowing.

The most notorious section of Las Vegas was called "Block 16," an anything-goes red-light district in the downtown area. Dating back to 1905, Block 16 and its gambling parlors were ahead of their time; Gov. Fred Balzar didn't legalize gambling until 1931. But that was a mere formality. Gambling, in fact, had

INSIDERS' TIP

If you're looking for the world's largest hotel, try the MGM Grand. It has 5,005 rooms and a 171,500-square-foot casino.

been legalized once before, in 1869, and then outlawed in 1910. Gambling operators had, of course, continued to ply their trade through the years. True to their independent and entrepreneurial spirit, Nevadans hadn't waited for politicians to tell them what to do.

Still, no other state had dared to go as far as legalizing gambling. Now, with legal cover, gambling halls began to come out of the shadows and promote their dice games, card tables and slot machines, known affectionately as one-armed bandits. The transition from sawdust joints to full-service hotel-casinos was inevitable.

Also in 1931 came the Hoover Dam project, the biggest single kick to the southern Nevada economy. The project, embraced as a part of President Franklin Roosevelt's Works Progress Administration, was seen as a way to create jobs and bring water to the southwest desert. Over a four-year span, this massive federal project brought 5,000 workers and a veritable cascade of money into the area. For Las Vegas, the damming of the mighty Colorado River was indeed a watershed event. The Hoover Dam provided the first reliable source of water, along with cheap electricity to meet the growing city's prodigious demands. It left the region with a recreational jewel called Lake Mead and a quaint suburb named Boulder City. Sixty years after the dam was completed, this quiet community remains the only one in Nevada that prohibits gambling, a holdover from the feds' anti-gaming fervor. Perhaps more than any other Nevada town, Boulder City has retained a conservative, patriotic and religious flavor from its dam-building days. Camp Sibert was established in 1941 to guard against sabotage at Hoover Dam. Retired veterans and true-believing Mormons have long played significant roles in town politics.

Uncle Sam helped boost the local economy again five years later when a Las Vegas airfield was converted into the nation's premier training school for pilots and gunners. Industry sprang up to fuel the war machine. Along with the Army Air Corps gunnery school (now named Nellis Air Force Base) was an industrial complex called Basic Magnesium Inc. This plant, built 15 miles southeast of Las Vegas in Henderson, manufactured munitions and bomb components. Being far enough inland, the federal government figured that

INSIDERS' TIP

Did you know that Clark County has more than one slot machine for every 10 residents? In 1996, the county licensed 130,452 slots and 4,042 table games.

southern Nevada was a safe place to train pilots and make weapons.

Beginning in 1950, the newly created Nevada Proving Ground, 100 miles to the north, would shake Las Vegas' foundations. The atomic era had arrived. At one point, atomic bomb tests were conducted on a monthly basis — above ground. School children would be herded off the playgrounds during detonations, but most townfolk took patriotic pride in the sound of freedom. The proving ground, later renamed the Nevada Test Site, grew along with its mission to ensure that America's nuclear stockpile would always be ready. Opening with 680 square miles of desert scrub, the site expanded to 1,350 square miles, slightly larger than Rhode Island.

While the military was busy north of town, the casinos were spreading south. Gambling was the city's No. 1 business, and the downtown casinos were evolving into larger hotel resorts on Las Vegas Boulevard ("The Strip") south of town. The famed thoroughfare, also known as the Los Angeles Highway back then, got its name from a former L.A. police captain who bought the Pair-O-Dice Club along the barren stretch in 1938. He said the road reminded him of the Sunset Strip.

Motel-style resorts started popping up. The El Rancho opened in 1941. The Western-themed Last Frontier opened in 1942, using a stagecoach to bring gamblers from the airport.

Meantime, Washington was encouraging Las Vegas to clean up its act. Block 16 was shut down in 1941 when the War Department threatened to bar service personnel from the entire town. "Sin City" was learning that it had better play by the rules, and the rewards were forthcoming.

Boomtown

The '50s and '60s in Las Vegas marked one of the nation's biggest building booms. With the advent of air conditioning, interstate highways and transcontinental travel, Las Vegas was becoming a destination resort. For the gambler, it was like Palm Springs and Palm Beach — only better.

The nine-story Riviera hotel became the first high-rise resort in 1955. It was followed by the 15-story Fremont hotel downtown. Elvis, the Rat Pack and Wayne Newton became regular headliners at The Strip resorts, and lounges featured such household names as Don Rickles, Buddy Hackett, Shecky Greene, Alan King and Louis Prima, all for the cost of a drink.

Among the cowboys and the construction crews, the city started to become more urbane. KLAS, the valley's first TV station, went on the air in 1953. An extension of the University of Nevada was established and eventually became known as University of Nevada, Las Vegas.

By 1960, the city's population had grown to 65,000. One of the newcomers was Howard Hughes. The eccentric billionaire started buying up casinos, including the Desert Inn (where he lived), Sands, Landmark, Silver Slipper, Castaways and Frontier. Paying top dollar for the properties ($14 million for the Sands and $13 million for the Desert Inn), Hughes sparked an intense round of speculation and opened the door for corporations to get into the gambling business. Such companies, sensitive about their image, tried to push smaller and less savory operators aside (see our close-up in this chapter).

The MGM Grand was built in 1973, and its 2,100 rooms made it the largest hotel in the world at that time. With funding from the deep

INSIDERS' TIP

Want to get rich at Las Vegas casinos? More likely, your play will help to build new resorts and pay local taxes. Clark County casinos generate nearly $6 billion in taxable revenue each year.

The Rise and Fall of the Mob

Vice and dice . . . they roll together. And from the beginning, organized crime has had its hand in Las Vegas. Called an "open town," Las Vegas became a magnet for syndicate bosses from Kansas City, Chicago, Cleveland, New York and other Eastern cities. Sniffing easy money, the underworld families saw new profit centers in this new city.

In the late 1930s, Meyer Lansky and Benjamin "Bugsy" Siegel consolidated a bookmakers' national network in Las Vegas, meaning that betting lines and cash were wired through town. After dabbling in downtown casinos, Siegel set his sights on creating a full-fledged resort. Construction of the Flamingo began in 1946, but cost overruns taxed the patience of his mob financiers. When the casino finally opened and immediately flopped, Siegel was a marked man. Suspected of siphoning money for himself, he was gunned down at his Beverly Hills home, and a Las Vegas legend was born.

The mob didn't skip a beat. Phoenix boss Gus Greenbaum took over the Flamingo, and the second opening was a big success. The $5 million property was years ahead of its time as the state's first full-service resort. Others would quickly spring up, bankrolled by organized crime and the Teamsters' Central States Pension Fund.

Union president Jimmy Hoffa wielded the $167 million Teamsters fund. Money supported casino owner Moe Dalitz's enterprises along The Strip, including the Dunes hotel. The fund helped purchase golf courses and real estate, and even built Sunrise Hospital, the city's first private-care facility.

Convicted in 1964 on mob-related charges, Hoffa disappeared after he served his time. But the "wise guys" were running free in Las Vegas.

The Thunderbird, the Stardust, the Aladdin and other smaller joints were well-known fronts for the mob. Ostensibly regulated by Clark County officials, the operators

— continued on next page

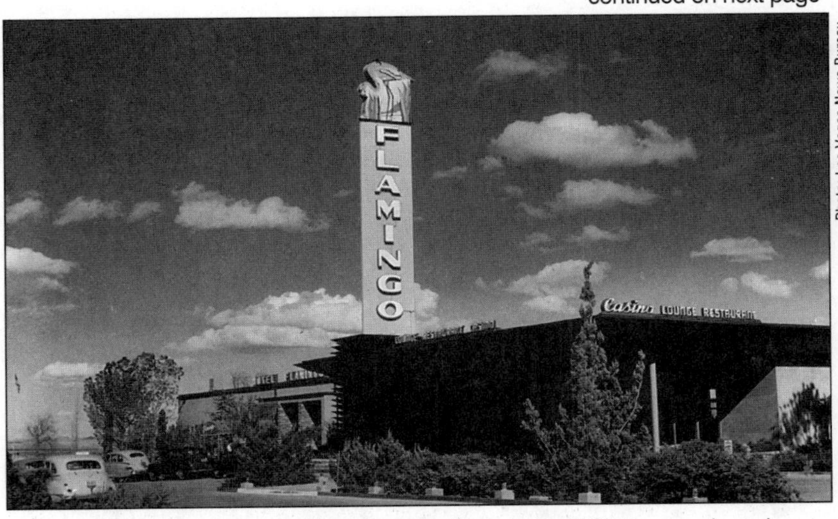

Photo: Las Vegas News Bureau

Bugsy Siegel's Flamingo Hotel got off to a troubled start in 1947. Its second opening, after Siegel was gunned down, was a big success.

routinely skimmed profits and flaunted the law. As depicted in the recent movie *Casino*, gangland activity included shakedowns, beatings, bombings and, of course, slayings. The streets of the "open city" at times resembled a shooting gallery as rival Mafia families settled scores.

News accounts of organized crime caught the eye of Tennessee Sen. Estes Kefauver. His organized-crime investigation zeroed in on the corruption and forced the state to step up its regulatory presence. The threat of intervention (not to mention taxation) by Washington was to be avoided like the plague. With millions of dollars pouring through casinos each year, it behooved the state to take control and ensure that it got its share of the action.

In 1960, the State of Nevada compiled its first List of Excluded Persons, popularly known as the Black Book. The original issue named 11 people who were barred from casinos, and consorting with known hoodlums was a sure way to fall into disfavor with state gaming regulators. Among those on the list was Mafia chieftain Sam Giancana. When Frank Sinatra hosted Giancana at Lake Tahoe's Cal-Neva Lodge in 1963, the singer effectively aced himself out of any casino ownership opportunities.

Sinatra and Las Vegas' burgeoning Italian-American community were a source of pride and frustration. The "chairman of the board," as Sinatra fashioned himself, was a big hit on The Strip. He and other top entertainers were earning $100,000 a week, a record-setting amount in those days. His crowd brought glitz and excitement as they gamboled and gambled along The Strip. But there was a darker side. The entourage included the flotsam and jetsam of society, heightening concerns about corruption and illicit activity.

Nevada cultivated the bad-boy image. Politicians accepted free rooms, booze and prostitutes from mob-operated casinos. Crime families placed their people into innocuous-sounding positions at hotels, thereby circumventing the rigorous employment screenings required for top-level jobs. In reality, the titles were meaningless. In some cases a food and beverage manager would be running the entire property. The result: The mob was raking in a minimum of $10,000 a day from some of the larger casinos.

In an effort to untangle and expose these backroom dealings, two governors in the '60s and early '70s beefed up Nevada's policing powers. Gov. Grant Sawyer refined the investigative and enforcement arms of the Gaming Control Board by creating a State Gaming Commission with wide-ranging authority to approve or reject gambling licenses. Gov. Paul Laxalt followed by pushing through a law permitting corporate licensing of gambling operations — hitherto not allowed. This brought the strict eye of the U.S. Securities Exchange Commission into the regulatory picture.

Billionaire Howard Hughes attempted to clean up the casinos he purchased. He hired straight-arrow, college-trained executives. He marshalled large security forces armed with the latest surveillance gadgets. Ultimately, however, his efforts failed. His money kept disappearing.

Despite the efforts of state regulators in the '60s and '70s, reputed mobsters managed to keep their gaming licenses. Front men such as Allen Glick, a San Diego businessman, were installed at resorts such as the Stardust. The real operators were in the shadows.

Eventually, though, the influence of corporate America began to loosen the mob's grip on casinos. In the 1980s these companies began implementing tighter cash accounting rules in their gambling halls. This gave state regulators the impetus to insist on the same statewide. Wall Street sharpies dictated that profit margins were to be rated and analyzed as never before. No one, including wise guys, would be allowed to drag down the bottom line. In 1993 Hilton Corp. razed Bugsy Siegel's fortress-like suite, with

— continued on next page

its false stairways and bulletproof office. The mob, it seemed, was no match for the likes of MGM, Bally and Circus Circus.

America, too, was changing Las Vegas. Amid the brighter lights and the hordes of tourists, the city was becoming a family destination. Mob mayhem was no longer part of the program. The business that Bugsy started was now under new ownership.

---

pockets of well-known corporations, such as Hilton, and local start-ups like Circus Circus, gambling projects have been getting bigger ever since. In 1990, Circus Circus opened the Excalibur with 4,032 rooms to claim the distinction of being the world's largest. In 1994, a new MGM Grand was built with 5,005 rooms, and the hotel recaptured the world's-largest honors.

Free of the slow-growth ordinances enacted by its northern neighbor Reno, Las Vegas boomed unabated. While burnishing its reputation as an entertainment capital, it became home to a growing legion of full-time residents. Sunny skies, cool casinos and no state income tax have made Las Vegas the country's fastest growing city.

In 1995 Clark County surpassed the 1 million population mark, attracting newcomers at the rate of 4,000 to 5,000 a month. Tract home developments sprawled toward the mountains, giving Las Vegas the feel of a new Los Angeles. In fact, nearly half of the new southern Nevadans came from recession-wracked Southern California in the 1990s.

One of the newest chapters in Las Vegas history is being written by Steve Wynn. Arriving in the late '60s from New Jersey, the son of an East Coast gambler is credited with taking Las Vegas gaming to the next level. With financing from junk-bond king Michael Milken, Wynn built The Mirage for $610 million and set new standards for opulence and cash flow. He is now erecting the $1.3 billion Bellagio resort. It will rise on the land once occupied by the Dunes.

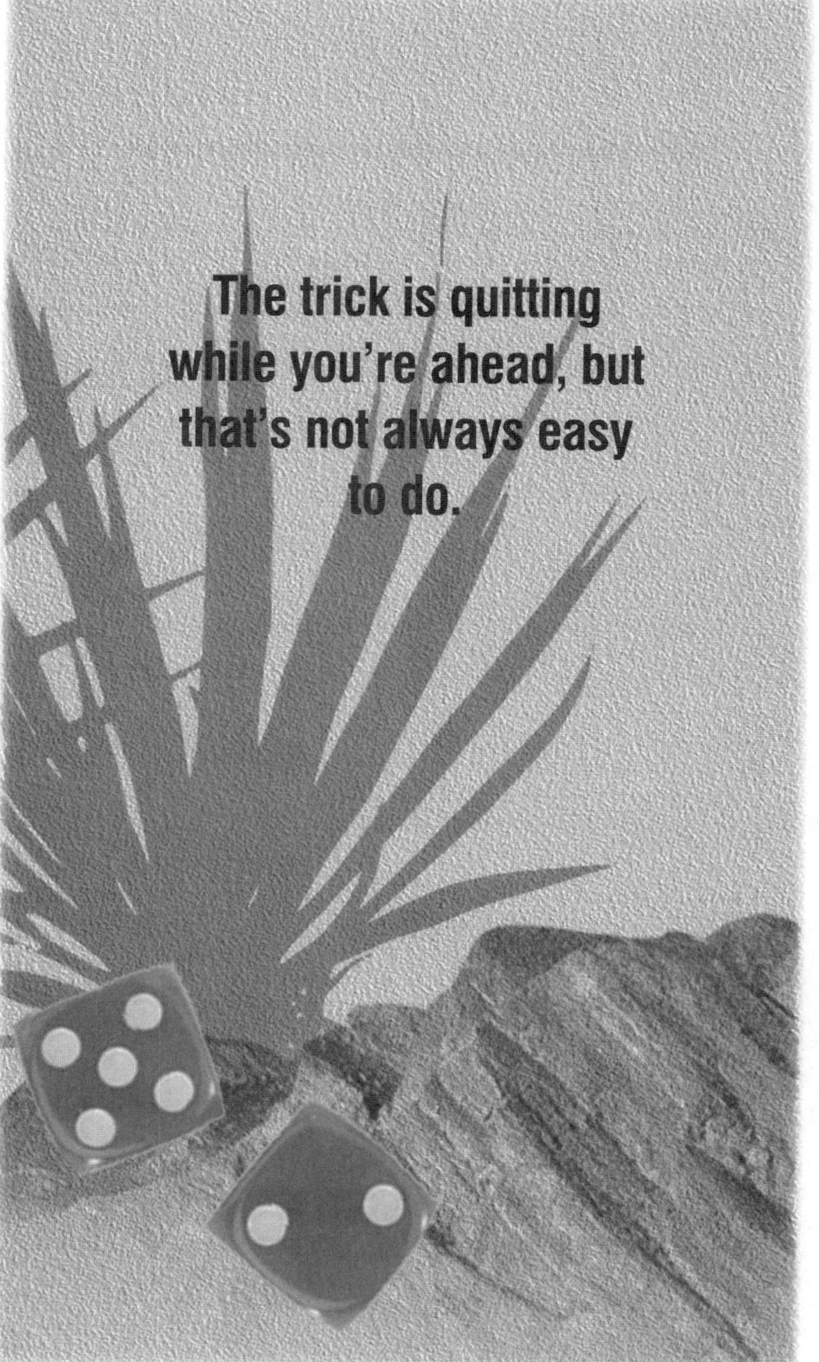
The trick is quitting
while you're ahead, but
that's not always easy
to do.

Gaming Guide

There's never been anything subtle about a Las Vegas casino. When Monte Carlo opened its first casino in 1879, Sarah Bernhardt recited a symbolic poem. The debut of Las Vegas' first modern gambling resort featured Abbott and Costello at the Flamingo Hotel in 1946. And it's been a comedy of manners ever since.

While the city's casinos have remained an outrageous sanctuary of fantasy, luxury and utter madness, they have evolved from rooms of green-felt craps and blackjack tables to incredible electronic arcades. The Caesars Palace casino, for instance, has 12 craps tables, 64 blackjack tables, 13 roulette wheels, eight baccarat tables, two Big 6 wheels — and 2,000 slot machines! See our Independent Casinos chapter or our Gaming Resorts and Accommodations chapter for information on specific casinos in Las Vegas.

The result is a sort of high-tech fairyland with electrified sights and sounds that relentlessly hammer the senses, all the while beckoning visitors to defy the odds and take a shot at becoming a winner, if not an instant millionaire.

Instant millionaires? As electronic games have evolved, so has the size of their jackpots. It's not uncommon for slot jackpots to reach into the millions of dollars. Some of the more popular ones include Megabucks, High Rollers, Fabulous Fifties and Dollars Deluxe. While most pay their awards in installments (usually over 20 years), one jackpot, Cool Millions, pays the first million instantly.

All Las Vegas casinos deal in the same basic commodity: a chance to beat the odds. But one thing every astute gambler understands is that winning is a hit-and-run proposition. Because the casino enjoys a statistical advantage in every game, the longer you expose yourself to it, the greater your chance of losing.

The house advantage is the result of a combination of things — the odds or percentages inherent in the game, rules tailored to favor the casino, payoffs at less than actual odds, or predetermined payoffs like those in slot machines. The casino's edge may be small — as in baccarat and sports betting — or enormous — as in keno and the wheel of fortune. But it generates billions of dollars a year in gambling profits.

If the casino has an advantage in every game, why gamble at all? Well, gambling can be fun and exciting, and it's now recognized as a viable form of entertainment. In rare instances it can be profitable. The casino's advantage plays out over the long run, over a large number of events, bets or games. But dramatic fluctuations in lady luck can occur over a short span, and people actually win.

The trick is quitting while you're ahead, but that's not always easy to do. It's difficult to leave the blackjack or craps table in the middle of the evening, even though you've doubled your initial bankroll. It's also difficult to stop playing a slot or video poker machine, especially after you've hit some pretty substantial jackpots. There's excitement in watching the machine light up and in hearing the coins pour into the metal tray.

But to be successful you must understand that no matter how well the cards are falling, no matter how hot the dice, no matter how "loose" the slot machines, the trend will eventually reverse itself. And when it does, you must have the will power to recognize the change in fortune and to react to it by altering or stopping play.

Most visitors come to Las Vegas with the intention of making their bankroll last as long as possible. They do this by finding a game in which they lose at a slow pace. If that's entertainment, fine. But why not play the games, and if you get lucky and win a jackpot or two, take a break from the casino. Do some shopping or sightseeing or find a magazine and relax by the pool. You might find that coming home with your "mad money" intact actually made the trip more fun.

Anatomy of a Casino

At virtually every Las Vegas resort, the casino is the hotel's focal point. Oftentimes you can't even reach the front desk without passing through the casino, which gives first-time visitors the impression they've landed in the middle of a prison riot. But, believe it or not, there's method to the madness taking place around you. Here's a quick tour of what to look for in a Las Vegas casino, how to get around and how to get the most out of it.

First of all, you must be at least 21 years old to gamble in Las Vegas. Any underage person caught gambling or loitering in a casino will be asked to leave and, more importantly, if he or she wins a jackpot the casino won't pay it! Be sure to have valid identification when gambling because casinos are carding players more frequently than ever before. The reason? The state Gaming Control Board has begun assessing heavy fines on casinos that allow underage gambling.

You'll also need your I.D. if you hit a substantial slot jackpot. The IRS requires a W2G form to be filled out on all jackpots of $1,200 or more, so the casino will ask you for two forms of identification, usually a driver's license and Social Security card. Nonresident aliens are subject to a withholding tax of 30 percent to be deducted from the jackpot before payment.

Even if you're not a big-time gambler, you should know about the **main cashier**, which is also called the main cage by casino personnel. If your luck is good, you'll spend a lot of time there, redeeming chips, coins and tokens for cash. You can also establish credit, cash checks and purchase coins or tokens for play in slot machines. The cage, however, won't sell you chips, which you must purchase from the dealers when you "buy in" at the various tables.

In addition to the main cage, most casinos have other satellite cashiers or **change booths** where you can purchase coins for play in slot machines or redeem your overflowing buckets of quarters for cash. To keep the machines humming, cashiers on wheels or "change persons" usually circulate throughout the casino selling coins to slot players.

Every casino in Las Vegas is required to have an electronic surveillance system commonly called the **eye in the sky**, which monitors and records activity in the casino. The number of TV cameras hidden in the ceiling under plastic bubbles may be as few as four at a small place like the Key Largo Casino or as many as 100 at the Las Vegas Hilton. The video cams are connected to VCRs that tape every game and bank of slot machines in the house. The tape recordings, which are saved for three days, are used as a check against cheats, thieves and dishonest employees. They are also used to investigate complaints from customers and settle disputes between gamblers.

Nearly every casino has a **slot club**, which awards its members freebies, including cash, for a required amount of play. Ordinarily, slot club members accumulate points while playing, and then redeem their points for cash, complementaries, room discounts, merchandise or other benefits. Although the amount of trade-off between coins played and points earned varies, a typical slot club may award 15 to 20 points for every $100 played through a machine. Note that this does not mean you have to shell out $100. If you spend $5 worth of coins on a machine that continues to spit it back in small amounts so you can continue playing, you are credited with the amount of coins that pass through the machine, which could be much more than your original stake of $5.

Using the same example, the player would be able to begin redeeming points when he or she reaches 100 points and at that time get $1 back. As you can see, it takes considerable play to build up the points in a slot club. The slot club tracks its members' play with a plastic card, which must be inserted into the machine before you begin play. There's no cost to join a slot club, and many players sign up at several casinos.

The same principle of accumulating points at the machines is often available to players at the table games. What was once offered only to so-called high rollers is now available to average gamblers. In fact many slot clubs allow their members to simply present their cards at the blackjack or craps table in order to accumulate points.

Most casinos have hosts and hostesses or a promotions desk. The hosts are like floating concierges who cater to the wishes of the casino players and promote the casino's programs. These can include play for points, contests and special events. The hosts and hostesses also serve as representatives for the casino's slot clubs. If there are no hosts and hostesses on the casino floor, you can check in at the **promotions booth** and find out about the slot club and other programs.

Nearby you may find a **redemption booth**. But rather than offering salvation for your soul, the redemption booth gives out prizes and other gifts when you redeem your slot points. They also often give away coupons that are good for discounts in the casino, restaurants and box office.

You can expect to find automated teller machines (ATMs) for Plus, Cirrus or Instant-Teller networks throughout most casinos. The In Casino Cash and ATM systems are part of the Instant Teller, Star, Plus and Inn systems. These also accept Visa, MasterCard and American Express for a $1 to $2 service charge.

Don't expect to see any clocks in the casino. The hotel executives want their customers for the duration, so clocks are never part of the decor. The same is true for windows: You won't glimpse a sunset through a plate-glass window because the casinos want time to stand still during the gambling experience.

The casino bosses even went so far several years ago to try out a type of perfume that was supposed to make the gambling experience so pleasant you wouldn't want to leave your seat at the roulette wheel. But saner heads prevailed, if not the Food and Drug Administration, and the system was scrapped.

Casino Etiquette

It's natural to be confused by all the fast action in a Las Vegas casino. After all, most newcomers have little or no gambling experience, except for their Friday night poker games or office football pools. While there are no hard-

and-fast rules of conduct, these guidelines will help you enjoy your casino experience.

Perhaps the most intimidating area of the casino is the pit, where you'll find clusters of blackjack tables, roulette wheels and other table games. The area behind the tables is reserved for pit bosses (supervisors) and other casino personnel, so avoid walking into these areas unless invited by the bosses. While dealers will be willing to explain the games to you, it would be helpful to review the rules of the more popular games (listed later in this chapter) ahead of time or attend one of the free lessons offered by the larger casinos.

Most table games — blackjack, poker, craps, roulette and baccarat — use chips for play, so you must buy in, that is, purchase chips for cash or a marker (credit voucher). The chips come in various denominations starting at $1. These can be used at different games and may be redeemed for cash at any time. When choosing a table game, always check the minimum table bet, which is usually displayed on a small plate. For instance, the casino's blackjack tables may have minimums ranging from $5 to $500 a hand. Generally, the table minimums are higher on The Strip than at downtown casinos.

Feel free to ask the dealer for help during the game. Besides explaining rules, odds or procedures, dealers will often advise the proper strategy, such as when to hit, stand or double down in blackjack. If a dealer is rude or unwilling to help, find another table or leave the casino. You should never be made to feel embarrassed just because you're a newcomer. Playing the slots is a lot simpler than gambling at the tables: You can play at your own pace, move around freely and never have to confront dealers, bosses and other gamblers. Well, almost never. Despite the hundreds if not thousands of machines in a casino, you may find some patrons playing more than one machine at a time. The casinos are divided in their policy of whether to allow one player to monopolize more than one machine, but don't expect a casino to tell a customer to stop gambling. Many more disputes among players arise when one leaves a slot machine — expecting to come back — and returns to find someone else playing the machine. The common practice to reserve a machine is to place a coin cup or bucket on the seat, but there's no guarantee other players will honor or recognize this significance. If you must leave a machine, ask a casino worker, such as a floor person or change person, to watch your machine for you. They seldom refuse this courtesy. If you want a break for dinner but feel attached to your particular machine, ask the floor person to shut it down until you return. This is not an uncommon practice if the machine won't be inoperative for more than hour or two. Under no circumstances should you leave a machine unattended when you have accumulated credits on it, nor should you leave buckets of coins or other valuables in the tray below the machine. There are scavengers looking for loose coins or unattended machines with unplayed credits.

Tipping is common in a casino, but it is never a requirement. Instead, it should always be a reward for friendly, quality service. When tipping at the tables, you can tip the minimum bet or place an extra bet for the dealer. For slot winners, the common practice is to tip the change person or whomever else you deem worthy (a cocktail server, casino host, etc.) an amount equal to 5 percent to 10 percent of your jackpot.

Glossary of Casino Terms

Action: Having a wager on the outcome of an event, usually a sporting event. Players are said to be in action when they have a bet riding on the game, race or fight.

Betting right: In craps, betting with the shooter that the dice will pass.

Betting wrong: In craps, betting against the shooter that the dice won't pass.

Boxman: In craps, the casino executive seated between the standing croupiers who oversees the game.

Buy-in: The amount of cash used to purchase chips before entering a table game: blackjack, poker, craps, roulette, etc.

Cage or casino cage: The main cashier

where you can redeem chips, coins and tokens for cash, establish credit or cash checks.

Carousel: A group of slot machines, usually of the same type and coinage, and often connected to a common progressive jackpot.

Change color: Exchanging casino chips for larger or smaller denominations. For instance, changing 20 red ($5) chips for one black ($100) chip.

Checks: A casino term for the chips or tokens used in table games.

Chips: The casino's tokens issued in various denominations and used in lieu of cash at the gambling tables.

Come out roll: In craps, the first roll of the shooter before a point has been established.

Comp: Short for complimentary, designates the freebies extended usually from the casino to players: drinks, meals, shows, rooms, etc.

Credit line: The amount of credit a player is allowed to gamble with.

Credits: In a slot machine, the amount of coins accumulated by the player. A common tourist mistake is leaving a machine before cashing out your coins or playing off the credits!

Drop: The total money (cash, chips and marker) taken in by a table, from the drop box, which receives all the money taken in at a table.

European Wheel: In roulette, a wheel with only a single "0" position, as opposed to American wheels with "0" and "00" positions. Players have better odds on European wheels, which are rare in Las Vegas.

Even money: When the odds are 1-to-1, and the payoff equals the amount wagered.

Eye in the sky: The casino's surveillance system that monitors and video tapes the casino floor.

Grind house or grind joint: A casino with mostly low table minimums and small denomination slot machines.

High roller: A big bettor, sometimes called a whale or premium player.

House advantage: The casino's advantage on a bet, that is, the difference between the casino's payoff and the actual odds, expressed as a percentage. For instance the casino enjoys a minimum 5.26 percent advantage on roulette, which means the payoffs are at least 5.26 percent less than the actual odds. The house advantage is 0 percent when the payoff is equal to the actual odds.

Juice: Influence; if you have friends in high places, you have access to juice. If you are in high places you have juice.

Junket: An organized tour of gamblers who receive low travel rates in exchange for gambling a predetermined amount of money.

Las Vegas Strip or The Strip: The section of Las Vegas Boulevard from Sahara Avenue south to Hacienda Avenue, which includes most of the major Las Vegas casino-resorts.

Loose slot: A slot machine that pays off freely.

Marker: Promissory notes or IOUs signed by players who have credit in casinos. Ordinarily, players exchange markers for chips at the table, not at the casino cashier.

Payoff, payout: The payment of a winning bet to a player, most often from a slot machine.

Pit: The area reserved for casino personnel inside a group or cluster of gaming tables.

Pit boss: The casino executive who oversees the action from inside the pit. He's sometimes called a pit bull.

Progressive or progressive jackpot: The payout on a machine or group of machines that increases with each coin played. Some progressive jackpots reach into the millions of dollars.

Rated players: Gamblers whose bets are tracked by the casino in order to determine the amount of complementaries that will be extended to them.

RFB: Short for room, food and beverage, and refers to complementaries extended to players who are rated by the casino.

Shill: A casino employee who gambles at the tables with the house's money, thus creating the semblance of action.

Tip: A gratuity given to a casino employee.

Toke: Casino personnel's term for a tip.

Vigorish or vig: Generally, the house advantage on a bet, expressed as a percentage. In sports betting, the vigorish is the amount the casino charges to place a bet: The average vigorish on a football bet is 10 percent, which means you must bet $1.10 to win $1.

Wise guy: This used to tab members of organized crime, but more recently casinos use it to refer to astute sports bettors.

Games People Play

Blackjack

Blackjack or "21" is the casino's most popular table game. The rules are simple to learn, and, if sound basic strategy is followed, the player can greatly reduce the casino's edge and possibly swing it in his favor.

The game is played with one or more decks of 52 cards. Cards are valued at face value, except for the aces, which can be valued at either one or 11 points. Face cards — jacks, queens and kings — are valued at 10 points.

The object of the game is to beat the dealer. A player does this by having a higher valued hand than the dealer, while not "busting" by exceeding 21 points. If either the player or dealer busts, the other wins automatically. A major advantage for the dealer is that the player must play his hand first. Even if a player busts and the dealer subsequently busts as well, the player loses. Ties are a standoff or "push," and neither wins.

If either the player or dealer is dealt an ace and 10-valued card, he has a blackjack. A blackjack is an immediate winner and pays the player at 3-2 odds. Other winning hands are paid at 1-1 or even money. If both the dealer and player are dealt a blackjack it is a standoff.

The play begins with the dealer distributing two cards to each player and two to himself, dealt one at a time with the first card going to the player. One of the dealer's cards is exposed to help the player decide whether to hit (take another card) or stand (play the ones he has). In addition to standing pat, the player may double down his hand or split pairs.

By doubling down, the player doubles his initial bet and accepts one additional card to complete his hand.

By splitting pairs, the player also doubles his bet but separates his two identical cards into two separate hands, to which he draws additional cards. Each hand is played separately, taking hits as needed. The only exception is that a player who splits aces is only allowed to take one additional card for each ace. If that additional card is another ace, however, the player can split again.

Doubling down and splitting are powerful techniques to increase your chances of winning.

The Rules

1. The player can double down on his first two cards. Some casinos allow doubling down only if the player's two-card total is 10 or 11. This is a disadvantage to the player, and he or she should find a casino where doubling is not so restricted.

2. The player can split any pair.

3. After splitting pairs, the player may not double down, except at a few casinos.

4. The dealer must stand on hands totaling 17 or higher. Some casinos, notably in downtown Las Vegas, require their dealers to hit a "soft" 17. A soft hand is one that contains an ace. Again, this is to the player's disadvantage; it's better to play against a dealer who will not hit a soft 17.

5. Insurance pays 2-1. When the dealer's up card is an ace, he or she will offer the player a chance to insure himself against the dealer's possible blackjack. The player can risk half his original bet and win 2-1 should the dealer hold a blackjack (the net result, if the dealer holds a blackjack, is the player breaks even). This is usually a bad bet, even when the player holds a blackjack of his own, because the casino is offering 2-1 for an event that should pay 9-4. Unless a player is an expert and counts cards, he or she should not take the insurance.

Basic Strategy

The basic winning strategy for Blackjack, based on computer-generated studies, is given below. It tells the player when to hit, stand, double down or split pairs, depending on the dealer's up card. Using basic strategy is not prohibited in casinos, and many dealers are allowed or even encouraged to advise gamblers as to how to properly play. In fact, most casinos don't mind if players use a "crib sheet" that charts the strategy.

Hit or Stand: With a hard hand (no aces) against the dealer's 7 or higher, the player should hit until he reaches at least 17. With a hard hand against the dealer's 4, 5 or 6, stand on a 12 or higher; if against dealer's 2 or 3, hit a 12. With a soft hand hit all totals of 17 or lower. Against a dealer's 9 or 10, hit a soft 18.

Doubling Down: Double down on any 11, no matter what the dealer shows. Double down on 10 when dealer shows anything except a 10 (dealer's "10" also includes face cards). Double down on 9 when dealer shows 2, 3, 4, 5 or 6. Double down on soft 17 (Ace-6) if dealer shows 2, 3, 4, 5 or 6. Double down on soft 18 (Ace-7) if dealer shows a 3, 4, 5 or 6. Double down on soft 13, 14, 15 or 16 against dealer's 4, 5 or 6.

Splitting Pairs: Always split aces and 8-8. Never split 5-5 or 10-10. Split 4-4 against the dealer's 5 or 6. Split 9-9 against the dealer's 2, 3, 4, 5, 6, 8 or 9. Split 7-7 against the dealer's 2, 3, 4, 5, 6 or 7. Split 6-6 against the dealer's 2, 3, 4, 5 or 6. Split 2-2 and 3-3 against the dealer's 2, 3, 4, 5, 6 or 7.

Craps

Craps is one of the most exciting and fastest games in the casino. And, because of its low house percentage against the player, it provides a chance to win large sums of money in relatively short periods of play.

It is also one of the least understood games, mainly because of the complicated table layout. The game, however, is very simple. A player or "shooter" rolls a pair of dice that determines the outcome of his and other players' bets.

The shooter's first roll of the dice is called the "come out" roll. If he rolls a 7 or 11 he, and those who bet with him, win. If he throws a 2, 3 or 12, that is "craps," and he and the other players who bet with him, lose.

If the dice turns up a 4, 5, 6, 8, 9 or 10, that number becomes the shooter's established "point," and he must continue rolling the dice until he makes the number again in order to win. If the shooter rolls a 7 before his point, he "sevens out" and loses.

Although the object of the game is very simple, craps is complicated by the myriad of bets available to the players. Most of those bets are heavily weighted in favor of the casino, and should be avoided.

The Bets

Pass Line: By playing the Pass Line, you're betting with the shooter. An immediate 7 or 11

INSIDERS' TIP

The seats at the gaming tables are reserved for players; friends and observers may watch the action while standing behind the players.

on the come out roll wins; a 2, 3 or 12 loses. If a point is established (4, 5, 6, 8, 9, or 10), it must be repeated before a 7 is thrown in order to win. The Pass Line bet pays even money and, with a house advantage of 1.41 percent, is one of the best bets at the table.

Don't Pass: The Don't Pass bettor bets against the shooter. He therefore wins his bet if the come-out roll is a 2 or 3 (a 12 is usually a push), and loses if the shooter throws a 7 or 11. If the shooter establishes a point, a 7 must be thrown before the point is rolled again in order to win. This even-money bet has approximately the same house advantage of winning as the Pass bet.

Come and Don't Come Bets: These bets are identical to the Pass and Don't Pass bets, except that they can be placed only after a point has been established. That is, an immediate 7 or 11 is a winner; a 2, 3 or 12 loses, and any other number becomes an established point for the Come bettor. The reverse is true for the Don't Come bettor. In addition, you can place as many consecutive Come/Don't Come bets as you like, while you are limited to one Pass/Don't Pass bet. The importance of these bets is that they allow players to increase their chances of winning during any given roll of the dice. They offer the same odds as the Pass/Don't Pass bets.

Place Bets: A bet on any or all of the Place numbers (4, 5, 6, 8, 9 or 10) is a bet that the number or numbers will be thrown before a 7. The 4 and 10 pay at 9-5 odds; the 5 and 9 at 7-5 odds; and the 6 and 8 at 7-6 odds. Placing the 6 and 8 is a fairly good bet because the house edge is 1.52 percent. However, placing the 5 and 9 and the 4 and 10 are less attractive because the house edge jumps to 4 percent and 6.73 percent, respectively.

The Field: This is a one-roll bet that any number in the Field — 2, 3, 4, 9, 10, 11 or 12 — will be rolled. If any other number — 5, 6, 7 or 8 — is thrown, the bet is lost. The house advantage on this bet is nearly 6 percent and too great to recommend it.

Big 6 and Big 8: A bet on either the 6 or 8, or both, can be made at any time, and either must appear before a 7 is thrown in order to win. Because the bet only pays even money, instead of its true odds of 6-5, the house enjoys an advantage of 9.09 percent.

Proposition Bets: These bets, which include the Hard Ways and One-Roll Bets in the center of the layout, are all poor betting propositions. Because the house advantage varies from 10 percent to 17 percent, they should never be made.

Free Odds: Although there's nothing on the table to indicate the existence of this bet, it is one of the most advantageous to the player. It is available to all Pass/Don't Pass and Come/Don't Come bettors after a point has been established. Once the shooter establishes a point, a player can make a bet equal to his previous bet and receive true odds (instead of even money) if the point is made. This amounts to 2-1 on the 4 and 10; 3-2 on the 5 and 9; and 6-5 on the 6 and 8. If the casino offers "double odds," the player can double his previous bet. It's always to the player's advantage to make the free odds bet, especially at double odds, because it gives you the chance to win more money at correct odds when the shooter is on a "hot" roll. With single odds, the house edge is reduced to 0.8 percent; with double odds it's reduced further to 0.6 percent.

Winning Strategy

As with other casino games, the goal in craps is to capitalize on the relatively short cycle of streaks that invariably occur. These are marked by prolonged passes of the dice by a given shooter. That is, the shooter continues to roll, often times for many minutes, without sevening out.

You can take advantage of these hot streaks by playing the Pass Line, backing that bet with Free Odds bets and placing multiple Come bets, also with Free Odds.

Professional gamblers disagree on the number of come bets to place. The most aggressive players make Come bets on every roll until all the point numbers are covered. This gives them the opportunity to win many bets in a short period of time, provided the dice stay hot and the shooter continues to roll without hitting a 7.

But that method is too risky. A sound strategy calls for placing a maximum of two Come bets, which, coupled with the original Pass Line bets, give the player three numbers always working for him. When one of the points is made and his bet is paid off, the player

Craps is one of the fastest-moving and most exciting games in a casino.

places another Come bet to keep three numbers working.

To recap:

1. Bet the Pass Line and back up the bet with a Free Odds bet.

2. Make two additional Come bets, also taking the Free Odds bets.

3. Stop betting after three points have been established.

4. If one of the Come bets is won, immediately place another Come bet. Similarly, if the original Pass Line bet is won, make another Pass Line bet.

This system lets the player capitalize during a shooter's hot streak while minimizing his losses when the dice eventually turn cold.

Roulette

In the United States roulette has never gained the popularity it has in Europe. The game is played at a relatively slow pace, and the house advantage of 5.26 percent makes it a difficult game to beat. Another drawback to roulette is the American-style wheel, which has 36 numbers plus 0 and 00. In Europe, roulette wheels have just a single 0. However, if you're a diehard roulette player, you'll find a few European-style wheels in Las Vegas casinos. When you play on a single-zero roulette wheel, the house advantage drops by almost half to 2.7 percent.

The game is simple to play; a roulette dealer spins the wheel and waits for the ivory ball to land on a number. Bettors have the option to guess which number out of the possible 38 the ball will land on, bet on a combination of numbers or pick whether the number will be red or black.

The various roulette bets and their payoffs are listed below:

Red or black	1 to 1
Odd or even	1 to 1
Numbers 1-18 or 19-36	1 to 1
Any one number	35 to 1
Groups of 12 numbers	2 to 1
Groups of 6 numbers	5 to 1
Groups of 4 numbers	8 to 1
Groups of 3 numbers	11 to 1
Groups of 2 numbers	17 to 1
Group of 0, 00, 1, 2, and 3	6 to 1

Basic Strategy

Roulette bets can pay handsomely. Pick the right number and your $5 bet, at odds of 35-1, is worth $175. But coming up with a winner takes tremendous powers of intuition, or blind luck. Neither lends itself to a sound betting strategy.

Serious players — the few who actually exist — like to bet "zones" of numbers, that is, groups or columns, rather than a single number, and hope the winning number falls within their zone. The most popular zones are the first, second or third 12 numbers, or a column of 12 numbers.

Also popular, perhaps because of the increased action, is betting red or black. A word of encouragement for color bettors: Lord Jersey once won 17 consecutive, maximum bets on black while playing in Monte Carlo, or so the story goes, and retired to the English countryside and never gambled again in his life.

Baccarat

Baccarat (pronounced bak-eh-rah) is the most glamorous, if not mysterious, game in the casino. The playing tables are usually roped off, and the croupiers staffing them are typically dressed in tuxedos. Three croupiers service the game. The one in charge is the callman, who handles the cards, decides the draw and announces the winning hand. The other two, who remain seated throughout the game, pay off winning bets and collect losing bets.

Because of the Monte Carlo aura surrounding the game, most players are intimidated from participating. However, baccarat offers one of the best percentages in the casino, with a house advantage of less than 1.4 percent on "bank" and "player" bets.

The Play

The object of the game is surprisingly simple. Baccarat is played with multiple decks of standard playing cards. Two hands composed of two cards each are dealt — one for the "player" and one for the "bank." Players can bet on either hand. The winning hand is determined by the point totals of the respective hands. All 10s and face cards are valued at 0. The rest of the cards retain their face value (the ace counts as one).

If the two-card total exceeds 10 points, you simply count the last digit of the number as your score. For instance, if a hand contains a 6 and 8 for a total of 14, the hand is valued at 4. The winning hand, either the "bank" or "player," will have a higher total value than the other.

The Rules

The rules determining whether additional cards are drawn are complicated, but it is not necessary for the player to memorize them. The croupier will decide if and when a draw is necessary; the player is never required to make that decision. They are included here so the player will understand the reasons behind the croupier's action.

1. If either hand has a value of 8 or 9 (these scores are called "naturals"), no further cards are dealt. The higher of the two hands is declared the winner. Should both hands have the same value, a tie is declared and neither wins.

2. If neither hand is a natural, a set of complicated rules comes into play. They are illustrated in the accompanying chart, but again, the croupier will make the decisions on drawing cards. Basically, the player's hand will take a third card if its value is from 0 to 5. It must stand on 6 or 7. The bank's hand must draw if its value is from zero to 2. When the bank has a value of 3 or more, draw is determined by the printed rules.

3. A bet on the player's hand pays even money. But, because the bank hand has a slightly higher percentage of winning (50.7 percent), winning bets on the bank hand are subject to a 5 percent commission paid to the casino. (In practice, the bank bets are paid at even money, and the accumulated commissions are paid to the house at the end of the deal or when the player leaves the table.)

4. Players can also bet that the hands will end in a tie. This bet pays at odds of 8-1, but it is a poor bet because the house has an advantage of nearly 15 percent.

Basic Strategy

Because players cannot decide when to draw cards, there is no skill involved in playing baccarat. It is purely a game of chance. However, streaks do occur, and a winning strategy can take advantage of these cycles.

A sound winning strategy calls for placing bets on the bank hands. This surprises many players because bank bets are subject to the 5 percent commission. However, the bank should win 50.7 percent of the time. And the 5 percent commission is paid only on winnings and not on losing bets. So, a player has a slightly better advantage by playing the bank.

As with other tables, games such as blackjack and craps, flat bets will, at the very best, even out over the long run. To be successful at baccarat, you should increase bets after winning hands in order to take advantage of short streaks that often occur. Conversely, losing bets should never be increased.

A sound betting system for baccarat calls for increasing your bets after a previous win over a cycle of five hands, according to the following schedule:

1. An initial bet of one unit is made.

2. The second bet is three times the original bet.

3. The third bet is four times the original bet.

4. The fourth bet is five times the original bet.

5. The fifth bet is six times the original bet.

After the fifth bet, the cycle reverts to the original bet. Although this system calls for increasing bets in the ratio of 1-3-4-5-6, no bet beyond the second one is ever double the previous bet. This prevents the player from being wiped out by a losing bet.

Keno

Keno has one of the highest house percentages against the player — a minimum of 22 percent — yet the game remains popular. The reasons are that it is an inexpensive way to gamble — you can play a keno ticket for as little as 40¢ (most casinos have a $1 minimum ticket); and there's a possibility of hitting a huge jackpot.

Anyone who plays keno should think of the game as a form of lottery or bingo and not a serious form of gambling. Therefore, any money bet on keno should be for fun, without any great expectancy of return.

The Game

Keno is played on a blank ticket, which you obtain at the keno parlor or at other places throughout the hotel-casino. A player selects from one to 15 numbers out of a possible 80, and marks them on the ticket. The marks are called "spots," and the number of spots determine how much the ticket is worth.

The operator of the game turns on a machine that randomly selects 20 numbered balls out of the possible 80 and calls out the numbers. If the player's numbers match most or all of the numbers selected, he wins a payoff based on how many spots he marked, how many spots he hit or "caught," and how much he bet.

Most casinos offer keno at the rate of $1 per ticket. Some hotels in downtown Las Vegas offer lower prices, while some Strip resorts have a $1 minimum. The accompanying chart gives sample payoffs for a 70¢ keno ticket.

If a player has a winning ticket, he must present it to the keno operator before the next game begins. Failing to do so voids his winning ticket.

Basic Strategy

The most common keno ticket played is the straight ticket, on which a player marks from one to 15 numbers and bets 70¢ or a multiple of 70¢. Little thinking and planning is necessary to play a straight ticket.

But to maximize your chances of winning at keno, serious players should play a "way" ticket. It is called a way ticket because you place your numbers in groups that give you various combinations or ways of winning. With way tickets you can have more numbers working for you, and you don't have to catch all of them to hit a good payoff. Basically, a way ticket consists of three or more groups of equal numbers. Each group of numbers is circled, and they are counted in different combinations, which increase the possibility of winning.

For instance, suppose you wanted to play 12 numbers. If you marked the numbers on a straight 70¢ ticket and caught eight of them, you'd win $150. Now let's see what happens when you mark the same 12 numbers on a way ticket. Because all way tickets require three or more groups of equal numbers, we will divide the 12 numbers into three groups of

INSIDERS' TIP

Many resorts have eased their restrictions against cameras in the casino. Ask a casino host about the policy for taking photographs.

four. We could have also divided the 12 into four groups of three or six groups of two. The choice is yours. We do this on the ticket by marking the numbers, as we did on the straight ticket, then circling the three groups. What we now have is something different from the original 12-spot straight ticket. Counting two groups of numbers at a time, we now have three groups of eight numbers, or the equivalent of three 8-spot tickets.

These combinations are easier to understand if you refer to the sample ticket. If we call the circled groups A, B and C, they can be grouped together in only three possible combinations: AB, AC and BC. The result is three groups of eight numbers, or a "three-way eight-spot." The fraction 3/8 on the side of the ticket indicates the three-way eight-spot. Because you now have three chances of winning, the cost of the ticket is three times a straight ticket, or $2.10, but the potential payoffs, as you will soon discover, far outweigh the additional cost. Now if your same eight numbers hit, you are paid on the eight-out-of-eight payoff scale, or a whopping $12,500, instead of the $150 the eight out of 12 ticket would have paid.

This system of betting way tickets may sound complicated, but all casinos that offer the game supply booklets and schedules that can help you mark your tickets.

Caribbean Stud Poker

Originally developed for Caribbean cruise ships, Caribbean stud poker has become popular in Las Vegas because of its progressive jackpot, which often reaches into six figures. The game is based on five-card stud poker and played on a blackjack-style table.

Players are dealt five cards face down after placing their ante bets — a minimum of $5 in most casinos — and their $1 progressive ante, if they choose to play for the escalating jackpot, the value of which is displayed on an electronic reader board at the table. The dealer receives four cards face down and one card up. If the player doesn't like his cards, he may fold and surrender his ante bet. If he thinks he can win, he places a "call bet" equal to double his original ante.

The house has an advantage because the dealer must have an Ace/King or higher to continue play. If he doesn't, the hand is over, and the players who remained in the game are paid even money on their original ante, but their call bets are returned.

If the game continues and the player's hand fails to beat the dealer's, he loses the ante and call bets. But if the player's hand beats the dealer's, he's paid even money on his ante, plus a bonus amount on his call bet according to the following schedule:

Ace-King high, 1-1
One pair, 1-1
Two pair, 2-1
Three of a kind, 3-1
Straight, 4-1
Flush, 5-1
Full house, 7-1
Four of a kind, 20-1
Straight flush, 50-1
Royal flush, 100-1

Whether or not the player's hand beats the dealer's, he wins the following payouts if he bet the $1 to enter the progressive pool:

Flush, $50
Full house, $75
4 of a kind, $100
Straight flush, 10 percent of progressive pool
Royal flush, 100 percent of progressive pool

Let It Ride Poker

This variation of five-card stud is interesting in that players don't compete against the dealer or each other. Instead, they try to get a good hand by combining three cards dealt to them with the dealer's two "hole" cards. To help their cause, players can remove up to two-thirds of their original bet during play to reduce the risk when chances for a winning hand seem bleak.

Here's how it works: Players make three equal bets and are dealt three cards. Then the dealer receives two cards face down. If the player's not happy with his deal, he can remove one of his bets or let it ride.

The dealer then turns over one of his cards, which is counted as the player's fourth card, and the player must decide whether to withdraw his second bet or let it ride. In either case, the dealer then turns over his second card, and all the players lay down their cards. The play-

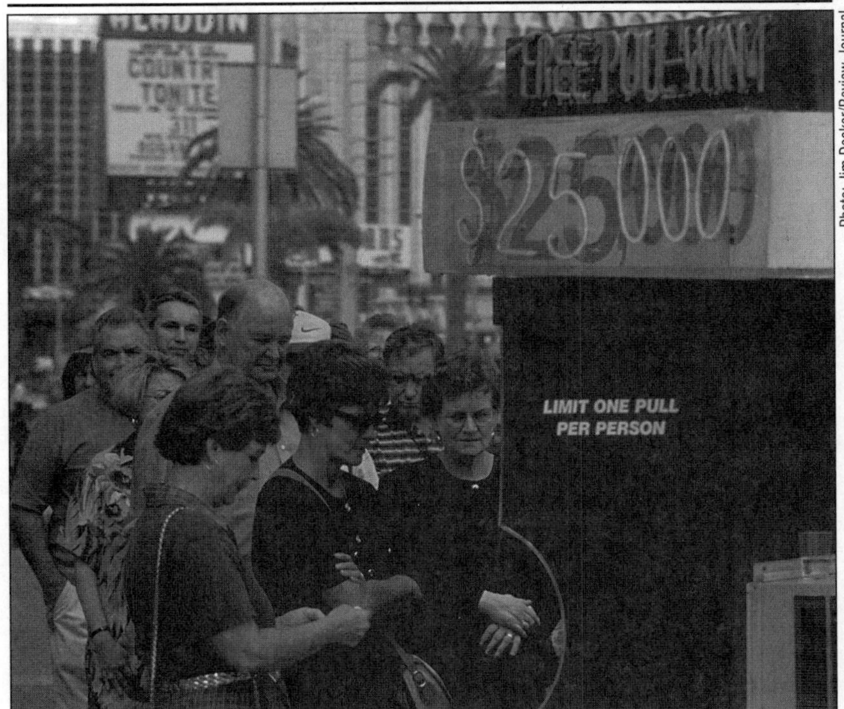

The free pull is a popular promotion designed to whet your appetite for the casino's slot machines.

ers' hands are determined by combining their three and the dealer's two cards. The minimum winning hand is a pair of 10s or better, which pays even money. If the player has a winning hand, he is paid on all his remaining bets according to the following schedule:

Pair of tens or better, 1-1
Two pair, 2-1
Three of a kind, 3-1
Straight, 5-1
Flush, 8-1
Full house, 11-1
Four of a kind, 50-1
Straight flush, 200-1
Royal flush, 1000-1

Pai Gow Poker

Despite its name, Pai Gow Poker bears little resemblance to its ancient Chinese namesake, which is played with 32 domino-like tiles. Rather, it's a kind of seven-card stud in which players arrange their cards into a five-card and a two-card hand, then try to beat the dealer's similarly arranged hand.

The game is played with a standard 52-card deck, and hands are ranked the same as traditional poker. After bets are placed, the dealer deals seven cards face down to the players and himself. Each player arranges his cards into a two-card and five-card hand, making sure the latter outranks the former. If the value of the five-card hand isn't higher than the two-card hand, the player automatically loses.

Because the game frequently ends in a tie with no money changing hands, players find they can play longer with a given bankroll than at blackjack, which actually enjoys a slightly lower house advantage.

Video Poker

No other casino game has gained the popularity that video poker has enjoyed over the past few years. In Las Vegas, electronic games — slot machines, video poker and video keno — now take up more than 50 percent of the casinos' floor space. And most of those machines are video poker machines.

There are several reasons for video poker's popularity. The first is that people can play at their own pace, without pressure from dealers, croupiers or other players. Secondly, there's an element of skill in video poker: Decisions must be made which, unlike slot machines, will determine whether and how much you can win. And, most important, there's always the chance of hitting a lottery-like jackpot.

The Play

The game of video poker is basically five-card draw poker. Machines offer several variations to the game, with more being developed every day, but the three that you should concentrate on are: 1) Jacks-or-better draw poker; 2) Joker's Wild poker; and 3) Deuces Wild poker.

Video poker machines are played with nickels, quarters, 50¢ pieces, $1 or $5 tokens. Most people play either the nickel, quarter or dollar machines.

The play begins after the player inserts coins into the machine. In order to win the highest royal flush jackpot or the progressive jackpot (which continues to grow as coins are played), always play the maximum number of coins, which is usually five.

After the coins are inserted, the machine "deals" five cards to the player, who must decide which cards, if any, to discard. You play your hand based on the payouts for winning hands, which are listed just above the video screen. Some machines indicate a possible winning hand, such as "Three of A Kind" on the video screen, but don't always rely on the machine to figure your hand for you.

After deciding which cards to keep, you press the "hold" button under each card, then press the "draw" button. (Some machines combine the deal and draw buttons into one.) The cards you've discarded will be replaced with new cards and, if you have a winning hand, its payoff will be indicated on the screen. At this point your winnings will drop into the coin bucket, or you will be given credit for the amount of the winning hand.

A note about credits: Credits allow you to play faster, without having to continually push coins into the slot. But always remember that the credits are yours, and you can collect your coins at any time by pushing the "Cash Out" or "Collect Winnings" button. It is not uncommon for players to move to another machine and forget their credits in the old machine.

Jacks-or-Better Basic Strategy

You'll have to decide between the two types of Jacks-or-Better machines: Full payout or progressive machines. The full payout pays a fixed amount of coins for a royal flush, usually 4,000 coins with the maximum bet. The progressive pays a jackpot that continues to grow until one of its machines hits the royal flush.

The progressive jackpot is higher than the fixed payout, but that is sometimes offset by lower payouts on the other hands, such as full houses and flushes. Always try to play a machine that pays the following jackpots for one coin bet:

Royal flush	800 coins
Straight flush	50 coins
Four of a kind	25 coins
Full house	9 coins
Flush	6 coins
Straight	4 coins
Three of a kind	3 coins
Two pair	2 coins
Jacks or better	1 coin

The primary objective at the Jacks-or-Better machine is to hit the royal flush. You'll also want to maximize your winnings if you don't hit the royal, which has odds of about 40,000 to 1 against it. In order to do that, follow this basic strategy:

1. Always draw one card to a royal flush, even if it means breaking a pat high pair (jacks or better), straight or flush. But don't break a pat straight flush for a one-card draw to a royal.

2. Draw two cards to a royal flush, unless you already hold a pat straight flush, straight, flush or three of a kind.

3. Draw one card to a straight flush unless you already hold a pat flush or straight.

4. Draw two cards to a straight flush unless you already hold a pat flush, straight, three of a kind, or high pair.

5. If you need one card for either a flush or a straight, draw for the flush.

6. If you need one card for either a flush or straight and already hold a high pair, keep the high pair.

7. If you need one card for a flush and already hold a low pair (10s or lower), break up the pair and draw for the flush. If you need one card for a straight and already hold a low pair, keep the low pair.

8. Always hold two pair and three of a kind.

9. Always draw to a low pair rather than holding a single high card.

10. Draw five cards when you don't have a single high card that can be paired and don't have four to a flush or straight.

Jokers Wild Basic Strategy

The addition of a joker to the deck results in more winning hands of three of a kind and higher but fewer high pairs because the even-money payoff is now on kings-or-better. Also, the overall winning payoff schedule is reduced, and the chances of hitting a "natural" royal flush are slightly less because of the addition of the 53rd card to the deck.

Nevertheless, Jokers Wild poker is very popular because hands such as straight flushes and four-of-a-kinds are more common, and the "mini-jackpot" paid on a five-of-a-kind is not out of reach. Once again, you must decide between the full payout and progressive machines. Whichever you choose, always try to find a machine that pays the following jackpots for one coin bet:

Royal flush (natural)	800 coins
Five of a kind	200 coins
Royal flush (joker)	100 coins
Straight flush	50 coins
Four of a kind	20 coins
Full house	7 coins
Flush	5 coins
Straight	3 coins
Three of a kind	2 coins
Two pair	1 coin
High pair (kings or aces)	1 coin

Because the joker complicates the playing strategy, it will be broken into two parts: hands dealt with a joker and hands dealt without.

Hands without the joker:

1. Always draw one card to a royal flush, even if it means breaking a pat high pair (kings or aces), straight or flush. But don't break a pat straight flush for a one-card draw to a royal.

2. Draw two cards to a royal flush, unless you already hold a pat straight flush, straight, flush or three of a kind.

3. Draw one card to a straight flush even if you already hold a pat flush or straight.

4. Draw two cards to a straight flush unless you already hold a pat flush, straight, or three of a kind.

5. If you need one card for either a flush or a straight, draw for the flush.

6. If you need one card for either a flush or straight and already hold a high pair, keep the high pair.

7. If you need one card for a flush or two cards for a straight flush and already hold a low pair (queens or lower), break up the pair and draw. If you need one card for a straight and already hold a low pair, keep the low pair.

8. If you're dealt two pair and one of them is a high pair, keep the high pair. If not, retain both.

9. Always draw to a low pair rather than holding a single high card.

10. Draw five cards when you don't have a single high card that can be paired.

Hands with the joker:

1. Always draw one card to a royal flush, unless you already hold a pat straight flush or joker royal flush.

2. Draw two cards to a royal flush, unless you already hold a pat straight flush, straight, flush or three of a kind.

3. Draw one card to a straight flush even if you already hold a pat flush or straight.

4. Draw two cards to a straight flush unless you already hold a pat flush, straight or three of a kind.

5. If you need one card for either a flush or a straight, draw for the flush.

INSIDERS' TIP

Many casinos offer incentives, such as a free dinner or the chance to win a car or other prizes, for simply cashing your paycheck at the main cage.

6. If you need one card for either a flush or straight and already hold a high pair, keep the high pair.

7. If you're dealt anything less than a high pair, or you can't draw to the hands listed above, hold the joker and draw four cards.

Deuces Wild Basic Strategy

Playing Deuces Wild can be a lot of fun because of the four wild cards circulating throughout the deck. When the deuces turn up, straight flushes, five of a kinds and even royal flushes become commonplace. But, because hands are easier to make, payoffs are substantially less, and the minimum hand for an even-money return is three of a kind.

But the game is popular because the wild cards ensure plenty of action, and the "mini-jackpot" paid on a hand of four deuces occurs quite frequently. Whether you're going to play a full payout or progressive machine, try to find one with the following minimum payouts:

Royal flush (natural)	800 coins
Four deuces	200 coins
Royal flush (deuces)	25 coins
Five of a kind	15 coins
Straight flush	9 coins
Four of a kind	5 coins
Full house	3 coins
Flush	2 coins
Straight	2 coins
Three of a kind	1 coin

Because the deuces are so important, playing strategy is evaluated according to the number of deuces dealt and the possible hands they may create.

Hands without deuces:

1. Always draw one card to a royal flush, even if it requires breaking a pat straight flush.

2. Always draw two cards to a royal flush, unless you already hold a pat straight, flush or straight flush.

3. Draw one card to a straight flush unless you already hold a pat flush or straight.

4. Draw two cards to a straight flush unless you already hold a pat flush or straight.

5. If you need one card for either a flush or a straight, draw for the flush.

6. If you need one card for either a flush or straight and already hold any pair, keep the pair.

7. Always hold three of a kind. When dealt two pair, discard one of them and draw.

8. Draw five cards when you don't have a pat hand and you don't have a chance at the hands listed above.

Hands with Deuces:

1. When dealt four deuces, hold all five cards to minimize the chances of "losing" one in the draw.

2. When dealt three deuces, hold them and draw for the fourth unless you already have a pat royal flush or five of a kind.

3. When dealt two deuces, hold them alone and draw unless you already have a pat four of a kind or better. Also, if you need one card for a royal or straight flush, draw for the one card.

4. When dealt a single deuce, hold any pat hand except break a flush or straight if you have a one-card draw for a royal or straight flush.

Poker

Casinos that offer poker simply provide the tables and dealers, and charge the players an hourly fee or take a percentage of the pot; players gamble against each other. The games usually offered are seven-card stud and Texas Hold 'Em.

Unlike video poker, where the goal is to get the highest paying hand, the object in "live" poker is to beat your opponents. Often times relatively weak hands, such as a pair of aces,

INSIDERS' TIP

Although slot machines are practically synonymous with Las Vegas, they first appeared in San Francisco's waterfront saloons during the 1890s. The originals were called Liberty Bells, and their players received free drinks when the winning symbols lined up.

two pair or three of a kind, are sufficient to win the pot. The skill in winning at poker lies in the ability to not only judge the quality of your hand but also that of your opponents' hands.

Although not every poker player is a novice-eating shark, many of the regulars are experts, so beginners should test the waters in low-stakes games or take a few lessons (most casinos offer them free of charge) before taking on the pros. Even after lessons, it's a good idea to watch a game for, say, 20 or 30 minutes, so you understand the method of play.

Seven-Card Stud

Most beginners start with seven-card stud. It's simple to learn, and the betting sequence provides for substantial pots. Play begins with the dealer giving each player two cards face down and then one card face up. The player with the lowest card showing makes the first bet. Other players can match the bet, increase the bet or withdraw.

Another card is dealt face up, and the player with the highest hand showing starts this round of betting. This is repeated until four cards have been dealt face up. The seventh and final card is dealt to the players who have remained in the game, and the final round of betting begins. During this "showdown," players may "raise" a bet up to three times. When the last bet is covered or "called," the dealer calls for the showing of hands, and the highest hand wins.

Recommended Strategy

Experts believe the first three cards dealt nearly always determine the outcome of the game. Therefore, playing the first three cards is the most important part of the poker game. If none of the combinations described below are dealt in the first three cards, drop out.

1. Three of a kind: The odds are about 400 to 1, but it does happen. Play the hand, covering all bets, but don't raise until the sixth card. You want the pot to build, as you have a winning hand in most games.

2. A pair of aces or kings: A good starting point, but watch the table for cards that will improve your hand. If they appear, your chances of winning are reduced. After the fifth card, if betting is heavy and you have not increased the value of your hand, drop out.

3. A pair of queens or jacks: An open pair (one card showing) reduces the value of your hand. Again, if betting is heavy after the fifth card and you have not bettered your hand, drop out.

4. Three cards to a straight flush: A very good start because there are several ways to improve it. Bet or raise during the first round. But after the fifth card, if you have not drawn a card to the straight flush, flush or straight, drop out.

5. Three cards to a flush: With this hand you should complete the flush in one out of six hands. Hold it until the fifth card is dealt. If you have not received another card in your suit, drop out.

6. A low pair (10s or less), three high cards (ace, king, queen or jack), or three cards to a straight: After the fourth card, if you have not increased the hand's value, drop out. You must have good cards to work with. Wait until the next hand; don't bet your whole bankroll on a losing hand.

Texas Hold 'Em

Texas Hold 'Em is considered the game of choice among professional poker players. High-stakes games are played daily in Las Vegas casinos, but the biggest of them all is the $1 million World Series of Poker held every year at Binion's Horseshoe in downtown Las Vegas.

The game is very similar to seven-card stud, except only two of the seven cards are dealt to the player; the other five are dealt face up and used collectively by all players.

The play begins with the dealer giving each player two face-down cards. The player next to the dealer is required to start the betting; the other players will match his bet or with-

INSIDERS' TIP

To ensure random rolls, the dice used at the craps tables are manufactured to a tolerance of 0.00002 inch (two ten-thousandths), or about 1/17 the thickness of a human hair.

draw. Incidentally, it's not uncommon in these high-stakes games to see players leave early, often after receiving only two or three cards.

The dealer discards or "burns" the top card from the deck, then deals three cards face up in the center of the table — this deal is called the "flop." Another round of betting is completed. The dealer then burns another card and adds a fourth face-up card to the center. Once again, there's a round of betting.

Finally, a fifth face-up card is dealt to the center. Each player can now determine his or her hand, based on the two face down cards and the five community cards in the center of the table. A final round of betting occurs, along with a showdown and revealing of hands. Once again, the highest hand wins.

Recommended Strategy

The strategy for Texas Hold 'Em is similar to seven-card stud, except it's based on your first two cards. If you're dealt none of the combinations below, drop out.

1. A pair of aces: This is the best starting hand. Hold and bet from the first round.

2. A pair of kings: Another very good hand. Hold and bet from the first round.

3. A pair of queens or jacks: Hold and cover all bets until the fourth up card is dealt. If you have not increased the value of your hand, drop out.

4. Two high value cards (ace, king or queen): Hold and cover all bets until the fourth up card is dealt. If you haven't bettered your hand, drop out.

5. Two high-value cards of the same suit: Hold until the fourth up card, and if you haven't increased the value of your hand, drop out.

6. A small pair (10s or less): Hold until the fourth up card; if you haven't increased your hand's value drop out.

Generally, if you haven't received a pair of aces or better — two pair, three of a kind, etc. — after the fourth up card is dealt, drop out. Seldom is a hand won by less than a pair of aces.

Big Six or Wheel of Fortune

There's no Vanna White but the Wheel of Fortune can be fun as a diversion from the more intensive table games. Also called Big Six because the ornate wooden wheel is six feet in diameter, the Wheel of Fortune is divided into nine sections, each of which is further divided into six pockets. This gives the wheel a total of 54 pockets, each holding one of the symbols you can bet on.

These symbols include U.S. currency bills of $1, $2, $5, $10 and $20 denominations and two other symbols, usually the casino's logo and a joker. The wheel symbols are reproduced on a table layout and determine the amount of the payoff when the wheel stops on them.

For instance, if the wheel stops on a $1 bill, the players who bet on the corresponding bill on the layout are paid 1-1. If it lands on the $10 bill, those players are rewarded at 10-1 odds. The two non-currency symbols, the casino logo and joker, usually pay at 40-1 or 45-1.

There's no standard wheel but most Big Six wheels have the following number of symbols:

Symbols	Chances
$1	24
$2	15
$5	7
$10	4
$20	2
House	1
Joker	1

Obviously, with odds of 53-1 of hitting either the house or joker symbol, the Wheel of Fortune is a difficult game to win. And with payoffs of only 40-1 or 45-1, the house advantage is among the highest in the casino.

Sports Betting

Sports betting is big business in Las Vegas, the only city in the country where you can legally bet on the outcome of a sporting event. But sports wagering doesn't generate the huge profits the machines and table games bring in. Casinos report that the "hold" at their sports books is less than 5 percent, which means they keep as profits about 5 percent of all the money wagered. In contrast, the hold for slot machines is more than 60 percent and about 15 percent for table games.

Because sports betting requires more skill than luck, astute gamblers and sports handicappers often find ways to beat the house. To compensate, sports books do everything possible to tilt the percentages in their favor.

The first method is charging a commission on a sports bet. Commonly referred to as the "house vigorish," the commission is usually 10 percent. This means that a bettor must risk $110 to win $100 betting football or basketball games. (If the bettor wins, the original $110 is returned to him.)

Sports books also set up point spreads to make predicting the outcome of a game more difficult. The point spread is the amount of points a favored team must overcome in order for a bettor to win his bet, used mainly for football, basketball and hockey betting.

For instance, if a football team is favored by seven points, the team must win by eight or more. If it wins by less than seven points, or loses outright, the bettor loses. If the final score falls on the number, say, 21-14, it is a "push" or tie and the bet is refunded.

The flip side is that underdogs receive the points and needn't actually win the game for the bettor to win his bet. In the above example, the underdog can either win the game, or lose by up to six points for its backers to win.

For baseball and hockey bets, the books set odds or a "money line." (For hockey, most players must contend with a point spread — usually not more than two goals — as well as a money line.)

The money line is a decimal version of betting odds. It is most commonly used in baseball and hockey betting, but it is frequently offered on football bets in lieu of the point spread. Instead of listing a team as a 3-2 favorite, or a 6-7 underdog, the sports books use a plus or minus dollar figure to represent a team's odds of winning.

A team with a negative money line is the perceived favorite and its payoff is less than the amount risked. Conversely, if a team has a plus money line, it is considered the underdog and pays more than the amount wagered.

For example, a team with a -1.80 money line means you must risk $1.80 in order to win $1, which, added to your original bet gives you a payoff of $2.80. If the team's money line were +1.80, a win is worth $1.80 for every $1 bet for a like payoff of $2.80, but at a risk of only $1.

If you're a mathematician you will have figured out that the plus money line represents odds on the underdog winning, and that the negative money line is the inverse of the odds on the favorite winning. In the above example, the odds on the underdog are 1.80 to 1, and the odds on the favorite are 1 divided by 1.80, or 0.55 to 1.

If this is as confusing to understand as it has been to write, just remember you have to bet the amount of the *minus* money line to win $1 (or multiples thereof), and that each $1 bet on a *plus* money line pays off at the stated amount.

Horserace Betting

Most sports books offer wagering on horseraces — thoroughbreds, quarterhorses and trotters — that are transmitted via satellite to Las Vegas from major tracks around the country. Since the early 1990s many of the race books joined the state's Pari-Mutuel Association, which pools bets made at the casinos with those at the participating racetracks. By pooling bets, casinos are able to book "exotic" bets such as the Trifecta or Pick Six offered at the racetrack, which often pay prizes in five and six figures. In addition to protecting casinos from paying huge jackpots from their own funds, pari-mutuel wagering provides casinos a steady return, usually a small percentage of the pool.

Some experts believe horserace betting is a poor proposition because of the taxes that reduce the pari-mutuel betting pool. For instance, of the total money wagered on California races, about 80 percent is returned as winning payoffs. The 20 percent taken for taxes, breeders' fees and operating costs is perceived as a "house advantage," far greater than any casino table game. However, veteran horse players believe handicapping — picking a winner — is a science and not a game of chance, and winning payoffs are just rewards for their knowledge and skill.

Las Vegas' resort hotels have evolved into today's fantasy-inspired mini-cities that offer all the amenities and services a visitor could want.

Gaming Resorts

Nothing characterizes Las Vegas like its gaming resorts. Ever since Bugsy Siegel built his Fabulous Flamingo in the middle of the desert, Las Vegas has been identified, if not defined, by its hotel-casinos.

When people think of Las Vegas, they think of its resorts: the Desert Inn's golf course and luxury bungalows, Caesars' fountains and toga-clad goddesses, Circus Circus' big top, the Sahara's camels, the Tropicana's swim-up blackjack table and the Mirage's volcano.

As the city has grown, so have the size and scope of its hotels. Starting with Siegel's modest pleasure dome and continuing with trend-setters like the Aladdin, Sahara and Caesars Palace, resort hotels have evolved into today's fantasy-inspired mini-cities that offer all the amenities and services a visitor could want. Those amenities — gambling, restaurants, nightlife and recreation — have become standard features. Look close and you'll see most hotels have a sprawling casino, a variety of restaurants and at least one production show or celebrity showroom. Recently, hoteliers have discovered tourists spend money outside the casino, so the trend is to add retail shops to the mix of hotel amenities. In addition, spas and health clubs typically charge for their various services — lockers, showers, massage, tanning booths, etc.

Because of hotels' focus on their attractions — the thrill rides, casino games, lounge singers and prime rib buffets — there is less emphasis on guest rooms. With a few exceptions whose rooms are a cut above the rest — Caesars Palace, Bally's, Desert Inn, Golden Nugget and Las Vegas Hilton — most gaming hotels maintain clean and modern guest rooms, but none that would rival the luxurious rooms in resorts in other parts of the country.

There are, of course, non-gambling hotels in Las Vegas that emphasize accommodations, including the Marriott, Courtyard, Alexis Park and St. Tropez, to name a few. These are included in our Nongaming Accommodations chapter, which also identifies quality motels and extended-stay accommodations.

In addition to the major resorts on The Strip and downtown, this chapter also will examine the increasingly popular "neighborhood" hotel-casinos, those built apart from the regular tourist centers. The idea behind these resorts was to provide a place where residents could gamble and otherwise entertain themselves in a less tourist-oriented environment. As it turned out, these hotels have become attractive to visitors as well because of their friendly atmosphere, budget rates and unique amenities.

Overall there are more than 102,000 hotel rooms in Las Vegas, the most of any American city. Plus the city is home to nine of the 10 largest (by room count) resort hotels in the world:

1. MGM Grand (5,005 rooms)
2. Ambassador City Hotel, Thailand (4,631 rooms)
3. Luxor (4,440 rooms)
4. Excalibur (4,032 rooms)
5. Circus Circus (3,744 rooms)
6. Flamingo Hilton (3,642 rooms)
7. Las Vegas Hilton (3,174 rooms)
8. Mirage (3,049 rooms)
9. Monte Carlo (3,004 rooms)
10. Treasure Island (2,900 rooms)

And the room count will continue to grow. New megaresorts — Bellagio, Paris, The Venetian and Marriott — are expected to be completed by the year 2000 and will add nearly 14,000 rooms to the city's total. With so many rooms it shouldn't be difficult to find a place to stay. But during some conventions and holiday weekends the hotels sell out, so it's a good idea to have a reservation before you arrive. Even if a hotel sells out and you failed to make a reservation, it's often possible to obtain a room. Some guests who book rooms never arrive, so you can sometimes find accommodations by approaching hotels after 6 PM. It's a little risky, especially with your family waiting in an overheated car, but you can often get a room at the last minute. If your hotel of choice is sold out, ask for a referral to another. Most hotels refer customers to other properties when they can't accommodate them.

No matter where you stay, you'll find hotel prices here among the country's lowest, running a good 20 to 30 percent below those of other resort and convention cities. Weekday rates are usually 20 to 40 percent lower than on weekends, so ask the hotel about its prices for Monday through Thursday arrival. Also, rates at downtown hotels are typically 30 to 50 percent lower than their Strip counterparts.

FYI

Unless otherwise noted, the area code for all phone numbers listed in this chapter is 702.

Price Code

Each hotel's listing in this chapter includes a symbol indicating a price range for a double occupancy, one-night stay on a weekend.

$	**$50 or less**
$$	**$51 to $100**
$$$	**$101 and more**

Note: Hotel rates can fluctuate and are typically lower from Sunday to Thursday, when it is also easier to find a room. Rates are often higher on holiday weekends, such as Memorial Day, Easter and Super Bowl weekend, and during the busiest citywide conventions, such as Comdex and CES (Consumer Electronics Show), which are held in November and January, respectively.

Rates vary seasonally as well. During the period from Thanksgiving to Christmas and during January, rooms are cheaper and easier to find. Conversely, the city is busiest during March so rates may be driven up considerably. It is always a good idea to make and confirm a reservation as far in advance as possible. And remember that room rates listed are based on information received from the hotels and are subject to change.

The Strip Area

Bally's Las Vegas

$$ • 3645 Las Vegas Blvd. S. • 739-4111, (800) 634-3434

Bally's was originally built as the MGM Grand in 1973 by Kirk Kerkorian, then controlling stockholder in MGM Studios, which also built the International Hotel (now the Las Vegas Hilton) four years earlier. In 1980 the hotel was the site of the city's worst disaster — a fire swept through the hotel killing 87 people and injuring 700. The hotel reopened nine months later with a new sprinkler system (they previously weren't required) and other safety devices, which were subsequently adopted into the city's building codes.

Bally Gaming Corporation, a slot manufacturing company, bought the hotel in 1986, changing the hotel's name but retaining the Hollywood motif — guest rooms have brass stars on the door, and photos of legendary MGM stars grace the hallways. The 2,832 guest rooms, including 265 suites, are contained in two 26-story towers. Most are primarily decorated in California modern — overstuffed furniture and mushroom coffee tables — and are among the largest in the city.

Expansion at the hotel in the 1990s added Colorful Plaza, a space-age entryway of palm trees, neon columns and cascading fountains, and moving sidewalks that bring customers in from the street.

The step-down casino at Bally's is the size

INSIDERS' TIP

The stretch of Las Vegas Boulevard south from Sahara Avenue was nicknamed The Strip in the 1950s after Hollywood's famed Sunset Strip, by gambling executive Guy McAfee, a former Los Angeles police officer.

of a football field, and the tables and machines are well-spaced so players never feel cramped. The race and sports book has tiered, arena-like seating and is apart from the casino in the downstairs shopping arcade. The shopping arcade is home to about two dozen shops, including several art galleries, apparel stores, a Hollywood memorabilia shop and a delightful ice cream parlor.

There are three showrooms that host a variety of headliner and production show entertainment. The 1,450-seat Celebrity Room presents headliners such as George Carlin, Anne Murray and Penn & Teller, while the 5,000-seat Events Center has hosted concerts for Joe Cocker, the B-52s and Michael Bolton. Bally's ongoing production show, *Jubilee*, is a lavish cabaret that features remarkable special effects such as the sinking of the *Titanic* and Samson destroying the Temple of the Philistines (see our Nightlife chapter).

Among the dining options are continental cuisine at Seasons, Italian fare at Al Dente, Bally's Steakhouse, 24-hour coffee shop, Las Olas Mexican restaurant (see our Restaurants chapter) and The Big Kitchen Buffet, a nonstop food-fest that has become popular with locals as well as tourists.

Other amenities include a large outdoor pool area, wedding chapel, tennis courts and a first-class health club. There's also a free state-of-the-art monorail linking the hotel with the MGM Grand down the street.

Barbary Coast Hotel

$$ • 3595 Las Vegas Blvd. S. • 737-7111, (800) 634-6755

Turn-of-the-century San Francisco is the motif at the Barbary Coast. If you can get one of the hotel's 200 rooms, you'll be charmed by the Victorian wallpaper and paintings, floral carpeting, etched mirrors and white-lace curtains. Some rooms even have four-poster brass beds, mini bars and whirlpools.

Although usually crowded, the casino has a friendly atmosphere. The Nob Hill theme continues with crystal globe chandeliers, carved oak and a stained-glass mural depicting, appropriately, The Garden of Earthly Delights. Measuring 30 feet long and 5 feet high, it is the world's largest stained-glass mural, and it took more than 8,000 hours to complete.

For fine dining, Michael's, specializing in fine continental cuisine, is one of the best restaurants in town (see our Restaurants chapter). But if you prefer simpler culinary pleasures, there's also a McDonald's.

Boardwalk Holiday Inn Hotel-Casino

$$ • 3750 Las Vegas Blvd. S. • 735-1167, (800) 635-4581

Sandwiched between the Monte Carlo and soon-to-be-completed Bellagio megaresorts, the world's largest Holiday Inn is possibly the strangest as well. The massive Cyclone roller coaster out front is strictly for show, as are the Ferris wheel and parachute drop. Adding to the Coney Island chaos is a 30-foot tall jack-in-the-box that pops up every couple of minutes.

Walk past the midway games and shooting gallery and you'll find a casino that is bright and cheerful with low-minimum table games: $1 blackjack, $2 craps and $3 roulette, Let it Ride poker, Big Six, Pai Gow poker and Mini baccarat. Slot lovers will find 600 machines, and sports fans will flip over the Del Mar Race and Sports Book, which features a VIP lounge, self-betting terminals, weekly golf match-ups, NASCAR wagers and a variety of proposition bets.

When it's time to refuel, The Deli is noted for its Castle burgers and foot-long half-pound Coney Island Hot Dog. The Surf Buffet has a variety of cheap eats, and Coney Island Ice Cream is a nice place for a sweet treat.

After the sun goes down, Elvis impersonator Trent Carlini stars as The Dream King, and you can catch comedians in the Boardwalk Comedy Club nightly except Mondays. For a taste of close-up magic, check out *Dixie Dooley's World of the Unreal*, a magic show for kids of all ages.

Caesars Palace

$$$ • 3570 Las Vegas Blvd. S. • 731-7110, (800) 634-6661

The grandeur that was once Rome's exists at Caesars Palace. Marble statues, Roman fountains, imported cypress trees and toga-clad cocktail waitresses help the megaresort realize its Roman-opulence theme. Outside the palatial entrance and to the right of the main fountain — the one Evil Knevil's son vaulted with his motorcycle in 1989 — is a Brahma Shrine, where visitors from the Far East actually worship and leave offerings of fruit and flowers. Nearby, the people-moving sidewalks carry you *into* but not out of the casino. As the walkway glides between Roman aqueducts, booming martial music heralds your arrival and a recorded voice assures you the slot machines are friendly.

The casino, one of Las Vegas' most ornate, attracts more than 17 million visitors annually. It is accented by coffered ceilings and decorated with Olympian wall art, deep carpeting and Roman statuary. A graceful trellis crowns the table games, and the latest in slot and video machines await the adventurous.

Adjacent to the main casino, the Omnimax Theater is a gigantic dome designed to envelop movie audiences with sound and pictures. The futuristic theater features 98 speakers and several projection screens, even on the ceiling, creating an incredible movie experience. Other first-class entertainment options include: the 1,000-seat Circus Maximus Showroom, home to such showbiz illuminaries as Johnny Mathis, Julio Iglesias, Celine Dion and David Copperfield; the new Caesars Magical Empire, a subterranean adventure that takes guests on a mystical, dazzling journey through the realms of magic and mystery while they feast on a four-course gourmet dinner; and the always-rockin' Cleopatra's Barge Nightclub (see our Nightlife chapter for complete listings on all three).

Dining at Caesars is nothing short of, well, a Roman Holiday. The Bacchanal features a six-course feast where "wine goddesses" pour vintage beverages from shoulder height and Middle Eastern dancers sway to modal melodies (see our Restaurants chapter). The Palace Court restaurant serves haute cuisine in the atmosphere of a private, European courtyard, and the Empress Court has been named by *USA Today* as one of the country's top Cantonese restaurants. Ah'So Restaurant is a Japanese steakhouse with a waterfall, arched bridges and flowing streams (see our Restaurants chapter), and the elegant Neros steak and seafood restaurant serves fresh seafood and prime, dry-aged beef steaks. Rounding out Caesars' dining choices are Primavera Italian restaurant, a 24-hour coffee shop, an all-you-can-eat buffet and La Piazza Food Court for quick meals and late-night snacks.

The Forum Shops at Caesars is a shopping and dining Riviera wrapped in historical touches that make conspicuous consumption seem sacred. More than 100 stores and restaurants are housed in the 500,000-square-foot, marble and granite promenade, including Gucci's, Versace, FAO Swartz, Fendi, Planet Hollywood, the Palm restaurant and Wolfgang Puck's Chinois (see our Shopping chapter).

The 1,500 guest rooms and suites are among the finest in the city and are appointed with features such as armoires, marble European-style bathrooms, dressing rooms, velvet chaise lounges and platform beds. Suites feature circular beds, private dining rooms, wet bars, in-room saunas, steam rooms and elaborate audiovisual systems. Caesars also offers ultra-luxurious suites to its best customers (a.k.a., biggest gamblers) such as the Via Suites with their lush Italian garden atmosphere and the two-story Roman and Greek Fantasy Suites, which are like the one shared by Tom Cruise and Dustin Hoffman in the movie *Rain Man*. By early 1998 Caesars will complete its new 29-story tower adjacent to the Garden of the Gods pool area. This will add 1,200 guest rooms to the property, which will feature a variety of floor plans from 500 to 750 square feet. There will also be two floors devoted to luxury "high roller" suites, plus a 20,000-square-foot health spa and two floors of convention and meeting rooms.

The action continues outside with Caesars Sports & Entertainment Arena, which regularly features championship boxing and other sporting events. Also, the 4.5-acre Garden of the Gods pool area is the most extravagant in Las Vegas with fountains, landscaped courtyards, marble statues, manicured shrubbery, private cabanas, four large swimming pools and two whirlpool spas. Overall, Caesars Palace remains one of Las Vegas' top architectural marvels as well as one of the city's best destination resorts.

Circus Circus Hotel/Casino

$ • 2880 Las Vegas Blvd. S. • 734-0410, (800) 634-3450

The first thing most people notice at Circus Circus is the pink-and-white, clown-shaped marquee out front. Then it's the tent-shaped casino under a pink-and-white big top. Inside, there are free circus acts, a carnival midway, arcade games and Grand Slam Canyon theme park. Put it all together and you have the No. 1 hotel choice for families with children — which makes the hotel a perpetual three-ring scene.

The casino, spread over three separate gaming areas, is best compared to Times Square on New Year's Eve. Throngs of slot players congregate, and the clamor of coins and bells is nearly deafening. A haven for low rollers, the casino under the big top features low-limit table games, but how a blackjack player can concentrate while a trapeze artist in spangled tights flies overhead is beyond belief.

Thankfully, the rooms are off the midway. After several expansions there are 3,744 rooms and suites, with most of the decor featuring soft blue carpeting, light-wood furniture, pastel spreads and upholstery and just a few hot-air balloons painted on the wall.

Grand Slam Canyon — fully enclosed and completely climate controlled — is one of the most popular attractions in Las Vegas for kids. Designed to resemble a classic desert canyon, hand-painted rock gives way to caverns, pinnacles and steep cliffs while a stream flows through the stark landscaping, cascading over a 90-foot fall. Adding to the setting are eight life-size dinosaurs dwelling among two 140-foot peaks, a fossil wall, an archeological dig and Pueblo Indian cliff dwellings. The park's rides appeal to kids of all ages and include a double-loop, double-corkscrew roller coaster, a wild water flume ride and a futuristic laser-tag arena. See our Kidstuff chapter for a complete rundown.

Other amenities at Circus Circus include a very good steakhouse, an all-you-can-eat buffet, pizzeria, swimming pools, a wedding chapel and a 384-space RV park with hook-ups, convenience store, laundry facilities, pool, Jacuzzi, playground and disposal stations.

Continental Hotel

$ • 4100 Paradise Rd. • 737-5555, (800) 634-6641

The Continental will take you Back to the '50s, which will become the name of the hotel later this decade, according to its new owners, Crowne Ventures Inc. For now the oldies theme is carried out through memorabilia in the restaurant and casino — neon signs, James Dean posters, metal Coke trays and more. You can even take some of the Fabulous Fifties home with you — the gift shop sells a complete line of T-shirts, gumball machines, jewelry, Coke signs and other reproductions.

At Big Daddy's Diner the '50s mood is set with the checkerboard floor, red-and-white dinette tables and chairs, a Wurlitzer juke box, Coke glasses and other memorabilia. You can feast around the clock on counter favorites such as burgers, fries, shakes, meat loaf, onion rings and patty melts (see our Restaurants chapter for a complete listing).

Most of the Continental's 400 guest rooms were remodeled in 1996 and 1997, and the large pool area has a landscaped courtyard in the center of the property.

Debbie Reynolds Hotel-Casino & Movie Museum

$$ • 305 Convention Center Dr. • 734-0711, (800) 633-1777

Movie buffs can glimpse Hollywood's Golden Age at Debbie Reynolds Movie Museum, which displays memorabilia from Reynolds' fabled MGM prop and costume collection. In the hotel lobby, Baccarat crystal chandeliers (from *The Great Waltz*) glow above marble-topped consoles (from *Camille* and *Marie Antoinette*), a brocade, high-back ottoman (from *Grand Hotel*) and Harold Lloyd's vintage Steinway player piano, one of only four in existence. You can also check out costumed figures of Laurel and Hardy and Mae

West, in an elegant, black velvet evening gown, low-cut, of course, along the "Hollywood Walk of Fame."

Debbie Reynolds bought the hotel, which was previously called the Paddlewheel, in 1992 and refurbished the 193 rooms that include 23 two-room suites. The rooms feature wet bars, dark wood furniture, spa-size tubs and king beds.

Reynolds performs weekly in a musical stage show, alternating with female impersonator Kenny Kerr, who previously starred in Boy-Lesque.

Desert Inn Hotel and Country Club

$$$ • 3145 Las Vegas Blvd. S. • 733-4444, (800) 634-6906

During the 1960s the Desert Inn was where billionaire Howard Hughes hid from the world in his ninth-floor penthouse. In 1996, when Hughes and his nongambling Mormon entourage were asked to give up their suites customarily reserved for high rollers, Hughes bought the hotel for $13.25 million. Over the next four years he proceeded to buy half the hotels on The Strip, although it is rumored he never left his two-room penthouse.

Today, the Desert Inn is Las Vegas' only true resort hotel. Topping the list of its country club amenities is its famous 18-hole Desert Inn Golf Course. The par 71 course has hosted PGA, LPGA and Senior PGA tour events for more than four decades. Recent additions include an 18-hole putting course and brand-new clubhouse. Other recreational facilities at the 200-acre resort include five lighted tennis courts, a jogging track, workout room and a European spa, which features saunas, steam rooms, whirlpools, massage, skin care and other pamper stations.

The 821 guest rooms include 60 suites and are among the finest on The Strip, featuring chaise lounges, armoires and country English furnishings, all in cool lavenders or quiet pastels. You can choose from rooms in the 14-story tower, but for a taste of the hotel's glamorous past, try the rooms in the older garden wing.

The casino — small by today's megaresort standards — is still one of the classiest in town with its plush carpeting, tasteful wall coverings and 30 circular brass chandeliers that look like Saturn's rings. The table minimums are slightly higher than most casinos on The Strip, but the race and sports book attracts a lot of medium-level players.

Rounding out the hotel amenities are five restaurants, including the classic French Monte Carlo, the Hong Kong delicacies of Ho Wan and the popular Mediterranean tastes of the Portofino (see our Restaurants chapter). The Crystal Room hosts headliner performers from Smokey Robinson to Dana Carvey and is widely celebrated by visitors and locals alike.

Excalibur

$$ • 3850 Las Vegas Blvd. S. • 597-7700, (800) 937-7777

Built to resemble an old English castle, the Excalibur's entrance features turrets, spires and a 265-foot-high bell tower that stands guard over the moat. To keep pace with the exploding volcano and pirate battle up the street, Merlin the Magician battles a dragon every night in a free laser light show beneath the castle's drawbridge. Inside, the medieval theme is further reflected in the cobblestone foyer and rock-walled atrium with a three-story-high fountain. The massive registration desk is flanked by suits of armor and decorated in red-on-red carpeting and wall coverings. Like its cousin Circus Circus, the Excalibur caters mostly to families and is usually packed.

The 100,000-square-foot casino is one of the city's largest, and the action is usually fast and frenzied. In fact, during busy weekends the red-on-red monstrosity can sound like a tin-can factory in an earthquake. At least the race and sports book is separated from the 2,600 slot machines, so sports bettors can watch their football games in relative peace.

On the mezzanine level above the casino, there's a medieval shopping village where jugglers, musicians, magicians and assorted minstrels provide a roving Renaissance Faire. On the level below the casino you'll find a dungeon "fun zone" for kids, complete with video arcade, games, and a Magic Motion Simulator that takes you on the high-tech thrill ride of your life.

With six restaurants, finding sustenance should be easy. Sir Galahad's serves a delicious Yorkshire pudding along with the house specialty of prime rib, while Wild Bill's offers steaks, ribs and chicken specialties (see our Restaurants chapter). There's also an Italian restaurant, continental restaurant, 24-hour coffee shop and Round Table buffet.

The hotel's main show, King Arthur's Tournament, takes place in a 900-seat, basement arena, featuring jousting knights, Merlin the Magician and a three-course dinner you consume with your fingers.

The 4,032 guest rooms are done in bold reds, blues and greens and feature dark wood furniture and wrought-iron fixtures. Other hotel amenities include a wedding chapel, beauty salon and two pools.

Flamingo Hilton Hotel

$$ • 3555 Las Vegas Blvd. S. • 733-3111, (800) 732-2111

Many people consider the original Flamingo Hotel, built in 1946 by Benjamin "Bugsy" Siegel, as the predecessor to modern commercial gambling in Las Vegas. Unfortunately, Siegel's original suite and garden wing was plowed over to make room for expansion in the mid-1990s, and all that remains in tribute to the Chicago-mobster-turned-Vegas-hotelier is a stone pillar and small plaque in the rose garden behind the casino.

Surrounding the rose garden are lush grounds and walking paths that take you on an expedition through live African penguins, Chilean flamingos, Mandarin ducks and Koi fish swimming in ponds under three-story-high waterfalls. Adding to the resort atmosphere are the tennis courts, swimming pools and a world-class health spa.

The expansions have increased the hotel's room count to 3,530, making it one of the 10 largest hotels in the world. As you might expect, it caters to plenty of tour groups and is usually crowded and bustling. Bought by Hilton Hotels from Kirk Kerkorian in 1970, it is the most profitable hotel in Hilton's entire chain. The facade facing The Strip is decorated with neon-pink flamingos against a mirrored backdrop. The theme is carried throughout the hotel, but the rooms have a more Hilton influence, done in conservative blues and greens with modern wood and rattan furnishings.

INSIDERS' TIP

Three times in his career Kirk Kerkorian built the world's largest resort hotel: the International (now the Las Vegas Hilton) in 1969; the MGM Grand (now Bally's) in 1973; and the current MGM Grand in 1995.

In keeping with its Miami modern heritage, the casino features tropical pink, magenta and tangerine neon accents in a rambling, bustling casino, which is usually overflowing. In addition to the normal mix of table games and slot machines, the Flamingo features sic bo, an Asian dice game where players try to pick the numbers or combination of numbers on three rolled dice. The most fascinating part of the game is the colorful Chinese table layout, which looks like a Hong Kong test pattern gone berserk.

In the Flamingo Showroom, the Radio City Rockettes kick up their well-formed heels nightly, accompanied by singers and variety acts. In the smaller Bugsy Celebrity Theater, the heartwarming tribute to the 1950s, *Forever Plaid*, plays nightly. (See our Nightlife chapter.)

Diners can choose from nine restaurants serving a variety of cuisine including Chinese, Italian and Japanese. There's also a steakhouse, garden buffet, coffee shop and deli.

Frontier Hotel

$$ • 3120 Las Vegas Blvd. S. • 794-8200, (800) 634-6966

The massive marquee that once advertised Siegfried & Roy now touts single-deck blackjack and multiple odds on craps, a testament to the hotel's current dedication to serious gambling. The original Last Frontier opened in 1942 and was only the second hotel on The Strip. But it was demolished in 1966 to make way for the current Frontier. Before it opened in 1967, Howard Hughes bought the hotel, and his Summa Corporation sold it in 1988 to the current owner, Margaret Elardi.

The Elardi family also bought the old Silver Slipper Casino next door and demolished it to make room for expansion in 1990. That expansion included a 15-story tower that raised the room count to 986 and added a state-of-the-art race and sports book. At press time the Elardis had agreed to sell to Kansas businessman Phil Ruffin for $167 million.

There are only two places to eat in the Frontier, but they both serve excellent food at bargain prices — Margarita's Mexican Cantina and Michelle's Village Cafe.

Hard Rock Hotel & Casino

$$$ • 4455 Paradise Rd. • 693-5000, (800) 473-7625

The Hard Rock Hotel takes its rock 'n' roll theme beyond interior decoration — the place is a shrine to rock and its superstars. Throughout the circular-shaped casino are priceless treasures, such as Elvis' jumpsuit, Elton John's piano, a round bar that Kiss performed on and a gold-plated 32-saxophone chandelier. There are also dozens of museum-like displays of rock memorabilia, such as Beatles collectibles, vintage records, guitars, drum sets and much more. Selected as one of the top 25 coolest places to stay in the world by *Condé Nast Traveler* magazine, the Hard Rock Hotel is geared to the stylishly hip crowd. The casino is well-placed in the center of the hotel, with other amenities and services located around it. Players will find the usual table games and machines, but with a rock 'n roll twist — some of the slots have guitar necks for handles, and the gambling chips have Jimi Hendrix on them.

Reflecting a Southern California influence, the Hard Rock's pool area has a sandy beach lagoon and hillside gardens plus a row of tent cabanas. You'll also find spas and whirlpools and rock music piped underwater.

True to its mission, the Hard Rock's showroom — The Joint — is one of the best places in town to experience a rock concert (see our Nightlife chapter for full listing). The atmosphere is more of an intimate club than a concert hall, and the acoustics and lights shows are outstanding.

The 340 guest rooms and suites are bright-and-airy, California modern with French doors, dark wood furniture, crimson bedding and tropical drapes. An expansion will more than double the number of rooms in 1998.

Other amenities include two restaurants (see our Restaurants chapter for a listing on Mortoni's), a cocktail lounge, an athletic club with exercise equipment and men's and women's steam rooms and showers, and a retail store that sells a wide variety of Hard Rock merchandise.

Harrah's Las Vegas

$$ • 3475 Las Vegas Blvd. S. • 369-5000, (800) 634-6765

What was once the world's largest Holiday Inn is now Harrah's Las Vegas. Although Harrah's has owned and operated the 1,725-room resort since 1983, the name was changed in 1992 to enhance the corporation's image in the gaming industry. An expansion in 1997 scrapped the hotel's original riverboat motif in favor of a European carnival theme, complete with a lush Carnaval Court, strolling performers and colorful exterior murals.

The casino, which always seems in a state of renovation, meanders over nearly 100,000 square feet. Always crowded and noisy, the casino has about 2,000 slot and video machines, 44 blackjack tables and a good mix of craps, roulette, baccarat, poker and Caribbean Stud games. You can also play keno and bingo and bet in the race and sports book.

The hotel's featured production show, *Spellbound*, is a fantasy-filled magic show, and the Improv showcases seasoned comedians and up-and-comers (see our Nightlife chapter).

The modern rooms contain plush teal carpeting, peach print upholstery, white wood furniture and blue bamboo-style chairs.

Other amenities include six restaurants, four bars, a health club, pool and cluster of retail shops.

Imperial Palace Hotel

$$ • 3535 Las Vegas Blvd. S. • 731-3311, (800) 634-6441

The small, blue-roofed pagoda at the front of the hotel is only the tip of the iceberg to this sprawling 2,700-room complex behind its modest Strip facade. The hotel features an Oriental theme with an entry marked by crystal and jade, bamboo and curved wood accents.

The Asian look continues into the well-stocked casino, which is tastefully done in bamboo and rattan furnishings under a dragon-motif ceiling. While most of the action is from double-fisted tourists pouring coins into the 2,000 machines, the race and sports book up the escalator draws plenty of bettors with its frequent promotions that include favorable point spreads and lower vigorish, and the football handicapping contest is among the city's most popular.

Also popular is the hotel's Antique & Classic Auto Collection, which contains 200 rare and historic vehicles, including Al Capone's 1930 V-16 Cadillac, Elvis' '76 Eldorado, Hitler's '36 Mercedes and John F. Kennedy's 1962 Lincoln "Bubbletop," to name a few. There is also a room full of rare Duesenbergs worth in excess of $50 million.

The hotel's *Legends in Concert* production (see our Nightlife chapter) remains vibrant as new entertainers are added to the revue and continues to play to a packed showroom. In addition to live impersonations of music's superstars, the show is backed by a live orchestra, which is fast-becoming a rarity in Las Vegas.

Also worth seeing is Hawaiian Hot — a Polynesian revue and all-you-can-eat luau, which is presented from spring through fall. The show features sword and fire dancers, Tahitian hula dancers and other Polynesia performers plus a finger-licking luau with roast pig, poi, coconut hai pei pudding and much more.

Among the hotel's seven restaurants, the best are Ming Terrace for Cantonese and Mandarin specialties, the Embers for steak and seafood and The Seahouse for fresh seafood. There's also a buffet, coffee shop, pizza palace, rib house and burger joint. (See our Restaurants chapter.)

Other amenities include a wedding chapel, health club, video arcade, shopping promenade and Olympic-size swimming pool.

Las Vegas Hilton

$$$ • 3000 Paradise Rd. • 732-5111, (800) 774-1500

Elvis may not have built the Hilton, but he certainly enhanced its station during the last 8 years of his life when he performed here. When the Hilton opened in 1969 as the International Hotel, Barbra Streisand christened the new showroom, but Elvis followed a month later and continued his reign until he died in 1977. Purchased by Hilton Hotels in 1971, the Las Vegas Hilton is the flagship in the chain's fleet. Adjacent to the convention center, the hotel is favored by conventioneers and business travelers as well as tourists who seek a self-contained resort.

About a block from The Strip, the 3,174-room property has a 10-acre outdoor recreation deck that features six tennis courts, a putting green, shuffleboard and a large pool area. The Hilton also has its own country club with a par 71 course, just 2 miles east on Desert Inn Road.

The hotel's 100-foot registration desk and lobby area are separate from the step-down casino and are decorated with tropical colors, Grecian bas-reliefs, crystal chandeliers and neon rainbows. The large guest rooms feature upholstered easy chairs, marble-top dressing tables, wood-frame mirrors and deep closets. Room colors tend toward cool blue and green pastels.

Like everything else at the Hilton, the casino is well-designed and well-appointed. It's in the center of the hotel with restaurants and entertainment venues surrounding it. Table games are at the center, flanked by slot machines and a keno lounge. The popular race and sports SuperBook is one of the most popular in the city, catering to locals as well as tourists. Because of the upscale clientele, table limits have higher minimums, usually $5 at blackjack and craps, and most of the slots are of the $1 variety. If you're into the big-ticket machines, tuxedo-clad change personnel dispense $100 and $500 slot tokens in a canopied slot gazebo.

When the sun sets, the Nightclub lounge — Las Vegas' finest — rocks with regular entertainers such as Kristine W and The Sting, and the showroom showcases celebrity headliners (see our Nightlife chapter).

Dining at the Hilton is superb with an international flavor. The award-winning Bistro Le Montrachet serves classic French cuisine, and Benihana's offers two rooms — the Village for hibachi dining and the Seafood Grille. (See our Restaurants chapter.) Other excellent dining rooms include Andiamo's for Northern Italian fare, Barronshire for steak and prime rib, the Hilton Steak House, Margarita Grille for Mexican and Southwest specialties, a 24-hour coffee shop and the Buffet of Champions.

The hotel's latest addition is Star Trek: The Experience, an interactive attraction from Paramount Parks. Among the features is a motion simulator, TurboLift to the shuttlecraft launch bay and film images during the craft's "voyage." There's also a museum with costumes and memorabilia and Spacequest Casino with futuristic slot machines.

Luxor Hotel

$$ • 3900 Las Vegas Blvd. S. • 262-4000, (800) 288-1000

Architecturally speaking, the Luxor, with its pyramid design and Egyptian theme, is the most unique resort in Las Vegas. The entrance is marked by a sandstone obelisk etched with hieroglyphics that towers over Karnak Lake, a lagoon surrounded by reeds, palm trees, rock formations and statues of pharaohs. The hotel's porte-cochere is a 10-story sphinx that crouches above a rock-and-stone entrance. At night, green laser beams from the sphinx's eyes strike the obelisk and lake, causing the water to boil and rise in a water curtain, on which video holograms of ancient Egypt are projected.

Built by Circus Circus Enterprises in 1993, the 30-story (350-foot) pyramid is shrouded in dark glass, with its apex containing a 40-billion-candlepower beacon (the world's strongest), which sends a shaft of light more than 10 miles into space at night. Inside, the pyramid's atrium is large enough to stack nine Boeing 747s and features three levels of dining, entertainment and gambling.

Guest rooms are built into the pyramid's sloping walls and are reached by "inclinators," elevators that rise at a 39-degree angle, leaving passengers feeling like they're on an enclosed ski lift. The interior of the pyramid is tastefully decorated with deep-red carpeting, sandstone walls, faux palm trees, Egyptian statues and hieroglyphic-inscribed tapestry.

For a peek into Egypt's past, visit King Tut's Tomb and Museum, an accurate reproduction of Howard Carter's 1922 find, often called the most significant archaeological discovery of modern history. After you watch a five-minute video of Tutankhamen's life, guides escort you through the tomb's antechamber, burial chamber and treasury room, where you'll see more than 500 replicas of mummies, Egyptian furniture, a chariot, pottery, baskets, jewelry, linens and other artifacts. The gift shop sells Egyptian antiquities and keepsakes. *Secrets of the Luxor Pyramid* is an hourlong adventure spread over two venues. Episode One, "In Search of the Obelisk", uses a motion simulator to send you through a wild chase that begins with a plummeting elevator. "Luxor Live" in Episode Two

The Golden Gate Hotel: Las Vegas' Birthplace

For a glimpse of what Las Vegas was like before it became a fantasy-filled Land of Oz, take a trip downtown and visit the Golden Gate Hotel. Built in 1906 at the corner of Fremont and Main streets, the Golden Gate is the city's oldest hotel. More importantly, it's one of the city's few links to its colorful past, retaining much of the charm and character that defined the city before reality became virtual and hype replaced history.

When the hotel first opened, it was called Hotel Nevada. Rooms cost $1 per night and included electric lighting, ventilation and steam heat radiators. There was no air conditioning, of course, and guests shared common bathrooms at the end of the hall. The hotel's ground floor had a lobby and a few offices but no casino; yet there was gambling — a roulette wheel and a few poker tables — until it was outlawed in 1909.

Over the years, the hotel expanded. A year after the hotel opened, it installed the city's first telephone in the office of pioneer newspaper publisher Charles "Pop" Squires. During the 1920s, a third floor was added, and in 1931 — the same year gambling was legalized again — the hotel was renamed Sal Sagev, or "Las Vegas" spelled backward.

The hotel was renamed the Golden Gate in 1955 when a group of San Francisco investors took over the hotel and opened the casino. Four years later, the new owners introduced Las Vegas to the shrimp cocktail — a tasty little treat they discovered in an Oakland deli. The dish caught on and has been a Golden Gate tradition ever since. That tradition, of course, has spread throughout the city. In fact, the consumption of shrimp

— continued on next page

Photo: Golden Gate Hotel

The Golden Gate Hotel & Casino, built in 1906, is the city's oldest hotel, though it looks a little different today.

in Las Vegas has grown to more than 60,000 pounds daily — more than the rest of the country combined. Forrest Gump would love it.

During the '50s and '60s, the Golden Gate enjoyed the reputation of serving good food, including a 50¢ sandwich and 50¢ giant shrimp cocktail. It also became a gathering place for local business professionals, news reporters, judges and lawyers such as Richard Bryan and Bob Miller, who currently serve as Nevada senator and governor, respectively.

Today, while the Golden Gate has modernized to keep with the times, it retains much of its historic charm. Many of the original 10-foot by 10-foot guest rooms remain, though they've been updated with air conditioning, private baths, cable TV, coffee makers, voice mail and even computer ports! The rates have increased to about $50 a night, which includes breakfast and a newspaper, but the mahogany doors, plaster walls and tiled bathroom floors remind guests of the hotel's rich history. (For more about the hotel, see our write-up in this chapter.)

Downstairs, the decor suggests turn-of-the-century San Francisco: mahogany panels, countertops, ceilings and baseboards; brass railings and fixtures; checkerboard tile floors and leaded-crystal chandeliers. In the San Francisco Shrimp Bar & Deli, you can still enjoy a shrimp cocktail — served with a wedge of lemon in a tulip glass — even though the price has soared to 99¢. Or you can feast on huge deli-style sandwiches of corned beef, pastrami or chopped liver. For heartier appetites, the Bay City Diner is one of the better eateries downtown, specializing in thick steaks, broiled seafood and other American favorites, delivered in ample portions.

The Golden Gate's casino contains all the modern games — blackjack, craps, roulette, Let it Ride poker — as well as slot and video machines. But there are reminders of the days before computer chips controlled the slots: a few vintage slot machines like a Jennings War Eagle, historic photographs and antique artifacts from the hotel's early days, including a replica of the first telephone.

The casino also contains a black baby grand piano that sings its snappy tunes starting around noon daily. At times the joint sounds like an old silent movie house with the piano player pounding out melodies that rise and fall with the film's plot.

But perhaps some of the best reminders of the Golden Gate's golden years are the patrons who continue to come here. Look closely among the clientele, and you might find a couple who has celebrated their anniversary in the hotel ever since they were married here in 1946, or a local 95-year-old woman who traditionally starts off her week with a pancake breakfast and a few pulls on a one-armed bandit.

The Golden Gate has withstood the test of time, and it has endured the whims and ravages of a market-driven economy. For Las Vegas, the Golden Gate is a step backward. A most welcome step.

---

takes on the format of a live TV talk show and ends up with more 3-D wizardry. See our Attractions chapter for more information.

In the main pyramid building, there are 2,526 rooms and suites that cling to the inside of the pyramid. Each room has a sloped wall and bank of windows with views of The Strip and surrounding mountains and a door that opens to overlook the pyramid's interior atrium. There are 1,950 more rooms in the recently-completed tower just north of the pyramid. The rooms are accented with wooden furniture that's etched with Egyptian characters.

The casino is among the largest on The Strip and one of the most attractive with its sandstone walls decorated with colorful Egyptian murals and bas-relief sculptures of ancient kings and queens. In addition to the usual mix of slots and table games, the casino features quick and friendly cocktail service from servers who all miraculously have black Cleopatra-like hair.

Hotel amenities include a pool, retail shops

and seven restaurants — the Isis for continental dining (see Restaurants), Papyrus steakhouse, the Sacred Sea Room for fresh- and saltwater seafood, a 24-hour coffee shop, buffet, deli and ice cream parlor.

MGM Grand

$$ • 3799 Las Vegas Blvd. S. • 895-1111, (800) 646-7787

An emerald monolith that appears like layers of Legos blocks, the MGM Grand with its 5,005 rooms is the world's largest resort hotel. To live up to its lofty billing, the MGM offers a plethora of attractions, entertainment venues, restaurants and casino space.

The world's largest hotel is home to the world's largest casino — it sprawls over 171,000 square feet and is actually larger than the field at Yankee Stadium. Although touted as having four theme areas — Emerald City, Hollywood, Monte Carlo and Sports — they all blend together in a collage of rainbow-colored carpeting, floral wall coverings and neon-studded, marquee-style lighting.

The hotel has a variety of showrooms and arenas, where events have ranged from Bette Midler and Barbra Streisand concerts to Tyson-Holyfield championship fights. Jay Leno and NBC's *Tonight Show* frequently broadcast from the hotel, and the ongoing production show *EFX* starring David Cassidy is rated among the city's best productions (see our Nightlife chapter for a complete listing).

Dining is a smorgasbord with choices ranging from the California nouveau tastes of Wolfgang Puck (see Restaurants) to the classic specialties of the Brown Derby. In between you'll find the Southwestern treasures of the Coyote Cafe (see Restaurants), Chinese specialties at Dragon Court, Cajun cuisine at Emeril Lagasse's New Orleans Fish House, French cuisine at Gatsby's and upscale Italian dining at La Scala. There's also a New York-style deli, 24-hour coffee shop, buffet and fast food court.

The massive lobby features a brass registration desk, behind which sits an 80-panel video screen that flashes panoramic images of desert scenes, baseball stadiums and advertisements. Waiting guests can sit beneath a circular dome adorned with gold panels and bright red ceiling, while high rollers can follow the red carpet to a glassed VIP registration area.

The 5,000-plus rooms are honeycombed in four emerald-green towers. Most follow the hotel's *Wizard of Oz* motif, with emerald carpeting, gold-crown moldings, red poppy linens and prints of scenes from the movie. Of the hotel's 750 suites, about half are really oversized guest rooms with a sofa and two TVs; others perch on the 29th floor, fill 3,000 square feet in a split-level design and are served by one butler and up to 27 telephones.

FYI

Unless otherwise noted, the area code for all phone numbers listed in this chapter is 702.

MGM Grand Adventures is the city's only amusement park, featuring 33 acres of adventure rides, shows, theme streets, shops and restaurants. Built by Duell Corporation, the architect of non-Disney theme parks such as Sea World and Six Flags Magic Mountain, Grand Adventures was inspired by MGM's famous back lot in Los Angeles. Allow five to six hours for the rides and shows. Expect less walking than in most theme parks — the park is about one-tenth the size of Disneyland. See our Attractions chapter for a complete description of the park.

Other hotel amenities include a pool area the size of four football fields, two headliner theaters, a 15,000-seat events arena, tennis courts and the amusement park. Families will like the King Looey Youth Activity Center, a day-care facility open to the 3- to 16-year-old children of hotel guests. In addition to adult supervision, the center has every toy imaginable, from Duplo building blocks for preschoolers to Ping-Pong and Super Nintendo for preteens.

The Mirage

$$ • 3400 Las Vegas Blvd. S. • 791-7444, (800) 347-9000

With its gold-mirrored facade glistening in the desert, The Mirage stands out among Strip hotels. It is also a major tourist attraction. Nearly half the visitors to Las Vegas find their way to the 100-acre, 3,054-room resort.

Conceived as a Polynesian theme resort,

this hotel is Jungleland gone wild. Outside the entrance there's a lagoon with waterfalls and grottos as well as an erupting volcano. The spectacle takes place atop a 54-foot-tall man-made mountain, and you can watch it from the sidewalk. The eruption, which begins after dark and runs every half hour, spews fire and smoke onto the mountain's waterfalls, palm trees and into the surrounding lagoon.

Inside, behind the marble-and-brass registration desk, you'll find a wall-length, 20,000-gallon aquarium with pygmy sharks, rays and other sea life. If the air feels heavy at the casino entrance that's because of the tropical rainforest, climate-controlled for the orchids, Canary Island date palms and other tropical plants. A short walk from the atrium is a glass-enclosed habitat for Siegfried and Roy's white tigers.

The hotel's casino suggests an island atmosphere theme with its colorful tropical prints and canopies over the gaming areas. A separate casino behind a gold door is reserved for players who are willing to play blackjack at a minimum $1,000 a hand (on average, that's about $50,000 an hour of bets). The race and sports book is one of the largest on The Strip, featuring an adjoining tropical bar with TV carousels for easy viewing and a nearby California Pizza Kitchen for a fresh supply of munchies.

Since its opening The Mirage has been a major player in the high-roller market. The top five floors of the hotel contain penthouse suites earmarked for big-spending gamblers, and there is a cluster of exclusive villas, each with its own pool and putting green, behind the hotel.

The guest rooms are done in tropical color schemes and contain rattan and cane furnishings and floor-to-ceiling headboards crafted from white louvered panels.

Hotel amenities include four international restaurants — French, Chinese, Japanese and Italian — a seafood restaurant, 24-hour coffee shop, buffet and the Siegfried and Roy magic show (see our Nightlife chapter), the most expensive production show in town. And there's more: The pool area features tree-lined islands, grottoes, waterfalls and lagoons.

Monte Carlo Hotel Casino

$$ • 3770 Las Vegas Blvd. S. • 730-7777, (800) 311-8999

A joint venture between Mirage Resorts and Circus Circus Enterprises, the Monte Carlo is a blend of European refinement and Vegas glitz. The architecture features stately columns, cascading fountains and Renaissance-style statues, yet it resists lapsing into overstated baroque.

Most of the hotel's attractions were designed for guests who like to participate. Outdoors lovers can bask in the glow of six pools in a lush garden setting, dip in the wave pool and take a leisurely raft ride on Easy River. Next to the water park are four lighted tennis courts and pro shop for rentals and lessons. For the young at heart, the Street of Dreams has an arcade and midway where you'll find a motion simulator, virtual reality golf game and other attractions.

The casino features 2,200 slot machines in coinage from 5¢ to $100, 95 table games, poker tables, a 550-seat bingo parlor, keno lounge and race and sports book.

When it's time to eat, the Monte Carlo has six restaurants and a food court to choose from. Blackstone's Steak House serves aged Midwestern beef prepared over an open-hearth charcoal broiler, the Dragon Noodle Company offers exotic Asian dishes prepared exhibition style, and the Tea Emporium demonstrates the ancient art of the tea service. The Italian restaurant, Market City, has a huge antipasto bar with selections such as marinated fennel, grilled eggplant and fresh mussels, and the Southern Italian fare of homemade pastas, pizzas and grilled entrees comes in whopping portions. The popular Monte Carlo Pub & Brewery has six fresh brews to quench the palate. You can also indulge in fresh pizzas, pasta and sandwiches in an old warehouse atmosphere. And when the live entertainment stops, there are 35 big screen TVs and surround sound to keep the adrenaline flowing.

The Monte Carlo's main production show is one of the best in town. Performing in a 1,200-seat showroom custom-built for his unique show, Lance Burton, Master Magician, is the only winner of all four major international magic awards (see our Nightlife chapter).

Finally, the hotel's 3,002 rooms include 256 suites and are decorated with cherry furniture and turn-of-the-century decor, tastefully accented with brass fixtures, Italian marble and polished granite.

New York-New York Hotel Casino

$$ • 3790 Las Vegas Blvd. S. • 740-6969, (800) 675-3267

Start spreadin' the news: There's a slice of the Big Apple in Las Vegas. At the core of the new resort are replicas of New York City landmarks such as the Empire State Building, Brooklyn Bridge and a Coney Island roller coaster, which soars over Fire Island and around a blushing Statue of Liberty.

Adding to the Manhattan flavor of the 2,035-room hotel are Vegas versions of three popular New York eateries — the lively America restaurant, Gallagher's steak house and Gonzalez Y Gonzalez, which, like its East Coast counterpart, features a well-stocked Margarita bar. For more street-friendly fare, you can even wrap your fingers around a genuine Nathan's hot dog at the Coney Island Food Pavilion.

For nighttime fun, the 1,045-seat Madhattan Theatre hosts a fast-moving production show, *MADhattan*, a frenzied combination of dance, song and physical comedy (see our Nightlife chapter). And the Motown Cafe and Nightclub features star-studded memorabilia such as original gold records and rhinestone costumes worn by groups such as The Four Tops, Temptations, Supremes and Boys II Men. You can also enjoy the live sounds of the Motown Cafe Moments and after 11 PM, dance the night away to the hits of yesterday, today and tomorrow. For a flavor of the Great White Way, swing and sway to the Big Band sounds in the Empire Bar, or if raucous sing-along is more your number, visit the dueling pianos in The Bar at Times Square.

New York-New York's 12 skyscraper-like towers house 2,034 guest rooms and suites, which feature 63 different floor plans and themes. Most are decorated in warm earth tones with light-wood furniture and polished chrome lamps.

Riviera Hotel

$$ • 2901 Las Vegas Blvd. S. • 734-5110, (800) 634-6753

When the Riviera opened in 1955, it changed the face of The Strip. Not only was it the first high-rise (nine stories), but it also broke from the city's predominant dude-ranch architecture. Because it has never had a themed appearance, the Riviera has been popular with film makers shooting on location in Las Vegas. The 1961 classic *Oceans 11* was shot here, as was Martin Scorsese's 1994 *Casino*, a dark look at the Vegas of the 1970s.

Today the 2,100-room hotel's claim to fame is its entertainment. The best show is in the Riviera Comedy Club, which hosts top comics such as Pauly Shore and Drew Carey as well as fresh newcomers. The other production shows — *Splash*, *La Cage* and *Crazy Girls* — are essentially unchanged since their debut in the mid-'80s.

Coupled with its large gambling casino, the hotel is always bustling. Fortunately the rooms are far from the casino din and feature rich blue and black velour upholstery, dark wood furnishings and magnificent views of the city.

Other amenities include five restaurants, two lighted tennis courts, an Olympic-size pool and a mini shopping arcade.

Sahara Hotel

$$ • 2535 Las Vegas Blvd. S. • 737-2713, (800) 634-6666

Opened in 1952, the Sahara Hotel quickly burst into the city's emerging entertainment scene. Ray Bolger (famous as the scarecrow in the *Wizard of Oz*) and singer Lisa Kirk headlined the Congo Room on its inaugural night. Since then the Congo Room has hosted countless other stars such as Ann Margret, Judy Garland, Johnny Carson, Liza Minnelli and Tina Turner as well as Broadway musicals, circus acts and sporting events. One of its most famous headliners was The Beatles, who made their Las Vegas debut at the Sahara in 1964. Today, popular comedians such as Rich Little, Jackie Mason and Jeff Dunham can still be seen on the Congo stage nearly every night of the week.

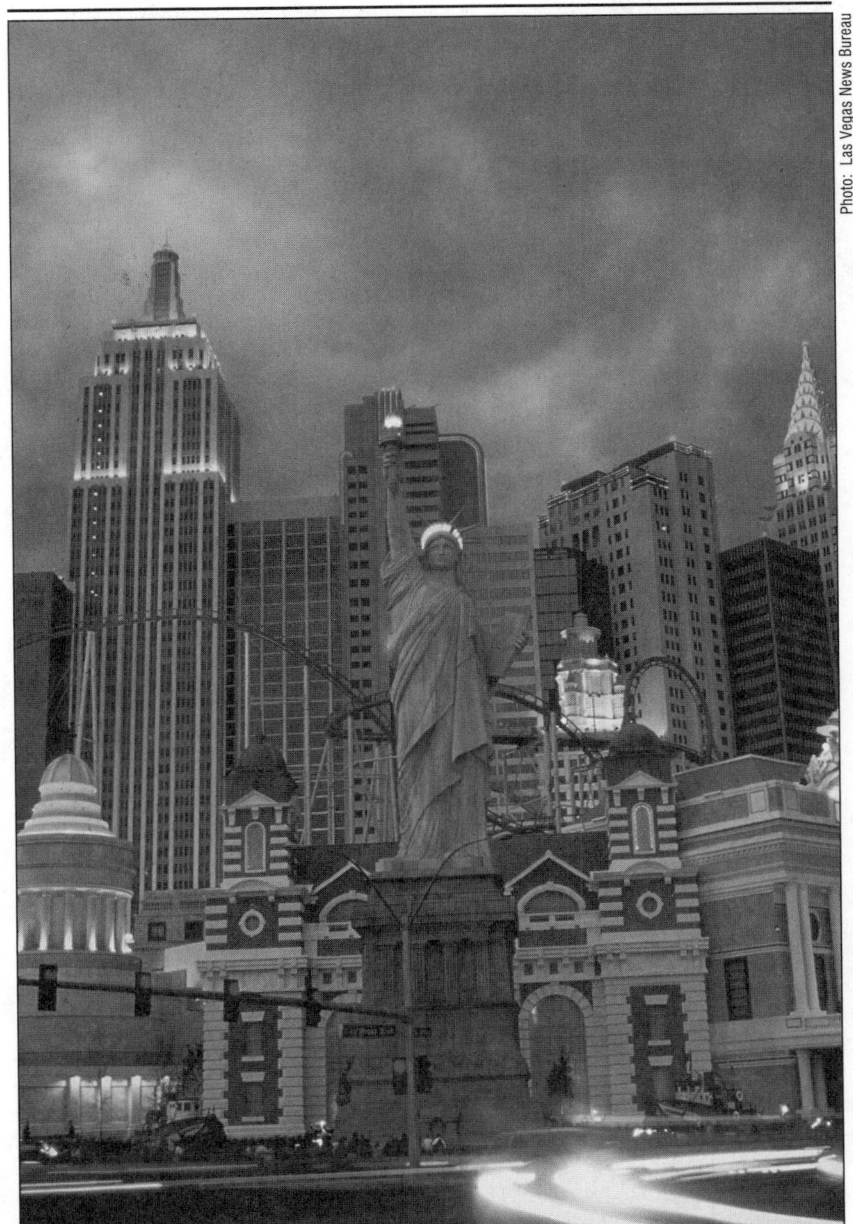

Photo: Las Vegas News Bureau

New York-New York Hotel Casino brings a slice of the Big Apple to Las Vegas.

Through several expansions, the Sahara has taken on a new look. Its famous vertical sign — once the world's tallest freestanding sign — is gone. In its place is a 160-foot neon marquee and electronic reader board. New towers and Moroccan-style arches, along with palm trees and cascading fountains, have replaced the original two-story garden buildings. The renovations have helped revitalize the aging resort and made it a popular destination for tour groups and conventioneers. It has also boosted the room count to 2,033, which includes 70 suites. The new and renovated rooms have a sunny disposition with tan carpeting and drapes, earthtone upholstery and wooden desks with brass lamps.

The Sahara's casino is one of the brightest and roomiest in town, with slot and video poker machines on one side and table games — guarded by statues of sultans — on the other. Daily slot tournaments and other promotions keep the casino hopping.

Hotel amenities include two pools, one with landscaped gardens and a thatched-hut bar, five restaurants, a cabaret lounge and a high-tech, interactive Grand Prix motion simulator, which gives its riders the experience of driving a powerful race car without ever leaving the hotel.

San Remo Hotel

$$ • 115 E. Tropicana Ave. • 739-9000, (800) 522-7366

In the shadow of the MGM Grand across the street, the San Remo Hotel offers an affordable alternative to the impersonal hustle and bustle of the much larger Vegas resorts. A high, arched ceiling and crystal chandeliers in the casino help the hotel live up to its Southern Riviera namesake. All the usual games are available — blackjack, craps, roulette, Caribbean Stud, Pai Gow and Let it Ride — as well as more than 600 slot and video poker machines. The San Remo also has one of the city's more popular slot clubs, the Money Club, which awards points for slot play that can be later redeemed for cash, comps and merchandise.

The 711 rooms in the twin silver-and-gold towers are modern affairs with plush blue carpeting and dark hardwood furniture.

The hotel has five restaurants, including a steakhouse, Italian trattoria, buffet, coffee shop and an outstanding sushi bar. There's also a Parisian-style cabaret show called *Showgirls of Magic* (see our Nightlife chapter) and a large heated pool.

Stardust Hotel

$$ • 3000 Las Vegas Blvd. S. • 732-6111, (800) 824-6033

For more than 40 years the Stardust has exemplified Las Vegas style and flash. From the days of mobster Tony Spilotro and gambling mogul Lefty Rosenthal (who were both inspirations for Martin Scorsese's *Casino*) to the famous *Lido de Paris* revue to today's *Enter the Night* production show, the hotel has remained an adult playground, unencumbered with family attractions. The casino is large and filled with gamblers, not sightseers.

The hotel's casino meanders through several large sections of machines and gaming tables, and the sports book is perhaps the most popular in town, especially during the football season, when the book sets early betting lines and offers odds on "nonboard" football games, that is, contests between smaller schools such as Ivy League universities.

The Stardust recently opened a 1,500-room, 32-story tower, bringing its guest room total to 2,431. Another 1,500-room monolith is planned for the late 1990s. The new rooms, among the better buys on The Strip, are decorated with earthtone carpets, red and black upholstery, glass or marble tables and wicker furniture.

Diners have a good choice of restaurants to choose from, including the popular Mexican cafe Tres Lobos, the nifty '50s-style Ralph's Diner and the upscale steakhouse, William B's (see our Restaurants chapter). The Stardust's lavish production, *Enter the Night* (see our Nightlife chapter), has been dazzling crowds since it replaced the venerable *Lido de Paris* in 1992, and the hotel lounge frequently hosts quality acts such as Susan McDonald and The Coasters. Rounding out the amenities are eight bars, two pools, a video arcade and a cluster of retail shops.

Treasure Island

$$ • 3300 Las Vegas Blvd. S. • 894-7111, (800) 944-7444

Long John Silver and his plundering pals would approve of this pirate-themed resort that proclaims its presence with a 60-foot-high skull and crossbones over the readerboard marquee. But that's just the start. The hotel fronts The Strip with a replica of an 18th-century sea village, surrounded by rock cliffs, shrubs, palm trees and nautical artifacts, all perched atop Buccaneer Bay, a blue-water lagoon. Two fully rigged ships — a pirate galleon and a British frigate — moored and anchored in the bay, play out for a mock sea battle every 90 minutes beginning in the late afternoon. The show fills the sidewalk with onlookers, who marvel at the cannons blazing, masts toppling, powder kegs exploding and stunt actors leaping into the lagoon.

The hotel's pirate theme continues inside with 18th-century bas-relief art on the ceilings, overflowing treasure chests on the walls and black carpet decorated with colorful images of jewels, gold doubloons and rope chains. Slot machines and gaming tables are tightly grouped in the casino, but players don't seem to mind the close quarters, as the casino is always packed.

Like the Mirage, its cousin next door, the hotel is built in a Y-shaped configuration with three coral-colored, 36-story towers. There's a glint of gold throughout the lobby, which features black corkscrew pillars, marble floors covered with Oriental rugs and a chandelier made of gold-plated skulls and bones. Waiting guests will enjoy the pirate-theme murals behind the onyx registration desk.

The 2,900 rooms are decorated with light carpeting, brass fixtures, white-washed wood furniture, 17th-century nautical paintings and floor-to-ceiling windows.

The hotel's ongoing production show, Cirque du Soleil's *Mystere*, is staged in a specially built, 1,500-seat theater that is typically sold out. The reason? The show is perhaps the best in town (see our Nightlife chapter). Restaurant choices include a Mexican cantina, mesquite grill, steak and seafood house, sandwich shop, buffet and continental restaurant. Hotel amenities include a spa with sauna, whirlpool and exercise room, a beauty salon, a pool area with a 200-foot slide and cabanas covered with blue awnings and two wedding chapels.

Tropicana Hotel

$$ • 3801 Las Vegas Blvd. S. • 739-2222, (800) 468-9494

An island paradise might describe the Tropicana Hotel. At the entrance to the 1,900-room resort are two 35-foot-tall Maori gods, a waterfall, outrigger canoes, palm trees, a lagoon and a Polynesian longhouse, which often hosts Hawaiian entertainment. Between the hotel's twin towers is a 5-acre water park featuring three pools, a 110-foot waterslide, five spas, two lagoons, tropical plants and exotic flowers. The guest rooms are decorated with colorful prints and wood-and-bamboo furnishings.

The Trop's casino is a refreshing change from the usual red-on-red motif with its tropical flower prints and lush green carpets. In addition to the usual poker room and sports book, you'll find poolside video poker machines and swim-up blackjack tables, which have a special waterproof layout and money dryers.

The hotel's long-running production show, *Folies Bergere*, is a musical tribute to the Parisian cabaret and has been enthralling audiences for more than three decades. Another popular nightspot at the Trop is the Comedy Stop, a classic comedy club that presents some of the best stand-up comics in the country. Dining choices include Pietro's classic continental cuisine, El Gaucho steak and seafood house, Calypsos coffee shop, an all-you-can-eat buffet and Mizuno's Japanese steakhouse for specialties prepared tableside. Other amenities include a wedding chapel, health club and a small cluster of retail shops.

Vacation Village

$ • 6711 Las Vegas Blvd. S. • 897-1700, (800) 338-0608

The first hotel motorists from California see upon entering the city is this low-profile, Southwestern-style, 360-room resort about 3 miles south of the actual Strip. Because it is so far from the action, the hotel relies on budget-priced rooms and inexpensive food to attract guests.

The bright and airy rooms feature Southwestern patterns and pastels, light wood furniture and a plastic Saguaro cactus for authenticity. The casino has plenty of room to maneuver and features a wide variety of slot, video poker and keno machines, 10 blackjack tables, roulette, Let It Ride and a race and sports book. Restaurant choices include a Denny's coffee shop, a taco stand, Italian restaurant and a very good all-you-can-eat Chinese buffet. Other amenities include three bars, a cabaret lounge and an outdoor pool overlooking the surrounding desertscape.

Westward Ho

$ • 2900 Las Vegas Blvd. S. • 731-2900, (800) 634-6803

The colorful casino facade with its weeping-willow light fixtures conceals a sprawling, 800-room motel-like property in back. Popular with families, the Westward Ho has guest parking outside the rooms, which are furnished with clean but simple furnishings.

The casino attracts a fair amount of traffic from The Strip and is most popular for its nickel slots and video poker machines. There are also blackjack tables, craps, roulette, keno, Caribbean Stud and Let it Ride Poker. The lounge/showroom features a modest production called *Hurray America*, which features various headliners including Marty Allen and his wife, singer Kate Blackwell. Except for a small deli counter, there's only one place to eat: a combination coffee shop and buffet, which is quite good, especially the steaks, prime rib and salad bar.

Downtown

Binion's Horseshoe

$ • 128 Fremont St. • 382-1600, (800) 237-6537

The first thing you notice about Binion's Horseshoe is the bustling, elbow-to-elbow casino. The emphasis here is on gambling, Wild West style. Day or night, the casino is usually packed. Every seat at the blackjack tables is filled, dice shooters crowd two deep around the craps tables, and slot players feverishly work the row upon row of machines as if possessed. The hotel boasts a no-limit gambling policy, but if your stake isn't in the high roller category, you can have your photo taken with $1 million in cash — 100 $10,000-bills encapsulated in a gold horseshoe-shaped vault. The hotel is also the site of the annual World Series of Poker, which guarantees at least $1 million to the winner.

Founded by Texan Benny Binion, the hotel's decor is true to its frontier heritage and reflects an Old West theme with darkwood panels, etched glass chandeliers and antique furnishings. The ceilings are low, as is the lighting, creating the feeling you've stepped back into the Horseshoe of the 1960s. Add the dealers in string ties and polyester-clad gamblers, and it's like you're caught in a retro time warp.

Of the 380 guest rooms, 80 are part of the original hotel and feature Victorian wallpaper, brass or painted-iron beds and quilted spreads. The 300 tower rooms, which were annexed from the defunct Mint Hotel next door, are more modern in decor, featuring plush carpeting, velvet headboards and white-enameled furniture.

Besides the fast and loose casino action, Binion's has a nice mix of dining choices. The buffet serves the usual prime rib fare but adds a nightly theme such as Tex Mex, Bayou, Italian and barbecue. There's also a first-rate steakhouse and a Chinese restaurant staffed with talented chefs. But your best dining bet is the 24-hour coffee shop, where the late-night $2 steak dinner and all-day $2.99 farmers breakfast are legendary. Other specialties include homemade chili and a hearty stew.

California Hotel

$ • 12 Ogden Ave. • 385-1222, (800) 634-6255

Despite its hip Hollywood implications, the California Hotel speaks of the tropics in a

FYI

Unless otherwise noted, the area code for all phone numbers listed in this chapter is 702.

INSIDERS' TIP

During the busiest conventions such as Comdex and CES (Consumer Electronics Show), hotels may raise their room rates by as much as 300 percent or more.

resounding "Aloha." As part of the Boyd Gaming family of resorts, the 781-room hotel has been a mecca to the Hawaiian tourist market since it was built in 1975. About 90 percent of the clientele are Hawaiians booked on special tour packages, so hotel staff wear aloha shirts, the restaurants offer Polynesian and Oriental specialties, and the bars serve tropical drinks. The casino, which is decorated with crystal chandeliers, etched glass and Italian marble, even has slot and video poker machines with Hawaiian names and themes. There's also a live keno lounge and an upstairs sports book.

The hotel's best restaurant is the Pasta Pirate, a casual seafood and pasta cafe decorated like a Monterey fish cannery. Prices are fair, and you can feast on a variety of fresh seafood such as mahimahi, salmon, shrimp and tuna (see our Restaurants chapter). For more formal dining, the Redwood Bar & Grill has a cozy lodge atmosphere highlighted by a massive fieldstone fireplace and serves steaks, seafood, chops and chicken specialties. The reliable Market Street Cafe is a 24-hour coffee shop with bargain-priced daily specials such as teriyaki beef, sweet-and-sour chicken and an authentic Hawaiian lau lau. The mezzanine level has a Waikiki-style bar, a Wiki Wiki ("hurry hurry") cafe for quick-serve Hawaiian specialties and a cluster of shops. As part of a 1996 expansion, a pedestrian walkway was built over Main Street to connect the California with Main Street Station, which is also owned by Boyd Gaming.

El Cortez

$ • 600 Fremont St. • 385-5200, (800) 634-6703

Built in 1941, the El Cortez is the oldest hotel-casino in town. The southwest wing retains the original adobe brick building, tiled roof and neon marquee that once stood three blocks from the nearest paved street. Since then a 14-story, 200-room tower has been added, but the original walk-up rooms with wooden floors and tile baths remain. The hotel was once owned by Benjamin "Bugsy" Siegel and sold when he needed to raise cash for his Fabulous Flamingo Hotel on The Strip. Today, El Cortez caters mostly to budget travelers, seniors and slot players.

Video poker is the name of the game in the casino, which caters to a large, loyal contingent of locals, many of them senior citizens. Here you'll find every nook and cranny of the split-level casino crammed with machines of every type and coinage. Because there are so many nickel poker and keno machines, the action is often intense. But be patient and you'll find a comfortable spot to join the fray.

There are only two places to eat: the Emerald Room, a 24-hour coffee shop that serves mammoth portions at bargain prices, and Roberta's, a steak and seafood house that specializes in prime rib, New York steak and Alaskan crab legs.

Fitzgerald's Hotel

$ • 301 Fremont St. • 388-2400, (800) 274-5825

Every day is St. Patrick's Day at the 34-story Fitzgerald's Hotel, the tallest building in downtown Las Vegas. Commonly referred to as the "Fitz," the 650-room hotel has a playful Luck of the Irish theme — shamrocks, leprechauns, and four-leaf clovers along with emerald green carpeting and wall coverings. Even the hotel staff dons green uniforms.

Coinciding with its merger with Holiday Inn in 1996, the hotel underwent a $17 million expansion that included remodeled guest rooms, expanded casino, new restaurants and a gigantic neon rainbow with a pot of gold over the hotel's Fremont Street entrance. Also standing guard is Mr. O'Lucky, a jolly green leprechaun who is supposed to spread good fortune to those who pass beneath him.

The dining choices are very good at the Fitz, including Molly's, a combination coffee shop and buffet that serves the usual fare plus fresh-baked goods in an Irish cottage setting. Pasta lovers will like Vincenzo's Cafe, where you can feast on Northern Italian cuisine. And Limerick's steakhouse (see our Restaurants chapter) specializes in well-aged steaks and prime rib plus fresh seafood, lamb and veal in an Irish castle-like dining room.

The budget-priced rooms have dark-green carpeting, but the wall coverings and furnishings are more subdued in light pastels and earth tones. Other hotel amenities include a McDonald's, bakery, sports bar, ice cream shop, coffee pub and cocktail lounge with live entertainment nightly.

Four Queens Hotel

$$ • 202 Fremont St. • 385-4011, (800) 634-6045

Reflecting a New Orleans motif, the Four Queens is the Grand Old Dame of downtown. Built in 1966, it was named for the owner's four daughters. It was later bought by Hyatt Corporation, and today it's owned by the Elsinore Corporation.

The lobby decor suggests the French Quarter with its carved wood registration desk, brass trim and hurricane-lamp chandeliers. The 720 bright, cheerful rooms feature plush tan carpets, dark polished wood furniture, brocade wallpaper and Victorian four-poster beds.

If you've got pull, try the world's largest slot machine (certified by Guinness) in the casino. Appropriately dubbed the Queen's Machine, the one-armed beast is 9 feet high and 18 feet long and accommodates six players who sit in chairs, shovel dollar coins into the slot and pray all eight reels line up with queens. If their prayers are answered, the jackpot pays $300,000. More prudent gamblers can get craps or poker lessons in the chandeliered casino.

Hotel amenities include two restaurants — Magnolia's Veranda coffee shop and Hugo's Cellar, a first-rate steakhouse and wine cellar (see our Restaurants chapter) — two cocktail lounges and an ice cream parlor.

Fremont Hotel & Casino

$ • 200 Fremont St. • 385-3232, (800) 634-6460

Built in 1956, the Fremont Hotel was downtown's first *carpet* joint (as opposed to the rural *sawdust* joints). It was also where Wayne Newton made his singing debut.

Today, its block-long neon sign helps light up the Fremont Street Experience and, like its sister hotel across the street (The California), it features a tropical island motif while also catering to a large contingent of travelers from Hawaii.

The hotel's 452 guest rooms are modern and comfortable and feature floral patterns in hues of emerald and burgundy. Most units have safes; some have mini-bars.

The sprawling casino is always busy, as bucket-toting gamblers flit from machine to machine, like hyperactive honey bees fluttering from flower to flower. And, during football season, the sports book is one of downtown's busiest.

Dining choices at the Fremont Hotel are very good. The upscale Second Street Grill is a good spot for steaks, seafood, chicken and lamb chops, while the Lanai Express serves up Chinese and Polynesian specialties. Seafood lovers will like the Paradise Buffet's Seafood Fantasy, which is offered Tuesday, Friday and Sunday, and baby back rib eaters will enjoy a branch of Tony Roma's.

Gold Spike Hotel & Casino

$ • 400 E. Ogden Ave. • 384-8444, (800) 634-6703

For an authentic look at the lower end of the gambling spectrum, check out the Gold Spike, a block north of Fremont Street. A throwback to the old sawdust joints, the Gold Spike's casino has plenty of $1 blackjack tables, nickel slot, poker and keno machines and penny slot machines. Actually, the penny slots are found only in Jackie Gaughan-owned properties: the Plaza, Western Hotel and the Gold Spike. Other gambling bargains include 40¢ live keno, 10¢ roulette and a coffee shop. There are 116 rooms.

Golden Gate Hotel

$ • One Fremont St. • 385-1906, (800) 426-1906

Built in 1906, the Golden Gate is the city's oldest hotel. (See our close-up in this chapter for the hotel's colorful history and how it influenced Las Vegas' growth.) It also had the distinction of introducing Las Vegas to the shrimp cocktail, which was brought here

INSIDERS' TIP

Sports fans can track the latest scores and betting lines 24 hours a day by calling the Stardust Sports Line at 220-9000.

from San Francisco by its owners during the 1950s.

While the hotel has been expanded and modernized over the years, the casino and public areas retain a feeling of turn-of-the-century San Francisco. You can still get a great shrimp cocktail served in a tulip glass with a wedge of lemon, or feast on huge deli sandwiches in the San Francisco Shrimp & Deli Bar. For heartier appetites, the Bay City Diner (see Restaurants chapter) serves up thick steaks, broiled seafood and other American favorites.

The hotel's 106 rooms have come a long way since the days of horse-drawn carriages. They've been updated with air conditioning, private baths, cable TV and voice mail, and the $50 per-night rate includes a breakfast and *USA Today* newspaper.

The casino contains about 500 slot and video poker machines, plus all the usual table games. Scattered throughout are a few vintage "one armed bandits" from the '30s and '40s.

While the Golden Gate may be the smallest hotel-casino in town, it's not short on history and charm. Located at the head of the Fremont Street Experience, it's definitely worth a visit.

Golden Nugget

$$ • 129 Fremont St. • 385-7111, (800) 634-3454

With its facade of polished white marble, gold trim and white canopies, the Golden Nugget stands out as the jewel among downtown hostelries. It's also the only downtown hotel *without* a neon sign. Inside, the posh hotel does have everything else, including the world's largest gold nugget — a 61 pounder — in a display case just outside the gift shop.

The hotel's elegant lobby features leaf-glass chandeliers, white marble floors and columns, etched glass panels, gold and brass accessories and red Oriental rugs. The white-marble and gold-trim decor is carried throughout the casino, restaurants and common areas.

The best restaurant is Lillie Langtry's, which features gourmet Asian cuisine (see our Restaurants chapter). The California Pizza Kitchen is also popular, and the 24-hour coffee shop has a surprisingly extensive menu with a number of California-chic specialties.

The 1,907 guest rooms, which include 27 luxury apartments and six penthouse suites, are among the most luxurious in town and feature cream-colored carpets and wall coverings, light-wood tables and club chairs, tropical-print bedspreads and drapes.

The hotel's elegance continues in the posh casino with plush carpet in tropical colors and white marble walls accented by brass and gold trim. Despite appearances, you can still find plenty of nickel slot machines and $2 blackjack tables. There's also a race and sports book and keno lounge.

The hotel's Theatre Ballroom once hosted celebrity headliners but is now home to the ongoing *Country Fever*, a country music revue (see our Nightlife chapter). Other amenities include his and hers beauty salons, a video arcade, a health spa and an outdoor pool surrounded by mature palm trees.

Jackie Gaughan's Plaza Hotel

$ • 1 Main St. • 386-2110, (800) 634-6575

Jackie Gaughan's Plaza Hotel is the only caravansary in town, with a built-in train depot and Greyhound bus station. Bus travelers can step off the platform into the hotel's casino.

The hotel's 1,037 rooms include 136 suites and are open and airy, featuring plush green carpeting, walnut veneer and colorful patterns in the draperies and bedspreads. Make sure you ask for one that faces Fremont Street rather than the railroad yard behind the hotel.

The complex has three restaurants, including one serving excellent Chinese-Thai cuisine and Center Stage Restaurant, which serves

INSIDERS' TIP

At 1,149 feet, the Stratosphere is the tallest observation tower in the country and the fourth-tallest building behind the Sears Tower (1,454 feet), World Trade Center (1,377 feet) and Empire State Building (1,250 feet).

continental fare with a front-row view of Glitter Gulch's neon pyrotechnics. Other amenities include a topless production show called *Xtreme Scene* and a sports deck with a pool, jogging track and the only tennis courts in the downtown area.

Lady Luck Hotel

$ • 206 N. Third St. • 477-3000, (800) 523-9582

The charter buses out front are a tipoff — the Lady Luck is favored by tour groups because of its budget-priced rooms and bargain restaurants. The hotel also has one of the brightest casinos in town, featuring 800 machines to keep the decibel level high and a good mix of table games — craps, blackjack, roulette, Caribbean Stud, Let it Ride and Mini Baccarat. If you plan a lot of gambling, check out the Mad Money Slot Club, which has one of the higher payback rates in town.

The hotel's 791 rooms include 132 junior suites, seven master suites and two Presidential suites. They are bright and open and feature light-wood furnishings and pastel color schemes. All are equipped with an in-room TV, remote control, digital alarm clock, refrigerator and full-length dressing mirror. Junior suites have a Jacuzzi bath, larger rooms, separate vanity and sitting area.

When it's time to eat, the Banquet Buffet has a variety of hot and cold selections, and the 24-hour coffee shop features daily specials such as a $4.49 prime rib special. For a quality dining experience, try the Burgundy Room (see our Restaurants chapter), which features a gourmet menu and magnificent wine list in a room filled with original art by Dali, Erte and Poucette.

Las Vegas Club

$ • 18 Fremont St. • 385-1664, (800) 634-6532

One of the best-kept secrets in town is the Las Vegas Club. Despite its glittery neon and mirrored exterior, the hotel has a friendly, small-town atmosphere. The lobby is separate from the casino, with potted plants and comfortable chairs for relaxing. The hall leading to the casino is decorated with sports memorabilia such as autographed photos, baseballs, bats and gloves and vintage programs and ticket stubs.

The casino's mirrored ceiling creates an open feeling — even when it's packed — and it's seldom noisy. Blackjack players love the Las Vegas Club because of its liberal rules: double down on any two, three or four cards; split and re-split any pair; surrender your original hand for half your bet; and win on six cards totaling less than 21. The sports book is also one of the most popular with local bettors. During football season it's a madhouse on game days.

Through a 1996 expansion, the hotel now has 409 guest rooms, mostly modern affairs with Southwestern color schemes, white wood furniture and ceramic lamps. The hotel has a good steakhouse and an excellent coffee shop, which usually draws a line of people for breakfast and lunch sittings.

FYI

Unless otherwise noted, the area code for all phone numbers listed in this chapter is 702.

Main Street Station

$ • 200 N. Main St. • 387-1896, (800) 465-0711

Main Street Station originally opened in 1991 but closed after a few months because of severe financial problems. But since it was bought and reopened by Boyd Gaming (Stardust, Sam's Town, Fremont and California hotels), it has evolved as one of downtown's classiest destinations. The architecture suggests 1890s New Orleans with its brick promenade, magnolia trees, wrought-iron fences and Victorian street lamps from pre-World War I Brussels.

Inside, the hotel makes liberal use of hardwood and tile floors, gas lamps, brass fixtures and enough antiques to fill a Southern mansion. For instance, the lobby contains authentic hardwood railroad benches and bronze, dropped-dome chandeliers from the El Presidente Hotel in Buenos Aires. The stained-glass window greeting casino visitors is from Lillian Russell's mansion, and the carved mahogany cabinetry behind the registration desk came from a Kentucky apothecary. You'll also find Theodore Roosevelt's Pullman railroad car and a section of the Berlin Wall.

Visitors will find great places to wine and

dine. Among them are the Pullman Grill, a moderately priced steakhouse with a cigar and martini bar located inside a rail car that once belonged to Louisa May Alcott; and the Garden Court Buffet, whose food stations serve up delicious doses of designer pizza and pasta, Mexican medleys, Chinese favorites and Hawaiian luau treats. But the best place to indulge is the Triple 7 Brewpub (see our Restaurants chapter for complete details), which follows a 1930s warehouse motif with rich hues of mahogany and cherrywood accented by brass and copper patinas. The featured fare includes oysters on the half shell, chile verde, gourmet pizzas and a serving of garlic french fries that will take your breath away. Any of the four ales are worth a visit, and save room for the World's Greatest Bread Pudding.

Stratosphere

$$ • 2000 Las Vegas Blvd. S. • 380-7777, (800) 99-TOWER

No one misses the Stratosphere: Its space-needle tower is visible from anywhere in the Las Vegas valley. In fact, the 1,149-foot tower is the tallest observation tower in America. If you want to rise above it all, it costs $5 to take the ride to the top ($4 for Nevada residents), where you'll get a sweeping view of the valley and surrounding mountains. There are two observation decks — one indoors and one outside. For those with stomachs of steel, there are two thrill rides at the top: a roller coaster and the Big Shot, which shoots upward 180 feet then free falls back to the launching pad.

Getting back to earth, the hotel hosts an afternoon show, now a rarity in Las Vegas, called *Viva Las Vegas*. After dark, the *American Superstars* take over in the main showroom and stage drop-dead impersonations of superstars like Madonna, Gloria Estefan and Michael Jackson, to name a few (see our Nightlife chapter). Note that the impersonators perform live, as opposed to the lipsynch impressionists at some other shows.

The Stratosphere has a good selection of dining options. For continental cuisine and a view of the world from every angle, try the Top of the World restaurant, which rotates 360 degrees every hour. The Big Sky Steak House, also at the top of the tower, serves steaks, prime rib and seafood off a fixed-price menu. But our favorite places to eat are Ferraro's Italian restaurant, which has been serving innovative dishes to Las Vegans for decades, and Roxy's Diner, a retro eatery where ballroom-dancing waiters swing as they serve.

At 97,000 square feet the Stratosphere's casino is one of the largest in town. Spread over several split levels you'll find all the popular table games and nearly 2,500 slot and video machines. There's also a keno lounge and race and sports book.

Other hotel amenities include three wedding chapels in the tower pod — talk about taking the plunge! — and a 200-seat cocktail lounge. The Stratosphere's 1,500 guest rooms, which include 120 suites, are modern affairs and are equipped with creature comforts such as hair dryers, coffee makers, clock radios and floor safes.

East Valley

Boulder Station

$$ • 4111 Boulder Hwy. • 432-7777, (800) 683-7777

Like the other Station hotel-casinos, Boulder Station focuses on offering a variety of eating and gambling choices favored by local residents. The massive casino has more than 120,000 square feet of casino space where you'll find 3,000 slot, video poker and keno machines plus all the popular table games, highlighted by single-deck blackjack and 10X odds on craps.

INSIDERS' TIP

Many casinos offer free funbooks for their guests. They typically contain discount coupons for drinks, food, shows and car rentals as well as match play coupons, which can be wagered like cash at the tables.

There are 11 restaurants and quick-serve outlets, plus eight bars throughout the property. One of the best is the Guadalajara Bar & Grill, which serves overflow portions of hot sizzling fajitas, traditional burritos and elaborate combination plates. And don't miss the one-of-a-kind Mild to Wild Salsa Bar, where you can dip yourself silly on your favorite salsas and bean dips. For prime-grade steaks and seafood, try The Broiler, while the Pasta Palace serves Italian favorites in a vineyard setting. Boulder's Feast buffet has hundreds of items to choose from, including a novel flambé dessert station. For diners on the run, the quick-serve outlets offer everything from burgers to yogurt to pizza to pretzels.

From headline acts to first-run movies, Boulder Station is also one entertaining place. *The Railhead*, an intimate cabaret, features live entertainment from blues bands to improvisational groups to karaoke nights. It also hosts concerts for mostly country stars such as Rick Trevino, Hal Ketchum and John Berry.

Sam's Town

$$ • 5111 Boulder Hwy. • 456-7777, (800) 634-6371

If you want a taste of the Old West, saddle up and head for Sam's Town. Starting with the Western movie-set exterior, everything here emphasizes the spirit of the Old West. There's a gambling hall, 14 saloons and 10 restaurants offering up "home-style chuck."

A recent addition is Mystic Falls Park, a spectacular indoor atrium with a nine-story glass roof and 25,000-square-foot indoor park filled with live trees, brooks, waterfalls, footpaths and animated birds and squirrels.

Despite its Dodge City ambiance, the casino is a complete and sophisticated gambling hall. There are nearly 3,000 slot machines in all shapes and sizes in the tri-level casino, plus dozens of blackjack tables, craps tables and a European-style roulette wheel (no double zero). The poker room offers Texas Hold'em and Seven Card Stud, and the bingo parlor hosts several sessions a day that include free continental breakfast at the early bird (7:30 AM) session.

Other amenities include a Western dance hall, 56-lane bowling alley, horseshoe-shaped swimming pool, ice cream parlor and a Western emporium that's the largest in Nevada (see our Shopping chapter). At the Final Score sports bar, patrons can take a shot at an indoor basketball court, electronic darts, and other virtual reality games. Outside, the recreation area features a pool with waterfalls, sand volleyball court and whirlpool spas. You can also watch a free water and laser show, the Sunset Stampede, four times daily.

Showboat Hotel, Casino & Bowling Center

$$ • 2800 E. Fremont St. • 385-9123, (800) 826-2800

A Vegas landmark since 1953, the Showboat opened as a somewhat rickety 100-room motel and casino. Through expansions, the hotel now has nearly 500 modern guest rooms, a 106-lane bowling center, an 80,000-square-foot casino, four restaurants, showroom and the city's largest bingo parlor.

Because of its many attractions, the Mardi Gras-theme hotel has become a mecca for low rollers who flock to the bowling alley and the bingo parlor. They also like the 1,600 slot and video poker machines, which are spread across a casino that is bright and spacious and accented by plantation murals, flower boxes, plants and chandeliers. Also popular with parents is the supervised day-care center, which gives kids a safe place to play for three free hours.

Of the 495 guest rooms, six are suites. The newer ones are in the 19-story tower and feature dark wood furniture and plush carpet, color coordinated in pleasing earth tones. The older garden rooms by the pool are less luxurious but still clean and comfortable.

INSIDERS' TIP

The first major resort built on The Strip was the El Rancho in 1941. It burned down in 1960 and its site at the corner of Sahara Avenue and The Strip remains vacant.

Sunset Station

$$ • Sunset Rd. at U.S. 95, Henderson • 547-7777, (888) 786-7389

The latest and largest in the Station Casinos family, Sunset Station, which opened in June 1997, is set on 100 acres across the street from the Galleria Mall in Henderson.

Like its Station cousins, Sunset Station has a full slate of dining choices: Rosalita's for Mexican specialties; Capri Italian Ristorante; Costa del Sol seafood restaurant and oyster bar, which serves fresh selections in a fishing village setting (see our Restaurants chapter); a 24-hour coffee shop and international buffet; and a Gordon Biersch microbrewery specializing in German-style lagers. If you're in a hurry, you can get quick service at Viva Salsa, Capri Pizza Kitchen, Fat Burger, Manhattan Bagel, Kenya's Bakery and Ben & Jerry's Scoop Shop. In addition to six full-service restaurants, Sunset Station's amenities include a celebrity showroom, lounge, 10-screen movie theater and game arcade.

The 80,000-square-foot casino has more than 2,500 slot and video machines, of which more than 700 are of the 5¢ variety, a testament to the local patronage. There are also 40 table games, a spacious race and sports book, keno lounge and live poker parlor. The hotel's 470 guest rooms, which include 70 suites, are contained in a 20-story tower that's adjacent to a Mediterranean-style swimming pool.

West Valley

Arizona Charlie's Hotel & Casino

$ • 740 S. Decatur Blvd. • 285-5200, (800) 342-2695

The Wild West is a popular theme for Vegas resorts, but Arizona Charlie's takes it a step further — this is "Where the West Gets Wild." And who's to dispute them with bars like the Naughty Ladies Saloon and restaurants like the Yukon Grill?

Historically, Arizona Charlie was a frontiersman who raised cattle in Mexico, mined for gold during the Klondike Gold Rush and roped steers in Buffalo Bill's Wild West Show. So the casino that bears his name is probably more mild than wild, compared to his amazing adventures. Nevertheless, you can seek your own motherlode in the saloon-like gambling hall, where you'll find 1,600 slot and video machines, blackjack, craps, roulette, Let it Ride and a 24-hour poker parlor. You can also play bingo and bet the broncos in the race and sports book.

When it's time for chuck, the Yukon Grill serves charbroiled steaks, chops, chicken and seafood, or you can chow down on a variety of grub in the 24-hour Sourdough Cafe coffee shop. The Wild West Buffet is good for hearty appetites, and Chin's Chinese Restaurant brings a taste of the Far East to the Wild West.

After the sun sets, the aforementioned Naughty Ladies Saloon stages a bawdy dance hall revue, or you can look for your favorite entertainers in the Palace Grand Theatre, which has booked top acts such as Ambrosia and Tower of Power.

The hotel's 258 guest rooms include seven suites and feature Western artifacts, Native American art and light wood furniture. Rounding out the amenities are a sparkling pool and banquet facilities for up to 600.

Boomtown

$ • 3333 Blue Diamond Rd. • 263-7777, (800) 588-7711

Whether or not you strike it rich, you can stake your claim in this Gold Rush-themed resort about 3 miles southwest of The Strip. Boomtown's decor is surprisingly tasteful, if not authentic, from the gaslight lamps and rough-hewn beams to gold-panning sluices and leather-trimmed furniture.

Bring an appetite because the Chuckwagon Buffet has plenty of ribs, steak and chicken for hearty diners, or you can grab a bite 24 hours a day in the Comstock Coffee Shop. You can wet your whistle in the Whiskey River Bar, or belly up to Peedoodles Long Bar for a monstrous 60-ounce Margarita (if you drain it, you can keep the glass). For the adventurous, Rattlesnake Ricky's gives new meaning to "lounge lizards," who can dance and carouse in the glow of state-of-the-art video sound walls. For more civilized entertainment, try the Opera House Theater, which frequently hosts country-western stars like Ricky Van Shelton and Aaron Tippin.

The casino is reminiscent of the old Longbranch Saloon, but the only Kitty you'll encounter is on the Seven Card Stud and Texas Hold'em tables. Otherwise, you have to be content with about 1,200 slot and video machines and a good mix of table games.

Boomtown's 300 guest rooms are tastefully done with light-wood furniture, wrought-iron lamps and brass headboards, but the more popular accommodations are at the 460-space RV park, which offers phone and cable TV, picnic areas, clubhouse and swimming pool.

Gold Coast

$ • 4000 W. Flamingo Rd. • 367-4700, (800) 331-5334

One of the most popular neighborhood hotels is the Gold Coast. The complex has a tasteful, understated (a rarity in Las Vegas) Spanish flair with a white adobe exterior and red-tile roof. The registration area features tiled floors, an arched entry, carved-wood doors and stained-glass windows. The 750 rooms are large and bright, with plush blue carpet, light adobe walls with wood trim and Southwestern-style curtains and spreads.

The list of hotel amenities are of the something-for-everyone variety and include four restaurants, five bars, two large casinos, a 72-lane bowling alley, a country-western dance hall and a cabaret lounge for other live bands. If you get tired of shooting dice or playing the slots, you can bowl a line or two, catch a movie in the twin-screen theater, learn the Texas two-step or simply relax in the ice cream parlor and watch hotel guests struggle with their luggage.

Unless you're a bingo player, avoid the mezzanine level, where hundreds of serious bingo nuts gather 10 times a day for sessions that resemble after Christmas sales.

There's more: The pool is surrounded by landscaping, waterfalls and a tropical bar; the two movie theaters are the only ones in town to screen foreign and offbeat art films; and the tiny shopping arcade has a wine-and-spirits shop with more than 200 collectible miniatures.

Palace Station

$$ • 2411 W. Sahara Ave. • 367-2411, (800) 634-3101

Originally built in the mid-1970s as a motor court and bingo parlor, Palace Station has evolved through a series of expansions into a modern resort hotel. The bingo room is still one of the busiest in town, but the hotel now boasts five excellent restaurants, a piano bar, live entertainment, a new 22-story tower and a huge casino that caters to die-hard slot and video poker fanatics.

In addition to launching the Station Casinos chain as one of the most successful in the gaming industry, Palace Station served as a model for other "neighborhood" casinos. Its formula, which couples a mix of popular dining choices with a large casino filled with video poker machines, has been repeated by practically every other locals-oriented casino in Las Vegas and beyond.

The tried-and-true dining choices include The Feast buffet, the 24-hour Iron Horse coffee shop, The Broiler seafood restaurant, the Pasta Palace and the Guadalajara Bar & Grill for happy-hour Margaritas and tasty Mexican specialties.

The casino has more than 2,200 machines, 50 gaming tables, a 600-seat bingo room, two live keno games, a nine-table poker room and spacious race and sports book. The casino also has been a pioneer in locals-oriented promotions, including its Car-A-Day in May giveaway that started in 1985 and its Great Giveaway Football Contest that has been the citywide standard since it was introduced in 1986.

The 600-room tower has a marbled lobby accented with chrome and polished brass. The rooms are decorated in warm colors against bold-print bedspreads and feature carved wood furniture, overstuffed easy chairs, built-in dressing tables, floor-to-ceiling windows and brass wall and ceiling lamps. The 400 older

INSIDERS' TIP

Las Vegas is home to nine of the 10 largest resort hotels in the world.

rooms in the original section of the hotel are basic but clean and pleasant with earth tone color schemes

Rounding out the hotel's amenities are two cocktail lounges; the Loading Dock Lounge, which offers nightly entertainment; a gift shop; two swimming pools; and a video arcade.

The Rio

$$ • 3700 W. Flamingo Rd. • 252-7777, (800) 752-9746

Bring your party masks because it's a Brazilian carnivale at The Rio, an upbeat, fast-paced all-suite hotel about a half-mile west of The Strip. The hotel is easily identified by its brightly lit sign that resembles a geyser erupting neon streams of water and the red- and purple-neon accented towers.

Through expansion the Rio's casino has grown into one of the largest and noisiest in town. The calypso theme continues with confetti colors, thatched huts and faux coconut palms. In addition to the foliage, you'll find the usual casino games and machines plus a bright and spacious sports book and Jackpot Jungle, a slot and video poker arcade equipped with TV monitors for viewing old movies and hotel information while gambling. In the registration area, guests are greeted by brass parrots, colorful ribbons of neon, nautilus shells on the ceiling and plush carpeting that suggests a floor of confetti and streamers.

The 2,563 suites are at least 600 square feet in size and feature rich earth tones accented by tropical print spreads and curtains, smoked glass tables, velour furnishings in the sitting area and floor-to-ceiling windows for panoramic city views.

The most recent expansion (completed in 1997) added a 41-story, 1,037-suite tower and Masquerade Village — a $200 million shopping, dining, entertainment and gambling complex, woven together in an ongoing carnivale atmosphere. Visitors to the Village are treated to a daily Masquerade Show in the Sky, in which five fantasy floats glide high above the village floor to an orchestration of music and dance. A cast of 36 specialty performers including musicians, aerialists and costumed stilt walkers add to the festivities, and guests can participate by traveling on one of the floats. Other amenities in Masquerade Village include six restaurants, a wine-tasting cellar, about 30 retail shops and galleries (see our Shopping chapter) and wedding facilities that feature two decorated chapels, catering and reception areas and two 1,200-square-foot honeymoon suites.

Among the hotel's best dining bets are the Village Seafood Buffet, the Voo Doo Cafe for Cajun specialties, Asian favorites at The Mask, Mexican dishes at Babloeo, Buzios for a popular oyster and seafood bar, a rotisserie grill for poultry, steaks and seafood and the always-crowded All American Bar & Grill, a Manhattan-style eatery with great food and a broad selection of American beers.

For after-hours fun, Club Rio is one of the hottest discos in town, and the showroom's featured performer, ventriloquist/comedian Danny Gans — the man with a thousand voices — has been acclaimed as one of the best all-around entertainers in the city (see our Nightlife chapter). Outdoors lovers will find the pool area to their liking. A sandy beach lies at the edge of a tropical lagoon, complete with waterfalls and three swimming pools. There's also an entertainment gazebo and two sand volleyball courts.

Santa Fe Hotel

$ • 4949 N. Rancho Dr. • 658-4900, (800) 872-6823

Surrounded by open desert and mountains in burgeoning northwest Las Vegas, the Santa Fe Hotel is far from The Strip's madding crowd. Because of its remote location, the farthest from the action, guests enjoy a more relaxed pace, and facilities are seldom crowded. As you'd expect from the name, the low-profile hotel has a Southwestern flavor with white stucco walls and a red-tile roof. The rooms are colored with cool pastels accented by Navajo-pattern prints and white wood furniture.

The casino is noted for its user-friendly layout — there's plenty of room to spread out — and friendly dealers, change persons and cocktail servers. But what would you expect from a casino whose managers host picnics and barbecues in the parking lot?

Although the gentle pace here is laid back, it's not comatose. The bowling alley and ice-skating rink keep the place jumping, and the lounge often hosts Dixieland and jazz musicians. Among the dining choices are a steak and seafood house, French restaurant, Italian restaurant and a Mexican/Southwestern restaurant. There's also a buffet, coffee pub and a Ben & Jerry's Ice Cream parlor.

North Valley

Fiesta Casino Hotel

$$ • 2400 N. Rancho Dr., North Las Vegas • 631-7000, (800) 731-7333

The self-proclaimed "Royal Flush Capital of the World" is obviously geared to a specific market — video poker players! So naturally most of the casino's 1,200 machines are video poker. Because of the broad variety of poker machines — Double Bonus, Double Double Bonus, Deuces Wild, Aces Bonus, Deuces Wild Bonus, to name a few — the Fiesta gives free lessons that teach you how to play all the latest machines. The lessons are held once a week (call for day and times) in the casino. If poker isn't your game, you can still gamble on video keno and reel slot machines or play live keno, bingo and table games. You can also bet the ponies and your favorite teams in the race and sports book, which features a drive-through window for making bets from your car.

Following the neighborhood casino recipe for success, the Fiesta offers a multitude of eating options including a Chinese restaurant; the Old San Francisco Steak House, made famous by blocks of aged Swiss cheese and the "Girl on the Red Velvet Swing"; and the Albuquerque-based Garduno's Restaurant & Cantina, famous for its Margaritas and guacamole prepared tableside. But perhaps the highlight of the dining rooms is the Festival Buffet, which features 11 serving stations, including a fire-pit barbecue, where each day an entire side of beef or pig is spit-roasted over a mesquite wood barbecue and a wood-burning rotisserie cooks 90 chickens. There are also separate cookers for ribs, fish and shish kabobs. Other specialty stations include a wood-burning pizza oven, Cajun kitchen with open-flame burners, chowder bar, high-pressure woks for Asian specialties and a specialty coffee bar (see our Restaurants chapter).

Like most of the other locals-oriented casinos, the Fiesta is short on guest rooms (100) and entertainment and long on slots and video poker machines. So if poker's your game, the Fiesta's your name.

Texas Station Gambling Hall & Hotel

$$ • Rancho Dr. at Lake Mead Blvd., North Las Vegas • 631-1000, (800) 654-8888

Squeeze into your Wranglers and lace up your Ropers for some Western-style fun. Built in mid-1995, Texas Station continues the family of Station Casino clones started by Palace Station in the mid 1970s. But it's the first to veer from Station's railroad motif in favor of a Wild West theme. Like its Station predecessors, Texas Station targets local gamblers and entices them with an array of first-rate dining choices and a sprawling casino stocked with a myriad of gambling machines.

Restaurants include the Stockyard Steak & Seafood House, San Lorenzo Italian restaurant, 24-hour Yellow Rose Cafe and Laredo Cantina & Cafe (a great spot for Margaritas), a fresh salsa bar and Mexican and Southwestern specialties. The Market Street Buffet may not be deep in the heart of Texas, but its deep-pit barbecue should satisfy cravings for cattle-country cuisine.

The casino has nearly 2,000 slot and video machines, plus the usual complement of table games — blackjack, craps, roulette, Let it Ride and Pai Gow Poker. You can also try a new game called Royal Match or return to old favorites like keno, bingo, horse racing and sports betting.

INSIDERS' TIP

Casinos that cater to tourists have a heavier mix of reel slot machines than video poker and keno machines. The opposite is true at casinos for locals, who seem to prefer games with an element of strategy.

There are only 200 guest rooms (including two suites) at Texas Station, but they are hardly afterthoughts. The rooms are bright and spacious and well-appointed with oak furnishings, wrought-iron fixtures, dark carpeting and brocade upholstery.

Nighttime attractions at Texas Station include 12-screen movie theaters and two popular watering holes: The Garage Bar for cognac and fine cigars and the Armadillo Lounge for throwing down Bloody Marys and all-night honky-tonkin'.

It may come as a surprise, but there are local hotels and motels that don't have so much as a slot machine.

Nongaming Accommodations

If you're not a gambler, or just don't want to fight your way through the casino crowds on the way to the front desk, you don't have to stay in a huge gambling-centered megaresort when visiting Las Vegas. It may come as a surprise, but there are local hotels and motels that don't have so much as a slot machine.

This chapter is dedicated to establishments that leave the gaming to others. These accommodations run the gamut from old-style motor lodges to swanky upscale resorts. We have crisscrossed the Las Vegas Valley to highlight some of the best choices here.

First, a few pointers.

Rates in Las Vegas fluctuate from week to week and month to month. Part of the variation is due to the seasons. The demand for rooms is strong almost year-round but tends to be heaviest in spring and fall. Peak periods occur during all holidays and around major conventions, such as the COMDEX computer trade show in mid-November and the Consumer Electronics Show in early January. It's not unusual for hotels and motels to triple or quadruple their regular room rates during these events, which span up to a week.

When looking at advertised rates, note that hotels may advertise a great price — such as $18 — but that's almost always a per-person rate based on double occupancy. So that actually adds up to a minimum charge of $36. You'll also want to be mindful of the local sales and room taxes that are tacked on, boosting the bill by 9 percent. We take all this into account in our listings.

Price Code

As with our Gaming Resorts chapter, this section uses a three-tier price code. Rates are quoted for a single-night, double-occupancy stay on a weekend night. The prices are for typical weekends — excluding holiday weekends and the peak convention periods mentioned above. A word of advice: Some Strip hotels, in an effort to discourage visits by children, will give no price break to families. So the customary discounts for minors indicated in this chapter may make nongaming motels and hotels a better deal.

$	**$50 and less**
$$	**$51 to $100**
$$$	**$101 and up**

Unless otherwise noted, the accommodations in this chapter have outdoor pools, free local phone calls, cable television and rooms for nonsmokers. Major credit cards are accepted, and reservations are encouraged, especially on weekends. Pets are not permitted unless we tell you otherwise.

This chapter is divided into four styles of lodging: hotels and motels, extended-stay properties, bed and breakfasts and RV parks. The categories are further divided into geo-

INSIDERS' TIP

Looking to ring in the New Year here? You had better make your reservations at least two months in advance. The New Year's holiday has become the most popular in Las Vegas.

graphic regions around the valley. (For accommodations in Boulder City, see our Daycations chapter.) The rate symbols for extended-stay units, where lodgers may dwell for weeks, are converted to daily charges.

As this chapter was being compiled, a number of new nongaming hotels were on the drawing board and promised to bring added variety and sophistication to resort life here. Marriott Corp. entered the market and is building two full-size hotels. The first opened for business in the fall of 1997 and is listed in this chapter. The other, a 1,500-room Marriott Marquis at the MGM Grand, is scheduled to debut in 1999. These hotels — along with Marriott's existing Courtyards, Residence Inns and a Fairfield Inn — will make the company a major player on the Las Vegas hospitality scene.

Another newcomer to town is the Ritz Carlton, which is planning a 500-room luxury hotel. Also on the grounds of the MGM Grand, this Marriott-owned resort is not expected to open until 2000. A half-mile farther south on The Strip, a Four Seasons Hotel will rise at Circus Circus' new development south of its Luxor pyramid. Tentatively slated to open by 1999, the Four Seasons will have 400 rooms in a 25-story tower. Each of these projects will be accompanied by large-scale convention and banquet facilities.

The arrival of these elite newcomers suggests a paucity of quality nongaming hotels. Statistically, that's true. Nearly 90 percent of Las Vegas' 100,000 hotel rooms are attached to casinos. And while there are scores of motels, many are small and decrepit affairs. Scattered north and east of downtown, these types of motels are often poorly maintained. Their vacancy signs speak volumes about their business, which tends to pick up only when every other room in town is filled. You won't find any flophouses in this chapter.

The lion's share of nongaming hotels are, ironically enough, just off the casino-packed Strip. We list a number of presentable properties in this area. They run the gamut from budget specials to pricey resorts. However, good lodging at any price can be tricky to find in other parts of the valley. Read on and we'll show you the way.

FYI

Unless otherwise noted, the area code for all phone numbers listed in this chapter is 702.

Hotels and Motels

The Strip Area

Alexis Park Resort Hotel

$$$ • 375 E. Harmon Ave. • 796-3300, (800) 453-9000

This is a perfect spot for conventioneers and families who want a full-service retreat from Las Vegas' noisy hustle and bustle. The all-suites, two-story complex features a refreshing water garden on 20 lushly landscaped acres. Every one of its 500 newly remodeled suites has a refrigerator, mini-bar and VCR. Some of the larger units (up to 1,200 square feet) have fireplaces or Jacuzzis. Alexis Park has a 24-hour lounge and a gourmet Italian restaurant. For fitness buffs, there are three pools, a spa, two tennis courts, a well-appointed workout room and a nine-hole putting green on the grounds. Hair styling and massages are available. For business get-togethers, 44,000 square feet of meeting space is available in a variety of configurations. For families, youngsters through age 18 stay free. Valet laundry service is offered, and free coffee is perking in the elegant Spanish-tiled lobby each morning. Alexis Park stays busy year-round, so reservations are a necessity.

Algiers Hotel

$$ • 2845 Las Vegas Blvd. S. • 735-3311, (800) 732-3361

Opened in 1953, the Algiers qualifies as a Las Vegas landmark. Offering guests bargain rates for a Strip location, the small, centrally located hotel has a large pool, and the 105 rooms are clean and well-maintained, even

INSIDERS' TIP

The average daily cost for a room in the Las Vegas area is $54, according to the Las Vegas Convention and Visitors Authority.

though the furnishings are dated. The service is friendly and homey without the hustle of newer establishments. The two-story layout is an oasis of simplicity among The Strip high-rises and allows visitors to park near their rooms. A barbecue restaurant is off the lobby, but don't expect such spiffs as free coffee or complimentary hors d'oeuvres. The Algiers calls itself a hotel, but it's really a no-frills motel that lets its neighbors do the entertaining.

Carriage House

$$$ • 105 E. Harmon Ave. • 798-1020, (800) 777-1700

A half-block east of The Strip, the Carriage House is often overlooked by visitors. But the 154-suite hotel offers some of the best accommodations in the city. The rooms are among the best buys in town and feature plush carpeting, overstuffed sofas, kitchenettes and VCRs. The relaxing lobby is decorated in cool grays and blues and furnished with sofas and tables. The ninth-floor restaurant, Kiefer's, has unobstructed views of the city and the neighboring MGM Grand Hotel and Theme Park. Outside, the tennis court, pool, Jacuzzi and sun deck are surrounded by pine trees. Free airport shuttle service is available, and coin-operated laundries can be found on each floor.

Courtyard by Marriott

$$-$$$ • 3725 Paradise Rd. • 791-3600, (800) 321-2211

The Courtyard is popular with business travelers because of its fax machines, meeting rooms and large work desks in the 149 guest rooms. The rooms, decorated in tasteful earth tones, range from Spartan single-bed quarters to spacious suites that include separate living rooms. The cable TV has pay-per-view first-run movies, and the telephone is conveniently cordless. You'll find an exercise room, whirlpool and swimming pool. Special facilities are available for handicapped travelers. Located across Paradise Road from the Las Vegas Convention Center, Courtyard is a hot ticket during the city's nonstop trade shows, so reservations are essential. Like most Marriott properties, this Courtyard is clean and well-maintained, and the grounds are manicured. The staff is efficient. Discounts of up to 30 percent are available on some of the slower summer weekends. Lodgers who stay over for seven nights or more can also get a cut rate.

Crowne Plaza Hotel

$$$ • 4255 Paradise Rd. • 369-4400, (800) HOLIDAY

This upscale member of the Holiday Inn corporation features 200 suites set in a six-story atrium. New and ensconced in glass, this hotel is bright and airy. A waterfall tumbles through the central atrium. The rooms are comfortable and spacious with modern furnishings. It's friendly to families (each suite has two TVs, and kids younger than 18 stay free) as well as business executives (9,000 square feet of convention space and three big conference rooms). In-room dataports, VCRs and refrigerators make for an enjoyable, self-contained stay. And this is one of the few luxury hotels that allows pets.

Fairfield Inn

$$ • 3850 Paradise Rd. • 791-0899, (800) 228-2800

The least expensive of Marriott Corp.'s properties, Fairfield Inn still knows how to pamper guests. Each room has a large, well-lit work area and desk. Complimentary continental breakfasts, airport shuttles and free incoming fax service are among the perks at the 129-unit complex. Data ports are installed in every room, and specialized suites for handicapped travelers are available. Just 2 miles north of the airport and within walking distance to topnotch restaurants, Fairfield Inn is a clean and modern hotel that's a consistent bargain, especially if you have youngsters — they stay free.

Inns at McCarran

$$ • 5100 Paradise Rd. • 798-2777, (800) 634-6439

The closest lodging to McCarran International Airport, the Inns at McCarran is actually a combined Days Inn and Howard Johnson. If you like light and airy rooms, check into the Days Inn. If you favor dark woods and a subdued ambiance, try HoJo. Either way, you'll find yourself in a clean and comfortable room since all 327 units have been recently remodeled. If you're going to stay for a couple of days, ask for one of the selected rooms that has a refrigerator and microwave. In addition to tourists who prefer distance from the action, the motel caters to business travelers and conventioneers. It's also popular with local companies because of its Inn Club, which guarantees a corporate rate 365 days a year, even during conventions like COMDEX. Families like the Inns, too, because kids stay free. A deli restaurant is on site, as are a coin-operated laundry and cocktail lounge.

La Concha Motel

$$ • 2955 Las Vegas Blvd. S. • 735-1255

The Moroccan-style architecture is no accident. La Concha took over the neighboring El Morocco a few years back and retained the theme for its circular lobby. Bringing the multi-ethnic theme to the next level, there's a Korean restaurant at the motel. Check out the sushi bar; it's all you can eat — so long as you eat it within an hour. Two- and three-story motel complexes from the '60s extend out back, leading to a modern nine-story tower. In all, there are 351 rooms that run a bit larger than the typical shoebox-size rooms common at so many motels. Decorated in light wood, the motif is clean and contemporary. But aside from the two swimming pools, the amenities are sparse, so don't plan on doing any cooking, laundry or HBO viewing. Just put the chores on hold and walk to The Strip from this nice central location.

La Quinta Inn

$$ • 3970 Paradise Rd. • 796-9000, (800) 531-5900

La Quinta Inn is a 228-room, Mediterranean-style building with white stucco walls, red-tile roof and black ironwork, all surrounded by tall palm trees and lush landscaping. The lobby, which is a cross between a Swiss chateau and a country farmhouse, features exposed beam ceilings, tile floor, arched windows and leather wing chairs for relaxing. The step-up dining room, which doubles as a reading room or den, features open-beam ceilings, country English wood tables and chairs and a cozy fireplace. The rooms, which are light and airy, are above-average size and include balconies, VCRs, microwaves, refrigerators and whirlpool tubs. The three-story building contains banquet and meeting rooms that will accommodate up to 100 people in each. A 24-hour complimentary shuttle service runs to the airport and to designated stops along The Strip.

Marriott Suites

$$$ • 235 Convention Center Dr. • 650-2000, (800) 228-9290

Located midway between the Las Vegas Convention Center and The Strip, the Marriott Suites are the hotel giant's first foray into southern Nevada. The 278-room, 17-story tower, just completed in the fall of 1997, is an all-suite facility. Separate bedrooms and sitting rooms, pragmatically decorated in business-like greens and mauves, span 650 square feet. Each suite has a refrigerator and coffee maker. Room service is available, and a copy of *USA Today* is delivered every morning. The hotel, which caters to corporate travelers, runs a free shuttle to and from the airport and has valet laundry. A well-appointed Business Center on the top floor comes equipped with personal computers, printers, copiers and fax machines. An attendant is on site to assist with the equipment, and the front desk can tell you about any charges that apply. Downstairs, 2,800 square feet of meeting space is available. Overall, the suites are relatively light on recreational amenities, providing just a basic pool and workout room. A restaurant and grill called Alleys serves up basic American fare, but if you're looking for lounge entertainment or late-night dining, you'll want to take the two-block walk to The Strip.

Motel 6

$ • 195 E. Tropicana Ave. • 798-0728, (800) 4MOTEL6

The largest Motel 6 in the United States, this budget-priced chain motel has 877 rooms just a mile east of The Strip. Sprawling as it may be, this place is always packed with families and children and is booked well in advance. But unlike Motel 6s of bygone days, this inn will accept credit card reservations. The two-story U-shaped building wraps around a pool and features a playground and whirlpool. Coin-operated washers and dryers are available. The rooms are typical of Motel 6 — sparsely appointed but clean and functional.

St. Tropez Hotel

$$$ • 455 E. Harmon Ave. • 369-5400, (800) 666-5400

The St. Tropez looks like a Palm Springs resort with its pink stucco walls, red-tile roof and palm trees. Inside, the mission-style hotel features luxurious rooms that have everything from refrigerators and ironing boards to blow dryers and bathrobes. Half of the 149 suites have been refurbished in light avocado greens and pastels. The others retain an old world flavor with dark woods and furnishings. All rooms come equipped with VCRs. The inviting pool area is surrounded by trees and gardens. The lobby has a rich European ambiance, fitting for St. Tropez's upscale clientele. Business travelers appreciate the in-room dataports, available fax services and daily delivery of *USA Today*. A ballroom and meeting rooms are on site. A restaurant also is on the premises, and limited room service is available. Free shuttle service runs to the airport and The Strip. Speaking of free, kids 12 and younger stay gratis. You'll enjoy the complimentary continental breakfast buffet off the lobby. At 5 PM, adults can replenish their caffeine levels at an open cappuccino and espresso bar.

Downtown

Days Inn Downtown

$$ • 707 E. Fremont St. • 388-1400, (800) 325-2344

With 147 rooms, this is the largest Days Inn in the region and a perfect motel for budget travelers who still want decent lodging. Kids younger than 18 stay free, and as many as five people can stay in a room for the regular double-occupancy rate. The bathrooms are ample, and the room decor is muted, with the color scheme ranging from browns to blacks. Located across Fremont Street from the El Cortez Hotel-Casino, the motel is just a short two blocks from the Fremont Street Experience. A restaurant on the premises serves generous portions at reasonable prices. Small pets are allowed with the manager's permission.

Econo Lodge Downtown

$ • 520 S. Casino Center Blvd. • 384-8211, (800) 223-7706

Three blocks south of Fremont Street, this Econo Lodge has 48 remodeled rooms decorated in light colors and modest furnishings. Each unit is equipped with a coffee maker and a refrigerator. HBO is on cable, and a coin-operated laundry is on site. Weekday rates are a bargain, but you had better get a reservation if you want to stay on a weekend. Kids younger than 18 stay free. There is no pool.

East Valley

Courtyard by Marriott

$$-$$$ • 2800 Green Valley Pkwy., Henderson • 434-4700, (800) 321-2211

You know the drill. This Courtyard is a virtual clone of its sister hotel on Paradise Road — and hundreds of others nationwide. The rooms are clean, light and modern. The grounds and common areas are well-maintained. Still, there are a few welcome touches to this brand-new hotel that opened last fall. Covered areas have been included for casual outside dining. These cabana-style retreats are equipped with cool-stream misters and fans to beat the heat. Slightly larger than the Paradise Road Courtyard, there are 155 rooms. And the location is within easy walking distance to Green Valley's trendy commercial center that contains movie theaters, arcades and a growing number of restaurants.

Sunrise Resort

$$ • 4575 Boulder Hwy. • 434-0848, (800) 362-4040

Located on the "Boulder Strip" midway between Sam's Town and Boulder Station hotel-casinos, this executive suite hotel has 300 units. The rooms, furnished in cheery peach and teal tones, have kitchen facilities (but bring your own silverware and plates). There are 230 two-room suites, each measuring a spacious 400 square feet. Each comes with two televisions, two telephones, a fold-out queen-size bed and a full king-size bed. These suites are bargain-priced at the same rate as the one-bedroom units and, needless to say, they are the first to fill up, so reservations should be made well in advance. Corporate group discounts can trim as much as 20 percent off the price of rooms. Families get a break, too, because kids 18 and younger stay free. For group gatherings, Sunrise Resort has two meeting rooms, suitable for parties of 50 to 70 people. Coin-operated laundry and dry-cleaning services are available too. A deli restaurant is on site, and free shuttle service is provided to the airport, The Strip and to nearby Boulder Highway resorts.

West Valley

Bonnie Springs Motel

$$ • 1 Bonnie Springs Ranch Rd. • 875-4400

If you want to get away from it all, this is the place to go. Eighteen miles west of town off Charleston Boulevard, this bucolic resort is a throwback to the old days. Among its 50 rooms are five themed suites dressed up in the motifs of American Indians, Spanish, Chinese, covered wagons and the Gay '90s. If you're not into period pieces, there are suites with indoor Jacuzzis, fireplaces and mirrors on the walls and ceilings. Yow! And for more conventional family fare, 13 larger suites contain full kitchens (with utensils) and televisions in both bedrooms. VCRs can be rented and that might be a good idea because Bonnie Springs doesn't have cable. Kids younger than 13 stay free, and they will enjoy the free petting zoo and miniature train on site. Cowpokes ages 7 and older can saddle up for morning horseback rides ($20 per hour). Next door is Old Nevada, a rustic Western village with turn-of-the-century shops, an opera house and a wax museum of notable Western figures on the main street. Daily gunfights and shootouts are staged to keep things lively. (See our Attractions chapter for details.) Meeting rooms on the grounds accommodate up to 1,000 people for conventions and retreats. A restaurant a half-mile away at Bonnie Springs Ranch serves excellent food. Any steak on the menu is excellent! In keeping with the old West flavor, there are no nonsmoking rooms at the motel. Pets are accepted with a $50 cash deposit.

Holiday Inn Express

$$ • 8669 W. Sahara Ave. • 256-3766, (800) 4HOLIDAY

Located in the high-rent district next to The Lakes subdivision and across the street from Canyon Gate Country Club, this Holiday Inn has 59 rooms in a modern three-story tower.

Some of the spanking-new suites include full kitchens, complete with dishwashers, ovens and all utensils. Others feature six-person Jacuzzis and are decked out in Native American or Egyptian themes. Three restaurants, an ice cream parlor and a pizza parlor are within walking distance. Children younger than 19 stay free with their parents, and the youngsters can frolic on the grassy park areas surrounding the hotel. Corporate customers are pampered, too, with complimentary fax service and a theater-style meeting room that is equipped with audiovisual equipment, which can also be used at no extra charge. When the weekday travelers leave, the hotel discounts weekend rates. Every morning, guests wake up to a full continental breakfast in the lobby. From 5 to 6 PM on weekday evenings, cookies, coffee and other beverages are served. The upscale surroundings provide a welcome sense of comfort and security for travelers, and the hotel is favored by many women executives for that reason.

North Valley

Comfort Inn North

$$ • 910 E. Cheyenne Ave., North Las Vegas • 399-1500

Just west of Interstate 15, this modern 59-room motel caters to lodgers who want to put some distance between themselves and The Strip. Three kitchenette suites and three spa suites allow families to stretch out. While all rooms have computer dataports installed, a special business suite makes a good temporary office with a fax, a large desk and working areas. A meeting room accommodates groups of up to 50 and comes equipped with an overhead projector, white boards and a VCR. The Comfort Inn North is popular with families waiting to move into nearby neighborhoods. A full continental breakfast is served daily, and the weekend fare is especially scrumptious, including waffles and breakfast burritos. The motel has chess boards, jigsaw puzzles, dominos and coloring books for the youngsters (who stay free if they're younger than 18). And the adults may appreciate the fact that there are no noisy video games on the premises. If you need a gambling fix, however, the Fiesta Hotel-Casino's free shuttle stops here daily. A coin-operated laundry is on site, and pets are welcome without a deposit.

Nellis Motor Inn

$$ • 5330 E. Craig Rd., North Las Vegas • 643-6111, (800) 528-1234

Less than 2 miles from Nellis Air Force Base and the Las Vegas Motor Speedway, this 52-unit motel is as unassuming as its blue-collar neighborhood. But don't sell it short. The inn, part of the Best Western chain, has all queen-size beds and newly refurbished rooms dressed up in light colors and oak furnishings. The rooms have coffee makers and HBO. Kids 12 and younger stay free, and there is a playground for them to burn off all that youthful energy. Bring along Fido because pets are allowed. A coin-operated laundry is on the premises.

Vegas Chalet

$ • 2401 Las Vegas Blvd. N., North Las Vegas • 642-2115

Clean and most affordable, the Vegas Chalet is close to North Las Vegas' downtown civic center. It's white and red exterior is well-maintained, as are its 50 rooms, which can be rented at weekly discounts. Half of the units have small kitchenettes (no microwaves, silverware or plates, however). There is no pool, but you'll have HBO in your room and a coin-operated laundry on the premises. Pets are allowed for a $10-a-day additional charge.

Extended-stay Hotels

The Meridian

$-$$ • 250 E. Flamingo Rd. • 735-5949

Live like a local at this 685-unit luxury apart-

INSIDERS' TIP

If you decide to stroll up Fremont Street at night, use caution. While police, including bike patrols, are prevalent, Las Vegas, like most downtowns, has its unsavory elements.

ment complex that has 100 apartments available for rent by the day, week or month. One- and two-bedroom flats come with all the creature comforts: housewares, linens, full kitchens, telephone answering machines and washers and dryers. The units have spacious 9-foot ceilings and private balconies and are ensconced inside security gates. The modern Spanish-style complex, set on manicured grounds, blends recreation with business. Two lagoon-size pools and spas, tennis and racquetball courts and a health club are on the grounds just a half-mile east of The Strip. Conference rooms and meeting facilities also are available, and corporate residents can take advantage of a concierge desk that handles faxes, photo copying and video equipment. A 21-seat mini-theater is an ideal venue for screening training films. Weekly maid service also is available.

Polo Towers

$$$ • 3745 Las Vegas Blvd. S.
• 261-1000, (800) 935-2233

Travelers can spend days or weeks on The Strip at this 479-room complex. Studio and one-bedroom suites are designed for business travelers and families alike. Decorated in Southwest pastels, Berber carpet and light wood, each suite has sliding doors that open to a private balcony. All units have refrigerators, and the one-bedroom flats have full kitchens, complete with all the cooking and dining utensils. Video players, full stereos, closet safes and computer dataports are in all rooms. A pool and spa are on the roof; a fitness center, steam room and salon, with masseurs and hair stylists, are on the ground floor. Though the Polo Towers doesn't have its own restaurant, the Polo Plaza out front houses a Marie Callendar's, Chevy's (Mexican) and a Starbucks. Business meetings can be accommodated in four convention rooms, ranging from 700 to 2,000 square feet. The front desk provides fax and copy service and can even produce transparencies for overhead projectors. When you're all done for the day, try the 19th-floor bar for a cool drink and a great view. It's open 24 hours.

Residence Inn by Marriott

$$ • 3225 Paradise Rd. • 796-9300
$$ • 2190 Olympic Ave., Henderson
• (800) 331-3131

Like Marriott's Courtyard, its stablemate next door, the Residence Inn on Paradise Road is situated neatly across the street from the Las Vegas Convention Center. This townhouse-style hotel serves a complimentary breakfast and a complimentary weekday dinner buffet. The 144 studio units and 48 two-bedroom suites have kitchens, complete with microwaves and dishwashers. VCRs, generous closet space and coin-operated laundry provide the comforts of home. Curbside parking and nicely landscaped grounds add to the relaxed feel. The quiet lobby features wing chairs for relaxing around the fieldstone fireplace. Rounding out the hotel amenities are a pool, three spas and a grocery-shopping service. If you're in Henderson, a new 126-unit Residence Inn recently opened at 2190 Olympic Avenue. Comparably equipped, it offers easy access to Green Valley's commercial and retail centers. And it, too, is next to a Courtyard by Marriott.

Sun Harbor Budget Suites

$$ • 3684 Paradise Rd. • 699-7000
$$ • 4855 Boulder Hwy. • 433-3644
$$ • 4625 Boulder Hwy. • 454-4625
$$ • 2219 N. Rancho Dr. • 638-1800
$$ • 1500 Stardust Rd. • 732-1500
$$ • 4205 Tropicana Ave. • 889-1700
$$ • 4975 Polaris Ave. • 227-8377

Located around the valley — but always within walking distance of casinos — every room at these 200- to 300-unit complexes is a minisuite with a living/dining room and kitchen. The buildings are laid out like large apartment complexes, with a dozen or so units in each block. Sun Harbor offers discounted monthly packages. Maid service is available, but you can save the expense if you bring your own linens and towels. Self-serve laundry facilities are on site. Also, second- and third-floor units run less than ground floor rooms. One- and two-bedroom units are available, and all suites come with satellite television service. The pool areas include barbecue pits shaded by palm trees. Lighted tennis and volleyball courts are nearby. Complimentary coffee and snacks are provided in the lobby. Though Sun Harbor

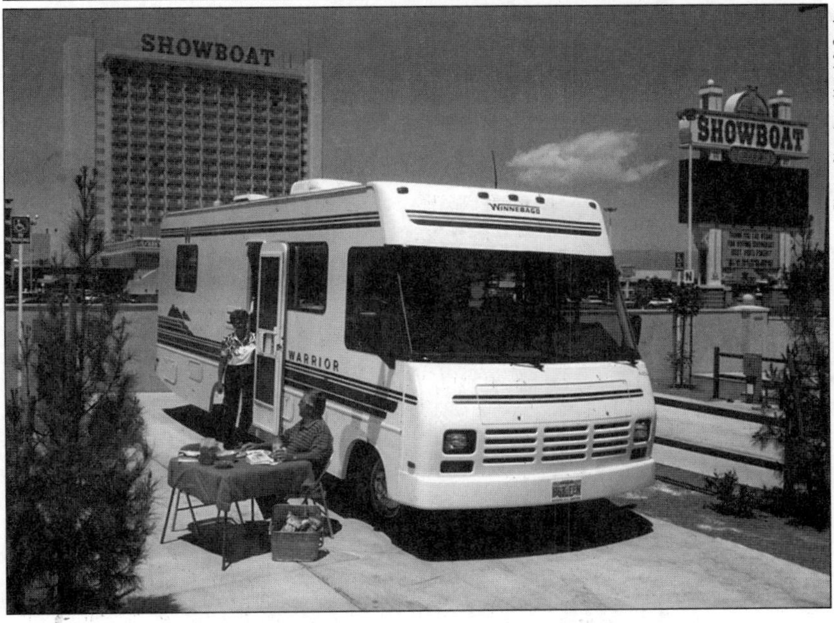

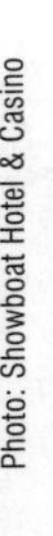

Several of the gaming resorts have RV parks complete with hook-ups and facilities for RV travelers.

complexes are nicely landscaped and relatively new, their proximity to casinos and fun-loving clientele are not necessarily conducive to family-oriented vacations. The toll-free number is (800) 752-1501 for all locations.

Bed and Breakfast Inns

With so much emphasis on gaming, bargain buffets and Strip-centered entertainment, Las Vegas' bed-and-breakfast business is almost nonexistent. In fact, you have to head for the hills to find one. There are, however, a couple that have succeeded in cultivating a quiet and exclusive hospitality niche. And their off-the-beaten-track locations make them a particularly enjoyable respite from all the hustle and bustle.

Almost Heaven

$$$ • 123 Rainbow Canyon Blvd., Mt. Charleston • 872-0711, (888) 636-5398

Located 7,000 feet above sea level at Mount Charleston, Almost Heaven pampers guests with crisp pine-scented air and a lavish turn-of-the-century motif. Forty-five minutes northwest of Las Vegas (take Nev. 157 W. from U.S. 95), this is a cozy place with just four suites. Maryjane Falls is the name of the honeymoon suite. The others are named Robber's Roost, Charleston Peak and Bristlecone Pine. Each has distinctive decor that includes feather beds, elaborate floral tapestries, claw-foot bathtubs, fresh-cut flowers and in-room fireplaces. A 3,000-square-foot Victorian parlor is a gathering place for breakfasts and afternoon hors d'oeuvres. Personalized butler service and in-room dining are available for couples who prefer privacy. The entire 10,500-square-foot home — along with its service staff — can be rented for group gatherings or meetings. A spacious Jacuzzi room with marble flooring provides soothing relief after a day of skiing or hiking. A new 9-hole golf course is just 2 miles down the road.

Chateau Spaulding

$$$ • Sunrise Mountain • 437-1606, (888) JGATSBY

Talk about exclusive. This modern Mediterranean villa near the top of Sunrise Mountain so zealously protects its privacy that visitors must call ahead to get the address. Set on 2 acres 20 minutes east of The Strip, the 10,000-square-foot Chateau Spaulding features four suites. The top of the line is the 1,200-square-foot Great Gatsby suite, which has a private patio, balcony, Jacuzzi and dining chamber, his-and-her showers, a sunken marble bath and a fireplace. All suites offer spectacular views of the valley. Guests are treated to Ralph Lauren robes and Waterford crystal. Butlers serve breakfasts in-room. For an additional charge, the staff will order in gourmet dinners and can arrange for tennis, golf, horseback riding, bicycling and sightseeing outings. The chateau, which provides free pickup and drop-off at the airport, also makes its limousine and yacht on Lake Mead available to guests for an added fee. Chateau Spaulding's entire facility can be rented by the day or weekend — a popular option for some elaborate weddings.

RV Parks

Recreational vehicles have many ports of call in the valley. Rates are competitive, with many costing less than $20 a day. The parks listed here all have full hookups and accept pets unless otherwise indicated. Most parks do a brisk business and encourage reservations.

Boomtown

$ • 333 Blue Diamond Rd. • 263-7777, (800) 588-7711

If you're coming in from California, this is a good place to drop your anchor. Just a couple of miles south of The Strip off Interstate 15, you can settle in here before braving the craziness of Las Vegas traffic. Boomtown's 460 spaces are, well, spacious, measuring 60 feet by 12 feet. And each is cable and phone ready. There's a mini mart, pool, showers, laundry and shuttle to the hotel.

California Hotel-Casino and RV Park

$ • 100 Stewart Ave. • 388-2602, (800) 634-6505

This freeway-close location, at the junction of I-15 and U.S. Highway 95, is a great place for downtown visitors. It's an easy two-block walk to the Fremont Street Experience and its 10 casinos. The 220-space lot is gated and includes a swimming pool, Jacuzzi, showers and laundry.

Circusland RV Park

$ • 500 Circus Circus Dr. • 794-3757, (800) 634-3450

Just off The Strip next to the Circus Circus hotel-casino, Circusland is a favorite for families. With the hotel's indoor amusement park, Grand Slam Canyon, just steps away and scores of casinos within easy walking distance, you won't have to do much driving once you pull in. The 369-space facility has a monorail to the casino and a fenced run for pets, plus a pool, Jacuzzi, supply store and laundry facilities. Because Circusland is so popular, it limits its visitors to two-week stays.

KOA Kampground

$ • 4315 Boulder Hwy. • 451-5527

Set up camp here for a day, a month or more. Discounted long-term rates are available at this 240-space facility that has a store, showers, a pool and Jacuzzi. Kids will enjoy the playground, and adults will like the free shuttle to casinos. This is one of the very few parks that allows tents too.

Oasis Las Vegas RV Resort

$ • 2711 Windmill Dr. • 258-9978, (800) 566-4707

Across I-15 from Boomtown, this south-end park is another convenient port of entry for RV campers coming up from California. With a mind-boggling 700 spaces, the Oasis

INSIDERS' TIP

If you are a member of AAA or the American Association of Retired Persons (AARP), be sure to mention that when booking a room. Most local hotels and motels offer discounts to those groups.

has a resort-style clubhouse with banquet facilities and a ballroom. The pool is accompanied by a sandy beach, and duffers will enjoy the 18-hole putting course. A large store and a children's playground make the Oasis almost a city unto itself.

Sam's Town RV Park

$ • 5111 Boulder Hwy. • 454-8055, (800) 634-6371

Along the old eastern entrance to town, Sam's Town RV Park offers 291 spaces, along with a pool, showers, store and laundry. The facility is a treat for country-western fans who enjoy the boot-scooting musical entertainment offered by neighboring Sam's Town hotel-casino. And since Sam's Town is on the way to Lake Mead, this is also a good staging area for anglers and boaters.

Sunrise Resort RV Park

$ • 4575 Boulder Hwy. • 434-0848, (800) 362-4040

Just up the road apiece from Sam's Town, Sunrise Resort offers a 239-space lot. The facility features a modern recreation room with pool tables and exercise equipment. A pool and barbecue area are also on the grounds. And you can leave the driving to others by taking Sunrise's free shuttle to casinos along Boulder Highway.

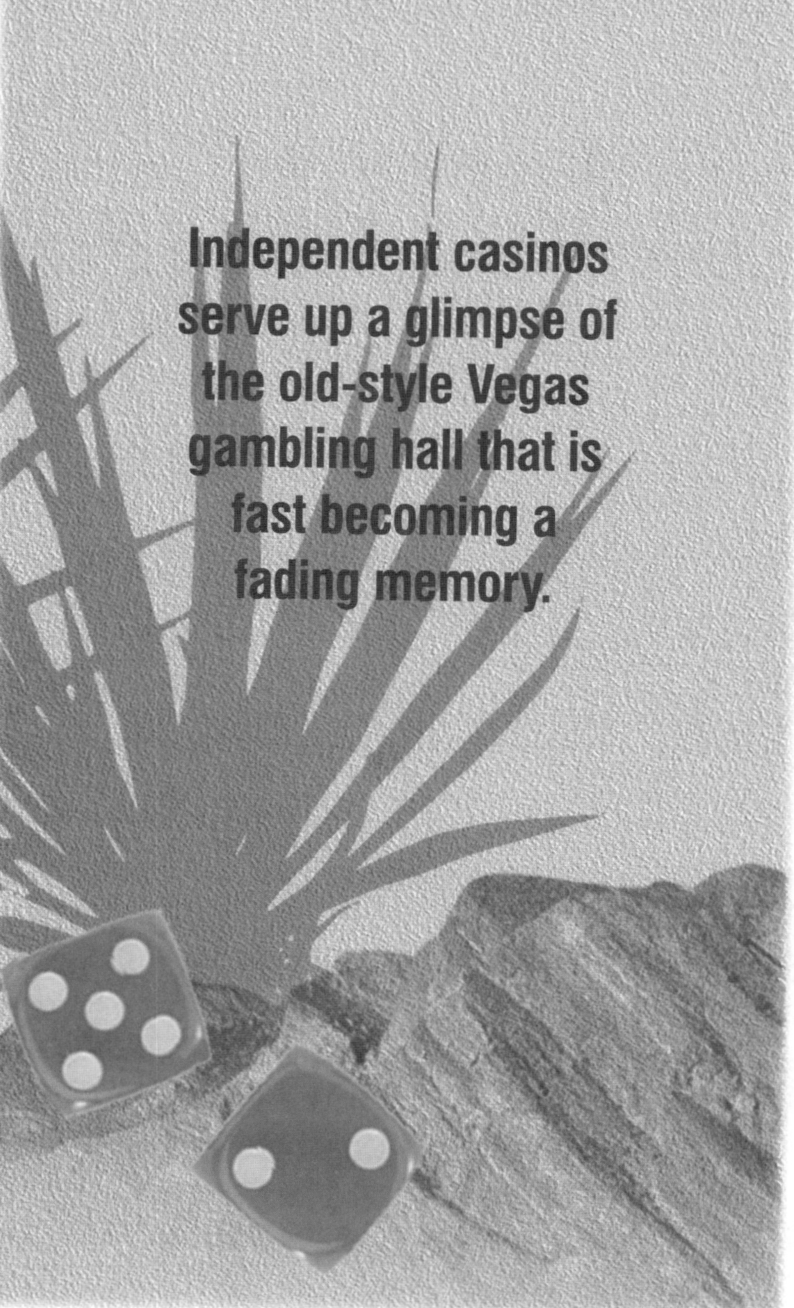
Independent casinos
serve up a glimpse of
the old-style Vegas
gambling hall that is
fast becoming a
fading memory.

Independent Casinos

The independent, stand-alone casino is fast becoming an endangered species in Las Vegas. Ever since the powerful Nevada Resort Association in 1989 pushed through legislation that required every new casino to have a 250-room hotel attached to it, very few have been built. And many of them, especially in downtown and along The Strip, have closed their doors, unable to compete against the megaresorts that offer a smorgasbord of amenities beyond card tables, slot machines and keno parlors.

For this book we've classified independent casinos as those gambling halls that have cashiers on the premises but don't offer accommodations. This differentiates them from bars, convenience stores and other establishments that have gambling devices but do not pay jackpots directly to the players. Instead, these establishments usually rely on a slot route operator to come out and make the awards, fill the machines with coins when they run dry and repair them when they crash. (See our Gaming Guide chapter for inside tips on playing.)

Many of the long-lost casinos were an essential part of Las Vegas' colorful history — the Pioneer Club in downtown erected the landmark Vegas Vic neon cowboy on Fremont Street, and Little Caesars on The Strip was legendary for accepting high-stakes bets on sporting events, including a $1 million bet on the 1978 Super Bowl (the casino lost).

Nevertheless, there are a couple dozen independent casinos remaining in town, many of them serving up a glimpse of the old-style Vegas gambling hall that is fast becoming a fading memory. Many of these casinos are patronized by local gamblers, so visitors can also mingle with the locals and gain a feel for life in Las Vegas. While most tourists probably have never visited or even heard of these casinos, they remain an intrinsic aspect of Las Vegas' ambiance. Venture outside the marble walls of the megaresort, and you'll discover why.

The Strip Area

Ellis Island Casino

4178 Koval Ln. • 733-8901

You can't miss the Ellis Island Casino with its green-and-white canopy awnings, brick veneer front and English Tudor gables. Enter the front door, and you're standing in the middle of the sports book, where a bank of TV monitors stare intently at you from their ceiling perch. The entry is only fitting — the sports book with its various proposition bets and liberal betting lines has been the main attraction at Ellis Island Casino for years. Move a few feet to the right, and you're in the modest casino dominated in the center by a horseshoe bar that's surrounded by about 200 video poker and slot machines. Rounding out the amenities is a 24-hour restaurant that serves value-priced steaks and seafood plus pasta specialties.

Eureka Casino

595 E. Sahara Ave. • 794-3464

The Eureka is a popular gathering spot for casino personnel who work at the nearby Sahara, Riviera, Stardust and Circus Circus hotels. On any given night, you can find dozens of them, nursing their Margaritas and piña coladas while clustered around the U-shape bar or hunkered down over their favorite video poker machines. Because it caters to locals, the Eureka's 225 machines are mostly of the video poker and keno variety, in nickel and quarter denominations. There are also a few reel slots and dollar machines plus a few progressives. The Eureka also serves good food at fair prices in its coffee shop and regularly stages drawings for valuable prizes such as Hawaiian vacations and new cars.

O'Shea's Casino

3555 Las Vegas Blvd. S. • 792-0777

Next door to the Flamingo Hilton, O'Shea's is in a modern brick-and-stucco building reminiscent of an upscale Tudor-style restaurant. Like most on The Strip, the casino floor is noisy with the constant clank of coins and slot machines. There are more than 500 electronic games here, split evenly between reel slots and video poker and keno machines. All coin denominations are available, with a lean toward the lower-end nickel and quarter machines. Players will also find all their favorite table games — craps, roulette, the Big Six wheel, Let it Ride, Caribbean Stud poker and blackjack, which occasionally opens a $3 minimum table, a rarity on The Strip. In addition to a 24-hour restaurant, O'Shea's has a fast food court with a Burger King, Subway, Orient Express, Jay's Pizza, Baskin Robbins and a few specialty shops including Ethel M Chocolates. Upstairs is O'Shea's Magic & Movie Hall of Fame (see our Attractions chapter), an exhibit of show business, ventriloquism and magic memorabilia. You can also see a live comedy-magic show and browse in a magic gift shop.

FYI

Unless otherwise noted, the area code for all phone numbers listed in this chapter is 702.

Silver City Casino

3001 Las Vegas Blvd. S. • 732-4152

With its barn-red panels, wraparound porch and swinging doors, Silver City could pass for a large saloon in a John Ford Western. Inside, there are more Western artifacts — mining pick axes, lanterns, branding irons, hurricane lamp chandeliers and more. There are even Western scenes painted on the ceiling above the casino floor. The pit runs the length of the casino and contains a full complement of games — blackjack, roulette, craps, poker and Let it Ride. About 600 electronic games surround the pit with many more to the rear of the casino. At the rear of the casino you'll find a few 10¢ slot machines, which are quickly becoming a rare breed in Las Vegas. A large alcove to the side of the pit is dedicated to mostly 5¢ slot and video machines.

Among the casino's popular promotions are a daily free play on a giant poker machine for a chance to win a new car and a scratch-card game for cashing your paycheck. Prizes range from free drinks, food and two-for-one dinners to cash awards up to $5,000. Night owls will like the restaurant's graveyard specials that include a 99¢ Belgian waffle and $3.99 steak dinner.

Slots-A-Fun

2880 Las Vegas Blvd. S. • 734-0410

Slots-A-Fun, next door to Circus Circus, will give you a taste of what casinos in Las Vegas were like 25 years ago: The casino is wide open to the sidewalk with raucous gamblers crowded around the craps tables, seemingly oblivious to the pedestrians and traffic on the street. Adding to the ambiance are 50¢ hot dogs, 99¢ shrimp cocktails and a free-pull promotion in which you pull a slot handle on a special machine for a chance at a new car. There are also hundreds of machines crammed tightly into the long, narrow casino, plus all the popular table games — blackjack, craps, roulette, Caribbean Stud, Let it Ride and Red Dog. There's even a kitschy souvenir shop where you can buy T-shirts and caps with tasteless slogans about what you didn't do in Las Vegas.

Town Hall Casino

4155 Koval Ln. • 732-1499

The aging Town Hall Casino has a loyal following of players who love the casino's selection of IGT Fortune video poker machines. Unlike the modern credit and bill-accepting models, these older machines dump coins without building credits and usually offer the hard-to-find 9-to-1 payoff on full houses. The IGT Fortunes may not be the fanciest poker machines in town, but some of the old-timers swear by them and will play nothing else. In the split-level casino you'll also find a fair number of reel slots, three blackjack tables and a 24-hour restaurant. Helping to entice patrons are bonus payouts on blackjack and video poker, and a double-your-paycheck check-cashing promotion.

Downtown

Coin Castle Casino

15 E. Fremont St. • 385-7474

Above the Coin Castle's entrance is a 10-foot-high king, although the statue looks more like Merlin the Magician peering down from his castle-top perch. Out front, barkers attract players by hawking a free spin on a big electronic slot machine. The free spin leads to other promotions inside, such as free drawings and bonus payouts while you gamble on one of the Castle's 101 slot and video poker machines.

Sassy Sally's Casino

32 Fremont St. • 382-5777

The barkers in front of Sassy Sally's use a different tactic to get you in: You get a free souvenir photo of yourself, but it takes 15 minutes to process. So why not gamble inside while you wait? There are about 150 slot machines to choose from, including the progressive Nickels Deluxe and Quarters Deluxe as well as a variety of video poker machines. If you aren't interested in the machines try the bar, which has a nice oak counter top, oak bar stools and cold beer.

East Valley

Alystra Casino

333 W. Sunset Rd., Henderson • 564-8555

At first glance, it's hard to believe the Alystra is a casino. With its Cape Cod gables, paneled exterior, shake roof and wraparound porch, it looks more like a Victorian estate in

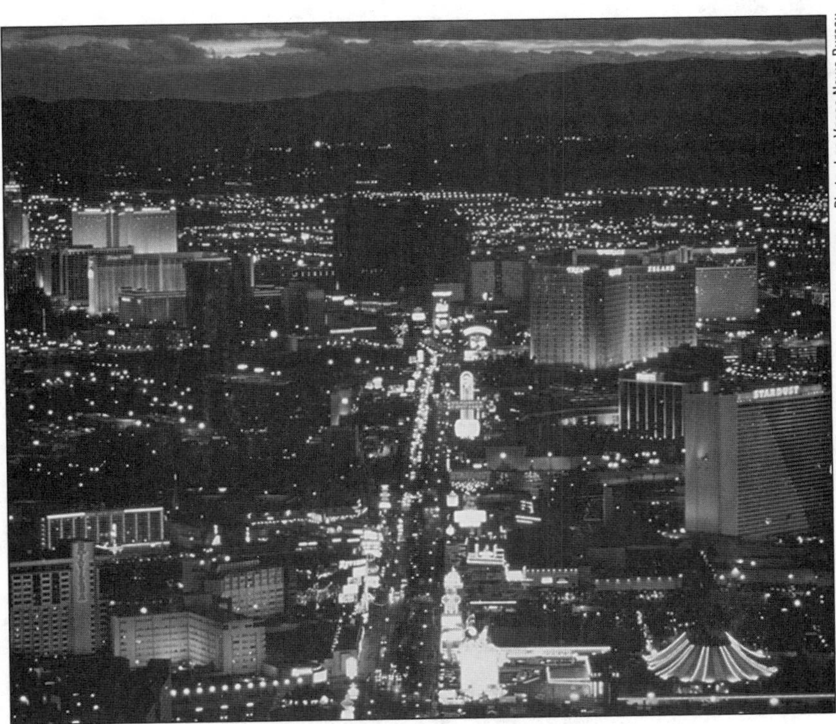

Photo: Las Vegas News Bureau

The Strip illuminates the heart of the valley at night.

old Pasadena than a gambling hall. Inside, the casino rambles through several rooms and split levels, culminating in a center hall that is flanked by a sports book and a cocktail lounge. The latter features a large TV screen, which can be seen from anywhere in the casino. In addition to the four blackjack tables ($2 minimum), gamblers will find a wide variety of video poker and keno machines plus reel slots such as Quarters Deluxe, Nevada Nickels, Cool Millions and Megabucks. The Alystra also has a slot club that rewards members with cash and merchandise such as caps, T-shirts, jackets and more. There are also weekly cash drawings for Club Alystra members and seasonal promotions, such as the summer Jet Ski giveaway. Rounding out the amenities are a restaurant and gift shop that sells logo merchandise.

Barley's Casino & Brewing Co.

4500 E. Sunset Rd., Henderson • 458-BREW

If there were a casino for the X generation, Barley's would be it. In fact, it's so modern it doesn't even resemble a casino. The floors are hardwood, the open ceilings have cannery-style ducts, the walls are accented with brick and wood paneling, and there are actually windows that allow sunlight to make everything bright and visible! In the center of the casino are eight blackjack tables ($2 minimum), which are surrounded by about 200 machines, most of which are video poker including several $5 video poker machines. Although there are just a handful of reel slots, you can chase the large jackpots such as Quarters Deluxe. Rounding out the gaming amenities are a sports book and keno lounge, which gives keno bettors 48 hours to cash in their winning tickets. This is a first for Las Vegas, since nearly every other keno game in town requires winning keno tickets to be cashed prior to the start of the following game — a time span sometimes as short as three minutes.

When it's time to tap into a different kind of action, the brew pub serves a robust range of lager, Oktoberfest and Bavarian beer, and the restaurant serves a stylish blend of Southwest and California cuisine. There's even a patio dining area to escape to when the din of machines becomes too much.

El Dorado Casino

140 S. Water St., Henderson • 564-1811

On the outside the El Dorado sports a 1950s-style building facade that may have once served as an old movie theater. But everything is neon modern inside the casino, which among our stand-alone casinos is most like those on The Strip. You'll find a large number of machines — more than 600 — spread across a vast area of about 16,000 square feet. Among the reel slots are the popular Wild Cherry, Double Diamond and Red, White & Blue, plus linked progressives such as Nevada Nickels and Megabucks. You can also try for a new car on a 5¢ Red, White & Blue progressive. At the center of the casino is a pit with about 10 blackjack tables, craps, roulette, Caribbean Stud and Let it Ride. Flanking the pit are a live keno lounge, 200-seat bingo hall and a sports book. Rounding out the amenities are a coffee shop, Mexican restaurant and cocktail lounge with live entertainment.

Gold Rush Casino

1195 E. Sunset Rd., Henderson • 454-0544

With fewer than 200 machines, the Gold Rush is small compared to most casinos but has enjoyed a loyal following for many years. Patrons are of the "low roller" variety who enjoy playing the Deuces Wild, Joker poker and Bonus Poker machines. And they find plenty in the 5¢ denomination. There are also lots of video keno machines, another hit with the local crowd.

INSIDERS' TIP

Keno players find lower rates — as low as 40¢ and 50¢ a game — in the smaller independent casinos, while rates on The Strip begin as high as $1.20 to $2 per game.

Also popular is the Gold Rush's paycheck cashing promotion, which awards scratch cards that pay up to $1,000 instantly. When it's time to refuel, the restaurant serves hearty meals at rock-bottom prices, such as a 99¢ breakfast special and $4.95 prime rib dinner.

Joker's Wild

920 N. Boulder Hwy., Henderson • 564-8100

The Joker's Wild is another of The Strip clones with its circus tent exterior — blue-and-white stripes on a white building accented by neon and runner lights. The casino is dominated by row after row of slot and video machines, including the popular Wheel of Fortune, Quartermania, Megabucks, Double Diamond and Wild Cherry. In the pit, gamblers can play blackjack for $1 to $3 a hand as well as roulette, craps, Let it Ride, Caribbean Stud and keno. You'll also find a sports book, 24-hour restaurant and buffet, and a lounge with live entertainment. One of the more popular attractions is the Joker's paycheck cashing promotion in which check-cashers try for $5,000 in cash plus other prizes on a ceiling-reaching Paycheck Tower.

Ligouri's Restaurant & Casino

1133 N. Boulder Hwy., Henderson • 565-1688

The adobe brick and stucco building may be aging, but players don't seem to mind. They keep coming for the vintage video keno and poker machines, especially the hard-to-find Fortune poker machines from IGT. Patrons also find a few slot machines, a live poker game and a '50s diner-style restaurant.

Longhorn Casino

5288 Boulder Hwy. • 435-9170

Neon signs and cowboy silhouettes in the window greet visitors to this roadhouse-style gambling hall that features more than 200 slot and video machines and four blackjack tables ($2 minimum). In addition to the popular Joker poker, Deuces Wild and Bonus Poker, the games include a good mix of reel slots such as Wild Cherry and Red, White & Blue. With a lean to the low-stakes gambler, many of the machines are in the 5¢ denomination. Also popular with a solid base of regular customers are the Longhorn's Chuckwagon restaurant and a lounge that serves up live entertainment on the weekend.

Pot O' Gold Casino

120 Market St., Henderson • 564-8488

Don't let the alabaster, penitentiary-like exterior deter you. The Pot O' Gold is much more appealing inside with its high ceilings and cozy alcoves. It's even more desirable if you like video poker because nearly every type of machine is represented — Bonus Poker, Bonus Deluxe, Double Bonus, Triple Bonus, Multi Poker, Powerhouse Poker, Deuces Wild and Loose Deuces, to name a few. Slot players won't sit idly with all the Wheel of Fortune, Double Diamond and Five Times Pay machines around, and there's an entire room filled with video keno machines. For those who prefer to interact with live bodies, the casino has a 150-seat bingo hall and blackjack and Let it Ride poker.

Rainbow Club Casino

122 S. Water St., Henderson • 565-9776

The nondescript pink stucco exterior conceals a fast-paced casino with more than 500 slot and video machines. Spread over several areas, the casino is like a forest of electronic games, from the older coin-dumping keno machines to the latest, touch-screen multigame marvels. Also a hit with the patrons who pack the joint are twice-weekly cash drawings plus vacation giveaways to the casino's sister resort, the Oasis Hotel & Casino in Mesquite, Nevada. The 24-hour restaurant is popular, especially with its daily and graveyard specials that include a T-bone steak for $5.95, baby back ribs for $4.49 and "mom's special" pot roast for $3.99.

Renata's

4451 E. Sunset Rd., Henderson • 435-4000

If you like the "dark side" of gambling, try Renata's. The casino has the ambiance of a modern cocktail lounge, dimly lit with plenty of dark corners in which to escape. The casino has 200 slot and video machines. All the popular machines are represented, with an emphasis on video poker: Triple Bonus, GameMaker and the hard-to-find Caribbean Stud poker. For gamblers looking for a shot at the big jackpots, there are also linked progressives, Quartermania and Cool Millions.

When you're ready for a break from the machines, try the cocktail lounge, which is slightly elevated and overlooks the casino floor.

Roadhouse Casino

2100 Boulder Hwy., Henderson • 564-1150

The Roadhouse is a fun house, starting with the rustic 1950s-style architecture of the building — corrugated tin walls, a roof with twin spires and a winged monument in front. The name of the joint is even painted on the roof, just like in *Green Acres*. Inside, the ambiance is laid-back in a blue-collar sort of way — country-western is the music of choice, if not in the lounge then on the Wurlitzer jukebox. The casino consists of about 200 machines, mostly video poker and keno along with a few reel slots, many of which back right up to the small dance floor: Swing your partner then draw to an inside straight!

Among the other amenities is a small lounge-showroom that hosts a variety of entertainment, ranging from rock and blue grass bands to ventriloquists and hypnotists. There is also the Roadhouse Restaurant, a genuine '50s-style diner complete with vintage counters and stools, fountain, coke machines, syrup dispensers, metal signs and much more. Of course, the featured fare is food from the Fabulous '50s — juicy hubcaps, cruiser burgers, patty melts, sandwich baskets, fountain treats and much more (see a complete listing in our Restaurants chapter).

Roadrunner Casino

154 S. Boulder Hwy., Henderson • 566-9999

As a hangout for the country-western crowd, the Roadrunner has everything but sawdust on the floors. In addition to the jukebox blaring achy-breaky favorites, the Roadrunner greets visitors with lots of wrought iron and leather artifacts, distressed-wood wall panels and hurricane-lamp chandeliers. The gambling is confined to about 100 machines, mostly video poker and keno. There's also a restaurant that specializes in steaks and barbecue favorites.

Skyline Casino

1741 N. Boulder Hwy., Henderson • 565-9116

Evidenced by the elbow-to-elbow crowds that gamble here, the Skyline has become one of the most popular casinos in the competition-rich East Valley. Among its attractions are 400 slot and video machines, many of which are of the popular 5¢ and 25¢ variety, three blackjack tables ($2 minimum), a Let it Ride table, poker parlor and a sports book. There is also a lounge with live entertainment, and an always-busy restaurant specializes in hearty, full-course meals at dirt-cheap prices (see our Restaurants chapter).

Tom's Sunset Casino

444 W. Sunset Rd., Henderson • 564-5551

As one of the first casinos built in Henderson, Tom's Sunset Casino has cultivated a loyal following of gamblers who can bet blackjack at $1 minimum per hand, play Texas Hold'em and Seven Card Stud poker, and back their favorite teams in the sports book. Machine players like the older, upright video keno machines and the 5¢ progressive joker poker machines. You'll also find a nice mix of reel slots and periodic promotions such as bonus payoffs for any four-of-a-kind. Completing the amenities are a 24-hour restaurant, all-you-can-eat buffet and cocktail lounge.

Triple J Bingo Hall & Casino

725 S. Racetrack Rd., Henderson • 565-5555

The Triple J is built like a large warehouse or airplane hangar — 20-foot-high ceilings, open steel beams and a corrugated metal roof. The largest portion of the casino is an exhibit hall that in the past has served as a 1,600-seat bingo parlor and kick-boxing arena. Someday the owners will decide its permanent fate. The

INSIDERS' TIP

Players who hit a jackpot of $1,200 or more on a slot or video machine or $1,500 on a keno ticket are required to sign and file a form W-2G with the IRS. The casino provides the form and fills it out, and they won't pay you until you sign it.

casino features four blackjack tables ($1 minimum), a sports book and about 20 machines, mostly video poker and keno. You'll also find a snack bar and cocktail lounge with live entertainment on the weekends.

North Valley

Jerry's Nugget
1821 Las Vegas Blvd. N. • 399-3000

Totally remodeled and expanded in 1996, Jerry's Nugget has evolved as the jewel of the North Valley casinos. Among the additions are a porte-cochere and 15-foot-high fountain at the entrance, a tiled foyer, fresh carpeting and soft lighting throughout, a new restaurant and an overall indoor promenade effect that makes moving from venue to venue pleasant and effortless. Also new to Jerry's Nugget is its Royal Street Theater, an intimate lounge and dance hall with split-level seating and space-age lighting, and a delightful bakery and sweet shop where you can blow your diet on pastry treats, ice cream and frozen yogurt. Gamblers can whet their appetite on roulette, craps and blackjack ($2 minimum on some tables) in the pit or in the live poker room, keno lounge, bingo parlor and full race and sports book. All the popular electronic machines are available, including a variety of poker and keno machines and the new Wheel of Fortune slot machines that seem to have taken The Strip casinos by storm. Rounding out the amenities are a very good 24-hour coffee shop, one of the few in town that serves vegetarian specialties, a formal steak house and an innovative paycheck promotion where your possible winnings flash across a video wall. Incidentally, Jerry's old oil derrick sign out front was untouched by the renovation. It's nice to see a casino owner who believes in nostalgia and knows it isn't always necessary to blow up your landmarks.

Mahoney's Silver Nugget Casino
2140 Las Vegas Blvd. N. • 399-1111

The exterior of Mahoney's Silver Nugget is a bizarre combination of neon tubes, glass panels, painted pictures and flashing lights, all presumably intended to attract customers from the street. Inside, the Silver Nugget is as much an active neighborhood recreation center as a casino. There are teenagers and families everywhere but mostly in the bowling alley, which is very dark, very noisy and very trippy with its space and planetary scenes painted above the alleys. There is also a garden cafe and small lounge that often hosts karaoke sing-alongs. The casino features $2 minimum blackjack tables, craps, live poker with bad beat jackpots, a keno lounge and sports book. Machine freaks have their video poker and keno machines, with the better selection toward the rear of the casino, where it almost becomes quiet enough to hear oneself think.

Opera House Saloon & Casino
2452 Las Vegas Blvd. N. • 649-8801

Despite the tony name, the Opera House more closely resembles a pink stucco saloon. Actually it's a clean cozy little affair with a small pit in the center where you can play on one of four $2 blackjack tables. Most of the action is on the video poker machines, including the popular Bonus Poker, Deuces Wild, Joker Poker and Double Bonus Poker models. There are also plenty of keno machines and a 24-hour restaurant and cocktail lounge.

Poker Palace
2757 Las Vegas Blvd. N. • 649-3799

Looking like something out of Disney's Fantasyland, the Poker Palace facade features a castle skyline outlined in multicolored neon lights. But inside, normalcy prevails in a casino accented by wood-paneled walls, indirect lighting and crystal chandeliers. The main casino offers blackjack ($1 minimum), Let it Ride, roulette, live poker, a race and sports book plus plenty of reel and video machines. In addition to popular poker machines such as Double Bonus and Bally's GameMaker, you'll find reel slots such as the Wheel of Fortune, Nevada Nickels and Quartermania. Nonsmokers will love the separate nonsmoking casino (it even has its own front entrance), where you can play all the popular slot, video poker and keno machines. Another big attraction at the Poker Palace is its paycheck promotion, not only because you can win up to five times your paycheck ($10,000 limit) but also because your chances ride on the spin of a huge wooden wheel of fortune rather than a computerized random number generator.

Las Vegas dining is no longer condemned to prime rib, shrimp cocktails and steak and eggs. Hundreds of restaurants across town serve exciting, innovative and oftentimes award-winning cuisine.

Restaurants

Benjamin Franklin once advised, "Eat not to dullness; drink not to elevation." He never lived in Las Vegas.

The fact is the consumption of food and drink has been a cornerstone of this city's resort industry for more than 40 years. Tourists often cite cheap food — the all-you-can-eat buffets, $4.99 prime rib dinners and 99¢ breakfasts — as among the reasons for taking a Las Vegas vacation. Moreover, new residents frequently credit lower food costs as incentives to move to the southern Nevada desert. And who can blame them? In what other city can you go out to dinner and consume enough food to sustain a small municipality, all for the price of a Happy Meal?

Serving inexpensive food in massive volumes is a by-product of the gaming industry: Resorts have traditionally operated food and beverage departments at a loss in order to entice gamblers with cheap prices. If that doesn't sound like a formula for culinary success, it isn't. Historically, Las Vegas has never been known for great restaurants. Inexpensive, yes. Five-star dining, not quite.

But times change. Many hotels, especially the newer resorts, are reversing the loss-leader philosophy by making restaurants pay for themselves by offering quality food and service at more representative — that is, higher — prices. So far tourists haven't flinched at pricier tabs, according to recent surveys, though increases may not be perceptible except to those who track such things. Those surveys also indicate the Vegas tourist of the 1990s is spending less money in the casino and more on food and shopping trips.

Besides offering better food at higher prices, hotels are now leasing out restaurant space to seasoned restaurateurs. Check out the restaurants in the MGM Grand (Coyote Cafe, Wolfgang Puck, Gatsby's) and New York-New York (Motown Cafe, Gonzalez y Gonzalez, Gallagher's Steak House), and you'll find most are high-end eateries that have proven success records in other locales. A note about calling hotel dining rooms. While many have their own direct phone number, we've listed the main hotel telephone number, which you can call any time for information and reservations.

Also contributing to the changing face of Las Vegas dining is the expanding population. With the influx of seasoned diners from other cities, local developers have begun to add new and different types of restaurants throughout the city. Many of these — a reflection of the newcomers' diverse backgrounds — offer a variety of ethnic cuisine. For instance, we've even seen Middle Eastern restaurants, once a rarity in town, open up across the street from each other!

The upshot of all this is that Las Vegas dining is no longer condemned to prime rib, shrimp cocktails and steak-and-eggs. Hundreds of restaurants across town — in and out of hotel casinos — serve exciting, innovative and oftentimes award-winning cuisine.

In this chapter we've included the best of the hotel restaurants as well as the exemplary and unusual neighborhood eateries. The restaurants are grouped first by location, then by type of cuisine.

Price Code

Our price-code rating reflects the cost of entrees for two, without cocktails, appetizers, wine, dessert, tax and tip.

$	**less than $20**
$$	**$20 - $30**
$$$	**$31 - $50**
$$$$	**more than $50**

Most restaurants, except for the upscale, ultradeluxe dining rooms, have very casual dress requirements, so you can expect to be seated nearly everywhere, even though you might be dressed in Bermuda shorts and sneakers. Most restaurants (and all of the hotel dining rooms) accept major credit cards, but we'll let you know the ones that don't. And most have a nonsmoking section.

The restaurants listed in this chapter are open for dinner only, unless otherwise indicated.

Take the time to browse through this chapter, and you'll discover a marvelous world beyond the shrimp cocktails and all-you-can-eat buffets. Of course, if you're a buffet fanatic, check out our close-up on Las Vegas' buffets near the end of the chapter. You may be surprised at some of the bigger and better all-you-can-eat extravaganzas. Good hunting and good eating!

FYI

Unless otherwise noted, the area code for all phone numbers listed in this chapter is 702.

The Strip Area

American

All Star Cafe

$$ • 3785 Las Vegas Blvd. S. • 795-8326

The All-Star Cafe is supposed to be a popular haunt of tennis star Andre Agassi, who lives in Las Vegas when not globetrotting with Brooke Shields. Even if he's not here you can rub shoulders with photos of Andre and other celebs and feast on Agassi linguine pomodoro, Joe Montana's three-cheese ravioli and Monica Seles' chicken Caesar salad. If you're not into name-dropping, try the penne chicken and broccoli, sausage lasagna or roast chicken pizza with broccoli florets and diced fresh tomato. It's open for lunch and dinner.

Club Cappuccino

$ • Harrah's Hotel, 3475 Las Vegas Blvd. S. • 369-5000

You can get a coffee fix 24 hours a day at Club Cappuccino, which serves specialty drinks such as Almond Joy Espresso, Monkey Mocha and Brandy Alexander. Java traditionalists will like coffee made from beans from Colombia, Brazil, Guatemala and several African nations. There's also fresh-baked pastry when you need to reach a sugar high.

Country Star American Music Grill

$$ • 3724 Las Vegas Blvd. S. • 740-8400

If you like to eat in front of the TV, you'll feel at home here, where more than 100 video monitors (they're even in the bathrooms) constantly play country music videos and interviews with country stars. The chili and corn bread are staples, but you can also get into the spirit with Reba's garden pasta or a Vince Gill burger. Other tasty tidbits include beef and baby back ribs, buffalo and beef steaks and hickory chicken with rattlesnake sauce. It's open for lunch and dinner.

Dive!

$ • Fashion Show Mall, 3200 Las Vegas Blvd. S. • 369-3483

Steven Spielberg's nautical-theme restaurant features the hull of a submarine jutting out from the side of the Fashion Show Mall. Although it looks like it's ready to launch a torpedo at Treasure Island, it only drips water from the bow. Inside, you'll find dozens of burgers and submarine sandwiches and house specialties such as grilled garlic toast with tomato basil salad, fajita sub cucina and periscope pot pie. Dive! is open for lunch and dinner.

Fog City Diner

$$ • 325 Hughes Center Dr. • 737-0200

It may not be Fisherman's Wharf, but the diner has the feel of a classic dining car with its dark wood furnishings, brass fixtures and booth seating. Because of Fog City's upscale menu, fresh oyster bar and pricey wine list, it attracts a yuppie crowd, but you can find a booth away from the cellular phone fanatics. In addition to great appetizers — fresh oysters on the half-shell, chilled snow crab, mu shu pork burritos and the garlic oregano bread — the restaurant serves "small plate" dishes, which are mini entrees that, when combined, form a great meal. The best include crab cakes, Manila clam chowder and Mighty Meat loaf, which is enhanced by a sweet apricot chutney topping. It's open for lunch and dinner.

Hard Rock Cafe

$$ • 4475 Paradise Rd. • 733-8400

If you don't mind a heavy dose of VH1 with your meal, hip hop over to the Hard Rock Cafe at the corner of Paradise and Harmon. You can't miss the place with its 77-foot guitar out front. Inside, it's rock and roll memorabilia — signed photos, posters, programs, guitars and the like. The Hard Rock is big on sandwiches, which include a chicken Caesar sandwich made with sliced breast of roast chicken and Caesar dressing; a Club Rap, a sort of club sandwich wrapped in a wheat tortilla; and a grilled vegetable sandwich made with zucchini, yellow squash, roasted red peppers and the usual condiments. Two excellent choices are the big country club sandwich, piled high with roasted turkey, crisp bacon, lettuce and tomato on a lightly toasted french roll; and the "Pig" sandwich, one of the house specialties, made from hickory-smoked (for 14 hours) pork shoulder that is hand-pulled and shredded and topped with a sweet and tangy barbecue sauce. It's open for lunch and dinner.

Kiefer's

$$$ • Carriage House Hotel, 105 E. Harmon Ave. • 739-8000

This romantic hideaway atop the Carriage House Hotel has one of the best views of The Strip. Grass wallpaper, rattan club chairs and dozens of plants create a tropical atmosphere in the heart of the desert. You'll dine on moderately priced spicy Louisiana seafood gumbo, steak au poivre, veal saltimbocca or the house specialty, orange roughy Oscar — fillets topped with crabmeat and asparagus spears and finished with Béarnaise sauce. Kiefer's is open for dinner only.

Mr. Lucky's

$$ • Hard Rock Hotel, 4455 Paradise Rd. • 693-5000

This is a great spot to refuel on designer burgers, chicken salads, grilled steaks and seafood and Tex-Mex specialties. The room is bright and open, decorated with light-wood furniture and massive rock posters on the wall. The Generation X crowd and rock music videos can become deafening, but after hours the joint winds down and becomes a nice place for a late-night rendezvous. It's open 24 hours.

Planet Hollywood

$$ • Forum Shops, 3500 Las Vegas Blvd. S. • 791-7827

Probably the best of the celebrity-themed restaurants, Planet Hollywood is a great place to eat, drink, hang, people-watch or buy leather bomber jackets. Pick a spot among the movie and TV memorabilia downstairs, or grab a quiet table upstairs where you can oversee the action. When there isn't a band or musician playing, there are plenty of video monitors running footage of heaven-knows-what, accompanied by music from a turbo-driven audio system. The food is California chic: gourmet pizzas, pasta, fish, burgers, salads and fajitas. Save room for a chocolate mousse that's worth the splurge. Planet Hollywood is open for lunch and dinner.

Ralph's Diner

$ • Stardust Hotel, 3000 Las Vegas Blvd. S. • 732-6111

For a taste of the Fabulous Fifties, visit Ralph's Diner, where dancing waitresses often be-bop to jukebox oldies across the checkerboard floor. From the old-fashioned soda fountain, you can gorge yourself on milk shakes, banana splits, sundaes, burgers, fries, malts and daily blue-plate specials. Ralph's is open for breakfast, lunch and dinner.

Chinese

Beijing

$$ • 3900 Paradise Rd. • 737-9618

The Beijing restaurant resembles an Oriental gallery with its rare art works, embroidered silk pictures, jade, cloisonné and ivory carvings — many of which are for sale. Signature dishes at reasonable prices include the sweet-and-sour pineapple duck, fish steak with plum or curry sauce, lobster with electronic eyes, sizzling steak and tender shrimp with pine nuts. In addition there is a unique selection of vegetarian dishes, including the banquet, which uses soy-based substitutes to create kung pao "chicken" and imitation pork. Beijing serves lunch and dinner.

Chin's

$$ • 3200 Las Vegas Blvd. S. • 733-8899

Lots of glass and polished metal beams accent this upscale Chinese restaurant popular with the business lunch crowd. The dim sum lunch, a house specialty, is fancy and appetizing — shrimp puffs, minced chicken, spicy chicken and sweet rice buns filled with chicken, beef or pork. Among the innovative entrees are strawberry chicken, spicy Manila clams in the shell and raspberry and strawberry shrimp with fruit sauce. Chin's is open for lunch and dinner.

Dragon Noodle Company

$$$ • Monte Carlo Hotel, 3770 Las Vegas Blvd. S. • 730-7777

For a hotel dining room, Dragon Noodle Company does a good impression of a Hong Kong eatery. Many of the foods are displayed for diners' inspection, and the food is prepared on special Teppan broilers out in the open. A house specialty is the air-dried roast duck that offers the traditional flavors of Peking duck without the high fat and oil content. Fans of Far Eastern teas will also like the restaurant's Tea Bar, where you can sample a range of exotic teas. It's open for dinner only.

Empress Court

$$$$ • Caesars Palace, 3570 Las Vegas Blvd. S. • 731-7110

For Hong Kong-style Cantonese cuisine without equal, take the brass-railed staircase that encircles a koi pond to Empress Court. The house specialty is Peking duck, prepared tableside by a white-gloved carver who transforms the entire duck to filling for small rolled crepes covered with a rich hoisin sauce. Other specialties include golden crisp squab, sauteed prawns with walnuts, abalone, shark's fin and bird's nest soup, and jade chicken with Yunnan ham. Fresh seafood — kept in fresh- and saltwater aquaria — vary with the season and often include rock cod, Dungeness crab and lobster. Vegetarians don't despair, the tofu dishes and Buddhist Vegetarian Feast will make you glad you gave up meat. The restaurants serves dinner only.

Garden of the Dragon

$$$-$$$$ • Las Vegas Hilton, 3000 Paradise Rd. • 732-5111

For some of the best Chinese food accented by fresh fish and seafood, come to this tea house-style restaurant that overlooks the Benihana Village gardens. Some of the specialties include steamed whole flounder, live shrimp, abalone with oyster sauce, fresh clams with black bean sauce and fresh steamed Dungeness crab. You can also sample duck, chicken, beef, pork, vegetable and noodle favorites as well as a unique sizzling lamb dish prepared tableside with fresh garden vegetables. It's open for dinner only.

Ho Wan

$$$ • Desert Inn Hotel and Country Club, 3145 Las Vegas Blvd. S. • 733-4444

Ancient Chinese clay pictures, tapestry and artifacts decorate this upscale dining room where Asian high rollers hang out and Hong Kong-trained chefs create seafood dishes such as steamed trout with ginger and scallions and exotic soups such as birds' nest, shark's fin and seaweed with cabbage. Other house favorites include prawns in black bean sauce and Peking duck. For dessert try the chilled black-leaf lychee. Ho Wan serves dinner only.

Moongate

$$$ •The Mirage, 3400 Las Vegas Blvd. S. • 791-7352

Classical Chinese architecture is used to create an open courtyard surrounded by structures with rooflines punctuated by leaves and cherry blossoms. In the dining rooms, sculpted wall panels frame the backdrop of Oriental murals while soft lighting beneath a dark summer sky adds to the Asian mystique. Classic Szechwan and Cantonese cuisine includes fillet of salmon, roast duck and black peppered beef. Moongate serves dinner only.

Papyrus

$$$ • Luxor Hotel, 3900 Las Vegas Blvd. S. • 262-4822

Maybe this place should be called "papaya" for its tropical motif — ferns, palm trees and waterfalls. The food is a delightful blend of Chinese and Polynesian, cooked tableside on Otemanu hot rocks. Don't miss the steamed fish and Szechwan chicken, which are cooked lau lau-style, and the fried ice cream dessert. Papyrus is open for dinner only.

Peking Market

$$ • Flamingo Hilton Hotel, 3555 Las Vegas Blvd. S. • 733-3111

For a Chinese feast, the Peking Market will overwhelm you with its nine-course dinner that features lemon chicken, Mongolian beef, seafood, Chinese vegetables and banana fritters. The Asian decorations — miniature pagoda lamps and carved jade figurines — add an artistic touch while the twinkling lights above the 800-gallon aquarium mimic a clear night sky. The restaurant serves dinner only.

P.F. Chang's

$$ • 4165 Paradise Rd. • 792-2207

For Chinese food with a European accent, try this popular eatery across from the Continental Hotel at the corner of Flamingo Road. Influenced by 12th-century Chinese art, the bistro is decorated with wall murals and reproductions of lions and other sculpture unearthed in the ancient city of Xian. Some of the innovative dishes include pan-fried Peking raviolis, sesame shrimp, kung pao scallops, catfish with black bean sauce, Malaysian chicken and Szechwan beef. For dessert be sure to sample the pear almond custard torte. It's open for lunch and dinner.

Continental

Bacchanal

$$$$ • Caesars Palace, 3570 Las Vegas Blvd. S. • 731-7110

For a Roman dinner banquet, guide your chariot to Bacchanal, where you'll be treated to a lavish, six-course feast in a garden setting around a fountain. The fixed-price meal features fruit and crudites, seafood, soup, salad, pasta, entree and dessert, followed by coffee and petit fours. Allow about two hours for the experience, which is highlighted by toga-clad wine goddesses and belly dancers.

Isis

$$$ • Luxor Hotel, 3900 Las Vegas Blvd. S. • 262-4773

You'll feel like you're dining with the pharoahs in this elegant room guarded by Caryatid statues and gold-embossed "wings of Isis" on the glass doors. Inside, you'll find displays of reproductions of Egyptian artifacts — many from King Tutankhamen's tomb — and a vaulted ceiling decorated with gold Egyptian stars. The chef's favorites are the marinated shrimp and lobster, grilled veal scallopine and oysters and beef Wellington. Try one of the many specialty coffees with your dessert. Isis serves dinner only.

Kokomo's

$$$$ • The Mirage, 3400 Las Vegas Blvd. S. • 791-7111

At this tropical bistro you can dine in a tropical rainforest cooled by the mist of a cascading waterfall and nestled among banana trees, royal palms, orchids and other exotic flowers. Diners can choose from seafood, beef, lamb and pork specialties. For an appetizer try the crabmeat taco with pineapple salsa, and save (or make) room for the chocolate raspberry mousse cake. Kokomo's serves dinner only.

Michael's

$$$$ • Barbary Coast Hotel, 3595 Las Vegas Blvd. S. • 737-7111

One of the finest restaurants in the city, Michael's is an elegant room featuring finely upholstered decor and a stained-glass dome ceiling that creates a feeling of turn-of-the-century San Francisco. Among the house favorites are imported fresh Dover sole, rack of lamb, veal Française and chateaubriand for two. In addition to a number of tempting pastries, Michael's serves a complimentary tray of fruit slices dipped in white and dark chocolate at the end of the meal. Dinner only is served.

Palace Court

$$$$ • Caesars Palace • 3570 Las Vegas Blvd. S. • 731-7110

For a touch of Roman decadence, head for the award-winning Palace Court, which is adorned with lush green plants, objets d'art and a magnificent stained-glass dome ceiling. Distinctive appetizers include caviar, French onion soup and smoked Scottish salmon carved tableside. The house specialties are steak Diane, rack of lamb, breast of duck and prime sirloin. True to the genre, knowledgeable sommeliers will assist in the selection of a wine that may cost slightly less than a domestic automobile. Palace Court serves dinner only.

Pegasus

$$$$ • Alexis Park Hotel, 375 E. Harmon Ave. • 796-3300

For the ultimate in fine dining, it's Pegasus, where dark-glass panels, mirrored walls, silver champagne stands and a custom crystal chandelier help create a sophisticated ambiance. Imaginative appetizers include lobster medallions with quail eggs, red caviar in sauce imperial and mushrooms baked in puff pastry. The house specialty is lobster prepared with black truffles and wine in a bordelaise sauce, served flaming. A harpist adds to the romantic atmosphere during the dinner hour. Pegasus serves lunch and dinner.

Spago Restaurant & Cafe

$$$ • Forum Shops, 3500 Las Vegas Blvd. S. • 369-6300

This chic cafe reproduces Wolfgang Puck's famous Hollywood hangout with a California chic decor of warm wood panels, beamed ceiling, marble pedestal tables and rattan-backed chairs. Among Puck's lunch and dinner specialties are a duck sausage and spicy chicken pizza, Peking duck spring roll, steamed Maine lobster with saffron fettuccine and basil, almond-ginger-crusted salmon and Sonoma lamb tacos with Wolfgang's fresh tomato salsa.

French

The Bistro

$$$$ • The Mirage, 3400 Las Vegas Blvd. S. • 791-7111

Fine French cuisine and the mood of Paris during the time of the impressionists are the featured fare at Bistro, where Cezanne, Lautrec and Degas are represented with prints and lithographs. Specialties are as carefree as the atmosphere and include escargot en brioche, breast of muscovy duck in Zinfandel sauce, hot Charlotte of forest mushrooms with Madeira cream in toasted brioche, and a delightful Chambord bonnet parfait. The Bistro serves dinner only.

Gatsby's

$$$$ • MGM Grand, 3799 Las Vegas Blvd. S. • 891-1111

If there can be such a thing, the featured fare at Gatsby's is French cuisine with a California flair. Prepared in a special Bonnet kitchen, the specialties include farm-raised ostrich, pâté de foie gras and Gatsby's signature dish, ahi tuna. Also featured are Dover sole, rack of lamb, prime meat, fish and game along with vegetarian specialties. Wine lovers will want to explore the three wine cellars, each regulated for whites, reds and champagnes. More than 600 wines from every region of the world are stocked. Gatsby's serves dinner only.

Le Montrachet

$$$$ • Las Vegas Hilton, 3000 Paradise Rd. • 732-5111

The Las Vegas Hilton next to the Convention Center has several first-rate restaurants, topped by Le Montrachet, an intimate, European-style room accented by soft peach lighting, elegant floral arrangements and formal table settings. The cuisine is presented by an attentive staff and features poached fillet of John Dory, medallions of venison and rack of lamb. You can make a gourmet meal of such appetizers as chilled foie gras of duck, pheasant breast mousse and the hot duck and spinach salad. All the desserts are works of art, notably the white espresso ice cream shaped in a chocolate swan. The restaurant serves dinner only.

Monte Carlo Room

$$$$ • Desert Inn Hotel and Country Club, 3145 Las Vegas Blvd. S. • 733-4444

The decor speaks of a French villa with its oil paintings and garden setting. Some of the time-tested specialties — often prepared tableside by legions of fawning waiters — include scampi with lemon garlic sauce, striped sea bass en croûte for two, duck à l'orange, filet mignon Rossini and steak Diane. For a real treat try the baby veal chops stuffed with Gruyère, prosciutto, caramel and ginger and the chocolate mousse with raspberries for dessert. This restaurant serves dinner only.

Pamplemousse

$$$ • 400 E. Sahara Ave. • 733-2066

For a romantic hideaway only a block off The Strip, visit Pamplemousse, which means "grapefruit" in French. This intimate, candlelit bistro is in a converted house. There is no menu; the waiter simply recites the daily specials. You start with a French Riviera-style salad: a large basket of fresh vegetables and a vinaigrette house dip. Among appetizer choices are fresh shrimp scampi, scallops, soft-shell clams, escargots, shallots and an outstanding fettuccine. Entree choices may include prime New York filet, milk-fed white veal, Norwegian salmon with orange curry sauce or roast Wisconsin duckling with cranberry sauce, cream of garlic sauce, green pepper corns or fresh fruit. This restaurant serves dinner only.

Pietro's

$$$-$$$$ • Tropicana Hotel, 3801 Las Vegas Blvd. S. • 739-2222

For elegant dining, try this softly lit, art deco-style dining room where you can feast on French cuisine such as breast of capon estragon and roast duckling à l'orange. Other favorites are chateaubriand bouquetiere and rack of lamb printanière. Harpists add to the ambiance during the dinner hour and Sunday brunch.

Seasons

$$$$ • Bally's Las Vegas, 3645 Las Vegas Blvd. S. • 739-4651

Your menu in this French Provincial dining room changes with the seasons and may feature roast duckling Grand Marnier; Chilean sea bass; grilled chicken breast with foie gras and cognac sauce; and chateaubriand bordelaise for two. Fresh fish prepared in a variety of ways and lobster with smoked salmon mousse are served throughout the year. Dinner only is served.

Italian

Alta Villa

$$ • Flamingo Hilton Hotel, 3555 Las Vegas Blvd. S. • 733-3434

Fronted by a terra-cotta fountain, this restaurant resembles an Italian village with its trellised grape arbors, flagstone floors and vaulted ceiling. Some of the tasty entrees — prepared in a ceramic-tiled exhibition kitchen — include osso bucco and chicken piccata. All dinners and pasta dishes are served with a hearty minestrone soup and fresh-baked ciabatta bread. Alta Villa serves dinner only.

Battista's Hole in the Wall

$$ • 4041 Audrie Ln. • 732-1424

The first time we walked into Battista's, the young host put his arm around our shoulders and said, "Let's eat!" This is a fun, friendly place, with a wandering accordion player who guarantees he can play a tune connected with anyone's hometown. Among the appetizers, the calamari and steamed clams are the best. The pasta is homemade and includes lasagna, manicotti and fettuccine with meatballs, sausage and seafood. Specialties are the veal (picante, Marsala, Milanese, Bolognese and parmigiana), steak and chicken. Dinners include all the wine you can drink and a cup of cappuccino. Battista's serves dinner only.

Bertolini's

$$$ • Forum Shops, 3500 Las Vegas Blvd. S. • 735-4663

In addition to serving passable Italian cuisine, Bertolini's is a great place to people-watch. Located at the edge of the Fountain of the Gods in the upscale Forum Shops, the traffic into and out of the expensive designer shops is like a passing parade. If you feel you should be part of the show, grab a table out on the patio so everyone can get a load of you. When not preening for the cameras, try some of the pasta and gourmet pizzas. Bertolini's serves lunch and dinner.

Cafe Milano

$$ • 3900 Paradise Rd. • 732-1884

One of the better Italian delis in town, Cafe Milano features a cozy storefront dining area and ice cream parlor. The best selections are lasagna and penne pomodoro, arabiata (tomato, garlic, red pepper) with meatball plus spaghetti aglio colio and carbonara. Also

INSIDERS' TIP

Buffet lines can be a problem. Rules of thumb to avoid them: early for breakfast, late for lunch, early for dinner.

popular are the cannelloni stuffed with veal ricotta cheese and antipasto misto with salami and cheese. The ice cream parlor has a huge selection of Italcream gelato and tartufos. A good bet is the refreshing lemon Italian ice. Cafe Milano serves lunch and dinner.

La Strada

$$ • 4640 Paradise Rd. • 735-0150

In addition to subdued lighting, quiet booths and mirrored walls, La Strada often features a pianist to help with the romantic ambiance. The antipasto platter of calamari, gazpacho, chicken liver pâté and buffalo mozzarella makes a great beginning. Moderately priced entrees include chicken and veal dishes and seafood choices such as calamari Provençale, scampi Napoleone, Norwegian salmon, sauteed orange roughy and mussels peasant style. La Strada serves dinner only.

Lance-A-Lotta Pasta

$$ • Excalibur, 3850 Las Vegas Blvd. S. • 597-7777

A pasta joint in King Arthur's Court? Don't knock it until you've tried one of the dozens of different pasta dishes made with traditional antipasto and minestrone al parmesan. You can also choose from entrees such as veal piccata, shrimp scampi and frutti di mare. The restaurant serves dinner only.

Market City Caffe

$$$ • Monte Carlo Hotel Casino, 3770 Las Vegas Blvd. S. • 730-7777

As soon as you walk into this Naples-influenced trattoria, you're greeted by the smells of wood-fired pizza and handmade pasta. Specials of the house — created by the owner's grandmother from Naples — are lasagna alla salsciccia, pollo alla Diavola and salmon al pesto. Diners may also feast at the huge antipasto bar or choose from a variety of pastas, pizzas and grilled entrees. Market City Caffe serves lunch and dinner.

Primavera

$$$ • Caesars Palace, 3570 Las Vegas Blvd. S. • 731-7586

Surrounded by the Garden of the Gods pool complex, Primavera is a light and cheerful bistro where patrons dine in fan-back chairs amid pistachio green and bright pink color schemes. The menu spotlights Northern and Southern Italian specialties such as linguine alle vongole — chopped clams with spices served over pasta and fettucine primavera, hand-cut pasta tossed with seasonal vegetables. For a refreshing cocktail try the Casanova Cream Fizz, a rich blend of lemon and lime juice with cream and apricot brandy. Primavera serves dinner only.

Tre Visi & La Scala

$$$ • MGM Grand, 3799 Las Vegas Blvd. S. • 891-7220

Tre Visi features dishes from restaurateur Franco Nuschese, famous for his Cafe Milano in Washington, D.C., which blends Italian favorites from Tuscany and Milan. Open for breakfast, lunch and dinner, the cafe features homemade pastas, chicken, veal, fresh fish, pizzas and fresh-baked breads. The restaurant's fine dining room, La Scala, models the famous opera house in Milan with dining booths patterned after a theater balcony. Open for dinner only, La Scala serves a tasty pasta seafood ravioli and grilled lamb chops with saffron-flavored mashed potatoes. If you want to eat light, try the Parma prosciutto with Bosc pear and gorgonzola or the arugula and fennel salad with shaved Parmesan and lemon vinaigrette.

Japanese

Ah'So

$$$ • Caesars Palace • 3570 Las Vegas Blvd. S. • 731-7731

Tucked away from the bustling casino,

INSIDERS' TIP

Reservations aren't accepted at coffee shops and buffets, but they're a good idea when dining in other restaurants, even for lunch.

Ah'So has the atmosphere of a serene Japanese garden, complete with a cascading waterfall, arched bridges and quiet ponds. The fixed-price, six-course meal is prepared teppan yaki style, which is both culinary art and entertainment. Following the soup and appetizers the master table chef will prepare tempura seafood and vegetables, followed by entree — lobster, beef or chicken. The feast is topped with kudamono — fresh fruit, fruit torte or ice cream. Ah'So serves dinner only.

Benihana's

$$$-$$$$ • Las Vegas Hilton, 3000 Paradise Rd. • 732-5801

The Benihana Village meanders through gardens, streams, fish ponds, tea houses and two floors of dining rooms. The hibachi dinners are prepared by master chefs at tables shared by eight people. With the skill of a surgeon, the chefs carve and prepare the dinner entrees — steak, salmon, chicken, filet, shrimp and vegetables — then cook them on the tabletop grills for appreciative patrons. The dinners are served with Japanese onion soup, salad with ginger dressing and steamed rice. Save room for the green tea ice cream or Mandarin cheesecake dessert. Benihana's serves dinner only.

Mikado

$$$ • The Mirage, 3400 Las Vegas Blvd. S. • 791-7111

With its placid streams, delicate gardens and exquisite murals, Mikado suggests the quiet elegance of a private Japanese home. Even before you've entered the restaurant, you'll savor the aroma of lobster, steak, chicken and shrimp cooked and served teppan yaki style. In addition, a complete selection of specialties is available from an à la carte menu as well as a sushi bar in the garden area. Dinner only is served.

Mexican/Southwestern

Coyote Cafe

$$ • MGM Grand, 3799 Las Vegas Blvd. S. • 891-1111

The Vegas version of Mark Miller's famous Santa Fe restaurant is decorated extensively with hand-painted coyotes, lizards and other desert artwork — the scene is like a Georgia O'Keeffe landscape gone wild. The Southwestern specialties include black beans, blue-corn enchiladas and jerk chicken tacos topped with homemade guacamole and sweetened with mild salsas. If you would rather drink your lunch or dinner, try the Margaritas and custom-blended pineapple rum. Coyote Cafe is open for lunch and dinner.

Margarita's Cantina

$$ • Frontier Hotel, 3120 Las Vegas Blvd. S. • 794-8200

Margarita's features colorful booths and Mexican decor in a bright and cheerful setting. Specialties of the house are polle en mole, carne asada and shrimp in Mexicali sauce. Steaming tortillas served immediately after you're seated is a nice touch. For a special treat try the tropical burrito dessert. It's open for lunch and dinner.

Paco's Hideaway

$$ • Sahara Hotel, 2535 Las Vegas Blvd. S. • 737-2111

This colorful restaurant on the mezzanine above the casino has booth seating accented with Mexican tile and giant, rhinestone-studded sombreros. Specialties include tequila pollo, steak picado and fajitas served on a tabletop brazier. Also recommended are the chimichangas, tostadas, tamales and enchiladas. Paco's serves dinner only.

Tres Lobos

$$ • Stardust Hotel, 3000 Las Vegas Blvd. S. • 732-6111

This place serves some of the best Mexican food in town. All the traditional favorites are here — fajitas, enchiladas, chimichangas, burritos and the like. Or you can sample one of the innovative house specialties such as camarones puerto penasco — jumbo shrimp sauteed in garlic and shallots, laced with romano cheese, artichokes and pine nuts, all spread over a bed of Spanish rice. Go easy on the chips and salsa so you'll have room for the chimichanga banana split, a diet-busting concoction of ice cream, whipped cream, sauces and fresh bananas wrapped in a flour tortilla and deep fried and rolled in cinnamon sugar. It's open for lunch and dinner.

All-You-Can-Eat Buffets

In Las Vegas gluttony isn't a sin; it's a religion. And the temples of worship are the all-you-can-eat buffets. Virtually every hotel-casino has a buffet. Some are fancier than others, some are pricier than others, some serve better food than others. But they all work the same way — you pay once price, sometimes as low as $4.99 for dinner, and you can eat yourself into oblivion.

The concept of the buffet started in the early 1940s at the original El Rancho Las Vegas Hotel, where owner Beldon Katleman was looking for a way to keep customers in his hotel after the hotel's late stage show. Katleman ultimately dreamed up the "Midnight Chuckwagon Buffet — All you can eat for a dollar." His idea of treating guests to an elaborate feast for a small price was soon copied by other hotels, and the Vegas buffet boom was born.

It didn't take long for other hotel operators to figure out that if the Midnight Chuckwagon Buffet was such a great customer-holder, why not offer it at breakfast, lunch and dinner as well? They did, and the rest is history.

Today the average dinner buffet features about 45 food selections per meal that include salads, fruits, roast beef, baked ham, roast turkey, fried chicken, vegetables, potatoes, rolls, coffee and all the desserts imaginable. Some hotel-casinos also offer international choices such as Mexican, Brazilian, American, Chinese and Italian specialties served at specific "food stations."

In addition to breakfast, lunch and dinner buffets, many hotels feature weekend champagne brunch buffets for a slightly higher price. Others offer theme buffets highlighting different cuisines such as seafood, Italian or Greek food, usually on different days of the week.

Buffet prices vary, but they average from $3 per person for breakfast to $7.50 for dinner at the major resorts. It sounds cheap, but those small tabs can add up. For instance, Circus Circus, which serves more than 4 million buffet meals a year, once fed more than 17,600 people on one incredible day.

In recent years, the resorts that are patronized by local residents — so-called neighborhood hotel-casinos — have been slowly but surely raising their buffet prices. A price check of four properties that have been hosting all-you-can-eat affairs at least a decade — Palace Station, Golden Nugget, Showboat and Caesars Palace — shows the upward trend. At locals-oriented hotels, dinner prices may range from $7.50 at the Showboat up to $13.95 at Caesars, with Palace Station and the Golden Nugget taking the middle ground at $8.99 and $10.25 per person, respectively. Add them together, divide by four, and you get an average dinner cost of $10.17 per person.

Of course, today's buffets are a whole new ballgame with higher labor and food costs and a public expecting better quality all the time. When you choose a buffet, look for that quality, whether it takes the form of additional carving stations or better-quality foods such as crab legs, shrimp, breast of turkey, etc. And by all means shop around. In Las Vegas, the competition has created a buyer's market.

If you haven't the time to shop the hotel buffets, here are a few worth trying. **The Feast at Palace Station**, 2411 W. Sahara Avenue, 367-2411, set the standard for hotel buffets starting in the early 1990s. It pioneered the use of manned carving stations and custom omelette makers, and its salad and dessert bars are among the largest in the city. Other casinos in the Station chain (Boulder Station, Sunset Station) also offer their own versions of The Feast.

— continued on next page

Photo: Main Street Station

The Garden Buffet at Main Street Station is an elegant affair.

Recently, the **Carnival World Buffet at The Rio**, 3700 W. Flamingo Road, 252-7777, has challenged The Feast as the city's most popular eat-a-thon. If you can stand the long lines, you'll be rewarded with fresh and tasty Brazilian, Chinese, Mexican and Italian food. Hint: If you join the Rio's slot club, you can pass through a much shorter line.

A room with a view has never been a buffet amenity, but if you like to watch and eat at the same time, head to **Treasure Island Buffet**, 3300 Las Vegas Boulevard S., 894-7111. Here you can view the nightly pirate battles while gorging yourself on Asian, Italian and American food.

— continued on next page

Perhaps at the top of the buffet food chain is the **Palatium Buffet at Caesars Palace**, 3570 Las Vegas Boulevard S., 731-7110, which serves quality food with an Italian accent. The best stations are the heaping pasta bar and rich dessert table.

Buffet prices downtown are a solid 20 to 30 percent cheaper than The Strip buffets. One of the best is the **Garden Buffet at Main Street Station**, 200 N. Main Street, 387-1896. Besides an elegant, classy setting, the Garden Buffet features a variety of ethnic food stations, including Mexican, pizza, Hawaiian, Chinese and American, of course. There is also a very good Friday seafood buffet. The **Paradise Buffet at the Fremont Hotel**, 200 E. Fremont Street, 385-3232, is also highly recommended for its Friday seafood feast, famous for its mounds of Alaskan king crab legs.

Z'Tejas Grill

$$ • 3824 S. Paradise Rd. • 732-1660

This hyperactive eatery is a good place to sample the nouveau Southwestern cuisine — traditional Tex-Mex imaginatively mixed with Continental dishes or Southwest specialties prepared with improbable ingredients. For example, there's a filet mignon brushed with Hatch red chili, a roast duck quesadilla and oysters with guacamole salsa. Just about everything is adorned with rich and not-too-spicy sauces, and the daily specials feature fresh fish and chicken. It's open for lunch and dinner.

Middle Eastern

Gandhi

$$ • 4080 Paradise Rd. • 734-0094

If you like fire and spice, Gandhi serves some of the finest Indian food this side of New Delhi. Begin with an appetizer of chooza pakora or vegetable samosa. The roti (barbeque bread), also makes a good beginning. Tandoori offerings, cooked in a charcoal clay oven, include chicken, boneless leg of lamb and minced lamb blended with spices and herbs. The curry dishes are incendiary but won't put you in an altered state. But if you find your temperature rising, cool down with a bottle of Golden Eagle Lager Beer, India's No. 1 beer. Don't leave without trying one of the cold desserts, such as homemade Indian ice cream or rice pudding with almonds and pistachios. It's open for lunch and dinner.

Marrakech

$$$ • 3900 Paradise Rd. • 737-5611

Besides traditional Moroccan cuisine, Marrakech offers the ambiance of the North African desert. First you're seated at low, brass-inlaid tables with decorated pillows for reclining. Waiters dressed in traditional caftans and slippers perform the sacred hand-washing ritual. (The not-so-sacred belly dancers arrive later.) Then the deluxe-priced, seven-course dinner starts with Itarira soup and Moroccan salad. Pastilla — phyllo dough over a mixture of ground chicken, almonds and scrambled eggs — is next. But you're not through because the real eating is just beginning: Flaming lamb brochette is followed by roast chicken or lamb shank and honey-covered chabakia.

Patio Cafe

$ • 3900 Paradise Rd. • 866-6300

One of the better finds for breakfast and lunch is the Patio Cafe in the Citibank Business Park. Though small, the cafe is bright and airy and tastefully appointed with a Spanish tile floor, oak captain's chairs, ceiling fans and lithographs of Mediterranean resorts and seascapes. True to its name there's an outdoor patio with wrought-iron furniture and vine-covered trellises. The cafe features the usual mix of eggs, omelettes, salads, sandwiches, burgers and the like. But the best lunch dishes are the Middle Eastern specialties, which include roasted eggplant salad with sesame sauce; Israeli salad, a hearty helping of diced cucumber, tomatoes and onions in a light lemon and olive oil dressing; and falafel, ground chickpeas and vegetables, deep fried and served with sesame sauce in a warm pita. Patio Cafe is open for breakfast, lunch and dinner.

Shalimar

$$ • 3900 Paradise Rd. • 796-0302

Northern Indian cuisine prepared in tandoori ovens is the specialty here. Appetizers include samosa (deep-fried pastry stuffed with vegetables); tandoori-cooked chicken tikka; marinated lamb kabob; and shish kabob. The chicken curries are prepared with almonds, spinach, dried fruit, sauteed onions and scallions. Seafood curries are made with prawns and fresh fish. Complete vegetarian dinners with eggplant, cauliflower, okra, spinach and tomatoes are also offered. Basmati rice, imported from Punjab, is prepared with saffron and vegetables. Shalimar serves lunch and dinner.

Seafood

Emeril Lagasse's New Orleans Fish House

$$ • MGM Grand, 3799 Las Vegas Blvd. S. • 891-7374

Celebrity chef and author Emeril Lagasse brings his signature blend of New Orleans Creole/Cajun cooking to Sin City. Spotlighted is his signature barbecue shrimp as well as favorites such as double-cut pork chops and fresh seafood that is flown in daily from around the world. Don't forget to try his famous banana cream pie with banana crust and caramel. It's open for lunch and dinner.

Sacred Sea Room

$$$ • Luxor Hotel, 3900 Las Vegas Blvd. S. • 262-4772

Murals and hieroglyphic reproductions of fishing on the Nile line the walls, and a wave-like ceiling mosaic creates the illusion of feasting in an Egyptian fishing village. The featured fare, of course, is fresh- and saltwater seafood flown in daily. Landlubbers can try the veal chops, New York steaks and poultry dishes. It's open for dinner only.

Steakhouses

Beef Baron

$$$ • Flamingo Hilton Hotel, 3555 Las Vegas Blvd. S. • 733-3111

While the venerable hotel is famous for its Miami modern decor, its most popular restaurant is the Old West-style Beef Baron, decorated with longhorn chandeliers, mounted deer heads and vintage rifles. The menu features sizzling steaks, prime rib, rack of lamb, chateaubriand, roast duckling and fresh seafood. It's open for dinner only.

Embers

$$$ • Imperial Palace Hotel, 3535 Las Vegas Blvd. S. • 794-3114

Red leather booths, mahogany tables, brocade chairs and ribbons of red neon create a stately but subdued atmosphere for fine dining at reasonable prices. Among the house favorites are the 24-ounce porterhouse steak, chateaubriand for two, filet mignon with Alaskan crab legs, fresh salmon and New York steak. Even the supporting cast is first rate, including a house salad of garden greens and artichoke hearts and a hearty French onion soup. For a real treat splurge on the cherries jubilee, prepared tableside. It's open for dinner only.

Lawry's the Prime Rib

$$$ • 4043 Howard Hughes Pkwy. • 893-2223

This is only the fifth Lawry's to open worldwide since the original was founded in 1938 on La Cienega Boulevard in Los Angeles. The art-deco-style restaurant is famous for its rolling stainless steel carts for tableside beef carving, waitresses in crisp '30s uniforms and, of course, prime rib of beef available in several cuts, the largest being the Diamond Jim Brady slab complete with bone. If you have a bone to pick with beef, the fresh seafood selections often include grouper with lemon herb butter and Atlantic lobster tails. Of the accompaniments, don't miss the spinning salad bowl and the traditional Yorkshire pudding baked in small sheets and served in pie-shaped slices. It's open for dinner only.

Rosewood Grill

$$$$ • 3339 Las Vegas Blvd. S. • 792-9099

With its dark-wood panels, leather booths, red carpet and starched white tablecloths, this sophisticated room is reminiscent of Las Vegas 30 years ago. The dinner menu is built around the classics — filet mignon, steaks, prime rib and fresh seafood that might include a grilled fillet of Pacific tuna. The restaurant has also become famous for its huge Maine lobsters that are flown in daily. Many of these contenders tip the scale at more than 10 pounds, so be careful when ordering. Market price can push one of those to $200. Rosewood Grill serves dinner only.

The Steak House

$$$ • Circus Circus Hotel/Casino, 2880 Las Vegas Blvd. S. • 734-0410

If you like your steaks large, thick and juicy, bring a hearty appetite to The Steak House. Don't let the high-wire acts and throngs of kids on the midway at Circus Circus discourage you; The Steak House is a quiet, oak-paneled dining room where you can enjoy mesquite-broiled New York, sirloin, porterhouse or filet mignon. It's open for dinner only.

William B's Steakhouse

$$$ • Stardust Hotel, 3000 Las Vegas Blvd. S. • 732-6111

If you like dining in 1890s elegance, William B's features a turn-of-the-century motif with its polished mahogany wall panels, etched glass, brass fixtures and sepia-toned photographs. Traditional American cuisine includes prime rib, steaks, fish, veal, rack of lamb and a classic onion soup. It's open for dinner only.

Yolie's Steakhouse

$$$ • 3900 Paradise Rd. • 794-0700

Brazilian-style cooking is featured at Yolie's Steakhouse, where you can eat in the high-ceilinged dining room or on the rooftop terrace. The fixed-price house specialty begins with soup or salad, then continues with a procession of waiters bearing sausage Ipanema, turkey breast wrapped in bacon, young spring chicken, New York sirloin, brisket of beef and leg of baby lamb. Side dishes include fried potatoes, polenta, bananas, vegetables and rice. If you prefer to order from the menu try scampi, orange roughy, rack of lamb for two or daily seafood specials. Yolie's serves dinner only.

Downtown

American

Bay City Diner

$ • Golden Gate Hotel, One Fremont St. • 385-1906

Located in the city's oldest hotel, Bay City Diner retains the aura of turn-of-the-century San Francisco with its mahogany walls, ceilings and baseboards, brass fixtures and leaded-crystal chandeliers. Famous for introducing the shrimp cocktail to Las Vegas in the 1950s, Bay City Diner serves bargain-priced breakfasts, porterhouse steaks and chicken specialties 24 hours a day.

Enigma Garden Cafe

$ • 918½ S. Fourth St. • 386-0999

Peace, love and flower power are alive and well in this converted-house-turned-hippie-hangout a block west of Las Vegas Boulevard. Pass through the wrought-iron gates to the back patio where you'll find a garden gathering place for loners, Krishna types, artists and poets and a few local business people. The 24-hour menu features health-oriented egg dishes, sandwiches, salads and a mish-mash of Middle Eastern specialties. You can also enjoy a variety of espresso drinks, mochas, cappuccinos, lattes, fruit smoothies, amalfis, sodas, egg creams and more.

Holy Cow! Casino, Cafe & Brewery

$$ • 2423 Las Vegas Blvd. S. • 732-2697

The first microbrewery to open in town, Holy Cow! is known by its distinctive black-and-white Holstein cow logo that is plastered everywhere, from the billboard over the building to the T-shirts of the wait staff. They serve four types of beer, each with its own unique flavor, including the Rebel Red ale, which won

INSIDERS' TIP

Use discount and two-for-one coupons to save on dining costs. You can find them in free visitor magazines, the entertainment section of the *Las Vegas Review-Journal* newspaper and in funbooks given away by the resorts.

a people's choice competition for pale ales, cream ales, brown ales and oatmeal stouts. The 24-hour restaurant serves steaks, burgers, sandwiches, breakfast and Wisconsin bratwurst. Also worth trying are the rotisserie chicken, pork ribs and walleye pike.

Liberty Cafe

$ • White Cross Rexall Drugs, 1700 Las Vegas Blvd. S. • 383-0101

The old-fashioned drugstore lunch counter is nearly extinct, but there are a couple of relics remaining in town, and this is one of them. In addition to the monster breakfasts (try the Greek omelette), greasy burgers and chicken-fried steak, the day-to-day clientele with their retro duds help play out the time warp. But don't laugh, they know where to find the best double vanilla malted.

Roxy's Diner

$$ • Stratosphere, 2000 Las Vegas Blvd. S. • 380-7777

For a taste of Vegas' version of "Happy Days," pop in a Buddy Holly tape and cruise to this blast from the past where everything — the fountain decor, crisply-starched uniforms and Golden Oldies music — replicates the vitality of the Fabulous Fifties. Home-style favorites include chicken fried steak, Mom's meat loaf with red pepper gravy, burgers, malts, shakes and Po'Boys. Roxy's is open 24 hours.

Triple 7 Brewpub

$$ • Main Street Station, 200 N. Main St. • 387-1896

This is a classy joint that follows a 1930s warehouse motif with high ceilings, parquet floors, rich mahogany and cherry wood accented by brass and copper fixtures. The bar itself is one of the most attractive in town with etched, beveled glass and more mahogany panels. Although the pub's menu by necessity leans toward party-style selections, you can choose from a fair variety of salads, sandwiches, burgers, pizzas and Southwest specialties such as chile verde, pork tostada and sirloin and black bean chili. It's open for lunch and dinner as well as late-night suppers.

Your Place or Mine for Lunch

$ • 622 Carson Ave. • 386-6060

This venerable lunch counter has been feeding downtown office workers for decades. The reason? They make fantastic sandwiches at bargain prices. Choose from the usual suspects — ham, turkey, cheese, beef, egg, tuna, chicken salad, etc. — or try one of the specialties: the "sprout special" with avocado, alfalfa sprouts and egg, tuna, seafood or chicken salad; the all-veggie sub with cucumber, green peppers, onions, avocado, sprouts and soy baco-bits on a soft roll. For a change of pace try the stuffed avocado, green pepper or tomato. The date-nut bread with cream cheese is out of this world.

Chinese

Emperor's Room

$$ • Lady Luck Hotel, 206 N. Third St. • 477-3000

An eclectic blend of Chinese cuisine and rare Oriental art are featured in the Emperor's Room. Mainstays include Mandarin garlic chicken, shrimp and scallops in a nest and Peking duck. After dining, be sure to check out the Soldiers of Xian replicas, dating from 2000 B.C. during the Quin dynasty. It is open for dinner only.

Fong's Garden

$$ • 2021 E. Charleston Blvd. • 382-1644

Fong's, which opened in 1933 as the Silver Cafe, is one of the city's few remaining culinary landmarks. The big neon pagoda, Chinese-red booths and Buddha rock shrine are slightly out of date but nevertheless reminiscent of simpler times. Traditional Chinese fare includes moo goo gai pan, almond duck, Chinese sausage with vegetables and abalone Cantonese. The drinks, served in the Trader Vic manner with skewered pineapple and colorful parasols, are generous and potent — try the Scorpion, Zombie and Fong's Special. Fong's is open for lunch and dinner.

Gee Joon

$$ • Binion's Horseshoe, 128 E. Fremont St. • 382-1600

In the ancient Chinese game of Pai Gow, "gee joon" is the highest ranking hand and translated means "supreme" or "excellence." Located on the mezzanine above the casino, Gee Joon aspires to its lofty namesake by serving an array of Cantonese dishes, including the house specialty, Peking Duck, which is marinated overnight in plum and hoisin sauce and basted with honey. Gee Joon is open for dinner only.

Komol Kitchen

$$ • 827 Las Vegas Blvd. S. • 387-0570

Located between a wedding chapel and topless adult bookstore, Komol draws a spicy clientele. Which is appropriate for the cafe's Thai style of cuisine — the panang curry, rice and pad thai are hot enough to elevate anyone's temperature. Other tasty favorites available for lunch and dinner include satay, chunks of pork on skewers with a spicy peanut sauce, and beef larb, a concoction of ground meat with rice flour, cheese and lime juice served with cabbage wraps. The restaurant is open for lunch and dinner.

> **FYI**
>
> Unless otherwise noted, the area code for all phone numbers listed in this chapter is 702.

Lillie Langtry's

$$$ • Golden Nugget Hotel, 129 Fremont St. • 385-7111

Posh and cozy describe this bistro that is adorned with draped booths, Venetian-glass chandeliers and a domed ceiling. House favorites include the great combination plate appetizer (ribs, shrimp, egg roll), moo goo gai pan, dragon eye fruit, beef with oyster sauce and seafood tofu soup. For more exotic tastes try the shark-fin soup, crab with black bean sauce and abalone with oyster sauce. Lillie Langtry's is open for diner only.

Continental

Burgundy Room

$$$ • Lady Luck Hotel, 206 N. Third St. • 477-3000

Plush burgundy velour ensconces diners in this intimate bistro, where you can also view art by Salvador Dali and sculptures by Max Le Verrier. The house specialty is live Maine lobster, chosen from the tank at the room's entrance. Other upscale entrees include fresh swordfish, salmon and seafood kabobs and Black Angus beef selections. For a real treat, try the seafood served over angel-hair pasta. It is open for dinner only.

Frogeez on 4th

$$ • 300 S. Fourth St. • 380-1122

From hot dogs to escargot, you can have it all in this ground-floor eatery. Breakfast and lunch are served for the working-class crowd, and starting in the afternoon and continuing until the wee hours of the morning, choose from the Bistro Menu, an eclectic array of grilled chicken and fennel sausage, anjou pear and Roquefort, Muscovy duck and crème brûlée.

Hugo's Cellar

$$$ • Four Queens Hotel, 202 E. Fremont St. • 385-4011

Another classy downtown restaurant is Hugo's Cellar. A fresh rose handed to each female guest sets the tone for dining in this intimate, brick- and brass-accented room. A waiter prepares your salad tableside from a well-stocked cart, and you can select from entrees that include prime steaks, veal, lamb, duck, chicken and seafood. A compote tray of chocolate-dipped fruits precedes the pastry cart, which tempts you with cheesecakes, strawberry torte and Black Forest cake. Hugo's Cellar is open for dinner only.

Redwood Bar & Grill

$$$ • California Hotel, 12 Ogden Ave. • 385-1222

The Redwood Bar & Grill features a cozy lodge atmosphere accented by decorative wood paneling, copper fixtures, country English furniture and a fieldstone fireplace. The upscale dinner entrees feature time-tested favorites such as steak Diane, veal Oscar, chicken with apricot sauce, roast prime rib and an 18-ounce porterhouse steak special. Only dinner is served.

Second Street Grill

$$ • Fremont Hotel & Casino, 200 E. Fremont St. • 385-3232

For traditional dishes with a Pacific Rim influence, try this elegant eatery in the Fremont Hotel. The spacious dining room has a neo-Roman flourish with faux-marble columns, indirect lighting and white-wood furniture with dark upholstery. In addition to seafood, veal, beef and poultry entrees, you can sample interesting specialty dishes such as deep-fried lumpia with basil peanut dip, Mongolian hot seafood pot, pan-fried crab cakes, asparagus bisque, veal medallions and rack of lamb. Second Street Grill serves dinner only.

Top of the World

$$$$ • Stratosphere, 2000 Las Vegas Blvd. S. • 380-7777

Top of the World lends new meaning to "upscale" dining — your table is more than 800 feet above the ground in a room that rotates so you have a 360-degree view of Las Vegas over the course of your meal. Some of the imaginative dishes include chicken satay, cioppino San Francisco, lobster fettuccine and chicken breast with lobster Thermidor sauce. The restaurant serves dinner only.

French

Andre's

$$$-$$$$ • 401 S. Sixth St. • 385-5016

If you think the best restaurants are found in the most expensive hotels, Andre's will prove you wrong. Here, in a converted wood-frame house on a Downtown side street, Andre's serves classic French cuisine for dinner only. There are several intimate dining rooms, all dimly lit, discreet and furnished with country antiques. As you would expect, the service is impeccable. Appetizers include smoked baby coho salmon with dill sauce; smoked trout with remoulade sauce; three pâtés with black currant sauce; and snails en croûte maison or bourguignonne. Main entrees include frogs' legs; imported Dover sole served à la facon du chef; stuffed Australian lobster tail; and stuffed pork tenderloin with apple and walnuts. The dessert cart adds the perfect touch: almond chocolate cake, fruit tarts or fresh berries. There's also an extensive wine cellar for the well-seasoned connoisseur.

Italian

California Pizza Kitchen

$$ • Golden Nugget Hotel • 129 E. Fremont St. • 385-7111

Located in a quiet, split-level setting far from the chaotic din of slot machines and other annoyances, CPK takes the foods people love and puts them on pizza. Among the more innovative toppings are Thai chicken, eggplant Parmesan, goat cheese, Peking duck, tuna melt, shrimp scampi, BLT and barbecue chicken. You can also dine on pasta dishes and salads — the romaine and watercress salad and the barbecue chicken chopped salad are the best. CPK is open for lunch and dinner.

Chicago Joe's

$$ • 820 S. Fourth St. • 382-5246

A favorite with locals for decades, Chicago Joe's is a delightful restaurant built in a converted home near the downtown courthouse. The dining areas, separated by the bar, are cozy but not cramped. Specialties include snails and pasta, lobster, veal, eggplant Parmesan, lasagna, cheese ravioli, linguine with calamari, clams (fresh steamed or baked) and meatball sandwiches. It's open for lunch and dinner.

Stefano's

$$$ • Golden Nugget Hotel, 129 E. Fremont St. • 385-7111

For Italian specialties visit this cheerful room accented by colorful murals, hand-blown glass chandeliers and tiles from Salerno. Some of the chef's favorites include linguine with clams, scampi fra diavolo and veal piccata, or create a meal with appetizers such as fresh mussels, calamari alla Luciana and steamed clams. The cioppino is a meal in itself, and the chocolate pasta with ice cream will change your outlook on world events. Stefano's is open for dinner only.

Vincenzo's Cafe

$$ • Fitzgerald's Hotel & Casino, 301 Fremont St. • 388-2462

This bright and airy room is accented by a hardwood floor and light-wood tables and chairs. The open exhibition kitchen lets you watch chefs prepare wood-baked pizzas, homemade pastas and seafood. For a Naples-inspired treat, try the large grilled prawns and Italian sausage poured over handmade mostacciolli with fresh tomatoes. Vincenzo's is open for lunch and dinner.

Mexican/Southwestern

El Sombrero

$ • 807 S. Main St. • 382-9234

From the outside this tiny cantina looks like a Tijuana jail, complete with bars on the windows. It doesn't improve much on the inside — six booths, six tables, a loud Mexican juke box and a garish mural on the wall. But the food is good and plentiful. Try the menudo, chili Colorado, natillas and dinner specials — shrimp on tomatoes, scrambled eggs with Mexican sausage and diced beef with red chili sauce. In addition to hearty dinners, the breakfast and lunch items are among the best bargains in the city.

Dona Maria

$ • 910 Las Vegas Blvd. S. • 382-6538

This family-run cantina specializes in bargain-priced tamales with a variety of stuffing — pork, beef, chicken and cheese. Other standard offerings include tacos, enchilladas, burritos and chimichangas. It's open for lunch and dinner.

Los Tres Amigos

$ • 1919 E. Fremont St. • 383-8566

Housed in a tiny shack between two motels, this cozy, dimly lit eatery is difficult to spot. Keep a sharp eye, and you'll be amply rewarded. As are the rules with most mom-and-pop Mexican restaurants, the portions are enormous, and the prices are low. Instead of starting with the traditional salsa and chips, try the botuva compuestra, an assortment of taquitos, nachos and mini chimichangas. The chile verde (diced pork with green sauce) and chile Colorado (diced beef with red sauce), are the best entrees. It's open for lunch and dinner.

Macayo Vegas

$$ • 1741 E. Charleston Blvd. • 382-5605

This popular eatery has been serving traditional Mexican dishes since 1960. The dining room is accented with Southwestern art and furnishings, while the cuisine has a Southern Mexican flavor. Entrees include chicken Maximilian, crab enchiladas and shrimp à la Vera Cruz. Traditional fajitas, tamales, chimichangas and chili relleno are also expertly prepared. It's open for lunch and dinner.

Salvadoreno

$ • 720 N. Main St. • 385-3600

Just a few blocks north of the Fremont Street Experience you'll find authentic Salvadoran cuisine in a hole-in-the-wall eatery. Although the juke box is sometimes loud enough to wake the dead, and the walls are covered with maps and posters of chaotic El Salvador, the cuisine is both politically correct and fiscally prudent. Seating is of the early dinette school of design. The pupusas (tortillas filled with cheese, beans and pork), platanos (fried bananas in milk) and pastelles de gallina (chicken and vegetable pies) are budget priced. Other hearty entrees include carne guisada, beef stew with carrot, potato, rice and refried beans; and pollo encebollado. The thick, homemade corn tortillas are of the I-dare-you-to-eat-just-one variety. Salvadoreno is open for breakfast, lunch and dinner.

Seafood

Great Moments Room

$$$ • Las Vegas Club, 18 Fremont St. • 385-1664

Dark leather booths, mahogany furnishings and soft lighting create a nice spot for close encounters in the shadow of the Fremont Street Experience. If you like seafood you'll love the house specialty — a hearty bouillabaisse — as well as other ocean favorites such as sauteed scalone, salmon, filet mignon and scampi. The restaurant serves dinner only.

INSIDERS' TIP

Casino restaurants lose money — from 9 percent a year on The Strip to 36 percent Downtown — because of low prices and liberal comp policies.

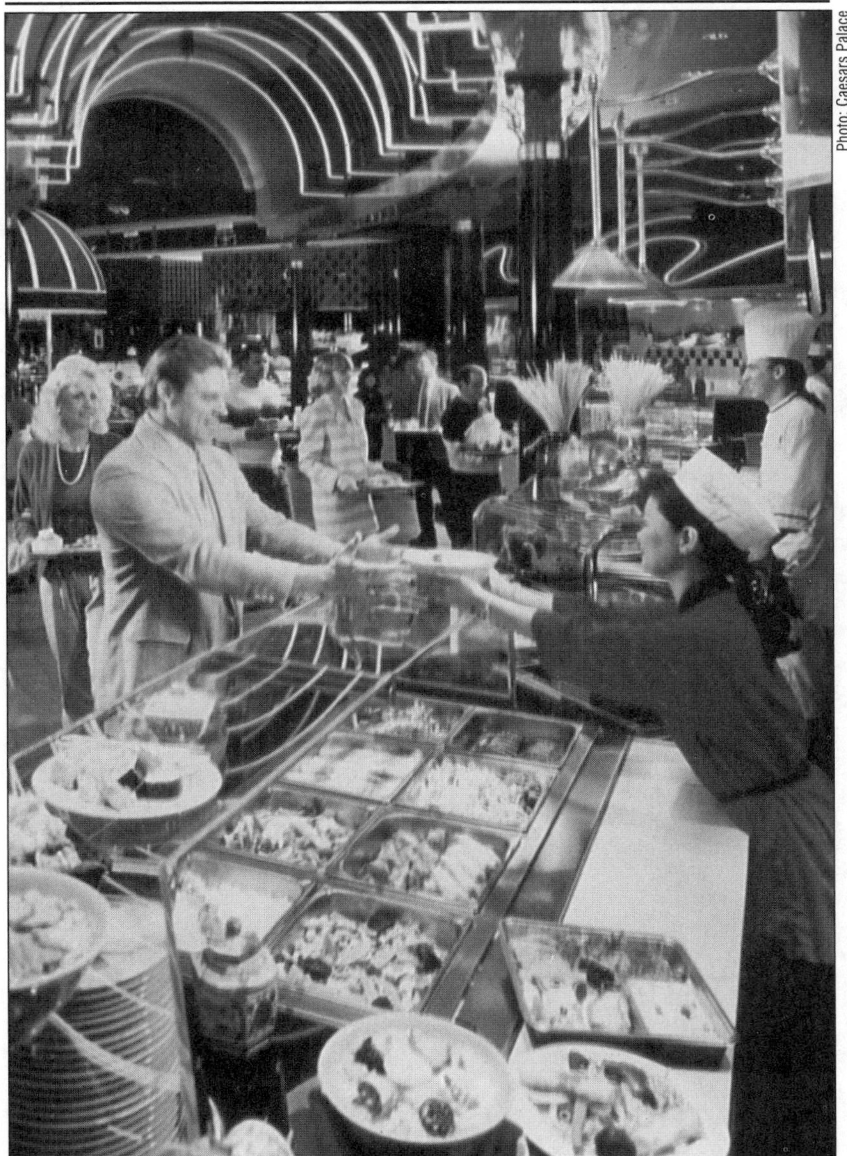

Photo: Caesars Palace

Most hotels have a food court or pavilion for diners who want to refuel on the run.

Pasta Pirate

$$ • California Hotel, 12 Ogden Ave. • 385-1222

The aroma of mesquite-broiled seafood greets visitors to this cozy restaurant just off the bustling casino. Patterned after a dockside fish factory, the intimate room features open ventilator ducts, a brick floor, tin walls, fishnets and neon signs. The house specials include steamed clams, Australian sea bass and snow crab legs. Ask about the fresh catch of the day, which can include Atlantic salmon, swordfish, halibut and orange roughy. It is open for dinner only.

Steakhouses

Big Sky Ranch Steakhouse

$$$ • Stratosphere, 2000 Las Vegas Blvd. S. • 380-7777

What better way to enjoy a sizzling steak than in an Old West setting with chuckwagons, log hand rails, wooden floors, branding irons and tack on the walls. Grilled favorites include beef brisket, rotisserie chicken, Carolina pulled pork, T-bone and filet steaks and prime rib. If you're *really* hungry, go for the fixed-price Feast — barbecue pork ribs, beef brisket, Southern fried chicken, Carolina pork, bottomless salad, corn muffins, baked beans, coleslaw and ranch house fries. If you're still standing, try a wedge of the apple cobbler. Big Sky is open for dinner only.

Binion's Ranch Steakhouse

$$$ • Binion's Horseshoe, 128 E. Fremont St. • 382-1600

Meateaters will like this joint. Brocade-covered booths and oil paintings highlight the restaurant's Old West theme. Be prepared for a dramatic view of the city after your ride in the outside glass elevator. You'll get generous portions of prime rib, lamb chops, New York steak, filet mignon or a 23-ounce porterhouse steak. Fresh fish and chicken dishes are also served.

Limericks

$$ • Fitzgerald's Hotel & Casino, 301 Fremont St. • 388-2460

Art deco meets Moorish castle in this black-and-gold accented room that specializes in dry-aged beef (14 to 21 days) as well as lobster, lamb, veal, fish and chicken. Among the unique appetizers are a shrimp cocktail in which the sauce is made with a light marinara and the escargot that is accented with a tomato conncasse. Limericks is open for dinner only.

Pullman Grill

$$$ • Main Street Station, 200 N. Main St. • 387-1896

True to its name, this place is reminiscent of an old-time dining car with its wood panels and richly appointed parlor seating. Among its specialties are Black Angus steaks and prime rib, but you can also order fresh seafood — ahi tuna sashimi and Maryland crab cakes that will make you forget the Chesapeake Bay. Save room for the scrumptious bread pudding with pineapple rum caramel sauce. It's open for dinner only.

East Valley

American

Country Inn

$$ • 2425 E. Desert Inn Rd. • 731-5035

Every day is Thanksgiving at the Country Inn, where the speciality is a complete turkey dinner with all the fixings. The Inn — a little white cottage protected by large shade trees about 3 miles east of The Strip — also serves turkey steaks, roast beef and pork. The country breakfasts are also popular on the moderately priced menu. Country Inn serves breakfast, lunch and dinner.

Cyber City Cafe

$$ • 3945 S. Maryland Pkwy. • 732-2001

This shopping center coffee pub weds the worlds of espresso and e-mail. That's right, in addition to sipping designer coffees you can access the Internet on one of the computers. After a morning of surfing and downloading, try the Virtual Reality — a veggie burger with cheese, sprouts, tomatoes, cukes, red onions, Dijon mustard and mayo on seven-grain bread. There are also a variety of espressos and fresh roasted coffee, plus juices and other smart drinks. Cyber City serves lunch, dinner and late-night snacks until 1 AM.

Green Shack

$$ • 2504 E. Fremont St. • 383-0007

As the oldest restaurant in Las Vegas, this little diner with the wagon-wheel front originally opened as the Colorado in 1929, when Jimmie Jones and her mother, Effie, sold fried chicken from the window of their two-room house. A railroad barracks was later converted and used as a dining room. The main part of today's dining room is that same barracks.

The restaurant is clean and homey — handmade crafts and memorabilia from the early days adorn the dining room. A bar and cocktail lounge have been added, and a one-man band plays on weekends in the glow of the year-round Christmas tree. The specialty is still Southern fried chicken. There are also gizzards, liver, fish and steak and homemade bread pudding or strawberry shortcake for dessert. It's open for dinner only.

Jazzed Cafe & Vinoteco

$$ • 2055 E. Tropicana Ave. • 798-5995

Tastefully elegant by coffee pub standards, Jazzed Cafe features cabaret tables with fresh-cut flowers, candle lighting and European lithographs on the walls. In addition to a robust house java, Jazzed has an extensive wine list and tasty menu items, especially the eggplant Parmesan, cioppino, rigatoni and other Italian favorites. Jazzed Cafe serves dinner only, but is open for late-night (early morning) tete-a-tetes.

Jerome's

$$ • 2797 S. Maryland Pkwy. • 792-3772

The owners of Jerome's wanted to bring a taste of San Francisco to Las Vegas so they decorated the restaurant with mahogany furniture and white butcher-paper tablecloths. The food selections come closer to hitting the Bay City's mark and include fresh sourdough bread, clams Sausalito, Russian oysters, and mussel saffron soup topped with puff pastry. Also featured are grilled sea scallops, blackened swordfish, grilled yellowfin tuna plus chicken, veal, beef and pasta dishes. Jerome's serves dinner only.

Jerusalem Restaurant & Deli

$ • 1305 Vegas Valley Drive • 735-2878

As far as we could find, this is the city's only strictly kosher restaurant, serving solid, mainstream dishes in portions that would warm any Jewish mother's heart. The dinner feast includes soup or salad, stuffed cabbage, meatballs, kebab and baked chicken served with rice and vegetables. Other entrees are suniyeh, chicken schnitzel and beef Carmel — hummus topped with chopped beef and pine nuts. For lunch there's salami and pastrami sandwiches, falafel, kebabs, tuna and potato salads, and potato and vegetable latkes.

Kiefer's Downtown Henderson

$$ • 15 E. Lake Mead Dr., Henderson • 565-0122

In the same location as onetime landmark, Nick's Supper Club, this is a good place to feast on seafood in a Caribbean setting. There's an oyster bar with two large aquariums (for decoration only), where you can order shrimp cocktails (three kinds of shrimp) and oysters Rockefeller. The house specialty is the Kiefer's Catch — poached orange roughy topped with crabmeat, butter, jack and cheddar cheese, all encased in a pastry shell shaped like a fish.

Moose McGillycuddy's

$$ • 4770 S. Maryland Pkwy. • 798-8337

True to its name, there's a moose head inside this Southern California-inspired pub and restaurant. Other shades of California include hundreds of photos of bikers, bikinis and music memorabilia on the walls plus Monterey cannery-type ducts in the ceiling. For lunch and dinner you can dine on ribs, burgers, grilled chicken and Beefeater sandwiches, fish and chips, mushroom fettuccine, chicken and Mexican dishes.

The Roadhouse

$$ • 2100 N. Boulder Hwy., Henderson • 564-1150

This is a throwback to the old-time roadhouses that Cary Grant and Myrna Loy used for their rendezvous in those classic Golden Age films. There's even a rustic ambiance to the building's post World War II architecture — corrugated tin walls, a roof with twin spires and a winged monument in front. The name of the place is even painted on the roof in case you arrive by light aircraft. Inside, it's a genuine diner complete with vintage counters and stools, a soda fountain, Coke machines, syrup dispensers, a juke box, metal signs and much more. Of course, the featured fare is food from the Fabulous Fifties — juicy hubcaps, cruiser burgers, patty melts, sandwich baskets, fountain treats and the like. The Roadhouse also serves hearty breakfasts at bargain prices (the rib-eye steak and eggs is only $5.95) as well as home-style dinners — steaks, pot roast, pork chops, meat loaf, fried chicken and liver and onions, none of which costs more than $7.95. The Roadhouse serves breakfast, lunch and dinner.

Souper Salad

$ • 4020 S. Maryland Pkwy. • 792-8555

If you're in need of a good place to unclog your arteries, this is it. The cafeteria-style restaurant has a salad line that features leafy greens — spinach, romaine and iceberg lettuce — plus all the condiments for a great, healthy salad: green peppers, cucumbers, celery, mushrooms, sprouts, tomatoes, zucchini and more. There's also a soup station, dessert bar and stuff-your-own potato station. Open for lunch and dinner, Souper Salad will also prepare sandwiches — ham, turkey, club, chicken salad — for eating in or take out. It's open for lunch and dinner.

FYI

Unless otherwise noted, the area code for all phone numbers listed in this chapter is 702.

Chinese

China Doll

$ • 2534 E. Desert Inn Rd. • 369-9511

This storefront eatery with its plastic dinette tables is a good spot for traditional Chinese favorites such as kung pao chicken, fresh squid with vegetables, beef with broccoli, lemon chicken, sweet and sour pork and crispy Peking duck. A house favorite is the double-cooked pork with cabbage. China Doll serves lunch and dinner.

Ichi Ban Gai

$ • 1801 E. Tropicana Blvd. • 736-2828

This is a friendly, neighborhood restaurant that does a flavorful rendition of all the classics at a crisp tablecloth setting. Try the sushi and sashimi bar, gomaae (spinach salad), yaki soba, salmon shioyaki or teriyaki or beef curry over rice. The delicate shrimp puffs, lettuce chicken and mu shu pork are tasty appetizers. Desserts of glazed bananas or fried pudding are satisfying finales. The restaurant serves lunch and dinner.

Mandarin Court

$ • 1510 E. Flamingo Rd. • 737-1234

This modest storefront cafe is tastefully decorated with Chinese hanging tapestries and brocade. The extensive menu, which can be explained by the wait staff, features specialties such as honey-garlic chicken wings, crispy duck, beef and pork in hot garlic sauce and clams with black bean sauce. The restaurant serves lunch and dinner.

Wo Fat

$ • 3700 E. Desert Inn Rd. • 451-6656

If you're familiar with the Hawaiian Islands, the name may sound familiar — it's the same as the famous Chinatown restaurant in Honolulu. But the local chef at Wo Fat brought more than the name of the restaurant to Las Vegas. He brought many dishes that made the Hotel Street restaurant so popular in the islands. You can sample such island chicken dishes as cold chicken in onion sauce, mushroom boneless chicken and pot roast chicken. From the sea, there's lobster with black bean sauce, abalone with black mushrooms and clams with black bean sauce. If you're adventurous try the watercress pork soup, braised pig's foreshank or stuffed bittermelon. The hot-and-sour soup is also tasty, if not incendiary, so be forewarned. Wo Fat is open for lunch and dinner.

Continental

Anthony's

$$$ • 1550 E. Tropicana Ave. • 795-6000

For more adventuresome game than you'll ever find in a casino, try this lively restaurant decorated with brass fixtures and etched glass — it has the widest selection of fresh game in the city. Specialties include lion with port sauce, camel steak in Bordeaux sauce, buffalo steak in bordelaise sauce and alligator steak. Less exotic selections include orange roughy, broiled swordfish steak and quail stuffed with mushrooms. Anthony's serves dinner only.

Cafe Michelle

$$ • 1350 E. Flamingo Rd. • 734-8686

This is a popular spot for outdoor dining, except during July and August when you can saute mushrooms on the sidewalk. Dining al fresco in a shopping center may not compare to the Champs Elysees, but think of all the francs you're saving. Besides you might spot a celebrity while you dine on fresh fish, veal, pastas, crepes, braised calf's sweetbreads financiere, asparagus and spinach omelettes and frittatas. It's open for lunch and dinner.

Crown & Anchor

$$ • 1350 E. Tropicana Ave. • 739-0281

For a taste of Merry Olde England, try this British-style pub, enhanced by dark wood furnishings, wooden staircases and nautical artifacts throughout. There's even a buxom blonde figurehead over the bar, which offers nearly three dozen draught beers, ales and stouts imported from the Continent. The clientele includes many U.K. expatriots, who reminisce about the Commonwealth while watching soccer matches between Liverpool and Newcastle on the satellite TV. Traditional English fare includes fish and chips, steak and kidney pie, chicken curry, Lancashire hot pot, Cornish pastie and bangers and mash. Crown & Anchor is open for breakfast, lunch and dinner.

Old Heidelberg

$$ • 604 E. Sahara Ave. • 731-5310

For award-winning Bavarian cuisine try Old Heidelberg. Traditional fare includes veal bratwurst, knockwurst, potato pancakes, gulash soup, zieguner with mushrooms in wine and yager schnitzel. If the sauer bratten, which is marinated for two or three days, is missing from the menu, ask for it. Desserts include fresh Black Forest cake, crepes and apple strudel. Warsteiner German beer is on tap; 30 other varieties of beer are available. Dinner only is served.

Plantation Room

$$ • Showboat Hotel & Casino, 2800 Fremont St. • 385-9123

The Plantation Room plants you in a Southern mansion with its hardwood floors, antebellum murals and veranda-like seating. So ensconced, you have your choice of grilled steaks, poultry and fresh seafood. Chef's favorites include the chicken pontchartrain and roast duckling with orange sauce. The restaurant serves dinner only.

Delis

Bagelmania

$ • 855 E. Twain Ave. • 369-3322

In a city short on delis, Bagelmania is a welcome find. The New York-style deli with its massive counter and Formica-top tables features nine varieties of bagels served with lox or nova, sturgeon, sable, chub, herring, white fish or just plain cream cheese. Sandwiches are mainstream deli: corned beef, pastrami, roast beef, ham and turkey, to name a few. Bagelmania serves breakfast, lunch and dinner.

Bagels and More

$ • 2405 E. Tropicana Ave. • 435-8100

This is a lively little affair that does a pretty good impression of a Bronx deli. A nice touch is the mezzanine level, in which booths and tables encircle the loft and overlook the counter and main floor below. You can feast on deli favorites such as corned beef, pastrami, turkey, beef tongue, chopped liver, kosher salami and brisket of beef, to name a few. Breakfast fare includes eggs, omelettes, cheese blintzes, waffles and, of course, the signature bagels served with nova lox, whitefish, chopped herring and other condiments. It's open for breakfast, lunch and dinner.

Celebrity Deli

$ • 4055 S. Maryland Pkwy. • 733-7827

This little cafe has tile floors, Formica-topped dinette tables and wooden chairs, all surrounded by chilly pastels of pink and lavender. The menu features traditional deli favorites such as corned beef, pastrami, turkey and salami, with dinner entrees such as smoked fish, stuffed cabbage, brisket of beef and Eomania steak. Among the fresh baked goods are bagels, knishes, kugels and danishes. The Celebrity Deli serves lunch and dinner.

Siena Deli

$ • 2250 E. Tropicana Ave. • 736-8424

This is one of the best Italian delis in town, but sticklers for grand decor and sophisticated service should look elsewhere. Here, you place your order at the deli counter, then take a seat at one of the few tables at the front of the store and wait. The massive meatball sandwich and a Sicilian (square) pizza are specialties of the house, but you won't go wrong with sandwiches made from sausage and peppers, prosciutto, mortadella and Genoa salami, to name a few. If you're planning a party or simply want to pig out, Siena will prepare cold cut and antipasto trays and submarine sandwiches up to 6 feet long. Siena Deli serves lunch and dinner.

Italian

Bootlegger Ristorante

$$ • 5025 S. Eastern Ave. • 736-4939

This family-run cafe is famous for its pasta selections: eggplant and broccoli parmigiana, baked rigatoni, lasagna, baked mostaccioli or baked meat ravioli. There's also a wide variety of seafood, beef, veal and chicken dinners. The house specialty is seafood diavolo made cioppino-style with jumbo shrimp, clams and calamari in marinara sauce, served over a bed of linguine. The restaurant serves dinner only.

Carluccio's Tivoli Gardens

$$ • 1775 E. Tropicana Blvd. • 795-3236

Just a few steps from the Liberace Museum, Carluccio's Tivoli Gardens serves generous portions of home-style Italian food. Inviting appetizers such as mussels, shrimp scampi, crab-stuffed shrimp, calamari and clams served steamed or baked on the half-shell are the best offerings. House specialties include chicken Florentine, shrimp fra diavolo, zuppa de clams, linguine with red or white clam sauce or seafood diablo. Carluccio's serves dinner only.

Cipriani

$$ • 2790 E. Flamingo Rd. • 367-6711

Don't let the silly lighthouse and beached lifeboat outside fool you. Inside, the dining room's crystal chandeliers, French doors and salmon-colored drapes create a posh atmosphere where you can feast on innovative southern Italian cuisine. Signature dishes include fettuccine with caviar and salmon, veal Montebianco, chicken frascati and scampi imperiale. The five-course special dinner features osso buco, seafood, veal or chicken. Cipriani serves dinner only.

Piazza D'Angelo

$$ • 2895 N. Green Valley Pkwy., Henderson • 451-8886

Opened in mid-1997, this charming bistro has become a favorite with the Green Valley crowd. Decorated with Southwestern tile and light-wood furnishings, D'Angelo offers diners a view of The Strip skyline and the mountains that surround the valley. Specialties of the house include fresh pasta, seafood dishes, wood-fired pizza, veal scaloppine, chicken and pork chops. For a treat try the baked eggplant with pesto, mozzarella and tomato sauce or the grilled, marinated portobello mushrooms. Piazza D'Angelo is open for lunch and dinner.

Japanese

Fuji

$$ • 3430 E. Tropicana Ave. • 435-8838

Hibachi dinners are the specialty here, where carved masks, paper lanterns and colorful pillow-cushions take guests from a modern shopping center to Old World Japan. Select from chicken, shrimp, New York steak and yakitori. Or opt for a combination dinner such as the sesame chicken, beef teriyaki, shrimp tempura and yakitori. Dinners are served with soup, salad, shredded pickle, rice, vegetables, green tea and ginger ice cream. Connoisseurs might find the sushi selections limited, but you can't beat the tangy wasabi and ginger slices. Fuji serves dinner only.

Geisha Steakhouse

$$ • 3751 E. Desert Inn Rd. • 451-9814

A scaled-down version of Benihana, Geisha Steakhouse serves complete Japanese dinners at six hibachi tables. Begin with beef and mushroom soup and then watch your chef orchestrate dinner on the hot table. Entree choices are sesame chicken, thin New York steak, samurai New York steak, shogun filet mignon, scallops, shrimp and lobster — all served with hibachi shrimp, vegetables and

INSIDERS' TIP

The best bargain breakfast in town is the $2.50 "Natural" at Binion's Horseshoe, where you get two eggs, potatoes, toast, coffee and a slice of ham that covers the plate.

fried rice and a glass of plum wine. Dinner only is served.

Ginza

$$ • 1000 E. Sahara Ave. • 732-3080

Come in from the bright desert sun and discover a colorful, Far Eastern setting behind the anemic storefronts of Sahara Avenue. The sushi bar features octopus and tuna as well as other traditional selections. The specialty is yosenabe, a Japanese bouillabaise with shrimp, crab, fish and clams served in a covered stone bowl, but you can also choose from entrees such as pork, beef, chicken and seafood. Ginza serves dinner only.

Kabuki

$$ • 1150 E. Twain Ave. • 733-0066

In addition to a sushi bar and traditional teriyaki and tempura dishes, there's an intriguing selection of broiled squid legs, dried whitefish on ground radish, squid with smelt eggs and three kinds of rice balls wrapped in seaweed. For the less adventurous the house specialty is the Love Boat dinner for two — sushi, beef teriyaki, yakitori, mixed tempura, tea and ice cream. Kabuki serves dinner only.

Nippon

$$ • 101 Convention Center Dr. • 735-5565

Sushi lovers must visit Nippon, where they can feast on 30 varieties of raw fish in the restaurant's long, narrow dining room or cozy sushi bar. The house specialty is the nabe yaki udon — fish cake, cabbage, shrimp tempura, onion, mushrooms and udon noodles, all served in an iron kettle. Beef sukiyaki and shrimp tempura with vegetables are also recommended. Nippon serves dinner only.

Tokyo

$$ • Commercial Center, 953 E. Sahara Ave. • 735-7070

Tokyo gives you a choice of dining at two large hibachi tables, a 14-seat tatami room or the sushi bar. There are dozens of entree choices, but the best bet is cooking your own dinner on the tabletop hibachi — beef, chicken, seafood and vegetables on skewers — served with soup, pickles, rice, dessert and green tea. Start with one of the many interesting appetizers: Octopus with vinegar seasoning and fish cakes with hot green mustard are two of the best. Tokyo serves dinner only.

Korean

Seoul Korean BBQ

$$ • Commercial Center, 953 E. Sahara Ave. • 369-4123

This small but well-maintained cafe specializes in barbecue thin-sliced beef, boneless short ribs, yellow corvina, saury, adka or sliced chicken — all prepared over gas-fired braziers. Or you can opt for one of the popular "food bowls" such as sliced pork or seafood casserole with kim chi. If you burn easily, ask for the mild seasoning — the Korean hot spicy sauces are just that. The restaurant serves lunch and dinner.

Mexican/Southwestern

Chapala's

$$ • 3335 E. Tropicana Blvd. • 451-8141

South-of-the-border specialties are featured in this hacienda-style restaurant with paintings on the walls, a fountain in the dining room and pepper ristas framing the windows. House specials include seafood chimichanga, steak tampiquena and enchilada, breast of chicken tamiquena with hot salsa, and relleno stuffed with crab and shrimp among its blackboard specials. The combination dinners feature corn-chicken enchiladas, tamales with red chile, beef tacos and relleno with green chile. Mexican and domestic beer and a wide variety of Margaritas are available. It's open for lunch and dinner.

Chevy's

$$ • 4090 S. Eastern Ave. • 731-6969

Exuding the promise of an impending fiesta, Chevy's is like a Spanish courtyard with splashy colors accenting the heavy adobe-like walls. The usual chips and salsa are anything but usual — the chips are parchment thin, and the salsa is thick and chunky with a smoky flavor. In addition to the usual burritos, fajitas and tostadas, you might try the fresh salmon tacos or the green spinach enchiladas. Incidentally, the tortillas that accompany the meal are made on a device that sits under a corrugated tin roof near the kitchen. It's a fascinating, Rube Goldberg contraption that flattens the dough balls, drops them onto rotating discs, bakes them along the way and spits them out like little puffer fish. The machine can crank out about 900 tortillas an hour. And if they're not served within three minutes, they're thrown out. Chevy's is open for lunch and dinner.

Lindo Michoacan

$$ • 2655 E. Desert Inn Rd. • 735-6828

Named for the Mexican state of Michoacan in central Mexico, Lindo Michoacan is a cheerful place that meanders through several rooms, decorated with woven rugs and serapes, south-of-the-border artifacts, tile floors and tables surrounded by multicolored chairs. If you sit in the main room, you can watch fresh tortillas being handmade at an old-style tortilleria. Owner Javier Barajas, who learned to cook in his native Michoacan, brought dozens of specialties from his homeland, including fresh beef tongue prepared in green molé sauce and jalapeño; roasted goat with a red molé sauce; and napolitas — Mexican cactus served with onions, cilantro, tomatoes and jalapeños. Other great dishes include chile rellenos and chile verde — chunks of pork marinated and simmered in a mild red sauce, then served with fresh flour tortillas, rice and beans. All meals are served with traditional chips and salsa and a tasty bean dip. The salsa is on the incendiary side, but you can request a milder green tomatillo salsa. On the other hand, you can ask for extra hot salsa — if you can stand it, your sinuses will be forever grateful. Lunch and dinner are served.

Ricardo's

$$ • 2380 E. Tropicana Ave. • 798-4515

For a fiesta, complete with strolling Mariachis and waiters dressed like flamenco dancers, come to this south-of-the-border cantina. In addition to traditional Mexican specialties — steak picado, carne asada, enchilada Puerto Vallarta — the Margaritas here are among the largest Las Vegas has to offer. Ricardo's serves lunch and dinner.

Willy and Jose's

$$ • Sam's Town, 5111 Boulder Hwy. • 456-7777

Helping to add the flavor of Old Mexico to this cantina are rough-hewn tables, adobe walls with "peeling" wallpaper, tile floors and faux broken windows. House specialties include steak picado, flautas, enchiladas, shrimp quesadillas and beef or chicken fajitas. From the lounge you can sip three kinds of tequila, and for dessert take a shot at the deep-fried ice cream. The restaurant, which serves dinner only, offers a free-meal-on-your-birthday promotion.

Middle Eastern

House of Kabob

$$ • 4110 S. Maryland Pkwy. • 732-2285

This shopping center cafe, decorated with wall murals of desert landscapes and a Turkish marketplace, features fine Middle Eastern dishes for lunch and dinner. Signature specialties include a range of kabobs — kafta (minced ground beef), chicken, mushroom, lamb and eggplant — served over rice with hummus, pita and grilled tomato and onions. Other favorites include tabouli salad, lamb curry, vegetarian pita pockets, falafel and mousakka. It's open for lunch and dinner.

Mediterranean Cafe & Market

$$ • 4147 S. Maryland Pkwy. • 731-6030

One of the best finds in town is this restaurant and grocery, situated in a nondescript shopping plaza near the university. Vegetarian specialties include baba ganoush, baked eggplant with fresh garlic, grape leaves, hummus and tabouli. Meaty offerings include kibbe, kabob sandwich (the house specialty) and gyros salad. Several varieties of Middle Eastern coffees are available as well as Morroccan and chamomille teas. Complete your feast with the homemade rose water, saffron and pistachio ice cream and a cup of sweet Turkish coffee. The market offers a variety of packaged goods you can take with you. It's open for lunch and dinner.

Seafood

The Tillerman

$$$ • 2245 E. Flamingo Rd. • 731-4036

The city's well-heeled "now" people congregate here. But you don't need a cellular phone to enjoy this bistro's skylight, central atrium or balcony seating. Famous for its seafood specials, the catch of the day could include Pacific salmon, swordfish, Chilean grouper, Norwegian salmon, shark or fresh tuna. Prime rib, New York strip and beef brochette are also popular entrees on the deluxe-priced menu. More than 200 labels are stocked in the wine cellar. The Tillerman serves dinner only.

Steakhouses

Billy Bob's Steak House & Saloon

$$ • Sam's Town, 5111 Boulder Hwy. • 456-7777

Leave your fancy meetin' clothes at home when you come to this casual Western-style room, where you're invited to kick back for frontier-sized dinners. The portions are generous, and specialties include mesquite-grilled Angus beef, chicken and seafood. For the heartiest of appetites there's a 28-ounce rib eye, and if you're still standing, Grand Canyon cake for dessert. After dinner you can belly up to the Silver Dollar Bar to drain a few tall ones. Dinner only is served.

Thai

Lotus of Siam

$ • Commercial Center, 953 E. Sahara Ave. • 735-4477

Lotus of Siam features inexpensive Thai cuisine served in a quiet setting among traditional Thai art. The food is milder than most experienced diners expect. The secret is blending each course with seasonings — ginger, lemon grass, fish sauce, lime leaves and hot red and green peppers — to create varying degrees of sweet, sour, bitter or salty flavors. Appetizers include mee krob (the national dish of Thailand), a semisweet combination of fried crispy rice stick and shrimp. The chicken, beef, seafood and catfish entrees are served with a spicy red curry sauce, and the traditional noodle dishes — wide Thai noodles or rice noodles — are served with seafood, beef or chicken. It's open for lunch and dinner.

West Valley

American

Coffee Pub

$ • 2800 W. Sahara Ave. • 367-1913

For a California-style breakfast or lunch, try this stylish little bistro with mosaic-top tables and patio dining. The featured fare is basically "California-with-it": sandwiches named for the Golden State's in-spots, spinach salad, quiche, a crab souffle roll and soup and salad combinations. The natural shakes are made with fresh fruit juices and sorbet. Save room for dessert because the carrot cake, chocolate mousse and homemade muffins are out of this world. The white chocolate cheesecake, especially with a cup of Kenya coffee, is sinful. Breakfast specials include omelettes, quiche, croissants, fresh fruit and muffins, bagels, pastries and Belgian waffles.

The Egg and I

$ • 2533 W. Sahara Ave. • 364-9686

Hearty breakfasts are served here, where customers line up early on weekend mornings. But the wait is seldom long, and it's tempered by complimentary coffee or tea. Egg specialties include a variety of omelettes, huevos rancheros, eggs Benedict and a vegetarian version with sliced tomatoes, avocado and two poached eggs, smothered in hollandaise sauce. All are served with ranch potatoes and a choice of toast or English muffin. Other favorites are the frittatas (open-faced omelettes served in its skillet), Belgian waffles served with blueberries or strawberries and french toast. The plate-sized pancakes are wonderful, especially the apple-and-cinnamon ones served with an applesauce syrup. A nice touch is the pitcher of iced water, garnished with lemon slices, and pot of hot coffee on the table. The Egg and I serves breakfast and lunch.

Omelet House

$ • 2150 W. Charleston Blvd. • 384-6868

Hungry for a hearty ranch-style breakfast? The Omelet House, a longtime favorite of the nearby medical center crowd, is a rustic eatery with wooden booths and tables. Their specialty — can you guess? — is omelettes, a whopping 32 at last count. Unique varieties include ham, pineapple, coconut and cheese; and crab stuffed with broccoli and smothered with cheddar cheese. All are accompanied by a heaping order of breakfast spuds. Although not as famous as the omelettes, the hamburgers are among the best in town. The homemade chili, vegetable soup and ham and beans are also popular. The Omelet House serves breakfast and lunch.

Poppa Gar's

$$ • 1624 W. Oakey Blvd. • 384-4513

This venerable restaurant has been a popular gathering place for more than 30 years. As a testament to its popularity, the walls are adorned with dozens of photos of city officials, judges, celebrities and prominent business people. There are also numerous big game trophies — bison and deer heads — so don't expect sprouts and tofu. The seven-page menu lists breakfast, lunch and dinner offerings that range from wild buffalo burgers to fried quail with eggs to pan-fried trout to roast loin of pork. If you stop by for breakfast, try the french toast, which is made from a thick Texas slice of bread that's dipped in a batter made from corn flakes, eggs and half-and-half.

Chinese

Bamboo Garden

$$ • 4850 W. Flamingo Rd. • 871-3262

Hidden in a nondescript shopping center, Bamboo Garden is seldom crowded. Owner Jack Tong, formerly of Caesars Palace, has put together an imaginative menu that features hot braised pineapple fish; sizzling fish Shanghai-style stir fried with vegetables; grandfather's chicken sauteed in honey sauce; firecracker beef made with a spicy hot pepper sauce, and Hunan eggplant. You can also enjoy Mongolian lamb and Oceania — seafood served in a nest. It's open for lunch and dinner.

Cathay House

$$ • 5300 Spring Mountain Rd. • 876-3838

Dim sum is the name of the game here. Choose shrimp puffs, pork-filled sweet buns, rice-paper chicken, pan-fried dumplings and shrimp tempura, to name a few of the more than 40 items offered on passing carts. The flaming pineapple chicken is one of the house specialties. Others include prawns with spinach sauce, scallops with orange sauce, duck (almond and orange), Peking lobster covered in a red honey-glazed sauce, and ocean velvet — seafood sauteed in a silky wine sauce. Save room for one of the flaming desserts or the sugarcoated fried apple. It's open for lunch and dinner.

King City Seafood

$$ • 4670 S. Decatur Blvd. • 876-9588

Usually packed with Asian diners, King City Seafood is among a few eateries that offer dim sum, in which dozens of appetizer-like specialties are served from passing carts. Some of the cart choices include a sweet rice bun stuffed with barbecue pork, steamed wonton with shrimp, bean curd wrapped meat, a tasty green pepper with shrimp paste and a light and airy fried taro cake. Some of the more exotic offerings include jelly fish, stewed chicken feet, curry dry squid and shark's fin dumpling soup. It's open for lunch and dinner.

Continental

The Aristocrat

$$$-$$$$ • 850 S. Rancho Dr. • 870-1977

Fine dining in a supermarket shopping center? Despite its storefront location, the Aristocrat is an intimate bistro that seats about 50 people. Dinner specialties include rack of lamb, North Atlantic Salmon, veal rib chops and prime tenderloin, plus an array of delightful appetizers such as steamed black mussels in a Chardonnay sauce and black ravioli stuffed with lobster mousse. A popular hangout for power lunches, the Aristocrat features a tasty mushroom soup; beef Stroganoff Romanoff made with prime tenderloin tips and served in a puff pastry; an avocado boat stuffed with crab; and almond-crusted Atlantic salmon with lemon dill cream sauce. Owner Jan Leenders will also prepare any dish for a customer when given ample notice. It's open for lunch and dinner.

Cafe Nicolle

$$ • 4760 W. Sahara Ave. • 870-7675

If you enjoy dining al fresco come to Cafe Nicolle, where the outdoor tables are accented by palm trees and flower boxes and misted with a fine spray during the hotter summer days. Inside, it's New York modern, black and gray lucite tables accented with brass fixtures and red upholstery. Appetizers include Italian prosciutto melon, French escargots bourguignonne and mushrooms stuffed with crabmeat. Entrees, served with either Caesar or garden salad, include filet mignon with Béarnaise sauce, lamb chops à la Greque with oregano; chicken served française, veal piccata or scallopini. Also good are the crepes, omelettes and homemade pecan pie. Cafe Nicolle is open for lunch and dinner.

Napa

$$$$ • The Rio, 3700 W. Flamingo Rd. • 252-7777

This new upscale dining room — part of the Masquerade Village expansion — features a retractable central skylight, wrought-iron sculpture, colorful artwork and light-wood accents. Among the pricey specialties are roasted pear and pecan with fried blue cheese, corn soup with Manila clams and scallop quenelles and wood-grilled veal chops with truffled gnocchi. Napa has also become known for its extensive wine cellar, which houses, among others, a $1 million collection of Chateau d'Yquem dessert wines (1855 to 1990) and thousands of rare and exotic wines that include a 1950 bottle of Chateau Lafite Rothschild worth more than $20,000. Napa serves dinner only.

Italian

Beach Pizza

$$ • 8512 W. Lake Mead Blvd. • 255-8646

Lean and low-fat California-style pizzas are the attractions here. Sun-dried tomatoes, oven-baked eggplant and shrimp scampi are a few of the toppings. Pasta dishes range from tortellini in Alfredo sauce to lighter dishes such as lemon chicken pasta. A few vegetarian and specialty salads are also available. Beach Pizza, which is mostly a take-out place but has a few tables, is open for lunch and dinner.

East Side Mario's

$$ • 6750 W. Sahara Ave. • 227-4040

Although more than 3,000 miles from Canal and Mulberry streets, Mario's will give you a taste of New York's Little Italy with its fruit and vegetable stands and stringed-light replica of the Brooklyn Bridge. The all-Italian menu includes pasta specialties such as angel hair primavera, fettuccine Alfredo, garlic mushroom rigatoni and penne with sausage and hot peppers. For a good sampling of New York-style antipasto try the New York Combo — hand-battered marinated artichoke hearts, mozzarella sticks and Buffalo-style chicken wings, served with blue cheese dressing and hot Pomodori sauce for dipping. The restaurant serves lunch and dinner.

Ferraro's Cafe

$$$ • 5900 W. Flamingo Rd. • 364-5300

This is a favorite hangout of Jerry Lewis when he's in town. George Kirby, Paul Anka and a host of hotel executives also regularly feast on the Southern Italian cuisine at this westside bistro. It's also a hit with locals, who make an entire meal of the appetizers such as the artichoke stuffed with bread crumbs, garlic, Romano cheese and black olives in light wine sauce, or the deep-fried squid in a spicy tomato and onion sauce. Other house favorites include bowties alla checca, rigatoni amatriciana, linguine pescatore and osso bucco in burgundy sauce. It's open for dinner only.

North Beach Cafe

$$ • 2605 S. Decatur Blvd. • 247-9530

Decorated with the work of local artists, North Beach Cafe in the Sahara Pavilion has become a popular haunt for power lunches with westside business types. The innovative pasta-oriented menu features such specialties as empanadas Argentina, chicken Veneziana, linguine pescatore, penne with grilled chicken and spinach and charbroiled ahi tuna. The cafe is open for lunch and dinner.

Ti Amo

$$ • Santa Fe Hotel, 4949 N. Rancho Dr. • 658-4900

In a courtyard setting with a domed ceiling,

a sky mural and Tuscan landscapes on the walls, Ti Amo serves personal-size pizzas including cheese, vegetarian, BLT, tomato basil and Hawaiian. Specialties of the house are fettuccine primavera, cheese manicotti, cheese ravioli, lasagna and spaghetti carbonara with sauteed pancetta and prosciutto in light cream. Ti Amo serves lunch and dinner.

The Venetian

$$ • 3713 W. Sahara Ave. • 876-4190

Don't judge this place by the ghastly, studio-set mural on its facade. It is a longtime favorite of Vegas residents. Since the mid-1950s, the Venetian has served savory dishes such as neck bones à la Venetian — pork bones and meat marinated in wine, vinegar, capers and pepperoncini, then simmered until tender. Veal (Milanese, scallopini, parmigiana, Française and Marsala) and chicken (cacciatore, Angelo, Marsala and à la dentino) are the dinner mainstays, along with fresh seafood. The Venetian serves dinner only.

Japanese

Kifune

$$ • 2202 W. Charlston Blvd. • 366-9119

While some restaurants hang photos on the wall as testimony to their popularity, authentic Japanese houses such as Kifune collect wooden boxes with their customers' names on them. Judging by the stack of "sake" boxes at the rear of the restaurant, Kifune has a loyal following. During the day, the sushi bar is overflowing with medical workers from the nearby hospital. But you can also take a seat in the dining room and indulge in specialties such as fried noodles with meat and vegetables, Japanese omelette with chicken and fish stew with vegetables. Kifune serves lunch and dinner.

Osaka

$$ • 4205 W. Sahara Ave. • 876-4988

Osaka offers three ways to dine on its Japanese cuisine: the sushi bar, the main dining room, or the tatami room, where you remove your shoes and sit on the floor at low tables. Sushi offerings include Inari cone, octopus, cucumber roll, flying fish eggs and a California roll of crab, shrimp, avocado and cucumber. Ask for low-sodium tamari sauce instead of soy sauce if you're health-conscious. Some of the exotic seafood selections are broiled eels teriyaki, yakisakana and breaded oysters — all accompanied by soup, rice and tea. Osaka is open for lunch and dinner.

Steakhouses

Philips Supper House

$$$ • 4545 W. Sahara Ave. • 873-5222

A Southern-style mansion sets the stage for this popular steakhouse that features three dining rooms, bay windows, upholstered walls and a cozy bar. The menu features oysters Rockefeller, steamed clams, oysters on the half-shell, scampi and artichoke hearts Française. Among the popular entrees are lamb chops, steaks, veal and an enticing selection of seafood: blackened whitefish, scalone (a combination of scallops and abalone), halibut picante, scallops, swordfish steak, salmon, trout, sand dabs and Alaskan king crab legs. The dinner salads are of the knife-and-fork variety, and the hot-baked bread is always fresh. Philips serves dinner only.

Bob Taylor's Ranch House

$$ • 6250 Rio Vista Rd. • 645-1399

Bring an appetite to Bob Taylor's Ranch House, an Old West steakhouse, complete with tack and cowboy memorabilia on the walls. This place is famous for its steaks — thick, aged New York, filet mignon, T-bones, porterhouse — all cooked on a mesquite grill. If you have an unabashed appetite, there's a 28-ounce Diamond Jim Brady cut (it should be Diamond John Candy cut). The slab takes a half-hour to cook (medium rare) and who knows how long to eat. The menu also offers seafood and chicken dishes. Dinner only is served.

Vietnamese

Saigon

$$ • 4251 W. Sahara Ave. • 362-9928

Authentic Vietnamese food is featured in

this small, storefront cafe with dinette-style seating. The food can be spicy hot, so insist on full disclosure from your waiter. Signature specials are squid with traditional hot sauce, sauteed shrimp with broccoli, carrots, onions and mushrooms, and hot sauteed beef with lemon grass. Although Vietnam is not famous for desserts, do try the sweet yellow bean and coconut pudding. Saigon is open for lunch and dinner.

North Valley

The North Valley area, which encompasses most of North Las Vegas, has always been a kind-of suburb to Las Vegas. Therefore, there hasn't been the commercial growth that would spawn a great many restaurants like there has been in other parts of the valley. The three casino-hotels in the area — Jerry's Nugget, Fiesta and Texas Station — have become popular gathering spots to eat. Here are few of our favorite restaurants in the North Valley.

Memphis Championship Barbecue

$$ • 4379 Las Vegas Blvd. N. • 644-0000

Whether you're here for lunch or dinner, the specialty is Blue Ribbon baby back ribs, served tender enough to cut with a fork and drenched in a sweet barbecue sauce. The smoked chicken wings and homemade chili make a satisfying meal. If you like appetizers with your Miller Genuine Draft, try the onion loaf and crispy potato skins.

Garduno's Restaurant & Cantina

$$ • Fiesta Casino Hotel, 2400 N. Rancho Dr. • 631-7000

Famous for its restaurants in New Mexico, the Garduno family now serves great Mexican seafood, homemade tortillas, sopapillas and sweet corn cakes at the Fiesta. Also popular is the guacamole prepared tableside, nine types of fajitas, and generous Margaritas served in a glass rimmed with coconut shavings. Garduno's is open for lunch and dinner.

Old San Francisco Steak House

$$ • Fiesta Casino Hotel, 2400 N. Rancho Dr. • 631-7000

The restaurant chain based in Texas is known for its trademark blocks of aged Swiss cheese served with every entree, which include Angus beef, steaks, prime rib and chateaubriand. If you want to dine beefless, try the duck à l'orange, rack of lamb and seafood specialties such as live Maine lobster and cold water lobster. While dining you can watch the Girl on the Red Velvet Swing trying to ring the bells over the bar. Early bird specials are served from 5 to 6:30 PM. The restaurant serves dinner only.

San Lorenzo

$$ • Texas Station, 2101 Texas Star Ln. • 631-1000

Deep in the heart of Texas you can feast on great Southern Italian cuisine. Among the house specialties are gnocchi marinara, champagne fettuccine with shrimp and gorgonzola-filled filet mignon with Chianti wine sauce. You can also choose from seafood, chicken and veal specialties. No matter what you eat, save room for the crème brûlée or tiramisu. San Lorenzo is open for dinner only.

Magnolia Room

$$ • Jerry's Nugget, 1821 Las Vegas Blvd. N. • 399-3000

Jerry's Nugget's expansion and renovation in 1996 did wonders for the popular northside casino. Its Magnolia Room, with its grotto-like ambiance, would rival any continental restaurant on The Strip. Among the innovative appetizers are the potato pancakes with smoked salmon and crab cakes with pepper chutney. Some of the house specialties include chicken Florentine en croûte and veal piccata with brandy caper sauce. The Magnolia Room is open for dinner only.

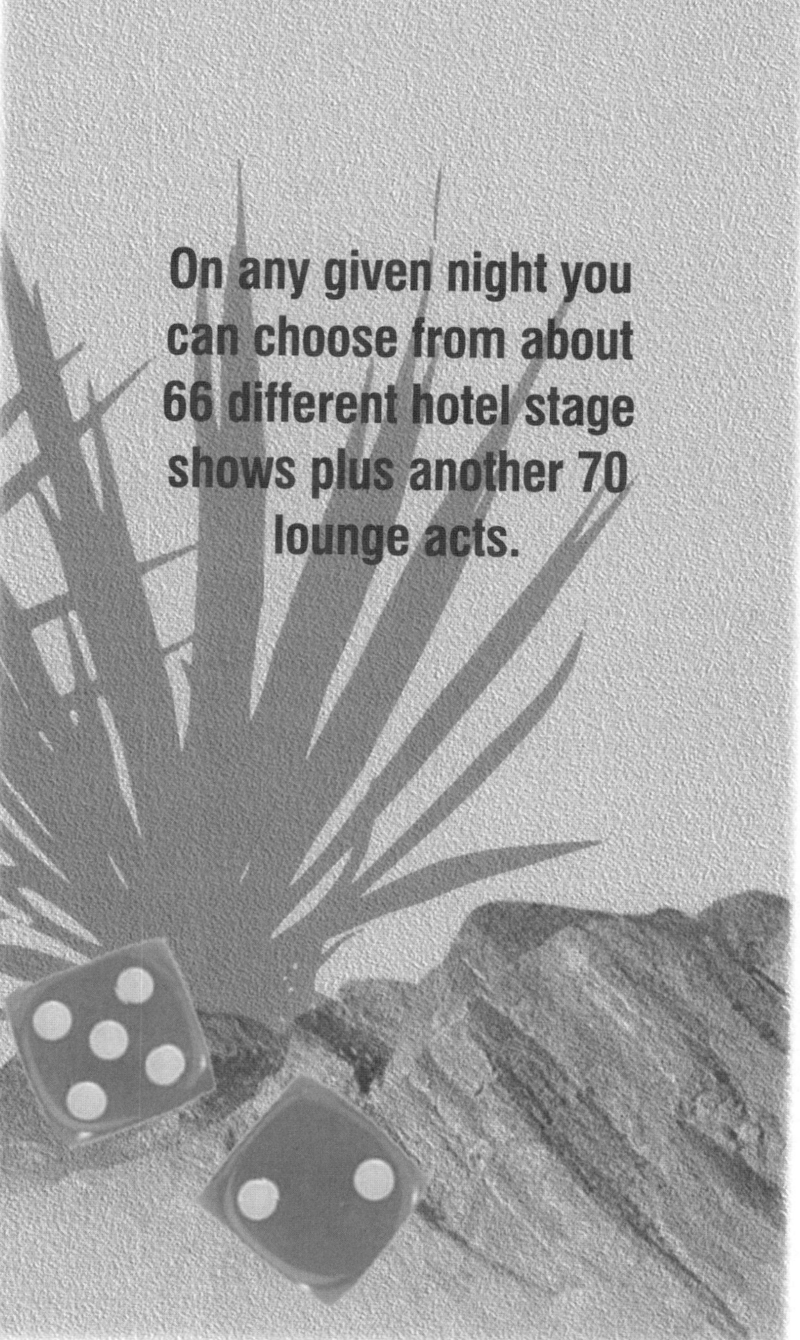
On any given night you can choose from about 66 different hotel stage shows plus another 70 lounge acts.

Nightlife

No city in the world offers more after-dark excitement than Las Vegas. As a 24-hour adult amusement park, Las Vegas has something for every night crawler — from the flashy hotel shows to the sleazy biker bars to the punk nightclubs to the yuppie singles bars to the flashback dance hops. It's all here, basking in neon, blinking until dawn.

Much of the city's nightlife revolves around the hotel-casinos with their lavish stage productions, celebrity concerts, cable TV comedians, topless revues and free lounge shows. On any given night you can choose from about 66 different hotel stage shows plus another 70 lounge acts. Hotel shows range from star-studded productions such as MGM Grand's *EFX* starring David Cassidy to awesome stage spectaculars like Siegfried & Roy's space-age fantasy at the Mirage to Cirque du Soleil's surreal *Mystere* at Treasure Island. There are less presumptuous revues, such as the thoroughly entertaining *Country Fever* at the Golden Nugget and the people-pleasing *La Cage*, a drag show at the Riviera.

As an alternative to the stage extravaganza, some hotels book celebrity headliners such as Lionel Ritchie, George Carlin, Paul Anka, Liza Minnelli, Tony Bennett, Kenny Loggins, Luis Miguel, Huey Lewis & The News — the list eventually includes anyone in show business, past or present. Other hotels — in an effort to attract new customers — seek different kinds of entertainment, ranging from circus acts to jugglers to topless magicians to jousting medieval knights to dancing dogs . . . well, the list is endless. The list of acts in hotel lounges is equally as varied, ranging from sloppy ventriloquists to one-woman bands to game-show bits to polished groups such as the Fortunes and The Coasters. But most of the time, the lounge acts are up-and-coming musicians or singers putting on an entertaining show.

Staging nightlife is no longer the exclusive province of the gaming resorts. As the city of Las Vegas has grown, so has the number of community nightclubs, sports bars, brew pubs, dance halls, cowboy saloons and other after-dark haunts.

In this chapter we'll introduce you to the best the Vegas night has to offer. In a city that immodestly bills itself as The Entertainment Capital of the World, we'll explore the best showrooms, brew pubs, cigar bars, nightclubs, dance halls, blues bars, jazz joints and comedy shops.

Pricing

Throughout the chapter we've avoided giving specific prices for shows, concerts or nightclubs because they often change without notice or reason.

All comedy clubs charge nearly the same for admission — between $13 and $16 a seat, which usually includes 2 drinks.

The nightclubs in town often have a small cover charge, usually not more than $5. However, when a band is playing, the cover may jump to $10 or $15.

The prices for production shows change often, so we've included a price code with these write-ups to let you know about how much you'll spend. Most production show prices include tax and either one or two drinks. Following a trend that started earlier in the decade, most seats are sold by reserved ticket, which effectively eliminates the worn-out practice of tipping an usher or captain for a better seat. Our price code for an adult ticket is:

$	**less than $25**
$$	**$25 - $40**
$$$	**$41 - $55**
$$$$	**more than $55**

While Las Vegas nightlife can be as exciting as anyplace in the world, take care and caution in planning your evening. Helping to fuel Las Vegas' all-night nightlife scene are the city's liberal liquor laws, which allow consumption and sale of alcohol 24 hours a day if you're 21 years and older. So it is crucial to observe the no drinking and driving laws and to watch for those who don't observe them. Equally important is to behave responsibly as a pedestrian, especially after a night of consuming alcohol. This is a city where many people ignore the signs and lights that control intersections, and, unfortunately, many pedestrians are killed every year because they didn't heed the "Don't Walk" light or stop sign. With those simple caveats in mind, put on your sensible dancing shoes, grab some bail money, and let's do the town.

FYI

Unless otherwise noted, the area code for all phone numbers listed in this chapter is 702.

The Strip Area

Comedy Clubs

Catch A Rising Star

$ • MGM Grand, 3799 Las Vegas Blvd. S. • 891-7777

The glass-enclosed theater houses the national Catch A Rising Star comedy club, which helped shape the careers of some of the country's favorite comedians, including Robin Williams, Billy Crystal, Jerry Seinfeld and Elayne Boosler. In addition to scheduled comics, guests are occasionally treated to impromptu appearances from visiting celebrities. The Catch presents stand-up comedy — usually two or three comedians — twice nightly. Wednesdays are local appreciation nights, with local residents receiving ticket discounts.

Comedy Max

$ • Maxim Hotel, 160 E. Flamingo Rd. • 731-4300

Comedy Max is smaller than most clubs, but this puts the patrons closer to the comics' barbs. Like most clubs, seating is on stools grouped around small tables. Comedy Max hosts about three comics per show — one headliner and two supporting acts — whom you have probably seen on cable TV. Shows are presented twice nightly.

Comedy Stop

$ • Tropicana Hotel, 3801 Las Vegas Blvd. S. • 739-2714

One of the oldest venues for comedy in Las Vegas, the Comedy Stop is also one of the largest with more than 400 seats. Seating in the club is at banquet tables, though some patrons toward the rear of the room may have a problem seeing the stage. Typically, three comedians are presented twice nightly.

The Improv

$ • Harrah's Las Vegas, 3485 Las Vegas Blvd. S. • 369-5111

Although The Improv is relatively new to Harrah's (it moved here from the Riviera in 1995), the Budd Friedman-owned club traces its roots to the old cellar comedy stores of New York and Chicago. The Improv presents three or four first-rate comedians twice nightly except Mondays.

Riviera Comedy Club

$ • Riviera Hotel, 2901 Las Vegas Blvd. S. • 794-9433

To gain control over its bookings and show content, the Riviera booted out the very popular Improv in 1995 and opened its own shop, cleverly called the Riviera Comedy Club. The new shows are no different from the old ones, however, with the Club presenting three to four comics twice nightly (a third show is staged on Friday and Saturday nights). The Riviera has ventured into new waters with its all-gay comedy revues and its XXXtreme Comedy — mostly shock comedians who talk nasty about bodily functions and social disease.

Nightclubs

The Beach

365 Convention Center Dr. • 731-1925

Surfboards and plastic palm trees are the fare at this popular nightspot across the street from the Convention Center. But you won't need a beach towel, just a little energy to schlep among the two levels of lounges, dance floors, singalong piano bar and (are you surprised?) a race and sports book. In addition to the betting parlor, you'll find games upstairs — an arcade and the inevitable slots. The crowd is mostly postpubescent, so don't expect anyone dressed beyond jeans, tank tops and muscle Ts. The Beach often hosts intimate concerts of mostly rock bands, and the all-male Chippendales revue plays selected nights during the week.

Cleopatra's Barge

Caesars Palace, 3570 Las Vegas Blvd. S. • 731-7110

For one-on-one encounters, climb aboard Cleopatra's Barge for dancing to live bands, usually rock or rhythm and blues. The lively lounge is more like a crayon-colored Viking vessel, complete with oars, furled sails and a buxom mermaid figurehead, but it floats in real water and bobs when the dance-floor action heats up. Be careful crossing the gangplank; inebriated revelers have been known to take a dive into the drink.

Drink and Eat Too!

200 E. Harmon Ave. • 796-5519

Locally known as The Drink, this is one of the city's hottest nightclubs, where you can go crazy in a maze of six party rooms, a sunken courtyard dance floor and eight bars, including a stand-up martini bar and smoky cigar lounge — all serving drinks in crazy containers such as baby bottles and miniature buckets. Wild colors, flowers, exposed pipes and ducts create a psychedelic '70s warehouse effect, while the music ranges from local rock bands to national touring groups plus the incredibly popular Boogie Knights disco-revival group once a week. The Drink's core clientele is from the sublime to the ridiculous — well-dressed conventioneers, sloppy tourists and insufferably skinny hipsters.

The Nightclub

Las Vegas Hilton, 3000 Paradise Rd. • 732-5111

The Nightclub is perhaps the best bargain in live entertainment with the Emeralds, Kristine W. and the Diva Dancers plus dancing until 4 AM. Art deco styling give this upscale lounge a true, well, nightclub feel. Space-age light and sound systems provide atmosphere, and an elevated "balcony" area allows for a view from the top.

Utopia

3765 Las Vegas Blvd. S. • 736-3105

Leave your silk tie and alligator purse at home if you plan an evening in Utopia. This is a popular Generation X hangout, so the crowd's apparel can range from grunge to Guess jeans. Located at the back of a small Strip shopping center, Utopia really rocks on the weekend with its 20,000 watts of Euro power linked to a high-tech light display. Of course, what good are all those decibels without a dance floor, and Utopia has a huge one — split level, so if you want to stand out, you can boogie 2 feet above the crowd. For closer encounters, there are private booths and high-top seating on a mezzanine level overlooking the dance floor and a balcony patio flanking The Strip and the Monte Carlo Hotel across the street.

Production Shows and Celebrity Showrooms

Bally's Celebrity Room

$$$ • Bally's Las Vegas, 3645 Las Vegas Blvd. S. • 739-4567

Right next door to the Jubilee! theater, the 1,400-seat Celebrity Showroom presents some of the biggest stars in show business, from Liza Minnelli and George Carlin to Paul Anka and Barbara Mandrell. The showroom has also hosted offbeat artists such as shock comic Andrew Dice Clay and schlock acts like Regis and Kathy Lee.

Congo Showroom

$$ • Sahara Hotel, 2535 Las Vegas Blvd. S. • 737-2111

The Sahara's Congo Showroom enjoys a colorful history of showcasing four decades of Las Vegas entertainers. From Mae West to George Burns to Judy Garland to Tina Turner, the Congo Showroom has hosted them all, including the Beatles in 1964. Today, the Congo Showroom searches for an identity to carry it into the 21st century. After a few failed attempts at presenting ongoing production shows, the Sahara seems content to offer B-grade and up-and-coming headliners, such as Judy Tenuta, Rich Little, Jackie Mason and The Smothers Brothers.

The Debbie Reynolds Show

$$ • Debbie Reynolds Hotel & Movie Museum, 305 Convention Center Dr. • 733-2243

Despite financial problems that threaten to close her hotel, Debbie Reynolds proves she is indeed unsinkable by performing five nights a week in her 500-seat Star Theater. The petite star of stage, screen, TV and Broadway sings, dances and jokes with audiences throughout her 90-minute performance without missing a beat. She also taps her acting skills when she impersonates such stars as Barbra Streisand and Zsa Zsa Gabor. Following the show, Reynolds meets with members of the audience, signs autographs and poses for snapshots. *The Debbie Reynolds Show* plays Monday through Friday. Children age 6 and younger are not admitted.

Lance Burton: Master Magician

$$ • Monte Carlo Hotel Casino, 3770 Las Vegas Blvd. S. • 730-7777

Though magicians have become commonplace in Las Vegas, Lance Burton remains the city's premier illusionist. His show is an entertaining blend of intimate cabaret and high-powered Vegas extravaganza. He even involves audience members, who help bring the illusions up close and personal. The show consists of about 17 illusions, some of them quite majestic in size, such as his levitating and disappearing white Corvette and his "off to the gallows" stunt in which he somehow escapes the noose and ends up in the middle of the audience. Burton is backed on stage by a winsome sextet of dancers plus comic juggler Michael Goudeau, who elevates the art of physical comedy to new and hilarious levels. *Lance Burton: Master Magician* is performed twice nightly except Sunday and Monday in the Lance Burton Theatre.

Caesars Magical Empire

$$$$ • Caesars Palace, 3570 Las Vegas Blvd. S. • 731-7333

Breaking from the format of traditional stage shows, *Caesars Magical Empire* is a multichambered magical mystery tour that blends fine dining with the world of illusion. It begins with a kind of intimate supper show, where a magician performs for a group of about 15 diners. After feasting you are guided through subterranean catacombs to a seven-story-high Sanctum Secorum, where you can explore the Forbidden Crypt of Ramses, watch a brief Lumineria show or quench your thirst in the Sanctum bars. After refueling, you move on to one of two theaters that spotlight the talents of master magicians who perform on rotating schedules. Among the previous performers are Kevin James, The Pendragons, Sultan & Co. and Scott Grocki. Ticket price includes a four-course dinner.

Circus Maximus Showroom

$$$ • Caesars Palace, 3570 Las Vegas Blvd. S. • 731-7333

From Jack Benny and Judy Garland to Diana Ross and Jerry Seinfeld, the roster of headlining celebrities in Caesars' Circus Maximus room has included show biz's best. In the past, the 1,000-seat room with four tiers of seating has also hosted productions such as Juliet Prowse in *Sweet Charity* and the original *Odd Couple* starring Tony Randall. While Broadway shows are no longer staged here, the showroom hosts TV specials such as NBC's *World's Greatest Magic*.

Crazy Girls

$ • Riviera Hotel, 2901 Las Vegas Blvd. S. • 794-9433

This long-running topless show debuted in 1985 and continues to jiggle twice nightly in the hotel's Mardi Gras Plaza. The show features eight showgirls who dance to canned music and act out silly skits on a small stage. There are, however, some talented cast members. Debra Sills is a gifted singer (she actually sings live on-stage), and Karen Raider — the leader of the pack — is an accomplished real estate broker. The show is dark on Monday. No one younger than 18 is admitted.

Photo: New York-New York Hotel Casino

The street-smart *MADHattan* show at New York-New York deviates from the traditional Vegas extravaganza.

The Dream King

$ • Boardwalk Holiday Inn Hotel Casino, 3740 Las Vegas Blvd. S. • 730-3194

If you want to "Shake, Rattle and Roll," stop by the Lighthouse Showroom for Trent Carlini's *The Dream King*. As one of the city's top Elvis impersonators, Carlini has the look, the moves and the voice to create a drop-dead impression of Presley in his prime. The Dream King plays once a night, Tuesday through Sunday. Children younger than 12 are admitted free.

EFX

$$$-$$$$ • MGM Grand, 3799 Las Vegas Blvd. S. • 891-7777

David Cassidy has come a long way since playing the teenybopper heart throb on *The Partridge Family* in the 1970s. Today, with warmth, wit and a dashing dose of exuberance, Cassidy has made *EFX* one of the city's top production shows. A high-tech musical odyssey through time and space, *EFX* has Cassidy embarking on a humorous, emotional journey to rediscover his power of imagination. Along the way he discovers worlds beyond reality and encounters legendary characters like Harry Houdini, H.G. Wells and Merlin the Magician. The diverse musical score incorporates everything from Gregorian chants and traditional Irish music to hard rock and Broadway ballads. Plus the show's special effects are truly spectacular, derived from film and theme park technology. *EFX* is presented twice nightly, Tuesday through Saturday. Children's ticket prices are available.

Enter the Night

$$ • Stardust Hotel, 3000 Las Vegas Blvd. S. • 732-6325

Another of the large-scale Vegas revues, *Enter the Night* celebrates the mystery and intrigue of the night through explosive dance numbers, dynamic music, variety acts and incredible laser special effects. The show stars Jennifer Page as lead singer, with music by Jon Brielle, who won a Tony Award for his *Foxfire* musical score. An intrinsic part of the show are its specialty acts, including ice skaters Cindy Landry and Burt Lancon, who perform a picturesque adagio number; Argentinian folk dancers, who combine a boleadora with lasers and special effects; and an amazing duo called The Scott Brothers, who use their robot-like movements in a human cartoon sequence. *Enter the Night* plays twice nightly Tuesday through Thursday and Saturday and once a night on Sunday and Monday nights. The show is dark on Friday.

An Evening at La Cage

$ • Riviera Hotel, 2901 Las Vegas Blvd. S. • 794-9433

La Cage is the city's best female-impersonator revue, a.k.a. "drag queen" show. Starring Frank Marino as a catty Joan Rivers, *La Cage* also features lip-sync impersonations of Liza Minnelli, Dionne Warwick, Madonna, Diana Ross and others. A great moment is the "Sister Act" number with a dozen hip-hopping "nuns" grooving on and off the stage. The show is very well-choreographed (the supporting female dancers are superb), and the music (taped) and lighting tastefully enhance the show. It may be a bit kinky, but it's a solid production. *La Cage* is presented twice nightly with a third late show added on Wednesday; it is dark on Tuesday.

Folies Bergere

$$$ • Tropicana Hotel, 3801 Las Vegas Blvd. S. • 739-2411

Las Vegas' longest-running production show, *Folies* was retooled in 1997 with new numbers, costumes and sets. Still, it remains the city's premier showcase for exquisite showgirls. Like previous editions, the show is a tribute to the Parisian Music Hall and the women who made it famous. The new show highlights changing French fashion, music and social codes of the past 100 years, including a royal ballroom segment, a beach scene set on the Riviera in the 1920s, a jazzy 1950s number and a Contemporarily Yours finale that catapults the show into the 1990s. Other memorable moments include a 1940s jukebox number with jitterbugs and flying acrobats; a Hollywood glamour number from the '30s; and, of course, a signature can can routine from turn-of-the-century Paris. *Folies Bergere* is presented at twice nightly, except Thursday, in the Tiffany Theatre.

Forever Plaid

$ • Flamingo Hilton Hotel, 3555 Las Vegas Blvd. S. • 733-3333

This former off-Broadway show had everything going against it when it debuted in 1994 — no showgirls, no magic acts, no pyrotechnics, outdated music and a quirky, if not bewildering, plot. To wit: four glee clubbers — the Plaids — return from the dead (they died in a car collision with a bus carrying girls from a Catholic school), and seek to perform the perfect show while overcoming their own shortcomings. As bizarre as it sounds, the show has become something of a cult favorite in town. Part of the allure is the late '50s and early '60s music, performed live in the intimate, 200-seat Bugsy's Celebrity Theater. *Forever Plaid* is presented twice nightly except Monday.

The Great Radio City Spectacular

$$$ (early dinner show) $$ (late cocktail show) • Flamingo Hilton Hotel, 3555 Las Vegas Blvd. S. • 733-3333

The high-kicking Radio City Rockettes star in this whimsical tribute to New York's Radio City Music Hall. The show also features soloist Paige O'Hara, whose incredible voice brought Belle to life in Disney's animated classic, *Beauty and the Beast*. Among the more interesting variety acts are comedy juggler Nino Frediana, magicians Tim Kole and Jenny-Lynn, and Stacy Moore and his madcap mutts. *The Great Radio City Spectacular* is presented twice nightly with an early dinner show and late cocktail show; the show is dark on Friday.

Hollywood Theatre

$$$ • MGM Grand, 3799 Las Vegas Blvd. S. • 891-1111

This intimate theater features an old-fashioned movie house entrance and 630 seats in a tiered, horseshoe arrangement around the stage. It has hosted entertainers such as Randy Travis, Sheena Easton, Smokey Robinson, Rita Rudner and the Go-Gos. It is also home to Jay Leno and his *Tonight Show* during Las Vegas tapings.

Jubilee!

$$$-$$$$ • Bally's Las Vegas, 3645 Las Vegas Blvd. S. • 739-4567

This long-running show, revamped with new costumes, sets and production numbers in 1997, features a spectacular musical extravaganza with a huge cast of dancers and dazzling stage effects ranging from sinking the *Titanic* to a World War I aerial dogfight to Samson destroying the Temple of the Philistines. The 16-minute opening number, based on Jerry Herman's *Hundreds of Girls*, sets the pace with dozens of dancers and singers in beaded costumes and feathered headdresses. *Jubilee!* plays twice on Tuesday, Wednesday, Thursday and Saturday nights and once on Sunday and Monday; the show is dark on Friday.

The Kenny Kerr Show

$ • Debbie Reynolds Hotel & Movie Museum, 305 Convention Center Dr. • 733-2243

Longtime Vegas female impersonator Kenny Kerr presents his *Women of Hollywood*, a slightly sinful drag show that pays tribute to such superstars as Barbra Streisand, Cher, Diana Ross and Marilyn Monroe. While the show is tastefully done, it sometimes draws a rowdy crowd of gays and straights as well as a generous sampling of curiosity seekers from the Midwest. The show is presented at 10:30 PM Monday through Saturday in Debbie's Star Theatre. Because the drag queens present the nasty-talking side of their alter-egos, no one younger than 18 is admitted.

King Arthur's Tournament

$$ • Excalibur, 3850 Las Vegas Blvd. S. • 597-7600

King Arthur's Tournament, held in a multitiered theater, is a medieval-themed dinner show that features jousting, magic acts, singers and laser special effects. Jousting? Yes, armor-clad knights ride thundering steeds and engage their cohorts in realistic jousts; knights also fight each other with battle axes and swords. But the show retains a Las Vegas flavor — maidens dance in Broadway-style formation, and a courtly king lapses into a version of "Viva Las Vegas." Because King Arthur's Tournament is a dinner show, you can eat your Cornish game hen dinner with your fingers. The show is presented twice nightly.

Legends in Concert

$$ • Imperial Palace Hotel, 3535 Las Vegas Blvd. S. • 794-3261

This venerable celebrity-impersonation revue has been entertaining audiences since the mid-1980s. The secret to its success lies in the accomplished performers who re-create the talents of superstars such as Elvis Presley, Roy Orbison, Buddy Holly, Liberace, Madonna and The Blues Brothers, to name a few. Note that these impersonators perform live — rather than lip-sync — and are backed by a live band. Adding sparkle to the show are the obligatory showgirls/dancers, backup singers and a Krypton red laser and projection system that creates mystifying patterns and special effects. *Legends* comes to life twice nightly except Sunday.

MADHattan

$$$ • New York-New York Hotel Casino, 3790 Las Vegas Blvd. S. • 740-6969

The city's newest production show is also the freshest. Neither traditional nor predictable, *MADHattan* is hip, original, primal and emotionally charged. Carried by its ethnic and youthful performers, *MADHattan* is a raw, fast-paced excursion into the mean streets of New York. There's actually a story line that unfolds through a series of sequences and production numbers, told with the help of a six-piece live band, hip hop and break dancers, a smooth sounding quartet of singers and a bizarre comedy duo. Even the theater is a rollicking tour of New York neighborhoods with its collage of taxis, buses, subway platforms and steps of the New York Public Library; moreover, the theater walls are decorated with authentic graffiti murals created by a genuine New York "tagger," Rober Gastman. The show plays twice nightly except Wednesday and Thursday.

Mystére

$$$$ • Treasure Island, 3300 Las Vegas Blvd. S. • 894-7111, (800) 392-1999

Of the city's best production shows, *Mystére* is the most artistic. It is also the most visual, the most innovative and the most original. Despite that, *Mystére* is also difficult to define, since it is performance art without boundaries, ballet without gravity, theater without actors. A product of Cirque du Soleil, the creative theater company that holds the patent on imagination-bending, *Mystére* is a surrealistic celebration of music, dance, acrobatics, gymnastics, mime and comedy. *Mystére* takes audiences on a metaphorical journey that starts at the beginning of time — symbolized by a powerful opening of Japanese Taiko drums sent from the heavens — with a blend of music, dance and stunning display of athleticism. From the mesmerizing aerial bungee ballet to the dazzling Korean plank and from the precision Chinese poles performance to the awesome trapeze artists, *Mystére* is a dynamic presentation of art in perpetual motion. Cirque du Soleil presents *Mystére* twice nightly Wednesday through Sunday. Children's ticket prices are available.

Showgirls of Magic

$ • San Remo Hotel, 115 E. Tropicana Ave. • 597-6028

Magic, comedy and cleavage are staples of Vegas entertainment, and *Showgirls of Magic* exploits all three in this bawdy burlesque-style revue just off The Strip. The show features three bouncy showgirls/magicians who dance and otherwise undulate their way through several parlor illusions and magic tricks. Adding to the fun are the slapstick antics of Los Latin Cowboys, crazy gauchos whose marvelous routine is highlighted by out-of-control boleros. Stealing the show is Antonio Hoyos, a 3-foot-tall Charlie Chaplin lookalike who, among other things, plays a diminutive Sonny to a 450-pound Cher. Their duet, "I've Got You Babe," sends audiences into hysterics. The show plays twice nightly (topless scenes in late show) except Monday.

Siegfried & Roy

$$$$ • The Mirage, 3400 Las Vegas Blvd. S. • 792-7777

The hottest ticket in town is for the *Siegfried & Roy* show, which also commands the most for any show — about $90 a ticket. Despite the price, the illusionists' show is always packed and features space-age illusions, a fire-breathing dragon, exotic white tigers and even a live elephant who vanishes into thin air then reappears on-stage. While some of the illusions are variations of time-tested tricks, such as levitating a man or sawing a woman in half, they are performed with such flair and pizazz that they even Stephen Spielberg would be impressed. The illusionists are supported by a large-scale production company of dancers and acrobats as well as state-of-the-art sound, lighting and special effects. Performances are held twice nightly Friday through Tuesday in the Siegfried & Roy Theatre.

Spellbound

$$ • Harrah's Las Vegas, 3475 Las Vegas Blvd. S. • 369-5222

In a town that can't have enough wizardry, *Spellbound '97*, starring Mexico's leading illusionist, Joaquin Ayala, is presented in a cozy theater with every seat close to the action. While the illusions aren't as mind-boggling as Siegfried & Roy's, Ayala and his capable assistants combine pyrotechnics, dance and gravity-defying illusions into a well-staged show that keeps audiences, well, spellbound. Their levitations and saw-a-woman-in-half stunt are interesting variations on traditional tricks. As always, the backdrop

INSIDERS' TIP

Las Vegas has a curfew for unchaperoned youths younger than 18. Youths must be off the streets by midnight on weekends and holidays and 10 PM on weeknights (Sunday through Thursday).

is lavish sets, dazzling costumes and leggy dancers. The show plays twice nightly in the Spellbound Theater.

Splash

$$$ • Riviera Hotel, 2901 Las Vegas Blvd. S. • 794-9433

Splash is an aquatic revue staged around a 20,000-gallon aquarium complete with mermaids, high divers and synchronized swimmers. The show, which debuted in 1985 and reached its popularity peak in the early 1990s, has revamped its music and dance numbers in recent years to try to keep current. At last glance the showroom was transformed into a submarine, and the show took audiences on a cruise to the Abyss, Shangri La and other freaky ports of call. In addition to the signature mermaid aquacade, the show features daredevil motorcylists, magic acts, music, dance and an outstanding juggler, Wally Eastwood. Children are admitted to the early show only — some topless numbers are held during the late show. *Splash* plays twice nightly.

The World of the Unreal

$ • Boardwalk Holiday Inn Hotel Casino, 3740 Las Vegas Blvd. S. • 730-3194

This campy one-man show stars magician Dixie Dooley, a cross between Houdini and P.T. Barnum, whose late-afternoon show includes sleight-of-hand tricks, seances, ghost writing and other nonconventional parlor-room feats. Although the show doesn't have the range and scope of large-scale Strip productions, Dooley is an engaging performer who keeps audiences entertained. In one of Dooley's seances, tables float, ghosts appear and objects appear to fly through the air, as if hurled by angry goblins. In another illusion, he brings to life a tiny wooden man and makes him talk, sing and flirt with women in the audience. Dixie Dooley performs twice daily except Monday.

Pubs, Sports Bars and Microbreweries

Betty Boop Lounge

MGM Grand, 3799 Las Vegas Blvd. S. • 891-7777

When you need a break from slot machines, try the Betty Boop lounge, which features a wall-length mural of the perky cartoon character perched atop a garden of flowers. Near the entrance a robotic Foster Brooks slurs one-liners and party jokes.

Catch A Rising Star Lounge

MGM Grand, 3799 Las Vegas Blvd. S. • 891-7777

If you're looking for an after-hours party on the weekend, check out the lounge near the Catch comedy club on Friday and Saturday nights. The action usually starts about 1 AM with a show called *Fierce*, which is more an impromptu jam session with Strip musicians, dancers and singers. And since most of the audience members are off-duty Strip entertainers, the place really rocks. Plus, there's no cover charge and only a one-drink minimum.

Hamilton's

New York-New York Hotel Casino, 3790 Las Vegas Blvd. S. • 740-6969

This trendy club is reminiscent of big-city hideaways such as L.A.'s Bat Rack and New York's Stork Club, places dedicated to time-tested pleasures like a good cigar, single-malt scotch, the tinkling of martini glasses and the velvet strains of Nat King Cole in the background. The brainchild of tanned wonder George Hamilton, the pricey pub serves aged cognac and other potables in an art deco setting. You can also enjoy accompaniments such as Beluga caviar, smoked trout salad and a canape plate with salmon, shrimp and ham.

INSIDERS' TIP

For a complete listing of the city's shows, concerts and other events, check the Friday edition of *NEON,* the tabloid section of the *Las Vegas Review-Journal*.

Double Down Saloon

4640 Paradise Rd. • 791-5775

It's appropriate that renegade director Tim Burton hung out here during filming of *Mars Attacks*. The bar has a freaked-out feel with its psychedelic murals (on the walls and ceiling) and retro, mix-and-mismatch furnishings — a velvet sofa, overstuffed club chairs and plastic dinette chairs. Once you become acclimated to the environment, there's a pool table, electronic darts, TV monitors and poker machines.

Hard Rock Cafe

4475 Paradise Rd. • 733-8400

You can't miss the trendy restaurant/lounge at the corner of Paradise Road and Harmon Avenue — there's a 77-foot-high guitar out front. Inside, it's rock and roll memorabilia, signed photos and lots of university students. The bar is lively, and the food is excellent, though the continuous sounds of old and new rock can reach deafening decibel levels, especially if you sit in the sunken dining area.

Holy Cow!

2423 Las Vegas Blvd. S. • 732-2697

The first microbrewery to open in town, Holy Cow! is known by its distinctive black-and-white Holstein cow logo. But don't expect any milk here; Holy Cow! serves only fresh-brewed, hand-crafted European-style beers, about 500,000 pints per year. There are four types of beer, each with its own unique flavor, including the Rebel Red ale, which won a people's choice competition for pale ales, cream ales, brown ales and oatmeal stouts. The Holy Cow! restaurant serves steaks, chicken, burgers, sandwiches, breakfast and Wisconsin bratwurst. The casino has about 60 slot and video machines, and they are usually humming. There's also a popular logo shop where you can buy T-shirts, hats, sweatshirts, mugs, steins and other merchandise, all emblazoned with the ubiquitous black-and-white moo cow.

Kiefer's

Carriage House Hotel, 105 E. Harmon Ave. • 739-8000

One of the best views of The Strip is from this cozy restaurant and lounge atop the Carriage House Hotel. Grass wallpaper, rattan club chairs, coral-colored furnishings and dozens of plants create a Caribbean atmosphere in the heart of the desert. The piano bar adds the proper amount of ambiance for romantic escapes from the frenzy below.

Monte Carlo Pub & Brewery

Monte Carlo Hotel Casino, 3770 Las Vegas Blvd. S. • 730-7777

Even if you're not an avid beer drinker you'll like the unique atmosphere here — huge copper beer barrels and antique furnishings create an elegant atmosphere. Live piano entertainment is featured nightly, and there's an outdoor patio that overlooks the hotel's lavish pool area. If you're a student of the brewing process, you can get a bird's-eye view of the operation from the microbrewery's catwalk. Six different styles of Monte Carlo-labeled beer are produced, including a light beer, an India pale ale and an American-style, unfiltered wheat ale. The pub also features a traditional Irish stout, a rich amber ale and a regular brewer's special. Some of the food specialties created to accompany the beer are brick-oven pizzas and sausage platters. The menu also contains a full line of salads and sandwiches.

Peppermill

2985 Las Vegas Blvd. S. • 735-7635

For a Strip tavern, the Peppermill is surprisingly restrained. Candle-lit tables and a fireplace surrounded by plush sofas create the feeling of a living room cocktail party. The waitresses' long evening gowns are a refreshing change from the skimpy outfits worn at the nearby casinos. If you're hungry for more than the jar of peanuts on the table, a full menu in the dining room is served around the clock.

The Still

9495 Las Vegas Blvd. S. • 361-7012

For a taste of an old-time roadhouse, try this little joint 8 miles south of Tropicana Avenue on the old Los Angeles Highway. Drive south on The Strip past the old McCarran Field terminal and aged motels waiting for guests who never arrive. When The Strip skyline is just a blur in your rearview mirror, look for the Still's peaked, corrugated tin roof and brick walls. Inside, you'll find cedar paneling, par-

Photo: Jim Decker/Review-Journal

The Canadian-French *Mystere* at Treasure Island weds the worlds of art and performance.

quet floors, a copper-clad still and an upstairs banquet room designed as a jail. The music is usually easy listening rock from the '50s and '60s, but it could be jazz or rhythm and blues. If you're hungry, try the 2-pound Jethroburger, a monster hamburger that makes a Whopper look like a Wheat Thin.

Downtown

Comedy Clubs

Comedy Fun House

$ • Four Queens Hotel, 202 Fremont St. • 634-6045

The only comedy club downtown, the Comedy Fun House opened in mid-1997 in a converted meeting room on the hotel's second floor. But the small room, which seats about 200 people, and its makeshift stage, put the comics up close and personal and within easy heckling distance of the most distant customer. The stand-up comics include circuit performers such as Bruce Baum, Marty Rackham and Jimmy Wiggins.

Nightclubs

Huntridge Performing Arts Theatre

1208 E. Charleston Blvd. • 477-7703

For a jolt of alternative and underground rock, visit the Huntridge, a converted art deco style movie house built in the 1940s that now hosts dance parties and concerts featuring mostly local bands. The building was closed in 1995 after the roof caved in (the building was unoccupied) and reopened in 1997. Featured groups have included Lagwagon, Limp Atari, Goldfinger, Shelter and Voodoo Glow Skulls.

Production Shows

American Superstars

$ • Stratosphere, 2000 Las Vegas Blvd. S. • 380-7711

This rock 'n' roll celebrity tribute features impersonations of superstars such as Madonna, Diana Ross, Michael Jackson, Gloria Estefan and Charlie Daniels as well as up-and-coming stars like the Spice Girls, the British rock imports who skyrocketed to fame with singles "Wannabe" and "Say You'll Be There." The celebrity impersonators are supported by a live band and Superstar Dancers, who perform with each act in the show. *Superstars* is presented twice nightly except Thursday; children's ticket prices are available.

Country Fever

$$ • Golden Nugget, 129 Fremont St. • 386-8100

Like everything else at the Golden Nugget, *Country Fever* is a first-class act. The show features a live country band, engaging dancers and eye-catching choreography. But don't expect the traditional Bob's Country Bunker sets. Among the show's highlights are a gospel singing sequence; a revealing dance number; and a Garth Brooks impersonator. The price of admission even includes a basket of deep-fried munchies. *Country Fever* is presented twice nightly except Friday in the Theatre Ballroom.

FYI

Unless otherwise noted, the area code for all phone numbers listed in this chapter is 702.

Marshall Sylver

$$ • Stratosphere • 2000 Las Vegas Blvd. S. • 380-7711

Immodestly billed as "The World's Greatest Hypnotist," Marshall Sylver stars in a show that is more nightclub act than production show. Over the course of 80 minutes, he extracts willing subjects from the audience, places them under a hypnotic spell and induces them to perform weird stunts such as beeping like a roadrunner, laughing uncontrollably, swatting invisible flies, turning into an extraterrestrial — well, you get the picture. The show is entertaining if you enjoy laughing at fellow audience members, but Sylver's pitch for his self-help tapes and books at the end of the show is completely uninspired. Sylver performs twice nightly Wednesday through Sunday.

The Xtreme Scene

$ • Jackie Gaughan's Plaza Hotel, 1 S. Main St. • 386-2444

The Xtreme Scene is a fast-moving cabaret with scintillating showgirls and dancers, the lyrical voice of Andy Fullen and the Tabak motorcycles, a troupe of daredevils who race at breakneck speeds inside a steel Thunder Dome. No stranger to staging spicy revues, the Plaza had the distinction of hosting a topless ice-skating show called Nudes On Ice, and a forgettable Crazy Horse tribute, Xposed. Now it's topless dancers doing cartwheels.

Pubs, Sports Bars and Microbreweries

The Bunkhouse

124 S. 11th St. • 384-4536

Despite its somewhat seedy location, The Bunkhouse is a great Western-style bar that serves perhaps the coldest beer in town. Outside, it's split rail accents on the roof and above the entrance; inside it's more of the same plus branding irons, tack and saddles, horseshoes and other cowboy memorabilia as well as dozens of posters of old-time Western movie heroes — Tom Mix, Hoppalong Cassidy, Roy Rogers and John Wayne, to name a few. The service is always friendly, the room is well-lit and there's comfy seating at tables or in booths. Occasionally the bar hosts live bands, bike runs and outdoor barbecues.

Triple 7 Brewpub

Main Street Station, 200 N. Main St. • 387-1896

One of downtown's best spots to indulge, Triple 7 follows a 1930s warehouse motif with high ceilings, parquet floors, rich mahogany and cherrywood accented by brass and copper fixtures. The bar itself is one of the most attractive in town with etched, beveled glass and more mahogany panels. Throughout are 40-inch TV screens for viewing sports and music videos, or you can watch the vats, kettles and ferment tanks brew the four homegrown microbrews, which range from a light German ale to a smooth, dark malty porter. The pub's menu is actually good, with selections in the party-food category — burgers, pizza, Southwest specialties, buffalo wings, sushi and raw oysters.

Siegfried & Roy

The storied history of Las Vegas entertainment can be recorded in just a few names. Liberace, of course, during the 1950s, and Elvis — the King — through the 1960s and '70s. In the decade following Elvis' death in 1977, others tried to take the mantle — Wayne Newton, Engelbert Humperdinck, Tom Jones, Julio Iglesias, Liza Minnelli and even Frank Sinatra — but none could carry it as high or hold it as tenaciously as their predecessors.

Close-up

It wasn't until the 1990s that people around the world would come to recognize two names, Siegfried & Roy, as synonymous with Las Vegas entertainment. Siegfried & Roy emerged during an era when there were only shows but no show men. And they did it by becoming architects of illusion, creators of fantasy.

The hottest ticket in Las Vegas since 1990 has been Siegfried & Roy's show at the Mirage Hotel. Even though the ticket commands the highest ticket price for any show — about $90 a ticket — dozens of people line up at the box office every night hoping for a canceled reservation.

— continued on next page

Photo: The Mirage

Seigfried & Roy play with three of their white lion cubs, Quest, Passion and Destiny.

Working twice a night before a packed theater, Siegfried & Roy stage a spectacular show, featuring space-age illusions, high-tech special effects, mesmerizing music and a large-scale production company of dancers and acrobats. Among the totally mind-boggling visual illusions are a beautiful woman transformed into a 600-pound rare white tiger; a full-sized elephant that vanishes into thin air; and a fire-breathing dragon that battles the dynamic duo to the death (you figure out who dies).

Even the "little" illusions are spectacular, though they don't seem like it at the time because they seem dwarfed by the enormity of the full-scale illusions. For instance, in one sequence Siegfried is on stage talking to a member of the audience when a skeleton — bones and all! — walks out from the wings pushing a tea cart. It's easy to take what's happening for granted because it is happening so naturally, yet later on you wonder, "How could that happen?" The same can be said for a sequence in which two "talking" white tiger tails flutter about the stage, in and out of a water bottle, singing and talking to each other. The stunt is truly amazing, but it almost goes unappreciated because you're lulled into believing that it is actually happening!

Siegfried & Roy's signature white tigers and lions are used in several illusions throughout the show. There's even a five-minute video during the show that shows the animals at home with the illusionists. Over the years the animals have become more than stage props for the German-born superstars. The animals have become a symbol of Siegfried & Roy's passion to aid and assist in the planet's ecological balance. In fact they are always striving, whether on stage or in TV interviews, to raise America's awareness of animal preservation.

Toward that end, Siegfried & Roy established the Secret Garden at the Mirage, a palm-shaded sanctuary that is home to a collection of the world's rarest and most exotic creatures. Here you can find snow white tigers, striped white tigers, heterozygous tigers, white lions, heterozygous white lions and the Asian elephant that appears and disappears on stage.

"Conservation comes from within for Siegfried and myself," says Roy. "What man has destroyed, we are attempting to resurrect in the Secret Garden."

Siegfried adds, "We are blessed to be in a position to create something unique and enduring so that future generations can see with their own eyes the beauty, the majesty and the nobility of these animals. But it's only a beginning, only a sample."

East Valley

Nightclubs

Carollo's

2301 E. Sunset Rd. • 361-3712

At Carollo's, darkwood paneling and oil paintings of the New England countryside make a strange backdrop for live rock music, but it works. The dance floor is packed on the weekend. The Wednesday night talent contests and Thursday ladies' nights are also popular.

Dylan's Dance Hall & Saloon

4660 Boulder Hwy. • 451-4006

Although it's not as large as some of the western dance halls on the Boulder Highway Strip, Dylan's attracts locals who are serious line dancers. Thursday through Saturday they two-step in full gallop to DJ-driven new country.

The Hop

1650 E. Tropicana Ave. • 736-0042

If dances like the Twist and the Stroll turn you on, pony down to The Hop. This is one of the best clubs for serious dancing — a large dance floor, state-of-the-art sound and light systems and live music from the '50s and '60s have made this a popular spot with a mostly 30-and-older crowd. The Hop is also one of the classiest joints in town with its black and jade enameled bars, salmon-shaded walls, indirect lighting and open, airy seating areas furnished with comfy club chairs and cocktail tables. The bars and seating areas surround the step-down dance floor so traffic congestion is kept to a minimum. The DJ starts the evening at 7 PM, then fills in during the band's breaks.

Moose McGillycuddy's

4770 S. Maryland Pkwy. • 798-8337

True to its name, there's a moose head inside this Southern California-inspired pub and restaurant that rambles through several split levels and dining areas. Other shades of California include hundreds of photos of bikers, bikinis and music memorabilia on the walls, plus Monterey cannery-type ducts in the ceiling. The main bar is trimmed in oak and dispenses Bass, Guinness Stout, Newcastle, Pyramid and Samuel Adams Boston Lager on tap. There's a step-down dance floor surrounded by high-top seating and a couple of booths. Frequented by undergrads from UNLV across the street, the pub and dance floor swings into gear on the weekends.

The Railhead

Boulder Station, 4111 Boulder Hwy. • 432-7777

There's always something happening in this intimate cabaret-style club on the Boulder Strip. The booking agent shows no favoritism in choosing his acts, which have ranged from retro rock stars like Chubby Checker, R&B's Sonny Turner and country's Charlie Daniels. When headliners aren't lighting up the stage, customers find the spotlight during the frequent karaoke nights.

Rockabilly's

3785 Boulder Hwy. • 641-5800

The cow skulls and branding irons are the tip off: This is a Western saloon and dance hall. But most of the cowboys are of the suburban variety — they prefer driving Broncos to riding them. Good food is served around the clock, and if you don't know how to do the two-step, take a free dance lesson.

Sam's Town Western Dance Hall

Sam's Town, 5111 Boulder Hwy. • 456-7777

For a taste of "Gilley's of Las Vegas" come to the country-flavored Western Dance Hall. Surrounded by buffalo heads, branding irons and Remington-style prints, you can line dance or clog your way into oblivion. There are dance lessons for city folk not up to speed on the latest steps, including traditional line dancing as well as a Vegas-style "Electric Slide" or "Tush Push."

Silver Saddle Saloon

2501 E. Charleston Blvd. • 474-2900

One of the most popular country spots in town, the Silver Saddle features a large dance floor and a stage for the resident Silver Saddle Band. During the day you can sit at the large horseshoe-shaped bar or play pool and listen to Shenandoah and Eddie Raven on the jukebox.

Tom & Jerry's

4550 Maryland Pkwy. • 736-8550

Housed in a long, red-tile building, Tom & Jerry's attracts party animals from the UNLV campus across the street. The dance club features a sunken, octagon-shaped dance floor flanked by a small riser stage for live bands. Cafe tables and chairs surround the dance floor, and high-top seating is against the walls. For disco authenticity there's even a mirror ball. If you want a break, there's a pub apart from the action — a nice bar with tables and a few leather booths.

Pubs, Sports Bars and Microbreweries

Barley's Casino & Brewing Co.

4500 E. Sunset Rd., Henderson • 458-2739

Even though this place is a casino, it doesn't look and feel like one — the floors are hardwood, the open ceilings have cannery-style ducts, and the walls are accented with brick and wood panels. The brew pub serves a stylish blend of Southwest and California cuisine, and you can sit on the outside patio when the weather cooperates. The microbrewery produces three hand-crafted brews: Blue Diamond Beer, a classic garden-style lager; Red Rock Beer, an original

Oktoberfest beer that's full bodied with an amber color; and Black Mountain Beer, an unfiltered dark beer whose taste is a careful blend of dark and caramel malts.

The Bomb

3015 Boulder Hwy. • 384-2655

You might want to bring bail money to The Bomb, or at least a friend who has an attitude. This is the loudest, most raucous rock club in town. It has all the trappings of an indoor rock festival. It often books national rock stars as well as up-and-coming local talent.

Cafe Michelle

1350 E. Flamingo Rd. • 732-8687

Strip entertainers, visiting celebrities and white-collar suits who like to be seen come to this popular shopping-center hangout for an after-show drink in the quiet, intimate lounge portion of this popular cafe. The piano bar and the outdoor patio are popular during the week. There's jazz on the weekends.

Chuckster's

4632 S. Maryland Pkwy. • 736-7808

Although across the street from the UNLV campus, the atmosphere here is quiet and restrained. Perhaps that's why it's an early-evening meeting place for university types, who gather to discuss cognitive dissonance, Maxwell Planck's Theory and other light topics. The tavern has a small platform presumably for live musicians and a big screen TV presumably for televised chess matches. There's also a jukebox that seems to play the proper tunes, making Chuckster's a nice place for a quiet drink and relaxing conversation.

Crown & Anchor

1350 E. Tropicana Ave. • 739-8676

Like any good British-style pub, the Crown & Anchor has a warm neighborhood feel enhanced by dark wood furnishings, wooden staircases to the two lofts, and masts, rigging, nets and other nautical artifacts throughout. There's even a buxom blonde figurehead over the bar, which serves up nearly three dozen draught beers, ales and stouts including, among others, Bass, Abbot Ale, Whitbread, Woodpecker and John Courage. The seating around the bar is comfortable, and the stools are often filled with U.K. transplants, who reminisce about the Commonwealth while watching soccer matches between Liverpool and Newcastle on the satellite TV. One of the lofts has a pool table and other games, while the other has parquet-top tables with brocade-back chairs — a quaint setting beneath the tulip ceiling fans, peaked ceiling and skylight. There's another dining area in front, a homey parlor with similar tables and chairs that view the street through French doors.

Favorites

4110 S. Maryland Pkwy. • 796-1776

The band is too loud and the dance floor too small at this popular center near UNLV, but that's probably why it's so popular with the university crowd — the dancing is toenail to toenail. Or maybe it's the reggae and alternative bands that occasionally take over the round stage. The pace relaxes when jazz and rhythm and blues are featured, and swing-era types have their day when Sherman Gunn's Big Band takes over once a week.

Final Score Sports Bar

Sam's Town, 5111 Boulder Hwy. • 456-7777

If you play as hard as you work, try the Final Score, which is as much a gymnasium as a sports bar with its indoor basketball court, pop-a-shot, shuffleboard, sand volleyball pit, pool, Jacuzzi, pinball, electronic darts, air hockey, video games, funky sports memorabilia and more than 30 TV monitors. Oh, yes, there's a bar when you're ready to knock down a few cold ones.

INSIDERS' TIP

The legal drinking age in Las Vegas is 21, and there is no curfew for sale or consumption of alcohol.

Paddy's Pub

4160 S. Pecos Rd. • 435-1684

For a taste of Ireland, try Paddy's Pub. The colonial yellow building with white pillars belies the quaint Irish pub inside. Guinness, Harp and Bass are on tap, and Shamrock, Schnapps and Bushmill Irish Whiskey are among the bar offerings. Irish stew, corned beef and cabbage, fish and chips and a lively game of darts round out the Dublin-like experience.

Pepper's Lounge

2929 E. Desert Inn Rd. • 731-3234

Arthur Murray would have had a field day at this hoppin' place just off Pecos Road. Live entertainment varies from contemporary rock and Big Band to Latin salsa and easy listening. But the dancers — many in the 50-and-older category — seem like they know what they're doing.

Sneakers

2250 E. Tropicana Ave. • 798-0272

Sneakers is everything a sports bar should be: laid back and friendly, at times raucous, with everything from golf clubs (wood shafts!) and hockey sticks on the wall to satellite dishes on the roof. And with 10 big screens for optimal viewing and the best burgers in town, this is couch-potato heaven. Another thing: After the games have ended, they turn up the music and have a block party in front of the place.

The Stake Out

4800 S. Maryland Pkwy. • 798-8383

The Stake Out has a movie-sized television screen that can be seen from anywhere in the bar, but the best spot is the upstairs lounge. Here, you can enjoy a cold beer and bucket of wings, watch your favorite team, then shoot a game of pool if the action slows down. Breakfast, lunch and dinner are served 24 hours a day.

TGI Friday's

1800 E. Flamingo Rd. • 732-9905
4570 W. Sahara Ave. • 889-1866

Despite its chain-store heritage, TGI Friday's is one of the city's more popular singles bars. If you can ignore the nonstop trading of phone numbers, the atmosphere is casual, not desperate, and the emphasis is on fun. There's also an extensive menu and a nice dining area.

Tommy Rocker's Cantina and Grill

4275 Industrial Rd. • 261-6688

When Tommy moved from his previous digs on the west side, he scrapped his shrine to rock'n'roll motif and set up a Caribbean-style *Cocktail*-ish beach bar, sans Tom Cruise. If you're courageous try the Proud Mary, a straightforward Bloody Mary that's just hot enough so you won't stop breathing or the Moody Blues Blast From the Past, a crazy concoction of rums, liqueurs and fruit juices. Tommy and his band play regularly — old time rock 'n' roll — and he encourages the crowd "to get rowdy" and have fun.

The Wet Stop

4440 S. Maryland Pkwy. • 791-0977

Another university-driven bar, The Wet Stop reminds one of an old speakeasy with its low ceilings and close-in seating. Although mostly dark and minimalist, the pub has colorful bar stools and half-moon windows that overlook the street and UNLV. Live bands vary from rock to alternative to reggae throughout the week, and day-trippers can drink two-for-one from 10 AM to 6 PM.

West Valley

Nightclubs

Club Rio

The Rio, 3700 W. Flamingo Rd.
• 252-7776

A teeth-rattling sound system and walls of video monitors should get your dancing juices flowing in Las Vegas' largest nightclub. The music is hard rock most of the week, but the mirror ball comes out on Wednesday nights when Boogie Knights, complete with overblown Afro wigs, bell bottoms and platform shoes, unleash their disco mania. There's a $10 cover charge for men, $5 for women, though local women get in free. Also, dress appropriately; they won't let you in if you're wearing a tank top and cutoffs.

Gold Coast Dance Hall & Showroom

Gold Coast, 4000 W. Flamingo Rd. • 367-7111

The Dance Hall & Saloon is a huge, barn-style room with wood-grain walls, a high red ceiling and wrought-iron chandeliers. The music varies from rock to country-and-western. If you aren't up on the latest country craze, they'll even give you free dance lessons. Once a week a Harry James-style Big Band takes the stage, and fox-trotters take over the large, oval dance floor.

Production Shows

FYI

Unless otherwise noted, the area code for all phone numbers listed in this chapter is 702.

Danny Gans

$$$ • The Rio, 3700 W. Flamingo Rd. • 252-7776

Impressionist Danny Gans, known as the "Man of Many Voices," has built a repertoire of nearly 300 characterizations from which he chooses about 75 for each of his one-man shows. Among his incredible impressions are Al Pacino in a scene from *Scent of a Woman* and an emotionally charged exchange between Henry Fonda and Katherine Hepburn from *On Golden Pond*. Blessed with a powerful singing voice, Gans also impersonates singers. He delivers renditions of stars such as Billy Joel, Rod Stewart and Tom Jones, then switches to a dead-on replica of Sarah Vaughan. He also pulls off Willie Nelson and Julio Iglesias singing their famous duet. Danny Gans performs at 8 PM Wednesday through Sunday in the Copacabana Showroom.

The Orleans Showroom

$$ • The Orleans Hotel & Casino, 4500 W. Tropicana Ave. • 365-7111

Every seat in this 827-seat concert theater has a perfect view of the stage. Plus the room's amphitheater-style design and high-tech sound and lighting systems make it a great place to see celebrity headliners, who have included Everly Brothers, Crystal Gayle, Eddie Money, the Beach Boys and Frankie Valli and the Four Seasons.

Pubs, Sports Bars and Microbreweries

Big Dog's Cafe & Casino

6390 W. Sahara Ave. • 876-3647

You can't miss this place: A two-story-high mural of a St. Bernard adorns the front wall; the side walls have Dalmations and pointers. No, this isn't a kennel, even though beer flows from red fire hydrants, bar snacks are served in dog dishes and canine artwork is plastered everywhere. Obviously, this is a fun place, owned by the same folks who run the Holy Cow! microbrewery. In fact, the beer is from the Holy Cow! (see our write-up in The Strip section). If you get hungry, Big Dog's has a full kitchen that serves up steaks, ribs, bratwurst, burgers and the usual party favorites such as fried calamari, pizza and quesadillas.

Bourbon Street Cabaret

The Orleans Hotel & Casino, 4500 W. Tropicana Ave. • 365-7111

With the quiet feel of a courtyard club in New Orleans' French Quarter, the Bourbon Street Cabaret is a nice spot to enjoy your favorite drink while listing to classic jazz, blues and zydeco. Part of the club's decor includes huge replicas of grand and baby grand pianos suspended from the ceiling.

The Inferno

3340 S. Highland Ave. • 734-7336

This relatively new club, formerly the Hob Nob, a hangout for local musicians, is now a popular gathering spot for the city's gay scene.

INSIDERS' TIP

The first celebrity headliner to appear in Las Vegas was Sophie Tucker, who starred at the Last Frontier in 1944.

Studio 54 it ain't, but the dance floor is huge, and the resident DJ, Rick, keeps the place hopping. Besides full-frontal dancing, The Inferno features large-screen TV monitors, pool tables, the inevitable slot machines and funky stone griffins behind the bar.

Leroy's Satellite Sports Lounge

Howard Johnson's, 3111 W. Tropicana Blvd. • 798-1111

One of the great sports bettor hangouts was the original Leroy's Sports Book downtown, a shoddy smoke-filled place where cigar-chewing old men sat for hours at a time playing the ponies or parlaying baseball bets. The original Leroy's is gone, but we now have this fairly reasonable facsimile — a hole in the wall with a handful of tables, a two-tray buffet of free food and a beer display as the backdrop for the live entertainment, usually a singer and piano player. What better environment to pull for your team while sipping a Bud Light?

L.J.'s Sports Bar & Grill

4405 W. Flamingo Rd. • 871-1424

If L.J.'s looks too cavernous to be a sports pub, it's because it used to be a disco called Tramps. Well, the mirror ball and Donna Summer tapes are gone, but you can watch your favorite teams on the large-screen TVs in a setting any couch potato would love — cold beer on tap, great finger food and autographed sports photos and memorabilia on the surrounding walls.

Loading Dock Lounge

Palace Station, 2411 W. Sahara Ave. • 367-2411

This is a popular spot with local hotel and casino workers who like to hang out after work. The bands begin playing in the afternoon, usually rock or rhythm-and-blues, but the dance floor doesn't heat up until mid-evening.

Mambo's Lounge

The Rio, 3700 W. Flamingo Rd. • 252-7777

If you have a taste for a Latin beat — or even if you don't — check out the salsa and merengue sounds at Mambo's in the Rio. The live bands perform with flair and gusto, and they've recently expanded the lounge to accommodate the flashy lambada-style dancers. While the music and clientele are authentic, the Mambo's decor lapses into Vegas' version of a Jimmy Buffet Bar — thatched roofs, rice-paper fans and bamboo furnishings.

Naughty Ladies Saloon

Arizona Charlie's Hotel & Casino, 740 S. Decatur Blvd. • 258-5200

Old West hospitality is the fare at this saloon that looks like it's straight from a *Gunsmoke* TV set. Sorry, there's no Miss Kitty tending bar, only frontier-style Western music with (who else?) The Naughty Ladies, who get the place whooping and hollering. Attire is mostly tight jeans, boots and Peterbilt caps. The place is friendly, and the drinks are cold.

North Beach Cafe

2605 S. Decatur Blvd. • 247-9530

If you want to blend in, bring your business card and cell phone to this yuppie conclave on the west side, where you can bend elbows with lawyer and real estate types while listening to pretty good jazz two nights a week. When you become tired of listening to dissertations on wraparound mortgages and other light banter, take a shot at the open-mike showcase. Here you move into the spotlight and provide the vocals for the three-piece combo, who will gently lead you to a new and better existence.

Play It Again Sam

4120 Spring Mountain Rd. • 876-1550

It's not exactly Rick's Place, but Play it Again features candle-lit tables in solarium booths that surround the low-key lounge. Live piano, blues and jazz attract celebrity regulars such as Walter Matthau and David Brenner, who like the fajitas.

Sand Dollar Lounge

3355 Spring Mountain Rd. • 871-6651

A waterfront bar in the desert? That would be the Sand Dollar Lounge. Fish nets and mooring poles create a nautical ambiance at this popular lounge tucked into the corner of a nondescript business complex. Despite the atmosphere, there are no clambakes or fish fries, only the popular resident Boogieman Blues Band. When the band stops there's a jukebox, pool table and dart board.

Skinny Dugan's

4127 W. Charleston Blvd. • 877-0522

At this well-designed pub, you can listen to the live band while sitting around the U-shaped bar or find a quiet booth. The parquet dance floor is seldom crowded, so, if you like to dance, be prepared to be part of the show. If not, amuse yourself with pool, games, video poker machines or cribbage one night a week.

North Valley

Pubs, Sports Bars and Microbreweries

Draft House Barn & Casino

4543 N. Rancho Dr. • 645-1404

This big barn with the silo on the side is a popular hangout for Cheeseheads — a.k.a. Green Bay Packer fans. When the Pack is playing, arrive early to get a seat at the bar or in the beer garden. When the game ends you can sample some of the fine Wisconsin bratwurst, roasted chicken, steak or walleye, or try your hand at one of the 35 video poker machines. Two of them are the brand-new IGT poker machines that take from one to 100 quarters on a single hand. A hundred quarters per hand? What do you do when your elbow locks up and you can't shovel in any more coins?

Jerry's Nugget Royal Street Theater

1821 Las Vegas Blvd. N. • 399-3000

This intimate lounge and dance hall has split-level seating and space-age lighting and frequently hosts live entertainment such as Magaly and the Vamps when it isn't staging a Latin Dance Party.

Texas Station Gambling Hall & Hotel

2101 Texas Star Ln. • 631-1000

When you want to go bar-hopping, you can do it within the cozy confines of Texas, gambling hall, that is. One of the bars, Crazy Mary's, is known for its Bloody Mary and infused vodka, while you can catch Margarita madness at the Laredo Cantina. If you're feeling slightly more sophisticated, point your upturned nose to the Garage for cognac and fine cigars from the pub's own humidor.

Men's Clubs

The adult entertainment scene is found primarily in clubs away from the resort hotels, which are too tame for the bump-and-grind, runway shows, whether or not they're topless or completely nude. Despite the city's liberal liquor laws, these clubs have strict rules regarding alcohol. To wit, no alcohol is served if the club stages nude dancing. So you may pay up to $10 for a Snapple in a nude club. The one exception is the Palomino Club in North Las Vegas, which was grandfathered in to allow alcohol sales even though they have nude shows. Listed below are some of the more popular men's clubs in town. For a more extensive listing there are dozens of tourist publications — as well as billboards and taxi posters — that advertise these clubs, so it shouldn't be hard to extend the list. Expect to pay a cover charge for admission to all men's clubs.

The Can-Can Room, 3155 Industrial Road, 737-1161

Cheetah's, 2112 Western Avenue, 384-0074

Club Paradise, 4416 Paradise Road, 734-7990

INSIDERS' TIP

If you decide to stroll up Fremont Street at night, use caution. While police, including bike patrols, are prevalent, Las Vegas, like most downtowns, has its unsavory elements.

Crazy Horse, 4034 Paradise Road, 642-2984

Crazy Horse Saloon Too, 2476 Industrial Road, 382-8003

Girls of Glitter Gulch Gentlemen's Club, 20 Fremont Street, 385-4774

Larry's Villa, 2401 W. Bonanza Road, 647-2713

Little Darlings of Las Vegas, 1514 Western Avenue, 366-1633

Olympic Garden, 1531 Las Vegas Boulevard S., 385-9361

Palomino Club, 1814 Las Vegas Boulevard N., 642-2984

Discover Nevada's Largest Mall

The Boulevard isn't just Nevada's largest, it's also Las Vegas' favorite. With four major department stores and over 140 other unique stores and boutiques, it's easy to see why.

Also for your convenience:

- Hair salons
- Travel agency
- 1-hour photo processing
- Shoe Repair
- Optometrists
- 3 Covered Parking Garages
- Free Valet Parking
- Automotive Repair
- Restaurants
- Acres of Self Parking

The Boulevard

Nevada's Largest Mall

Minutes from the Strip
Convention Center and Downtown
Maryland Pkwy. & Desert Inn Rd.
732-8949
www.blvdmall.comm

Shopping

If Las Vegas truly is Sin City, then shopping here could be an outlet for all seven Deadly Sins: Avarice and Gluttony, of course; Sloth as you stroll in the afternoon sun; Pride when you discover a bargain others have overlooked; but Envy and Wrath when you hesitate on a Frank Lloyd Wright-style lamp and lose it to another sharp-eyed shopper; even Lust, for the upscale malls are as much fashion runways as marketplaces.

Besides satisfying basic needs, shopping can be a form of entertainment and relaxation, and it's a great way to get to know the city. The choices range from upscale boutiques and emporiums, such as Gucci's, Saks Fifth Avenue and Neiman-Marcus, to offbeat clothing stores, antiquarian bookstores and hip art galleries. The history and culture of the region are reflected in the Southwestern and Indian art, crafts and jewelry sold at several well-stocked shops. Local rock and gem dealers specialize in quartz crystals and polished jewelry mined in nearby states.

Las Vegas even has its own antique guild, made up of dozens of shops, most within a few blocks of each other. Their treasures range from Victorian jewelry and collectibles to juke boxes, German clocks and retro-chic clothing. There's also a cartel of vintage music stores that sell an intriguing array of albums and tape recordings such as the early Beatles and Fats Waller. A growing Asian population has created shopping districts where you can browse through shops specializing in Chinese, Japanese and Korean art, crafts and curios.

If you want authentic gambling souvenirs, or if you want to set up your own "casino" at home, visit one of several dealers who recondition and sell slot machines. You can also buy craps and blackjack tables, roulette wheels, cards, dice, chips — even authentic clothing worn by card dealers, keno runners and croupiers.

Retail sales — always a part of the tourism business — have grown by leaps in the 1990s. Casinos are finding that, while hotel rooms remain filled, visitors are dumping less of their travel dollars into slot machines and more into retail purchases. Thus, the gaming resorts have expanded their shopping opportunities. For instance, in 1997 the Rio Suite Hotel opened a new tower and wing called Masquerade Village, which includes 60,000 square feet of retail space and is home to dozens of high-end theme shops such as Alegre, Orvis, Speedo Fitness Wear and Money Magnetz. About the same time, Coca Cola opened a retail store in the Showcase Mall just north of the MGM Grand Hotel on The Strip. In late 1997, the Forum Shops — the nation's highest-grossing shopping center with average revenue of $1,200 per square foot — added 280,000 square feet of space and new tenants such as FAO Schwartz, NikeTown, Virgin Records Megastore, Fendi, Polo and Hugo Boss.

Expansion of retail space on The Strip will continue. The Fashion Show Mall, already the city's premier shopping mall between Treasure Island and the Frontier, will double in size to 1.8 million square feet by spring 2000 and add two major department stores, Bloomingdale's and Lord & Taylor.

While shopping on The Strip is easy — just grab your billfold and a good pair sneakers — shopping around the valley takes more planning. This city, unlike, say, San Francisco or Washington, D.C., is spread over a vast area. So, other than The Strip, there is no North Beach or Georgetown neighborhood ideal for browsing. Therefore, we've identified the city's best shopping destinations — the malls, commercial centers, shopping districts and unique specialty shops — and grouped them by geographic location. This way, you'll be able to quickly and easily locate the city's best shopping sites. So, with that in mind, unleash the plastic, and let's shop.

Antiques and Collectibles

Downtown/East Valley

Little-known to most tourists — as well as many residents — are the antique and collectible shops on E. Charleston Boulevard, just a couple of miles southeast of the downtown area. There are about two dozen of them, and most belong to an informal guild that promotes their stores. Many of them retain the charm of the converted homes they occupy. Their treasures range from Victorian jewelry and antique German clocks to vintage pipe organs and retro-chic clothing. Charleston Boulevard may not have the panache of Los Angeles' Melrose Boulevard, but shoppers won't be intimated by overbearing salespeople or outlandish prices.

FYI

Unless otherwise noted, the area code for all phone numbers listed in this chapter is 702.

Antique Square
2014-2026 E. Charleston Blvd.
• 386-0238

The square is home to a dozen stores. The owners of the square, Nicolas & Osvaldo have several rooms and a long hall lined with cabinets to show off the large range of antiques. A mix of periods, styles and tastes are reflected in the crystal, china, decorative tea cups, clocks, chandeliers and silver tea sets. One cabinet is filled with tiny sterling silver pieces: salt and pepper shakers, spoons, thimbles, tea strainers, pickle forks, cream pitchers, baby spoons, coasters and napkin rings. Or there's the bronze deco table lamps, statuettes, busts and statues that dot the shop's landscape. If metal statuary doesn't appeal, try the palace urn from the Meissen region of Germany, the Civil War battle flag or the 17th-century rosewood desk ornately carved with fire-breathing dragons.

Fancy That features a variety of china and porcelain, including elegant Chinese tea services and milk glass kitchenware. There's also quite a collection of purple Depression glass pieces that line several shelves — bowls, goblets, trays, candlesticks and more. Rhinestone costume jewelry and an occasional piece of furniture, such as a tiger-oak display cabinet, round the selection at Fancy That.

American collectibles are the specialty at Yana's Junke. Yana's displays items such as a hand-crank ice cream maker, a pierced-tin cabinet, Ball canning jars and Coca-Cola ice chests and old bottles. Etcetera offers gold and silver coins, Oriental and primitive artifacts, Early Americana and a few artistically carved walking sticks. On display are coins and old costume and real jewelry. The shop contains a collection of tin boxes, coffee grinders and butter churns, some 100 and 200 years old, including a glass Dazey churn with wooden paddles.

Treasures found at Granny's Nook might include an upholstered bench, marble-top and tiled washstands, an oak desk with red inlaid leather and a pair of converted carriage lamps for $600. Other possibilities include handmade quilts and embroidered linens, a cupid photo in a double heart-shaped frame and a white Denmark telephone from the 1930s. Dishes include Fiestaware and Blue Willow.

If you enjoy sifting through boxes of classy junk, check out Bonnie's Antiques and Collectibles, where you may unearth letter-openers, Oriental carvings, hat pins, postcards and tea wades — all set among country furnishings and Tiffany lamps.

Nicholas Antonio Antiques has an unending selection of swords, knives and daggers as well as such jade and ivory pieces as a 12-inch square carved ivory box, a 3-inch-high Chinese ivory horseman, ivory-headed walking sticks, armies of 2-inch lead soldiers, a collection of silver pocket knives and a shoebox of old postcards. You'll also find Native American artifacts, clocks and old paintings.

Your pocketbook may not be able to stand it, but most of the items at Buzz & Co. Fine Antiques are breathtaking. You might find a 19th-century French d'ore bronze chandelier; an inlaid leather-top, brass-trimmed cherry desk; or a pair of Italian frosted green glass horses weighing 60 pounds each — originally made for royalty and signed by the artist.

Miniatures are the specialty at Celeste And

Company. The shop also has glassware, rugs, dolls, decorative plates, silver spoons, upholstered furniture, a mint gramophone and a U.S. Navy microscope. Estate Antiques sprawls over several large rooms offering such items as a white porcelain Christmas crèche, panels of stained glass, a collection of china animal salt and pepper shakers and a set of yellow Federal glass dishes, c. 1935-37. You may also find a collections of tiny clocks, Hummels or Wizard of Oz plates as well as bed and armoire sets and an Estey reed organ.

B. Bailey & Company

1636 E. Charleston Blvd. • 382-1993

Bailey's is a classy little shop that does a nice job presenting its fine Lenox china, sterling silver, porcelain figures, costume jewelry, handmade quilts, vintage clothing and other collectibles. There are also a few quality pieces of furniture. When we last visited we found a hand-carved armoire, ivory-inlaid secretary and beveled-glass hutch. Unique to the shop is a selection of quaint metal door stops designed as, among other things, curled up cats and high-hat penguins.

Hub Cap Annie's

2112 E. Charleston Blvd. • 387-1148

This isn't really an antiques store, but it is within the antique guild's district, and the stock can be considered collectible. Anyway, Annie claims to have the world's largest collection of hub caps. Where she got them, or why she kept them, is a mystery, but if you have a need for a hubcap for a '53 DeSoto, she probably has one.

Maude's Antique Cottage

3310 E. Charleston Blvd. • 457-4379

Maude's is a converted house fronted by a white picket fence. Inside, you'll find Victorian-flavored American antiques along with gifts, new and antique dolls and Teddy bears. All of the furniture has been refinished, from marble-top hall tables and wash stands to pine and oak Hoosiers. Doll collectors can find

Maud Humphreys, Bessie Pease Gutmans, Madame Alexander, Jennys, a 1930s bisque Kewpie-like doll and a Victorian baby doll. Fiestaware, Jewel-T dinnerware, Minnie Mouse pieces and dancing animal pitchers are among the other collectibles.

Showcase Antiques

1632 E. Charleston Blvd. • 384-1117

For upscale antique hunters, Showcase Antiques tends toward well-designed and unusual furniture and china, with an accent on the Oriental. In this clean, airy shop, with Oriental rugs underfoot, you'll find such items as an elegant small desk with hidden compartments; a fringed silk grand-piano shawl with superlative Oriental embroidery; a fine rush-seat ladder-back bench; a small foldaway dining table with cane-seat chairs; and a sleek mahogany hall table and matching beveled mirror. Look in the back rooms where the owner has collected antique organs with pipes and foot pedals.

Silver Horse Antiques

1651 E. Charleston Blvd. • 385-2700

This charming little shop sells all categories of antiques and collectibles, from ebony dresser sets, cast-iron skillets, glassware, china, old bottles and cruets to oak sideboards and dressers — with prices ranging from a few dollars for an old glass-stoppered bottle to a thousand for a dining table. A special feature of the store is the functioning, one-chair (vintage, of course) barber shop, complete with wall cases displaying straight razors, shaving mugs and brushes.

Also under the store's roof is the Sunshine Clock Shop, 363-1312, a collection in the back room with a genuine Calumet wall clock, German-made and Tiffany grandfather clocks, mantel clocks like your grandmother owned and black-iron clocks from the 1930s. Ray Emery, one of eight certified clock-makers in the United States, collects clocks from around the country to display here and can also restore or repair yours.

Sugarplums

2022 E. Charleston Blvd. • 385-6059

Sugarplums is a treasure chest of collectibles, featuring fancy crystal and china, decorative wall plates, dolls, porcelain figurines, silverware, perfume bottles and evening bags from the 1920s and 30s and even the late 1800s. Although the furniture in this exquisite shop is for sale, the owner uses it to display miniatures such as salt-cellars and tiny spoons, thimbles, deco rings and Victorian cameos. In 1988, a perfume and scent-bottle society was formed here with 18 people from across the nation, growing to an international membership of 12,000. Here you will see everything from the massive 24-ounce perfume bottles down to the tiniest scent bottle and art-glass atomizers. You may also find such treasures as the 1800-1830s French crystal and gold-plate scent box, containing six bottles and funnels.

Toys of Yesteryear

2028 E. Charleston Blvd. • 598-4030

This charming little shop is Valhalla for toy-lovers. Among the treasures are train sets, dolls, metal toys, pull toys and windup toys. Some of the specialties are a collection of '50s Dinkie toys, a variety of battery-operated contraptions and tin windup toys. Prices on the tin toys range from $100 to $200. There is also a lovely collection of carnival dolls, most from Coney Island. If you grew up in New York, you may recall breaking these dolls in half to use as chalk when you played hopscotch on the sidewalk.

INSIDERS' TIP

The Forum Shops at Caesars Palace has more sales per square foot, $1,200, than any mall in the nation. The national average is $300 per square foot.

Yesteryear Mart

1626 E. Charleston Blvd. • 384-6946

A few blocks east of Antique Square, Yesteryear Mart shows off exquisite art-glass pieces, bowls, lamps and a fine jewelry collection as well as some furniture.

West Valley

Red Rooster Antiques

1109 Western Ave. • 382-5253

In a cavernous two-story, multiroom warehouse, Red Rooster Antiques carries the country look in collectibles, furniture and hand-crafted gifts. Glass milk bottles, canning jars, hand-embroidered linens and old kitchen tools such as hand-crank nut grinders or orange presses are available in quantity. In furniture, you'll find dressers, hall trees, cupboards, sideboards, a weathered trunk or perhaps a horse-collar mirror. There's even a niche for old rusted farm implements and livestock harnesses.

Sampler Shops

6115 W. Tropicana Ave. • 368-1170

This indoor mall—a converted grocery store—has more than 40,000 square feet where 200 dealers display their wares. You'll find antiques, books, collectibles, dolls, furniture, glassware, jewelry, toys and much more. There's also a small cafe.

Books and Periodicals

There's something introspective — as well as adventurous — about browsing through a bookstore. You're intensely alone until you stumble upon the right selection and are transported to a new and exciting world.

Used-book stores offer a unique adventure. Poring over titles, it's hard to know what treasures you'll uncover. The Las Vegas Valley has a marvelous selection of used-book stores. Here are some of the better ones, plus a few unique new booksellers as well.

The major book chains are all represented in Las Vegas.

The Strip Area

Get Booked

4640 Paradise Rd. • 737-7780

Located in the heart of the city's Gay Quarter, Get Booked is Las Vegas' source for gay, lesbian and feminist print material, including books, magazines, journals, flyers and a newsletter. A couple of popular titles include *Beautiful Boys*, an extravagant collection of erotica edited by John Patrick, and *Lesbian Bedtime Stories 2*, a pulpy collection of intrigue, humor, erotica, fantasy, romance and adventure. There's also a gay and lesbian video collection (for rent or sale), or you can purchase Billy, the world's first out-and-proud gay doll. On weekends, you can even get a free psychic reading.

International Newsstand

3900 Paradise Rd. • 796-9901

Located in the Citibank Business Park, the Newsstand has a large number of domestic and international magazines and out-of-town newspapers. Local bettors like the collection of sports publications, especially those devoted to handicapping and beating the spread. The place also has a mini market, if you're dying for a Nutrageous bar or a bottle of Evian.

Waldenbooks

Fashion Show Mall, 3200 Las Vegas Blvd. S. • 733-1049

Meadows Mall, 4300 Meadows Ln. • 870-4914 (West Valley)

Bibliophiles will find a good selection of mainstream works as well as multimedia sections for tapes, CDs, audio books and videos. The store in the Meadows Mall also has a well-stocked children's book section.

Downtown

Gambler's Book Club

630 S. 11th St. • 382-7555

The ultimate gambler's bookstore is

INSIDERS' TIP

The Las Vegas Antiques Guild consists of two dozen shops on E. Charleston Boulevard, east of Maryland Parkway.

Gambler's Book Club, which has become a Las Vegas institution since it opened in 1964. There are thousands of titles dealing with horse racing, sports handicapping, poker, blackjack, casino games, slot machines, gin rummy and jai alai, just to name a few. You can also purchase gambling and sports magazines as well as special workbooks for tracking teams and recording outcomes. Just for fun, you can also buy a small "home" version of the team schedules that the real sports books use. For balance, there's even a section of books on compulsive gambling and how to lick it. If you don't have time to examine everything, take one of the tabloid catalogues — GBC does a tremendous mail-order business.

Gundy's Book World

1442 E. Charleston Blvd. • 385-6043

This tiny storefront bookstore has a fair collection of out-of-print and rare editions, mostly paperbacks, dealing with aircraft, movies, Western Americana and sports. You'll also find crates of old magazines — *Life*, *National Geographic*, *Playboy*, *Saturday Evening Post*, etc.

East Valley

Albion Books

2466 E. Desert Inn Rd. • 792-9554

With more than 50,000 titles, Albion is the largest and best-stocked used-book store in town. It also has the best collection of first editions with specialties in mystery, literature, science fiction, Americana and railroad and military history.

B. Dalton Bookseller

Galleria Mall, 1300 W. Sunset Rd., Henderson • 434-1331
Boulevard Mall, 3680 S. Maryland Pkwy. • 735-0008
The Meadows Mall, 4300 Meadows Ln. • 878-4405 (West Valley)

As mall outlets, B. Dalton stores are smaller than most book chains, but they should fill the needs of most book buyers. The stores carry a good selection of Las Vegas and Nevada travel guides, and there's a voluminous section of occult, metaphysical and New Age works.

Barnes & Noble Booksellers

567 N. Stephanie Rd., Henderson • 434-1533
2191 N. Rainbow Rd. • 631-1775 (West Valley)

Barnes & Noble has a bookstore ambiance; you don't feel like you're browsing through a discount store. Both stores have excellent history sections, perhaps the best in town. The stores are paired with Starbucks coffee shops so you can sip while poring over the titles.

Bookstar

3910 S. Maryland Pkwy. • 732-7882
4730 Faircenter Pkwy. • 877-1872 (West Valley)

This national chain may be the Wal-Mart of booksellers — lots of books in an aircraft-hangar-style superstore. Nevertheless, Bookstar has a great selection of bargain-priced and marked-down books. You'll also find well-stocked shelves of local history, Las Vegas lore and gambling guides. The Maryland Parkway store has a larger selection of magazines and periodicals than the West Valley store plus it also provides table space so local arts groups can put out their free publications.

Christian Supply Centers

1766 E. Charleston Blvd. • 382-7889
643 N. Stephanie Blvd., Henderson • 434-4020
2550 S. Rainbow Blvd. • 876-2212 (West Valley)

Nevada's largest retailer of Christian supplies is a veritable supermarket of Bibles, inspirational books, music, video tapes, greeting cards and gifts as well as church and Sunday school supplies.

Parkland Books

3661 S. Maryland Pkwy. • 732-4474

Tucked away in the aging Maryland Square shopping plaza, Parkland Books sells used and out-of-print books only. But there are some quality books here, including a fine section on collectibles as well as natural history, nature, geography, Americana, conservation and children's literature.

Psychic Eye

953 E. Sahara Ave. • 369-6622
3315 E. Russell Rd. • 451-5777
4810 Spring Mountain Rd. • 368-7785
6848 W. Charleston Blvd. • 255-4477

The Psychic Eye has books on astrology, yoga, tarot cards, psychic healing and other metaphysical subjects. Plus you can have a psychic reading or purchase New Age products here.

Rebel Books

4440 S. Maryland Pkwy. • 796-4141

Rebel is a popular source of new and used course books for UNLV students. Even if you're not an undergrad you may someday have the need for a manual on differential equations or a legal, medical, technical or other reference guide. If you're in a hurry for knowledge, take home a stack of Cliff's Notes.

Readmore Books & Magazines

2560 S. Maryland Pkwy. • 732-4453
2250 E. Tropicana Ave. • 798-7863
6154 W. Flamingo Rd. • 362-3762
4454 N. Rancho Dr. • 645-6644

If you're looking for some light reading for lounging around the pool or the flight back home, go to Readmore Books & Magazines. Besides thousands of paperback books — mystery, romance, science fiction, mainstream, best-seller, etc. — the stores carry the largest collection of magazines in town — thousands of titles, from *Alaska Men* and *Columbia Journalism Review* to *UFO* to *Details for Men*.

West Valley

Bertae Specialties

2401 W. Charleston Blvd. • 878-5113

This is a unique shop because it's hard to tell what they're selling — inspirational, self-help, metaphysical, Christianity and meditation. You can also take a class in dowsing, hypnosis or ESP. Or you can purchase a lawn sprinkler or garden trowel. This must be what they mean by "one-stop shopping."

Book Magician

2202 W. Charleston Blvd. • 384-5838

Book Magician — formerly the well-respected Amber Unicorn — is a bibliophile's dream. Here you can browse through thousands of well-organized used and antiquarian books, while sipping a cup of coffee or tea. Especially interesting is the collection of local history and lore. You'll also find several stacks of astrology, occult and metaphysics. The cookbook collection is one of the largest in the city.

Borders Books

2323 S. Decatur Blvd. • 258-0999

Borders has a large selection of books of local interest, comfy chairs and couches for relaxed sampling, frequent book signings and author lectures, and a coffee/juice bar with tasty snacks. In addition to the usual range of new books — fiction, nonfiction, business, high-tech, etc. — Borders has a carefully chosen section of children's books.

Dead Poet Books

3858 W. Sahara Ave. • 227-4070

Don't let the bookstore's small size deter you. Sift through the used general and out-of-print hardbacks, and you'll probably find a gem among the stacks, anything from Paul Bowles' *The Sheltering Sky* to William Congreve's *The Double-Dealer*. In addition to the sizable literature collection, you'll find Western Americana, fantasy and science fiction.

Family Bookstores

1230 S. Decatur Blvd. • 870-9550

This well-stocked store next door to Blueberry Hill restaurant features inspirational books, bulletins, T-shirts, jewelry, tapes, CDs, wall plaques and other gifts.

INSIDERS' TIP

You can grocery shop by computer through Mobile Mart; call 656-2780 for details.

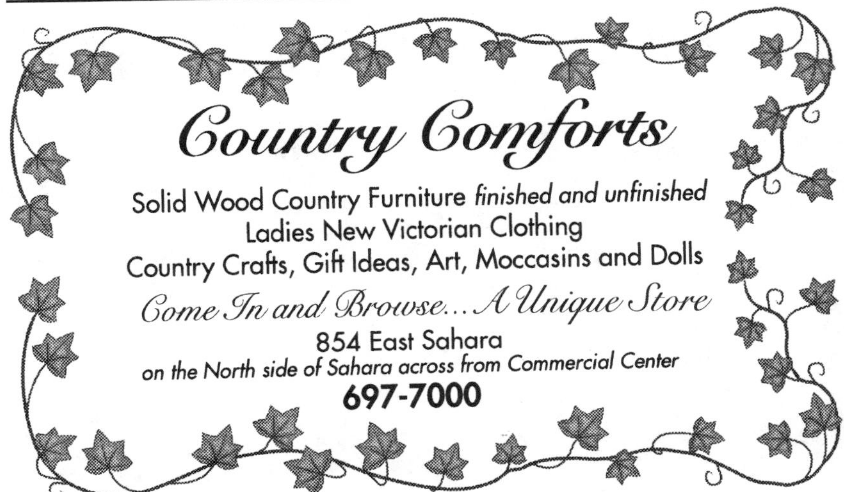

Lemstone Books
Meadows Mall, 4300 Meadows Ln.
• 870-9996

As part of a nationwide chain of Christian bookstores, Lemstone has a vast selection of inspirational books — Christian living, family, marriage, Bibles, devotional, current issues and fiction. You can also choose from greeting cards, tapes, CDs, jewerly and wall art. Among the popular gift items on hand are Precious Moments figurines and dolls, music boxes, banks, angels and the well-received Noah's Ark figures.

Mead Publishing
515 S. Commerce St. • 387-8750

For books on the history, restoration or collecting of slot machines come to Mead Publishing, two blocks west of Main Street. You'll also find a variety of books on pinball machines, juke boxes and other coin-operated collectibles as well as gambling-related publications. And Mead publishes a monthly magazine, *Loose Change*, for collectors of coin-op equipment, mostly slot machines.

Traveling Books & Maps
4001 S. Decatur Blvd. • 871-8082

Everything for the traveler — armchair or aisle seat — is in this store in the Renaissance Shopping Center at Flamingo Road. Of course, you can choose from hundreds of guidebooks, both foreign and domestic, but you'll also find specialty books, such as adventure and economy guides, and special language aides. You can also select from maps, globes, passport cases and travel accessories, and owner Jerry Netzky promises he will laminate anything.

Gambling Supplies and Memorabilia

Instead of stuffing coins into a slot machine (the casinos will hate us for this), why not buy one and take it home with you? They are legal in about 40 states (the dealers have updated lists), and local merchants usually guarantee their machines and ship them to your home. Most of the reconditioned, electronic slot machines start at around $600. Video poker machines are slightly higher. If you shop and haggle, you may save on the price. The mechanically operated antique slot machines, however, are more costly. A vintage War Eagle or a Bursting Cherry can cost between $2,500 and $3,000. The genuine antiques — 100 years and older — can command prices in five figures. Some of the better places to purchase gambling equipment are in or near downtown.

The Strip Area

C.J.'s Casino Emporium
2780 Las Vegas Blvd. S. • 893-0660

If you haven't had enough of slot machines,

C.J.'s will sell you a reconditioned reel slot or video poker machine from its inventory of more than 2,000. The machines come with a one-year guarantee but, best of all, they come with a key to the cash box. Also available are video keno machines, blackjack machines and other amusement devices — juke boxes, hand-held video games and gumball machines, to name a few. A 10- to 15-year old working slot machine may cost from $500 to $1,000, while a used video poker machine is slightly higher — an IGT Fortune costs about $800 and an IGT Deuces Wild or Bonus Poker will run about $1,500. The antique slots include Mills and Jennings classics, usually with new castings, wood cases and fully-operational (restored, if necessary) inside mechanisms. Typical prices for antique slots: a Mills Golden Nugget (Black), $2,695, and a Jennings Sun Chief, $3,595.

Downtown

Gamblers General Store

800 S. Main St. • 382-9903

One of the largest collections of slot machines — as well as other gambling supplies — is at Gamblers General Store. Here you can select from several dozen reconditioned and vintage slot machines. Also on hand are full-size blackjack, crap and roulette tables — complete with green-felt layouts — priced from $1,200 to $5,000. Or if you need a folding poker table for your friendly Saturday-night get-togethers, buy one for about $250. The General Store also stocks every type of gambling paraphernalia imaginable. In addition to hundreds of gambling books and videos and customized poker chips, you can buy playing cards, dice sets, coin changers, green visor shades, raffle drums, bingo cages and boards, a dealer apron (one size fits all), croupier sticks and felt layouts for every type of casino game. There are even dice-inlaid toilet seats.

House of Antique Slots

1236 Las Vegas Blvd. S. • 382-1520

This dealer has a museum-like collection of older gambling devices as well as antique vending machines, furniture and wall art. The kind of choice pieces you might find include a parquet wheel of fortune, Bird of Paradise jukebox by Wurlitzer, reconditioned gas station pumps, coin-operated candy machines and more. Some of the early slot machines, many from the 1920s and 1930s, include Jennings Chief, Mills Bursting Cherry and Mills Castle Top.

West Valley

Bud Jones Company

3640 S. Valley View Blvd. • 876-2782

You're in the chips when you come to Bud Jones, a supplier of official chips to the casinos. Bud Jones' custom chips for home use come in about 15 different colors and are gold embossed with up to three initials on both sides. You can also purchase fancy chip storage and carrying cases — vinyl covered with polished brass hardware — that hold from 300 to 1,000 chips.

Paul-Son Gaming Supplies

2121 Industrial Rd. • 384-2425

Paul-Son is a major supplier of gambling chips to the casino industry, but you can purchase customized chips for home use. The home versions aren't exactly the same as the casino chips, which have a special composition to defeat counterfeiters, but you'll barely tell the difference. Paul-Son also sells playing cards, dice, tabletop layouts for blackjack, craps and roulette and casino furniture.

The Poker Chip Store

4460 W. Reno Ave. • 365-1400

This is a great place to purchase new and used poker chips, especially collectible chips from defunct hotels such as the Dunes, Haci-

INSIDERS' TIP

Las Vegas started to become a family destination in 1968 with the opening of Circus Circus, site of the world's largest permanent circus. Since then, Circus Circus has built the Excalibur and Luxor hotels on the southern end of The Strip.

enda and the Silver Slipper. The store also has a large collection of gambling books, videos, computer software and other supplies. For a free mail-order catalog, call the above number or fax to 365-1408.

Hotel Shops and Souvenirs

Virtually every hotel and casino has a gift shop, usually a haven for souvenir T-shirts, coffee mugs, snow domes and salt and pepper shakers. But the gift shops at some of the resorts sell interesting, though often pricier souvenirs, of your visit. We've listed a few hotel shops that stand out for their unusual or bargain-priced mementos.

The Strip Area

Treasure Island
3300 Las Vegas Blvd. S. • 894-7111

For upscale artifacts try the shops at Treasure Island, where you'll find Moroccan chests inlaid with stone and camel bone and intricately patterned ceramic platters, bowls, pitchers and Tiffany-style vases.

Excalibur
3850 Las Vegas Blvd. S. • 597-7777

At Excalibur you can choose from medieval reproductions of Spanish weaponry, wizard sculptures, chess sets, paintings, lamps, pewter shields and axes.

The Mirage
3400 Las Vegas Blvd. S. • 791-7111

For gifts with a tropical flavor, visit the Mirage. You'll find a complete collection of carved fish from Bali, South Sea totems and feathered dolls.

Luxor Hotel
3900 Las Vegas Blvd. S. • 262-4000

The shops at Luxor specialize in Egyptian-made ceramic vases, hand-tooled leather boxes, hand-blown perfume bottles, games and Christmas ornaments. You can also buy reproductions of the jewelry, papyrus scrolls and other treasures found in King Tut's tomb.

O'Shea's Casino
3555 Las Vegas Blvd. S. • 792-0777

If you're in need of some Irish luck, stop at O'Shea's and try the gift shop, which is overflowing with shamrock pins, shirts, caps and four-leaf clovers — all in white and emerald green.

Frontier Hotel
3120 Las Vegas Blvd. S. • 794-8200

The Country Village gift shop at the Frontier Hotel has quirky, modern-day souvenirs. But they're displayed in antique hutches that are real collector's items, embellished with ornate carvings of fruit and flowers with curlicue legs signed by their talented maker.

Flamingo Hilton Hotel
3555 Las Vegas Blvd. S. • 733-3111

No other Vegas hotel has as many shops devoted to itself than the Flamingo Hilton. In addition to the "regular" logo souvenir shop, the Flamingo also has Flamingo Apparel, Flamingo Bazaar, Flamingo Toyland and Flamingo Kiddie Shop.

Toni Cats & Company at the Riviera Hotel
2901 Las Vegas Blvd. S. • 734-7447

At this shop you'll find irresistible treasures such as diamond-studded collars, velvet leashes, rubber and plastic toys, gourmet treats and a variety of thoughtful gifts for that special cat or dog in your life.

The Western Emporium at Sam's Town
5111 Boulder Hwy. • 454-8048

The Western Emporium has 25,000 square feet of Western wear, accessories, Southwestern art, gifts and more. See our Western Wear section for a complete listing.

INSIDERS' TIP

The Western Emporium at Sam's Town is the state's largest retailer of Western wear and accessories.

Hotel Shopping Arcades

Listed below are the few hotels that have a large enough cluster of shops to be classified as an arcade or mini shopping mall.

The Strip Area

Avenue Shoppes

Bally's Las Vegas, 3645 Las Vegas Blvd. S. • 739-4111

Downstairs at Bally's, the Avenue Shoppes include about 20 retail stores offering a variety of items including men's and women's apparel, gifts, art, collectibles and T-shirts. Also along the Avenue is a Bally's logo shop, the largest in the city. In addition to high-fashion boutiques — Marshall Rousso for women, Mort Wallin for men — you can pore over Far Eastern arts and crafts at Arts of Asia or discover authentic Indian and Southwestern art and jewelry at the Indian-owned TePee.

Appian Way

Caesars Palace, 3570 Las Vegas Blvd. S. • 731-7110

Though not as large as the Bally's arcade, Appian Way is home to some of the world's most exclusive shops. Designer women's shoes from France are sold at Del Monaco Shoe Salon, while Cuzzen's caters to the well-heeled man. Gucci's, famous for its crocodile shoes and handbags, is worth exploring, even if you don't buy one of their $6,000 purses or a pair of $900 loafers. Exclusive jeweler Cartier and Galerie Michaelangelo art gallery are also part of this scaled-down Rodeo Drive.

The Masquerade Village Shops

The Rio, 3700 W. Flamingo Rd. • 252-7777

The Rio's new Masquerade Village Shops invite visitors to stroll down replicas of 200-year-old Tuscan streets and browse among 26 retail stores. Among the interesting outlets are a Nicole Miller for designer silk sportswear for men and women; Speedo Authentic Fitness for running and swimming accessories; Reel Outfitter for the fly-fishing gear you've always dreamed about; and the Nawlins Store, for a taste of New Orleans favorites such as fresh-baked beignets and hot chickory coffee and a unique voodoo shop for amulets, charms and handmade voodoo masks.

Tower Shops

Stratosphere, 2000 Las Vegas Blvd. S. • 388-1130

This international-themed shopping promenade is one flight up the escalator leading to the 1,200-foot-high tower. The 30-plus shops are found along street scenes from Paris, Hong Kong and New York. Some of the popular stores include Kid Vegas, Victoria's Secret, Perfumania and Bernini Sport. When you're ready for a cool sweet treat stop in at Haagen-Dazs for a cup of coffee ice cream.

Malls

The Strip Area

Belz Factory Outlet World

7400 Las Vegas Blvd. S. • 896-5599

With more than 140 stores, the Belz Factory Outlet World ranks among the top-three shopping malls in Nevada and is the largest factory outlet mall in the United States. Located at Las Vegas Boulevard S. and Warm Springs Road, Belz is about 7 miles south of Tropicana Avenue. In addition to the myriad of shops, the mall has a carousel for kids plus two food courts. Nearly half the outlet stores sell men's, women's and children's clothing. Among the popular brand names represented are Bugle Boy, Geoffrey Beene, Jones New York, Levi's and Oshkosh B'gosh. Some of the more interesting shops include Blue Wave, for everything in tropical prints; the Hat Company, if you've been out in the sun too long; and The American Outpost, a kind of half-price version of Banana Republic, where you'll find a good selection of safari shorts, gingham shirts, cotton twill and other cool, though rough-hewn, clothes. Belz also has more than 30 jewelry and accessory shops to help accent your fancy new outfits, including After Thoughts, where you can pick up a glitzy bracelet, earrings, necklace or, heaven forbid, nose ring. If your ensemble is finally complete, but you lack a fragrance, go to Perfumania.

Here you'll find every type of designer perfume. The store even stocked Omar Shariff samplers when no one — except Bloomingdale's, his exclusive distributor — had them. But go easy on the samplers, or you'll leave the store smelling like a scratch-and-sniff card from hell.

Unlike many malls, where men pass the hours on "loser" benches while holding their wives' purchases, Belz has shops geared to the male's interest. Besides the usual offerings like Nike and Rockport, Belz has testosterone-stimulating outlets such as Bose, for turbo-powered, molar-rattling speaker systems; Casio and its myriad of hand-held electronic wizardry; and Black & Decker, an entire store devoted to the ultimate male diversion — power tools! Before you leave the mall, visit Flashbacks. This small shop is crammed with vintage collectibles and replicas. Some of the treasures include reproductions of military radios, black powder guns, juke boxes, popcorn machines, soft-drink dispensers, neon signs and old jewelry — all reconditioned to mint, working condition. There is also a magnificent collection of signed posters, newspapers and photographs of Hollywood's greats, including a boyish Paul Newman for $350, a hard-staring Clint Eastwood for $295 and a dynamite Whitney Houston for $295.

Fashion Show Mall

3200 Las Vegas Blvd. S. • 369-8382

The Fashion Show Mall is the jewel of the city's shopping malls, featuring more than 130 shops on two enclosed levels. Despite its Strip location (between Treasure Island and Frontier hotels), you'll find as many locals shopping here as tourists. The mall is anchored by five major department stores: Macy's, Dillard's, Robinsons-May, Saks Fifth Avenue and Nieman Marcus. And two major department stores, Bloomingdale's and Lord & Taylor, will be added before the year 2000 when the Fashion Show completes an expansion that will double its size to 1.8 million square feet. The mall is also home to dozens of upscale specialty and designer shops such as Louis Vuitton, Amici, Abercrombie & Fitch, Caché and Liz Claiborne, to name a few.

Some of the more interesting finds are at the smaller boutiques. For instance, have you ever found yourself in a shop where every item grabs your attention? Where everything looks like it was tastefully and painstakingly selected just for you? Carlan's Gifts is that type of shop — an enchanting little boutique that sells trendy house furnishings and classy gifts. If you're into leather, clothing that is, North Beach Leather sells nifty apparel, men's and women's, designed by San Francisco's Michael Hoban, who originally started his business making jackets for the San Francisco Police Department and Hell's Angels. Today they're worn by television celebrities such as Arsenio Hall and Chuck Woolery. Incidentally, this is the shop where Elvis spent $17,000 on his first visit and another $21,000 over the next few weeks. Many of his selections were gifts for friends. Ask store manager Joseph De Nucci to tell you the story.

The Mall is a great place to feed your foot fetish. Amici and the Brass Boot sell quality shoes for men, while Norman Kaplan and Joyce Selby offer the same for women. Footlocker sells outdoor hiking and walking shoes. For fun footwear, try Bianca. If the sequined tennis shoes and lizard pumps knock your socks off, walk down to the Gap and have your feet recovered with stretchy knee-highs. Among the two dozen women's fashion boutiques are the glitzy but tasteful Lillie Rubin for extravagant evening gowns and Mondi for that oh-so-chic upscale Third World look. Quality men's apparel is sold at Detour-Palzileri, Amici and Uomo-Uomo Sport, where you can still buy a designer linen suit for less than $800.

The Mall is home to several excellent commercial art galleries that often host exhibits from artists such as Picasso and Dali. Wyland Galleries and Centaur Galleries also carry works by people-pleasing artists like Erte and Leroy Neiman. History buffs will want to stop at the Serendipity Gallery of Collectibles, which specializes in rare manuscripts, letters and photographs of famous people, from Abraham Lincoln and Marilyn Monroe to John Lennon and Babe Ruth. For gadget-lovers there's Future Tronics for high-tech toys and electronic gizmos, while real kids can find treasures galore at Game Keeper.

The Forum Shops at Caesars Palace

3500 Las Vegas Blvd. S. • 893-4800

The upscale Forum Shops adjacent to

Caesars Palace is much more than a glitzy shopping mall — it's a major tourist attraction designed along the lines of an ancient Roman street with statues that talk, fountains that dance and a sky that changes from dawn to dusk. The mall features more than 70 unique shops and restaurants with an additional 37 new stores expected to open by the end of 1997 as part of a 283,000-square-foot expansion. Among the newcomers will be F.A.O. Schwartz, Fendi, Polo and NikeTown and two new restaurants including Wolfgang Puck's Chinois. The new wing to the Forum Shops will extend west from the hotel's Fountain of the Gods, with storefronts surrounding a central Great Hall where an Atlantis-themed attraction will entertain visitors with animated robotic figures and sophisticated special effects.

Among the unique shops worth visiting at the Forum is Bebe, a New York-style designer boutique specializing in moderately priced form-fitting suits with hot pants, linen jump suits and black leather vests with crystal pleats. For ultra-chic (and ultra-expensive) women's wear visit the French Room and Gianni Versace, where you might stumble upon a snakeskin bodysuit or a beaded leather jacket. More conservative and reasonably priced attire, such as linen and silk skirts and suits, can be found at Express. Men can walk next door to Structure and find excellent prices on linen shirts and slacks and silk shirts and ties. A fun spot to visit is Boogie's Diner, where you can grab a sandwich or buy a leather and denim jacket, sequined sweatsuit or any number of items from the Aspen-based boutique. For athletic wear it's Just for Feet, which features the largest selection of tennis shoes in town. You can even try out a pair of Air Jordans on the shop's wooden-floored basketball court.

No mall is complete without a sweet shop, and the Forum Shops has two: the Sweet Factory for colorful confections and the Chocolate Chariot for hand-dipped chocolate fruits and more. A unique gift store is West of Santa Fe, which sells genuine Southwestern and Native American art and jewelry. In addition to the Zuni turquoise and Hopi silver jewelry and bolos, there are hand-carved fetishes, kachina dolls, feathered headdresses, pottery and blankets. The Forum also has several excellent spots to refuel, including the always-busy Planet Hollywood, with two levels of dining, cocktail bars and Hollywood memorabilia; Bertolini's, when you're ready to dine al fresco on quality Italian food in full view of the masses; and The Palm, the campy import from L.A.'s hip Melrose district.

FYI

Unless otherwise noted, the area code for all phone numbers listed in this chapter is 702.

East Valley

Boulevard Mall

3528 S. Maryland Pkwy.
• 735-8268

After the Boulevard's recent expansion to more than 1.2 million square feet, the oldest mall in Las Vegas is now the largest as well. In addition to the 140-plus stores and elaborate food court, the Boulevard has a variety of services that cater to customers' needs. Among them are a foreign currency exchange; notary, fax and copy service; valet parking; a taxi stand; and a public bus stop. Along with a local radio station, seniors' magazine and medical clinic, the single-level mall also sponsors The Boulevard Walking Club, in which members take organized walks through the mall's climate-controlled confines twice weekly (see our close-up in the Retirement chapter). Members also benefit from blood-pressure checks and health counseling from nurses from the Kimberly Quality Care clinic. If you're interested, stop by the mall's customer-service booth.

The mall is anchored by four mid-priced department stores: Macy's, Dillards, Sears and JCPenney. Most of the men's and women's clothing stores are geared toward younger, mid-scale buyers. Stores include Casual Corner, The Limited, Lane Bryant and Contempo Casuals for women and Structure, Oak Tree, JW, Coda and Harris & Frank for men. The Boulevard also has a vast array of shoe stores, jewelers, sunglass boutiques, card shops, booksellers, a pet store, luggage shops, opticians, hair salons, travel agencies — retailers to nearly every product and service imaginable. However, some of the more intriguing stores for gifts and specialty items include The Nature Company, The Mole Hole and African

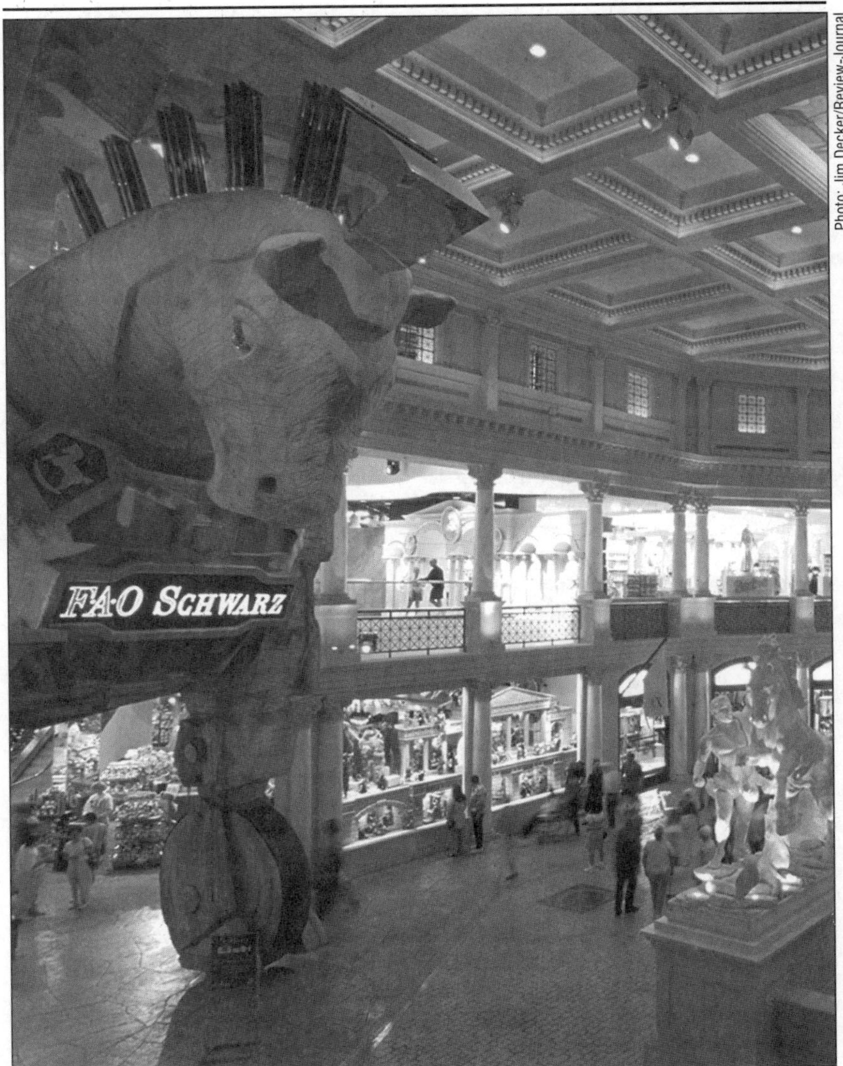

The recently expanded Forum Shops at Caesars Palace is the country's most successful shopping mall in terms of sales per square foot.

and World Imports for an assortment of figures, masks and wall art from Africa.

Galleria at Sunset Mall
1300 W. Sunset Rd., Henderson
• 434-0202

The two-level, million-square-foot mall is the newest in southern Nevada and is also the most attractive. There are fountains and pools throughout as well as indoor trees that reach toward the arched ceilings and domed skylights overhead. It all makes for a very pleasant shopping/browsing experience. The mall is anchored by four major department stores: Dillards, Mervyn's, JCPenney and Robinson's-May. In addition, the mall has about 110 stores that include the usual mix of men's and women's clothiers such as Miller's Outpost, J. Riggings, Victoria's Secret, Hot Topic and Lerner New York as well as a variety of gift boutiques and stores for shoes, home furnishings, sporting goods, jewelers, eyewear, accessories, books and records. Among the more interesting shops is Bebe, a voguish designer of stylish women's outfits such as a form-fitting, double breasted blazer with a crepe miniskirt. The only Eddie Bauer in town is here, along with its cutting-edge recreational clothing. Strangely lacking, however, are the variety "fun" products usually sold at Eddie's — backpacks, pocket knives, compasses, waterproof cases and other hiking, cycling and outdoor accessories. Instead, there's a small assortment of watches, sunglasses, penlights and other products in the corner of the store.

Other interesting shops include Nava Hopi, for Native American jewelry, kachina dolls, amulets, dream catchers, suede and leather clothing and other artifacts, and Pacific Sunwear, which is stocked full of tropical island products from flip flops and sunscreen to Hawaiian print shirts to puka shell necklaces.

West Valley

Meadows Mall

4300 Meadows Ln. • 878-4849

The westside version of the Boulevard Mall is the Meadows Mall, which is anchored by Macy's, Dillards, Sears and JCPenney department stores. The two-level mall offers shoppers about 140 stores, boutiques and eateries plus a huge merry-go-round for the kiddies. The Meadows is also the frequent site of weekend art festivals and antiques shows, and the massive food court is a popular hangout for neighborhood teenagers.

Among the usual complement of mall shops are Victoria's Secret, Express, Hot Topic, Coffee Beanery, Petite Sophisticate, Charlotte Russe and The Limited. As a convenience to customers, the mall provides its own trolley that shuttles to and from the CAT bus transportation center downtown. The trolley leaves every hour Monday through Saturday. Call 229-6012 for exact times.

Pawn Shops

If you have a sharp eye for a bargain, especially in jewelry, consider one of the local pawn shops. Gamblers frequently turn to them for quick cash, so you can often find an inexpensive VCR, guitar, desktop computer or gold ring. The most well-stocked shops are found in or near downtown.

The Strip Area

Bobby's Jewelry & Loan

626 Las Vegas Blvd. S. • 382-2486

Bobby's is one of the classiest pawn shops in town, offering jewelry ranging from smoke sapphire rings and tourmaline brooches to sterling silver Hopi bracelets. Bobby's is also one of the few shops that sells sports memorabilia, collectibles and trading cards, in addition to cameras, guns, golf clubs, TVs and VCRs.

Downtown

The Pawn Place

119 N. Fourth St. • 385-7296

Just a block north of the Fremont Street Experience, the Pawn Place is well-supplied with loose and set diamonds, silverware, watches, handguns, tools and musical instruments. There's also a roomful of electronic equipment such as amplifiers, TVs, VCRs, camcorders and other products. For late-night transactions, there's a 24-hour night window.

Pioneer Loan & Jewelry

111 N. First St. • 384-2970

This venerable shop across the street from Binion's Horseshoe has been doing business since the 1930s. In addition to the usual VCRs, handguns and saber saws, Pioneer sells Persian rugs, antique teddy bears and unusual art objects. If you're looking for something different, the shop has an interesting collection of antique jewelry. And the gemologist on premises will appraise your jewels or make jewelry repairs.

Stoney's Loan & Jewelry

126 S. First St. • 384-0819

Located across the street from the Golden

Nugget, Stoney's specializes in gold rings, rope chains and other jewelry. You'll also find a variety of diamonds and other precious gems, plus a nice selection of cameras and electronic equipment.

Shopping Centers and Districts

The Strip Area

Factory Stores of America
9155 Las Vegas Blvd. S. • 897-9090

Even though this horseshoe-shaped shopping center with 50 outlet stores and loads of parking is less than 10 years old, it looks like a ghost town waiting to happen. Despite the name-brand retailers, much of the center's business has been pulled away by the Belz Factory Outlet World — a newer, larger and fully enclosed and air-conditioned mall — just a couple miles away. Moreover, many of the retailers with outlets in Factory Stores have opened duplicate outlets in the Belz mall, making it more difficult for the Factory Stores shops to compete. Nevertheless, you may be able to find special bargains as these shops try to remain competitive. In any case, when you shop at Factory Stores there's never a parking problem or long lines. Stores include: American Tourister, Book Warehouse, Corn-

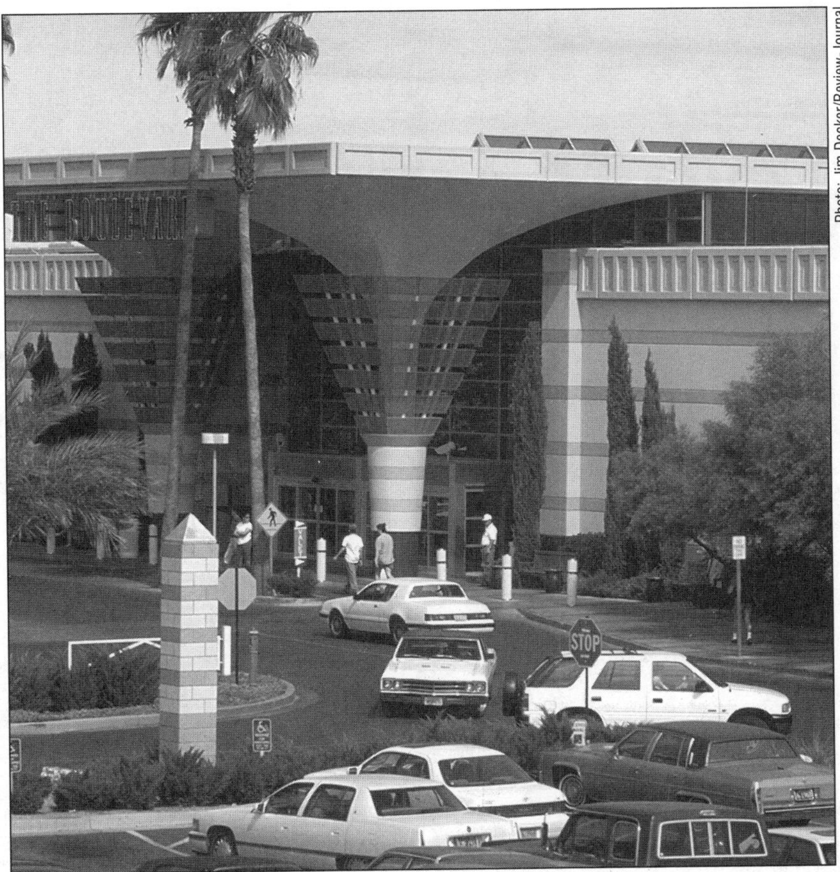

Photo: Jim Decker/Review-Journal

The Boulevard Mall on Maryland Parkway is the state's largest commercial mall.

ing Revere, Florsheim shoes, Geoffrey Beene, Izod, Jamaica Joe's, London Fog, Nine West, Rocky Mountain Chocolate Factory, Van Heusen and Westport Ltd.

Downtown/Glitter Gulch

The Las Vegas neighborhood known as Glitter Gulch, which stretches from Main Street to Las Vegas Boulevard, suffered a commercial decline during the 1980s, mainly because of the shift in tourism to The Strip's megaresorts and the growth of retail centers in the suburbs. The Fremont Street Experience has revitalized the downtown area and breathed new life into the shopping opportunities. Most of the shops on and around Fremont Street consist of souvenir and T-shirt shops, drug stores, check-cashing outlets, pawn shops and fast-food eateries. There are a few gems, however, hidden in the downtown cityscape.

Desert Indian Shop

108 N. Third St. • 384-4977

This shop is notable for its imaginative collection of Navajo, Zuni and Hopi jewelry and crafts. The turquoise-inlaid bolos and rings and etched-silver bracelets are particularly beautiful. If you're lucky, you might even meet some of the artists who come here from Arizona and New Mexico to sell their handiwork. Also on sale are artifacts of the Old West.

Turquoise Chief

1334 Las Vegas Blvd. S. • 383-6069

Just a few blocks south of Fremont Street, you'll find the city's largest selection of turquoise jewelry at the Turquoise Chief. It also handles Native American sand paintings, dolls, bolos and hand-carved fetishes.

Sunglass City

506 Fremont St. • 388-0622

Sunglass City has a huge assortment of designer sunglasses — everything from Ray Ban and Revo to Porsche and Serengetti. Even more fun than picking out a pair is haggling over the price. You can save considerably over what you would pay in a mall boutique if you're persistent. Sunglass City also stock thousands of men's and women's watches, from 14-karat gold Rolexes to $1.99 plastic models.

Ray's Beaver Bag

727 Las Vegas Blvd. S. • 386-8746

One of downtown's best shopping destinations actually defies description: This is the strangest and most interesting store in town. Billed as a pre-1840, black-powder gun shop, the store is more like a Yukon trading post. Of course, it does stock a complete line of black-powder muzzle loaders — all reproductions — and accessories. But there's so much more: hunting knives and tomahawks, cast-iron cookware, coonskin caps, snake skin-tanning kits, beeswax from Maine, handmade moccasins, leather pouches and bags and authentic Indian porcupine-quill jewelry. Even if you don't intend to go trapping or fur-trading, you'll want to look at the racks of pioneer and Western clothing. There are cotton frontier dresses, dusters, capotes made from Hudson Bay blankets, a full-length bearskin coat and the original calvary coat worn by actor Gary Cole in the film *Son of Morning Star*.

Four Aces Liquor

124 S. First St. • 386-9905

If you're looking for an out-of-town newspaper or want to buy a Daily Racing Form, go to Four Aces, where you can also buy the usual selection of cheesy T-shirts, packs of gum and packaged liquor.

Bonanza: World's Largest Gift Shop

2400 Las Vegas Blvd. S. • 384-0005

In the shadow of the Stratosphere Tower, this gift shop is right across the street from Holy Cow! Casino and Brewery. Stop and browse; even if you don't buy anything, you'll be amazed by the selection of souvenirs — dice clocks, jewelry, T-shirts, moccasins, plaques, tumblers, X-rated gags, windup animals, cactus, toys, UNLV paraphernalia, fudge and aspirin. Who knows, you may find the perfect gift for that not-so-perfect uncle.

Bell, Book & Candle

1725 E. Charleston Blvd. • 384-6807

If you need a change in your luck, or love life, there's this shop, which sells potions, charms, talismans, crystal balls and other "magick" supplies. Magick because the emphasis here is on sorcery and witchcraft, rather than New Age occult and metaphysics. The store also stocks rare candles, books and tapes; conducts classes in witchcraft; and has a black cat patrolling the display cases.

Valentino's Zoot Suit

906 S. 6th St. • 383-9555

A great spot to find a slinky 1930-40s evening gown is Valentino's Zoot Suit, where you may also discover a fox stole, sequinned party dress, satin nightgown or any other type of vintage clothing — ranging from the avant garde to the whimsical. Valentino also has a fabulous selection of men's ties from the 1920s, '30s and '40s, the kind you wish your dad would've saved.

The Attic

1018 S. Main St. • 388-4088

For a double dose of retro clothing, also check out this funky green brick building with two full floors of men's and women's clothes, shoes, accessories — even underwear — from the 1940s through 1970s. There's also a small collection of antiques, a jukebox, a '50s dinette, a floor-model radio, tables, appliances, Coke dispensers and more. But clothes take center stage, and some of the memorable blasts from the past might include a 1960s bandstand tuxedo with satin piping, a white go-go dress with yellow daisies, letterman sweaters and jackets, jeans, double-knit pants, military fatigues, flight suits, lamb broadtail jackets, matching pillbox hats and silk ties from the 1940s. For a 1970s look, try platform shoes and boots, some with rhinestones embedded in the heels. Don't overlook the glass display cases — they hold such treasures as 1960s cat-eye frames and rhinestone junk jewelry. There's no doubt you can burn a couple hours browsing and reminiscing, so try the upstairs cafe for designer coffees and fresh pastries.

East Valley

Commercial Center

953 E. Sahara Ave. • no phone

Constructed in 1962, Commercial Center is one of the oldest retail shopping centers in the city. Built like a U-shaped fort with parking in the center, it is a cluster of about 30 specialty shops and restaurants, flanked by Sahara and Karen avenues, a block west of Maryland Parkway. Although the Center is home to several clothing boutiques, an arts supply store, an athletic club and two pool halls, it is a good spot for Asian shops and restaurants. Here you can slurp noodles, shop for a kimono or find the perfect bonsai pot. Two markets, Oriental Foods and Asian Market are filled with Japanese and Chinese foodstuffs, from black seaweed-wrapped crackers to dried cuttlefish. These are excellent places to buy fresh fish, exotic mushrooms and other herbs. You'll also find shelves of inexpensive porcelain tea and saki sets, bowls, chopsticks, fans, magazines and videos. For a wider variety, consider David Ming Oriental Art Goods. Ming's is a fabulous source of bamboo and rattan furniture and hand-carved fish bone, ivory, jade, rose quartz, amethyst and lapis figures. There are also rice-paper scrolls, hand-painted screens and silk kimonos. Nearby is the Korean Art & Gift Shop, specializing in the calligraphy and ceramic art of Changpo. Considered a national hero in his native Korea, Changpo is a master of the ancient art of calligraphy. His work, which appears on scrolls and vases, captures the artistic spirit of the 5,000-year-old tradition. Also available are watercolor drawings of Korean landscapes, ceramics, Korean cosmetics, kimonos and silk jackets.

For serious or novice philatelists, Evans Stamps has a worldwide collection. Here you can buy single-issue stamps or complete collections. If your soul needs healing, and whose doesn't, consider the Psychic Eye. Here you can buy herbs, crystals and amulets, pyramid generators, meditation flutes, occult and New Age books, whose subjects cover astrology, Vedanta, Theosophy, Rosicrucian, pyramid power, crystal healing, tarot, Taoism, to name a few. You can also receive a psychic reading here. Before you laugh, let us say that one of us used to believe psychics were lucky prognosticators, with a gift of gab and an ear for fad. But that was before we had our fortune told by Patrice. Her predictions were uncanny; it was like sitting in the front seat with Mother Teresa. She's good, but you must call for an appointment. Other locations for this cosmic chain store include: 3315 E. Russell Road, 4810 Spring Mountain Road and 6848 W. Charleston Boulevard.

If you suffer from slot machine elbow, try Shiatsu Acupressure of Nevada, operated by licensed therapist Jin Shin Jyutsu. If words like "psychedelic" and "love-in" ring up good memories, you'll want to visit Vintage Madness. This funky little store is vintage 1960s, overflowing with racks of bell-bottoms, tie-dyed T-shirts, flower-power skirts, Jackie K. dresses, Nehru jackets, Madras shirts, Cuban-heel shoes, costume jewelry and much more. To enhance your shopping pleasure, rock music from the 1960s plays constantly, and the interior is a colorful psychedelic explosion.

Maryland Square Shopping Center

3661 S. Maryland Pkwy. • 734-7727

Built in 1965, this open-air shopping center has been upstaged over the years by the Boulevard Mall across the street. It usually runs about 50 percent occupancy, but some of the core tenants have remained and thrived. The center is anchored by Pay Less Drugs, a 24-hour pharmacy that sells a variety of home and electronic products, food, beverages, magazines and the like. The other large tenant is the Sports Authority, where you can purchase anything and everything related to sports, athletics, games, boating, etc. A fun place to browse is the Quilted Bear, a handmade-crafts mall where you can rummage through hand-crafted dolls, quilts, pot holders, wall hangings, ceramic and porcelain artwork, metal sculpture, wood boxes, decorative tins, milk cans, rubber stamp supplies and much more. Of special interest is a delightful room devoted year-round to Christmas ornaments and decorations. Some of the other tenants on The Square include Mr. Greengenes, a well-stocked health-food store where you can load up on vitamins and food supplements, natural health and beauty products, dried fruit and raw nuts, juices and other products. There's also a lunch stand for fresh sandwiches and fresh-squeezed juices.

You'll also find an arts and crafts boutique, Angels, that sells nothing but angels; the Needlenook for crewel, embroidery and knitting needs; Ed's Smoke Shop for tobacco and smoking supplies; and India Spices, a sweet-smelling Taj barbecue market where you can pick up fresh goat leg, lamb, poya, chutney as well as Indian videos and publications.

FYI

Unless otherwise noted, the area code for all phone numbers listed in this chapter is 702.

West Valley

Chinatown Plaza

4215 Spring Mountain Rd. • 221-8448

The growing Asian population in Las Vegas has spawned a few pockets of Chinese, Vietnamese, Philippine, Thai, Korean and Japanese stores and restaurants throughout the valley. Some, which are located in Commercial Center and along E. Charleston Boulevard, have become popular for their authentic food and exotic store products — produce, gifts, cultural wares, publications and videos. The Chinatown Plaza, built in the mid 1990s, is the city's first planned shopping center designed specifically for Asian tenants. Located just a couple miles west of the Strip, the Plaza has more than 28 stores and restaurants offering jade, gold and ivory jewelry, exotic herbs and medicines, hand-crafted furniture, Chinese literature and music, arts and more. You can even arrange an Oriental wedding in front of the Kuan-Yin in the wedding temple and culminate the ceremony by striking the 5-foot bronze wedding bell. Of course, if you enjoy Chinese food, the Plaza has several of the city's best Asian restaurants. Among the Plaza's more fascinating shops are 99 Ranch Market for live fish and crab, fresh vegetables and assortment of exotic condiments, spices and sauces; Chong Hing Jewelers, where you can pore over 24-karat gold, jade, pearl and semiprecious stones as well as hand-carved ivory; Mei Li Boutique, with a variety of silk kimonos, bamboo mats, Japanese thongs, ebony screens and other accessories; and T&T Ginseng for a dose of ancient herbs and other cure-alls from a Oriental medical doctor and herbalist. Some of the great places to eat include: Plum Tree Inn, where you can feast on dim sum, the midday appetizers that include rice bun dumplings, wan ton potstickers and other delights; Sam Woo BBQ, for Hong Kong-style barbecue duck and red pork; and Kim Tar Seafood for Oriental-style seafood and live lobsters and crab.

Sahara Pavilion
Sahara Ave. and Decatur Blvd. • 258-4330

The Sahara Pavilion shopping center sprawls over 450,000 square feet of retail space, anchored by Vons grocery, TJ Maxx, Sheplers Western Wear, Sports Authority and the Longs Drug Store. Other noteworthy chains include House of Fabrics, Gold's Gym, Michaels Arts and Crafts and Office Max. Some of the more intriguing, locally owned shops include the Stamp Oasis, where you'll find thousands of rubber stamps for sale as well as ink, paper, gold leaf for embossing and other supplies for creating your own art masterpieces. For the outdoor chef, try Barbecues Galore for an unbelievable range of grills, cooking utensils, charcoal, briquets, starter fluid and even tiki torches for that Labor Day luau. If you've got the hot dogs and chips but need beverages, go to Beverages & More for a head-spinning selection of things to drink: more than 3,000 wines and hundreds of beers as well as soft drinks, mixers, tonic and the like. There's also a section for gourmet foods such as fresh caviar and a supply of more than 250 types of cigars.

If your consciousness needs sustenance, try Psychic Age Bookstore, where you can get a psychic reading, have your astrological chart made while you wait, get a stress-relief massage or take a class in holistic healing. The bookstore also sells crystals, books, divination tools, meditation music and other New Age paraphernalia.

Tapes, CDs and Records

The Strip Area

Record City
555 E. Sahara Ave. • 369-6466

On the wall of Record City is a sign that reads: "Get A Life — Get A Turntable." Good advice, considering the store has the largest collection of used record albums in the city. Well-represented in hard-to-find vinyl are rare rock from the '50s, '60s and '70s as well as jazz, Broadway and movie soundtracks. You can also purchase bargain-priced cassette tapes and CDs, and they will take your worn-out music in trade. There are five other stores around town if this one doesn't have want you want.

Downtown

Odyssey Records
1600 Las Vegas Blvd. S. • 384-4040

Located in the shadow of the Stratosphere Tower, Odyssey is as much a community center as a record store; the place is always busy, even at 3 AM on a Sunday night. Besides having a huge collection of records, tapes and discs, the store is open 24 hours a day, seven days a week. It's the happening place to be on Christmas Day if you've got nothing to do and no one to do it with.

East Valley

Big B's CDs and Records
4440 S. Maryland Pkwy. • 732-4433

Once Las Vegas' largest dealer in eight-track tapes, Big B is slowly phasing them out as demand diminishes. So if you're still driving around with an old eight-track player or, better yet, a four-track Muntz Stereopak, get down to Big B's before the supply is gone.

J-Mars Records
2620 S. Maryland Pkwy. • 796-6366

If you've ever wondered what happened to all those 45-rpm singles, go to J-Mars Records. Here you'll find the largest selection of 45s in the city — from early pop and rock to classical. The store also has a huge collection of Beatles music — albums and tapes — as well as posters, buttons and other memorabilia. Plus, the selection of video movies is awesome, including the original *Mad Max* series and *Blade Runner* before the director's cut, to name a couple.

The Underground
1164 E. Twain Ave. • 733-7025

The music at The Underground is for the techno-punk-rave-tribal-progressive crowd. Specializing in alternative rock, imports and college radio, the store has a bizarre selection of albums, tapes and discs, from African Head Charge and the Young Black Teenagers to Bad Brains and the Butthole Surfers. You can also find a T-shirt, sticker or poster to go with your offbeat album.

Thrift Stores

Downtown

Charleston Outlet

1548 E. Charleston Blvd. • 388-1446

This place is always packed, mainly for the bargain-priced clothes that turn over as fast as they can stock them. For men, there are usually a fair supply of decent suits and sports coats, ranging in price from $15 to $40, as well as tons of pants and shirts. Women can wrangle over row upon row of dresses, skirts, tops and accessories. There's rarely any good furniture here, but sometimes you will pick up a nice set of golf clubs or garden tools.

St. Jude's Thrift Shop

1717 E. Charleston Blvd. • 386-0772

This tidy little store, which benefits children at St. Jude's Children's Ranch in Boulder City, is one-fourth the size of most thrift shops, but the merchandise is well-screened and reconditioned before being set out for sale. In addition to the nice selection of name-brand clothes for men and women, you'll find choice pieces of furniture that may include oak dining tables with Windsor or captain's chairs, rocker/recliners, overstuffed couches and glass-top cocktail tables.

East Valley

Junior League Repeat Boutique

1040 E. Twain Ave. • 731-2446

Adjacent to Maryland Square shopping center, the Repeat Boutique has plenty of women's sportswear, some of it actually newer than the '70s, plus men's shirts, shorts, jeans and jackets. There's also a good selection of used books on topics such as arts and crafts, how-to, cookbooks and the usual paperback pulp fiction.

New Vista Ranch Thrift Shop

4000 Boulder Hwy. • 457-4677

Located a few blocks from Boulder Station, this well-supplied shop meanders through several rooms with the largest containing a department-store-size collection of men's, women's and children's clothing. Moving to the rear of the store, you'll find a room not unlike a garage in need of cleaning — loads of household appliances, furniture, old bowling balls, tennis rackets, out-of-date Commodore computers, croquet sets and more. Be diligent, and you'll find something to take home, even if it's only a karate kick bag or crepe maker.

West Valley

Goodwill Industries Thrift Store

2560 S. Duneville St. • 251-1929

Located just off Sahara Avenue west of Decatur, this large store has the usual oversupply of clothing for men, women and kids plus a nice collection of wood and Formica tables, bookcases, desks, entertainment centers, computer desks and the like.

Salvation Army

4001 W. Charleston Blvd. • 878-8022

Some of the best furniture bargains can be found at the Salvation Army store near Valley View Boulevard. An entire showroom is devoted to furniture, which could include leather couches, velvet love seats, slider rocking chairs, roll-top desks, elegant dining suites and more. We've even found a rare recalmier and chaise lounge at this well-maintained store. Also on hand are many reconditioned TV sets, stereos, musical instruments and, sometimes, working computers.

North Valley

Elephant Walk

1767 N. Rancho Dr. • 646-2150

Located next to southern Nevada's only zoo (actually they call it a zoological park, but the animals still make loud noises), Elephant Walk has a variety of clean kitchen appliances, table lamps, bedroom sets and other reconditioned furnishings. Occasionally you can find a nice TV or VCR in its electronic collection, or even an IBM Selectric typewriter or Teac tape deck.

Western Wear

The Strip Area

Cowtown Boots

2989 S. Paradise Rd. • 737-8469

This is a great factory outlet for buying a pair of handmade leather boots in skins ranging from cowhide to snakeskin to Teju lizard to ostrich. Featured brands include the store's namesake, Cowtown, as well as other prominent brands. You'll find 7,000 to 10,000 pairs of hand-crafted boots.

East Valley

Western Emporium

Sam's Town, 5111 Boulder Hwy. • 454-8017

The largest Western Emporium in the state has 25,000 square feet of floor space in which to wander. Choose from name-brand boots, clothing, leather accessories, jewelry, gourmet coffees, Southwest accessories and original art. There's also a year-round cowboy Christmas shop and an old-time photo studio. Brand names include Wrangler, Levi's, Roper, Stetson, Lucchese, Acme, Tony Lama, Justin and Resistol. Starting the day after Thanksgiving, the Emporium holds a season-long Christmas tent sale offering bargain prices on Western wear, boots, hats and accessories.

West Valley

Adams Western Store

1415 Western Ave. • 384-6077

This tightly stocked store features Western and English riding apparel for men, women and children as well as coats, boots, belts, hats, Browning Sportsmen goods and tack (Colorado, Circle Y, Tex-Tan, Jack's Tack). For boots, you'll find brand names like Justin, Noconoa, Tony Lama, Laredo and Texas; hat brands include Stetson, Bailey, Resistol and Eddy Brothers; and clothing makers include H Bar C, Wrangler, Levi's, Panhandle Slim and Karman.

Attractions

Attractions in Las Vegas begin at — where else? — the casinos, where the gaming business has adopted the "entertainment store" concept. The larger hotel-casinos are designed as destination resorts for tourists and even locals. Growing legions of megaresorts are adding movie theaters, tot lots and other amusements for their nongambling clientele.

The hottest corner on The Strip may be at Tropicana Avenue, whose tenants include the MGM Grand, New York-New York and Excalibur plus the Tropicana Hotel. By taking the escalators and the elevated sidewalks, visitors can tour all fourproperties without using a car or having to cross a busy street.

Other attractions tend to be more spread out, although many are clustered along the 5-mile Strip. (Note that some of the featured destinations also appear in our Kidstuff chapter. A rundown on the casinos' nightly stage shows can be found in our Nightlife chapter.) Addresses for attractions in this chapter are in Las Vegas unless designated otherwise.

If you want to get out of town for a morning or afternoon, many splendid things lay within an hour's drive. One don't-miss attraction is Hoover Dam, just beyond the clean, green community of Boulder City. The 726-foot-high concrete edifice was dedicated in 1935. Its 17 generators produce enough electricity to serve a half-million homes a year, most of them in Southern California. The dam is also a great tourist spot. In fact, more than 32 million visitors have ventured inside so far. The National Park Service conducts informative and entertaining tours. As the guides say: "You can ask any dam question you want," and children 12 and younger get in free.

Behind the dam is Lake Mead, which offers boating, water skiing, fishing, boat touring and camping. There are six docking marinas with another half-dozen developed campgrounds along the 550 miles of shoreline.

To the north is Valley of Fire State Park. Eerie landscapes of hidden canyons and unique rock formations dot the landscape. The other-worldly feel of the place attracted the eyes of Star Trek movie producers, who filmed segments here. History buffs will appreciate the petroglyphs and other signs of Indian civilizations.

Mt. Charleston is a great destination for winter skiing and summer refreshment. Just 40 miles north of town off U.S. 95, this high point in the Toiyabe National Forest has ski lifts and a limited number of campgrounds.

And on the western edge of the Las Vegas Valley is Red Rock Canyon. You can see the stunning cliffs from the city, and you can get a closer look without even leaving your car by driving a 10-mile scenic loop.

For more details on these outlying areas, see our Great Outdoors and Daycations chapters. Meantime, let's do the town!

Adventure Parks

The Strip Area

GameWorks
3769 Las Vegas Blvd. S. • 895-7626

Call it the ultimate arcade complex. This 47,000-square-foot facility is the brainchild of movie mogul Steven Spielberg, Sega Enter-

INSIDERS' TIP

If you're going roller coasting at New York-New York Hotel Casino, you'll want to travel light. The double loop has a way of spilling change and other loose articles.

prises and Universal Studios. In its basement-like setting next to the MGM Grand are Vertical Reality and GameArc, where teams of players battle each other in mock warfare. Also included is a 75-foot rock-climbing wall, all the latest video equipment and more than 250 arcade games. And, for a high-tech touch, computer terminals with Internet access also are available. Games range from 50¢ to $4. GameWorks is open daily; call for hours of operation.

FYI

Unless otherwise noted, the area code for all phone numbers listed in this chapter is 702.

Grand Slam Canyon

Circus Circus Hotel/Casino, 2889 Las Vegas Blvd. S. • 734-0410

Local kids say this Circus Circus property is one of the best of Las Vegas' amusement parks. Adults will appreciate the air-conditioned comfort of this metallic pink domed indoor park and nearby casino. The park has a double-loop, double-corkscrew roller coaster, a water flume with a 60-foot free fall and one of the more elaborate laser-tag layouts. A carnival-style midway and lots of smaller rides (including bumper cars) appeal to visitors of all ages. See additional details in our Kidstuff chapter.

MGM Grand Adventure Theme Park

MGM Grand, 3799 Las Vegas Blvd. S. • 891-7777

Most of the rides here are oriented toward young children, so much of the fare tends to be on the tame side. But a more challenging addition is the SkyScreamer, which hooks you up to a line, lifts you 250 feet and sends you free-falling. Flyers are instructed to pull their own rip cords to begin their 70-mph dive. Reservations — pun intended — are required on the day of the flight. Cost is $10 to $20 (separate from the regular theme park admission) depending on the number in your group. Four can swing simultaneously, or you can fly solo.

Theme park rides include children's bumper boats, a log-flume ride, a free-floating raft that whirls through gushing white-water rapids and self-controlled paddleboats. Be prepared to get wet on the water rides.

A pirate-themed adventure show with breakaway masts, exploding towers, hungry sharks and hand-to-hand combat is performed several times a day in a 950-seat outdoor theater. Note: Though it doesn't cost anything to walk around the movie set-style streets, bring lots of cash if you plan spend much time at this theme park; the multitude of shops can empty you pockets in a hurry. And since most of the venues are outdoors, remember that sunblock in the summer!

The park is open every day, but hours and admission prices vary according to season. Doors open at 10 AM, and closing time varies. Wristbands, which permit unlimited rides, cost about $12. Kiddies under 42 inches tall are admitted free, and children younger than 13 must be accompanied by an adult. See our Kidstuff chapter for additional details.

Star Trek: The Experience

Las Vegas Hilton, 3000 Paradise Rd. • 732-5401

Space comes alive at the north tower of the Las Vegas Hilton, where Paramount Parks has developed an interactive Star Trek attraction. A motion simulator, designed by Iwerks Entertainment, provides thrills and spills for visitors of all ages. After receiving their mission instructions on the Bridge, passengers take the TurboLift to the shuttlecraft launch bay to board a virtual shuttlecraft. Film images immerse the craft during its "voyage." The whole trip takes about 30 minutes.

INSIDERS' TIP

Conventions are big business in Las Vegas. The 1.6-million-square-foot Las Vegas Convention Center is the largest single-level convention facility in the nation. When a major gathering is in town, such as the 110,000-member Comdex computer show in November, it's best to steer clear of the convention area.

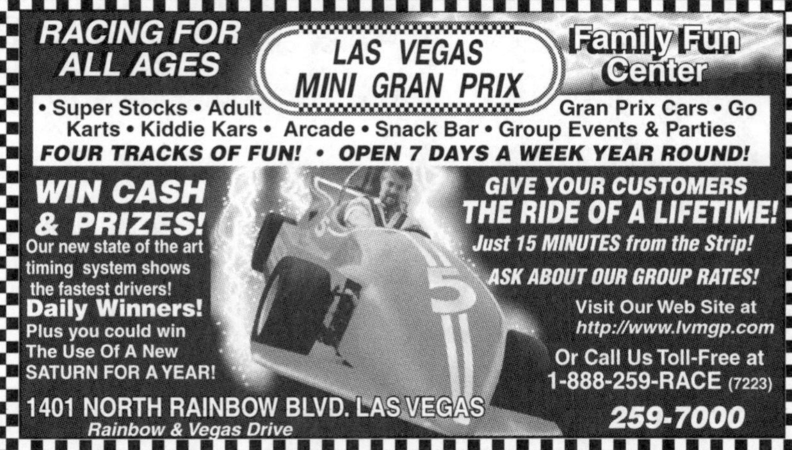

Veteran Trekkies will enjoy the museum loaded with costumes and memorabilia. For the gamblers, the Spacequest Casino features 24,000-square-feet of floor space and three space windows, which create the illusion of orbiting Earth. Distinctively futuristic slot machines and table games enhance the 24th-century ambiance, but they'll accept your old 20th-century money, of course. General admission to Star Trek: The Experience is $9.95. Call for hours of operation. It's open every day.

Derek Daly SpeedCentre

7000 Las Vegas Blvd. N. • 643-2126, (888) GODEREK

This is the ultimate thrill ride — taking a spin at up to 150 mph in a Formula One (Indy) racing car at the Las Vegas Motor Speedway. The program is structured in half-, one- and three-day racing schools tailored to your abilities and needs. And it's definitely for grown-ups with cash. The half-day programs, with classroom training and two driving sessions, run $475. A three-day regimen, which includes advanced racing techniques and long lapping sessions at the 1.5-mile oval, costs $2,195. Exclusive use of the race track is available for groups of 12 to 100 people. The SpeedCentre has specific reserved dates at the track, so call ahead for days of operation. For more information on the track, see our Spectator Sports section.

Factory Tours

Henderson (East Valley)

Cranberry World

1301 American Pacific Dr., Henderson • 566-7160

What could be a more refreshing break from the desert heat? Ocean Spray has put together a seven-minute show about cranberries and invites you to tour this plant southeast of town. Quaff samples of eight juices and snack on cranberry-soaked baked goods. Best of all, it's free. Hours are 9 AM to 5 PM daily.

Ethel M Chocolates

2 Cactus Garden Dr., Henderson • 433-2500

While you're in the southeast valley, stop by this sweet spot that draws about 2,000 visitors a day for self-guided tours. It's educational to learn about the birthplace of such delights at M&Ms, Milky Way, Three Musketeers, Snickers and Mars. And you'll please your palate with samples of candy and ice cream. Also enjoy a 2.5-acre garden with 350 species of rare cacti. Like the cranberry folks up the road, it's free. So what's not to like? Hours are 8:30 AM to 7 PM daily.

Kidd's Marshmallow Factory
8203 Gibson Rd., Henderson • 564-3878

Las Vegas and neighboring Utah are among the biggest consumers of marshmallows in the country. So why not make 'em here? Watch how corn starch and other polysyllabic ingredients are rolled smooth, cut into shapes, bounced in a drum and boxed into cartons. And then take a taste. Admission is free, and doors are open 9 AM to 4:30 PM Monday through Friday and 9:30 AM to 4:30 PM on weekends.

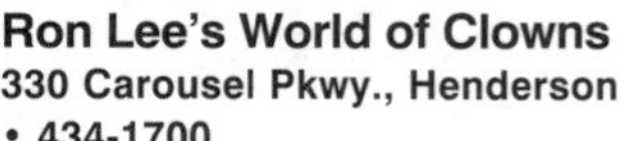

Ron Lee's World of Clowns
330 Carousel Pkwy., Henderson • 434-1700

Clowning around is business as usual at this factory. Open daily from 9 AM to 5 PM for free tours, the World of Clowns manufacturers more than 50,000 ceramic and pewter statuettes annually. Informative exhibits display the history of the craft. (See our Kidstuff chapter for additional details.)

Museums and Sightseeing

The Strip Area

Guinness World of Records Museum
2780 Las Vegas Blvd. S. • 792-3766

Life-size replicas, videos and even a computer data bank capture some of history's most compelling human feats. Visitors are greeted by a 9-foot-tall lifelike statue of Robert Wadlow, the world's tallest man. A special Las Vegas section details fun facts about the city. You want to know which stars were married here? Looking for some quick history on Las Vegas entertainment? A computer databank will provide the answers on demand. TV monitors show rolling video presentations throughout the museum. A dozen videos, including a five-minute tape of the world's longest domino fall, play constantly. The self-guided tour takes about a half-hour. It's all just up the street from Circus-Circus. Admission is $4.95 for adults, $3.95 for seniors, students and military and $2.95 for children 5 through 12. Hours are 9 AM to 6 PM daily.

Hollywood Movie Museum
Debbie Reynolds Hotel-Casino & Movie Museum, 305 Convention Center Dr. • 7-DEBBIE

See the dress that Marilyn Monroe wore in *The Seven Year Itch*, Elizabeth Taylor's *Cleopatra* headdress, Vivien Leigh's hats from *Gone with the Wind* and Doris Day's mermaid outfit from *Glass Bottom Boat*. These and 3,000 other costumes are showcased along with furnishings from celluloid classics. A half-hour show is narrated by Debbie herself. Admission is $7.95 for adults; children younger than 8 get in free. The museum, between The Strip and the Convention Center, is open daily from 10 AM to 10 PM.

Imperial Palace Auto Collection
3535 Las Vegas Blvd. S. • 731-3311

This place has big-name wheels from Adolph Hitler's to John F. Kennedy's. With nearly 200 cars on display (as part of a rotating collection totaling around 750), the IP houses some of the most famous and infamous vehicles from across the globe. Der Fuhrer's 1936 Mercedes was armored and mine-proofed. JFK's 1962 Lincoln was the bubbletop version — not the one that took that fateful turn in Dallas a year later. Other mobile classics belonged to Al Capone, Max Baer, W.C. Fields and, of course, such Las Vegas icons as Howard Hughes, Liberace and Elvis Presley.

INSIDERS' TIP

When visiting outdoor attractions, pack along a bottle of water or two. Las Vegas' summer heat can dehydrate you in minutes.

Admission is $6.95 for adults and $3 for seniors and children ages 5 to 12. Kids younger than 5 and AAA members get in free. Discount coupons are widely distributed in entertainment and tourist magazines. Daily hours are 9:30 AM to 11:30 PM.

Magic and Movie Hall of Fame
3555 Las Vegas Blvd. S. • 737-1343

The life and times of big-name illusionists and magicians are on display here, including levitation master Harry Kellar and Mephistoplhelian Dante, who concocted the terms "hocus-pocus" and "abracadabra." Located at O'Shea's Casino, the Houdini Theatre has stages half-hour magic shows at 2,3 and 4 PM. More than 120 exhibits are on display in this 20,000-square-foot hall that's open from 10 AM to 6 PM Tuesday through Sunday. Admission is $9.95 for adults and $3 for children 12 and younger.

Downtown

Las Vegas Natural History Museum
900 Las Vegas Blvd. N. • 384-3466

From dinosaurs to present-day wildlife, this museum takes its visitors on a journey through time. The collection of fossils includes skeletons of prehistoric creatures, cave bears and a skull and foot from a Tyrannosaurus Rex — all displayed in a real-life setting. Children are fascinated by the nine animated dinosaur exhibits, two of which are part of a traveling Smithsonian program. An auditorium for special shows and a children's museum is part of the complex. The museum is open daily from 9 AM to 4 PM. Admission is $5 for adults, $4 for seniors, students and military, and $2.50 for children ages 4 through 12. Children younger than 4 get in free. (For additional information, see our Kidstuff chapter.)

Lied Discovery Children's Museum
833 Las Vegas Blvd. N. • 382-3445

This is an interactive place with exhibits in the arts, humanities and sciences. It's a fun venue that lets families collaborate on problem-solving projects, experiment with a variety of contraptions and experience hands-on displays. From pulleys and electromagnetic fields to a pint-size grocery store and bank, the museum (pronounced "leed") provides learning experiences at a number of levels. (See our Kidstuff chapter for more details.) The museum also sponsors an Artist-in-Residence program in which artists from visual arts, dance, music, photography, puppetry, theater, creative writing and multidimensional art conduct workshops for children in the fall and spring. Admission to the museum is $5 for adults; $4 for seniors, military and children ages 12 to 17; $3 for children 3 to 11; and free for toddlers 2 and younger. For residents, the best deal is an annual membership, which allows unlimited visits, workshop discounts and invitations to members-only events. Base price is $30, with an additional $5 for each person added to the membership. Hours vary by season, but the museum is closed on Mondays. It is inside the main Las Vegas Library just north of downtown.

Mormon Fort
908 Las Vegas Blvd. N. • 486-3511

Formally titled the Old Las Vegas Mormon Fort State Historic Park, this is Las Vegas' oldest building. The fort, built by Mormon settlers in 1855, was purchased by the state from the city in 1990 for $300,000. Unfortunately, visitors can see only remnants of the original structures. Still, it's a quiet taste of history not far from the hustle and bustle of downtown. Admission is $1 for adults and 50¢ for children ages 6 to 12. Daily hours are 8:30 AM to 3:30 PM.

INSIDERS' TIP

Keep your eye out for the omnipresent "fun books." Casinos distribute the books, which may contain coupons for a free pull on a slot machine with a million-dollar jackpot. Other featured freebies include complimentary drinks, discounted meals and assorted memorabilia.

Fremont Street Experience

Arguably the most famous four blocks in the nation, the downtown section of Fremont Street was covered up and turned into a walking mall in December 1995. But the entertainment is far from pedestrian.

A 90-foot-tall "space frame," a tight, white lattice overhang that spans the street, stretches 1,400 feet along Glitter Gulch from Main Street to Fourth Street. Embedded in the vaulted ceiling are 2.1 million lights and 208 speakers capable of producing 540,000 watts of sound and concert-quality music. Each night, computer-generated light and sound shows are displayed overhead, with fanciful images ranging from streaking jets to boot-scooting country-western dancers. Fremont Street's three-story, 1,430-space structure, a half-block south on Fourth Street. The $70 million project is a joint partnership between the city, the Las Vegas Convention and Visitors Authority and the Fremont Street Experience Co., comprised of 10 downtown casinos.

The outdoor mall is cooled by a misting system, which makes Fremont Street a refreshing outdoor oasis in the summer. Strolling entertainers and food carts provide a festive atmosphere. Parking also is free and easy. If you use a casino lot, remember to get your ticket validated at the cashier's cage. You usually get up to three hours on the house.

If you have kids, it's OK to take them. Fremont Street Experience is clean and cleared of the panhandlers who were omnipresent in bygone days. There are a growing number of shops of interest to all ages. But have no illusions: This is still primarily a gaming venue, with 10 casinos and 500,000 square feet of gambling space lining each side of the street. Also in the mix is a topless lounge and a tavern that touts more than 100 beers from around the world. So pick your spots.

While you're there, you'll want to take in a couple of Las Vegas' most enduring icons. After 46 years, "Vegas Vic," the animated metal cowboy, is still waving atop the Pioneer Club. And you might stop by the city's oldest hotel, the Golden Gate, for one of its 99¢ shrimp cocktails served in classic glass dishes. Cocktails are often accompanied by live piano music, and the players even take requests.

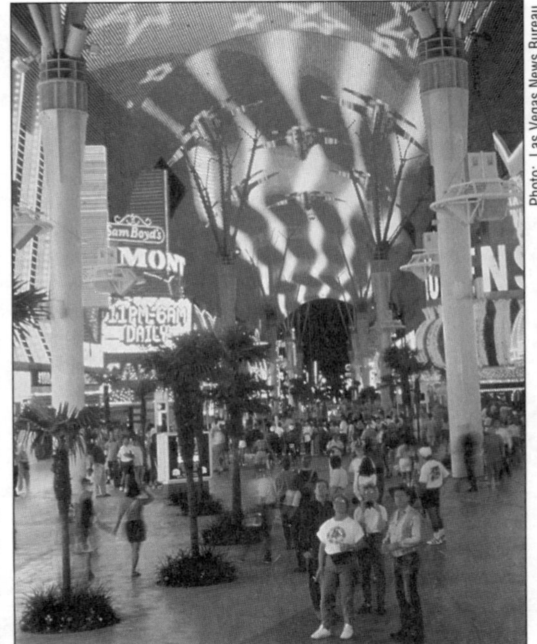

Photo: Las Vegas News Bureau

The Fremont Street Experience downtown provides nightly light shows and entertainment.

East Valley

Clark County Heritage Museum

1830 Boulder Hwy., Henderson • 455-7955

Southern Nevada's roots are exposed here. Historic structures, including pioneer homes, are set along Heritage Street. Regional memorabilia and artifacts fill an 8,000-square-foot exhibit center. Railroad cars, along with the original Boulder City train depot, are featured in a special display re-creating an 1880s-era ghost town. This is an easy and affordable morning or afternoon jaunt from town. Admission is $1.50 for adults and $1 for seniors and children. Doors are open daily from 9 AM to 4:30 PM.

Liberace Museum

1775 E. Tropicana Ave. • 798-5595

Mr. Showmanship comes to life at this glittering showcase 2 miles east of The Strip. Spectacular cars, fine pianos and outrageous costumes fill this one-man museum. Don't miss the world's largest rhinestone, a 50.6-pound gem presented to Liberace by the Austrian company that supplied all his costume stones. Admission is $6.50 for adults, $4.50 for seniors older than 60, $3.50 for students and $2 for children ages 6 to 12. Doors are open Monday through Saturday 10 AM to 5 PM and Sundays from 1 to 5 PM.

Marjorie Barrick Museum of Natural History

University of Nevada, Las Vegas, 4505 S. Maryland Pkwy. • 739-3381

This Southwestern collection features exhibits of live desert reptiles, mammals and insects, plus many Mojave desert fossils. Among the highlights is a skeleton of an ichthyosaur, a whale-size sea lizard that is Nevada's state fossil. The museum regularly hosts traveling exhibits, including those from the Smithsonian Institution. In front of the museum, an arboretum displays indigenous plants and a demonstration garden. Shaded benches line the paths and provide a peaceful and relaxing refuge just steps away from the college quad. The museum is open from 8 AM to 4:45 PM Monday through Friday. Admission is free.

McCarran Aviation Heritage Museum

McCarran International Airport, 5757 Wayne Newton Blvd. • 455-7968

This permanent display highlights southern Nevada's airborne history, from the first flight in 1920 through the introduction of jet aircraft. The main exhibit is open 24 hours a day and is above baggage claim on Level 2 of the main terminal. An additional exhibit on corporate aviation is on display at the Signature Flight Support building, which must be accessed separately. Signature is at 6005 Las Vegas Boulevard S. and its hours are 9 AM to 5 PM Monday through Friday. Both exhibits are free. Aviation buffs who like to watch the airport operations can park in a designated area south of the airport on Sunset Road and actually listen to the tower's communication with the aircraft. Just tune your radio to 1610 AM and you can follow the traffic controllers' conversation.

Thunderbirds Nellis Air Force Base

Las Vegas Blvd. N. and Craig Rd. • 652-9902

The Air Force's precision flying team is based here and offers tours every Tuesday and Thursday at 2 PM year round. The one-hour guided trip into one of America's largest air bases includes a movie, a visit to the Heritage Hall history museum and an up-close inspection of a Thunderbird F-16. Private groups of 20 or more may reserve a special tour between 8 AM and 4 PM on weekdays. All programs are free.

West Valley

Nevada State Museum

700 Twin Lakes Dr. • 486-5205

Ensconced in Lorenzi Park, an oasis from the urban glare, this museum contains graphic

INSIDERS' TIP

Sunset Park, just a few minutes from The Strip southeast of McCarran Airport, has a 13-acre lake stocked with up to 500 pounds of catfish and trout year round.

displays of southern Nevada's ancient history. A Colombia mammoth graces the 35,000-square-foot complex that's filled with archeological exhibits. Also on the premises is the Cahlan Library, which features an extensive collection of books, manuscripts, newspapers and maps — all about southern Nevada's bygone days. Curator Frank Wright is an excellent source on local history. And bring your picnic basket along. You can you feed the ducks at Lorenzi Park's lake, and the kids can frolic on the playground. Admission to the museum is $2 for adults. Children younger than 18 get in free. Daily hours are 9 AM to 5 PM (the library is closed on Saturdays and Sundays). The park is free.

Southern Nevada Zoological Park
1775 N. Rancho Dr. • 648-5955

Just a few blocks northwest of downtown is Las Vegas' only zoo — for animals, that is. But be aware that this is a much smaller venue than you'll find in most large cities. There are no wild animal park or safari rides here. For families with young children, the petting area is more than sufficient entertainment. Look for hours and admission prices in our Kidstuff chapter.

Ultimate Balloon Adventure
2013 Clover Path St. • 221-9199

Hot-air balloons are a great way to get a bird's-eye view of the valley. This company offers hour-long rides for $125 per person, and the balloon baskets can comfortably accommodate groups of six. Peak season is October through February, though balloons will fly year round. Early morning is the best time to fly because that's when the thermal lift is best. The large and colorful balloons cruise between 500 and 1,000 feet. You don't need any special clothing, but shutterbugs ought to bring along an extra roll of film (or two) and videocam shooters should carry spare batteries. Upon landing, riders are treated to champagne and finger food. Note: Hot-air balloons are registered aircraft, and pilots must have a license from the Federal Aviation Administration. If you decide to fly with one of the competing companies, you might want to check the credentials before leaving terra firma.

Resort Attractions

The Strip Area

Excalibur
3850 Las Vegas Blvd. S. • 597-7777

Are you in the mood for something medieval? King Arthur's Las Vegas-style court performs here daily from 10 AM to 10 PM. Every 30 minutes, jugglers, musicians, magicians and assorted minstrels take the stage on the floor above the casino to display their talents. The acts delight youngsters and adults alike — and are free of charge. On the floor below the casino, the "Fantasy Fare" arcade offers a more modern touch for game-minded youngsters.

Mirage Dolphin Habitat

The Mirage, 3400 Las Vegas Blvd. S. • 791-7111

Dolphins in the desert? Casino mogul Steve Wynn has seven bottlenosed dolphins swimming in a special 2.5 million gallon habitat behind his Mirage Hotel. Visitors can view these playful mammals from above and below surface level. A 15-minute tour is included. Admission is $3 and free for children younger than 10 (all children younger than 12 must be accompanied by an adult). Hours are 11 AM to 7 PM Monday through Friday and 9 AM to 7 PM Saturday and Sunday.

By the way, Wynn's ode to nature attitude extends to his gambling hall and shops. No fur is sold at the Mirage boutiques, and only dolphin-safe tuna is served in the restaurants.

While you're on the premises, see the royal white tiger habitat near The Strip-side entrance. These cats perform with Siegfried and Roy, and they're free for the viewing. Behind the hotel registration desk is a 53-foot, 20,000-gallon aquarium filled with 1,000 species of sea life from such exotic locales as Tonga, Fiji and the Marshall Islands.

Luxor Hotel

3900 Las Vegas Blvd. S. • 262-4000

If you want to walk like an Egyptian, this 30-story pyramid at the southern end of The Strip is the place for you. King Tut's Tomb and Museum features a full-size re-creation of the burial chamber. Tutankhamen's golden throne and sarcophagus — all handcrafted by Egyptian artisans in historically correct materials — are among the notable artifacts that are part of a 20-minute audio tour. Admission is $4. Doors are open 9 AM to 11 PM Sunday through Thursday and 9 AM to 11:30 PM Friday and Saturday.

For the daredevils, Secrets of the Luxor Pyramid is an hour-long adventure spread over two venues. Episode One, "In Search of the Obelisk," uses a motion-simulator to propel you through a wild chase that begins with a plummeting elevator. "Luxor Live" in Episode Two takes on the format of a live TV talk show and ends up with more 3-D wizardry. Hours are the same as King Tut's Tomb. Tickets cost $5 for the first show and $4 for the second. The hotel warns that this attraction may startle young children. For them, the IMAX movies, also on the premises, may be more appropriate.

New York-New York Hotel Casino

3790 Las Vegas Blvd. S. • 740-6969

Gotham never saw the likes of this — a roller coaster soaring over Fire Island and around Miss Liberty. The Manhattan Express twists, loops and dives out in front of this resort. It features the first-ever heartline roll, which creates the sensation a pilot feels when going through a barrel roll in an airplane. The 4½-minute ride costs $5. Riders must be at least 46 inches tall.

Treasure Island

3300 Las Vegas Blvd. S. • 894-7111

This is the one must-see free attraction on The Strip. Every 90 minutes from 4 to 11:30 PM, a live sea battle spills out in front of the Treasure Island hotel-casino. Acrobatic sailors and pyrotechnic explosions fill the air as pirates battle the British in a large lagoon. If you haven't already heard how the confrontation ends, we won't tell you. But here's a hint: Las Vegas is a pirate kind of town. Be sure to arrive at least a half-hour early to get a decent view. But if the winds are gusty, take a rain check because the high-flying actors won't be sailing.

Downtown

Stratosphere Tower

2000 Las Vegas Blvd. S. • 380-7777

This tower, the tallest observation tower west of the Mississippi, offers a great panoramic view of the Las Vegas Valley. With the area's relatively clear air, 100-mile visibilities are not unusual. If that's not enough, try the two rides overhead. Flying 100 stories above ground, the Let It Ride roller coaster circles the tower in a series of tight twists and rolls. Because of the limited space, don't expect high speeds — and you may not want to look down either! Even more pulsating is the Big Shot. Sit down and get rocketed 160 feet up the tower's spindle. Then experience a freefall back to the launching pad.

A quick elevator ride to the observation deck (which has shops and fast-food restau-

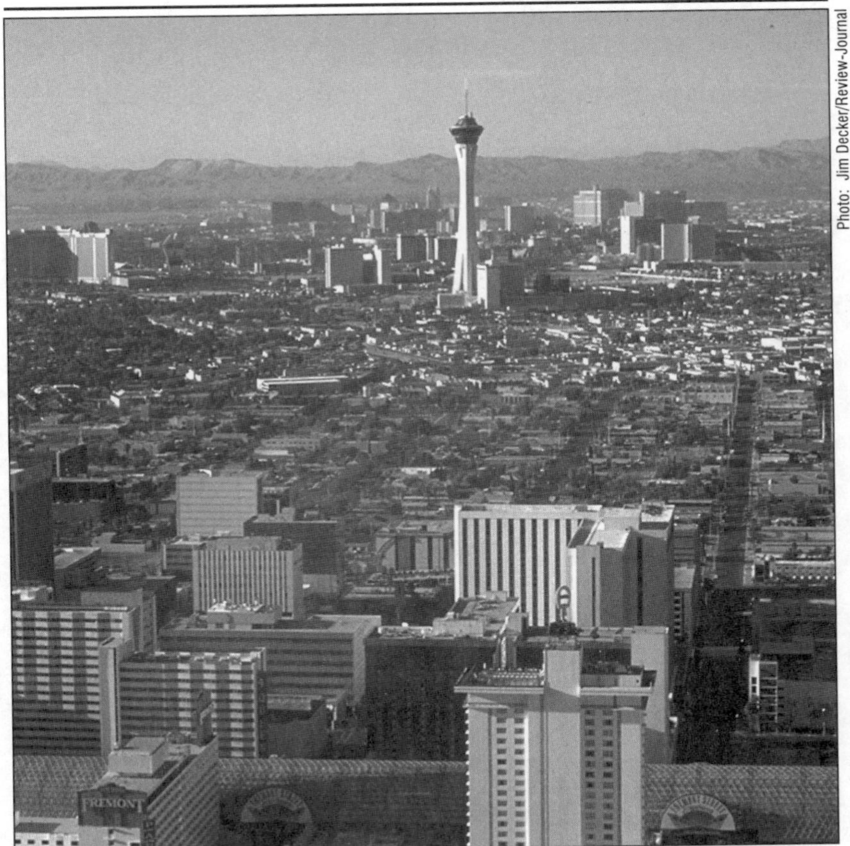

Photo: Jim Decker/Review-Journal

Rising more than 1,100 feet above the valley floor, the top of the Stratosphere Tower provides great panoramic views and a couple of thrill rides.

rants) runs $5 ($4 for Nevada residents). Rides also are $5. The tower and rides are open 10 AM to midnight daily. The rides don't operate if winds top 35 mph — a common occurrence in spring and summer.

Beyond Las Vegas

Buffalo Bill's

Primm • 382-1212

Thrill-seekers will find it's worth an hour's drive south of town to the stateline to take on the Desperado, one of the world's tallest and fastest roller coasters. The ride climbs to 209 feet and then plummets 225 feet at speeds exceeding 80 mph. Some low overhead clearances give riders the sensation they're going to lose their heads as the coaster hurtles through Buffalo Bill's casino. Whew! Cost is $5 and hours are 10 AM to 9 PM Sunday through Thursday and 10 AM to 11 PM on Fridays and Saturdays.

If that's not enough for you, try the Turbo Drop. This sadistic ride climbs 200 feet and then, without warning, yanks you and your fellow thrill-seekers earthward at 45 mph, bouncing you on a cushion of air just before you hit. Admission is $5, and riders must be at least 52 inches tall. Buffalo Bill's also offers a $25 wristband for unlimited rides, a movie, a hot dog and a soft drink (if your stomach can handle it). See our Daycations chapter for more about the town of Primm.

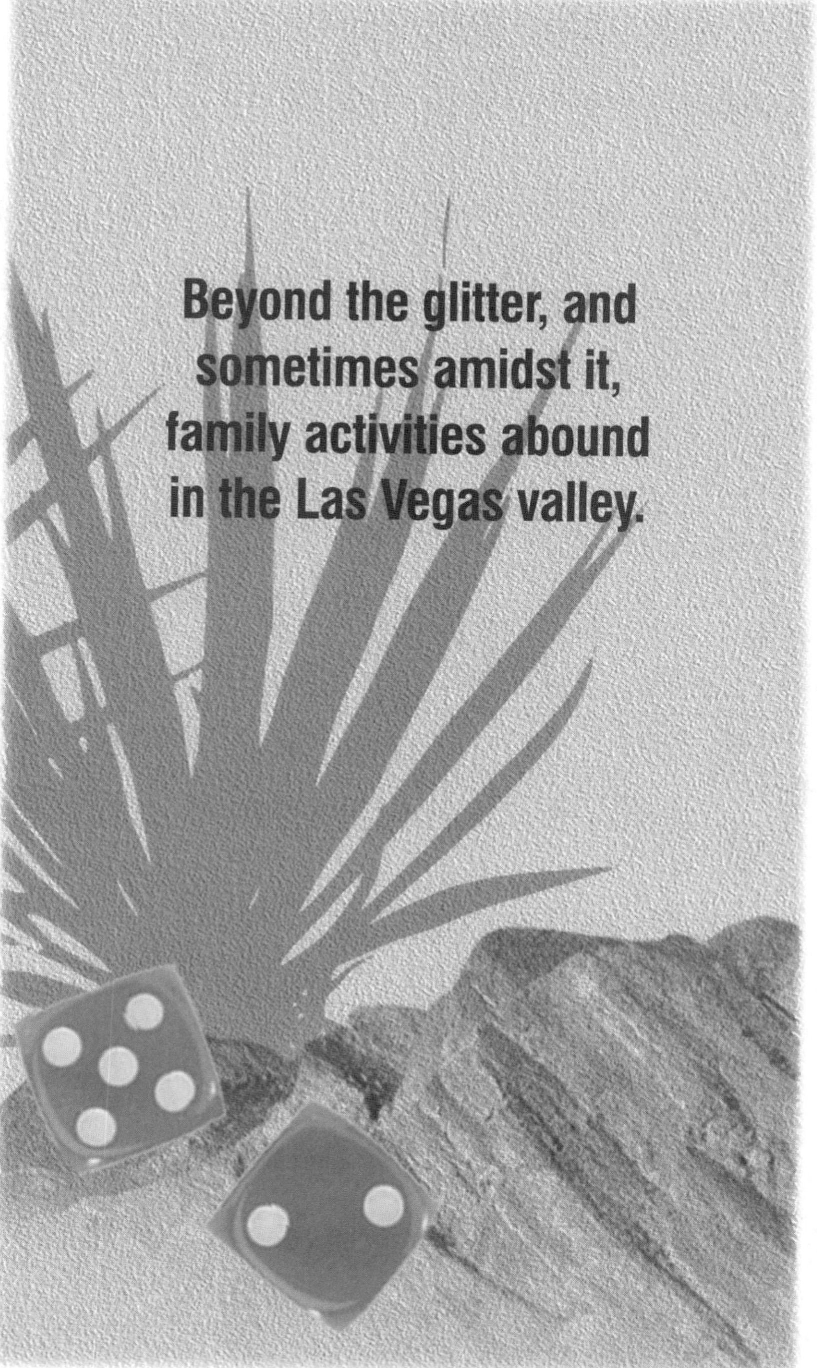
Beyond the glitter, and
sometimes amidst it,
family activities abound
in the Las Vegas valley.

Kidstuff

Las Vegas is, first and foremost, an adult playground. Games of chance beckon everywhere — from the slots at the corner 7-Eleven to the baccarat rooms at the megaresorts.

So what's a kid to do? Lots, actually.

Beyond the glitter, and sometimes amidst it, family activities abound in the Las Vegas valley. This chapter guides parents and children to the most family-friendly destinations.

Be aware that some of the most popular places are in and around casinos. The gambling halls attempt to keep these fun zones separate from the adult games, but, invariably, the trip requires a walk through parts of the casino. Visitors younger than 21 cannot tarry, so the stroll needs to be brisk. Moms and Dads aren't permitted to wager while youngsters are in tow. Also noteworthy is the fact that swimming pools at most hotel-casinos close around dusk (they would rather have customers gambling). This can be a problem for overheated youngsters in the summer, when it's still 90 degrees at 10 PM.

To help families determine their own comfort levels, this chapter is divided into two parts: Around Casinos and Around Town. Included in the Around Town section are programs for tourists and residents alike. Each section is organized alphabetically. For further information, you'll want to check our Attractions and Parks and Recreation chapters, which contains additional details about family-oriented fun. Of special note in the Attractions chapter are the four factory tours in Henderson, 15 miles southeast of Las Vegas — Ocean Spray, Ethel M. Chocolates, Kidd's Marshmallows and Ron Lee's World of Clowns.

For updates and special promotions on activities around the valley, *Las Vegas Kidz* magazine is a good source of information. The monthly publication carries an extensive month-to-month calendar of kid-oriented events that are free or low cost. The magazine, which is free, can be picked up at any local library and at Lucky grocery stores.

So, let's begin our tour of Kidstuff.

Around Casinos

Circus Circus Hotel/Casino

2880 Las Vegas Blvd. S. • 734-0410

In this most family-friendly of casinos, kids can play their own games at a video arcade, grab a snack at McDonald's or ride the monorail to the Grand Slam Canyon adventure park next door (see separate listing below). Youth-oriented fun is found on the second floor of the main casino. Free circus acts are performed throughout the day in a center ring from 11 AM to midnight.

Excalibur

3850 Las Vegas Blvd. S. • 597-7777

Bygone days come alive beneath the casino floor. Puppets, mimes, magicians and jugglers perform continuously from 10 AM to 10 PM at Medieval Village. Shows are free and last about 20 minutes. Elsewhere, carnival games entice youngsters in games of skill, while a Magic Motion Machine puts visitors in hydraulically activated seats for a rollicking ride through a runaway train and an outer space demolition derby directed by George Lucas. This ride costs $3.

Forum Shops at Caesars Palace

3500 Las Vegas Blvd. S. • 369-4008

Grab your toga! This Roman-themed shopping complex alongside Caesars Palace blends entertainment and upscale retailing. Animated statues, Planet Hollywood and the Warner Bros. store operate under an azure vaulted ceiling that lightens and darkens every hour to imitate the rising and setting sun.

Cinema Ride offers a wild 3-D experience. Four different rides give you the sensation of probing the ocean's depths in a submarine, riding a wild, runaway roller coaster, taking an intergalactic flight or riding through a graveyard on a bicycle. Riders must be at least 21 inches tall. Cost ranges from $7 for one ride to $14 for all four.

The Mall is open from 10 AM to 11 PM Sunday through Thursday and from 10 AM to midnight on Friday and Saturday.

Grand Slam Canyon

2889 Las Vegas Blvd. S. • 734-0410

Beat the heat under this pleasure dome behind Circus Circus. Ride the Canyon Blaster, a looping, corkscrewing roller coaster. Get wet on a water flume ride called Rim Runner. Also available: laser tag, net climbing, bumper cars and carnival midway games. Admission is $4, and rides cost $2 to $4 extra. Unlimited-ride wristbands cost $15.95 if you're more than 48 inches tall, $11.95 if you're not. The park is open Sunday through Thursday from 10 AM to 6 PM. On Fridays and Saturdays, hours are 10 AM to midnight.

FYI

Unless otherwise noted, the area code for all phone numbers listed in this chapter is 702.

MGM Grand Adventure Theme Park

3799 Las Vegas Blvd. S. • 891-7777

Disneyland on The Strip? MGM has put together a mixture of rides and shows reminiscent of the world of Disney. Among the attractions: a rapids ride, a flume ride, a river ride and a Space Mountain-style roller coaster.

Then there's showtime. "Dueling Pirates" combines dancing, tumbling and comedy. "You're in the Movies" gives audience members a chance to perform alongside pre-filmed scenes. Costumed characters from some MGM classics greet visitors among the shops and restaurants.

Admission rates vary according to season, but youngsters 13 and older are charged the adult rate (around $18). Kids taller than 42 inches generally can purchase an all-day, all-ride pass for $9 if they're hotel guests or Nevada residents. The price goes to $11 if you're not in those categories. Children less than 42 inches get in free. Children younger than 13 must be accompanied by an adult. Doors open at 10 AM and closing times vary with the season. In the summer, it's wise to get an early start since the afternoon heat can be brutal.

Santa Fe Ice Rink and Bowling Alley

Sante Fe Hotel-Casino, 4949 N. Rancho Dr. • 658-4900

About 20 minutes northwest of downtown, this neighborhood casino has a hockey rink and 60-lane bowling alley that are open to the public. Children can skate for $4, adults for $5. Skate rentals are available. The rink is open daily from 10 AM to 10 PM, but you should call ahead for public ice times because the rink is frequently booked. Bowlers should do the same, or risk waiting in line while leagues fill the lanes. Bowling rates are set by the hour, with rates ranging from $8.50 on weekdays to $12.50 on weekends. There are no discounts for juniors.

Star Trek: The Experience

3000 Paradise Rd. • 732-5401

Beam me to the Las Vegas Hilton, Scotty. In this brand-new attraction, visitors board the Starship Enterprise and battle alien vessels in a motion simulator. Youngsters can become members of Starfleet by assuming the identity of a Star Trek character at the Morphing Station. Also on the premises is a museum loaded with costumes, special effects gadgets and other Trekkie gear. General admission is $9.95. A themed restaurant and licensed shop are outside. Call for hours of operation.

Stratosphere

2000 Las Vegas Blvd. S. • 382-4446

The world's highest roller coaster, the High Roller, runs 900 feet above the ground

INSIDERS' TIP

Metro Police enforce a nightly curfew on The Strip. Minors (those younger than 18) must be off the street by 10 PM or accompanied by a legal guardian or parent.

at this hotel-casino between The Strip and downtown. It's a short circular ride that's fairly tame — you just may not want to look down over the edge of the tower. More gut-wrenching is the Big Shot, which shoots riders 160 feet above the observation deck. This catapult-style device runs up a steel tower and leaves you suspended momentarily. Then, in herky-jerky fashion, your seat jumps up and slips down. It's a three-minute ride that may seem a lot longer.

Rides cost $5 for adults and $4 for children — plus $5 admission to ride to the top of the tower. But the admission charge is waived for Nevada residents and it's frequently discounted for visitors. Call the hotel for details on special rates. Rides run from 10 AM to midnight on weekdays and until 1 AM on weekends, though gusty winds will halt both attractions. You have to be at least 48 inches tall to climb aboard.

Treasure Island

3801 Las Vegas Blvd. S. • 739-2222

A British Man O' War and a pirate ship do battle every 90 minutes on The Strip. Roaring cannons and stunning pyrotechnics fill the air in this free spectacle that runs daily, except during gusty winds. Inside the hotel, an 18,000-square-foot Mutiny Bay entertainment center has video games and electronically simulated rides that cost $3.

Around Town

Boys and Girls Club

2850 Lindell Rd. • 368-0317
1011 Dumont Blvd. • 792-1388
2801 Stewart Ave. • 388-2828
817 N. North St. • 646-8457
2530 E. Carey Ave. • 649-2656

Sports, crafts and field trips are some of the programs offered at this club for local youngsters after school and during the summer. Memberships are required, but the prices are unbelievably affordable. After-school programs run $32 for the whole school year from September through May. The centers are open from 2:30 PM to 8:30 AM, and they even pick up students at selected campuses.

In the summer, two-week programs run all day. Costs range from $25 to $75, depending on family income. Both programs run periodic field trips to area theme parks. Call the center near you for shuttle schedules and specific program information.

Clark County Parks and Recreation

2601 E. Sunset Rd. • 455-8200

For residents, this is a veritable one-stop call for activities ranging from biddy basketball to camping programs. Campuses and neighborhood centers around the valley provide after-school and summer fun, including crafts, sports and field trips. (See our Recreation chapter for center locations.) Want to cool off from the heat? Kids can swim at any county pool for just 50¢ a day. Two-week sessions of swimming lessons cost $20. Individual or family season passes also can be purchased at a discount.

Weeklong camps for young artists, scientists and outdoors lovers are conducted in cool and refreshing Lee Canyon each summer. Costs run around $250. These programs are very popular, so it's a good idea to reserve early in the spring. A series of boys' and girls' sports leagues run throughout the year. Ages range from 3 to 18. Classes and day outings start at $5. These can be fun for the whole family.

Special venues include an archery range, a radio controlled car track, an airfield for radio-controlled planes, Nellis Meadows BMX track and Dog Fancier's Park. The general information number can provide the latest schedules and activities.

Club Funtime Pizza 'N Play

3665 S. Rainbow Blvd. • 222-0300

Kids can burn a few calories and consume them too. Parents can enjoy an adult-style salad bar while the youngsters romp around in a 3,000-square-foot play area. Video games and a prize redemption center are on site. Admission to the play area is free from 11 AM to 4 PM; a $2.99 charge is imposed on evenings and weekends. Pizza 'N Play is open until 10 PM Sunday through Thursday and until 11 PM on Fridays and Saturdays.

Crystal Palace Skating Center

3901 N. Rancho Dr. • 645-4892
4680 Boulder Hwy. • 458-7107
1110 E. Lake Mead Dr. • 564-2790

Public in-line and roller skating is available most evenings at these skating centers around the valley. The musical fare tends to be family oriented, steering clear of rap and heavy metal medleys. Cost is $5 with skates, $6 without. Selected dates are designated family nights, when the whole brood can skate for $10. The centers are usually open nightly from 7 to 9:30 PM, but it's best to call ahead because the rinks are sometimes booked by private parties. The centers also offer roller hockey programs.

Disc Golf Course

2601 E. Sunset Rd. • 455-8281

Want to play a round through the air? Bring your Frisbee or a reasonable facsimile and toss it around this 18-hole, par 70 layout at Sunset Park. This free 5,491-yard course is open seven days a week and is designed for all ages. Scorecards are available.

Discovery Zone

2020 Olympic Ave., Henderson • 434-9575

Kids 12 and younger can crawl through 500 feet of tubes and bounce into seven big ball pools here. Parents get in free when accompanying their children and must remain on the premises. Kids 3 and older get in for $5.99; youngsters 1 to 2 are $3.99. The Discovery Zone is open daily 11 AM to 7 PM and from 10 AM to 9 PM on weekends.

Gymboree

918 S. Valley View Blvd. • 877-0074

Parents and toddlers younger than 6 will do some playful bonding at this indoor playground. Exercise classes and family game activities area a fun way for Mom, Dad and the young ones to break the home-bound routine. Classes are just $10, or $91 for a 13-week session. Out-of-town Gymboree members can get one class free. Hours are 9:30 AM to 12:30 PM and 6 to 8 PM on Tuesday, Wednesday, Thursday and Saturday.

Las Vegas-Clark County Library District

833 Las Vegas Blvd. N. • 382-3493

Las Vegas' 10 city libraries and 11 rural branches offer reading and a whole lot more — for free. Seasonal programs feature hands-on computer technology workshops, holiday concerts, a cinema series and weekly story-time sessions. Many libraries feature galleries and other special facilities that make for fun family outings. For example, the Summerlin branch, 1771 Inner Circle, 256-5111, has elaborate model airplanes dangling from the ceiling of its children's section. Libraries are open daily, including Sundays. A full schedule of events can be picked up at any branch or by calling the Young People's Library at any branch.

Las Vegas Mini Grand Prix

1401 N. Rainbow Blvd. • 259-7000

If you're at least 54 inches tall, you'll be able to take a spin around four miniature race tracks. For more horsepower, visitors 16 and older can step up to speedier Gran Prix racers and Nascarts. Rates are $4 a ride or $17.50 for five rides. Toddlers who don't measure up to the height requirements can try the kiddy carts or ride with others. Tracks, which are lighted, open every day at 10 AM and run until midnight.

INSIDERS' TIP

The Omnimax Theater at Caesars Palace wraps you in high-tech sound and images every day except Monday. Call 731-7900 for ticket information. Many of the presentations are educational, but you don't have to tell the kids that . . . they'll be enjoying the show too much.

Las Vegas Municipal Pool

431 E. Bonanza Rd. • 229-6309

This is the best deal for year-round swimming — and it's a well-kept secret. Youngsters through age 3 are admitted free. Four-to 6-year-olds swim for 50¢ and 7- to 17-year-olds get in for 75¢. Families can buy five-month season passes for $60 and use the pool for an unlimited number of trips. Centrally located downtown, the Olympic-size pool is clearly visible from U.S. Highway 95 in the winter months when its big air-filled bubble dome is up. The top comes off in the summer. The life-guarded pool opens for public swimming at 10 AM, though hours will flex according to season and periodic programs (many local high school teams train here after school).

There are a few drawbacks. The pool has no diving board, poolside seating or other amenities that you might expect at a facility of this size. And it's closed on Sundays. But, hey, it's a bargain, and there's rarely a crowd.

Las Vegas Natural History Museum

900 Las Vegas Blvd. N. • 384-DINO

Living sharks, 35-foot dinosaurs and other scary creatures lurk here. A Young Scientists' Center has hands-on displays, and daily workshops are open to children ages 6 through 12. Kids can pet a 13-foot-long python, dissect a cow's eye and dig for fossils in the

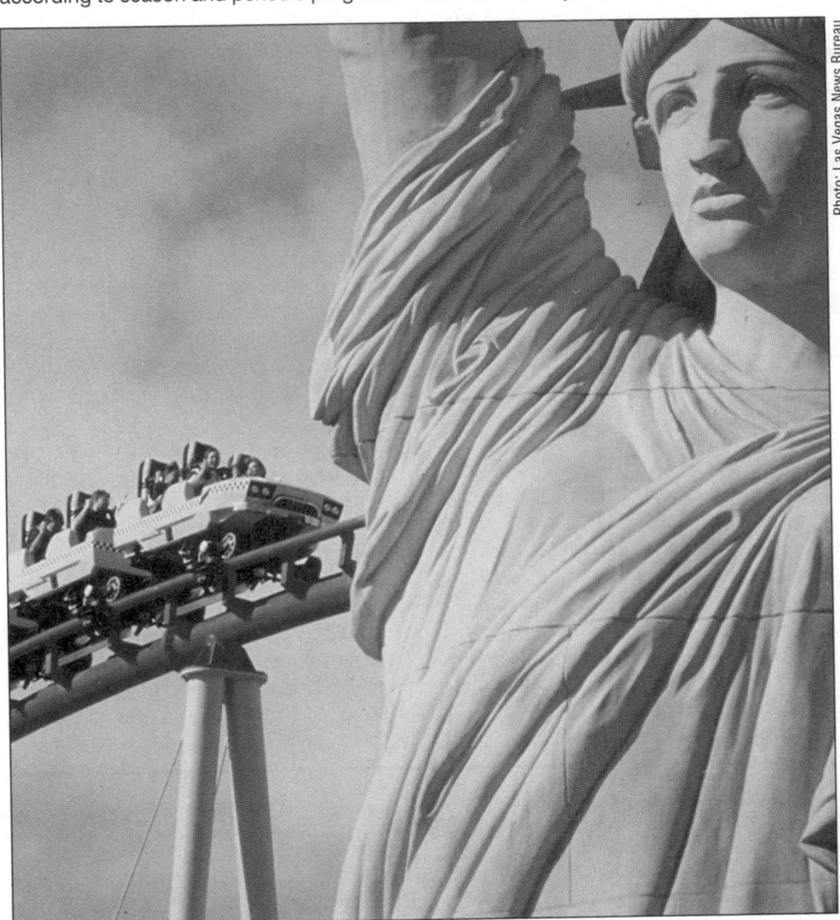

Photo: Las Vegas News Bureau

A roller coaster soars past the Statue of Liberty at New York-New York Hotel Casino.

museum's workshop. The museum is open daily from 9 AM to 4 PM. Admission is $5 for adults, $4 for seniors, students and military, and $2.50 for children 4 through 12. Children younger than 4 get in free. (See our Attractions chapter.)

Las Vegas Parks and Leisure Activities

749 Veterans Memorial Dr. • 229-6297

If the county programs don't meet their needs, Las Vegans can try their city's recreational offerings. Like the county, many of the programs piggyback onto local schools after classes. Seven "community schools" offer more than 200 classes ranging from beginning tae kwon do to ballet. Fees rarely exceed $20 for a two-month session.

The city also has 10 community centers scattered among neighborhoods. These facilities offer additional youth programs, classes and a slew of athletic opportunities. An adaptive recreation program for handicapped children is at Lorenzi Park, 3333 W. Washington Avenue, 229-6727 or 386-9108 for the hearing impaired. (See our Recreation chapter for a list of centers.)

Some programs coincide with track breaks (nearly half of Las Vegas' elementary schools are on year-round schedules). The three-week programs cost $50 a week. A special municipal sports information line can be reached at 229-2256.

Lied Discovery Children's Museum

833 Las Vegas Blvd. N. • 382-3445

Art, science and a whole lot more come alive at this hands-on museum that's anything but stuffy. More than 100 exhibits are found in this downtown facility, and workshops and activities are often scheduled. One of the most popular stops is called Everyday Living, where youngsters earn a paycheck, use a bank ATM machine and shop for groceries in a pint-sized store.

Kids can sing along with the hits at K-KID, an in-house radio station, or take a spin in the Gyro Chair. The eight-story Science Tower, laden with a weather station, a computerized hurricane exhibit and a keyboard-activated fiber-optic sculpture, is another interesting exhibit. Most of the activities are geared to elementary-age children, though preschoolers and teens will find enough to keep them entertained.

Admission is $5 for adults, $4 for seniors, military and children 12 to 17, $3 for children 3 to 11 and free for toddlers 2 and younger. For residents the best deal is an annual membership, which allows unlimited visits, workshop discounts and invitations to members-only events. Base price is $30, with an additional $5 for each person added to the membership. Hours vary by season, but the museum is closed on Mondays. It is across the street from the Natural History Museum.

Mountasia Family Fun Center

2050 Olympic Ave., Henderson • 898-7777

A cool hangout for teens, Mountasia features mini racing cars, a sizable roller rink and lots of arcade games. The darkened skating facility has strobe lights and the latest hits playing on a powerful sound system. Skate rentals are $4 and include all rink privileges. Cars are $4 a ride or 3 trips for $10.

Hours are 2 until 10 PM Monday through Thursday, 2 PM to midnight on Fridays; 10 AM to midnight on Saturdays and 10 AM to 10 PM on Sundays. Movie theaters and a number of family-oriented restaurants are just a few steps away in the adjacent Green Valley shopping center.

Old Nevada

1 Gun Fighter Ln. • 875-4191

Hey, pardner, are you in the mood for pistol fights, melodramas and other Wild West happenings? Old Nevada, part of Bonnie Springs Ranch, is 30 minutes west of town. It's open daily at 10:30 AM, but its weekend

INSIDERS' TIP

Buffalo Bill's Hotel-Casino at Primm on the California-Nevada state line has a roller coaster with the tallest drop in the world. The Desperado plummets 225 feet at speeds of up to 80 mph. (See our Daycations chapter for more about Primm.)

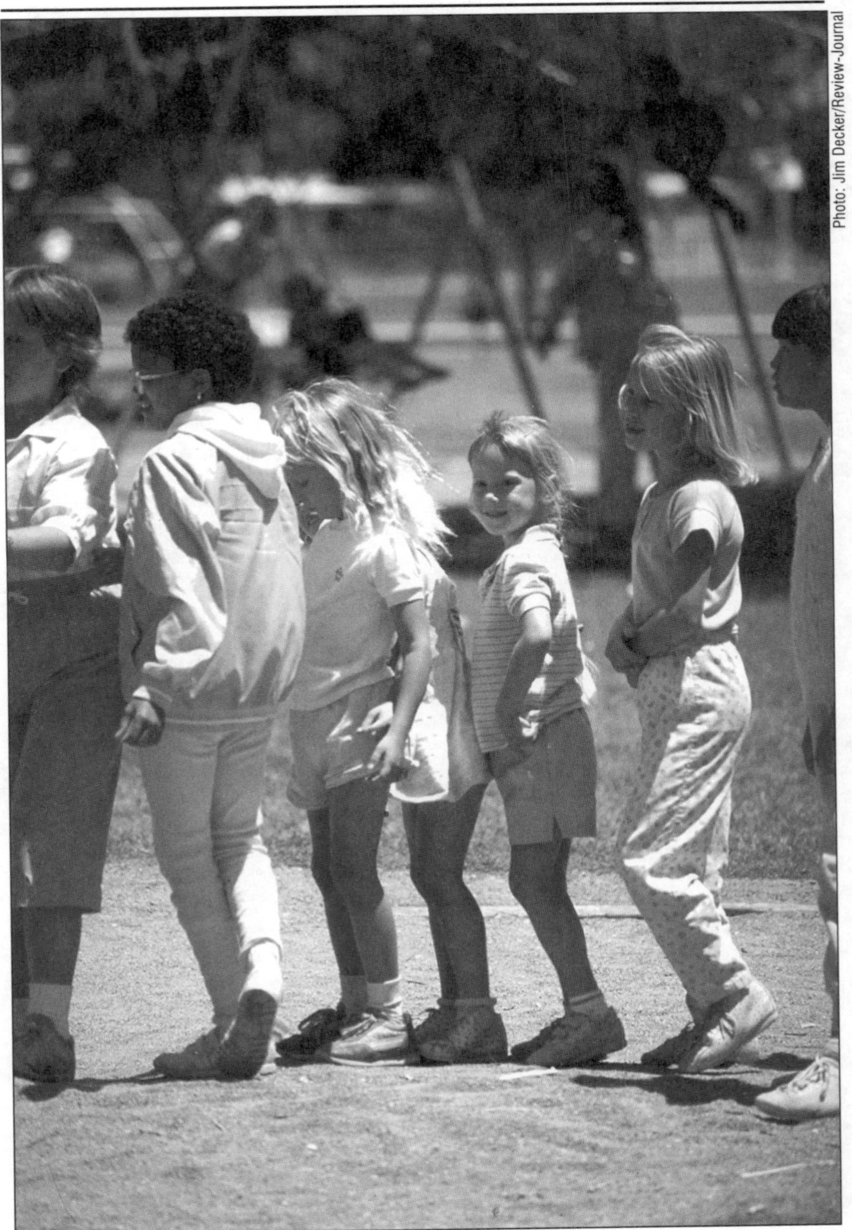
Photo: Jim Decker/Review-Journal

Sunset Park is one of numerous city and county parks in the valley that provides free family fun.

fare is especially fun, with train and stagecoach rides and a posse show that deputizes young'uns and lets them throw the bad guys in jail. For the kinder and gentler set, there are horseback rides and a petting zoo.

A restaurant serves up home-style food until closing at 5 PM (6 PM in the summer). Admission is $4 for children and $6.50 for adults.

Peter Piper Pizza

701 S. Decatur Blvd. • 877-8873
3430 E. Tropicana Ave. • 454-6366
350 Nellis Blvd. • 459-1200
2401 E. Lake Mead Blvd. • 399-1115

A local favorite for birthday parties, these pizza parlors offer much more than pies. Each restaurant has the feel of a big top, with carousels, kiddie rides and plenty of video and arcade games to go along with the food. With a minimum group of six, each party-goer gets pizza, cake, ice cream, drinks, balloons, party favors and game tokens. Rates vary slightly according to location, but party packages generally run $4.95 per child Monday through Thursday, $5.45 Friday through Sunday. Either way, moms and dads love it, because the house stays clean.

If you're not celebrating a birthday, eat and play anyway. Tokens cost 25¢ apiece. Winners receive coupons redeemable at the gift counter.

Rad Trax

3650 S. Decatur Blvd. • 253-7568

This place is Mecca for slot-car enthusiasts. With four tracks, including a new 155-foot layout, Rad Trax offers the best such facilities in the valley. Bring your own car and pay $1 for 15 minutes of track time or $5 for four hours. Cars can be rented for $2.50 for 15 minutes. Youngsters 15 and younger get half-price discounts Monday through Friday. The shop opens at 2 PM on weekdays and noon on weekends. Tracks are open until 10 PM on weekdays and 11 PM on weekends.

Ron Lee's World of Clowns

330 Carousel Pkwy., Henderson
• 434-1700

If you've seen a clown figurine, chances are it was made here. Free 35-minute tours are conducted at the plant from 9 AM to 5 PM daily. Youngsters can ride a carousel for $1, and visitors can clown around in the gallery and exhibits. It's best to go on a weekday, when you can see workers at this 30,000-square-foot plant work with pewter statues. About 200 are produced per day. (For more about factory tours, see our Attractions chapter.)

Scandia Family Fun Center

2900 Sirius Ave. • 364-0070

Miniature golf, batting cages, bumper boats, Indy race cars and lots of arcade games provide day-long entertainment . . . if you bring enough change. Three separate golf layouts offer varied degrees of difficulty. Golf costs $5.95 a round; the cars and boats go for $3.95. Kids 5 and younger can play and ride for free. For everyone else, the best deal may be a day-long pass for $15.95, which gives visitors the run of the park. Hours are 10 AM to 10 PM on weekdays and 10 AM to 11 PM on Fridays and Saturdays.

Southern Nevada Zoological Park

1775 N. Rancho Dr. • 648-5955

A family of rare Barbary apes calls this zoo home. So do a host of other mammals, birds and reptiles. Botanical displays also are found at the zoo, which is open daily from 9 AM to 4:30 PM. This is a compact zoo set on 2½ acres. But it nevertheless accommodates 150 species. Adult admission is $5, and children ages 2 to 12 get in for $3.

Ultrazone

2555 Maryland Pkwy. • 734-1577

Laser tag is the name of the game here. Players wearing vests and armed with laser guns can fire at each other for points in this 5,000-square-foot, two-story indoor facility. It's not painful, but it can be a bit pricey. Fifteen minutes in the arena costs $7.95. Group rates are available. Ultrazone is open Wednesday through Sunday and closed Monday and Tuesday.

INSIDERS' TIP

The Belz Factory Outlet World Mall is more than just shops. This mall at the south end of The Strip features a laser light show with synchronized music every hour at the center court and 585,000 square feet of walking space.

Wet 'n Wild

2600 Las Vegas Blvd. S. • 737-3819

From May to September, this 16-acre water park may be the coolest place on The Strip (it's next to the Sahara Hotel). Refreshed by 1.5 million gallons of water, Wet 'n Wild features a variety of rides ranging from a gentle kids' pool to the pulsating Black Hole ride. Teens love the Der Stuka, a seven-story freefall, and the Bomb Bay, which sends passengers screaming down a 76-foot slide. Coolers are permitted, but to maintain a family ambience, no alcohol is allowed. And be ready for crowds — on blazing summer days, folks are belly button to belly button.

All-day admission, which includes all rides, is $22.95 for adults and $16.95 for youngsters 3 to 11. Children younger than 3 get in free, and seniors get a 50 percent discount on all charges. Discount coupons frequently are available at local grocery stores.

YMCA

4141 Meadows Ln. • 877-9622

Hey, it's not just a song. For residents, the Y has some of the best kids' programs in town. In addition to the customary mix of gym and pool offerings, the Las Vegas facility runs dozens of camp-style programs. From toddlers to teens, participants can try their hand at computers, fine arts and even golf. Day-long sessions usually can be booked by the week, which is particularly helpful in the summer and during school track breaks. There also are after-school programs. For tourists, the Las Vegas YMCA offers up to 10 free visits to members who have "Y-Away" sticker on their cards.

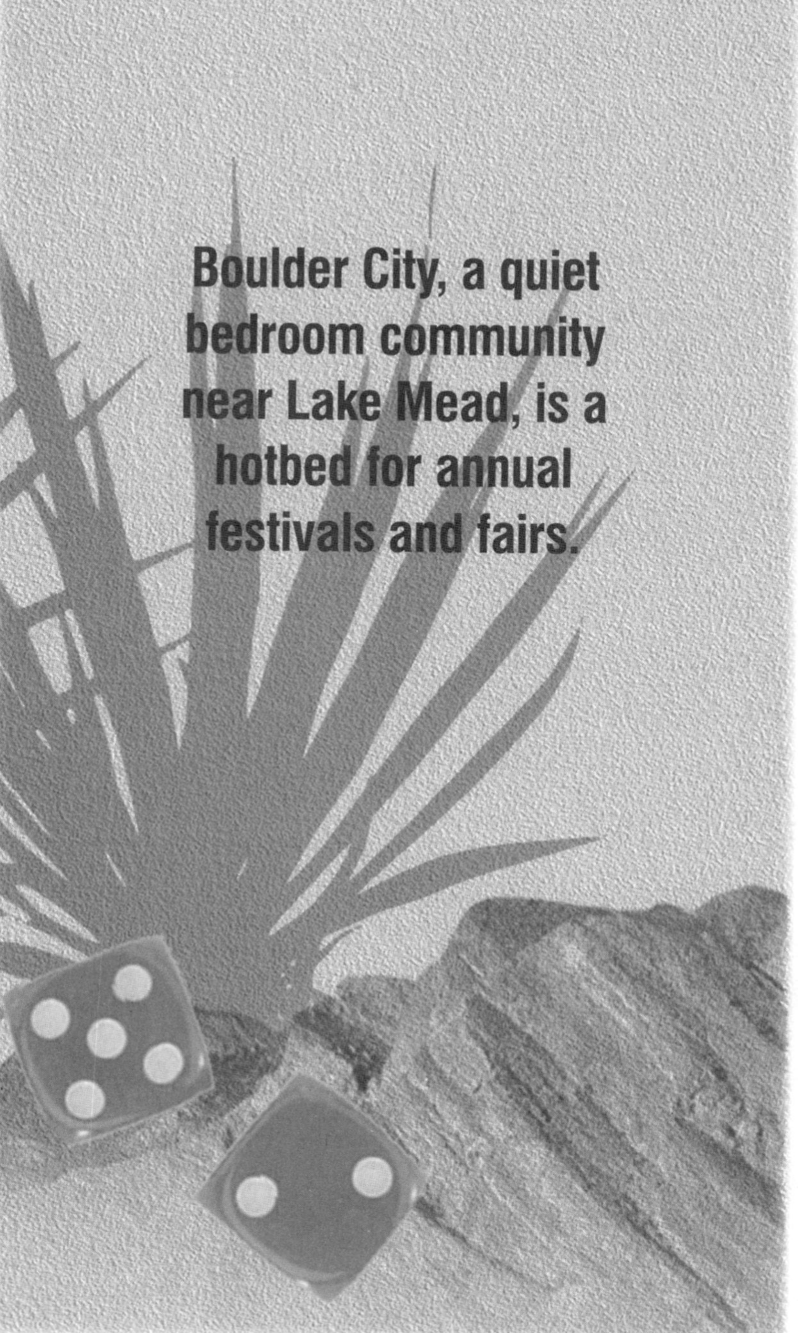
Boulder City, a quiet bedroom community near Lake Mead, is a hotbed for annual festivals and fairs.

Annual Events

Las Vegas' tourism industry runs 24 hours a day, seven days a week, but there's another, less frenetic side to the town. Like cities everywhere, Las Vegas has an annual cycle of time-honored celebrations and festivals, many of which are designed by and for local residents. That doesn't mean, however, that tourists can't join in the fun — and get a glimpse into the "regular" lifestyles of southern Nevada's not-so-rich and famous.

This chapter is dedicated to the events that come around each year. Some are world-class sporting contests (which have expanded descriptions in our Spectator Sports chapter). Others are offbeat, but most are down-home affairs that bring friends, families and neighbors together.

Included here are a few activities that go beyond the city limits. Boulder City, a quiet bedroom community near Lake Mead, is a hotbed for annual festivals and fairs. As the only town in Nevada without legalized gambling, Boulder City and its people are something special. Other rural events, such as desert road races, are worthy of mention as they draw spectators from throughout the region.

Regrettably, a few events were not pegged on the calendar as of our press time, so they didn't make the cut. For example, the Professional Bowlers Tour and the Senior Pro Bowlers Tour come to Las Vegas each year, but not always in the same month. (If you're curious about the latest dates, you can contact the Showboat Hotel at 385-9123 or the Professional Bowlers Association in Akron, Ohio, at (330) 836-5568.)

Unless otherwise noted, each of the following events is free to spectators.

January

Super Bowl High Rollers

Showboat Hotel, 2800 Fremont St. • 385-9150, (800) 257-6179

Amateur bowlers 50 and older compete for $1.3 million in prize money at this weeklong tournament in late January. Up to three bowlers can roll with a $750 entry fee. Seating is available for about 500 spectators. (See our Spectator Sports chapter.)

Chinese New Year

Asian Pacific Cultural Center, 4215 Spring Mountain Rd. • 252-0400

Celebrate the new year, Oriental style. The year begins on January 31 (1998 is the Year of the Tiger), and the occasion is marked by day-long festivities at this center 2 miles west of The Strip. Entertainers from throughout Asia and Hawaii perform authentic dances, including the Lion Dance, which chases out evil spirits. On tap are cultural exhibits, food and mahjong tournaments, where players match wits and numbered titles. The day's festivities also include fireworks.

OKC Gun Show

Cashman Field Center, 350 Las Vegas Blvd. N. • (800) 333-GUNS

This is one of the larger gun shows in the West, and it convenes in late January. Around 1,500 sales booths attract more than 20,000 attendees for this display of guns, ammo and military gear. Rifles and other long guns can be purchased on the spot. Handgun sales require a five-day waiting period, and purchases can only be made by Nevada residents. The event is usually held in conjunction with the manufacturing dealers' Shooting, Hunting and Outdoors Show. No weapons are sold at that event. Known as the S.H.O.T. Show, it's open to anyone who pays the $35 admission and has a federal firearms license.

Admission to the OKC Gun Show is $7, with dollar discounts for NRA members and senior citizens. Discount coupons can be found in the local newspapers on the day of the event. Rental space costs $60 for an 8-foot display table, plus a $14 vendor fee.

February

Las Vegas International Marathon

S.R. 604 to Las Vegas • 876-3870

This 26.2-mile event, held during the first week of February, begins in the small southern Nevada town of Sloan and finishes at the south end of The Strip. A half-marathon and relays also are run during the two-day event. Participants pay a $30 entry fee for the half-marathon and $40 for the big race. Grandstands are erected for free viewing along The Strip portion of the route. (See our Spectator Sports chapter.)

FYI

Unless otherwise noted, the area code for all phone numbers listed in this chapter is 702.

Mardi Gras

Charleston Heights Arts Center, 800 S. Brush St. • 229-6383

It's all purple, green and gold at this longest-running Mardi Gras festival in town. Ballroom dancing and partying begin around 6:30 PM on the Saturday before Ash Wednesday. A big Cajun buffet is served throughout the evening. Advance tickets are $10 for adults and $8 for students. Costumes are encouraged.

March

Hoover Dam Weekend Dance

1200 Ave. G, Boulder City • 293-4918

If you're a serious round and square dancer, drive out U.S. 93 to Boulder City on the first Friday and Saturday in March. This two-day event draws fancy steppers from throughout the West. Dances are held at Garrett Middle School on Avenue G on Friday night with alternating round dances and square dances. On Saturday morning, dancers head for the Arizona border for a giant street dance atop Hoover Dam.

Kite Carnival

Freedom Park, Washington Ave. and Mojave Rd. • 229-6729

Get a free kite and fly it on the first Saturday in March. There are prizes for youngsters and high flyers. Spring weather in Las Vegas is almost always breezy, so you're bound to get a good lift. The Metro Police Department also hosts a bike rodeo and a fingerprinting I.D. session for youngsters. A mobile stage provides entertainment.

Western Athletic Conference Basketball Tournament

Thomas and Mack Center, Tropicana Ave. and Swenson St. • 895-3900

Hoop it up with some of the best college basketball in the West as the top 12 WAC teams tip off for league championship honors in early March. The tourney runs six days and includes men's and women's teams. (See our Spectator Sports chapter.)

Busch Grand National

300 Las Vegas International Speedway, 7000 Las Vegas Blvd. N. • (800) 644-4444

NASCAR's Busch Grand National Series 300 runs at the 1.5-mile oval in late March. Ticket prices range from $15 for youngsters to $45 for adults. The Northern Auto Racing Club revs up for the Budweiser Sprint Car Shootout on the dirt track next door. (See our Spectator Sports chapter.)

Adult and Senior Free Fishing Derby

Sunset Park Lake, 2601 E. Sunset Rd. • 455-8289

Bring your tackle box and drop a line here. Sunset Lake is stocked each spring with 3,000 trout in preparation for this Saturday event in mid-March. As the name implies, this friendly contest is only open to anglers 18 and older. And you'd better get up pretty early. Registration begins at 6:30 AM, with competition running from 7 to 11:30 AM. Prizes are awarded for the five largest catches in two age categories: 18 to 54 and 55 and older. If you come up short, don't despair. There's a casting contest too. Free dinners and fishing equipment are among the bounty. Though this event is free, participants must have a Nevada fishing license, which can be purchased at Wal-Mart, K-Mart and most sporting goods stores for $12.

Corporate Challenge

749 Veterans Memorial Dr. • 229-6706

Think of this as the Olympics, Las Vegas style. Beginning in mid-March and concluding on the last Saturday in April, 20,000 amateur athletes compete for themselves and their companies in 27 different sporting events throughout the city. Competitors are divided among four classes, based on the size of their employer. Companies ranging is size from less than 150 workers to more than 2,000 help finance the events by paying all entry fees. That allows participants to play for free. Games include sand volleyball, tennis, swimming, ping-pong, skeet shooting, bowling, golf, softball, cycling and all track and field events. More than 100 teams vie for championship trophies while top competitors earn gold, silver and bronze medals in individual events. Closing ceremonies are highlighted by a massive tug-of-war and picnic. In some hotly contested years, that tug-of-war has decided team champions.

Miller Lite King of the Beach Invitational

Hard Rock Hotel-Casino, 4455 Paradise Rd. • 693-5000

Top players on the pro volleyball tour each play for $250,000. Two-man teams spike and dig in round-robin style over three days. Spectator tickets run $10 to $30. All the action takes place in the parking lot, which is filled with fine beach sand for the event.

St. Patrick's Day Parade

Fremont St. • 363-7178

Wearing o' the green is obligatory in downtown Las Vegas every March 17. That morning more than 130 entrants and floats set off for a colorful and raucous parade. This is the city's biggest parade. Lots of casinos use the occasion to run specials on corned beef and cabbage and green beer. Gulp! The procession starts off at 8 AM and winds up its six-block trip about 90 minutes later.

America's Cup Landsailing Regatta

Ivanpah Dry Lake, Primm • 220-4340

Wheeled craft of all sizes and shapes set sail across a desert stretch next to Interstate 15 at the Nevada-California state line. (See our Spectator Sports chapter.)

Big League Weekend

Cashman Field, 850 Las Vegas Blvd. N. • 386-7200

Wind up March with a Major League Baseball game at Cashman Field. Each year on a weekend in late March, six big-league teams play a set of games here before heading off for opening day. Tickets cost from $12.50 to $15.

Easter Senior High Roller

Showboat Hotel, 2800 Fremont St. • 385-9150, (800) 257-6179

Amateurs 50 and older gather for an Easter week bowl-a-thon at the Showboat Hotel. Entry fee is $400 and prize money tops $500,000. The Showboat also sponsors a slot tournament to go along with the event. (See our Spectator Sports chapter.)

April

Mardi Gras

Orleans Hotel-Casino, 4500 W. Tropicana Ave. • 365-7111
Rio Hotel-Casino, 3700 W. Flamingo Rd. • 252-7777
Fremont Street Experience, Fremont St. • 678-5724

In early April, these three venues stage special Mardi Gras festivities. The Orleans, a Bayou-themed resort on the west side of town, hosts live Dixieland jazz and buffet specials featuring authentic Cajun cuisine. The Rio, just 2 miles to the east, has a street carnival attraction called the Masquerade Village. Admission is free and visitors are treated to New Orleans-style parades and entertainment. Downtown, the Fremont Street looks more like Bourbon Street, with a street parade and entertainment imported from New Orleans. Call the locations for specific show times.

Jaycee Easter Egg Hunt

Jaycee Park, 2100 E. St. Louis St. • 229-6511

This Las Vegas tradition, sponsored by the local Jaycees, attracts as many as 500 youngsters each Easter. Beginning at noon, children line up in five age groups (up to age 11) and hunt down Easter goodies. The Jaycees shell out 3,000 plastic, candy and genuine eggs for this annual event that's free and open to the public. And, folks, remember to bring along a basket to haul home all your children's new-found treasures.

Native American Arts Festival

Clark County Heritage Museum, 1830 S. Boulder Hwy. • 455-7955

The history and artistry of American Indian cultures is celebrated through dance, drama and music performances at the Heritage Museum's outdoor stage. An outdoor craft market features more than 40 vendors with Native American arts, crafts and foods for sale to the public. Festival admission is included with the price of a museum ticket: $1.50 for adults and $1 for children and seniors.

Laughlin Rodeo Days

Casino Dr., Laughlin • (520) 296-6725, (800) 227-5245

Cowboys in the Laughlin River Stampede PRCA Rodeo compete over four days. The event, held in the first week of April, is usually graced by Miss Rodeo America. It also features what's billed as the world's longest line dance. (See our Spectator Sports chapter.)

Clark County Fair

Fairgrounds, Whipple Ave. and Woodbury Way, Logandale • 398-3247

This four-day fair celebrates rural life during the second week of April. Carnival rides, rodeo events and a host of homespun activities are conducted at the fairgrounds, a 40-minute drive north of Las Vegas on Interstate 15. The fair features live music and dancing daily. Literally thousands of exhibits and crafts competitions — ranging from counted cross-stitch to canned juices and nectars — are juried in all age categories. And, of course, livestock is judged, so bring along your potbelly pig and small caged birds.

To get there, take Nev. Highway 169 (Exit 93) to Logandale and go left on Whipple Avenue. General admission to the fair is $6 for ages 13 through 59. Children 5 to 12 pay $3, and seniors pay $5. Kids younger than 5 get in free. Carnival and rodeo passes run $6 to $14.

Primm 300

Whiskey Pete's Hotel-Casino, I-15, Primm • (702) 386-7867, (800) FUNSTOP

More than 300 off-road vehicles run this 300-mile course in the Nevada desert. The event is held mid-month and is sanctioned by the Southern California Off-Road Racing association. (See our Spectator Sports chapter.) For the best view of the race, bring your folding chair out behind Buffalo Bill's Hotel-Casino across the interstate.

Henderson Heritage Days

Various locations, Henderson • 565-8951

This citywide celebration, held over nine days in mid-April, features street dances, beauty pageants, chili cook-offs and a carnival. Each event takes place at a different venue. One don't-miss attraction is the Heritage Days Parade down Water Street. It seems like the whole town turns out for this event! Another favorite is the Mayor's Heritage Days Barbecue at the Civic Center Plaza. Music and free food are on tap, along with face painting and lots of games. It's an afternoon full of fun, and it's just 15 miles southwest of Las Vegas.

Harley Davidson River Run

Laughlin • 298-2214, 454-1544, (800) 227-5245

More than 50,000 hogs roar into this Colorado River town for a four-day extravaganza during the third weekend in April. This premier motorcycle event features riding exhibitions, bike giveaways and a 100-mile poker run with prizes. Police departments and the Harley's Angels precision riding team are always crowd favorites, as is the Miss Laughlin beauty contest. Registration is $30 in advance and on-site. Participants are eligible to take a spin on the Harley of their choice, which is a great way to stay current with the latest factory designs and features.

Food and entertainment are in plentiful supply, with daily pancake breakfasts and nightly concerts. These events cost extra. Laughlin is a 90-mile drive south of Las Vegas via U.S. Highway 95 and Nev. Highway 163.

World Series of Poker

Binion's Horseshoe, 128 Fremont St. • 382-1600, (800) 93POKER

You've got to know when to hold 'em and when to fold 'em at this storied event. From mid-April to early May, more than 4,000 players match wits in 21 tournaments. Buy-ins range from $1,000 for the ladies' game to $10,000 for the big No-Limit Hold 'Em World Championship that carries a $1 million first-place prize and $3 million total winnings. That nerve-rattling, four-day game wraps up the three-week gambling orgy. This event is a poker aficionado's hall of fame, attracting the best in the business. In fact, 15 current players have topped $1 million in winnings. But true to its humble origins, the tournament's cash prize is delivered in an unassuming cardboard box. The whole event is free and open to the public, but space is limited.

Las Vegas Senior Classic

TPC at the Canyons, 1951 Canyon Run Dr. • 242-3000

Take a trip down memory lane with some of the best senior golfers in the country. Tickets are $15 per day for this mid-month event. (See our Spectator Sports chapter.)

Earth Fair

Sunset Park, 2601 E. Sunset Rd. • 642-3253

Think green! This annual environmental fest, held on the Saturday nearest Earth Day's designated April 22 date, draws 45,000 to 50,000 people for a day in the park. Some come for the free trees — 5,000 pine seedlings and thousands more potted plants and Joshua trees are given away — others just come for fun. Youngsters are entertained by a carnival, and they can try their hands at creating art objects from recycled products. For the more mature set, oldies entertainers and impersonators work stage routines throughout the day. Also on display: electric cars, alternative fuel demonstrations and the winning projects in the local schools' Science Fair competition. Note that not everything is environmentally correct here. If you still crave a hot dog or ice cream, there are vendors who serve those too. The event is sponsored by KVBC Channel 3 TV.

Earth Day

UNLV, 4505 S. Maryland Pkwy. • 895-1630

On April 22, UNLV hosts an educationally oriented Earth Day for 3,000 local students — and any environmentally aware adults looking to skip a day of work. Keepers of the Wild, a local animal conservation group, brings in rare and threatened species, while the water district conducts a conservation demonstration. Solar car manufacturers and recyclers also show their wares.

May

Art Walk in the Park

Hills Park, 9099 Hillpointe Rd. • 229-6511

Nearly 100 Western artists display their wares at this free show held during the first weekend in May. Running from 10 AM to 6 PM on Saturday and Sunday, the Art Walk features just about every objet d'art from oil paintings to ceramics. If the kids get bored, food vendors are on hand, and lots of playground equipment is nearby. During the walk, you might traipse through the fountain at the park's entrance. It that shoots water up through the pavement — very cool!

Cinco de Mayo

Freedom Park, Washington Ave. and Mojave Rd. • 649-8553

Las Vegas' large and growing Hispanic community turns out for this annual Mexican celebration held on the Sunday closest to May 5. Daylong festivities start at 8 AM and last until sundown. It's a predominantly local affair that feels like a giant community picnic. Marching bands, games and demonstrations by firefighters are among the highlights, along

INSIDERS' TIP

During Halloween and the winter holidays, the MGM Theme Park puts on special themed events to celebrate the seasons. But beware that some passes exempt such promotions.

with carnival-style games. A multitude of food and merchandise booths are on the grounds. Admission is $5 per person, with youngsters 12 and younger getting in free.

Fremont Street Experience

Fremont St. • 678-5724

Tourists and locals alike can enjoy a three-day bash hosted by the Fremont Street Experience around Cinco de Mayo. Mariachi music and Hispanic entertainers fill the four-block section of downtown on May 4, 5 and 6.

Jazz in the Park

Clark County Government Center, 500 Grand Central Pkwy. • 455-8242

From mid-May to mid-June, four traditional jazz concerts are held on alternating Saturday evenings at the Government Center's amphitheater downtown. The atmosphere is informal, and the admission is free. Bring the kids and a picnic basket for jazz under the stars. Performers come from around town and around the country, with the assemblage ranging from duets to big bands. Shows run from 8 to 10 PM.

Craft Fair and Rib Burnoff

Sunset Park, 2601 E. Sunset Rd. • 455-8206

Music (mainly country), food and crafts are the order of the day for this mid-month event at Sunset Park. More than 80 vendors sell their wares and tantalize your tastebuds. Admission is $3. The rib burnoff features some of the area's top restaurants working the grills. Prices range from $1.50 for a sample to $15 for a full rack of ribs with side dishes of salads, beans and biscuits. Hours are 10 AM to 6 PM.

Spring Jamboree and Crafts Fair

Bicentennial Park, Colorado St., Boulder City • 293-2034

Handcrafted artwork is judged and juried at this two-day event held on the first weekend in May. The entry fee for a booth is $100, and about 150 booths are available. Also on the grounds are a classic car show, a kiddie carnival and a business fair, so there's something for everyone in the annual crowd that numbers up to 30,000.

June

Helldorado Days

Thomas and Mack Center, Tropicana Ave. and Swenson St. • 870-1221

A six-decade tradition, the Helldorado Days rodeo blends good fun and good causes in early June. Appealing to the cowboy roots of southern Nevada, the four-day event features bull riding and nightly rodeos, outdoor barbecues, a dance hall and exhibits. Admission is $12 to the bull ride and $11 to the rodeo. Proceeds help to fund the Las Vegas' Elks charitable endeavors and youth activities.

Winston Cup West

Las Vegas International Speedway, 7000 Las Vegas Blvd. N. • (800) 644-4444

NASCAR's Winston Cup West Series comes to town for a 150-mile race under the lights. General admission prices range from $15 to $45. (See our Spectator Sports chapter.)

Children's Fishing Derby

Sunset Park Lake, 2601 E. Sunset Rd. • 455-8289

On the second Saturday in June, people younger than 18 are invited to test their fishing skills at this 26-acre Sunset Park Lake. Unlike their elders competing in the March fishing derby, children do not need a Nevada fishing license to participate in this free event. But they nevertheless are eligible for prizes valued at $3,000. Prizes are given for the five biggest fish landed in three age categories. Gifts include movie passes, Grand Slam Canyon theme park tickets, free pizzas and, of course, fishing gear. Such largesse attracts nearly 1,500 participants each year. In preparation, the lake is stocked with 3,000 catfish. The biggest catch on record is a 13 pounder! Registration begins at 6:30 AM and the competition runs from 7 to 11:30 AM.

International Food Festival

Cashman Field Center, 350 Las Vegas Blvd. N. • 258-8961

Call this the United Nations of food. More than 20 countries' culinary offerings are on the menu here. The fare ranges from flavorful

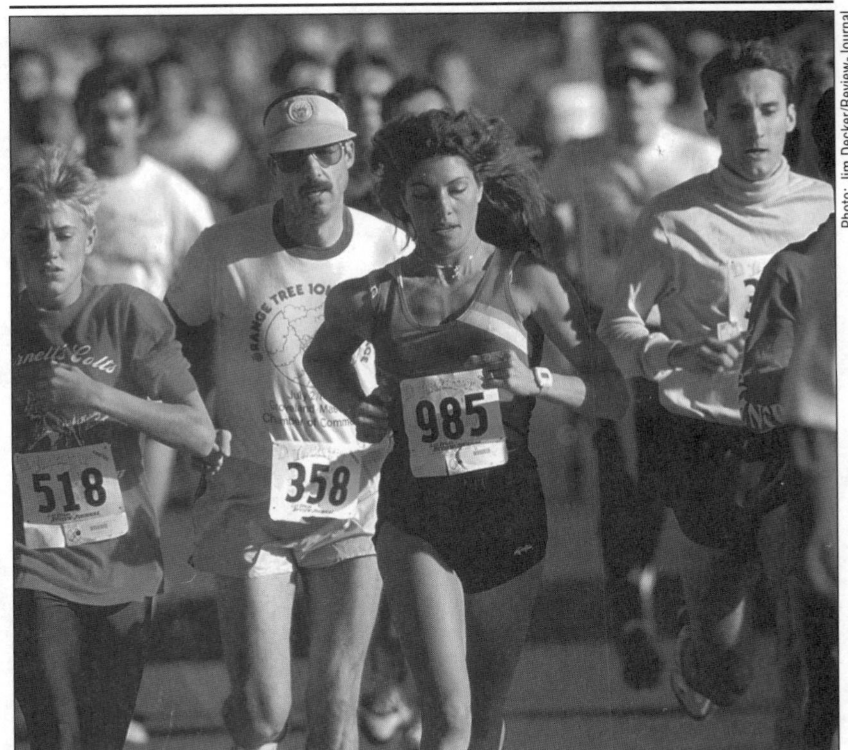

The Las Vegas International Marathon runs every February, attracting thousands of competitors and spectators.

Basque paella to red-hot Chilean dishes. Also popular is the local Irish Club's homemade Irish cream drink and a German beer garden. Meal prices range from $3 to $4, and admission is $2. Stage performances show off ethnic dances, and food booths have cultural displays. And whatever you do, don't eat before you go to this day-long Sunday food fest.

July

Boulder City Damboree

Central Park, Fifth and B Sts., Boulder City • 293-2034

Good old-fashioned Fourth of July fun is the order of the day in Boulder City. Festivities start with a pancake breakfast and a parade, followed by patriotic speeches and a band concert. Food and game booths are open all day at the park. At dusk, crowds gather at the old airport off U.S. 93 for a fireworks show.

A Star Spangled Celebration

Hills Park, Hillpointe Rd. and Glenside Dr., Summerlin • 792-4337

Patriotic music and a sing-along are featured at this alfresco affair in Summerlin. Playing under the lights, the Nevada Symphony Orchestra performs all the time-honored favorites, from "Stars and Stripes Forever" to the "Battle Hymn of the Republic" and the "1812 Overture." Bring along a picnic basket and spread out on the lawn, then stick around afterward for a panoramic view of the valley's Fourth of July fireworks shows. Tickets range from $15 to $25.

High Rollers

Showboat Hotel, 2800 Fremont St. • 385-9150, (800) 257-6179

The city's biggest amateur bowling event runs around the week of Fourth of July when the Showboat hosts the High Roller Tournament. A purse of $2.6 million is on the line, with $200,000 for first place. Entry fee is $1,100, but spectators always get in free.

Tour of World Figure Skating Champions

Thomas and Mack Center, Tropicana Ave. and Swenson St. • 895-3900

The ice heats up each July when the Campbell's Soups Tour of World Figure Skating Champions hits town. The biggest names in skating —including Michelle Kwan, Elvis Stojko, Oksana Baiul and Victor Petrenko — are among the performers. (See our Spectator Sports chapter.)

August

Sundown Bluegrass Concerts

Jaycee Park, 2100 E. St. Louis St. • 229-6511

Kick off your shoes and groove to the bluegrass tunes during this free concert series. Conducted during the first two Sunday evenings in August, the concerts begin at 7:30 each evening. Come early, bring a picnic basket and spread out on the lawn for a good time. There's some top-notch fiddlin' at these concerts, which showcase up and coming bands. A portable band shell provides excellent acoustics.

Kidzmania

Cashman Field Center, 350 Las Vegas Blvd. N. • 233-8388

By this time of the summer, many kids are going a little stir crazy in the summer heat. This two-day exposition, held in air-conditioned comfort, is a good antidote offering a wide variety of activities. There's a health and fitness area, where youngsters can try aerobics. Children can stop by the petting zone or join a kids-style game of "The Price is Right" or "Let's Make a Deal." There's even an essay contest in which the winner earns a trip to Disneyland.

Moms and dads can listen in on speakers discussing parenting issues from family discipline to college preparations. Exhibitors are on hand, representing preschools, dance schools, gymnasiums and karate clubs. Exhibitors can rent space for this Saturday and Sunday event for $575. Children are admitted free with one adult ticket that costs $5.

Police Olympics

Various parks • 259-6350

Law enforcement personnel from around the country compete in 22 events over five days in mid-August. Games range from bocce ball and arm wrestling to golf and volleyball (no handcuffs, nightsticks or weapons allowed). Entrants pay $40 to play in this annual sports fest that draws 3,000 participants annually — some from as far away as Germany and Australia. One of the biggest events is a round-robin softball tournament. Games are usually held under the lights and go until 1 AM. Needless to say, Las Vegas' Metro Police have a decided home-field advantage in the withering desert heat. Call the information number for venues.

Itty Bitty Baseball

Sunset Park, 2601 E. Sunset Rd. • 455-8206

Bring your future slugger to this one-day field event in late August. Youngsters ages 3 to 6 can try their hands at catching, throwing and hitting. For an $8 advance registration, participants get a free whiffle ball and bat to take home. This event is part of a larger Itty Bitty sports program

INSIDERS' TIP

If you're looking for an update on activities, try calling Las Vegas Events, which sponsors special tourism-oriented events. The number is 731-2115. Another good source for calendar information is the visitors center at the Las Vegas Convention Center and Visitors Authority, 892-2874.

that includes tennis, soccer, basketball — and even a Gran Prix with Big Wheels. Call the Clark County Parks Department for specific dates and registration information.

September

Chautauqua Festival

Bicentennial Park, Colorado St., Boulder City • 294-6224

Mingle, converse and dine with historic figures such as Thomas Jefferson, Abraham Lincoln, Brigham Young and Susan B. Anthony at this country-style cultural event. These reenactors know their history, and you will revel in the authentic setting. The two-day event, held during the second weekend of September, features a continental breakfast and daytime program for children on Saturday. Admission to the evening event is $2 ($1 for seniors and children). If you want to get up close and personal with the cast of Chautauqua scholars, while donating to Boulder City's arts programs, check out the dinner reception on the previous Thursday. Tickets are $25.

Las Vegas Cup Hydroplane Race

Boulder Beach, Lake Mead • 892-2874, (206) 870-8888

The world's fastest boats will make waves across Lake Mead during this two-day event. Also on tap is a propeller boat race. These jet-powered special crafts reach speeds of 200 mph. (See our Spectator Sports chapter for more information.)

Silver State Classic Challenge

S. R. 318, Lund • 385-9123

In mid-September, 100 cars roar up the Lund-to-Hiko route in pursuit of glory. The field includes foreign and domestic cars. The Showboat Hotel hosts a rally and car show before the race. A similar but smaller race, the Nevada Open, runs the same course in mid-May. (See our Spectator Sports chapter for more information.)

Greek Food Festival

St. John's Orthodox Church, 5300 El Camino Rd. • 221-8245

From luscious pastries to full-course meals, the food at this festival is sure to please all Greek food lovers. Held during the last week of September or in early October, this Friday-Saturday-Sunday event features authentic Greek music and entertainment on the lush grounds of this massive church located near Hacienda Road and Jones Boulevard on the far southwest side of the city. Admission tickets run around $2, with dining à la carte.

Rattlin' Rails Handcar Race

Yucca Street Rail Yard, Yucca St., Boulder City • 293-4857

Four-person handcars race up and down the tracks in this competition held during the last weekend of the month. Qualifying heats are run on Saturday. The races, run side-by-side on a rail spur, feature photo finishes just about every time, with most being decided by fractions of a second. How fast are they? Handcars have traversed the 450-foot distance in 16 seconds! Entry fees are $100 for five-person teams (someone has to push the handcar at the start of the race, and that person usually ends up face down in the middle of the tracks). The competitors enjoy a barbecue dinner at the trophy presentation on Sunday night. Spectators are welcome and can view all the action from bleachers equipped with a cooling mist system. Admission is free.

Shakespeare in the Park

Foxridge Park, Valle Verde at Warm Springs Rd., Henderson • 458-8855

The Bard's plays are staged for free at this end-of-September theater on the green. Bring the whole family and spread out on a blanket for three nightly performances. Friday and Saturday shows begin at 7 PM, with the Sunday performance starting at 6 PM. All of them are preceded by a show on the green, featuring jugglers, roving minstrel singers and assorted

INSIDERS' TIP

Nellis Air Force Base hosts an air show and open house on alternating years. Details on the schedule for the one-day event can be obtained by calling the public affairs office at 652-2750.

other acts. Local high school performers also turn out in Elizabethan-era costumes to sing and entertain. If you want to sit up front, a $150 pass will buy four folding chairs near the stage. Otherwise, it's first come, first served. Snacks are available.

Wurstfest

Gazebo Park California and Arizona Sts., Boulder City • 293-4151

Get a jump on Oktoberfest's bratwurst and beer here on the last Saturday in September. Festivities begin around noon and finish with a street dance in the evening. Also on tap is a motorcycle collection and a big auction of local collectibles. Among the recent items on the block was an Andre Agassi tennis racquet. Proceeds help fund the Sunrise Rotary Club's all-night party for Boulder City High School's graduating class.

October

Jaycee State Fair

Cashman Field, 350 Las Vegas Blvd. N. • 457-FAIR

One of the big events in the fall, this fair runs for six days during the first week of October. A carnival midway, exhibits and food booths fill this baseball and convention complex north of downtown. Some big-name bands provide entertainment, with nightly themes encompassing rock, jazz and Latin music.

The fair attracts about 60,000 visitors each year, with proceeds helping to fund the Jaycees' community work, including an Easter Egg hunt, clothes drives and meals for the homeless. General admission tickets cost $6 for adults, $4 for children ages 5 through 12 and $3 for seniors. The musical entertainment is included in the ticket price, but bring your change for the carnival rides and games.

Art in the Park

Bicentennial Park, Colorado St., Boulder City • 294-1611

More than 100,000 people descend on this quiet town during the first full weekend of the month to revel in arts and crafts. Some 300 booths display handiwork from throughout the valley, while the Boulder City Hospital Auxiliary provides the food. Shuttle buses are provided from remote parking lots.

Las Vegas 500K

Las Vegas International Speedway, 7000 Las Vegas Blvd. N. • (800) 644-4444

The Indy Racing League's 500-kilometer race runs under the lights. The IRL features big names in open-wheel racing. Tickets range from $15 to $45. (See our Spectator Sports chapter.)

Las Vegas Invitational

TPC at Summerlin, 1700 Village Center Cir. • 256-0111

Early October usually brings great weather to southern Nevada. It also brings great golfers, such as Tiger Woods, Greg Norman, Fuzzy Zoeller and Curtis Strange. Walk this immaculate stadium course — and take a peek at one of Las Vegas' most prestigious golf communities while you're at it. Daily tickets run $10 to $16. Five-day passes are also available for the event, which runs Wednesday through Sunday. (See our Spectator Sports chapter.)

Las Vegas Balloon Classic

Sam Boyd Stadium Park, Boulder Hwy. and Sunset Rd. • 434-0848, (800) 362-4040

More than 100 hot-air balloons fill the sky for this three-day event held in late October. Balloons come from all over the world and lift off every morning at 7 AM. On Saturday night the balloonists fire up their burners while tethered to the ground, giving the appearance of 100 giant glowing Christmas tree ornaments. Throughout the weekend, visitors can stroll among craft booths, vintage car displays, antique machinery and 14 food booths. On Sunday morning, wake up to a green chili cookoff. Competitors pay a $60 entry fee to vie for cash prizes and trophies ($30 for members of the Green Chili Association). Proceeds go to local charities.

Country Music Amateur Awards

Showboat Hotel, 2800 Fremont St. • 385-9150

Catch some of country music's rising talent in this three-day amateur competition in mid-October. This is the event where teenage singing sensation Lee Ann Rimes was discovered a couple of years ago. Performances are held from 8 PM to 1 AM, and they're all free.

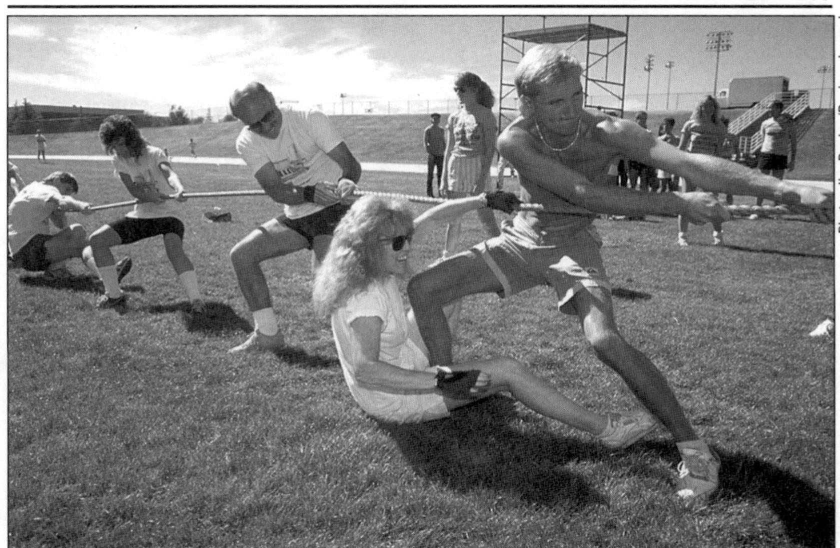
Photo: Jim Decker/Review-Journal

Corporate Challenge pits business vs. business each March and April, with 20,000 workers competing in 27 sports.

Rio's Italian Festival

Rio Hotel-Casino, 3700 W. Flamingo Rd. • 252-7777

Italian festivities at a Brazilian-themed resort? Well, that's Las Vegas for you. On the weekend preceding Columbus Day, the Rio hosts a celebration of Italian food and entertainment. This free event has the look of a variety show, with musicians, singers, bocce ball tournaments and children's face-painting booths. But the biggest draw is food — and lots of it. Dozens of Las Vegas' Italian restaurants offer samplings for $1 to $3. Some of these same eateries participate in a pasta-sauce contest, which is judged by the local media. The public can get involved, too, by bellying up to the table for a spaghetti-eating competition. There's even a grape-stomping contest. The event is held at the Rio's outdoors event center by the pool.

Creature Feature

Freedom Park, Washington Ave. at Mojave Rd. • 229-6729

For the youngsters, this is good, scary fun. Lots of games, prizes and sweet treats are available at this event, held two Saturdays before Halloween. Each year, roughly 4,000 people turn out to see live entertainment and to hear story tellers spin some scary tales. Dress the kids in their costumes, and they'll be eligible for prizes.

November

Craftsman Truck Series

Las Vegas International Speedway, 7000 Las Vegas Blvd. N. • (800) 644-4444

NASCAR Craftsman Truck Series and NASCAR's Winston West Tour each run 300-mile races in mid-November. Since the temperatures cool down about this time, both races are run in the daytime. It's a hoot to see more than 70 Chevy, Ford and Dodge pickups racing at speeds up to 160 mph. Tickets start at $25.

ITT-LPGA Tour Championship

Desert Inn Country Club, 3145 Las Vegas Blvd. S. • 733-4653

Las Vegas hosts the 30 top money winners on the women's tour during the week before Thanksgiving. Passes for the four-day event run $10 to $15 daily. (See our Spectator Sports chapter.)

Strut Your Mutt Day

Dog Fancier's Park, 5800 E. Flamingo Rd. • 455-8206

Have a dog-day afternoon at this uproarious event. Where else can you see stupid pet and human tricks such as a Dress Your Dog contest, a howling competition or a Puppy Love match to see how many times a dog will kiss its owner? And will any canine be able to fetch a hot dog without eating it? Winners of these and other events get Olympic-style medals—in the shape of dog bones. Held during the first or second Saturday of the month, Strut Your Mutt Day attracts as many as 300 pooches and thousands of family members. Admission for participants is $3. Spectators can join the fun for $1 or just bring a can or bag of pet food (which goes to the animal shelter).

Metro Police's K-9 unit also puts on a demonstration, and 30 booths are staffed by dog clubs and such groups as Canine Companions for Independence.

Thanksgiving Senior High Roller

Showboat Hotel, 2800 Fremont St. • 385-9150, (800) 257-6179

Like the Easter event, this weeklong holiday tournament attracts about 400 amateur bowlers age 50 and older. Participants pay a $400 entry fee and vie for more than $500,000 in prize money.

December

Western Athletic Conference Football Championship

Sam Boyd Stadium, Boulder Hwy. and Sunset Rd. • 895-3900

The first-place finishers in the Pacific and Mountain divisions battle for the league championship and a top bowl bid in the first weekend of the month. (See our Spectator Sports chapter.)

National Finals Rodeo

Thomas and Mack Center, Tropicana Ave. and Swenson St. • 895-3900

Las Vegas begins to resemble a cowtown in early December as the nation's richest rodeo rides in. And that's no bull. This 10-day event features the top 15 rodeo performers in seven different events: bareback riding, steer wrestling, team roping, saddle bronc riding, calf roping, barrel racing and bull riding. Prize money tops $3 million. (See our Spectator Sports chapter.)

Parade of Lights

Lake Mead Marina, 322 Lakeshore Rd., Boulder City • 457-2797

Get into the holiday spirit with this luminous lake event as 50 boats don special lights on the water. Trophies are awarded in nine classes of craft, including a Best of Show award for the most brilliant display. Past years have drawn 20,000 shoreline spectators, along with 350 other boats. Dress warmly for this night and bring along some food to cook at the beach. If you arrive early, stop by the marina and see the boats up close as they prepare for the show. From Las Vegas, take U.S. 93 south to the Boulder Beach exit and follow the signs to the marina.

Las Vegas Rugby Challenge

Freedom Park, Washington Ave. and Mojave Rd. • 656-7401

What do you call 1,080 guys chasing a pigskin? A rugby tournament, of course. And it happens during the first weekend of December when teams from around the world vie for prize money and trophies. The event is free to spectators. (See our Spectator Sports chapter for more details.)

Kwanzaa

West Las Vegas Library, 951 W. Lake Mead Blvd. • 647-8169

Celebrate the values of African-American

INSIDERS' TIP

During the first week of February, Clark County Community Centers host a "Going to Pieces Puzzle Contest." Puzzlers of all ages can test their skills on a timed jigsaw puzzle. There are individual and team divisions, with winners at each center moving on to compete in a playoff at the Meadows Mall. For dates and locations, call 455-8206.

life with a weeklong series of theater performances and workshops. Each day is themed to a specific value, ranging from self-determination and cooperative economics to creativity and faith. Many of the events revolve around family, so bring along the brood; they'll find that learning is fun!

Las Vegas Shootout

Thomas and Mack Center, Tropicana Ave. and Swenson St. • 895-3900

UNLV invites three top-20 teams for a holiday basketball tournament in late December. Tickets for the weekend tourney start around $15 per game. The teams come from across the country and provide a good early season test for the Rebels. (See additional details in our Spectator Sports chapter.)

Las Vegas Bowl

Sam Boyd Stadium, Boulder Hwy. and Sunset Rd. • 895-3900

Pitting a top Western Athletic Conference team against an at-large team from another major conference, the Las Vegas Bowl kicks off the bowl season. Usually held on the third Saturday of December, the Las Vegas Bowl awards $800,000 to each team. The bowl is sponsored by the Las Vegas Convention and Visitors Authority. Tickets begin at $25. (See additional details in our Spectator Sports chapter.)

New Year's Eve

Fremont Street Experience, Fremont St. • 678-5724

A 26-day-long Country Holiday Festival runs from December 1 through 26 along this four-block section of Fremont Street. A 50-foot Christmas tree is erected under the downtown canopy. Entertainment includes the March of the Toy Soldiers, live bands and a parade.

Then, on New Year's Eve, join a big street party in Glitter Gulch. The high-tech canopy overhead offers a dazzling light show while a high-powered sound system cranks out live music into the wee hours of the new year. Admission is $10.

With the growth of the city and the influx of a rapidly changing population, a burgeoning arts community has emerged in Sin City.

Arts and Culture

Art and culture in Las Vegas? The juxtaposition stretches the limits of believability. And why shouldn't it? The perception that Las Vegas culture is nothing more than Elvis lookalikes, dice clocks and rhinestone G-strings is not an uncommon one — and it isn't entirely unfair.

In fact, Las Vegas has supported that perception ever since Bugsy Siegel built his fabulous tangerine-magenta-fuchsia Flamingo Hotel in 1946. Since then Las Vegas has spoken, loudly at times, to the notions that high culture is no better than popular culture, that ballet is no better than burlesque, that the symphony is no better than stand-up comedy and that Vienna is no less vulgar than Vegas itself.

Yet, with the growth of the city and the influx of a rapidly changing population (about 5,000 people move to Las Vegas each month), a burgeoning arts community has emerged in Sin City. Admittedly, we have a long way to go before we'll threaten Stratford-on-Avon as an arts citadel, but our cultural community is making strides.

For instance, a typical itinerary for a cultural weekend in Las Vegas might include Renaissance madrigals by the nationally known Waverly Consort; David Mamet's *Speed-the-Plow*, staged by a local theater group; gallery hopping among everything from African artifacts to neon sculpture; a rehearsal of the resident opera theater at the University of Nevada, Las Vegas ; a film noir festival featuring Robert Siodmak's *The Killers*; and an evening of lively modern dance set to works ranging from Vivaldi to M.C. Hammer.

One of the problems our arts community faces is that the city is so young its art presence is being built from scratch. Another problem is that private funding for the arts is practically nonexistent in this town. Most of the arts support has come from the public sector, notably the City of Las Vegas and the University of Nevada, Las Vegas. Also contributing to the cultural enrichment of the community, although to a lesser extent, are Clark County's Cultural Affairs Division, the Community College of Southern Nevada and the Las Vegas-Clark County Library District.

Through the backing and encouragement of these and other institutions, Las Vegas is now home to dozens of resident arts groups and galleries, a nationally respected dance theater, symphony orchestras, an opera company, several community theaters, chamber music ensembles, a historical society and museum, an art museum and a natural history museum.

Moreover, some of the biggest names in classical music, from Itzhak Perlman to Leontyne Price, have visited Las Vegas as part of UNLV's Charles Vanda Master Series. International dance troupes and ensembles, such as the London Ballet and L'Orchestre de Chambere de Montreal, have been guests of the Southern Nevada Community Concert Association.

No culture in Las Vegas? Take time to look beyond the cleavage, craps tables and circus clowns. You might be surprised at what you find.

For a complete listing of music and dance recitals, concerts, plays, art galleries and exhibitions, book signings and other arts-related events, check Friday's edition of the *Las Vegas Review-Journal* newspaper, 383-0400. The

INSIDERS' TIP

From art exhibits to dance recitals to jazz concerts, tune in for all the latest arts news and information on the Arts Alive radio show every Friday on KNPR Public Radio 89.5 FM.

R-J also publishes close-ups and articles on featured events and artists. You'll also find arts listings and write-ups in the alternative weekly newspaper, *City Life*, 871-6780, and the weekly lifestyle tabloid, *Scope*, 256-6388. The latter two are distributed free of charge throughout the valley.

Support Organizations

Allied Arts Council of Southern Nevada

401 S. Fourth St., Ste. 110 • 386-4804

The Allied Arts Council reached its peak as a force on the cultural scene in the early 1990s, when it published a monthly magazine and coordinated the arts and artists in Southern Nevada and successfully lobbied for state and national funding for arts programs.

FYI

Unless otherwise noted, the area code for all phone numbers listed in this chapter is 702.

After a brief period of dormancy, the council in 1996 hired a full-time executive director, Constance DeVereaux, a part-time membership/events coordinator and a part-time publicist. Although the arts council no longer publishes a slick monthly magazine, the new staff has revived its "Arts Alive" datebook, a monthly arts newsletter and calendar and has established an Internet site (www.artsnevada.org) to disperse arts information.

The arts council also provides arts news on a weekly radio broadcast on KNPR, the city's National Public Radio affiliate. Besides enhancing the community's awareness of the arts, the council also has developed a Teaching and Learning the Arts plan for the local school district, and the Southern Nevada Arts Stabilization Initiative, a series of workshops for arts groups. The council also helps local artists with technical assistance and represents Southern Nevada at national arts conferences and workshops.

Cultural and Community Affairs Division - City of Las Vegas Parks and Leisure Activities

749 Veterans Memorial Dr. • 229-6297

The Cultural and Community Affairs Division sponsors a cultural season of performing arts, film series, artists and exhibitions. Recent events have included the American-Israeli contemporary dance troupe Keshet Chaim, classical guitarist David Richter and An Evening in Old Vienna by the Paragon Orchestra.

The division also stages the annual Choreographers Showcase, which features energetic new dances created by some of the city's best choreographers.

Musical touring artists recently hosted by the city include Bill Miller, singer/songwriter of Native American ballads and country rock; and the Women of the Calabash, a rhythmic explosion of music from Africa, Latin America, the Caribbean and Black America.

The division also hosts a variety of events and festivals like the Pacific Islands Festival, which features traditional dances, crafts, boutiques, games and a great luau. It also sponsors the open-air Farmers Market monthly at the Sammy Davis Jr. Festival Plaza in Lorenzi Park.

At the annual Art Walk in the Park at the Hills Park in Summerlin, you can see more than 100 artists and craftspeople from Nevada and throughout the Southwest present original work in oils, acrylics, watercolors, photography, etchings, batiks and sculpture (see our Annual Events chapter).

Musically, the city stages the Las Vegas Music Festival in June, when string, wind and upper brass students from around the world converge for 14 days of master classes, chamber music, concerto readings and concerts. Also in June the city parks are the setting for Sunday Concerts in the Park staged by the Las Vegas Summer Band, made up of professional and student musicians and educators. The Sundown Bluegrass Concerts are held in August, and the Concerts at the Hills Park in Summerlin feature an amphitheater-style atmosphere with seating on a sloped lawn.

Cultural Affairs Division - Clark County Parks and Recreation Department

2601 E. Sunset Rd. • 455-8200

Like its municipal counterpart, the county's Cultural Affairs Division offers programs spanning the visual, performing and media arts as well as historic preservation and museum services.

The division also incorporates a number of outreach activities into its programs that bring art into schools and underprivileged neighborhoods, enriching the lives of children and the mentally and physically handicapped.

The facilities operated by the Cultural Affairs Division include a community center, two fine arts galleries, an amphitheater and two museum sites — the Clark County Heritage Museum and the McCarran Aviation Heritage Museum (see our Attractions chapter).

Recent musical offerings include the county's annual Jazz in the Park series, which presents world-renowned jazz musicians at the Clark County Government Center Amphitheater; the award-winning Chestnut Brass Ensemble at the Winchester Community Center; and the best zydeco west of Louisiana by Nathan and the Zydeco Cha Chas.

The county's popular cinema series recently presented an in-depth study of film noir: *America in a Dark Mirror*. Some of the films viewed and discussed include *Murder, My Sweet*; *The Killers;* and *The Big Combo*.

Among the county's outreach programs is its Arts Train, in which professionals in the fields of dance, music, drama and the visual arts travel to school sites in low-income areas to help children develop and discover new artistic interests and skills.

The county also operates a summer Arts Camp in picturesque Lee Canyon, where youngsters 8 to 12 years old study visual arts, music, movement, theater and creative writing. It also has a fleet of Rec Mobiles that travel to disadvantaged neighborhoods, offering at-risk kids fun activities that include games and arts and crafts.

Community College of Southern Nevada

3200 E. Cheyenne Ave. • 651-5483

In the mid-1990s the Community College completed construction of its new Performing Arts Center, highlighted by the 524-seat Nicholas Horn Auditorium. The critically acclaimed Community College Theatre will put the new facility to good use with four annual productions. Also worth visiting on the campus are an art gallery with 1,500 square feet of intriguing architecture and dramatic natural lighting; an intimate 130-seat little theater; a 143-seat recital hall; and a planetarium (see our Recreation chapter for more about the planetarium).

Las Vegas Arts Commission

749 Veterans Memorial Dr. • 799-6074

Funded by the city of Las Vegas, the 10-member commission is staffed by arts professionals, practicing artists and others who are appointed by the city council. The commission's main mission is to promote and develop projects that put art in public places. Its first commission was the William Maxwell piece installed in 1991 on the curved south face of City Hall.

The commission's responsibilities include developing new art projects, reviewing project proposals, working with the private sector to encourage the inclusion of art in projects and developing community forums and outreach programs. It also provides speakers for organizations, communities and school groups interested in learning more about public art.

Las Vegas-Clark County Library District

833 Las Vegas Blvd. N. • 382-3493

The Las Vegas-Clark County Library District took a lead role in the local arts community in the early 1990s, when then-Director Charles Hunsberger spearheaded a movement to integrate cultural facilities and programming into the library system. A Midwest transplant with a background in museum administration, Hunsberger succeeded in directing a voter initiative that funded new libraries and galleries throughout the valley. In the process he redefined the role of libraries by making them cultural centers as well as information centers.

Using funding from the bond initiative, every new library built in the 1990s has included performing arts facilities and art galleries. Moreover, many of the city's older libraries have been remodeled to include new auditoriums or galleries.

Unfortunately, since Hunsberger's retirement in 1991, the library district's involvement in cultural programming and sponsoring events have diminished. The current crop of administrators has decided the district's role in cultural affairs should be a custodial one. The district no longer sponsors events but simply runs the facilities.

Thank goodness for the users — groups such as Actors Repertory Theatre, Las Vegas Little Theatre, the Las Vegas Jazz Society and the many others who stage their events at the library district's facilities throughout the valley.

Nevada Institute for Contemporary Art

The Cannery, 3455 E. Flamingo Rd. • 434-2666

The institute is a nonprofit group that promotes local artists, holds art classes and conducts workshops and seminars. It also has a studio-visit program to let art fans visit local artists in their studios. Its exhibit season at The Cannery includes open invitational exhibits. Since 1986 NICA has brought to Las Vegas more than 400 contemporary artists in 54 solo and group exhibitions. It also launched an outreach program that introduces students to fine art. The gallery is open 10 AM to 6 PM Tuesday, Wednesday and Friday, 10 AM to 8 PM on Thursday and 11 AM to 5 PM on Saturday and Sunday. Admission is free.

Nevada School of the Arts

315 S. Seventh St. • 386-2787

Nevada School of the Arts is in its 20th year of providing quality arts instruction in music, musical theater and the visual arts to residents of the greater Las Vegas area. The school is a nonprofit community arts school and is Nevada's only member of the National Guild of Community Schools of the Arts.

The school and its faculty subscribe totally to the idea that arts education builds numerous invaluable life skills in the lives of those who study. Nearly 50 faculty members provide instruction to about 400 students each term.

Instruction is made available at Clark County School District locations as part of the School-Community Partnership Program. Scholarships and financial aid are available.

University of Nevada, Las Vegas

4505 S. Maryland Pkwy. • 739-3535

Although UNLV was established in the last half of this century, it has rapidly become a major focal point in southern Nevada for concerts, recitals, theater, art exhibits and special programs. In addition to its modern Performing Arts Center on campus, UNLV's theater, music, dance and art departments present quality programs throughout the year.

The prestigious Charles Vanda Master Series brings outstanding international artists to Las Vegas. Recent guests have included the State Symphony of Russia, Itzhak Perlman, the Budapest Festival Orchestra, the Cincinnati Symphony and the Moscow Festival Ballet.

The university's Chamber Music Southwest Series was established in 1987 to bring nationally acclaimed ensembles and soloists to Las Vegas and to provide an outlet for outstanding musicians from Southern Nevada to perform. The list of recent performers includes Anthony Smith's cello recital, "A Musical Offering" by Ensemble Versailles and a concert by the Las Vegas Marimba Quartet.

The University Theatre presents two-week productions throughout the academic year. Recent efforts included *Ah, Wilderness*, *A Raisin in the Sun* and *A Midsummer Night's Dream*.

The university's Department of Dance presents several recitals throughout the season featuring jazz and modern dance and ballet. Often nationally known guest artists are invited for the fall and spring productions.

Also, the Donna Beam Fine Arts Gallery hosts touring art and photography exhibits and displays exhibitions of both faculty and student work.

Venues

Artemus Ham Concert Hall

UNLV Performing Arts Center, 4505 S. Maryland Pkwy. • 895-3535

Ham Hall is the city's best theatrical center, and its acoustics were once praised by violinist Isaac Stern as "warm and vibrant."

The 2,000-seat theater has moveable orchestra towers, an extensive lighting system and a Class A stage. It seats 1,500 patrons on the main floor and another 500 in the balcony.

Judy Baley Theatre

UNLV Performing Arts Center, 4505 S. Maryland Pkwy. • 895-3535

This 530-seat theater serves performing arts groups such as the Nevada Dance Theatre. In addition to a first-class stage and auditorium, the theater features a set-construction area, costume storage, dressing and makeup facilities and green rooms.

Black Box Theatre

UNLV Performing Arts Center, 4505 S. Maryland Pkwy. • 895-3535

This intimate, 175-seat studio theater is the setting for theatrical events staged by university departments and community theater groups.

Cashman Theatre

850 Las Vegas Blvd. N. • 386-7100

In the sprawling Cashman Field Center near downtown, this theater seats nearly 2,000 patrons and has been used for holiday concerts, speaker forums and gospel meetings.

Charleston Heights Art Center

800 S. Brush St. • 229-6383

The 365-seat theater is fully equipped with a proscenium stage and is the setting for touring dance, opera, music and theater companies and films.

Clark Country Library Theater

1401 E. Flamingo Rd. • 733-1139

The 399-seat auditorium has a modified thrust stage and is frequently used by community groups for recitals and conferences.

Community College of Southern Nevada

Nicholas Horn Auditorium, 3200 E. Cheyenne Ave. • 651-5483

The modern, 524-seat theater and auditorium has an excellent sound and lighting system and is used for CCSN theatrical productions several times a year.

Reed Whipple Cultural Center Theatre

821 Las Vegas Blvd. N. • 229-6211

Operated by the city of Las Vegas, this somewhat aging theater has 300 seats in a multipurpose auditorium, which is used by the Las Vegas Civic Symphony, the Civic Ballet and the Rainbow Company. Also on site are an intimate 80-seat theater, a dance studio, meeting and rehearsal rooms, a pottery studio and an art gallery.

Sammy Davis Jr. Festival Plaza

Lorenzi Park, 720 Twin Lakes Dr. • 229-2390, 229-2496

This 500-seat, Southwestern-style amphitheater features a fully equipped 28-by-56-foot stage with a basket-weave design floor, dressing rooms, projection booth, kitchen, restrooms and concession area. It is used for a variety of festivals and performances.

Spring Valley Library Auditorium

4280 S. Jones Blvd. • 368-4411

This intimate room seats about 200 people on retractable bleacher seating and is home to productions of the Las Vegas Little Theatre. The moveable stage has no curtains, but there is a modest light and sound system that's accessed by a catwalk.

Summerlin Library Performing Arts Center

1771 Inner Circle Dr. • 256-2217

This modern auditorium has theatrical seating for 284 and a fully equipped stage. It is used by Actors Repertory Theatre, Sign Design Theatre and Southern Nevada Musical Arts Society.

West Las Vegas Library Theater

951 W. Lake Mead Blvd. • 647-8169

The West Las Vegas Library Theater is a

INSIDERS' TIP

For up-to-the-minute information about cultural events, concerts, classes and lectures at UNLV call 895-3131.

modern, fully equipped auditorium that seats 299 and features opaque skylights and a nine-piece orchestra pit. It also has a fly tower to lower seats, props and lighting onto a 2,000-square-foot stage.

Winchester Community Center Theater

3130 S. McCleod Dr. • 455-7340

The 295-seat Winchester theater was opened in 1995 to a standing-room-only crowd for nationally acclaimed flutist and philosopher R. Carlos Nakai. The theater, with retracting seats, a stage and dressing areas, has enabled the county's Cultural Affairs Division to present local and national musicians, theater groups, storytellers, singing groups and guest artists.

Dance

Las Vegas Civic Ballet Association

821 Las Vegas Blvd. N. • 229-2415

Under the umbrella of the city's Cultural Affairs Division, the Civic Ballet teaches young dancers (8- to 23-years-old) by giving them a chance to work and perform with professional choreographers and guest artists. Rehearsals and two concerts a year are held at the Reed Whipple Cultural Center.

Nevada Dance Theatre

1555 E. Flamingo Rd., Ste. 112 • 732-3838

Founded in 1972 by artistic director Vassili Sulich, Nevada Dance Theatre is southern Nevada's only professional ballet company. Principal dancers are Claric Geissel and Sergie Popov. The group usually stages five or six productions a season, blending traditional ballet favorites such as *Carmen* and *Swan Lake* with innovative new works like Michael Smuin's *Dances with Song*. All performances are held at UNLV's Performing Arts Center.

Opus Dance Ensemble of Las Vegas

1600 E. Desert Inn Rd., Ste. 209-D • 732-9646

Founded in 1985, Opus Dance Ensemble provides a creative outlet for the many professional dancers and choreographers who work in local production shows. The ensemble stages two concerts a year — one in the fall and one in the spring — in either the main showroom of the Tropicana Hotel or UNLV's Judy Baley Theater, always playing to capacity audiences.

Simba Jambalaya Dance Theatre

1953 N. Decatur Blvd., Box No. 331 • 647-8808

Founded and directed by LaVerne Ligon, the dance theater offers dance classes for children (kindergarten through high school) and adult professionals in ballet, jazz, tap, African and hip hop. Ligon's multicultural dance troupe also gives performances, workshops and demonstrations in Clark County schools.

University Dance Theatre

UNLV, 4505 Maryland Pkwy. • 895-3827

As part of UNLV's Department of Dance Arts, University Dance Theatre is an opportunity for university students and Las Vegas community dancers to collaborate on spring and fall concerts as well as provide theoretical and technical preparation in ballet, modern, jazz and other dance forms. Other programs include master classes, workshops, guest artists and an artist-in-residence program.

Film

Charleston Heights Arts Center

800 South Brush St. • 229-6383

Film series and festivals sponsored throughout the year by the city's Cultural Affairs Division feature international films, classics, documentaries, and specialty, ethnic and animated films. Recent offerings include a *Dracula Retrospective: Count the Counts*, which traced the various incarnations of the world's favorite vampire. The first two films, *Nosferatu* and *The Cabinet of Dr. Caligari,* were accompanied by organist Jeff Weiler performing the original scores. The series continued with Bela Lugosi's *Dracula* of 1931, the disco Dracula of George Hamilton in *Love at First Bite* and Gary Oldman's portrayal of the Count in *Bram Stoker's Dracula*.

The city's International Film Series showcases critically acclaimed foreign films from

Photo: Jim Decker/Review-Journal

Community concerts in the park are popular outings for families in Las Vegas.

recent years and have included titles such as Germany's *Faraway, So Close*, France's *I Can't Sleep*, Romania's *An Unforgettable Summer* and France and Russia's *Window to Paris*.

Kids of all ages enjoy the Animated Film Series with such recent charmers as *Snow White and the Seven Dwarfs*, *Animal Farm*, *Yellow Submarine* and *The Hobbit*.

Clark County Cultural Affairs Division

Winchester Community Center, 3130 S. McCleod Dr. • 455-7340

Continuing film series and festivals are held in the community center's 295-seat theater. The film series are thoughtfully planned and presented with discussions conducted by a moderator, usually a local film critic or reviewer. The recent *Film Noir: America in a Dark Mirror* series featured a sequence of films that increasingly revealed the darker side of modern life in films such as *Murder, My Sweet* and *Out of the Past*.

Las Vegas Library

833 Las Vegas Blvd. N. • 382-3493

Frequent film fests are held in the library's 75-seat programming room. Many of the films highlight holidays and special events, such as the Christmas Holiday Film Fest, as well as topical events about black history and fighting the winter blahs.

Summerlin Library & Performing Arts Center

1771 Inner Circle Dr. • 256-5111

The Summerlin Library's continuing Cinema Series presents films based on literature. Accompanying the films are moderated discussions in the library's 284-seat theater. Recent offerings have included the film version of F. Scott Fitzgerald's *The Great Gatsby*, Steven Spielberg's *Empire of the Sun,* based on J.G. Ballard's best-selling novel, and *A Tree Grows in Brooklyn*, the splendid adaptation of Betty Smith's novel.

Music

Brown Bag Concerts

Performing Arts Society of Nevada, 5204 Las Cruces Dr. • 658-6741

This group sponsors escorted tours to concerts outside the Las Vegas area with transportation, room and concert tickets all included. The group also sponsors a monthly concert at Sun City Summerlin and holds weekly meetings at the Debbie Reynolds Celebrity Cafe.

Chamber Music Southwest Series

UNLV, 4505 Maryland Pkwy. • 895-3535

Faculty artists from UNLV along with national touring chamber musicians perform a wide variety of music, from jazz to classical, at Artemus Ham Hall. Recent soloists included Teresa Ling and Kelley Mikkelsen.

Charles Vanda Master Series

UNLV Performing Arts Center, 4505 S. Maryland Pkwy. • 895-3535

The late Charles Vanda founded this series in 1976 to bring classical and international artists to Las Vegas. The series annually presents symphonies, orchestras, soloists, chamber ensembles and dance companies. The concerts, all held in Artemus Ham Hall, have included Isaac Stern in recital, the Bolshoi Ballet Ensemble, flutist Jean-Pierre Rampal in recital and *The Pirates of Penzance*.

Henderson Civic Symphony

500 Harris St. • 565-2121

Sponsored by the Henderson Parks and Recreation Department, the symphony is a 50-member orchestra that presents four to five concerts a year, often with guest artists. Recent concerts featured Nikolai Rimsky-Korsakov's *Capriccio Espagnole*, with guest artists Manuel De Falla & Beethovan, mezzo soprano Rosemary Ricci and organist Douglas Wilson.

Las Vegas Blues Society

P.O. Box 27871, Las Vegas 89126 • 253-5252

The nonprofit group is dedicated to keeping the blues alive in southern Nevada. Its members perform in weekly jam sessions in area nightclubs, and the society sponsors two free outdoor "blues picnics" in the spring and fall. It also publishes a bimonthly newsletter and keeps members updated on events and jam sessions.

Las Vegas Civic Symphony

749 Veterans Memorial Dr. • 385-8948

Established in 1977, the Las Vegas Civic Symphony draws its talented members from local professional and student musicians. Performances are conducted by Alan Lewis and held at the Reed Whipple Cultural Center and Sammy Davis Jr. Festival Plaza.

Las Vegas Youth Orchestra

749 Veterans Memorial Dr. • 385-8948

Sponsored by the city's Cultural Affairs Division and the Clark County School District, the 85-member Youth Orchestra was formed in 1976 to give southern Nevada student musicians the opportunity to perform professional concert music. Students audition in the spring for seats in two orchestras. The advanced orchestra is directed by Karl Reinarz, and the intermediate orchestra is under the direction of John Sullivan. The orchestra holds four or five performances from September to May at the outdoor Sammy Davis Jr. Festival Plaza and Artemus Ham Concert Hall at UNLV.

Nevada Opera Theatre

4080 Paradise Rd. • 436-7140

Southern Nevada's major opera company, the Nevada Opera Theatre was formed in 1986 and is directed by Eileen Hayes. In addition to staging three major productions, an opera gala and midsummer opera festival, the group presents light opera, operetta and musical the-

INSIDERS' TIP

The brightly lit horse and rider at Fremont Street and Las Vegas Boulevard was originally a neon sign from the old Hacienda Hotel. Its restoration is part of an effort to save and display historic neon art from Las Vegas' early years.

ater for civic and community organizations throughout the year. A recent season included *The Marriage of Figaro, La Bohème*, *Maggio Fiorentino* and *Carousel*.

Nevada Symphony Orchestra

3667 S. Las Vegas Blvd. • 792-4337

Established in 1982, the 70-member orchestra led by conductor Virko Baley performs at UNLV's Artemus Ham Hall. Its Classical Series runs from November through April and includes four classical concerts, two holiday concerts, a new Sound Trek Series of four concerts and two special events.

Sierra Winds

UNLV, 4505 Maryland Pkwy. • 895-3332

Recognized as one of the nation's top chamber ensembles, the wind quintet consists of flute, oboe, clarinet, bassoon and horn. The group tours nationally and has performed at Carnegie Recital Hall in New York. It records under the Cambria label. Proclaimed by Mayor Jan Jones as cultural ambassador for the city of Las Vegas, the Sierra Winds was founded in 1982.

Southern Nevada Community Concert Association

1620 Stonehaven Dr. • 895-3801

The association works with Columbia Artists to bring a diversity of outstanding talent to Las Vegas at affordable prices. The season runs from October to April, with performances at UNLV's Artemus Ham Hall. A recent season included appearances by the New York Theatre Ballet, the Central Band of Her Majesty's Royal Air Force and Khenany, a seven-piece band from Mexico.

Southern Nevada Musical Arts Society

3950 Springhill Ave. • 451-6672

Founded in 1963 by musical director Doug Peterson, this society consists of an orchestra made up of local professionals, an 80-member chorus and the smaller Musical Arts Singers. The group presents the annual holiday "Messiah Sing-In" and concerts of major choral literature throughout the year at Artemus Ham Hall, Reed Whipple Cultural Center and the Community College of Southern Nevada.

Theater

Actors Repertory Theatre

1824 Palo Alto Cir. • 647-7469

Artistic Director Georgia Neu formed the group in 1987 as an outlet for community theater, and it has since become the city's only Actors Equity Association company. The professional repertory company is dedicated to classic, modern and musical theater with special emphasis on new works of merit. The group stages four productions a year in the Summerlin Library and Performing Arts Center. One recent offering was *My Fair Lady*.

Community College of Southern Nevada Theatre

3200 E. Cheyenne Ave. • 651-5483

Directed by Dick McGee, this energetic and creative community college theater has given Las Vegas critically acclaimed and award-winning productions since 1977. The intimate group stages four productions during the academic year, including plays such as *No, No Nanette* and *Inherit the Wind*.

Las Vegas Little Theatre

3844 Schiff Dr. • 362-7996

Founded by Paul and Sue Thornton in 1980, the Little Theatre is a nonprofit community theater that puts on five full-scale productions a season. Using local talent and open to volunteers, the Little Theatre also holds classes and workshops in acting and directing. A children's theater workshop is offered each summer. Performances are held in the Spring Valley Library auditorium.

New West Theatre

3540 W. Sahara Ave., Ste. 235 • 656-6600, 258-8022

Co-sponsored by the city of Las Vegas, New West Theatre has been producing quality popular and classic plays since it was formed in 1986. Plays are presented in the city's Charleston Heights Art Center, and some of them have included *Corpse!* by Gerald Moon, *Of Mice and Men*, *Driving Miss Daisy* and *Barefoot in the Park*.

The Off-Broadway Theatre

900 E. Karen Ave., Ste. D-116 • 737-0611

The newest theater group on the Las Vegas scene produces four plays a season and stages them in its own intimate, 90-seat theater. Some of its lively offerings have included *Squabbles*, *The Prisoner of Second Avenue* and *Some of My Best Friends are Jewish Husbands*. The group also offers afternoon and evening drama workshops and children's classes on Saturdays.

Rainbow Company Theatre

821 Las Vegas Blvd. N. • 229-6553

Children take center stage at the Rainbow Company, which is now in its 20th season of presenting quality theater for all ages. Sponsored by the city of Las Vegas, Rainbow Company consists of 35 members between the ages of 7 and 17. A full season of family-oriented productions is staged, including classics such as *Sleeping Beauty*, *Tom Sawyer*, *Cinderella*, *The Miracle Worker* and *Tales of Old Nevada*. The group also puts on awareness-raising productions, such as *Apologies*, a drama about teen suicide.

Sign Design Theatre Company

2718 S. Highland Dr. • 731-3738

The nonprofit children's theater company brings deaf and hearing children together to perform more than 200 shows annually, raising awareness about the deaf and enhancing self esteem. The group is open to children 4 to 17 years old, who learn sign language as well as dance, drama and the performing arts.

Signature Productions

3255 Mustang St. • 878-7529

With Karl Larsen as its president, Signature Productions is a nonprofit community theater group that provides the aspiring actor, producer, director or technical crew member a chance for growth and development in a variety of theatrical styles. With an emphasis on family-oriented theater, it also provides a wholesome and educational atmosphere for rehearsal and performance. The group usually stages two plays, often musicals, with open auditions for each.

Super Summer Theatre

3111 Bel Aire Dr. • 594-7529

The Super Summer Theatre hosts plays produced by local theater groups at the pastoral Spring Mountain State Park amphitheater. Typically, the theater runs from early June to late August, with Shakespeare and Broadway musicals the fare of choice.

Theatre in the Valley

693 Valley Verde Dr., Box 338, Henderson • 225-9160

The group was formed in 1992 to serve the Green Valley-Henderson communities. Its season usually consists of three plays presented at the Valley View Recreation Center in the fall, winter and spring.

UNLV's Department of Theatre Arts

4505 S. Maryland Pkwy. • 895-3666

The Department of Theatre Arts provides cultural enrichment for the university and the community through its University Theatre productions, which emphasize all forms of theater, especially new work and musical theater. Presentations are held in UNLV's Performing Arts Center. The department awards professional degrees in playwriting, musical theater, design and technology and also serves as a consultant in those areas.

Visual Arts

Museums

Las Vegas Art Museum

Sahara West Library, 9600 W. Sahara Ave. • 360-8000

Inside the newly constructed Sahara West Library, the Fine Arts Museum was built to Smithsonian specifications and features six major shows and three traveling exhibitions a year. Of the more intriguing exhibits were *Art After Post Modernism*, which featured 40 paintings by 15 artists, and the more traditional John Henry Wilson Collection of works by masters such as Rembrandt and Van Dyck. The gallery is open 10 AM to 5 PM Tuesday through Saturday and 1 to 5 PM Sunday. Admission is $3 for adults, $2 for seniors and $1 for students.

Photo: Jim Decker/Review-Journal

Community theater is well-represented in Las Vegas with several amateur and professional actors equity groups.

Galleries

Donna Bean Fine Arts Gallery

UNLV, 4505 S. Maryland Pkwy. • 895-3893

Shows by students and faculty of the university's Department of Art are presented here. A recent exhibition, *The Bombing of the American West*, included haunting photographs of crater-pocked land, bombed-out vehicles and live explosives. Hours are 9 AM to 5 PM Monday through Friday but are often extended for special exhibitions. Admission is free.

Charleston Heights Arts Gallery

800 S. Brush St. • 229-6383

Changing exhibits sponsored by the city's Cultural Affairs Division have included Kansas City artist Kathryn Arnold's large-scale oil paintings done in chaotic energy of color; Joe Smith's wall and standing ceramic works; and Jeff Key's wood sculptures that reflect his view that the bio-technical revolution and proliferation of toxins in the environment influence the course of evolution. The gallery is open from 1 to 9 PM Monday and Thursday, 10 AM to 9 PM Tuesday and Wednesday, 10 AM to 6 PM on Friday and 1 to 5 PM Saturday and Sunday. Admission is free.

Clark County Government Center

500 S. Grand Central Pkwy. • 455-7340

Changing exhibits from local artists can be viewed in the County Rotunda Room and have included The Nevada Clay Invitational, which featured ceramic creations by 15 artists.

Contemporary Arts Collective The Arts Factory

107 E. Charleston Blvd. • 382-3886

This nonprofit group is dedicated to modern art and local artists and recently put together an exhibition of southern Nevada artists. The group also has staged a runway fashion show and auction of wearable art. Hours are 11 AM to 4 PM Wednesday to Saturday. Admission is free.

Fine Art Gallery at the Community College of Southern Nevada

3200 E. Cheyenne Ave. • 641-4113

This contemporary gallery exhibits showings by local and out-of-state artists, such as *Ethnic Voices: A National Invitational Exhibition,* featuring various works by 16 artists from around the country. It is open Monday to Thursday from 10 AM to 10 PM, on Friday from 10 AM to 4 PM, and Saturday from 10 AM to noon. Admission is free.

Las Vegas-Clark Country Library District

Various locations • 382-3493

Many of the branch libraries have art space or complete galleries that exhibit work from mostly local or regional artists. Check with any branch library for a district programming guide, *Off the Shelf*, which lists art exhibits. For information about exhibiting work call District Gallery Manager Denise Shapiro at the number above.

The galleries are open from 9 AM to 9 PM Monday through Thursday, 9 AM to 5 PM on Friday and Saturday, and 1 to 5 PM on Sunday. (Las Vegas Library and West Charleston open at noon on Sunday). Admission is free.

The branches with galleries include:

Clark County Library (Flamingo Branch), 1401 E. Flamingo Road, 733-7810

Dana Marie Lull Gallery (Spring Valley Branch), 4280 S. Jones Boulevard, 368-4411

Enterprise Library Gallery, 25 E. Shelbourne Avenue, 269-3000

Green Valley Library Gallery, 2797 N. Green Valley Parkway, 435-1840

Las Vegas Library Gallery, 833 Las Vegas Blvd. N., 382-3493

Rainbow Library Gallery, 3150 N. Buffalo Drive, 243-7323

Sahara West Library Gallery, 9600 W. Sahara Avenue, 228-1940

Summerlin Library Gallery, 1771 Inner Circle Drive, 256-5111

Sunrise Library Gallery, 5400 Harris Avenue, 453-1104

West Charleston Library Gallery, 6301 W. Charleston Boulevard, 878-3683

West Las Vegas Library Gallery, 951 West Lake Mead Boulevard, 647-2117

Whitney Library Gallery, 5175 E. Tropicana Avenue, 454-4575

Reed Whipple Cultural Center Gallery

821 Las Vegas Blvd. N. • 229-6211

Programs often feature the artist in reception as well as a collection of works. Recent exhibitions included Carolyn Brookhart's intaglio prints of Arizona; New York artist Amy Zerner and her mixed media collages; and Kimberly Burleigh's graphite representations of the evolution of societal views of science and technology. The gallery is open 1 to 9 PM Monday, 10 AM to 9 PM on Tuesday and Wednesday, 10 AM to 6 PM on Thursday and Friday, 9 AM to 5 PM on Saturday and 1 to 5 PM on Sunday.

Winchester Community Center Gallery

3130 S. McCleod Dr. • 455-7340

The fine arts gallery in the county's community center houses touring arts programs that reflect various cultures and lifestyles. Recent exhibits included William Claxton's intimate photos of jazz greats Billie Holiday, Duke Ellington, Charlie Parker and more; an exhibit of 56 exquisitely crafted brooches from the Arizona Commission on the Arts; and a touring exhibit of the various techniques in woodturning. The gallery is open 9 AM to 9 PM Monday through Friday and 9 AM to 6 PM on Saturday. Admission is free.

Commercial Galleries

Art Affair

3871 S. Valley View Blvd., Ste. 9 • 368-7888

Art Affair holds an extensive collection of Hanna Barbera animation art, original production cels and sericels signed by Bill Hanna and Joe Barbera. It also has original serigraphs, etchings, lithographs and posters.

INSIDERS' TIP

To find out about local jazz happenings — concerts, parties, workshops and jam sessions — contact the Las Vegas Jazz Society at 457-9141.

Art Encounter

3979 Spring Mountain Rd. • 227-0220

Originals by more than 100 local and national artists are represented in oils, watercolors, sculpture, pottery and jewelry. Appropriate to Las Vegas are Lorne Cramer's neon sculpture. Also of interest are Alexa Pilcher's oils of African wildlife and Harumi Nakada's artistic tribute to domestic felines.

Crockett Gallery

2800 W. Sahara Ave., Ste. 7C • 253-6336

Contemporary fine art, limited editions and one-of-a-kind works in glass, sculpture, metal work, oils and watercolors are featured at this gallery. The gallery also hosts one-person shows showcasing artists such as Susan Pinue (wood sculpture) and Aurora Alvarez (watercolors and pastels).

DeWolf Fine Art

3311 S. Rainbow Blvd. • 255-8587

DeWolf features an extensive selection of original serigraphs, lithographs and etchings by masters from the 16th through the 20th centuries. Artists represented include Renoir, Cezanne, Cassatt, Tissot, Dali, Chagall, Rockwell and more.

Glass Artistry

4200 W. Desert Inn Rd. • 221-8494

Artist Rita Malkin and other local artists specialize in creating unique glass art in the form of sculpture, fused bowls and platters, stained-glass windows, and etched and carved mirrors. Work is done on site as artists prepare glass for the kiln to be fused. Classes and workshops on sculpting in glass are periodically offered.

Left of Center Gallery

2207 W. Gowan, North Las Vegas • 647-7378

Owner Vicki Richardson showcases minority artists and art that deals with minority experiences. Recent exhibits included Buena Johnson's celebration of Martin Luther King Jr.'s birthday. The gallery is also the permanent residence of After Images, a group of professional black artists.

Moonstruck Gallery

6322 W. Sahara Ave. • 364-0531

A wide array of fine crafts are on display and for sale, including jewelry, pottery, kaleidoscopes, handcrafted musical instruments, desk accessories, handblown glass and Native American flutes. Limited-edition prints by artists Bev Doolittle, Robert Bateman, Steve Lyman and Terry Redlin are also represented.

Studio West-Summerlin

8447 W. Lake Mead Blvd. • 228-1901

The gallery displays the original work of several southern Nevada artists, along with a large selection of limited-edition art. It is also the premier dealer for the works of Thomas Kinkade.

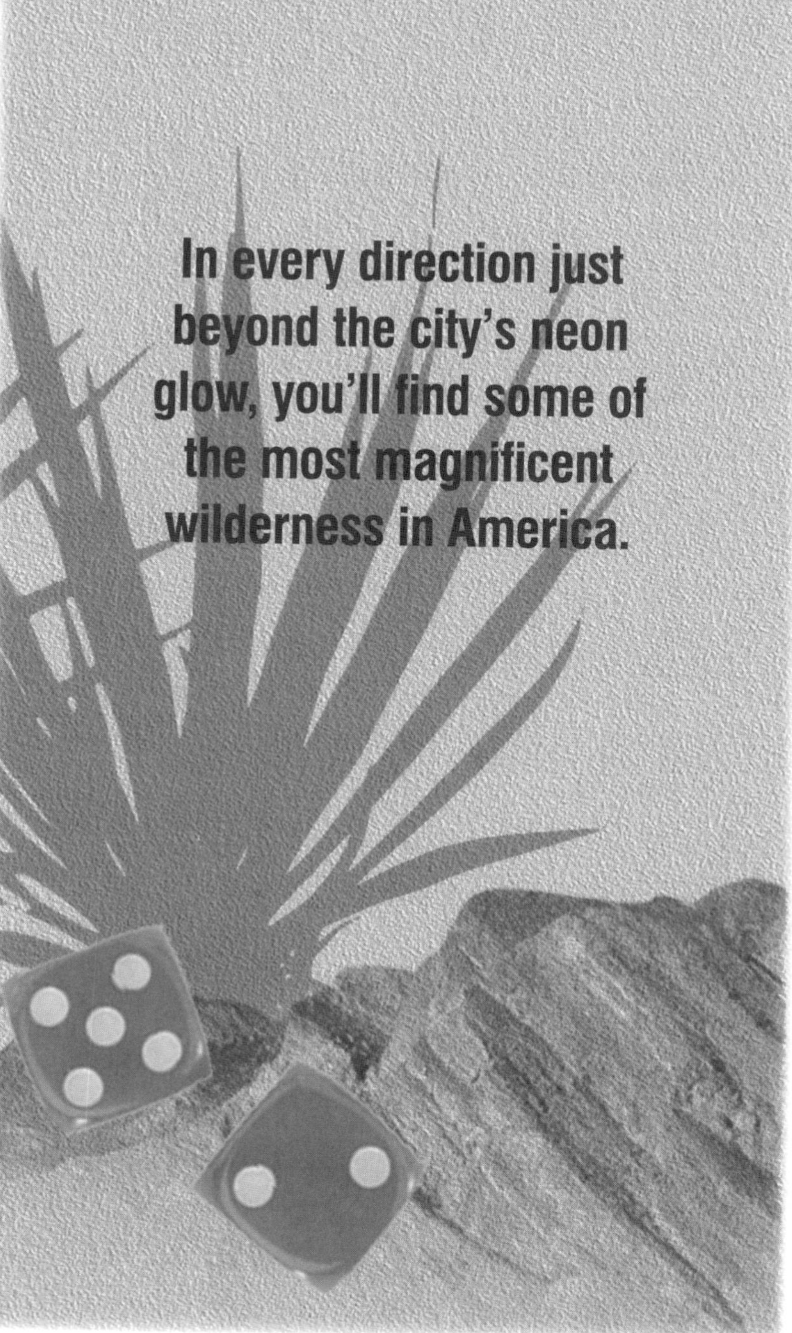
In every direction just beyond the city's neon glow, you'll find some of the most magnificent wilderness in America.

The Great Outdoors

Now that you've seen the exploding volcano, stuffed yourself silly on shrimp cocktails and developed a chronic case of slot-machine elbow, it might be time for a change of pace. Or maybe you've been hammered so hard at the craps tables that you need a renewal of body and spirit. If so, welcome to southern Nevada.

Beyond the neon pleasure garden of Las Vegas lies a land of mythic diversity and scenic treasures, free from the breakneck pace of Las Vegas' nonstop merry-go-round. The change from Lady Luck to Mother Nature is quick and easy in this part of the country. In every direction just beyond the city's neon glow, you'll find some of the most magnificent wilderness in America, waiting to be explored by hikers and rock climbers, boaters and anglers, skiers and birdwatchers, photographers and dreamers. But discovering nature's wonders doesn't mean renting a Land Rover, hiring a guide or buttoning up your Patagonias. Most of the destinations are within an hour's drive of Glitter Gulch; many are just a few minutes away. Just a few miles northwest of Las Vegas you'll find the sandstone escarpments of the Spring Mountains, the pine-fringed creeks and small springs of Red Rock Canyon, the alpine forestry of Mount Charleston and the winter ski resorts of Lee Canyon. Drive northeast and you can explore the ruins of ancient civilizations that lived here before any white settler set foot on the continent, or wander among the crimson rock formations of the Valley of Fire. Just a few miles south of Las Vegas is the blue-green grandeur of Lake Mead, the largest man-made lake in the United States. With 550 miles of shoreline and nearly 300 square miles of water surface, Lake Mead is a mecca for anglers, swimmers, boaters and water-skiers.

Most of the outdoor adventures described in this chapter can be enjoyed in less than a day, some in a few hours. Others may require more time to explore all the destination has to offer. Whatever your intention, you can only experience these wonders if you get away from the casinos and all-you-can-eat buffets, at least for a few hours.

Scenic and Recreation Areas

Corn Creek Field Station

Desert National Wildlife Range, U.S. Hwy. 95, 8 mi. west of Kyle Canyon Rd.
• 646-3401

A former working ranch and stagecoach stop, Corn Creek is now a field station for the vast Desert National Wildlife Range, which includes a special sanctuary of the once-endangered Nelson's Desert bighorn sheep. On a well-graded gravel road off U.S. 95, Corn Creek is only 22 miles north of Las Vegas. The natural springs of Corn Creek have formed upper and lower ponds connected by a gurgling brook. You can walk under the huge cottonwoods, mesquite, willows, fruit trees, cattails and tules clustered around the waterways. There's also a small picnic area with tables, canopies, grills, restrooms and water. Out of the thick, marshy underbrush, caretakers carved an area that includes houses and horse stables, trimmed lawns and fenced pasture, but these are not open to the public.

This small, rugged oasis is a marvelous site for bird-watching. So diverse is the birdlife here that the Audubon Society has included it as part of its Adopt a Refuge program. It is also on the edge of the California flyway and attracts an astonishing variety of birdlife from hummingbirds to hawks. The fruited mulberry trees attract evening, blue and rose-breasted grosbeaks, pine crossbills, western and summer tanagers and orioles. You might see other species such as black-and-white and Wilson's warblers, western bluebirds, flycatchers, thrashers, barn and great-horned owls, sharp-shinned and Cooper's hawks. If you take the footpaths around the ponds, keep an eye out for frogs, toads and lizards. You might even glimpse a coyote or fox on the perimeter of the cultivated area, and a jackrabbit, cottontail or ground squirrel may skitter from the underbrush as you approach. The ponds provide habitat for the endangered Pahrump poolfish. This minnow-size fish was transplanted here in 1971 when its native habitat at Pahrump Valley's Manse Spring was destroyed. A walk beyond the ponds takes you to mesquite-filled arroyos, where you may unearth arrowheads left behind by the ancient Indian tribes that once populated Corn Creek. (It is illegal, though, to take arrowheads out of the park.) Public restrooms, drinking fountains and a self-service information center are nearby. The area is open from sunrise to dusk. Admission is free.

FYI

Unless otherwise noted, the area code for all phone numbers listed in this chapter is 702.

Visitors with off-road vehicles may want to explore deeper into the refuge by taking a dirt road that leads east from the compound. About 5 miles from Corn Creek, the trail passes the southern end of the Sheep Mountain Range, an excellent bighorn habitat. Your best chance of spotting the sheep is during the cooler months, from late fall to early spring. Continue 2 miles along the trail to the agave roasting pits, which were used by ancient native peoples for slow-cooking meats and vegetables. Notice the mounds of blackened, fire-cracked rocks, which were discarded after each "barbecue" session. The roasting pits, sometimes called mescal pits, were used by prehistoric Native Americans including the Southern Paiute, Shoshone and Anasazi. The trail continues another 40 miles through several scenic canyons and washes. Throughout the Wildlife Range, you'll find picnic spots, campgrounds and horse riding trails. You can pick up a map of the refuge at Corn Creek. Before exploring the National Wildlife Range visitors are advised to check their vehicles' fuel, water and spare tire. You should also carry plenty of drinking water and sign the visitor book at the Corn Creek station, noting the time and date you enter the refuge. Except for the Corn Creek Field Station, the refuge is open 24 hours a day, seven days a week. Camping is allowed.

Lake Mead Recreation Area

U.S. Hwy. 95 • 293-8990

Created when the Colorado River was backed up by Hoover Dam from 1935 to 1938, Lake Mead is southern Nevada's second most popular attraction behind Hoover Dam. The sheer size of the lake — 550 miles of shoreline and nine trillion gallons of water — and the surrounding jagged canyons and desert sand dunes are reason enough to visit the largest man-made lake in the United States. But most people come for the recreational activities: swimming, boating, water-skiing, windsurfing, lying on the beach or exploring the hidden coves and inlets by houseboat. The lake is especially popular with anglers who take a run at largemouth bass, rainbow, brown and cutthroat trout, catfish and black crappie. Striped bass, which can reach 30 pounds, are the most popular game fish in recent years.

Lake Mead is part of the Lake Mead National Recreational Area, which also includes Lake Mohave (formed by Davis Dam about 67 miles downriver) and the land surrounding the lakes. Overall, the National Recreational Area covers 1.5 million acres (2,337 square miles) with 237 miles of surfaced roads in the park and 800 miles of unimproved back-country roads. There are a number of ways to reach Lake Mead, but the simplest is through Boulder City, about 20 minutes southeast of Las Vegas via U.S. 95. Other more remote jumping-off points are along the lake's northern finger at Callville Bay, Echo Bay and Overton Beach.

Admission to the National Recreational Area is $5 per vehicle, and you can stay for as

www.insiders.com
See this and many other Insiders' Guide® destinations online — in their entirety.
Visit us today!

long as a week. An annual permit costs $15. A good way to learn about the lake is to stop at the Alan Bible Visitor Center 601 Nevada Highway, Boulder City, 293-8990, midway between Boulder City and Hoover Dam. Movies, exhibits, books, brochures, topographic maps and nautical charts will help you plan your visit, plus there are restrooms and drinking water available. If you're inclined, the best place to spread a beach towel is at Boulder Beach, just a few minutes north of the visitors center. The 2 miles of sandy beach and the clear water of Lake Mead attract year-round sunbathers. Picnic areas, campsites, a snack bar and convenience store are nearby. The clear water and warm temperatures attract divers, who can explore the ill-fated yacht, *Tortuga*, near the Boulder Islands; *Cold Duck*, submerged in 35 feet of water; the remains of Hoover Dam's asphalt factory and the old Mormon settlement of St. Thomas.

About a mile north of Boulder Beach, **Lake Mead Marina**, 322 Lakeshore Road, 293-3484, has hundreds of boat slips and a popular floating restaurant, motel, coffee shop and cocktail lounge. Farther north, the **Las Vegas Boat Harbor** on Lakeshore Drive, 565-9111, has more boat slips, a picnic area, campground and restaurant. You can also camp or park your RV at **Callville Bay Resort Marina**, Star Route 10, off Northshore Road, 565-8958, which also features a coffee shop, store, marina and public showers. Deep beneath Callville Bay's sheltered waters lie the ruins of Callville, an 1864 river-port settlement and the head of steamboat navigation along the Colorado River for a few years. The town, deserted of course, was submerged by the lake when the river was dammed. The only motel on the north shore of the lake is at **Echo Bay Resort and Marina**, Star Route 89010, Overton, 394-4000. Along with a restaurant, coffee shop and lounge, the motel offers modern, budget-priced rooms, an RV village and an airstrip for light aircraft.

About halfway between Echo Bay and Overton Beach is Rogers Springs, an oasis created by a warm-water spring. Large Tamarisk trees shade the natural warm spring and gravel-bottom wading pool that prehistoric Indians once camped beside. Today you can enjoy a picnic in a shaded area next to the springs.

On the Arizona shore you'll find **Temple Bar Marina**, 1 Main Street, Temple Bar, (602) 767-3211, which features a modern motel and older cabins with kitchenettes, a cafe, cocktail lounge, campground, boat-launching ramp, fuel dock and store. This is the last outpost for supplies if you plan to boat north of Temple Bar.

For more information about recreational activities at Lake Mead, see our Parks and Recreation chapter. For information about Hoover Dam and Boulder City, see our Daycations chapter.

Lake Mohave

Nev. Hwys. 163, 164 and 165, off U.S. 95 • 293-8907

Lake Mohave is a long, slender body of water that extends 67 miles from just below Hoover Dam to Davis Dam, near Laughlin, Nevada, and Bullhead City, Arizona. The lake has 150 miles of shoreline and reaches its widest point — about 4 miles across — in the Cottonwood Basin. Lake Mohave provides a multitude of recreational activities, including boating, fishing, water-skiing, scuba diving and windsurfing. Landlubbing hikers will love the desert and canyons surrounding Davis Dam, which make for fascinating outings.

There are a number of jumping-off points along Lake Mohave's Nevada shoreline, which can be reached by driving U.S. 95 south of Hoover Dam. The first is at **Nelson Landing**, off Nev. Highway 165 about 55 miles from Las Vegas. Not much remains of the old resort and marina, which was washed away under a 45-foot wall of mud during a flash flood in 1974. None of the facilities was rebuilt, but you can park your car on the paved lot and walk down to the lake. You'll find facilities and provisions at **Cottonwood Cove**, 1000 Cottonwood Cove Road, Cottonwood Cove, 297-1464, a secluded desert oasis midway between Hoover Dam and Laughlin/Bullhead City, about 70 miles from Las Vegas. Open year round, the resort features a 24-room motel, convenience store, restaurant, RV park and full-service marina. To reach Cottonwood Cove, take U.S. 95 S. to the town of Searchlight, then turn east on Nev. 164. The only public beach at Lake Mohave is at **Katherine Landing**, Ariz. Highway 68, Bullhead City, (602) 754-3245, just 4 miles north of Davis Dam on the Arizona shore. The Landing also has a full-service marina, boat-launching docks, campground, motel, restaurant and grocery store. You can rent boats, fishing tackle and water skis here.

To reach Katherine Landing drive south on U.S. 95 to Nev. 163, then turn east and continue about 20 miles over Davis Dam, about 100 miles from Las Vegas. For more information about recreational activities at Lake Mohave see our Parks and Recreation chapter. If you want to explore the Laughlin area, check out our Daycations chapter.

Mount Charleston

Nev. Hwy. 157 • 872-5486

While the desert floor bakes below, the alpine wilderness of Mt. Charleston evolves with the colors and climates of four full seasons. Only 40 minutes north of Las Vegas, Mt. Charleston and the surrounding Toiyabe National Forest is a popular year-round destination for hiking, backpacking, picnicking, overnight camping and skiing during the winter months. The thick bristlecone pines clinging to limestone cliffs 10,000 feet above the desert floor create a stunning backdrop. A vast array of plant and animal life makes this unique environment home. After you turn off U.S. 95 and onto Kyle Canyon Road (Nev. 157), notice the change in vegetation as the elevation increases. Approaching the mountains you'll see Joshua trees, yucca and creosote bushes that have adapted well to the 120-degree summer temperatures and scant rainfall. In the spring the sides of the road are blanketed with a delicate layer of wildflowers. As you reach the 5,000-foot elevation, pinon pine and junipers take over the landscape, along with scatterings of sagebrush, rabbitbrush and scarlet trumpeter. You probably won't see them from the road, but deer and elk move into this region as the winter snows deepen at higher elevations. At about 6,000 feet, mountain mahogany, oakbrush and ponderosa pine replace the pinon pines and junipers. The pine stands grow larger as you progress up the mountain. Deer spend their summers in the area, which abounds with bluebell, snowberry and penstemons. At about this point you'll see a turnoff to the right. This is Deer Creek Highway (Nev. 158), which leads into Lee Canyon and its ski and snowboard resort. The paved roads end at roughly 7,500-feet, but you can see the forests of bristlecone pine, spreading across elevations of 9,000 feet and higher. Many of these gnarled veterans are more than 5,000 years old, predating the majestic redwoods and giant sequoias.

In addition to this varied plant life, the forest is home to the Palmer chipmunk (found nowhere else in the world), bighorn sheep and elk. The area's coyotes, bobcats, fox and cougar are seldom seen, but their tracks will alert you to their presence. Man, too, has found a niche here. On your drive up the mountain, you probably noticed cabins and rustic homes perched on sites carved out of the walls of Kyle Canyon. The area has become a colony for about 1,100 Las Vegans who don't mind the 30-minute commute into the city.

A good first stop is the Ranger Station on Kyle Canyon Road, 872-5486, where you can pick up maps and information on the area's ecology, sights and history. The large relief map is helpful in planning your outing, whether it be camping, hiking, picnicking or skiing. Drinking water and restroom facilities are nearby.

Exploring one of the hiking trails, which vary from easy, half-hour walks to two-day treks, is the best way to experience the mountain wilderness. Most of the trailheads are accessible by car and have water and restroom facilities. Check with the Ranger Station before starting. Most of the trails are open year-round, but some are closed during winter and early spring. Remember to stay on the marked trails, especially in the higher elevations, where vertical cliffs are dangerous and have claimed lives. Just a 15-minute walk off Deer Creek Highway, Desert View Scenic Outlook provides a breathtaking panorama of the valley and dry lake beds below. Due east is Sheep Mountain Range, and to the north is Paiute Mesa on the Nevada Test Site. During the 1950s, mushroom clouds from nuclear testing blasts were photographed from here. Bristlecone Trail begins just above the parking lot at the end of Lee Canyon Highway. The quarter-mile walk circles the ridge with views of the ski area and the spectacular white dolomite limestone cliffs of Mummy Mountain. Towering majestically at the end of Kyle Canyon Road, Cathedral Rock is accessible via a moderate, three-hour hike. You'll pass through stands of pine, fir and aspen on your way to the summit, offering breathtaking views of Kyle Canyon. Watch your footing because the trail ends with an abrupt drop of several hundred feet. Echo Cliff Trail also begins at the Cathedral Rock trailhead and climbs upward through the ponderosa pine and white fir forest above the picnic area. At the base of Echo Cliff, one returns along an old road, crisscrossing an avalanche path, where the aspen and brush are very colorful in the fall. The trail returns to the upper parking lot in the picnic area.

One of the most scenic areas to visit is Mary Jane and Big Falls, in upper Kyle Canyon. The 2-mile trail starts at the end of Kyle Canyon Road and should take less than four hours to complete. At the lower elevation, lofty pines and white fir are surrounded by vertical cliffs. Soon two trails lead to vantage points near a pair of waterfalls. The best time to view them is in early spring. During the summer there may be only a trickle of water from the cliffs. Deer Creek, one of the few streams in the Las Vegas District, flows through the Deer Creek Picnic Area in Lee Canyon, across the highway from the Mahogany Grove picnic area.

Mt. Charleston Peak rises to nearly 12,000 feet at the head of Kyle Canyon. If you're not content to simply gaze at its magnificence and you're an experienced backpacker, there are two trails leading to the summit. One begins in Lee Canyon (11 miles), the other at Cathedral Rock (9 miles). On either hike, plan at least one overnight camp to fully take in the trail's pleasures. (The 9-mile hike can be completed in one day, but you will have little time for exploring and will probably be descending the switchbacks in the dark.) Stop at the Ranger Station for trail maps, information and fire permits for the campground fire rings.

The Lee Canyon Ski Area, Nev. 156, 872-5462, may open as early as November or as late as January. The season may end with the warm March winds or last until May. There's good downhill skiing on bunny, intermediate and expert slopes, and snow-making equipment ensures the runs are in powder, not ice. There's also a ski school, rentals, lounge, snack bar and gift shop. For cross-country skiers there are some magnificent Nordic areas — Scout Canyon, Mack's Canyon, Bristlecone Trail — for touring and mountaineering. For more information about the ski resort, see our Parks and Recreation chapter.

If you simply want to enjoy the snow, the best spot to play is Foxtail Snow Play Area, just off the Lee Canyon Road. The slopes here have been cleared of obstacles and are open to sleds, toboggans and inner tubes. You'll also find restrooms, tables, grills and campfire areas, but you'll need to bring your own firewood.

During the winter, especially after a snowfall, snow tires or chains may be required in the Mt. Charleston area. Check road conditions by calling the Nevada Department of Transportation at 486-3116. A popular weekend getaway from Las Vegas, Mt. Charleston has overnight accommodations in the Mt. Charleston Hotel, 2 Kyle Canyon Road, 872-5500. Because of its elevation slightly below the timber line, most of the surrounding scenery is sagebrush and juniper trees, but the hotel's weathered-wood exterior, open-beam rafters, ponderosa pine pillars and open-pit fireplace all contribute to a mountain lodge atmosphere. The hotel also has a dining room, gift shop, cocktail lounge, and (for those who must) slot machines. You can also rent a cabin at the Mt. Charleston Resort, 386-6899, a very popular restaurant and bar at the top of Kyle Canyon Road. The resort's popular restaurant features a circular fireplace, an excellent menu offering game birds, sweeping views of the canyon and the charming Christmas Shoppe next door. For more information about facilities at Mt. Charleston, see our Daycations chapter.

Red Rock Canyon

Nev. Hwy. 159 • 363-1921

Red Rock Canyon is just a 20-minute drive from The Strip, but the distance is better measured in eons — the scene is a majestic mural of nature created over uncounted millennia. The centerpiece of the canyon is a nearly sheer escarpment more than 13 miles long and nearly 3,000 feet high. The escarpment is incised with numerous deep canyons, formed by snowmelt and rain runoff eroding along cracks in brittle cliffs. Perennial springs and seasonal streams encourage lush vegetation in relatively cool, shaded places that contrast with the dryness of the desert floor. To reach this colorful, enchanting wilderness area, press your sensible shoe to the accelerator and head west on Charleston Boulevard until you reach this national conservation area.

Now that you've left the suburban sprawl and found clean desert air, which is generally 10 degrees cooler than in the city, head to the Red Rock Visitors Center, 1000 Scenic Drive, 363-1921. Against the stunning backdrop of the red and yellow sandstone cliffs, the low-profile center blends into the surrounding desert. Inside, a recorded self-guided tour takes you through the geologic and wildlife history of the area, and park rangers are on hand to answer questions. (Nature books on indigenous flora, fauna and geology are for sale here.) The center is open from 8:30 AM to 4:30 PM daily. Outside the center, the desert landscape has been carefully set out with representatives of the region's plant life. Leaving the center, you may either return to the main road for a quick pass through the Joshua tree and yucca-dotted countryside or take the 13-mile one-way Scenic Loop. We suggest the latter. The Scenic Loop is open to traffic from 7 AM to dusk. Along the route, several vista points offer choice views of spectacular rock formations. The towering sandstone bluffs form a tapestry of colors — pink, red and purple. Experienced climbers, appearing like tiny marionettes suspended from threads, slowly dance their way up the tilted and folded layers of rock.

The spectacular rock formations, laid open like pages of a book, are the geologic result of the Keystone Thrust Fault, a fracture in the earth's crust where one rock plate is thrust horizontally over another. Scientists believe that about 65 million years ago two of the earth's crustal plates collided with such force that part of one plate was shoved up and over younger sandstones. This thrust contact is clearly defined by the sharp contrast between the gray limestone and the red sandstone formations. Either of the Calico Vista points offers a good

INSIDERS' TIP

Three kinds of venomous rattlesnakes as well as scorpions and Gila monsters live in the Red Rock area. Watch where you step and reach, especially along sandstone crevices.

vantage point for photographing the crossed-bedded Aztec sandstone. For a closer look, stop at the Sandstone Quarry parking lot, where you can walk to the large blocks of stone.

Additional pullouts on the loop, with views of wooded canyons and desert washes, are at Icebox Canyon, Pine Creek Canyon and Red Rock Wash. Picnic sites are at Red Spring and Willow Spring. Views from the vista points are magical, but to thoroughly experience the area, hike into one of the canyons, where there is a diversity of environments and scenery. One of the best hiking spots is Pine Creek Canyon. Give yourself about an hour and a half for the mild, 2-mile hike into the canyon, enjoy the scenery and return, packing in everything you want for refreshment and packing out everything you don't consume. Park at the top of the bluff and walk down the path along the creek-bed area. The creek water is potable except in the driest season when it turns stagnant. Follow the creek past a meadow to the ruins of a historic homestead, and continue to its source in the cathedral-like rocks. Growing along the bed are big sweet-smelling pinon pines. The desert plants are at their thickest here, with juniper trees, manzanita bushes, yucca, mesquite and Joshua trees in abundance. If your timing is right, you may glimpse a family of bighorn sheep, a coyote or a kit fox.

Birders should bring their field glasses, especially during the spring migration, to catch sight of Scott's, Bullock's and hooded orioles, California thrashers, summer and western tanagers, pine crossbills, golden eagles, white-throated swifts, black-throated gray warblers, blue-gray gnatcatchers, ladder-backed woodpeckers, bushtits, rufous-sided and green towhees, cactus wrens and black-throated hummingbirds, among other species. For a complete list, pick up a bird watcher's guide at the visitor center.

If you'd like a closer view of the region's geologic history, take the Keystone Thrust hike, a moderate 3-mile walk beginning at the White Rock Spring pullout. From the lower parking area, follow the dirt road to an abandoned vehicle trail that leads eastward. Follow the trail up the alluvial slope past a prominent hill called Hogback Ridge to the right, where you'll find an old car hulk and a well-preserved prehistoric roasting pit. Hike up the ridge for a grand view southward down the Red Rock valley and along the face of the Sandstone Bluffs. At the pass the trail forks; follow the right fork down into a small canyon to view the Keystone Thrust. As you descend, notice the sharp contrast in color between the older gray dolomite on top of the younger red and buff sandstone. This piggybacking of older crustal plates on top of younger ones is the distinguishing geologic feature of Red Rock Canyon. Near the end of the trail, you'll also notice three, rusted automobile bodies. Their origin is somewhat of a mystery, but local historians theorize that a nest of car thieves operated in the area during the 1930s and '40s, and these old hulks were once part of their cache.

The Calico Hills are riddled with natural water catchments called potholes or tinajas. After rains these natural water tanks may be home to small insects, larvae and fairy shrimp. Icebox Canyon has a maintained trail that leads for about three-fourths of a mile; the end of the canyon is reached after another half-mile of boulder-hopping in the canyon bottom. You can find shorter hikes along the loop. An easy trail to the bottom of the canyon at the second Calico Vista leads down to the Aztec sandstone and, after seasonal rains, to small pools of water. There is also good hiking at Sandstone Quarry where many small canyons offer a delightful escape from city life. Kids can learn about the wonders of nature on the Children's Discovery Trail in Red Rock Canyon. The half-mile path through Lost Creek Canyon leads to natural rock formations and overhangs that Indians once used as shelters. The trail entrance is near the Willow Spring Picnic Area on the scenic route, but stop at the Visitors Center for a guidebook before starting. The guide-workbook describes the trail's nine marked sites, where the kids are asked to examine the vegetation and listen to the "water music" of Lost Creek or smell the bark of a pine tree. It also points out and describes some of the animals that live near the trail.

A few points to keep in mind about hiking in Red Rock Canyon: Avoid dehydration by carrying water with you — most people need a gallon a day while hiking; be wary of flash floods, especially in the late summer months when thunderstorms occur with little warning; all natural and historic features such as plants, animals, rocks and Indian artifacts are protected — you may not disturb, damage or remove them. In Red Rock Canyon, all mountain bikes and bicycles are prohibited from hiking trails and must stay on the designated roads. The 13-mile Scenic Loop, however, is very popular with cyclists and provides a superb, if not strenuous, ride through the canyon's red sandstone cliffs. You can park your vehicle and start your ride from the Visitors Center, and remember to follow the one-way flow of traffic along the loop. On the first half of your ride you will gain about 1,000 feet of elevation, but most of the last half is downhill or flat. When you complete the loop, you're less than a 2-mile ride along Nev. 159 to the Visitors Center.

After leaving the Scenic Loop, you can turn left on Nev. 159 (Charleston Boulevard) and head back to the city or turn right and drive about 3 miles to Bonnie Springs Ranch, 1 Bonnie Springs Ranch Road, 875-4300. Built in 1843 as a cattle ranch and watering hole for wagon trains going to California, Bonnie Springs is now a mini-amusement park with a petting zoo, duck pond, bird aviary and riding stables. Next door, Old Nevada Village is a full-scale restoration of an old Western town. Although it looks like a movie set, there are no false fronts here — the weathered buildings contain country stores, a saloon, an ice cream parlor, an opera house, a sheriff's office, a shooting gallery, a silent movie house and a mini-train ride along the outside of the town. Throughout the day, there are "gunfights" in the street as well as other Wild West melodramas. For more information, see our Daycations chapter.

State Parks

Floyd Lamb State Park

9200 Tule Springs Rd. • 486-5413

Floyd Lamb State Park, also known as Tule Springs, is a scene D. H. Lawrence would love — a still, sylvan lake with ducks and geese on its banks, all surrounded by gently sloping hills and towering shade trees. This green oasis is only 15 miles north of downtown Las Vegas via U.S. 95. The park, open daily from morning until dusk, attracts anglers, birders, picnickers and hikers. You can feed the ducks on the large and small lakes connected by a stream, stroll around the trimmed lawns on sidewalks or set up your picnic on one of the many tables. Restrooms and drinking fountains are found throughout the park, and there's a trapshooting range nearby.

A variety of waterfowl pass through on the spring and fall migrations, including ruddy ducks, pintails, white-faced scaup, cinnamon and green-winged teal, Mandarin ducks, and Canada, snow and Ross' geese. Imported peacocks wander the grounds, punctuating the air with their squawks (you can hardly say "songs"; it's more like the rusty grate of an angry gate). Photographers will find inspiration in the pastoral setting and the buildings of the old Tule Springs Ranch. Built in the 1940s as a working ranch, it became a dude/guest ranch where guests waited out the six-week residency requirement for a quickie divorce. Now, the horse stables, tack rooms, a wooden water tower and barn provide a rustic backdrop for artists and photographers.

Named for the large reed-like plants indigenous to the area, Tule Springs is one of the few sites in the United States where evidence suggests the presence of man before 11,000 B.C. Fossils discovered at a site 5 miles southeast of the park show the presence of several extinct animals — the ground sloth, mammoth, prehistoric horse and American camel as well as the giant condor. Archaeologists continue working at the fossil site, though it has not been developed for public viewing. The park is open from 8 AM to 6 PM daily, and admission is $5 per vehicle.

Spring Mountain Ranch State Park

Nev. Hwy. 159, Blue Diamond
• 875-4141

For a close-up look at a ranch Howard Hughes once owned, drive 18 miles west on Charleston Boulevard (Nev. 159) to the Spring

INSIDERS' TIP

The Mt. Charleston area's temperatures are 20- to 30-degrees cooler than those in Las Vegas.

Photo: Jim Decker/Review-Journal

Mt. Charleston in the Toiyabe National Forest is an Alpine retreat only 45 minutes from The Strip.

Mountain Ranch State Park turnoff. After paying the $5-per-car entry fee, continue up the access road. Notice that the area appears tamer than the surrounding wild lands, thanks to the convergence of three climate zones and a year-round supply of water from Lake Harriet in the foothills above the ranch. The permanent outdoor stage on the south side of the access road was built by donations to the volunteer State Parks Cultural Board. During the summer months it features community theater and musical concerts, where audiences sit on their blankets and lawn chairs, spread out picnic-basket dinners and enjoy productions ranging from *The Sound of Music* to *Calamity Jane*. At the end of the access road you'll find a lush park with extensive lawns, oak trees, a couple dozen picnic tables, drinking fountains and indoor restrooms for those who prefer the comforts of home.

Across the rolling green pasture with its white rail fences stands an impeccably maintained New England-style ranch house. Built by radio star Chet Lauck (Lum of the "Lum and Abner" show), the ranch was later owned by Vera Krupp, of the German munitions family, and by billionaire Howard Hughes before it became part of the state park. You can enjoy a free tour of the ranch house, which has all its furniture in place, just as it was in the 1950s. Nearby is a sandstone-block farm house built in the mid-1800s and a reconstructed blacksmith shop, complete with old bellows, tools and cabinets. Guided tours to Lake Harriet above the ranch are also available. The reservoir, fed by Sandstone Spring, is surrounded by tall marsh grass and trees and is home to dozens of bird species, snakes, lizards, bighorn sheep and other wildlife.

The Spring Mountains just west of the park

were the site of a 1942 plane crash that killed actress Carole Lombard. On a flight to Los Angeles from Indiana, where she had been campaigning for war bonds, Lombard's plane had stopped for refueling in Las Vegas. A few minutes after takeoff, the DC-3 slammed into the snowy slopes near Mount Potosi, killing everyone on board. Lombard's husband, Clark Gable, immediately flew to Las Vegas and, after hours of waiting for word from search parties, set out for the crash site. But after traveling part of the way up the mountain he turned around, preferring to remember his wife as he had last seen her. Later that year, a black-spotted orange butterfly indigenous to the cliffs of the Spring Mountains was discovered and named the Carole's fritillary in honor of the actress.

The park is open from 8 AM to 6 PM daily. You can tour the main ranch house from noon to 4 PM Monday and Friday and 10 AM to 4 PM Saturday, Sunday and state holidays.

Valley of Fire State Park

Nev. Hwy. 169, Overton • 397-2088

The jagged sandstone mounds of vermilion, scarlet and mauve at Valley of Fire State Park create an eerie pallet, suggestive of a Martian landscape. Unlike Red Rock Canyon, which was created along shifting fault lines, the red sandstone formations here were formed from great sand dunes during the Jurassic Period. Complex uplifting and faulting of the region, followed by 100 million years of erosion, have carved this crimson-hued valley, 6 miles long and 4 miles wide, from the desert. A popular destination for rock hunters, the Valley of Fire is famous for its petroglyphs — ancient rock art left behind by the prehistoric Basketmaker people and the Anasazi Pueblo farmers, who are believed to be North America's earliest peoples.

In addition to exploring the majestic sandstone formations — spires, domes and serrated ridges — visitors can hike, camp and picnic. The state park is a 45-minute drive from Las Vegas via Interstate 15 or an hour's drive by Northshore Road along Lake Mead. The best time to visit is late September through early June since summer temperatures are ferocious. Photographers will capture their best images in the early morning and late afternoon because of the slanting light. A good first stop is the Visitor Center on Nev. 169 in Overton, 397-2088, where you can pick up maps, trail guides, displays, books and films on the geology, ecology and history of the region. The exhibits explain the natural forces that created this unusual spot. There's also a desert tortoise habitat where you can see the endangered animals at close range.

The driving tour through the valley takes only 15 minutes, but plan to stop at some fascinating sights along the way. You'll see about a half-dozen cabins that were built with native sandstone by the Civilian Conservation Corps in the 1930s as a shelter for passing travelers. Picnic facilities and restrooms are nearby. One of two sites where you can see close-up prehistoric Indian rock art is Petroglyph Canyon. Follow the self-guided tour along the sandy canyon bottom and watch for markings on the canyon walls. You should be able to see kachina figures tucked up and away from casual view as well as dancers holding hands, footprints, clan signs and various animals. Curved and straight lines tie some of the compositions together. The self-guided trail also leads to Mouse's Tank, named for a local Native American who hid from the law here at the turn of the century. The large rock catchment, or tank, at the trail's end collects and preserves rain water, providing a source for birds, reptiles, mammals and insects. Atlatl Rock is the Park's other major petroglyph site. Named for the ancient spear-throwing sticks depicted in many petroglyphs, Atlatl Rock has a stairway and scaffold for closer inspection of the extensive rock art. Excavations at the site have uncovered artifacts left by the Virgin Anasazi, Paiute and others who once lived along the Colorado River. Petrified Wood is a collection of 225-million-year-old logs and stumps washed into the area from ancient forests that

INSIDERS' TIP

For up-to-the-minute weather information in the Lake Mead Recreational Area call 736-3854.

once covered this now arid region. Two trails lead to the petrified logs, the most common local fossil. Other interesting rock formations are the Seven Sisters, a close grouping of seven upright "figures"; the Beehives, an unusual sandstone formation weathered by the eroding forces of wind and water; and the White Domes, a brilliant contrast of sandstone colors. On your drive to the Valley of Fire, you'll pass through Moapa Valley, a veritable oasis irrigated by the centuries-old Muddy River.

After exiting the interstate you'll discover alfalfa fields, horse ranches and milk dairies as well as two one-street towns. The first one is Logandale, a bedroom community on the site of St. Joseph, one of the first Mormon settlements in southern Nevada. Farther along Nev. 169 is Overton, whose main street spans several blocks of cafes, bars, markets, video stores and a movie theater. If you'd like a hawk's-eye view of the valley, take the paved road leading east out of Overton up the mountain to Mormon Mesa. The spot is a nice place to spread a picnic blanket and enjoy the panorama.

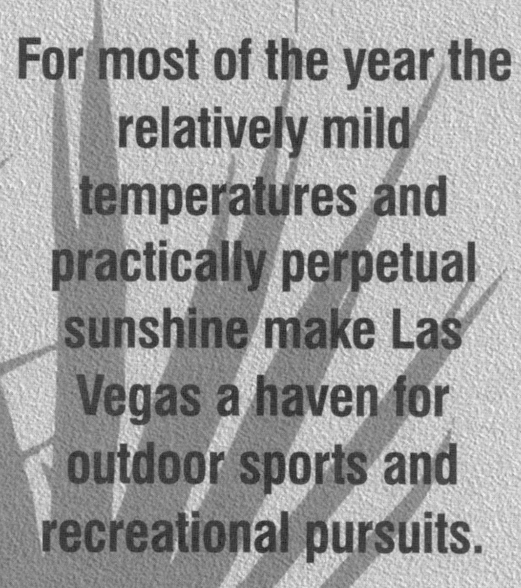

For most of the year the relatively mild temperatures and practically perpetual sunshine make Las Vegas a haven for outdoor sports and recreational pursuits.

Parks and Recreation

Many people imagine the southern Nevada desert to be a geographic purgatory, a scorching hot land seemingly unfit for habitation and possibly best suited as a place of exile. During the hottest summer months — July and August — Las Vegas lives up to those expectations with daytime high temperatures averaging well above the 100-degree mark. Yet for most of the year, the relatively mild temperatures and practically perpetual sunshine make Las Vegas a haven for outdoor sports and recreational pursuits.

Joggers, walkers and bikers find plenty of trails and paths to keep their cardiovascular systems humming, and tennis players are treated to top-flight facilities at the resort hotels, public parks and private clubs. And with nearly 40 golf courses, many of them championship quality, the region has become a golfer's dream — so much so that covering all that golf has to offer merits its own chapter (see our Golf chapter). Watersports enthusiasts can raft the Colorado River, scuba dive in Lake Mead or simply swim in one of the hundreds of pools in southern Nevada. You can even ice-skate 365 days a year, and during certain months, water ski at Lake Mead in the morning and snow ski at Mt. Charleston in the afternoon. For fishing, it's open season year round at Lake Mead, where lucky anglers hook into trophy-size largemouth or striped bass, catfish, trout and other freshwater species.

Lake Mead is also a valuable source of water that keeps the region's parks green. In fact, there are about 75 city and county parks with green belts, ball fields, towering shade trees, swimming pools, tennis courts, jogging tracks and much more. In addition to the usual sports and recreation, the municipal parks offer specialized activities and special-use areas, such as a radio-controlled boating pond and airfield, walk-through archery range, BMX bicycle track and an 18-hole Frisbee golf course.

For those who like their recreation indoors, the valley boasts several fine bowling alleys, some actually tucked within casinos, and dozens of billiard parlors. The city and county parks departments also maintain several well-equipped community centers, where visitors can take part in a variety of classes and activities, including yoga, dancing, table tennis, swimming, gardening, shuffleboard and basketball, just to name a few.

In addition to the community parks listed in this chapter, southern Nevada is home to several state parks, scenic and national recreational areas, which are all described in our chapter called The Great Outdoors.

Although Las Vegas has grown into a major city, the outdoors is never far away. Always remember we're in the middle of a vast desert, and it will get hot. Even in the milder months of March, April, May and June, temperatures

INSIDERS' TIP

The Las Vegas Parks and Leisure Activities Department forms seasonal leagues for basketball, soccer, golf and coed softball. To join or for more information call 229-2256.

can soar into the 90s and above, so be prepared with proper head covering, sunscreen and protection from the wind that often buffets in stinging gusts across the desert. Also remember that whenever you're playing or exercising outside, drink lots of water and carry a good supply when hiking, riding or walking. Dehydration and heat prostration can sneak up quickly in these parts.

Parks and Recreation Agencies

The area's rapidly growing population can find plenty of leisure-time and recreational activities at parks and community centers throughout the valley. All of these activities are administered through or supervised by the City's Department of Parks and Leisure Activities and the Clark County Parks and Recreation Department. Among the programs offered are sports leagues, aerobics classes, dance classes, martial arts, gymnastics, seniors activities and programs, teen and youth services, scuba diving, gun safety, fossil hunting and archery, to name a few.

FYI

Unless otherwise noted, the area code for all phone numbers listed in this chapter is 702.

In addition, the city and county parks departments offer specialized classes and programs, such as the city's Senior Outreach program, its Adaptive Recreation program for children with developmental disabilities and its Track Break program designed to keep students on the "right track" while on break from year-round schools. The county also sponsors numerous seniors programs and activities, plus a Track Break program of its own for children ages 6 to 12. Also for kids is the county's SafeKey Program, a before and after school recreational program that gives kids a chance to participate in sports, contests and tournaments, arts and crafts and other activities. Most of the classes and programs are available at little or no cost.

For more information, consult a city or county program guide, which you may pick up at any of the community centers listed below. Or you can receive more information by contacting the city's Parks and Leisure Activities Department and the county's Parks and Recreation Department.

City of Las Vegas Parks and Leisure Activities

749 Veteran Memorial Dr. • 229-6297

The department publishes "Beyond the Neon," a quarterly event calendar and program guide that lists classes, sports programs, description of facilities, locations and maps.

Clark County Parks and Recreation Department

2601 E. Sunset Rd. • 455-8200

For information on classes, activities and programs ask for the department's "Program Guide," which also lists facilities and locator maps.

City and County Parks

When viewed from the gondola of a hot air balloon, community parks dot the jumbled cityscape with splashes of green, like jagged brushstrokes in a colorful mosaic. Besides spelling relief from crowded casinos and clogged city streets, a visit to a community park can make you forget that southern Nevada is in the midst of an arid desert. There are about 75 city and county parks, most of which have restrooms, playgrounds, picnic areas, grills and ball fields (soccer, football, baseball). Many are also equipped with fitness stations, jogging tracks, tennis courts, horseshoe pits and basketball courts. Listed below are parks with special features and facilities.

East Valley

Dog Fancier's Park

5800 E. Flamingo Rd. • 455-8281

This one-of-a-kind park for pooches hosts dog shows, dog training and special events. The 12-acre park has a lighted grassy show area and spectators area. About 35 clubs, representing a variety of breeds, hold regular events at the park.

Freedom Park

Mojave Rd. and Washington Ave. • 229-6297

Picnickers can spread their blankets on the lush grass by a lake at the 30-acre Freedom Park, which also serves as the site for opening and closing ceremonies of the citywide Corporate Challenge games, held every spring. Volleyball courts, a jogging track, fitness center and playground are here to help jump-start your gambling-weary body.

Horseman's Park

5800 E. Flamingo Rd. • 455-8281

A complete equestrian center, Horseman's Park has two lighted arenas, 320 stalls, livestock pens and a cutting area. The main arena has seating for 2,500 spectators as well as bucking chutes and a practice arena. The park hosts some of the most prestigious horse show and rodeo events in the Western United States.

Jaycee Park

St. Louis and Eastern Aves. • 229-6297

Joggers will like the park's tree-lined, 1,088-yard track, which also features fitness and exercise stations along the way. You can also toss a few horseshoes or try the new bocce courts at this popular park located 3 miles east of The Strip. There's also a children's playground, picnic shelters, football/soccer fields and tennis courts.

Nellis Meadows Park

4949 E. Cheyenne Ave. • 455-8282

Cyclists love the 20-acre, lighted BMX (Bicycle Motocross) track, which is surrounded by green belts and playgrounds. BMX bicycle races are held throughout the year. Riders are required to join the National Bicycle League ($30 per year), and minors must have parents' written permission to compete in races.

Silver Bowl Sports Complex

6800 E. Russell Rd. • 455-8281

Next to the Silver Bowl stadium, the 40-acre park has six lighted ball fields, a playground and one of the better archery ranges in the state. It features 32 practice targets, with distances ranging from 10 to 70 yards. Also here is a radio-control car track for 1/4-, 1/8- and 1/10-scale model cars and a radio-controlled airfield, featuring a 100-foot by 700-foot east-west runway, pit areas for competition and two large shade shelters for spectators.

Sunset Park

2601 E. Sunset Rd. • 455-8200

The largest of the community parks, Sunset Park is a sprawling 300-acre park set amid towering shade trees, making it a favorite with joggers and power walkers. Among the amenities are a 13-acre lake, which is fully stocked for fishing with catfish and trout (license required for fishermen 12 years and older). There's also a model boat sailing area, archery course, horseshoe pits, over-the-line course and volleyball pits. The most recent addition to the park is a Frisbee Golf Course, a par 70 course of about 5,500 feet. You can pick up score cards at the park office daily. Tennis courts, lighted ball fields, fitness trails and a swimming pool round out the amenities.

West Valley

Angel Park

Westcliff and Durango Drs. • 229-6297

This lush 10-acre park is a relaxing stopover on the drive to Red Rock Canyon (see our chapter on The Great Outdoors). Facilities include a jogging track, tennis courts, physical fitness equipment and a picnic area with barbecue grills. Kids can enjoy a playground and cool off at the spray fountain.

Lorenzi Park

3333 W. Washington Ave. • 229-6297

Just a mile west of downtown, Lorenzi Park features tennis courts, softball fields, playgrounds and a 5-acre lake stocked with channel catfish and trout. Fishing is permitted, but you must have the required licenses (see our Fishing section in this chapter.) A carefully tended rose garden makes an aromatic spot for a picnic, especially after touring the Nevada State Historical Museum (see our Attractions chapter), located on the park grounds. Also here is the Sammy Davis Jr. Festival Plaza (see our Arts chapter) and the Durfelt Senior Center (see Community Centers, below).

Community Centers

Downtown

Dula Gymnasium

441 E. Bonzana Rd. • 229-6307

Activities in the newly renovated gymnasium for seniors include basketball, badminton, jazz dance and tap dancing. The gym's fitness room includes a treadmill, stepper, bicycles and weights, and you can play table tennis against a Ping Pong Robot (no kidding!). The gym is open from 8 AM to 5:30 PM Monday through Thursday and 8 AM to 4:30 PM on Friday.

www.insiders.com
See this and many other
Insiders' Guide® destinations
online — in their entirety.
Visit us today!

Las Vegas Senior Center

451 E. Bonanza Rd. • 229-6454

One of the largest community centers in the valley, the Senior Center has a fully equipped gym, swimming pool, billiards room, restaurant, library, banquet and meeting rooms. In addition to a variety of recreational and dance classes, the center sponsors health screenings and topical classes of interest to seniors such as tax preparation and living wills. The center is open from 9 AM to 10 PM Monday through Saturday.

Stupak Community Center

300 W. Boston Ave. • 229-2488

In an underprivileged area of Las Vegas once known as the "Naked City," the Stupak Center administers many crime prevention and community service programs such as Safe Haven, Family Youth Services, Positive Choices and Leadership/Citizenship classes. The center has a weight-training center and conducts classes in Parenting, Bilingual Computers and English as a Second Language. It's open 7:30 AM to 8:30 PM Monday through Thursday, 8:30 AM to 8 PM on Friday and 9:30 AM to 5 PM on Saturday.

East Valley

Chuck Minker Sports Complex

275 N. Mojave Rd. • 229-6563

The modern facility has a weight room, gym, sauna, lockers and showers and eight racquetball courts. In addition to exercise classes, you can participate in volleyball leagues, first aid classes, racquetball tournaments and wheelchair fitness categories. Daily rates are available, or you can become a member in one of several programs ($15 to $45 per month). The complex is open 7 AM to 9:30 PM Monday through Friday; 9 AM to 5 PM on Saturday and 10 AM to 4 PM on Sunday.

Orr Community Center

1520 E. Katie Ave. • 455-7196

Activities for all ages include sports, gymnastics, exercise and crafts. Orr is open from 10 AM to 7 PM Monday through Friday.

Paradise Community Center

4770 S. Harrison Dr. • 455-7153

Paradise offers programs and classes in sports, recreation, arts and crafts for all ages. It's open 7:30 AM to 9 PM Monday through Friday and 9 AM to 5 PM on Saturday.

Parkdale Community Center

3200 Ferndale Ave. • 455-7517

The Parkdale Center has an outdoor pool and basketball courts and administers the county's Track Break program for students,

INSIDERS' TIP

Clark County's Rec Mobiles are a fleet of vans that bring recreational fun to schools, housing projects and low-income neighborhoods. Games, sports, arts and crafts, and special events are all geared toward at-risk kids. Call 455-8272 for information and scheduling.

who are "off track" from their year-round classes. The center also conducts classes in arts and crafts, physical fitness and other recreational programs. The center is open 7:30 AM to 7 PM Monday through Friday and 10 AM to 2 PM on Saturday.

Rafael Rivera Community Center

2900 E. Stewart Ave. • 229-4600

Opened in 1996, this center is named for a Mexican scout who passed through the Las Vegas Valley in 1829, mapping the area and becoming one of the first to discover southern Nevada. In addition to classes in martial arts, CPR and first aid, outreach programs include bilingual classes, preschool programs, children's activities, teen workshops, services for seniors and activities for at-risk children. The center is open 9 AM to 8 PM Monday through Friday and 9 AM to 5 PM on Saturday.

West Valley

Derfelt Senior Center

3333 W. Washington Ave. • 229-6601

In Lorenzi Park, the center provides the active senior a range of activities and classes in yoga, tap dancing, cooking, mah jongg, fitness and more. It's open from 8 AM to 4 PM Monday through Friday.

Mirabelli Community Center

6200 Elton Ave. • 229-6359

The center conducts programs and classes for all ages, including basketball, aerobics, dance, judo/jujitsu and table tennis. The weight room has Lifecycles, stair climbers and weight machines, and the game room is a popular retreat for pinochle tournaments. It's open 9 AM to 7 PM Monday through Friday and 11 AM to 3 PM on Saturday.

Northwest Community Center

6841 W. Lone Mountain Rd. • 229-4794

Activities and classes for all ages include aerobics, table tennis, line dancing and shuffleboard. The center also administers the city's Track Break program designed for students on break from year-round schools. During these periods the center opens at 7 AM during the week and holds classes in arts and crafts and physical fitness programs. You can also enroll in one of the city's Lifetime Sports classes or Adaptive Recreation programs. It's open from 8 AM to 5 PM Monday through Friday.

North Valley

Doolittle Senior Center

1901 N. J St. • 229-6125

Bowling, table tennis, swimming, walking and line dancing are a few of the daily activities available for seniors. A popular program is the Community Gardening project in which seniors receive instruction then get hands-on experience growing vegetables, fruits and flowers. The center is open Monday through Friday from 9 AM to 3 PM.

Recreation

Archery

Archery Plus Inc.

1401 N. Decatur Blvd. • 631-4777

This well-supplied store has everything for the hunter and target shooter in its pro shop, including a bow-timing machine. Certified instruction on 30-yard indoor lanes costs $12 an hour (30 minutes of lessons and 30 minutes of shooting). Archery Plus is open from 11 AM to 9 PM Monday to Thursday, 11 AM to 5 PM on Friday and 10 AM to 5 PM on Saturday and Sunday.

Pacific Archery

4084 Schiff Dr., No. D-12 • 367-1505

Pacific Archery offers instruction on a 20-yard indoor range, with lessons costing $14 an hour. Pacific's pro shop has a large selection of target and bow hunting supplies and equipment. It is open from 9 AM to 9 PM Monday to Friday and 9 AM to 5 PM on Saturday.

Silver Bowl Sports Complex Archery Range

6800 E. Russell Rd. • 455-8200

Operated by the county's parks and recreation department, the range has 32 practice targets with distances ranging from 10 to 70 yards. It's open 24 hours, and it's free to the public.

Astronomy

Planetarium

Community College of Southern Nevada, 3200 E. Cheyenne Ave. • 651-4759

Stargazers should take a peek at the Community College's Planetarium, where you'll find interesting and educational movies on a 360-degree wraparound screen. The planetarium also conducts telescope viewing after the last performance, weather permitting. Many astronomical objects can be viewed, depending on the time of year and visibility. Presentations are at 6 and 7:30 PM on Wednesday and Friday and 5:30 and 7:30 PM on Saturday. Admission is $3.50; students, seniors and children younger than 12 pay $2.25.

Ballooning

There are several events and balloon races held throughout the year, including the Las Vegas Balloon Classic held every October at the Silver Bowl Park. The event usually attracts more than 100 balloons and features crafts and food booths, demonstrations and exhibits (see our Annual Events chapter for more information).

Balloon Safaris

2039 Civic Center Dr., Ste. 282, North Las Vegas • 259-6705

Licensed pilots will take you on hot-air balloon flights during the season, which runs from November to the end of May. Flights begin at $99 per person. The 90-minute flights end with a champagne celebration and start at $99 per person.

Blue Sky Balloons

3172 N. Rainbow Blvd., Ste. 102 • 243-4700

Licensed instructors guide your ascent into the cosmos at a cost of $150 for two people. Fights, which are offered from November to May, usually begin at dawn and last about 90 minutes.

Nevada High Inc.

6425 Tara Ave. • 873-8393

A licensed pilot will take you up, up and away for $125 per person, up to a maximum of four people. The voyage lasts for about an hour and you get a champagne celebration upon landing. The season runs from about November to April, depending upon the wind and temperature (gusty winds and hot temperatures ground balloon flights). Gift certificates and ballooning equipment also are available for sale.

The Ultimate Balloon Adventure

2013 Clover Path St. • 221-9199

The commercially licensed pilots will take you on flights that start before sunrise or just before sunset. Flights last from 60 to 90 minutes and culminate with a champagne celebration. The cost is $125 per person, double occupancy required. Predawn flights are $175 per person. The flight season is from November through May.

Bicycling

With ever-increasing traffic, road construction, narrow streets and virtually no bike lanes, the city streets are not exactly friendly for bike riders. In fact, one national magazine rated Las Vegas one of the worst places to ride in the United States. If you're not willing to brave city streets, there are some great parks and scenic areas for pedaling.

Nellis Meadows Park

4949 E. Cheyenne Ave. • 452-6053

Cyclists will find Valhalla at this park's 20-acre, lighted BMX (Bicycle Motocross) track, which is surrounded by greenbelts, ballfields and playgrounds. Serious riders can compete in BMX races that are held on selected weekends throughout the year. To compete, each rider is required to join the National Bicycle League ($35 per year), and minors must have their parents' written permission. Call the League at 254-5554 for more information.

Floyd Lamb State Park

9200 Tule Springs Rd. • 486-5413

Originally known as Tule Springs, this park has bike paths that meander among tree-

Photo: Jim Decker/Review-Journal

The Wet 'n' Wild water park on The Strip is a great place to cool off when the temperatures hit triple digits.

shaded groves, small fishing ponds, picnic areas, trimmed lawns and old buildings of the former Tule Springs Ranch. Be sure to brake for geese, ducks and peacocks, who roam freely throughout the park. Open from 8 AM to 6 PM, daily, the park charges $5 entry per vehicle (see our Great Outdoors chapter for more information).

Red Rock Canyon

Nev. Hwy. 159 • 363-1921

This is a popular spot for cyclers, even though bikes are prohibited from the hiking trails and must remain on the designated roads. The 13-mile Scenic Loop provides a superb, if not strenuous, ride through the canyon's red sandstone cliffs. Start your ride from the visitors center and remember to follow the one-way flow of traffic along the loop. On the first half of your ride you will gain about 1,000 feet of elevation, but most of the last half is downhill or flat. At the completion of the loop it's less than a 2-mile ride along Nev. 159 back to the visitors center (see our Great Outdoors chapter for more information).

Escape the City Streets

8221 W. Charleston, Ste. 101 • 596-2953

Fans of mountain bikes will love a guided off-road tour that takes you through Cottonwood Valley in Red Rock Canyon. The cost is $59 per person and includes the bike, helmet, gloves and a free T-shirt. For the same price there's a less strenuous on-road tour of Red Rock's 13-mile scenic loop. Tours include transportation to Red Rock Canyon and are available year round.

Downhill Bicycle Tours Inc.

1209 S. Casino Center Blvd., Ste. 122 • 897-8287

If you've got the stamina, try a bike tour through 18 miles of scenic beauty, while descending 8,000 feet through three ecological environments. Don't worry, a bus takes you up, your bike brings you down. The bus leaves The Strip at 9 AM and returns at 1:30 PM on Tuesday, Thursday and Sunday. The cost is $65 per person.

Billiards

Crystal Palace Billiards

2411 E. Bonanza Rd. • 384-6734

A favorite gathering place for families and casual players, the Palace has 22 pocket billiard tables, one snooker table and a snack bar. It's open 24 hours, seven days a week. Fees are $3 an hour for one person, $6 an hour for two, $8.10 an hour for three and $10 an hour for four people.

Cue Club

953 E. Sahara Ave. • 735-2884

In the aging Commercial Center shopping plaza, the Cue Club features 46 tables, two snooker tables, a few slot machines, a snack bar and a video arcade. You'll find a few sharp players here, and you can test your skill against them in periodic tournaments sponsored by the club. It's open 24 hours a day, and fees are $3.50 per hour per person.

Cue-Topia

860 E. Twain Ave. • 737-6998

This place is the quintessential pool hall — dimly lighted and populated with characters Raymond Chandler would love. If you don't have any luck on the tables, the sandwiches are pretty good. It's open 24 hours a day and costs $3.30 per person per hour.

Family Billiards

1089 E. Tropicana Ave. • 736-1568

Clean and brightly lighted, this parlor has 14 tables and a hamburger grill. It's open 24 hours a day and costs $2.50 per person per hour.

Lou Butera's Pool Sharks Billiards & Entertainment

3650 S. Decatur Blvd. • 222-1011

Many of the players here unpack their own custom-made pool cues, so carefully monitor the table stakes. Be especially wary of the owner, Lou Butera — he's a former world champion pool player! (See the close-up in this chapter.) There's a good selection of well-maintained tables: 15 4' by 9' tables and 11 bar-size tables. Open 24 hours, this facility charges $3.50 per person per hour or $7 per hour for two or more players.

Birding

Bird-watchers will enjoy pursuing their feathered targets in the state parks and wilderness areas near Las Vegas. For more information about these locations see our Great Outdoors chapter.

Pine Creek Canyon

Red Rock Canyon Nev. Hwy. 159 • 363-1921

In Red Rock Canyon, hike about 2 miles into Pine Creek Canyon, where you'll find sweet-smelling pinion pines along the creek bed. Especially during spring migration you might catch sight of Scott's, Bullock's and hooded orioles, California thrashers, golden eagles, cactus wrens and ladder-backed woodpeckers, to name a few. See our Great Outdoors chapter.

Floyd Lamb State Park

9200 Tule Springs Rd. • 486-5413

An oasis just 15 miles north of downtown Las Vegas, Floyd Lamb State Park has one large and several small lakes fed by natural springs, which attract a variety of waterfowl that pass through on the spring and fall migrations. Focus your field glasses and look for ruddy ducks, pintails, white-faced scaup, cinnamon and green-winged teal, Mandarin ducks, Canadian, snow and Ross' geese. You won't need any help finding the duck and geese wandering the park's grounds, or the imported peacocks who punctuate the air with their squawks (you can hardly say "songs"— it's more like the rusty grate of an angry gate). Open from 8 AM to 6 PM, daily, the park charges $5 entry per vehicle.

Corn Creek

Desert National Wildlife Range, U.S. 95, 8 miles west of Kyle Canyon Rd.

At Corn Creek, the fruited mulberry trees attract evening, blue and rose-breasted grosbeaks, pine crossbills, western and summer tanagers and orioles. For more information, see our chapter on The Great Outdoors.

Boating and Water Skiing

You can skip across **Lake Mead** in a power boat or simply relax under sail or on the deck of a houseboat. If you don't have your own boat or equipment, you can rent them at the places listed below.

In the Laughlin area, water skiing is permitted along the **Colorado River** from Laughlin south to Needles. The sparsely populated area just south of Bullhead City is the best choice. You can also water ski on **Lake Mohave** north of Davis Dam. For more information about the

Lou Butera: Pool Shark to the Stars

As a Hall of Fame pool player and former world champion, Lou Butera dislikes the term "pool shark." Even though, the name of his new pool hall at 3650 S. Decatur Boulevard is Lou Butera's Pool Sharks Billiards & Entertainment Center.

"I never liked hustlers or pool sharks — they give the game a bad rap," Butera says. "But those are just some of the stigmas that we can hopefully get rid of and make the game more respectable."

Making the game respectable has been a labor of love for "Machine Gun" Lou Butera, so-named because of his rapid-fire style of play, a style he used to earn the world record for running 150 balls in 21 minutes. The former world champion in straight pool has also won dozens of tournaments, such as the Midwest Open and Tournament of Champions, and holds several other records for running consecutive balls.

Butera has served as a consultant, choreographer and technical advisor on numerous TV shows and feature films, and he has taught celebrities the proper way to play pocket billiards.

Photo: Lou Butera

Former world champion "Machine Gun" Lou Butera owns a billiards hall in Las Vegas.

Last year, for instance, actress Nicole Kidman bought five two-hour pool lessons (at a cost of $3,750) for her husband, Tom Cruise, whom Butera calls a "nice young gentleman" with a "fairly nice game." He has also taught the likes of Arnold Schwarzenegger and choreographed Martin Sheen and Michael Douglas playing pool in a scene from the movie *American President*. Butera has worked on TV shows such as *The Fall Guy*, *Married With Children* and *Living Single*.

A 59-year-old native of Pittston, Pennsylvania, Butera played professional pool for about 30 years. He's been married to his wife, Caroline, for 40 years, and they have had seven children together. Butera moved to Las Vegas in late 1996 after living in Southern California for more than 20 years. Although he would never return to the grueling pro tour, Butera occasionally plays in a senior tournament or makes a special appearance. While he likes to keep his shooting skills sharp, Butera's current passion is to putter around his new pool hall, taking care of customers and making minor repairs.

One of the first things he did was put up a sign, "No foul language." Since then he's realigned and resurfaced all the tables, installed new pockets and purchased new balls and cues. He's also replaced the pool hall's outdated lighting system.

"I want to make my pool hall the nicest, friendliest, family-oriented pool hall in Las Vegas," he says. He will also take time out to offer free tips and impromptu lessons. And sometimes he'll dust off his pool cue and bring "some real hotshot" back to earth. After all, there's room for just one shark in Lou Butera's Pool Sharks Billiards and Entertainment Center.

Colorado River, Lake Mohave and Lake Mead, see The Great Outdoors chapter.

Lake Mead

Echo Bay Resort and Marina

Via Star Rt. 89010, Overton, NV 89040 • 394-4000

A good outpost for supplies on the lake's northern finger, Echo Bay has a general store, restaurant, campgrounds, RV park, motel and a small airstrip for light aircraft. At the full-service marina you can rent a fishing boat for $35 for four hours, $60 per day or $275 per week. Or you can get a ski boat for $225 per day and $1,050 per week. If you'd like a taste of boating's leisure life, try renting a houseboat — rates start at $650 for three-day, two-night packages and range up to $1,850 for seven days and six nights.

Lake Mead Marina

322 Lakeshore Rd., Boulder City • 293-3484, (800) 752-9669

About a mile north of Boulder Beach, this full-service marina will rent you a 20-foot skit boat for $225 a day or $45 an hour with a $225 deposit. You can also rent a fishing boat for $100 a day or $20 an hour and a patio boat for $175 day or $35 an hour. If you opt for the hourly rates there's a two-hour minimum, and the price doesn't include fuel. Other services at the marina include a general store, motel, floating restaurant and cocktail lounge. The marina is open from 8 AM to 4 PM daily.

Lake Mohave

Cottonwood Cove

1000 Cottonwood Cove Rd., Cottonwood Cove, NV 89046 • 297-1464

Cottonwood Cove is a secluded desert oasis on Lake Mohave's Nevada shoreline, midway between Hoover Dam and Laughlin/Bullhead City. Open year round, the resort features a 24-room motel, convenience store, restaurant, RV park and full-service marina. Here you can rent a fishing boat starting at $60 per day and a ski boat for $200 per day.

Katherine Landing

Ariz. Hwy. 68, Bullhead City, AZ 86430 • (602) 754-3245

Four miles north of Laughlin/Bullhead City, Katherine Landing is open year round and offers a sandy beach plus a free boat launch, swimming and picnic areas, restaurant, lounge, motel, campgrounds and RV park. At the full-service marina you can rent a fishing boat for $35 for four hours, $60 per day or $275 per week. A ski boat runs for $225 per day and $1,050 per week. If you'd like a taste of boating's leisure life, try renting a houseboat — rates start at $650 for three-day, two-night packages and range up to $1,850 for seven days and six nights. Boat rental hours are from 8 AM to 4 PM daily.

Bowling

Gold Coast Hotel

4000 W. Flamingo Rd. • 367-4700

Upstairs from the busy casino is this 72-lane alley that's open 24 hours, seven days a week. Fees Monday through Friday are $1.85 a game and $1.25 for shoe rental. Seniors 55 years and older pay $1.25; juniors 16 years and younger, $1.45. On Saturday, Sunday and holidays, it's $1.80 for all lanes.

Sam's Town Hotel

5111 Boulder Hwy. • 456-7777

This 56-lane alley features automatic scoring machines, a pro shop and a resident pro. Monday through Friday fees are $1.60 per game, $1.20 for juniors and seniors. Saturday, Sunday and holidays fees are $1.65 for all. It's open 24 hours a day except during league play, which is Sunday through Friday from 5:30 to 11 PM and Saturday from 5:30 to 9 PM.

Sante Fe Hotel

4949 N. Rancho Rd. • 658-4995

The modern facility has 60 lanes and Bowlervision, which tracks the speed and path the ball takes from the time it leaves your hand until it hits the head pin. It's open 24 hours. Fees are based on per hour per lane: Monday through Friday from 9 AM to 5:30 PM, adults play for $8, juniors and seniors, $7; Monday through Thursday from 6 PM to midnight, it's $10 for everyone; Friday and Saturday from 6 PM to midnight, it's $12; Saturday and Sunday from 9 AM to 5:30 PM, it's $12; all seven days from midnight to 8 AM, it's $7. Shoes rent for $1.50

Showboat Hotel
2800 Fremont St. • 385-9153

With 106 championship lanes, the Showboat is the largest bowling center in the state of Nevada. It is also the oldest stop on the PBA tour (see our Spectator Sports chapter). It's open 24 hours. Fees for adults are $2.05; juniors and seniors pay $1.55. Shoe rental is $1.75.

Sunset Lanes
4565 E. Sunset Rd. • 736-2695

This 40-lane center is a popular hangout for the teenage crowd. Hours are 8:30 AM to 1 AM Sunday through Thursday and 24 hours on Friday and Saturday. Fees are $1.50 before 6 PM and $1.95 after 6 PM. Shoe rental is $1.50.

Terrible's Town Bowling Center
642 S. Boulder Hwy., Henderson • 564-7118

The Mining Company has a country flavor with its 16 lanes, saloon-style bar, slot machines, snack counter and big-screen TV. It's open 24 hours a day. Fees are $1.75 Monday through Friday (younger than 12, $1.25) and $1.95 for everyone on Saturday and Sunday. Shoes cost $1.25.

Bungee Jumping

A.J. Hackett Bungy
Circus Circus Hotel, 810 Circus Circus Dr. • 385-4321

Take a leap from a steel tower 210 feet above the Las Vegas Strip, then free fall toward a sparkling pool (you run out of rope before you get there!). You receive a T-shirt and certificate with your first jump. The cost is $59 for first jump, $29 thereafter, and the fourth jump is free.

Camping

The scenic areas surrounding Las Vegas are home to some of the most magnificent wilderness in the Southwest. From the alpine forestry of Mt. Charleston and the blue-green grandeur of Lake Mead to the crimson rock formations of the Valley of Fire, nature's wonders abound and can be enjoyed up close by campers. All of the scenic areas and state parks are further described in The Great Outdoors chapter.

Mt. Charleston
Kyle Canyon Rd. • 878-8800, (800) 280-2267

About 40 miles northwest of Las Vegas, Mt. Charleston has six campgrounds open from May 1 through mid-September. Camping is limited to five days and is $10 per night for single-family sites and $20 for multi-family sites. Campground facilities include restrooms, water faucets, picnic tables and either a barbecue grill or open fire ring. Campsites are available on a first-come, first served basis, but some sites may be reserved by groups. Call the toll free number for information.

Lake Mead
U.S. 95 • 293-8906

There are eight campgrounds with 1,334 campsites at Lake Mead, which is open for year-round camping. The campgrounds offer water faucets, restrooms, picnic tables and barbecue grills. Campsites are $8 per night and available on a first come, first-served basis.

Valley of Fire State Park
Nev. Hwy. 169, Overton • 397-2088

At Valley of Fire State Park, you'll find 52 campsites with restrooms, water faucets, hot showers and picnic tables. They are available year round and cost $7 per night.

Climbing

Red Rock Canyon
Nev. Hwy. 159, 15 minutes west of Las Vegas • 363-1921

Rock climbers and rappelers love Red Rock Canyon for the sheer red-and-yellow sandstone escarpments that often reach heights of 3,000 feet. On any given day you can watch climbers, suspended like tiny marionettes, slowly dancing their way up the tilted and folded layers of rock. To learn more about Red Rock Canyon, see The Great Outdoors chapter.

Sky's the Limit

HCR 33, Box 1 Las Vegas, NV 89124
• 363-4533

Guide Randal Grandstaff will take you on a two-day climbing tour of Red Rock Canyon for $220, which includes transportation and all equipment. Or you can take a half-day course in climbing for $120.

Fishing

To get a resident fishing license, which is good for one year (March 1 to end of February), you must be a U.S. citizen and resident of Nevada for at least six months. It costs $21 for fishermen 16 years and older, $5 for ages 12 through 15 and for seniors 65 and older. Fishermen younger than 12 aren't required to have a license in Nevada. Visitors to the state may obtain a nonresident fishing license, which has the same license year as the resident's license. Fees are $51 for those 16 and older and $9 for juniors 12 through 15. You can also get a one-day fishing permit for $12.

Tackle Shops

Blue Lake Bait & Tackle

5485 E. Lake Mead Blvd. • 452-8299

At Blue Lake, you can pick up a fishing license as well as bait, lures, tackle, picnic supplies, cold drinks and ice. Owner Marvin Walker is also handy at repairing a rod and reel, especially spin casters. The shop is open from 5 AM to 7 PM daily.

Rainbows End Bass & Gas

1330 E. Lake Mead Dr., Henderson
• 564-5660

You can stock up on live bait, tackle, lures and other supplies and fill your tank with gas or diesel fuel at this well-stocked shop. You can also purchase a fishing license and get plenty of free advice from owner Mark Johnson. Rainbows End is open from 5 AM to 10 PM daily.

Fishing Spots

Lake Mead

U.S. Hwy. 95 • 293-8906

It's open season on all fish year-round at Lake Mead, where you'll find an abundance of catfish, bluegill, trout, crappie and striped bass, often tipping the scales at 30 pounds and more. One of the best spots for bass is near the Las Vegas Boat Harbor because of the waste-water nutrients that dump from the Las Vegas Wash into this section of the lake. Anglers consider the Overton arm of Lake Mead one of the best areas for striped bass, whose threadfin shad schools often churn the water in their feeding frenzies. For tips on other spots, ask any park ranger or try any of the marinas, which sell licenses, bait and tackle. For more information about fishing at Lake Mead, see The Great Outdoors chapter.

Colorado River

Fishing is excellent along the Colorado River near Laughlin and Bullhead City. Anglers can fill their creels with striped bass, rainbow trout, bass, catfish, bluegill and crappie. A good spot is the cold water below Davis Dam. There's also good fishing above the dam on Lake Mohave, noted for its rainbow trout and bass. For more information see the Laughlin listing in our Daycations chapter.

Lorenzi Park

3333 W. Washington Ave. • 229-6297

Closer to home, you can cast a line into Lorenzi Park's lake, which is stocked with rainbow trout in the winter and channel catfish during the spring and summer. There's a three-fish limit, and you must have a license to fish here.

Sunset Park

2601 E. Sunset Rd. • 455-8200

You can try your luck in Sunset Park's 13-acre lake, which is fully stocked with catfish and trout. There's a three-fish limit, and fisherman 12 years and older need a license.

INSIDERS' TIP

River running requires a permit from the U.S. Bureau of Reclamation, Lower Colorado Region, P.O. Box 299, Boulder City, NV 89005; phone, 293-8367. Apply at least two weeks in advance of your launch date.

Floyd Lamb State Park
9200 Tule Springs Rd. • 486-5413

In a pastoral setting D.H. Lawrence would love, you'll find a still, sylvan lake with ducks and geese on its banks. The main lake connects by stream with three smaller ponds, all of which are stocked with trout and catfish. Open from 8 AM to 6 PM daily, the park charges $5 entry per vehicle.

Hiking

Red Rock Canyon, Mt. Charleston and the Valley of Fire State Park have excellent hiking opportunities. You'll find additional information about these locations in The Great Outdoors chapter.

Red Rock Canyon
Nev. Hwy. 159 • 363-1921

Red Rock Canyon offers some of the most popular hiking in southern Nevada. One of the best spots is Pine Creek Canyon (2 miles), a trek past the creek and sweet-smelling pinon pines to a meadow with the ruins of a historic homestead. Or you can get a close view of the region's geologic history on the Keystone Thrust trail (3 miles), a moderate walk to the older gray dolomite on top of the younger red and buff sandstone. For maps and trail guides visit the Red Rock Visitors Center or call the number above.

Mt. Charleston
Kyle Canyon Rd. • 873-8800

Mt. Charleston has a multitude of hiking trails, which vary from easy, half-hour walks to two-day treks. Most of the trailheads are accessible by car and have water and restroom facilities. Check with the Ranger Station before starting. Most of the trails are open year round, but some are closed during winter and early spring. One of them, Echo Cliff Trail, begins at the Cathedral Rock trailhead and climbs upward through ponderosa pine and white fir forest above the picnic area. At the base of Echo Cliff, you return along an old road, crisscrossing an avalanche path, where the aspen and brush are very colorful in the fall. The trail returns to the upper parking lot in the picnic area.

Valley of Fire
Nev. Hwy. 169 • 397-2088

Hikers love to explore the Valley of Fire's jagged sandstone mounds of scarlet and crimson, which create an eerie palette suggestive of a Martian landscape. The state park is 45 minutes east of Las Vegas and best seen in late September through early June because of the ferocious summer temperatures. After you enter the park, stop at the visitors center, where you can pick up maps, trail guides, books and films on the geology, ecology and history of the region. The exhibits explain the natural forces that created this unusual spot.

Horseback Riding

Equestrians can challenge the rugged foothills of Mount Charleston and the surrounding Toiyabe National Forest, then marvel at the views of the desert floor below. Riders in Red Rock Canyon will enjoy the sandstone bluffs in a tapestry of color, and the spectacular rock formations that are laid open like the pages of a book. For more information about Red Rock Canyon and Mt. Charleston, see The Great Outdoors chapter.

Bonnie Springs Riding Stables
Nev. Hwy. 159, Red Rock Canyon • 875-4191

Take a guided ride into breathtaking Red Rock Canyon. Riders must wear closed shoes and weigh less than 250 pounds. Children younger than 6 are not allowed to ride. Hours are 9 AM to 5:45 PM daily, and rates are $16.50 per hour.

Cowboy Trail Rides
Red Rock Riding Stables, Marker 10, Nev. Hwy. 159 • 387-2457

Cowboy Trail Rides will take you on trail rides into Red Rock Canyon, Lovall Canyon,

INSIDERS' TIP

For information about joining a bowling league or forming one, contact the Southern Nevada Bowling Association at 362-5550.

Mt. Charleston and Valley of Fire. Choose hour-long rides to overnight trips, cattle drives, fishing trips, barbecues and more. Rates are $25 for the first hour, $20 for each hour thereafter. A half day is $105, and overnight trips cost $200.

Mt. Charleston Riding Stables

Nev. Hwy. 157, Mt. Charleston Rd. • 872-7009, 872-5408

The trail ride leaves daily at 10 AM for 3½ hour treks into Fletcher Canyon. The cost is $60 per person. No one heavier than 250 pounds is allowed to ride. Also available are hayrides and overnight wilderness rides into Fletcher Canyon for $150 per person.

Ice Skating

Santa Fe Hotel Ice Arena

Santa Fe Hotel & Casino, 4949 N. Rancho Dr. • 658-4993

Yes, you can ice skate in Las Vegas! This 17,000-square-foot ice skating rink includes a regulation-size hockey rink plus a 2,500-seat bleacher section for spectators. Hours vary because the rink is often pre-empted for hockey league games and other events, so call ahead. Admission is $5 for adults, $4 for children ages 3-12 and free for children younger than 3. Figure-skate rentals are $1.50, hockey skates are $2.

Jogging

Joggers usually require nothing more than a pair of running shoes and an uncrowded sidewalk for their daily fix. But if you prefer running on grass to pounding the pavement, try the athletic fields at the **University of Nevada, Las Vegas** (UNLV), 4505 S. Maryland Parkway, or any of the city and county parks listed above. You'll find paved jogging tracks as well as fitness courts at **Angel Park**, Westcliff and Durango drives, **Jaycee Park**, St. Louis and Eastern avenues, and **Sunset Park**, 2601 E. Sunset Road.

The Running Store

4350 E. Sunset Rd. • 898-7866

This is a good place to find out about and register for upcoming races and fun runs in town. There's also a good selection of footwear, clothes and other running accessories. The store is open from 10 AM to 6 PM Monday to Thursday, 10 AM to 8 PM on Friday, 10 AM to 6 PM on Saturday and 11 AM to 5 PM on Sunday.

FYI

Unless otherwise noted, the area code for all phone numbers listed in this chapter is 702.

Miniature Golf

Formula K Family Fun Park

2980 S. Sandhill Rd. • 431-7223

Watch out for the windmill on this 36-hole course. If you can't handle a putter, try your hand at the video arcade or grab the wheel of a go-cart. It's open seven days a week. The cost to play on either of the 18-hole courses is $3.50 per person. Formula K is open 3 to 10 PM Monday to Thursday, 3 PM to midnight on Friday, noon to midnight on Saturday and noon to 10 PM on Sunday.

Mountasia Family Fun Center

2050 Olympic Ave., Henderson • 898-7777

You can choose from two 18-hole courses and repair to the clubhouse for refreshments and video games afterward. Mountasia also has a roller-skating rink, bumper boats and go-carts. Admission is $5.50 for adults, $4 for children 12 years and younger and $4.50 for seniors. A family of four plays golf for a flat rate of $14. Mountasia is open from 2 to 10 PM, Monday to Thursday, 2 PM to midnight on Friday, 10 AM to midnight on Saturday and 10 AM to 10 PM on Sunday.

Scandia Family Fun Center

2900 Sirius Ave. • 364-0070

This 54-hole miniature golf course should keep you busy for a while. If not, take a few swings in the batting cages or take a turn with the bumper boats. It's open seven days a week. The three 18-hole courses are of varying difficulty and cost $4.95 per round. For a second round of 18 holes it's half-price. Children 5 and younger play free with an adult. Scandia is open from 10 AM to 10:30 PM, Sunday to Thursday and 10 AM to midnight on Friday and Saturday.

Paragliding

Thrillseekers Unlimited

3172 N. Rancho Dr. • 699-5550

Paragliding classes from beginners to Class III rating are available. In addition to instruction, Thrillseekers will supply the towing at several takeoff spots around Las Vegas. Price is $169, plus $75 for photos and video. Office hours are 10 AM to 6 PM Monday through Friday.

Racquetball

Caesars Palace

3570 Las Vegas Blvd. S. • 731-7110

If playing racquetball on vacation is important to you, stay at Caesar's Palace. Courts are in the health spas and are open to hotel guests only. It's open from 10 AM to 5 PM daily.

Green Valley Athletic Club

2100 Olympic Ave., Henderson • 454-6000

Open to members only, there are six racquetball courts and two squash courts, each with its own resident pro. Hours are 5 AM to 11 PM Monday to Friday and 6 AM to 9 PM Saturday and Sunday.

Las Vegas Athletic Club

1070 E. Sahara Ave. • 733-1919
3315 Spring Mountain Rd. • 362-3720

Players can choose from nine courts at the Sahara club and 11 courts at Spring Mountain. Cost is $10 an hour per person, which includes use of spa facilities. The clubs are open from 5 AM to 11 PM daily.

Chuck Minker Sports Complex

275 N. Mojave Rd. • 229-6563

Operated by the city of Las Vegas, the complex features seven racquetball courts, which are available for league play, lessons and tournaments. Fees are $7 per hour for two people with additional players paying $3 each. Memberships are available, from $35 per month to $150 annually. It's open 9 AM to 9:30 PM Monday through Friday, 9 AM to 5 PM on Saturday and 10 AM to 4 PM on Sunday.

University of Nevada, Las Vegas

4505 S. Maryland Pkwy. • 895-3150

With eight racquetball courts to choose from, UNLV students with an I.D. play for free, guests play for $2. It's open 6 AM to 9 PM Monday through Friday, 8 AM to 4 PM on Saturday and 10 AM to 4:30 PM on Sunday.

River Running

The Colorado River from Hoover Dam to Willow Beach is open year round to rafts, canoes and kayaks, but the best time to avoid extreme temperatures is spring and fall. The water moves relatively slowly along the 11-mile stretch, which is flanked by steep canyon walls, often with breathtaking scenery and a few wild burros and Big Horn sheep roaming the bluffs. A permit is required for both rafting and canoeing. There's no charge, but you must apply at least three weeks in advance of your launch date. To receive an application call the U.S. Department of Interior, Bureau of Reclamation, at 293-8204.

Black Canyon Raft Tours

1297 Nevada Hwy., Boulder City
• 293-3776

It's not exactly white-knuckle adventure, but you can float down the Colorado River on a raft from just below Hoover Dam to Black Canyon and see waterfalls, hot springs and geological formations. The trip, which is offered daily starting at 9:45 AM, takes about five hours to complete. Prices are $69.95 for adults, $35 for children younger than 12.

Boulder City Water Sports

1108 Nevada Hwy., Boulder City
• 293-7526

For a more thrilling run down the Colo-

INSIDERS' TIP

If you're traveling to Mt. Charleston for winter recreation, call 593-9500 for a local snow report; for road conditions call 486-3116.

rado River, you can rent a canoe, kayak or Waverunner. Make sure you have a trip permit (see information above). The shop is open from 8 AM to 6 PM daily.

Roller Skating

Crystal Palace

3901 N. Rancho Dr. • 645-4892
4680 Boulder Hwy. • 458-7107
4740 S. Decatur Blvd. • 253-9832
1110 E. Lake Mead Dr., Henderson • 564-2790

In addition to a spacious rink, each of the four locations offers classes in skating (in-line and traditional) and roller-hockey league play. It costs $4 to skate Monday through Thursday and $5 on Friday and Saturday. If you don't have your own skates you can rent them for $1. Hours are 7 to 9:30 PM Monday, Tuesday and Thursday, 3:30 to 6 PM on Wednesday and 7 to 11 PM Friday and Saturday. They're closed on Sunday, except the Boulder Highway location, which is open from 7 to 10 PM.

Mountasia Family Fun Center

2050 Olympic Ave., Henderson • 898-7777

Skate anytime at Mountasia's indoor rink, then challenge the arcade with its 100-plus video games. There's also miniature golf, bumper boats and go-carts. It costs everyone $4 to skate, which includes rental of regular or in-line skates. Mountasia is open from 2 PM to 10 PM Monday to Thursday, 2 PM to midnight on Friday, 10 AM to midnight on Saturday and 10 AM to 10 PM on Sunday.

Scuba Diving

At **Lake Mead**, the National Park Service has buoyed off a designated underwater trail at Boulder Beach, near the Pyramid Island Causeway. Call the National Park Service, 293-8906, for more information. Several local companies sell and rent diving equipment and/or offer instruction.

American Cactus Divers

848 E. Lake Mead Dr., Henderson • 564-3453

This business offers diving classes and scuba equipment sales and service. It's open Monday through Friday from 9 AM to 6 PM and Saturday and Sunday from 8 AM to 4 PM.

Neptune Divers

5831 E. Lake Mead Blvd. • 452-5723

Neptune offers instruction, sales, rental and service. Approximate cost for basic open-water instruction is $150 plus manuals. Hours are 10 AM to 5 PM daily except Wednesday.

Desert Divers Supply

5720 E. Charleston Blvd. • 438-1000

You'll find everything you need to explore the briny deep: fins, tanks, boots, regulators, wet suits and more. Open-water lessons are also available starting at $100 per session. Desert Divers is open from 10 AM to 7 PM Monday to Friday and 8 AM to 6 PM on Saturday and Sunday.

Shooting

Despite all the shot-up warning signs, it is against the law to fire a gun in metropolitan areas, national parks, wildlife preserves and conservation areas. In addition to the shooting ranges listed below, a few gunsmiths and sporting good stores have indoor ranges where you can test a new handgun or rifle. One shop will even let you shoot an Uzi. Just why you would want to is the question.

Desert Sportsman's Rifle & Pistol Club

Red Rock Canyon, P.O. Box 517, Las Vegas, NV 89125 • 642-9928

The private club has six ranges spread over 480 acres in the Calico Basin area of Red Rock Canyon. Membership in the NRA and an annual fee of $75 are required to join.

Las Vegas Gun Club

Floyd Lamb State Park, 9400 Tule Springs Rd. • 645-5606

In addition to paper targets, trap and skeet shooting with sporting clays are available. You can also receive instruction, rent guns, purchase shells or join a shooting league. Basic cost is $5 for a round of 25 targets. Hours are 9 AM to 5 PM daily and 9 AM to 10 PM on Wednesdays.

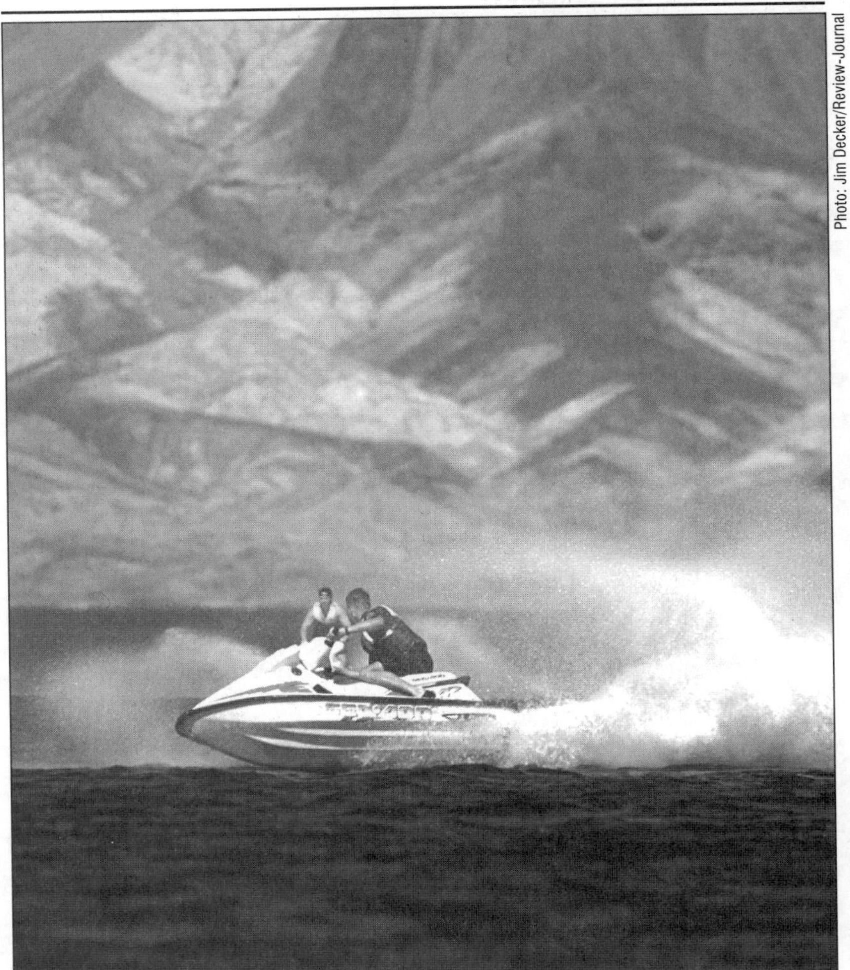

Photo: Jim Decker/Review-Journal

Because of its size, Lake Mead plays host to all types of watercraft, from Jet Skis to houseboats to paddlewheelers.

Skiing

Lee Canyon Ski Area at Mt. Charleston
Nev. Hwy. 156, Mt. Charleston

This ski area, which is only 47 miles from Las Vegas, offers good downhill skiing and snowboarding on bunny, intermediate and expert slopes as well as magnificent cross-country skiing at Scout Canyon, Mack's Canyon and Bristlecone Trail. There are also snow play areas, a hotel, lodges and a winter campground. The ski season, aided by snow-making equipment, runs from November through April, depending upon weather conditions. For more information about the Lee Canyon Ski Area and Mt. Charleston, see our Great Outdoors chapter.

Las Vegas Ski & Snowboard Resort
Nev. Hwy. 156, Mt. Charleston • 872-5462

Three double ski lifts carry skiers to more than 40 acres of maintained ski slopes surrounded by 600 acres of alpine forestry. Snowfall and snow-making equipment combine for an average pack of 80 inches. Nine 3,000-foot runs are available to beginner through advanced skiers, and vertical drop averages 1,000 feet. Snowboarding is restricted to certain days and hours; call for latest schedule. Other facilities at the resort include a ski shop, school, restaurant, lounge and day lodge.

All-day adult lift tickets are about $30, children's and seniors' tickets are about $20, and half-day and night-skiing tickets are available. Season passes are $540 for adults, $390 for seniors and children younger than 12 and $450 for students. During the season, the lifts run from 9 AM to 4 PM, daily plus 4 to 10 PM on Saturday.

Skydiving

Las Vegas Parachute Center

2772 N. Rancho Dr. • 877-1010

Take a dive from 12,500 feet in a tandem parachute with a licensed instructor, then freefall for about 6,000 feet while reaching speeds of 187 feet per second. The cost is about $175. Call about the center's other courses of instruction, including a 14-jump static line course and accelerated free falls.

Skydive Las Vegas Inc.

1401 Airport Rd., Boulder City • 293-1860

A licensed instructor teaches beginner, novice and expert. Learn skydiving with the tandem jump. After a half-hour lesson you'll jump with your instructor in a parachute built for two. Beginning jumps cost $159.

Skydiving, Indoor

Flyaway

200 Convention Center Dr. • 731-4768

Freefall in the only known skydiving simulator, an indoor 21-foot, vertical wind tunnel that generates air speeds of up to 115 mph. After about 15 minutes of instruction you get 15 minutes of flying time in the tunnel shared by five other flyers. Flights are videotaped, and copies can be made. Flyaway has an observation gallery, and the $2 admission applies to your flight. Hours are 11 AM to 7 PM Tuesday to Sunday. Cost is $24 for the first fall, $19.50 for a repeat flight.

Swimming

Swimming during the blistering summer months is a great way to keep cool while taking your daily dose of exercise. Practically every Strip hotel and neighborhood hotel-casino has a swimming pool, but the facilities are only open to hotel guests. Among the downtown resorts, the hotels with pools are Binion's Horseshoe, California Hotel, Golden Nugget, Jackie Gaughan's Plaza and the Lady Luck.

You can swim laps or take a dip in city-maintained pools. City-maintained pools are open from June through August; the Municipal Pool on East Bonanza Road is open year round. The Municipal Pool also has longer hours, from 7 AM to 3 PM and 7 to 10 PM Monday through Friday and 10 AM to 6 PM on Saturday and Sunday. The other pools typically open at 1 PM and close at 5 or 6 PM Monday to Friday. A variety of aquatics programs are offered at the pools, including swimming lessons, lifeguard training and aquacise. Admission is $1.50 for adults, 75¢ for juniors 7 to 17 years old and 50¢ for children 4 to 6 years old.

Municipal Pool, 431 E. Bonanza Road, 229-6309

Baker Swimming Pool, 1100 E. St. Louis Avenue, 229-6395

Brinley Swimming Pool, 2480 Maverick Street, 799-6784

Cragin Swimming Pool, 900 Hinson Street, 229-6394

Doolittle Swimming Pool, W. Lake Mead Boulevard and J Street, 229-6398

Garside Swimming Pool, 300 S. Torrey Pines Drive, 229-6393

Hadland Swimming Pool, 2800 E. Stewart Avenue, 229-6397

Trails Swimming Pool, 1920 Spring Gate Lane, 229-4629

Wet 'n Wild Water Park

2601 Las Vegas Blvd. S. • 737-3819

This 16-acre water park features more than a dozen chutes, slides, flumes, floats and plunges. Two of the most hair-raising are Der

Stuka, which is a seven-story free fall into a catch pool, and Bomb Bay, which sends its victims down a 76-foot slide like a missile projectile. The park's season runs from May through September. General admission price is $21.95 for ages 10 and older and $15.95 for ages 3 to 9. For more information see the Wet 'n Wild listing in the Attractions chapter.

Tennis

Most public parks have at least one tennis court that is open to the public; several are lighted for night play. Call the City of Las Vegas Parks and Leisure Activities department, 229-6297, or the Clark County Parks and Recreation Department, 455-8200, for a list of the parks that have tennis courts. Most public schools in Clark County have tennis courts that are open to the public when school is not in session. Most of the resorts have tennis courts for their guests, and some hotels open them to the public. If you're not staying at the hotel, call ahead to confirm policy or to make reservations. There are several private clubs with tennis courts, but since they are not open to the public, they are not listed here.

Las Vegas Sporting House

3025 Industrial Rd. • 733-8999

The two lighted outdoor courts are open 24 hours a day, and nonmembers may use all the facilities for $20 per day.

Twin Lakes Racquet Club

Lorenzi Park, 3075 W. Washington Ave. • 647-3434

Even though the eight, lighted outdoor courts are in a city park, they are operated under a lease with the Racquet Club. Cost to play is $2 per hour for singles play and $4 per hour for doubles play. Lessons are available for $25 an hour for individuals, $5 an hour for groups.

University of Nevada, Las Vegas

4505 S. Maryland Pkwy. • 895-4481

UNLV's modern tennis complex features 12 lighted outdoor courts, which are available to the public for $5 per person per day. Reservations are suggested.

Volleyball

Many of the city and county parks have volleyball courts and pits, including Alexander Villas, Charleston Heights, Freedom Park, Hidden Palms Park, Hills Park, Lewis Family Park, Paradise Park, Spring Valley and Sunset Park.

Las Vegas Volleyball Club

5277 Cameron St., Ste. 110 • 252-4244

This 17,000-square-foot indoor volleyball facility is available for league play, tournaments, clinics, private instruction, youth programs and open play. Open play is $5 an hour per person, or the court can be rented for $25 an hour. Hours to play are from 3 to 5:30 PM, daily. League play is reserved for the evenings, from 7 to 10 PM daily. Cost for league play ranges from $180 to $270 per team for a six-week session.

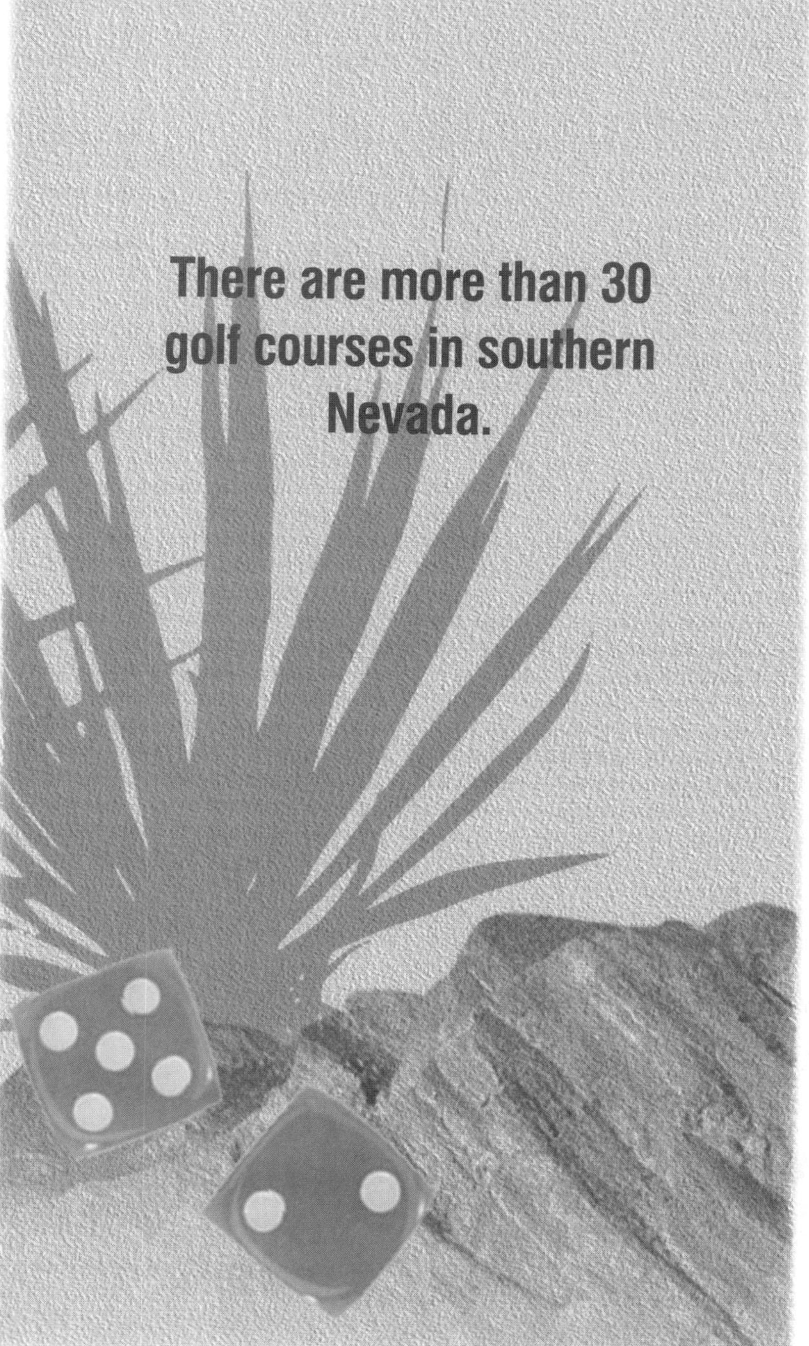
There are more than 30
golf courses in southern
Nevada.

Golf

Do you love golf? Las Vegas is your kind of town. It's the only city to host tournaments from all three professional tours — the men, the women and the seniors. It's also a place where you can play year round. And within easy driving distance (pun intended) there are regional resorts in every direction. These jaunts afford golfers the chance to see a little Southwest scenery away from the madding crowds of gamblers.

In all, there are more than 30 courses in southern Nevada. That may seem like a lot for a desert city where water is at a premium, but Las Vegas golf course operators are a resourceful bunch. To augment their wells, they use reclaimed water that is cycled back through the holding ponds and local water district treatment plants. You wouldn't want to drink out of the sprinkler heads, but this stuff is perfectly good for keeping the greens green.

Many newer courses also are scaling back their fairways without shortening them. Grassy stretches are interrupted by natural desert terrain. This saves on irrigation — and presents a challenge to duffers who don't always hit where they aim. On the plus side, there aren't so many water hazards. Anyway, plan on bringing some extra balls and a heavy-duty wedge if you venture onto these so-called "target courses."

If you're staying on The Strip, don't expect to find too many courses within walking distance. The Dunes and Tropicana courses are no more. That leaves only the Desert Inn and Las Vegas Hilton layouts, and they're both among the most expensive around. After all, they are sitting on some prime real estate.

This chapter walks you through the links that are open to the public. Don't expect to find too many bargains like the pitch-and-putt back home. Hordes of golf-crazy tourists keep Las Vegas courses busy virtually all year, and the supply-and-demand rule doesn't work in players' favor.

Many courses require players to use carts, which drives up the costs even further. There are, however, a few layouts where you can play for less than $30 a round. And some of the pricier ones are still worth the money, having been designed by world-renowned pro players. Hey, besides, you'd probably be sitting in a casino and spending more money anyway, right?

Most of the courses detailed here accept reservations seven days in advance. That doesn't mean you must call a week ahead, but it's wise to do so, especially if your party is larger than a foursome. Courses that accept longer-range reservations are specifically noted. Unless stated otherwise, each facility has a driving range, putting green, pro shop and restaurant.

To help you get your bearings, we've divided this chapter into four sections. The first three parts — encompassing regulation 18-hole courses and one par 3 course — are divided geographically. Close to the Hole, our first section, covers courses in Las Vegas. Courses in neighboring communities are found in the second section, A Chip Shot Away. Las Vegas' lone par 3 course, the North Las Vegas Golf Course, also is listed in this section. Golf venues outside the valley are

INSIDERS' TIP

Golf courses are almost always busy places in southern Nevada, so it's almost essential to get reservations. Most courses will issue tee times seven days in advance, but it doesn't hurt to call even further in advance. They may be willing to bend the rules.

listed under the third heading, Driving Distance. In all cases, course length and par data are for men's play.

The fourth section — Special Services and Organizations — rounds up specialized golf groups, schools and facilities, including 24-hour driving ranges, reservation services and amateur associations around southern Nevada. For miniature golf listings see our Kidstuff chapter, and for a rundown of golf tournaments see our Spectator Sports chapter.

Let's get started!

Close to the Hole

Angel Park Golf Club

100 S. Rampart Blvd. • 254-4653

This is a municipal course, but don't let that fool you. Angel Park is nicer and pricier than most. For starters, this club features two 18-hole courses designed by Arnold Palmer. There's also Cloud Nine, a 12-hole par 3 course with replica holes from the world's most famous par 3s. Then there's an 18-hole putting course and, of course, a driving range. All three of these specialty features are lighted, with play available until 10 PM (though only nine holes on Cloud Nine are illuminated).

> **FYI**
>
> Unless otherwise noted, the area code for all phone numbers listed in this chapter is 702.

The Palm Course, over 6530 yards of gently rolling terrain, is a par 70 layout. The other Palmer beauty is called the Mountain Course. With gorgeous valley vistas, it's a par 71 that plays 6722 yards. Each, with mandatory carts, runs $95 a round. But you can cut that price to $60 if you tee off on the twilight rate four hours before sunset. Cloud Nine spans 1341 yards for a par 36. Greens fees of $20 include a mandatory cart. Tee times can be reserved up to 30 days in advance. The clubhouse and restaurant are notably clean, modern and tastefully decorated with golf memorabilia.

Badlands Golf Club

9119 Alta Dr., 242-4653

Just down the street from Angel Park is Badlands. Built around scenic desert arroyos, this target course isn't for the faint of heart. Johnny Miller, with consultation from Chi Chi Rodriguez, designed this 6926-yard, par 72 masterpiece with accuracy in mind. If your tee shots carry well, you can have a lot of fun on this course. If not, you'll be roughing it. But you can always enjoy spectacular views of nearby Red Rock Canyon that looms immediately to the west.

Greens fees include a cart and a sleeve of balls for $90 Monday through Thursday. The rate goes up to $100 Friday through Sunday. Twilight rates on the weekdays run $35 after 1 PM. This is one of the few courses where you can book tee times 60 days in advance.

Desert Pines Golf Course

3401 E. Bonanza Rd. • 388-4400

One of the city's newest layouts, this Perry Dye design is the closest course to downtown. The layout features narrow fairways, undulating greens and some big fairway bunkers. It all makes for a challenging 6810-yard par 71. A double-deck, night-lighted driving range pops balls up on the tee for you.

Greens fees, including a mandatory cart, are $125 on weekdays and $145 Friday through Sunday. Twilight rates four hours before sundown are $65 Sunday through Thursday and $75 on Friday and Saturday. Locals can buy a resident card for $10, which entitles them to play anytime for $52. Club rentals are $50 for new Callaways. No metal spikes are allowed here, so the clubhouse offers a free changing facility that lets golfers screw in rubber cleats.

Desert Rose Golf Course

5483 Club House Dr. • 431-4653

Established in 1960, this county-run course is one of the more mature in the valley. It's flat, but the narrow fairways are lined with trees for a par 71 spanning 6511 yards. The course has recently undergone millions of dollars in renovation, which has improved the play. Also new is an expanded driving range. County residents get a break on greens fees, paying $35 on weekdays and $38 on weekends. Nonresidents are charged $60 anytime. Greens fees include carts. Clubs can be rented for $15.

Las Vegas Golf Club

4300 W. Washington Ave. • 734-1122

This is the city's counterpart to Desert Rose, but it's appreciably cheaper. No wonder it's so heavily played by locals. Opened in 1967, the Las Vegas Golf Club is a flat, tree-filled layout. It has several reachable par 5s on its 6631-yard, par 72 links. Monte Money, a Las Vegas golfing legend, holds the course record with a sizzling 59. Just minutes west of downtown, the club has a lighted driving range and offers lessons as well. Greens fees are the lowest around, with residents paying $12.25 to walk and $21 to ride. Nonresidents are charged $21.25 and $30 respectively. Club rentals are $18.

Las Vegas Hilton Country Club

1911 E. Desert Inn Rd. • 382-GOLF

The current home of three rounds of the PGA Tour's Las Vegas Invitational (the rest is played at the private TPC Summerlin), this resort course is accented by several lakes. Opened in 1961 as the Sahara Country Club, the course also is well-endowed with trees. There are some challenging par 3 holes on this 6815-yard, par 71 layout. Greens fees, including mandatory carts, run $125 Monday through Thursday and $145 Fridays through Sundays. Club rentals are $15 to $30.

Las Vegas Paiute Resort

10325 Nu-Wav-Kaiv Blvd. • 658-1400

As far as you can get without leaving Las Vegas, this Pete Dye-designed oasis is 20 miles north of downtown off U.S. Highway 95. The two courses here are sparsely vegetated and often windblown, but they're generally a few degrees cooler than the valley. The Snow Mountain course plays 7158 yards, while the Sun Mountain layout runs 7112. Both are par 72, but Snow Mountain, built in 1995, is particularly notable. *Golf Digest* magazine rated it as the best public course in southern Nevada.

Greens fees, with cart, are $85 at both courses. Club rentals run $35 to $45. Afterward, if you're looking to cool off, head for the forested hills of Mt. Charleston, just 15 miles west on Nev. Highway 157.

Los Prados Country Club

5150 Los Prados Cir. • 645-5696

A short course with five par 3s and narrow fairways, Los Prados runs just 5348 yards for a par 70. Many of the par 4s play around 300 yards on this course set amidst a residential community on the northwest side of Las Vegas. Greens fees include carts and cost $35 on weekdays, $45 on weekends. Club rentals are $20.

Painted Desert Golf Course

5555 Painted Mirage Dr. • 645-2568

One of the first desert target designs, this course features lush fairway landing areas weaving through an upscale residential community on the city's northwest side. The course runs 6840 yards with a par 72. Touring pro and Las Vegas resident Robert Gamez holds the course record of 62. Greens fees include a mandatory cart for $90 Monday through Thursday and $100 Friday through Sunday. Weekday rates after 1 PM are reduced to $48 on the weekdays and $53 on weekends. Clubs can be rented for $25 to $40.

Sheraton Desert Inn Country Club

3145 Las Vegas Blvd. S. • 733-4290

The only course left on The Strip, this legendary layout opened in 1952, making it the oldest in town. Home to more than 30 pro tour championships in past years, it continues to host the ITT/LPGA Championship. The course runs 7066 yards for a long par 72, making it a challenging day's work. Desert Inn lodgers can play for $115 on weekdays and $135 on weekends. Nonlodgers are charged $195. Club rentals go for $25 to $40.

Sun City Las Vegas Golf Club

9201-B Del Webb Blvd. • 363-4373

Two courses, established since 1989, meander through this retirement community in Las Vegas' northwestern hills. The Palm Valley Course features rolling terrain over 6849 yards. The Highland Falls Course, running 6512 yards, is more hilly and includes scenic waterfalls. Both are par 72, but quick and tricky greens can easily put you over that number. Residents get preference for play, but visitors can reserve tee times too. Greens fees are $95 on both courses with a mandatory cart. But if you're a Clark County resident teeing off after noon, the weekday rate falls to $50. Also available is a par 60 executive course called Eagle Crest. Measuring 4000 yards, it costs $55 with a cart and $45 without. A Sun City dress code prohibits T-shirts and cutoffs.

TPC at the Canyons
9851 Canyon Run Dr. • 256-2000

Raymond Floyd designed this course, which is home to the PGA Senior Classic. This desert dandy, opened in 1996, comes with lots of bare ground and rocks bordering, or encompassing, the fairways. It runs 6772 yards for a par 72. But that's a deceptively tough score because the greens are notoriously hard and fast. Monday-through-Friday rates are $115; Friday through Sunday costs $130. Carts are included. In June, July and August, greens fees dip to $50 on the weekdays and $60 on weekends. And half-price rates are in effect four hours before sundown.

A Chip Shot Away

Black Mountain Golf and Country Club
500 Greenway Rd., Henderson • 565-7933

A good course for beginners, this layout is challenging nonetheless, with plenty of sand bunkers and two large lakes. Distance is 6223 yards for a par 71. Established in 1959, the course is peppered with cacti and Joshua trees. The 6th and 9th greens also have been recently renovated. Greens fees are $40 Monday through Friday and $45 on weekends. A $10 cart fee is included, and carts are mandatory on weekends. Club rentals cost $13.

Boulder City Municipal Golf Course
1 Clubhouse Dr., Boulder City • 293-9236

Low-key and homespun, this quaint course is far off the beaten track and away from tourists. It's also one of the better deals around. Established in 1972, it features hundreds of mature trees along its wide, flat fairways. The 6561-yard, par 72 course can be played for $23 (walking) or $31 (riding). Club rentals cost $15.

Craig Ranch Golf Course
628 W. Craig Rd., North Las Vegas • 642-9700

A self-professed "poor man's course" — and proud of it — this club has been a North Las Vegas landmark since 1953. It's a narrow and short course, measuring just 6001 yards for a par 70. As such, it's a forgiving place to teach kids the game. But there are 7,000 trees of varying sizes to keep things interesting too. Craig Ranch does a lot of local repeat business, so it's obviously doing things right. Greens fees are $13, and carts are optional for an additional $7. Club rentals are just $5.

Desert Willow Golf Course
2020 Horizon Ridge, Henderson • 270-7000

If you don't have five hours to play, try this executive course in the retirement community of Sun City MacDonald Ranch. You don't need to be retired to walk this always-immaculate course designed by Billy Casper. And the 3811-yard, par 60 layout may make you feel years younger. Carts are optional here, with county residents paying $40 to ride and $30 to walk. Nonresidents pay $55 and 45 respectively.

Legacy Golf Club
130 Par Excellence Dr., Henderson • 897-2200

Rated among the top-100 courses in the country, this layout features wall-to-wall turf, two lakes, rolling terrain and plenty of trees.

INSIDERS' TIP

***Vegas Golfer* magazine is a good source of local golf news and can be found at most area courses.**

Notable is the "Devil's Triangle" on the back nine. A canyon creek runs through the 11th, 12th and 13th holes, spoiling many fine tee shots. Though they are each par 4s, this unholy trio of holes can make or break your game. Fortunate players walk away calling it the "Amen Corner."

Greens fees for this 6744-yard, par 72 course are $100, including mandatory cart. A $65 twilight rate is available four hours before sundown. Club rentals cost $25. The course will take reservations up to 60 days in advance.

Mt. Charleston Golf Resort

1 Kyle Canyon Rd. • 872-GOLF

Looking to cool off? When the valley is roasting in the 100s, the temperature here is usually about 85 degrees. Carved into Kyle Canyon, this new nine-hole layout would probably be the course of choice for rock climbers. This extremely hilly course features tee elevations of 150 feet. Hole 5 also has two lakes positioned in front of the green, making it a challenging par 4. Though this is a nine-hole par 70 course, players must pay for 18 (you go around twice). Carts, a necessity in this terrain, are included in the $99 greens fee. Clark County residents play for a discounted rate of $49. Opened in the fall of 1997, the course is snowed in for much of December and January, so be sure to call ahead to see if it's open. The clubhouse and pro shop are housed in a triple-wide trailer until a permanent building is erected.

North Las Vegas Golf Course

324 E. Brooks Ave., North Las Vegas • 649-7171

If you don't feel like playing 6000 yards or even 3000, how about 1158? This municipally run nine-hole, par 3 course's longest hole is 212 yards. Greens fees are a bargain at $5 on weekdays and $6.50 on weekends. Night play is available for $7.50 after 5 PM. Hand carts are $2.

Wildhorse Golf Club

2100 W. Warm Springs Rd., Henderson • 434-9009

Never heard of this one? How about Paradise Valley? Or Showboat? Or Royal Kenfield? Wildhorse has carried all these names. Now with a new $2.7 million clubhouse, the course is home to shimmering lakes, challenging holes and new bermudagrass greens that give a true roll. But true or not, this 7053-yard par 72 layout is one of the toughest around. The PGA rates it a 75.2, which is a couple of points higher than the average southern Nevada course.

Greens fees, including mandatory cart, are $110 Monday through Thursday and $125 Friday through Sunday. Club rentals are $20 to $40.

Driving Distance

Calvada Valley Golf and Country Club

1500 S. Red Butte St., Pahrump • 727-4653

This place is worth the trek to Pahrump, 60 miles west on Nev. Highway 160. The par 72 championship layout is inviting to players of all abilities. Good length from the back tees lets big hitters test themselves over the 7025-yard course. Weeping willows shade the property that was once an alfalfa field, and water hazards appear on 13 holes. The greens are very large and well-kept. Greens fees, with cart, are $42. Clubs can be rented for $15.

Calvada Executive Golf Club

2101 E. Calvada Blvd., Pahrump • 727-6388

An easy-walking course, this executive-style layout is 3587 yards for a par 59. The course is an excellent outing for beginners, seniors and families. No carts are allowed, but pull carts are available for just $2. Greens fees are $18, and clubs are available for $10.

INSIDERS' TIP

If you're a distance player, you'll want to check out these courses that exceed 7,000 yards: Calvada, Desert Inn, Palms, the Las Vegas Paiute Resort and Wildhorse.

Emerald River Country Club

1155 Casino Dr., Laughlin • 298-0061

The U.S. Golf Association rates this target course as Nevada's most difficult. Five holes border the Colorado River, and the course runs 6809 yards for a challenging par 72. Greens fees are $37 Monday through Thursday, $45 Friday through Sunday. Seniors get a $32 rate Monday through Thursday. All fees include carts. Clubs can be rented for $10. Note that summer temperatures in Laughlin routinely hit 110, so plan for an early start!

Furnace Creek Golf Course

Death Valley, Calif. • (619) 786-2301

How low will you go? This course, built in 1933, is the world's lowest layout at 214 feet below sea level. In Death Valley, 150 miles from Las Vegas, this resort course features flat terrain, grass bunkers and, surprisingly, tall trees. It runs 6105 yards for a par 71. Greens fees are $25. Carts cost $18 and are optional. Club rentals are only $6. And if you think Laughlin is hot, Death Valley regularly rates as the hottest place in America. Temperatures are most comfortable October through April.

Oasis Golf Club

851 Oasis Blvd., Mesquite • 346-7820, (800) 621-0187

Designed by Arnold Palmer and home to the Arnold Palmer Golf Academy, this course is an easy one-hour drive north on I-15. Sculpted into the hills, the Oasis has several elevation changes, and holes are played through desert gorges. There's also a glistening man-made lake to make your round enjoyable and challenging on this 6982-yard, par 72 layout. Though it's set in the casual town of Mesquite, players are expected to dress like they're on a resort course. That means no jeans or cutoffs. Greens fees are $99 for guests of the nearby Oasis hotel-casino. Nonguests pay $150. Both prices include a cart. An adjacent nine-hole course, the Vista, features a par 37 layout spanning 3524 yards. Hotel guests pay $30; nonguests are charged $40.

The academy offers half-day instruction for $150. Three- and five-day academies are $1,100 and $1,800 respectively. The fees include meals and accommodations.

Palms Golf Course

2200 Hillside Dr., Mesquite • 346-5232, (800) 621-0187

Ever heard of a course with a split personality? This is one of them. The front nine is played on flat land with several water hazards. The back side is full of ups and downs, with the par 5, 15th hole one of the most memorable stretches in the region. It's played off a cliff to the fairway several hundred feet below. Befitting the name, more than 200 palm trees grace the course, along with lakes and a prodigious number of sand traps. At 7008 yards, it's a long par 72. The course is more casual and affordable than the Oasis. Guests of the Oasis hotel-casino can play for $55 on weekdays and $75 on weekends. Nonguests pay $85 and $105 respectively. Carts are mandatory and are included in the fees. Club rentals are $15.

Primm Valley Golf Club

Primm • 382-1111

Affiliated with the Primm Valley Hotel-Casino, 60 miles south of Las Vegas on I-15, this course is actually across the state line in California. The 6945-yard, par 71 layout features wide fairways and quick, true greens. The back nine is refreshingly full of water in the form of lakes, brooks and a waterfall. Pros say the course is friendly for the beginner and fair to all players. Guests of Primm Valley, Buffalo Bill's or Whiskey Pete's hotel-casinos can buy a package that gives them two nights' lodging and a round of golf for $158 on weekdays or $178 on weekends. Nonguests can play a round for $160. Fees include carts. Clubs can be rented for $25.

If you were wondering, the course is in California because Mirage Resorts owner

INSIDERS' TIP

Hours for most courses are 6 AM to sundown. When reserving a tee time, it's best to call early and to have a credit card ready.

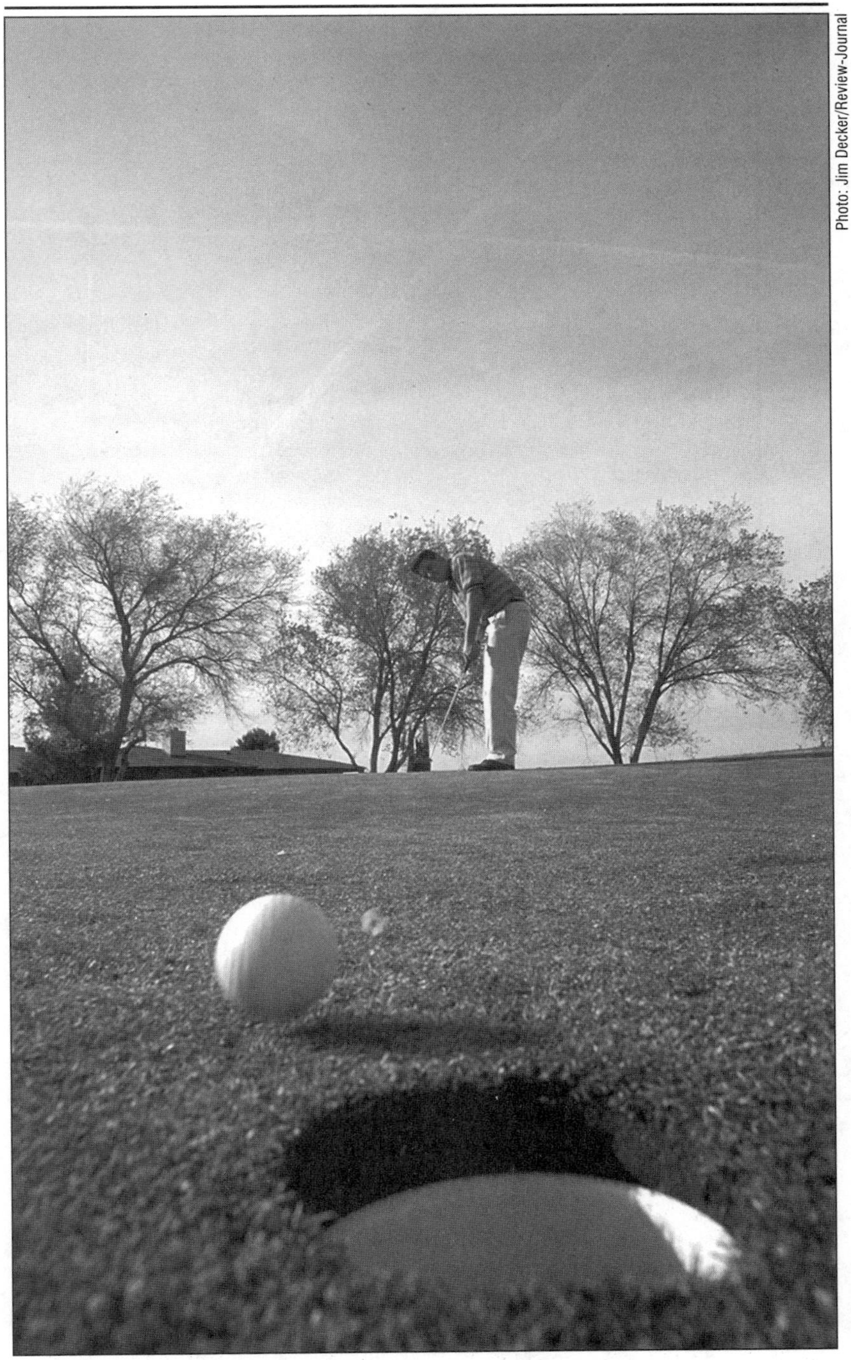

Photo: Jim Decker/Review-Journal

The valley's mild climate will keep you putting year round.

Steve Wynn stipulated that Tom Fazio, who designed Wynn's exclusive Shadow Creek golf course, could not build another course in Clark County. Only Wynn's invited guests are permitted to play Shadow Creek, located in North Las Vegas.

Special Services and Organizations

International Academy of Golf
4220 S. Maryland Pkwy., Ste. 210 • 792-8410, (800) 886-4651

At the Las Vegas Hilton Country Club, this golf school offers two-, three- and five-day packages, costing from $420 to $890. The prices cover all course fees, club cleaning and unlimited range balls. The shorter courses concentrate on fundamentals. Training aides, including video analysis, assist students in developing a more sophisticated feel of the game. The five-day regimen includes 18 holes of play with a golf pro. The student-instructor ratio is 4 to 1. Junior golf camps and player schools also are offered. Accommodations can be booked through the school.

Las Vegas International Golf Center
4813 Paradise Rd. • 798-8700

This practice facility, the largest of its kind in Nevada, offers two tiers of tees under the lights and a large, well-stocked golf shop. Spread over 44 acres at the corner of Paradise Road and Tropicana Avenue less than a mile east of The Strip, the center also has a pitching and chipping area as well as a 10,000-square-foot practice green.

Prices at the 120-stall driving range are $6 for 50 balls and $8 for 100. For an extra $4, players can swing away on natural grass tees. To putt and chip, the rate is $4 for every half-hour. The facility, which is open 24 hours a day, is the practice home of the UNLV golf team.

Las Vegas Women's Golf Association
4300 W. Washington Ave. • 870-9959

For $70 a year, female golfers can join this group that conducts team play year round. Twelve teams around the valley host a total of 12 tournaments at courses throughout the area. Invitational tourneys also are sponsored periodically, drawing golfers from Arizona and California.

Nevada State Seniors Golf Club
P.O. Box 42212, Las Vegas, Nev. 89116 • 255-0915

Open to male residents of Nevada 50 years and older, this group of 400 golfers plays monthly tournaments, including five out-of-town trips to regional courses. Prizes are awarded at each event. An annual championship match tees off at St. George, Utah, with the field divided into age categories ranging through 90. Annual dues of $75 fund a yearly dinner. Members receive rated handicaps through the Southern Nevada Golf Association.

Southern Nevada Golf Association
3918 Rhine Ct. • 242-4653

If you're a golfer with an established handicap and higher aspirations, you will want to joint this regionally recognized affiliate of the U.S. Golf Association. The 10,000-member group, founded in 1967, is an official arm of the USGA and ranks and classifies players in southern Nevada.

A schedule of 12 to 15 tournaments is sponsored by the northern and southern chapters each year, including two showcase events: the Nevada State Amateur Tournament and the Nevada State Match Play Tournament. The Amateur draws a field of 240 golfers, while the Match Play selects 48 competitors based on points earned during sanctioned tournaments. Tournament players receive discounts on greens fees and are eligible to win gift certificates. The group conducts meetings at Sunrise Country Club on the first Thursday of each month.

Southern Nevada Junior Golf Association
3430 E. Flamingo Rd., Ste. 20 • 433-0626

A nonprofit organization dedicated to the development of youth through supervised golf, social activities and tournaments, the association has 500 members ages 6 through 18.

For a $75 annual membership, youngsters of varying abilities can play in tournaments held throughout the year. A peewee bracket for children ages 6 to 10 participates in a nine-hole event. Other age groups are 11 to 12 and 13 to 18. Greens fees run $10 to $15 per event, with about 35 tournaments conducted throughout the year.

World Class Golf

1631 E. Sunset Rd., Ste. C-105 • 361-8778, (800) 332-8776

This reservation service can get you or your group onto just about any upper-end course in the area, including the private Sunrise and Canyon Gate country clubs. These consultants can help players find courses suitable for their ability and, if needed, book them into compatible foursomes. Another nice feature: Tee times can usually be arranged 60 days in advance for any size party. Unlike its competitors, World Class Golf does not tack a surcharge onto the standard greens fee. Club rentals and transportation are available for an extra charge. As with most services, World Class Golf will not book municipal course tee times.

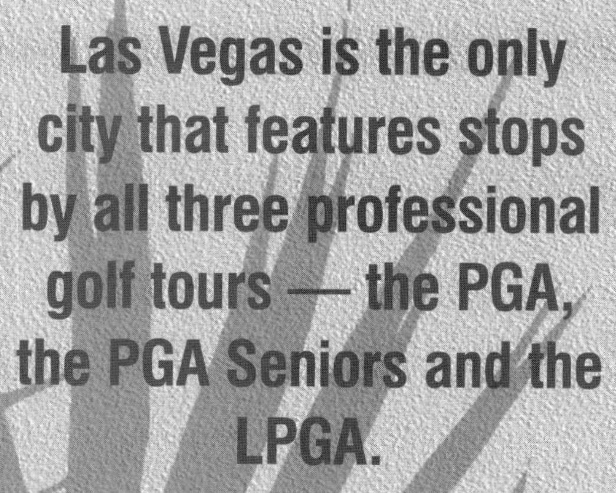

Las Vegas is the only city that features stops by all three professional golf tours — the PGA, the PGA Seniors and the LPGA.

Spectator Sports

Las Vegas is a game-crazy town. Just check out the sports books, those casino sports-betting parlors that are standing-room only on weekends. And during football season? It may be impossible to find a parking space! With a multitude of games beamed into every casino, bookmakers draw big crowds of action-hungry fans.

But what about seeing sports in person? Las Vegas has that too. From professional baseball to college basketball, the city offers spectator sports year round. Championship boxing matches and golf tournaments are held frequently. In fact, Las Vegas is the only city that features stops by all three professional golf tours — the PGA, the PGA Seniors and the LPGA. Even offbeat pursuits, such as windsailing and beach volleyball, are in the mix as well.

Alas, professional sports has had a spotty track record here. Since the 1970s, Las Vegas has been home to four soccer teams, three football teams, two basketball teams and a roller-hockey team — all of which have folded.

Still, there are some ongoing success stories. Professional baseball and hockey have thrived in the desert. And UNLV's athletic programs are competitive in a number of sports. Meantime, the city continues to build a reputation as a capital for prize fights, golf tournaments and rodeos. And, now, with the addition of a giant motor speedway north of town, auto racing is becoming a major player.

UNLV's strong sports program offers competitive teams and a clean, modern facility at the Thomas and Mack Center. The 18,500-seat arena on the southwest corner of campus is used for everything from ice hockey to bull riding — and, sometimes, it may be difficult to tell the difference!

So whatever sport you fancy, odds are Las Vegas will have something going on for you.

Baseball

Las Vegas Stars

Cashman Field, 850 Las Vegas Blvd. N. • 386-7200

The most enduring professional sports franchise in Las Vegas, the Stars came here in 1983 from Spokane, Washington. The AAA franchise of the San Diego Padres plays a 70-game home schedule at Cashman Field. This beautifully manicured diamond just north of downtown has 10,000 seats in a stadium that is clean and modern. Cashman has great sightlines and affords lots of chances to catch foul balls.

The Stars, locally owned by the Stickney family, annually attract more than 300,000 fans. The team has been competitive in Pacific Coast League play, winning championships twice in the '80s. It's not unusual for Pacific Coast League teams, which are just one step below the Big Show, to carry rehabilitating big leaguers on their rosters.

Virtually every game has some sort of theme or sponsor, so freebies and giveaways are common. Most games are at night, so heat is not usually a problem. For those Sunday afternoon games, however, be sure to bring plenty of sun block. You can also carry in your own plastic water bottles.

Ticket prices range from $4 to $8. Junior, senior and military tickets run $3. Games are played from the first week of April through the end of August.

During the week preceding the Stars' opener, six Major League teams wind up their spring training schedule with a block of games at Cashman. The lineup changes from year to year but generally includes a couple of West Coast teams. Tickets for those games run $12.50 to $15 apiece.

UNLV Baseball

Wilson Stadium, Swenson St. • 895-4176

The Hustlin' Rebels baseball team plays from late January to mid-May. The season schedule is sprinkled with tough regional teams, including Arizona State and UCLA. Wilson Field is on the north end of campus. Tickets start at $3.

Basketball

Las Vegas Shootout

Thomas and Mack Center, Tropicana Ave. and Swenson St. • 895-3900

The UNLV Rebels host three top-20 teams in a preseason basketball tournament in late December. Tickets for the four-game event start at around $15 per game.

UNLV Basketball

Thomas and Mack Center, Tropicana Ave. and Swenson St. • 895-3900

This is the 18,500-seat home that Jerry Tarkanian built. At the corner of Tropicana Avenue and Swenson Street about 2 miles east of The Strip, the T&M (or just the Mack) has one of college basketball's most dazzling pregame shows, complete with fireworks. There's a jumbo screen on the scoreboard, and when the Runnin' Rebels are playing, well, it's one of the loudest places in a not-so-quiet town.

The Rebels played their first game in 1958 and won their first NCAA basketball championship in 1990. The school won 10 out of 11 Big West Conference championships before joining the Western Athletic Conference, a sprawling 16-school league spanning four time zones. Upstairs tickets start at $12. Seats in the lower bowl range from $15 to $50, but the best seats are reserved for season-ticket holders. The Rebels' average attendance is 13,500, so seats are almost always available on game day. The season runs from November until early March.

Western Athletic Conference Basketball Tournament

Thomas and Mack Center, Tropicana Ave. and Swenson St. • 895-3900

March Madness comes to Las Vegas, with the WAC's top teams vying to be league champions. The 12 best men's and women's squads play a six-day schedule, Monday through Saturday. Full tournament passes for downstairs seats cost $120. Upstairs seats run $90. Daily tickets also are available. (See our Annual Events chapter.)

FYI

Unless otherwise noted, the area code for all phone numbers listed in this chapter is 702.

Bowling

High Rollers

Showboat Hotel, 2800 Fremont St. • 385-9150, (800) 257-6179

Amateur bowlers get rolling at four events scattered throughout the year. The Super Bowl High Roller Tournament runs for a week around football's biggest game in late January. This is an extremely popular event, usually selling out all 1,960 roster spots for a $750 entry fee (up to three bowlers can participate for that price). The winners get $100,000, and the total purse is $1.3 million. As if that weren't enough, the Showboat Hotel even throws in a blackjack tournament for bowlers and guests.

The Easter and Thanksgiving Senior High Roller tournaments run for five days around those holidays. Entry fee is $400, and the purse tops $500,000. The Showboat also hosts slot tournaments to coincide with those two events.

INSIDERS' TIP

The Stars and the Thunder frequently offer discount coupons for admission. Check local tourist magazines and newspapers for good deals. During baseball season, 7-Eleven stores often display free-ticket deals at the counter. And the Stars are almost always giving something away —from T-shirts to sports bags.

Photo: Jim Decker/Review-Journal

Hey, buckaroo! The National Finals Rodeo packs 'em in at the Thomas and Mack Center every December.

The biggest High Roller event convenes around the Fourth of July. More than 1,300 bowlers from around the world attend this annual event. The winner gets $200,000, and the total purse exceeds $2.6 million. But you have to pay to play; the entry fee is $1,100.

For spectators, the High Roller events are always free and very entertaining. The Showboat is a premier bowling facility with 106 lanes and a state-of-the-art Frameworks computerized scoring system. Bleacher seating is erected to accommodate about 500 fans. (See our Annual Events chapter.)

Boxing

Las Vegas, home of Mike Tyson, fashions itself as the professional boxing capital of the world. While the major world championship cards are seldom announced more than two or maybe three months in advance, look for September (for Mexican Independence Day) and November (between the World Series and the holiday season) as prime time for fisticuffs. Three hotels host the bulk of the bouts: Caesars Palace, The Mirage and the MGM Grand. The MGM, with its 16,325-seat Grand Garden Arena, attracts the largest number of top-line fights. UNLV's Thomas and Mack Center also is home to a few major matches each year. Whatever the locale, ticket prices for title fights are not for the faint of heart, usually starting at $200 and ratcheting up to $1,500.

For up-to-date schedules and information, call Caesars at 731-7110 or (800) 634-6698; MGM at 891-7777 or (800) 929-1111; The Mirage at 791-7111 or (800) 627-6667; or the Thomas and Mack at 895-3900.

Football

UNLV Football
Sam Boyd Stadium, Boulder Hwy. and Sunset Rd. • 895-3900

The Rebels play about six games at this

32,000-seat stadium each season. Seats on the south side of the stadium are preferable in the early part of the season because they tend to be shaded. The sunny north side may be a better ticket in November when the weather gets chilly. Seats start at $10. Because the Rebels have suffered through a string of losing seasons, tickets and good seats are readily available. The team opens its season in September and plays until December.

Western Athletic Conference Football Championship

Sam Boyd Stadium, Boulder Hwy. and Sunset Rd. • 895-3900

The top team in the Mountain Division squares off with the winner of the Pacific Division in this league championship game on the first Saturday in December. A victory means bragging rights in the 16-team Western Athletic Conference and an automatic bowl bid. The atmosphere is festive, with a pregame pep rally on Fremont Street downtown. Golfers will also enjoy a special WAC golf tournament on the links at Sunrise Golf Club. Ticket prices for the football game range from $40 to $100 (golf is extra).

Las Vegas Bowl

Sam Boyd Stadium, Boulder Hwy. and Sunset Rd. • 895-3900

In the first year-end bowl game, the Las Vegas Bowl matches a top Western Athletic Conference team with an at-large team from another major conference. Generally held on the third Saturday of December, the Las Vegas Bowl formerly matched the winner of the Big West Conference with the winner of the Mid-America Conference. In its new carnation, the bowl will award $800,000 to each team. The bowl is sponsored by the Las Vegas Convention and Visitors Authority. Tickets begin at $25. Fans should bring along heavy coats and blankets because the game starts at 5 PM, and temperatures will dip into the 30s after sundown.

Golf

Las Vegas Senior Classic

TPC at the Canyons, 1951 Canyon Run Dr. • 242-3000

Top players from the senior tour compete for $1 million at this course nestled in the city's western foothills. If you're looking to place a friendly wager, keep Las Vegas resident Jim Colbert in mind. He won the April 1997 event in a three-hole playoff and has been Player of the Year twice in the '90s. Other perennial favorites are Chi Chi Rodriguez and Raymond Floyd, who, incidentally, designed this course. Tickets begin at $15 per day.

Las Vegas Invitational

TPC at Summerlin, 1700 Village Center Circle • 256-0111

This is the premier golf event in the city, attracting some of the biggest names in the sport. Watch Tiger Woods, Greg Norman, Fuzzy Zoeller and Curtis Strange vie for $1.4 million in early October. Competition has been heated in recent years, with Woods winning the 1996 event in a sudden death playoff on the 18th hole. One of the richest stops of the PGA tour, the format is a five-day, 90-hole pro-am event. Galleries of up to 25,000 turn out at the three host courses: the TPC, the Sheraton Desert Inn and the Las Vegas Country Club.

The immaculate TPC stadium course is also home to some of the most prestigious dwellings in the valley, and representatives of the Summerlin community say they are inundated with calls from prospective buyers after each LVI telecast. For the privilege of walking the course, daily tickets are $20. But given the

INSIDERS' TIP

If you're interested in seeing the National Finals Rodeo — America's richest rodeo purse — get saddled up early. The 10-day event has been a sellout since 1985.

crush, it's better and cheaper to purchase passes in advance for $15.

ITT-LPGA Tour Championship

Desert Inn Country Club, 3145 Las Vegas Blvd. S. • 733-4653

Las Vegas hosts the 30 top money winners on the women's golf circuit during the week before Thanksgiving. See Laura Davies, Karri Webb, Nancy Lopez, Betsy King and Patty Sheehan tee it up for $800,000 in prize money. Passes for the four-day event run $10 to $15 daily.

Wendy's International Three-Tour Challenge

SouthShore Golf Club at Lake Las Vegas, Henderson • 735-1919, (614) 889-6781

Three golfers each from the LPGA Tour, the PGA Tour and the Senior PGA Tour face off during the last week of November at this exclusive Jack Nicklaus-designed course. Players have included Nicklaus, Hale Irwin, Fred Couples, Davis Love III, Payne Stewart, Patty Sheehan, Laura Davies and Annika Sorenstam. Tickets start at $15. All proceeds benefit the Dave Thomas Foundation for Adoption. (See our Annual Events chapter for more about these golf tournaments.)

Ice Hockey

Las Vegas Thunder

Thomas and Mack Center, Tropicana Ave. and Swenson St. • 798-PUCK

The cool game of hockey is thriving in the desert. The Thunder of the International Hockey League plays 41 regular season home games from October to April. The season usually extends into late April because the Thunder generally makes the playoffs. Some of the success is due to the team's aggressive personnel moves, which have brought National Hockey League players to Las Vegas for short-term rehabilitation. As an independent franchise, the Thunder isn't tied to any NHL team.

For purists, a Thunder game can be a bit distracting. The rink in the Thomas and Mack Center is 25 percent smaller than regulation. That shortens the space between the blue lines and sometimes makes for choppier play and passing. But it also can mean more scoring, which is fun!

The team draws about 7,000 fans per game. Tickets run $4 to $8. A special "4 for $40" package also is available and includes upgraded seating, free drinks, hot dogs and snacks for a party of four. Like the Stars, the Thunder is owned by the Stickney family.

Ice Skating

Tour of World Figure Skating Champions

Thomas and Mack Center, Tropicana Ave. and Swenson St. • 895-3900

Past and future Olympic medalists hit the ice in July for the Campbell's Soups Tour of World Figure Skating Champions. The show, often held on Independence Day, has featured some of America's biggest names on ice in recent years: Brian Boitano, Nicole Bobek, Todd Eldredge and Michelle Kwan. International greats such as Oksana Baiul, Viktor Petrenko, Elvis Stojko and Surya Bonaly have also performed. Tickets run $20 to $45. (See our Annual Events chapter.)

Landsailing

America's Cup Landsailing Regatta

Ivanpah Dry Lake, Primm • 220-4340

Sailing on bone-dry desert is the name of

INSIDERS' TIP

If watching TV and placing a bet is your brand of spectator sports, there are countless sports books to fulfill both desires. For sheer size and scope, three of the best are at the MGM Grand, Caesars Palace and the Las Vegas Hilton. These places are like living rooms on steroids, with wall-to-wall big screens displaying dozens of games.

this game. Sporting single sails, landsailers convene in late March to tack across a dry lake bed next to Interstate 15 at the Nevada-California state line. Scooting along at speeds up to 80 mph, these desert racers come in a variety of sizes and shapes. Spectators are welcome, but be sure to bring chairs and refreshments.

Marathon

Las Vegas International Marathon
S.R. 604 to the Las Vegas Strip • 876-3870

Distance runners from around the world gather in the first week of February to participate in this 26.2-mile event that begins in the small southern Nevada town of Sloan and finishes at the south end of The Strip. The race — along with a companion half-marathon and five-person relay event — attracts more than 6,000 competitors from all 50 states and 40 foreign countries. It is sanctioned by the U.S. Track and Field Association.

The course, along state highway 604 (the old Los Angeles Highway), saw its best recorded time in 1986, when Frank Plasso finished in 2:12:37. Marzena Helbik set the women's mark in 1997 with a time of 2:32:22. The event also hosts a number of specialty runners, including race walkers and "Clydesdales" — men weighing more than 200 pounds and women more than 160 pounds.

Entrants pay a $30 fee for the half-marathon and $40 for the full race. But spectating is free. Last year, more than 20,000 folks showed up, so it's a good idea to arrive early if you want to get a bleacher seat.

For kicks, a 5K International Friendship Run is conducted a day before the big race. Hey, that's just a warm-up for these folks!

Motor Sports

Las Vegas Motor Speedway
7000 Las Vegas Blvd. N. • 644-4444, (800) 644-4444

It's not Indianapolis' brickyard with a golf course on the infield, but for race enthusiasts, this sprawling $72 million, 1,500-acre complex may be a whole lot better. On the grounds are a 1.5-mile superspeedway, a 2.5-mile road track, a half-mile dirt track, a drag strip, go-cart tracks and even a racing school.

Major races are held throughout the year (see our Annual Events chapter), and plenty of seating is usually available, with the superspeedway's capacity topping 100,000. General admission tickets for the bigger events start at $15 for youngsters and $45 for adults. Three-day event passes go for $30 and $100 respectively.

Top events include: the Busch Grand National 500 and the Budweiser Sprint Car Shootout in March, NASCAR's Winston Cup West Series in June, the Indy Racing League's "LV 500K" in October and the NASCAR Craftsman Truck Series and Winston West Tour in November.

The **Richard Petty School** offers wannabe drivers a chance to get behind the wheel of a real stock car and rocket around the raceway at speeds up to 180 mph. You'll need a modicum of skill at shifting gears and a hefty wallet along with your valid driver's license. Behind-the-wheel packages begin at $330 for the "Rookie Experience," an eight-lap spin. More aggressive and intense programs include the "Experience of a Lifetime" (30 laps for $1,099) and the "Racing Experience" (80 laps for $2,199). The packages include in-depth looks inside the racing facility as well as one-on-one training. Teens 14 and older can ride along with a professional driver for $90. Res-

INSIDERS' TIP

During football season, many sports bars become unofficial team hangouts. Watch the local newspapers for up-to-date lists on which fans are going where. Also check out the ads for special food and drink deals. For example, the Colosseum, at 3645 S. Durango Drive, is a well-known Green Bay Packer bar that is particularly well-known for its good food and polite service (unless, of course, you're wearing the colors of a rival team).

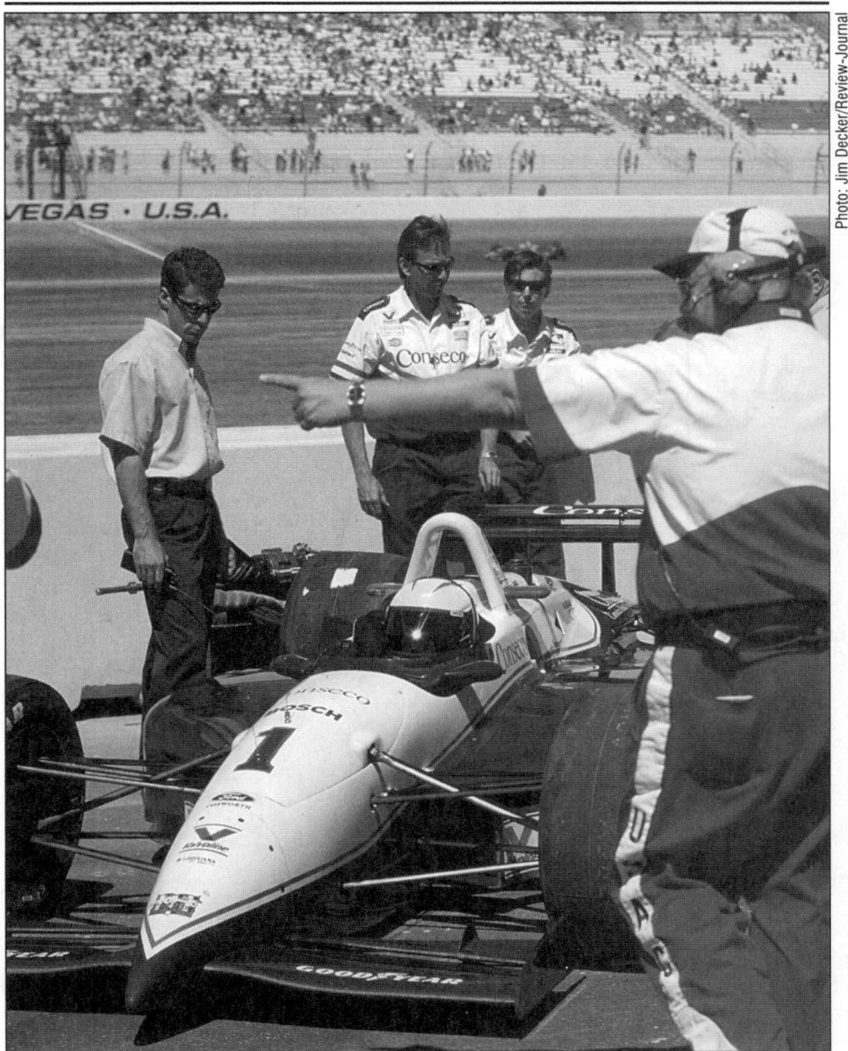

Photo: Jim Decker/Review-Journal

The Las Vegas Speedway hosts Indy car and stock car races year round.

ervations are required. Call 643-4343 or 800-BEPETTY for details.

To get to the track, take Interstate 15 north to Exit 54, north of Craig Road. For the large events, such as the Busch 500, you might consider taking a Citizens Area Transit bus to avoid the chronic congestion around the track. CAT runs nonstop lines from downtown.

Primm 300

Whiskey Pete's Hotel-Casino, Primm
• 386-7867, (800) FUNSTOP

This is a wild time in the desert: 300 off-road vehicles of all sizes and shapes running a 300-mile course in Nevada's wilderness. The event, once called the Mint 400, is held mid-April and is sanctioned by the Southern California Off-Road Racing association. The best vantage point for this six-hour gauntlet is behind Buffalo Bill's Casino.

Silver State Classic Challenge

S. R. 318, Lund • 385-9123

Where else but Nevada would the state close down a 90-mile stretch of highway to run a road race? Every September, 100 cars roar up the Lund-to-Hiko route in pursuit of glory. Speed classes, ranging from 95 mph to 180 mph, vie for prize money and trophies. Drivers from as far away as Saudi Arabia and Great Britain have participated in the field that features foreign and domestic cars of all makes and models. The Showboat Hotel hosts a rally and car show before the race and an awards ceremony afterward. A similar but smaller race, the Nevada Open, runs the same course in mid-May. Spectating is free at the roadside, just bring folding chairs and lots of liquid refreshment.

Rodeos

Laughlin Rodeo Days

Casino Dr., Laughlin • (520) 296-6725, (800) 227-5245

Cowboys competing in the Laughlin River Stampede PRCA Rodeo will vie for $200,000 in prize money, one of the richest purses on the circuit. The four days of rodeo, in a 6,000-seat arena, feature bareback riding, bull riding, team roping, steer wrestling, barrel racing, saddle bronco riding and calf roping. And cowpokes might want to keep their eyes peeled for Miss Rodeo America, who usually attends this event held during the first week of April. Daily tickets run around $30.

Wrangler Bull Riders Only World Championships

Thomas and Mack Center, Tropicana Ave. and Swenson St. • 895-3900

Also in early April, the world's best bull riders descend on Las Vegas. Big names like Terry Don West and Justin Andrade ride for $1 million in title money, taking on some of the most mean-spirited bulls. Bodacious, a legendary bull, has gotten the better of the cowboys in recent years, knocking the riders off in mere seconds. Needless to say, the action is fast and furious. Three-day passes go for $90 to $120. Daily tickets start at $30.

Helldorado Days

Thomas and Mack Center, Tropicana Ave. and Swenson St. • 870-1221

This four-day hoedown in early June features one night of bullriding and three nights of rodeo activity on the floor of the Thomas and Mack Center. Both events are sanctioned by professional organizations. Admission is $12 to the bull ride and $11 to the rodeo. In addition to the floor events, the sponsoring Las Vegas Elks Club offers exhibits and a small carnival midway outside.

National Finals Rodeo

Thomas and Mack Center, Tropicana Ave. and Swenson St. • 895-3900

Yahoo! This is the Super Bowl of rodeo — the top 126 money winners in the Professional Rodeo Cowboys Association circuit dueling for a $3 million purse. For 10 days in the first week of December, the NFR brings a decidedly cowboy flavor to Las Vegas. Most of the hotels trot out their country-western shows, and Cashman Field Center downtown hosts a western gift and apparel display.

Cabbies and valets love this show because these skilled cowpokes and their fans are known as big tippers. Casinos don't mind the action either. And they're pleased that the PRCA has extended its contract with Las Vegas through the year 2010. Daily tickets start at $24, but you'd better order at least 10 months in advance because NFR has been a sellout every year since coming to Las Vegas.

INSIDERS' TIP

Betting and sports go hand in hand in Nevada. More than $70 million is wagered each year on the NCAA Tournament and the Super Bowl. And for that reason, neither of those events are likely to be played in Nevada. Neither the NFL nor the NCAA permits wagering on collegiate games played in the state.

Rugby

Las Vegas Rugby Challenge
Freedom Park, Washington Ave. and Mojave Rd. • 656-7401

Let's scrum! Teams from around the world get together for a rough-and-tumble tournament during the first weekend of December. In recent years, squads from Russia, Somoa, Australia and Canada have been among the 72 teams vying for prize money and trophies. Entry fees, not yet established, help to raise money for local charities. Spectators can view all the two-day action for free.

Las Vegas Midnight Sevens
Sam Boyd Stadium, Boulder Hwy. and Sunset Rd. • 656-7401

Also, in June, is a downsized tourney called the Las Vegas Midnight Sevens. Instead of the usual 15 players, these seven-man teams play an even faster-paced game. The competition is held at the recreation fields outside Sam Boyd Stadium. And, as the name of the event implies, play runs continuously from 4 PM to 3 AM. That's one way to beat the heat. Spectators get in free, but bring along a folding chair because bleachers are in short supply.

Speed Boats

Las Vegas Cup Hydroplane Race
Boulder Beach, Lake Mead • 892-2874, (206) 870-8888

The world's fastest boats hit Lake Mead in September for two days of races. These 26-foot-long "unlimited" craft fly across the water at speeds of 200 mph. The pilot's perch is designed like an F-16 jet cockpit, which is fitting, since these boats barely skim the surface as they traverse the lake. About a dozen boats compete in this event each year.

These monster boat races are free for the viewing and draw big crowds (more than 300,000 took in a hydroplane race in Detroit in 1996), so be prepared for some heavy traffic. Take the Boulder Beach exit off U.S. 93 and follow the crowd to Lakeshore Drive. A separate race nearby features propeller boats that go half as fast as the unlimiteds.

Volleyball

Miller Lite King of the Beach Invitational
Hard Rock Hotel-Casino, 4455 Paradise Rd. • 693-5000

What do you get when you add 350 tons of sand to the back parking lot at the Hard Rocket Hotel-Casino? Beach volleyball, of course. The oh-so-hip resort hosts the annual stop on the Association of Volleyball Professionals tour each March. Playing for $250,000 in prize money are two-man teams playing in round-robin style over three days. Among the recent competitors were Mike Dodd, Whit Marsh and Karch Kiraly. Tickets run $10 to $30.

A museum without air conditioning, Death Valley National Monument is a giant geology lab displaying salt beds, sand dunes and multitiered hills containing layers that are windows on the history of the earth.

Daycations and Weekend Getaways

Most visitors are surprised, if not shocked, to learn there are destinations in southern Nevada beyond the bright lights of Las Vegas. But not far from the pulsating delirium of the gambling halls and showroom extravaganzas are dozens of quick escapes or "daycations" that are sure to stimulate your interest and revitalize your spirits.

Drive northeast and there are hamlets and farm towns, where you can belly up to the bar with working cowboys and catch the true flavor of the American West. Or if you prefer, you can laze around a health spa or play golf in the verdant Virgin River valley that Mormon farmers settled long before the resorts and interstates.

South of Las Vegas the charming hamlet of Boulder City will transport you to a slow-paced "Mayberry RFD" kind of community, free from the fast pace of modern civilization. And just 30 minutes from the city you can witness the awesome power of Hoover Dam from the inside tunnels that honeycomb its base, or explore the sparkling riverside resorts of Laughlin and the old mining camp of Searchlight, both less than 100 miles from The Strip.

Only 120 miles from Las Vegas, just across the Utah state line, are the magnificent Dixie National Forest and historic town of St. George, seemingly plucked from the New England countryside, complete with Victorian homes, church spires and emerald lawns. Soak up the inspiration at Brigham Young's summer home, or bask in the magnificence of southern Utah's geological marvels.

No matter which direction you turn, the diversity of uncommon sights and unique attractions create a mosaic of experiences for those curious enough to venture beyond the dimly lit casinos and air-conditioned hotel rooms.

Whether you're a visitor looking to detox from a busy convention or marathon gambling session or a local resident seeking a quick escape to recharge your batteries, head for one of these delightful destinations. Even if you've seen all the must-see attractions of Las Vegas, don't miss the little-known treasures as well.

Headin' West

Bonnie Springs Ranch, Old Nevada

A nice stopover after a visit to Red Rock Canyon or Spring Mountain Ranch State Park (see Great Outdoors chapter) is **Bonnie Springs Ranch** and **Old Nevada**, about 20 miles west of Las Vegas. If you've just completed the Red Rock Canyon scenic loop, you can turn right and drive 3 miles to Bonnie Springs Ranch and Old Nevada, 1 Gunfighter Lane, 875-4191. Or if you're driving from Las Vegas, take Charleston Boulevard west to the Bonnie Springs turnoff.

Built in 1843 as a cattle ranch and watering hole for wagon trains going to California, Bonnie Springs Ranch is now a mini-amusement park with a petting zoo, duck pond, aviary and riding stables. This is not your typical petting zoo; in addition to the goats and sheep there is a variety of interesting animals here — exotic birds, llamas, porcupines, buffalo, foxes and bobcat.

Next door, Old Nevada is a full-scale restoration of an old Western town. Although it looks like a movie set, there are no false fronts here — the weathered buildings contain country stores, a saloon, an ice cream parlor, an opera house, the sheriff's office, a shooting gallery and a silent movie house. A mini-train rides along the outside of the town (it also serves as a shuttle from the parking lot). Throughout the day, there are "gunfights" and "hangings" plus other Wild West melodramas in the streets.

After dark the grownups will like the saloon and supper house. But one caveat: Don't wear one of your good neckties into this joint. It may become one of the scissored clippings hanging from the rafters.

FYI

Unless otherwise noted, the area code for all phone numbers listed in this chapter is 702.

Mount Charleston

As described in our Great Outdoors chapter, the alpine wilderness of Mount Charleston, 40 minutes northwest of Las Vegas, is a popular recreational destination for hikers, campers, horseback riders and snow skiers during the winter months. But it can also be a quick and charming escape from the frenzied city life "down below." Counted among the mountain's amenities are a rustic resort hotel, a bed and breakfast inn, an alpine lodge, a cluster of log cabins and a new golf course that has been cut into the sides of Kyle Canyon.

The **Mt. Charleston Hotel**, 872-5500, is the first stop on the drive up Kyle Canyon Road (Nev. Highway 157). Because of its elevation slightly below the timber line, most of the surrounding scenery is sagebrush and juniper trees, but the hotel's weathered wood exterior, open beam rafters, ponderosa pine pillars and open-pit fireplace, all contribute to a mountain lodge atmosphere.

During the summer months, when Mt. Charleston enjoys temperatures 25 to 30 degrees cooler than in Las Vegas, the hotel is a popular spot for outdoor weddings and other encounters. The hotel's Canyon Dining Room features cathedral ceilings with open rafters, tree trunk pillars, walls decorated with mounted heads of game animals and a sweeping 180-degree view of the surrounding hills. Menu specialties include beef, veal, pasta, chicken and scampi. Across the partition is the hotel's Cliffhanger Lounge, where you can have a drink or dance to a live band on weekends.

Most of the guest rooms have dark earth-tone furnishings and salmon-colored walls, but the best ones are the suites on the top (third) floor with their wood-burning fireplaces and peaked ceilings with exposed beams. Rates range from $85 to $145 per night. The hotel also has a spa room with Jacuzzi, gift shop/newsstand, and (for those who must) slot and video poker machine arcade.

The most recent addition to the hotel is a nine-hole golf course that opened in mid-1997. The course traverses the canyons below the hotel and can be played twice for a par 70, 18-hole contest. Long-range plans would expand the course to a full 18 holes and add a clubhouse, driving range and other facilities.

If you prefer a more intimate spot for a rendezvous, drive farther up the mountain to **Almost Heaven Bed & Breakfast**, 123 Rainbow Canyon Boulevard, 872-0711. The converted 10,500-square-foot chalet has four large guest suites, each furnished with Victorian antiques, wood-burning fireplaces, claw-foot bathtubs and fresh-cut flowers. Because the bed and breakfast is built on the side of a mountain, each suite has a panoramic view of the canyon. Another nice feature is the wooden verandah, where you can enjoy breakfast among the tall pines. Rates are a bit pricey, running from $200 to $400 per night.

Near the top of the mountain you'll find **Mt. Charleston Lodge**, 872-5408, a very popular restaurant and bar at the end of Kyle Canyon Road. Despite the name, there are no accommodations in the lodge, although you can rent a nearby log cabin ($130 to $180 per night) equipped with fireplaces, king-size beds, whirlpool tubs and private decks. The lodge's dining room is dominated by a circular fireplace and features an excellent menu offering a variety of dishes with a specialty of wild game. The bar hops at night with live entertainment and a small dance floor. During the summer months the lodge hosts hay rides, and in the winter it offers horse-drawn sleigh rides.

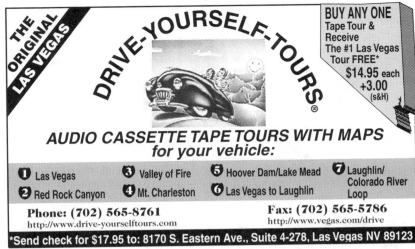

Primm

It wasn't long ago that drivers from California would cross the Nevada state line to find a weather-beaten wooden tower announcing Kactus Kate's, a ramshackle casino beneath it. Today, the tower and casino are mercifully gone, and in its place is a full-blown destination resort: the Primm Valley Resort and Buffalo Bill's Hotel Casino.

The pair of resorts on the east side of Interstate 15 along with Whiskey Pete's Hotel & Casino on the west side are now collectively known as the **Primadonna Casino Resorts**. And the border crossing isn't Stateline anymore; it's officially called Primm, in honor of the family that has developed the border town for the past half century. If you'd like to check out Primm, make a 40-minute run for the border on I-15 S. from Las Vegas.

While Whiskey Pete's has been here the longest, Buffalo Bill's has become the centerpiece of the three Primm properties. It is the largest with 1,243 rooms, it has the largest casino and it also has the widest selection of things to do. The most visible of the attractions is the Desperado, the world's tallest and fastest roller coaster, which actually begins and ends its thrilling, twisting and stomach-churning journey inside the hotel.

Thrill seekers will also like the Turbo Drop, a 200-foot-high gut-wrencher that shoots riders downward at speeds up to 45 miles per hour. The effect is strange, actually a negative one G, then a positive 4.5 Gs during braking. If you don't like the feeling of being left hanging, there's a tamer version called the Rodeo Rider in Buffalo Bill's Ghost Town arcade area.

If you're not into nausea, the Adventure Canyon Water Log Ride is for you. You'll cascade down the swirling waters of a roaring waterfall and enjoy a leisurely ride along Buffalo Bill's Indoor River while you test your marksmanship with laser-equipped pistols along the way.

Other more civilized pursuits include The Ghost Town Motion Simulator Theatres, where you can experience awesome rides that magically transport you into the heart of the action. There is also a state-of-the-art movie theater, Western Ghost Town Shops, video arcades and swimming pools.

The newest addition to Primadonna Casino Resorts is a championship golf course, Primm Valley Golf Club, designed by noted golf architect Tom Fazio. Open to hotel guests only, the 18-hole course plays to a par 71 at 6,950 yards. There's also a club house, 18-hole putting green and driving range — all about 4 miles south of Primm. Greens fees range from $110 to $140 Monday through Thursday and $135 to $165 Friday through Sunday.

When the sun goes down, the ultramodern 6,500-seat Star of the Desert arena hosts a variety of entertainment and special events — big-name concerts, dances, rodeos, boxing matches and much more. Recent concerts have featured Travis Tritt, Hank Williams Jr., Charlie Daniels and Jo Dee Messina, plus special events like "The Blues Music Festival" starring B.B. King, The Robert Cray Band, Jimmie Vaughan and Jay Gellis.

At the Primm Valley Resort you can take a spin on an authentic gondola-style Ferris wheel from which the views are spectacular. There's also an eight-lane bowling alley and a full-size carousel with colorful turn-of-the-century circus designs and brightly flashing lights.

At Whiskey Pete's you can stare slack-jawed at Bonnie and Clyde's bullet-riddled "Death Car," the original Ford that the 1930s gangster team of Bonnie Parker and Clyde Barrow were trapped and killed in by law enforcement agents. Also on display is the restored 1931 Lincoln built by gangster Dutch Schultz and later owned by Al Capone. Whiskey Pete's also has a 700-seat showroom that features top-name popular and country music stars. Headliners have included such great names as Crystal Gayle, Mickey Gilley, America and the Captain & Tennille.

The three hotel-casinos combined have 113,000 square feet of gaming space, which includes more than 4,000 slot machines and 107 table games. The Race & Sports Books offer betting lines on all professional and collegiate sports, plus parimutuel wagering and full track odds for horse players. If Poker is your game, you'll want to play Texas Hold'Em and Seven Card Stud, with free instruction available for beginners.

When it's time to refuel, you can get good Mexican food at The Baja Grill in Buffalo Bill's or Italian favorites in Prima Ristorante & Oyster Bar. When your appetite calls for serious beef, go to the Silver Spur Steak House in Whiskey Pete's.

On the drive from Las Vegas to Primm you pass two hotel-casinos — the Gold Strike and Nevada Landing — in the town of **Jean**, about 20 miles east of Primm. The sister properties are owned by Circus Circus and feature the usual fare: full casinos with 2,000 slots, a variety of table games, Keno lounge and sports book. There are also nine restaurants, a convenience store, a gift shop, a gas station and an airport that provides fuel and tie-downs for private aircraft. There's not much else in Jean, except for a minimum-security prison on the hill overlooking the Gold Strike.

For an interesting change of pace, drive west from Jean on Nev. Highway 161 to the former mining town of **Goodsprings**. In its heyday this little oasis consisted of several stores, saloons, a post office, a school, a hospital, a first-class 20-room hotel and a weekly newspaper. And with a population of about 1,000 people in the early 1900s, it was the largest city in Southern Nevada.

Today, Goodsprings is mostly a few dozen homes surrounded by mill foundations and abandoned mines. But standing defiant in the middle of "town" is the **Pioneer Saloon**, a genuine old-time saloon that hasn't changed much since it was built in 1913. The oldest and largest stamped metal building in the United States, the Pioneer Saloon looks like a set from a Spaghetti Western — dual swinging doors and a flat-roof canopy over its front porch, distressed wood floors and bartop inside and ancient mining tools, a bellied stove and other artifacts that serve as reminders of the establishment's pioneer roots. If you're thirsty, belly up to the bar; the service is friendly, and the beer is cold.

Gone South

Boulder City

Visitors usually discover Boulder City as a pit stop on the way to Hoover Dam or Lake Mead. But beyond the gas stations, gift shops and motels of Nevada Highway is an enchanting little town.

Although it's only 30 minutes from the Las Vegas Strip, the town has no high-rise hotels, bowling alleys, amusement parks and traffic lights. And because it is the only city in Nevada that prohibits gambling, there are no casinos, sports books or slot machines.

Instead, it is a slow-paced "Mayberry RFD" type of town, complete with a central hotel plaza surrounded by eucalyptus trees and water fountains, a historic hotel, ice cream parlor, antique shops — all seemingly lost in a time warp between its Great Depression heritage and the 21st century.

Created by the federal government to house the builders of Hoover Dam, Boulder City is a geometrically "perfect" city. It was designed by Saco D. DeBoer, an admirer of Pierre Charles L'Enfant, who designed Washington, D.C. L'Enfant's influence is apparent in the fanlike layout of the city. Government offices sit on the crest of a hill at the base of the fan; commercial, residential and industrial zones spread out from the base. Streets are designed so through-traffic does not transgress residential areas, and the entire town is buffered from the desert with greenbelts and parks.

Coming from Las Vegas via Nev. Highway 582 (Boulder Highway), you first pass restaurants, gift and souvenir shops and motels along the highway. If you're famished, slow down and look for **Two Gals Restaurant,** 1632 Nevada Highway, 293-1793, which will be distinguished by the line of people waiting to get in. Even though it serves only breakfast and lunch, you won't be disappointed with their tasty selections that include avocado and sprouts omelets, quiche and a number of California chic burgers and sandwiches.

To reach the central historic district, continue south and then turn right on Arizona Street. Park anywhere near the plaza, where you'll find a central fountain and dozens of shops and restaurants.

The historic district is a cultural and historic jewel comprising the very heart of Boulder City. Listed on the National Register of Historic Places, these six square blocks contain some of the finest original architecture of southern Nevada, including the Water & Power Building, the Boulder Theater, the Nevada Drug Store building, the fabulous Boulder Dam Hotel and the quaint shops along Nevada Highway.

The district's most famous landmark is the **Boulder Dam Hotel,** 1305 Arizona Street, 294-1666, a stately Dutch Colonial-style building with stepped gables and white pillars. Inside, the hotel remains virtually unchanged since it was built in 1933. The lobby is a cross between a museum and an antiques shop, cluttered with old photographs and tapestry, a massive front desk and dark gumwood stair banisters and railings. The hotel was once a hideaway for the rich and famous, and the names of early guests are engraved on brass room door plaques. A few of its illustrious guests have included Glenn Ford, Bette Davis,

Shirley Temple, Cornelius Vanderbilt, the Maharajah of India and Crown Prince Olav of Norway.

Guest rooms in the hotel are being renovated and are not available for rent. Call for their status. There are, however, a number of gift shops and arts-and-crafts boutiques worth visiting. Also within the hotel is the **Boulder City Chamber of Commerce**, 293-2034, a good source for information and maps of the city. The self-guided walking-tour brochure points out the sites that have been listed in the National Register of Historical Places. Nearby is the **Boulder City Art Guild Gallery**, 293-2138, which displays the works of about 65 artists. Most are Southwest drawings and paintings, with a focus on the southern Nevada wilderness. Because of its serenity, the town is fast becoming a haven for artists, and there are frequent art showings and festivals here.

Around the corner, on Nevada Highway, are several well-stocked antiques stores. **Ack's Attic**, 530 Nevada Highway, 293-4035, has a large collection of old kitchen utensils, dolls, metal toys and postcards. Next door, **Janean's Antiques**, 538 Nevada Highway, 293-5747, stocks beautiful crystal and porcelain figures as well as country kitchen utensils and collectibles.

If you've worked up an appetite exploring this area try **The Old Town Depot**, 561 Hotel Plaza, 293-6368, which serves simple but tasty dishes — eggs, hamburgers, french fries — and, with its long wood-topped counter, is a popular gathering spot for locals.

The best Mexican food in town is served at **Carlos**, 1300 Arizona Street, 293-5828. Though the service is a bit slow, you won't be disappointed with the bargain-priced fajitas and chili rellenos.

There's one restaurant, however, that epitomizes the flavor of this little town. **Happy Days Diner**, 512 Nevada Highway, 294-4637, is a genuine 1950s eatery, complete with soda fountain and waitresses in starched white uniforms. Everything in the place, from the checkerboard floor tile and Wurlitzer juke box, to the Coke glasses and cherry phosphates, is vintage Fifties. The food — burgers, rings, fries, chocolate Cokes, grilled cheese sandwiches — and even the prices ($2.99 for the lunch special, $3.99 dinner specials) seem to be caught in a time warp.

Before leaving Boulder City, drive up Nevada Highway to **Denver Street** and turn left for a glimpse of residential life during the 1930s. The row of homes on the right were built in 1932 for the Hoover Dam project's managers and supervisors. The modest though quaint Hollywood Spanish-style houses have changed very little since the Depression era — most have large fireplaces, hardwood floors, sun rooms with casement windows and a basement. There's nothing in Las Vegas to match these charming doll houses, and they've become popular with many Las Vegans who don't mind the 30-minute commute into the city.

If you like Boulder City so much that you decide to spend the night, you'll find several good accommodations options. The **El Rancho Boulder Motel**, 725 Nevada Highway, 293-1085, (800) 548-1034, built in 1955, is tile-roofed, brick-built classic with 39 cozy guest rooms updated in contemporary decor. Four suites that sleep six can be rented, and kitchenettes are available to visitors staying at least three nights. All units have refrigerators and door-front parking. Boaters enjoy the El Rancho's large lot that lets them stow their craft at the motel. Though not long on special guest services — free morning coffee is about it — this mom-and-pop operation has a lot of loyal repeat business.

The **Lake Mead Resort and Marina**, 322 Lakeshore Road, 293-2074, (800) 752-9669, dates back to the 1930s. But don't be fooled by the "resort" moniker. Built with unassuming concrete blocks, it began as a lodging house for construction crews working on Hoover Dam 7 miles away. Today, it is well-maintained and beautifully situated with stunning lake views. The 48-room complex is laid out in a U-shape and includes some three-bedroom suites equipped with full kitchens. While each room has cable TV, there are no in-room telephones. As you would expect of a beach-front resort, there are lots of chairs and gazebos as well as a large pool near the lake. Winter rates plunge with the temperatures, starting at $35. House boats also can be rented at the marina.

The **Super 8 Motel**, 704 Nevada Highway, 294-8888, (800) 825-0880, is by far the biggest lodge in Boulder City, with 115 rooms. Unlike many of your standard Super 8s, this one has a dozen "Jacuzzi suites" that feature two bedrooms and balconies. Some, including the Bridal Suite, even have round beds. All rooms have refrigerators and kitchenettes, but be sure to bring along your own silverware, stoneware and stemware. Handicapped guest rooms are available. A restaurant with a reasonably priced menu is on the premises and offers room service. Adjoining the restaurant is a cocktail lounge that's open past midnight — a rarity in this quiet burg. Free coffee provides guests a morning eye-opener, along with complimentary copies of *USA Today*. The large pool is indoors — another unique feature — and a conference room is available for meetings. The front desk offers fax and Western Union service, as well as valet laundry service if you don't want to bother with the motel's coin-operated washer and dryer. Pets are allowed, if their owners put down a deposit. Kids younger than 12 stay free.

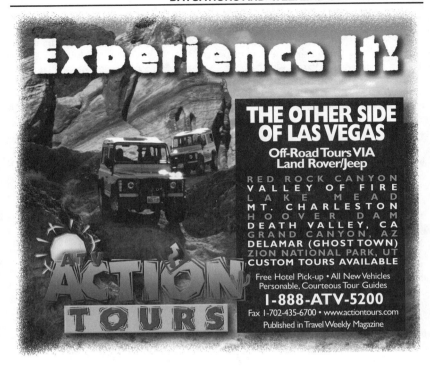

Hoover Dam

Long before gambling became king, Hoover Dam was the No. 1 tourist attraction in southern Nevada. Completed in 1935 — under budget and ahead of schedule! — the dam was touted as the Eighth Wonder of the World. And for good reason. The dam is one of the world's engineering marvels. The horseshoe-shaped plug that holds back two-years' flow of the mighty Colorado River is as tall as a 54-story building. The base is 600 feet thick and contains enough concrete to build a two-lane highway from San Francisco to New York. Inside there's as much reinforced steel as in the Empire State Building.

The dam took five years to build, at a cost of $175 million. At the peak of construction, 5,000 workers labored night and day. An average of 50 injuries a day and 94 deaths were recorded before the flood gates were closed and Lake Mead began to fill.

Today, Hoover Dam remains southern Nevada's top tourist attraction. Only 20 minutes south of Las Vegas via U.S. 93, the dam is open for tours every day of the year except Christmas.

Begin your visit at the **Exhibit Center** on the Nevada side of the dam. Notice the 30-foot-tall art nouveau figures outside — the Winged Figures of the Republic, cast in bronze by sculptor Oskar Hansen. Inside, you'll find further evidence of the 1930s architecture influenced by the WPA era: ornate railings and fixtures, floors and doors.

Across the street you'll find the new **Visitor Center**, a three-level, 110-foot diameter circular structure with a rooftop overlook. Admission is $6 for adults, $5 for seniors, $2 for juniors ages 6 to 16 and free for children 5 and younger.

The middle level of the center houses a reception lobby and a rotating theater divided into 120-seat sections. Interpretive exhibits detail the history of the Colorado River, the building of the dam and how it is used for electrical power, flood control and irrigation. In addition a 25-minute film on the construction of Hoover Dam is shown in one of the theater sections.

The level above the reception lobby features an exhibit gallery that contains static and interactive displays on the Southwest's environment, habitation and development, the people who built the dam and other related topics.

On the upper overlook level, an exhibit demonstrates the benefits of Hoover Dam and Lake Mead to the three lower basin states of Arizona, Nevada and California. Make sure your camera's loaded because the observation deck also gives visitors an unobstructed view of the dam and powerhouse, Lake Mead and the Colorado River.

The guided tour (included in price of admission), which takes about 35 minutes, begins with an elevator ride to the base of the dam. You'll feel the temperature drop as you descend — the interior of the dam averages between 55 and 60 degrees year-around. At the base you'll enter a monumental room housing the seven-story high turbines that took three years to build and assemble and that generate 4 billion kilowatt-hours of electricity.

The base of the dam is honeycombed with tunnels. One leads to a 30-foot diversion pipe; another leads to an outdoor observation deck where you enjoy a fish-eye perspective of the dam and the rugged canyon it bridges. Returning to the top you'll find a snack bar and souvenir shop. If you drive the two-lane road over the dam, you will find yourself in Arizona and will have lost an hour.

Laughlin

The resort town of Laughlin is a fascinating phenomenon. On the west bank of the Colorado River 100 miles south of Las Vegas, Laughlin was once a decrepit bait shop and eight-room motel that blossomed into a shimmering riverfront resort and the third-largest gambling center in the state.

Southern Nevada is full of rags-to-riches stories, but this is one of the best. The genesis of Laughlin lies in the energy and vision of its namesake, Don Laughlin, a former Las Vegas bartender and dealer who, in 1969, bought a bankrupt motel, bar and bait shop for $235,000 and parlayed it into the 660-room Riverside resort hotel and casino. The resort was so successful that Laughlin spent $10 million of his own money expanding the airport and building a bridge across the Colorado River. Corporate giants soon followed, and, by the mid-1980s, Harrah's, Ramada, Hilton and Circus Circus began their own building boom here. There are currently nine major hotels in Laughlin serving 5 million tourists a year.

Gaming, however, is not Laughlin's only attraction. The river and nearby Lake Mohave are major draws, offering year-round watersports such as swimming, boating, fishing and waterskiing. Also within short driving distance are ghost towns, historic mines and intriguing lost canyons waiting to be explored.

The "town" is actually a 2-mile strip of hotel-casinos, a scaled-down version of the Las

INSIDERS' TIP

The Mt. Charleston Golf Course covers such a wide range of terrain that players are required to use a cart.

Vegas Strip. But you won't see any stretch limos or Rolls Royces here; it's mainly RVs and pickup trucks. Known as the "Mecca of the Low Roller," Laughlin caters to budget-minded tourists and coin-toting gamblers, most of whom drive in from Arizona and California. Table stakes are the $2-a-hand variety, and hotel rooms are priced 30 to 50 percent less than their Vegas counterparts.

Most of Laughlin's working population lives across the river in Bullhead City, Arizona's fastest growing city. You'll find a small residential section, public library and shopping center west of the casinos in Laughlin, but most hotel workers commute from Bullhead City across two bridges and by ferry boat.

The best time to visit Laughlin is during the winter and spring months, when the daytime temperatures range from 65 to 80 degrees. Temperatures in July and August can reach an astounding 120 degrees or more, making this city the hottest spot in the nation.

If driving from Las Vegas via U.S. 95, stop on the way at the old mining town of **Searchlight** for a 10¢ cup of coffee at the Nugget Casino or a sandwich at the 49er Club. The rusting mining equipment and head frames on the hillsides are reminders of the days when the one-street town was once a booming gold rush town. During the 1930s, several Hollywood movie stars moved to this tiny desert community. The great costume designer Edith Head spent some of her childhood here, and Rex Bell and Clara Bow put Searchlight on the map when they bought the Walking Box Ranch just west of town on Nev. Highway 164. Today tours of the ranch are offered; contact the Walking Box Ranch, P.O. Box 68, Searchlight, NV 89046.

Just south of Searchlight, try the scenic route over **Christmas Tree Pass**. The marked 17-mile dirt road leaves U.S. 95 and climbs east through the Newberry Mountains, connecting with Nev. 163, about 6 miles west of Laughlin. As you climb toward Christmas Tree Pass, you'll see massive granite outcroppings and stacks of mammoth boulders. With the change in altitude notice that the sagebrush and cactus give way to pinon pines, for which the area was named. Don't be surprised to see some of the trees decorated with brightly colored cans, paper cups, glass balls or even items of clothing, presumably by local prospectors who never lost their Christmas spirit.

A few miles from Laughlin you'll reach a summit overlooking the river. From here the view of Laughlin is stunning, especially after dark when the hotel lights glow like burning embers against the dark river.

The hotels resemble small Las Vegas resorts. There are even a couple of theme hotels. One of the best is the **Colorado Belle**, 2100 S. Casino Drive, 298-4000, a 600-foot replica of a Mississippi steamboat, complete with three decks and four black smokestacks 21 stories tall. In the evening, the paddlewheel "turns" by strobe light. Inside, the decor is turn-of-the-century New Orleans, with lots of plush red carpeting, glass-globe lamps, brass railings and wrought-iron fixtures. The cluster of shops on the mezzanine level has several restaurants, an old-fashioned candy store and wandering clowns to keep your spirits up.

For a taste of Dodge City by the river try the **Pioneer Hotel**, 2200 S. Casino Drive, 298-2442, next door. The two-story hotel looks like a U-shaped fort, finished with weathered wood panels. The facade of the casino entrance suggests a Wild West boarding house. Swinging doors and a wooden porch lead into a hectic casino, decorated with darkwood floors and distressed paneling. On the river side of the hotel is a waving neon cowboy — River Rick — Laughlin's version of Vegas Vic. The hotel grounds facing the river have a lush flower garden, green grass and shade trees. There are also benches for relaxing and watching the ferry boats and jet skiers on the river.

Also worth visiting is the **Riverside Resort**, 1650 S. Casino Drive, 298-2535. Be sure to visit the antiques shop just off the casino. The small but interesting collection consists of slot machines, juke boxes, vintage radios and a variety of old neon signs. On display, but not for sale, are antique slots from Don Laughlin's personal collection, including a 1938 vest pocket slot machine and a 1931 slot that paid off in golf balls.

About 2 miles north of casino row is the **Davis Dam and Powerplant**, (602) 754-3628, built in 1953 to produce hydroelectric power and regulate water delivery to Mexico. The powerplant, downstream from the dam embankment on the Arizona side of the river, is open daily for self-guided tours, which include recorded lectures, illustrated maps and close-up views of the plant's turbines.

Behind the dam lies **Lake Mohave**, which extends 67 miles upstream to Hoover Dam. The long, narrow lake (4 miles across at its widest point) provides a multitude of recreational opportunities (see our Great Outdoors chapter for details).

Eastward Ho!

Mesquite

This small farming community in the verdant Virgin River valley now sprouts neon and cultivates slot-playing tourists. Like Primm at the California state line, Mesquite has enjoyed a modest boom as a gaming resort at the Arizona border, about 80 miles east of Las Vegas off Interstate 15.

Originally settled by Mormon pioneers in the 1880s, Mesquite is now home to four major gaming resorts that feature 2,700 guest rooms, a variety of restaurants, health spas, swimming pools, showrooms, lounges, RV parks, tennis courts and meeting rooms.

But rather than position itself as the next Las Vegas, Mesquite is rapidly emerging as a major golfing destination. **Si Redd's Oasis Resort Hotel Casino**, 897 W. Mesquite Boulevard, 346-5232, is home to three outstanding courses, including the magnificent Arnold Palmer-designed Oasis Golf Club, which was voted one of the 10 best new public courses in the United States by editors of *Golf Magazine*. The course features dramatic elevation changes and holes played through desert gorges and around glistening lakes.

Arnold Palmer also chose Mesquite for his prestigious golf academy, the only one in the Western United States. In addition to the Oasis, Si Redd's Resort is home to The Vistas, a nine-hole course, and the 18-hole Palms Golf Course, which features a par 5 15th hole that is played off a cliff to the fairway several hundred feet below.

Si Redd, incidentally, is somewhat of a legend in the history of Nevada gambling. He is credited with developing the video poker machine and is the founder of International Game Technology (IGT), the world's largest manufacturer of electronic gambling machines (slot, video poker and keno). In the early 1990s he sold his interest in IGT and purchased the old Peppermill Resort, which he renamed Si Redd's Oasis. Although now in his mid-80s, Redd continues to wheel and deal in the gaming industry.

FYI

Unless otherwise noted, the area code for all phone numbers listed in this chapter is 702.

At the **Casa Blanca Resort**, 930 W. Mesquite Boulevard, 346-7529, duffers can challenge the Cal Olson-designed Player's Golf Club, a picturesque 18-hole course cut through the area's wetlands.

Although it doesn't have a golf course, the **Virgin River Hotel/Casino**, 100 Pioneer Boulevard, 346-7777, attracts plenty of customers with its Western theme, 99¢ beer and $20 room rates. Much of its clientele are truckers and weary I-15 travelers who appreciate the barbecue and country flavor.

There are plenty of dining choices in the resorts, but one of the best outside a hotel is **Carrollo's**, 551 W. Mesquite Boulevard, 346-2818. Darkwood paneling and oil paintings of the New England countryside make a strange backdrop for the country-western music on the jukebox, but diners enjoy the porterhouse steaks, beef and seafood dishes.

To get a feel of life before greens fees and all-you-can-eat buffets, check out the **Desert Valley Museum**, 31 W. Mesquite Boulevard, 346-5705. Originally constructed as a library in 1941, the small stone building is something of a community attic, crammed with a variety of pioneer tools, utensils, bric-a-brac and other collectibles. Some of the oddities include a Native American rabbit fur cloak, a 1945 television set and a petrified tree stump with an egg buried in it. There is also a vast archives of old newspaper clippings, journals, publications and handwritten letters that reveal the human experience behind Mesquite's pioneer history.

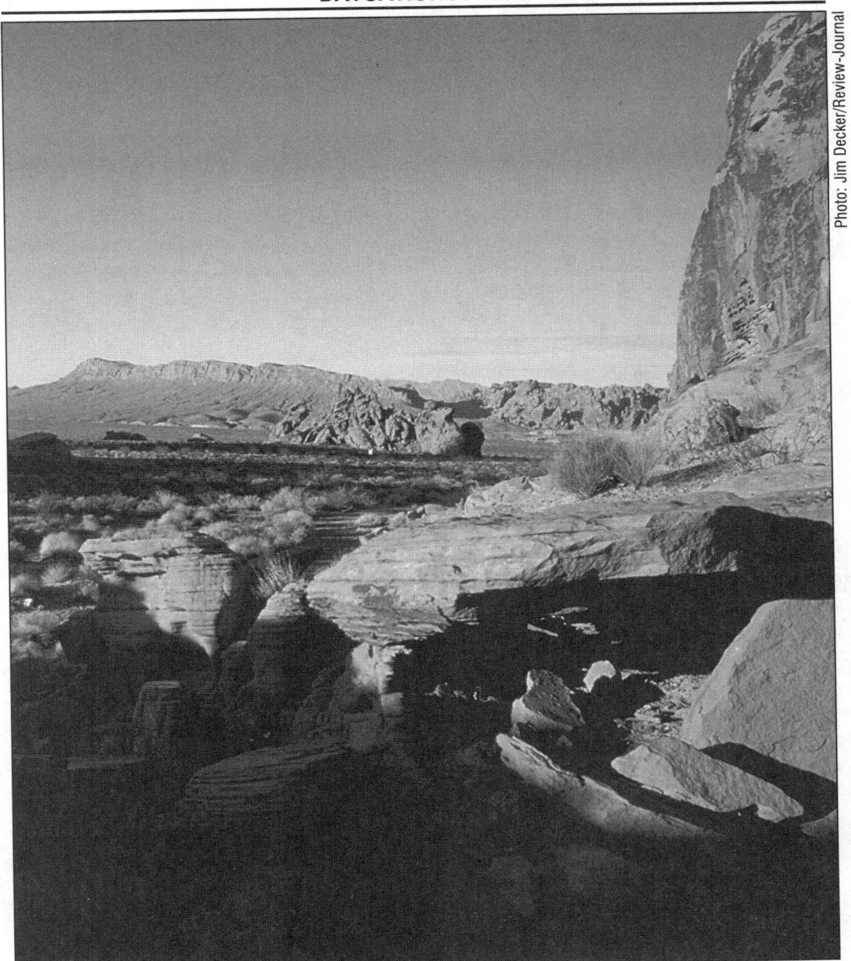

Photo: Jim Decker/Review-Journal

The eerie rock formations at Red Rock Canyon provide an interesting backdrop for hikers and rock climbers.

Moapa Valley

On your drive to the Valley of Fire (see our Great Outdoors chapter) you'll pass through Moapa Valley, a veritable oasis irrigated by the centuries-old Muddy River. After exiting I-15 about 60 miles east of Las Vegas, you'll discover alfalfa fields, horse ranches and dairy farms as well as two one-street towns.

The first one is **Logandale**, a bedroom community on the site of St. Joseph, one of the first Mormon settlements in southern Nevada. In the center of town is the **Aramus Arabians Ranch**, 398-3631, open to visitors who can admire, but not photograph, the roughly 70 prized horses.

Farther along Nev. Highway 169 is **Overton**, whose main street spans several blocks of cafes, bars, markets, video stores and a movie theater. If you'd like a hawk's-eye view of the valley, take the paved road leading east out of Overton up the mountain to **Mormon Mesa**. The spot is a nice place to spread a picnic blanket and enjoy the panorama.

If the drive has fueled your appetite, grab a pizza at **Tom's Pizza & Deli**, 397-8600, or immerse yourself in frozen dessert at the **Inside Scoop**, 397-2055.

At the south end of town is the **The Lost City Museum,** 721 S. Nev. 169, 397-2193, which features a fascinating collection of Anasazi artifacts. The Anasazi, or "Ancient Ones," settled the Moapa Valley centuries before any white man set foot in America. The remains of their settlement, which archeologists call the Lost City, was covered by the waters of Lake Mead, but representative buildings have been reconstructed at the museum. Museum exhibits consist of pottery, stone tools and weapons, baskets and household items from the Anasazi and other ancient Indian cultures. There's also a slab of sandstone decorated with petroglyphs (ancient rock drawings) similar to those in the nearby Valley of Fire. The museum also features exhibits relating to the Mormon farmers who settled the valley in 1865. The gift shop has an interesting collection of Hopi Indian cards, drawn by blind artist Jerry Mitchler.

St. George, Utah

Imagine a quaint, New England town, complete with emerald trees, wood-frame Colonial homes and churches with clock towers and spires, then add a backdrop that suggests a miniature, red-rocked Grand Canyon. What you'd have is the city of St. George, Utah, a delightful change of pace just across the Nevada state line, about 120 miles northeast of Las Vegas.

This little community is a key gateway to Zion National Park, Cedar Breaks National Monument and Snow Canyon State Park and it is also one of the best places in the country to retire. The attributes that make it a prime retirement location — mild weather, beautiful scenery and peaceful lifestyle — also make it a great travel destination. Throw in plenty of places to explore, shop, dine, stay and play, and you have a fascinating getaway a comfortable two-hour drive from Las Vegas.

For those with a yen for nostalgia, St. George is a treasure. There's a wealth of history on nearly every street in the city's central downtown area — the original town was settled by Mormon pioneers in the 1860s. Outdoor enthusiasts can hunt, fish, swim or boat at nearby parks and recreational areas, and golfers can tee off on one of eight city golf courses. And if you simply want to experience nature at its best, you will discover one of the planet's most varied landscapes — from lava crusted craters and billowing sand dunes to granite monuments and mountain meadows.

The city began when Brigham Young sent some 300 families from northern Utah to the southern Utah desert. Young envisioned a huge cotton mission that could supplement the West's supply during the Civil War, which had cut off shipments from the South.

Though initially successful, the cotton mission (and one to grow silkworms as well) ultimately failed because of an inability to compete in the marketplace after the end of the Civil War. However, a warm climate and bevy of recreational activities eventually made St. George the fastest growing city in the state, and one of the most popular retirement destinations in the country.

St. George is made for walking. Begin at the **St. George Chamber of Commerce**, 97 E. St. George Boulevard, (801) 628-1658, which was originally built in the 1870s as the Washington County Courthouse. Pick up brochures, a walking-tour guide and maps of the area. In the basement of the square, two-story, red-brick Colonial-style building are dungeon-like cells where cattle rustlers were once jailed. The large room on the second floor was used as a school and courthouse. Other interesting features include 18-inch thick interior walls, panes of original glass, old chandeliers, original paintings of Zion National Park and the Grand Canyon, an old vault, the exterior cornice work and the cupola.

INSIDERS' TIP

The Desperado roller coaster at Primm is America's tallest and fastest. It reaches speeds of nearly 90 mph and achieves G-forces of close to 4.0.

Directly behind the chamber offices is the **Daughters of the Utah Pioneers Museum**, 145 North 100 East Street, (801) 628-7274, which is filled with relics of the past, including children's toys, lace bonnets, worn tools, yellowed letters and photographs of pioneers. There is also a pioneer dress made from locally produced silk.

The **Mormon Tabernacle**, 2 S. Main Street, (801) 628-4072, was built in 1871 of red sandstone and has a four-faced clock on a square tower crowned by a slender white steeple. Tour guides explain how the limestone for 3-foot-thick basement walls was hand-quarried and the red sandstone blocks were hand-cut stone by stone from a nearby site. Take special note of the intricate, plaster-of-Paris ceiling and cornice work, all shipped to California by boat and then hauled by wagon team to St. George.

Only members of the Mormon Church may enter the **St. George Mormon Temple**, 450 South 300 East Street, (801) 673-5181, a dazzling white edifice that dominates the town. But an on-site visitor center does provide a pictorial history of the temple's construction and other background on the Church of Latter Day Saints. Built in 1871, it predates the Great Salt Lake City temple and is the oldest Mormon temple in use today. Free guided tours of the grounds are also available.

You can take a guided tour of **Brigham Young's Winter Home**, 155 West 200 North Street, (801) 673-2517, showcasing beautiful furnishing and memorabilia owned by the second president of the Mormon Church. Huge fruit and mulberry trees still cover the grounds.

Several historic buildings can be found in **Ancestor Square**, 42 West St. George Boulevard, along with dozens of shops and restaurants. The **Hardy House**, which is now a Mexican restaurant, was used by the sheriff of St. George during the 1870s. There's even a bullet hole in one of the doors. The **Gardener's Club Hall** served as a meeting place for club members and is still in use today. The one-room **Jailhouse**, believed to built by Sheriff Hardy in the 1880s, was constructed from black lava hauled down from the nearby Pine Mountains. The bars on the windows are original.

For a sweet taste of the 1890s, try **Judd's Store**, 62 W. Tabernacle Street, (801) 628-2596, a Western-style shop that hasn't changed much since it was built in the 1870s. Notice the gleaming polished wood floors, handmade display cases, pressed-tin ceiling and rippled-glass windows. Don't leave without sampling some of the baked goods, candies or a float, freeze or banana split from the marbled soda fountain.

St. George Art Center, 86 S. Main Street, (801) 634-5850, was built in the 1880s as the Dixie Academy, which grew to become today's Dixie College. The four-story, brick building is now used by the city to house art and leisure-related offices.

Twenty-five miles north of St. George on Utah Highway 18 is the town of Central and the turnoff to **Pine Valley**, a mountain hamlet with rustic cabins, brick cottages and Victorian homes. At the valley's center is a picturesque, satin-white chapel that's believed to be the oldest Mormon chapel still in continuous use.

Just north of the Pine Valley turnoff is a stone marker for the **Mountain Meadows Massacre Site and Memorial**. Here, in 1857, a group of emigrants — 120 men, women and children — en route to California was slaughtered by Mormons and Indians. The event is considered a dark period in Mormon history and one the church has tried to live down ever since.

After visiting Pine Valley, backtrack to Utah 18 and travel 12 miles south to the **Snow Canyon State Park** turnoff. Along the way are numerous extinct volcanic cones and lava fields, many beckoning to be explored. A small park, the canyon itself is a white-and-red mix of Navajo sandstone covered with black lava beds. Elevations range from 2,600 to 3,500 feet atop the cindercones. Snow Canyon has served as movie location for several films including *Butch Cassidy and the Sundance Kid*. Grasses, willows, cacti and other shrubbery peer through cracks. Evidence of early man's impressions of Snow Canyon can be seen at several pictograph sites within the park.

Leaving the canyon, you'll pass through Ivins and then connect with the rural community of **Santa Clara**, 3 miles west of St. George. Settled by Swiss immigrants, Santa Clara lays claim to the house built by noted missionary, Indian agent and colonizer Jacob Hamblin. Built in 1862, the rough-hewn, red sandstone

Jacob Hamblin Home, Utah Highway 91, (801) 673-2161, clearly demonstrates the sturdiness of frontier construction, designed to withstand Indian attack, and showcases a number of 19th-century furnishings and tools.

National Parks

As described in our Great Outdoors chapter, the wilderness area surrounding Las Vegas is magnificent. But it is only a sampling of what awaits visitors willing to venture beyond the Rand McNally lines that separate Nevada from its neighbors. The landscape and geological features in adjoining states are unlike anything else found on earth. And they're all within quick and easy access of Las Vegas.

In this land of astonishing diversity you'll find something new in every direction, from sheer sandstone cliffs and slickrock mesas to secluded beaches on bright blue lakes and vast deserts alive with giant cactuses and unusual animals. Within a few hours' drive of Las Vegas, you can explore high mountain peaks with lush rolling meadows and deep-slotted canyons with lost cities and hidden treasures.

Because Las Vegas is at the geographic center of four states — California, Nevada, Arizona and Utah — it is a convenient starting point for visits to some of the most varied, fascinating and beautiful national parks in the country. In this section we've selected four of them as possible getaways because of their proximity to Las Vegas as well as their many scenic and historic sights.

About a two-hour drive west of Las Vegas is the hauntingly picturesque Death Valley National Monument. Equal in size to the combined area of Connecticut and Rhode Island, Death Valley is one of the hottest regions on earth, second only to the Sahara Desert. Nevertheless, visitors are continually drawn to it, a region rich in history and diverse in landscape. A museum without air conditioning, Death Valley National Monument is a giant geology lab displaying salt beds, sand dunes and multitiered hills containing layers that are windows on the history of the earth. One level holds Indian arrowheads, another Ice Age fish, and beneath these deposits lies Precambrian rock.

In the opposite direction are the geological marvels of Southwestern Utah, a region of mythic diversity. From slickrock to ponderosa, from creosote to mountain valleys, the variety of scenery and natural wonders is unparalleled. No state has more national parks than Utah, and two of them are within an easy two-and-a-half hour drive of Las Vegas. At Zion National Park and Bryce Canyon National Park you'll find terrain of the Colorado Plateau — multicolored mesas, buttes, soaring cliffs, sandstone crags, alpine forests and mountain meadows. Besides magnificent sightseeing, visitors can fish, hike, cycle, enjoy winter sports or explore mountain trails on horseback.

To the southeast of Las Vegas is perhaps the grandest geological marvel of them all, the Grand Canyon. Awesome. Spectacular. One gropes for words when trying to describe the Grand Canyon. Nothing on the planet can compare to the immensity of this mighty chasm in northwestern Arizona. With more than 4 million visitors a year, the Grand Canyon is one of the most popular national parks in the United States.

Death Valley National Monument

Simply stated, Death Valley is the most famous desert in the United States. Renowned for exquisite but merciless terrain, Death Valley holds a bag of tricks even David Copperfield would envy.

One of the most hauntingly beautiful places in the world, Death Valley received its name in 1849 when a party of pioneers, intent on following a shortcut to the gold fields, crossed the wasteland, barely escaping with their lives. Later, prospectors stayed to work the territory, discovering rich borax deposits during the 1880s and providing the region with a home industry.

There are several entry points to Death Valley National Monument, 145 miles west of Las Vegas. You can enter the park along its eastern boundary at Death Valley Junction by driving northwest from Las Vegas on U.S. 95 and turning south on Nev. Highway 373 at Lanthrop Wells. But the approach we recommend is to take I-15 southwest to the town of Baker, California, (about 90 miles) then drive north on Cal. Highway 127, which leads to the park's south entrance.

And the pageantry begins even before you

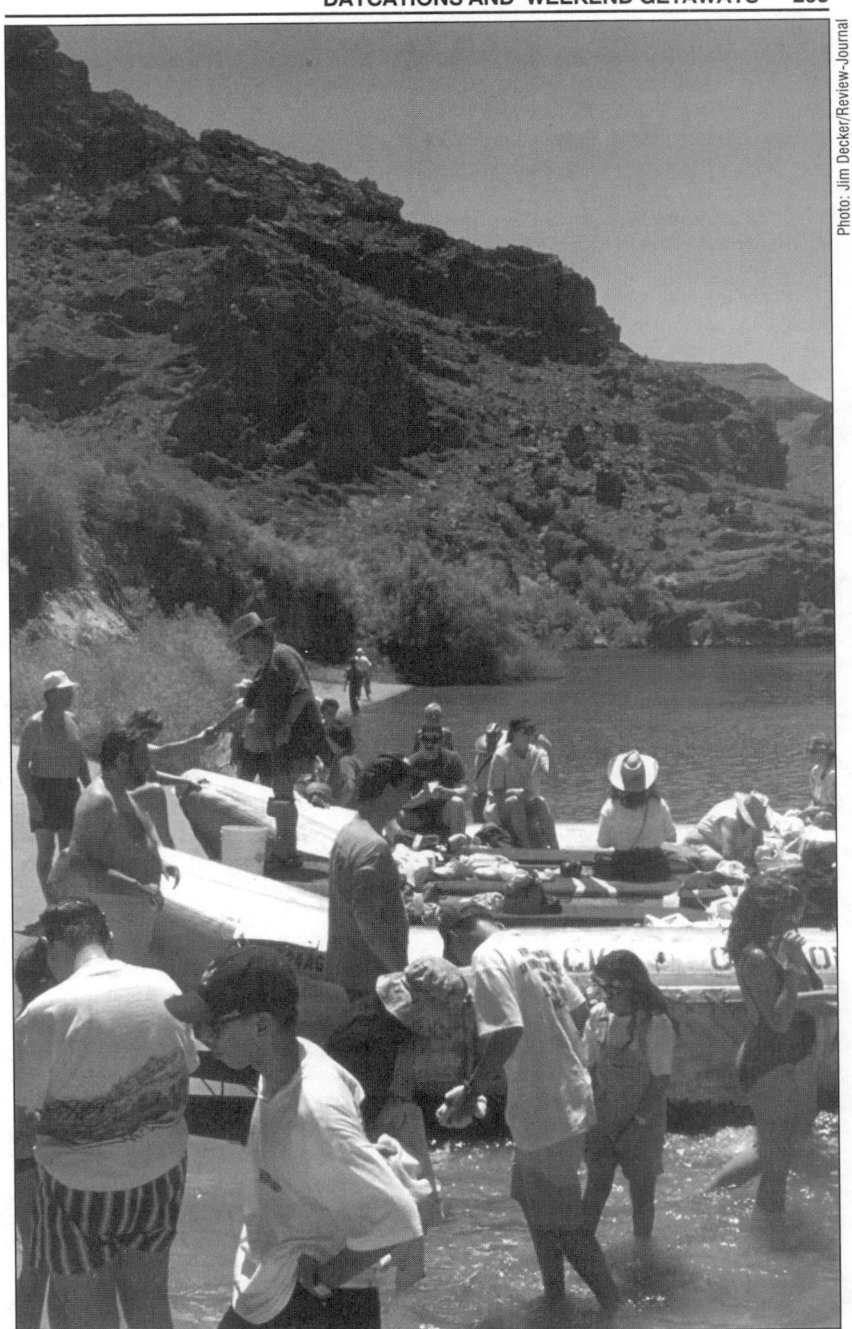

Photo: Jim Decker/Review-Journal

There are dozens of beaches and inlets along the Colorado River between Hoover Dam and Lake Mojave.

enter the national monument. On the highway leading from Baker, you'll descend into an ancient lake bed and pass **Tecopa Lake Badlands**, where erosion has carved fascinating formations from soft sedimentary rock. A side road leads several miles to **Tecopa Hot Springs**, a series of mineral baths once used by Native Americans. Today this natural resource has been transformed into a bizarre tourist mecca.

If there is a final outpost before the world ends, this is it. A white patina blankets the ground everywhere, as though salt had been shaken across the entire desert, and water stands in stagnant pools. Wherever you look, there are trailers with a background of rugged, stark, glorious mountains. Hundreds of trailers, like metal matchboxes against the Mojave sun, painted white like the desert and interspersed with satellite dishes. In a kind of desert Monopoly game, if you collect enough mobile homes you can hang out a sign and call it a motel.

The bathrobe-clad species that inhabits these tin domiciles is on permanent vacation. They wander from the private baths at the trailer parks and motels to the public hot-spring baths which, in the single saving grace to this surreal enclave, are free.

From the monument's south entrance, a good place to start your tour is along Cal. Highway 178. Within a couple miles lie the ruins of **Ashford Mill**, built during World War I when gold mining enjoyed a comeback. The skeletons of several buildings are all that remain of that early dream.

For a close-up of a cindercone, follow nearby West Side Road, a graded thoroughfare, downhill for 2 miles. That reddish-black mound on your left is **Cinder Hill**, residue from an ancient volcano.

The main highway continues through the heart of the region to **Mormon Point**. From here northward, Death Valley is one huge salt flat. Then continue to that place you read about in 3rd-grade geography, **Badwater**, 282 feet below sea level, the lowest point in the Western hemisphere. Legend has it the place got its name from a surveyor whose mule refused to drink here, inspiring him to scratch "bad water" on the map he was charting.

Take a stroll out onto the salt flats, and you'll find that the crystals are joined into a white carpet that extends for miles. Despite the brackish environment the pool supports water snails and other invertebrates. Salt grass, pickleweed and desert holly also endure here. Out on the flats you can gaze west at 11,049-foot **Telescope Peak** across the valley. Then be sure to glance back at the cliff to the west of the road. There high in the rocks above, a lone sign marks sea level.

About 3 miles from Badwater you'll find **Devil's Golf Course**. Rather than a sand hazard, this flat expanse is one huge salt trap, complete with salt towers, pinnacles and brine pools. The sodium chloride here is 95 percent pure, comparable to table salt, and the salt deposits are 3- to 5-feet thick. They were formed by a small lake that evaporated perhaps 2,000 years ago. Below them, earlier deposits from larger lakes reach more than 1,000 feet beneath the surface.

In this entire wasteland of wonders, the only major center of civilization is **Furnace Creek**, where a gas station, campground, restaurants and two hotels create a welcome oasis. The **Death Valley National Monument Visitor Center**, (619) 786-2331, is a good resource for maps and information. It houses a museum re-creating the history of Native Americans and early prospectors. You'll also see mineral displays and an oversize relief map of the valley.

The poshest place for many miles is **Furnace Creek Inn,** (619) 786-2345, set on a hillside overlooking Death Valley. This Spanish-Moorish-style building, built of stone and adobe, is surrounded by flowering gardens, palm trees and a stream that feeds three koi ponds. Both upscale restaurants at the inn serve fine food and enforce dress codes for

INSIDERS' TIP

Room rates in Laughlin run considerably lower than in Las Vegas. During the summer months and special promotions, they can be as low as $8 per night.

men and women. **Furnace Creek Ranch,** (619) 786-2345, is less formal than the inn and sprawls across several acres and features three restaurants, a saloon, general store and a swimming pool.

The nearby **Borax Museum** features the oldest house in Death Valley, a sturdy 1883 structure built by a borax miner. There's also a wonderful collection of stage coaches as well as a huge Rube Goldberg contraption once used to extract gold deposits from rock.

From Furnace Creek follow Cal. Highway 190 southeast to **Zabriskie Point**, a point at which nearly everyone inevitably arrives, as though it were a point of pilgrimage for paying homage to nature. What else can a mortal do, confronted with beauty of this magnitude? Toward the east amber-hued hills roll like waves toward the horizon. To the west lie badlands, burnished by blown sand to fierce reds and soft pastels. All around, the landscape resembles a sea gone mad, waves of sand breaking in every direction, with a stone tsunami, Manly Beacon, high above the combers, poised to crash into Death Valley.

Backtracking to Furnace Creek, Cal. 190 proceeds north toward the upper end of Death Valley. The history of the region's most valuable mineral is further revealed at the **Harmony Borax Works**. Surrounded by the ruins of Death Valley's most successful borax plant is an original 20-mule team rig.

At the very end of Death Valley, you'll find the strangest feature in the entire park — a castle in the desert. It's a place called **Scotty's Castle**, a wonderfully ridiculous building with wrought-iron detailing, inlaid tile, carved-beam ceilings, expensive antiques and nothing else for miles around. Somehow it reminds one of Hearst Castle in San Simeon, a place too gaudy to appreciate but too outrageous to ignore.

Ubehebe Crater, 8 miles from Scotty's lair, is another of the park's natural wonders. A half-mile in diameter and reaching a depth of 450 feet, this magnificent landmark was created by a single explosion. The force of the volcanic steam scattered debris over a 6-square-mile area and blew the crater walls so clean that one side retains its original sedimentary colors. Whether the crater dates back 10,000 years or is only a few hundred years old is currently being debated by geologists. They do agree that other nearby craters have been formed in the last few centuries.

From the crater, a winding gravel road leads 27 miles to **The Racetrack**, another of nature's magic acts. This 2-mile mud playa, set at the bottom of a dry lake, is oval shaped like a racecourse. In fact an outcropping at the north end of the valley is dubbed The Grandstand. The "racers," oddly enough, are rocks, ranging in size from pebbles to boulders. Pushed by heavy winds across the mud-slick surface, they leave long, faint tracks that reveal the distances they have raced.

Zion National Park

From its towering sandstone cliffs to its deep slot-like canyons, Zion National Park has it all. Sheer escarpments surround the verdant floor of Zion Canyon as lush hanging gardens and waterfalls stand in marked contrast to the desert-like terrain of stark rock formations and etched redrock walls. And this rewarding getaway is only 155 miles northeast of Las Vegas. To reach the park drive east on I-15 past St. George, Utah, about 120 miles. Then exit on Utah Highway 9 and drive to the park's main entrance, 1 mile north of Springdale.

It's easy to see why the popularity of Zion National Park, (801) 772-3256, has skyrocketed. Accessible year-round with an endless variety of hiking trails geared to all abilities, this "heavenly city of God" is a park for all people. Grandfather of Utah's national parks, Zion is packed with precipitous canyons and massive stone monoliths. Vividly colored cliffs, sheer-rock walls and unique formations make this park one of the state's most popular attractions.

This 147,000-acre park was carved almost single-handedly by the Virgin River, which flows along the canyon floor. Cottonwoods, willows and velvet ash trees line the river, providing an ever-changing kaleidoscope of colors as one season follows another. To avoid the summer-vacation crowds and traffic, plan to visit from November through April. Otherwise expect lots of cars, nonexistent parking and loads of other travelers.

Be sure to stop at the **Visitor Center** where rangers are happy to provide maps, brochures and backcountry permits. Naturalist-guided walks, evening programs and patio talks are scheduled from late March to November. Specific dates and times are posted at the center.

Depending on time and specific interest, you can drive, bicycle or take a guided tram tour through Zion. But don't miss out on the fabulous sights that await just off the roads. Zion is best appreciated close-up, and you'll miss the true majesty of the park if you don't explore.

Zion Canyon Scenic Drive takes visitors about 6.5 miles into the heart of Zion Canyon and its 2,000- to 3,000-foot-high walls carved inch-by-inch by the Virgin River cutting through the Markagunt Plateau. Just past the entrance you're likely to spot **West Temple**, the highest peak in Zion's southern section. Notice the delineated strata of rock as it rises 4,100 feet from base to peak.

One of the first places you might want to pause is **Court of the Patriarchs** vista point. From here you can see reverently named monuments like the Streaked Wall, the Sentinel, the Patriarchs (a series of three peaks called Abraham, Isaac and Jacob), Mt. Moroni, the Spearhead and the sheer-walled sandstone monolith Angels Landing, perched 1,500 feet above the canyon bed. To the east and above are two other monuments, Mountain of the Sun and the Twin Brothers.

The **Grotto Picnic Area** is the perfect spot to take a break from exploring the park. Here, in the cool shade of broadleaf trees and gamble oak, you'll find fire grates, picnic tables, water and restrooms.

Driving the road you'll spot **The Great White Throne** on the east side. Notice how this 2,400-foot megalith ranges in color from a deep red at the base to pink to gray to white at the top. The color variations arise because the Navajo sandstone has less iron oxide at the top than the bottom.

A bit farther is a short, paved walk that leads to **Weeping Rock**, where continuous rain "weeps" across a grotto. Even on a hot day, the spot remains cool. Like other parts of Zion, you should see lush, hanging cliff gardens thick with columbine, shooting-stars and scarlet monkeyflower. Pay close attention and you might spot the Zion snail, a creature found in the park and nowhere else.

The end of the road, so to speak, comes at **Temple of Sinawava**, perhaps the easiest area in the park to access. This huge natural amphitheater swarms with visitors enthralled by the sheer, red cliffs that soar to the sky and two stone pillars — the Altar and the Pulpit — in the center. There's a large parking area at the temple, but it fills quickly, so you may be forced to park up to a mile away alongside the Canyon Drive and hoof it back.

If you want to stay overnight, there are fine accommodations in the park or at nearby Springdale. Massive vermillion cliffs surround **Zion National Park Lodge**, (801) 586-7686, located in the heart of the park. A huge, manicured lawn and shade trees welcome guests to the property, which includes motel-style rooms, suites and cabins, which afford more privacy than guest rooms and feature fireplaces and private porches. Even if you don't spend the night, the lodge restaurant will satisfy every appetite with bountiful breakfasts, hearty lunches and gourmet dinners. Hamburgers, salads, seafood and steak are pleasantly presented amid the beauty of Zion.

In Springdale the rooms at **Flanigan's Inn**, 428 Zion Park Boulevard, (801) 772-3244, range from okay to very nice indeed. If you value spaciousness, splurge on the larger, suite-like spaces done in oak furnishings with tile baths, bentwillow wall hangings and ceiling fans.

American and English antique furniture fills **Under the Eaves Guest House**, 980 Zion Park Boulevard, (801) 772-3457. Constructed of sandstone blocks from nearby canyon walls, the home resembles a cheery English cottage. Full breakfast is served each morning, and guests can sip a cup of tea in the outdoor

INSIDERS' TIP

Adding to its collection of gangster memorabilia, Whiskey Pete's in Primm purchased the bullet-riddled, blood-stained shirt worn by Clyde Barrow (of Bonnie and Clyde) when he was killed by law enforcement agents.

gazebo that bursts with flowers or soak in the soothing outdoor spa.

In a quiet neighborhood, **Harvest House Bed and Breakfast**, 29 Canyon View Drive, (801) 772-3880, is sure to please even the most demanding guest. Expect bright, airy spaces full of wicker furniture, private baths, plush carpeting and balconies with an unparalleled view of Zion National Park. Beverages are available anytime from the dining room wet bar, and there's an extensive library of art and cookbooks.

When it's time for dinner, don't let the rustic appearance of **Bit and Spur Saloon and Mexican Restaurant**, 1212 Zion Park Boulevard, (801) 772-3498, fool you. Many consider this Utah's best Mexican restaurant. Besides standard favorites like chili rellenos and tostada supreme, the menu features deep-dish specials such as sour-cream and chicken enchiladas plus pasta diablo. Don't forget to take home one of their famous T-shirts.

Consistently good is the **Driftwood Restaurant,** 1515 Zion Park Boulevard in the Driftwood Lodge, (801) 772-3224, with its wraparound windows providing a glorious view of Zion. Utah mountain trout, crispy chicken and flame-broiled steaks top the dinner menu. For dessert there's a bountiful selection of homemade pies and cheesecake. Breakfast fare includes eggs, pancakes, muffins and the like.

If you have the time for some non-Vegas-like nightlife, the **Grand Circle Multimedia Sound and Light Show** is a treat for the senses at the O.C. Tanner Amphitheater in Springdale, (801) 673-4811. The production, which usually runs May through September, takes viewers on an odyssey through Zion National Park and other nearby national gems. The amphitheater also provides other top entertainment.

Bryce Canyon National Park

A child's jumbo-sized crayon box couldn't contain all the pastels, reds, violets, greens and blues found in the unspoiled land of Bryce Canyon National Park, about 210 miles northeast of Las Vegas in Southwestern Utah. Famous for its stupendous rock formations that seem to change color within the blink of an eye, Bryce contains a maze of trails that wind in and around its many wonders. To reach Bryce, drive east on I-15 past St. George, Utah, exit on Utah Highway 9 and drive until you reach Utah Highway 89. Exit here and drive north past the beautiful Cedar Breaks National Monument to Utah Highway 12, then exit and continue southeast until you reach Utah Highway 63, which leads to Bryce Canyon's main entrance.

Bryce is a national park on the jagged edge of the Paunsaugunt Plateau that really does defy superlatives. Even the gigantic summertime crowds can't distract from the natural amphitheaters, which are 50 million to 60 million years old, in the Pink Cliffs layer of the earth. Who'd have ever thought there were this many shades of red or shapes of rock? The sands and shales of Bryce, some softer than others, are the result of eons of erosion wearing away the limestone.

At sections of the parklike Silent City and other natural amphitheaters, the rock figures resemble chess pieces, a preacher, a woman playing the organ or faces that belong on Easter Island. Sculptured rock forms come in countless profiles, the most famous of which have been named "hoodoos." These, too, are ever-changing because of rainwater and snow seeping into the cracks of the rock, melting and thawing to wear away the layers.

Bryce Canyon's nooks and crannies are best explored on foot. But if time is a factor, it's wise to drive to the overlooks on the 21-mile park road for a sweeping look at the big picture. Start at the **Fairyland Point** lookout about 2 miles north of the visitors center to see the imaginary creatures, the looming **Boat Mesa** and mysterious **Chinese Wall** in Fairyland Canyon. The rather strenuous Fairyland Loop Trail also begins here.

For a concentrated collection of formations, head to the park's nucleus and either the **Sunrise** or **Sunset Point** lookouts to view the chess set-like "people" in **Queen's Garden**.

Walking along the Rim Trail, which skirts the canyon edge for a total of 11 miles, takes you to **Inspiration Point** and the eerie army of stone "people" called the **Silent City**. From the Rim Trail at this point it's possible to see the **Wall of Windows** and the majestic **Cathedral**.

Continuing south for another 2.5 miles takes you to **Bryce Point**, which allows breathtaking views of the whole Bryce Amphitheater. Three hiking trails, the Rim, Under-the-Rim and Peekaboo Loop, may be accessed from here. Horses share the Peekaboo Loop and take riders past profiles such as the **Alligator** and **Fairy Castle**.

From the main park road continue south for 7 miles to **Farview Point** to gaze at the natural wonders stretching hundreds of miles outside Bryce. The flat-topped mesa to the north is the **Aquarius Plateau**. South of the park are the distinctive **White Cliffs**.

Natural Bridge, with a huge opening in a rock, stands distinctly about 2 miles south of the Farview lookout. It's another 2 miles to **Ponderosa View Point**, where you can pick up the Agua Canyon connecting foot trail while seeing the lovely pink cliffs.

Drive the final 2 miles to **Rainbow Point** and **Yovimba Point** and end up at the park's highest points, towering at over 9,000 feet above sea level. A little more barren and rugged than other sections of Bryce, these two overlooks serve as trailheads for several hiking paths. It's worth the short jaunt on the **Bristlecone Loop Trail** to see the rare, gnarled trees up close and personal.

The closest real town to the park is **Tropic** — hometown to Ebenezer Bryce, the early park landlord who chose not to lose a cow here. There is a back route to Bryce from Tropic for foot travelers only, off the Peekaboo Loop trail. The easier way to go is by returning to Utah Highway 12 and traversing the 10 miles or so through lovely **Tropic Canyon**. A recently discovered natural bridge is on the east side of the highway about .3 mile north of the Water Canyon Bridge.

Once in Tropic, stop for a snack or to stretch your legs in this special village that remains true to its name. Flowers seem to dance in the gardens, and old trees stretch their limbs languorously. At the south end of town is **Ebenezer Bryce's old log cabin**, which houses Indian artifacts.

If you drove to Bryce Canyon by way of Springdale (Utah Highway 9) or Cedar Breaks National Monument (Utah Highway 14), consider returning through **Panguitch**, where Utah 143 will take you back to the interstate at Parowan. It's only a few additional miles, but the handsome, historic town is worth it.

A short walking tour through the center of town will give you a chance to see buildings left behind by early pioneers who founded the town in 1864. Begin the tour at the **Garfield County Courthouse**, 55 S. Main , built for just over $11,000 in 1907. Cross to the **Houston Home**, 72 S. Main, which was constructed of extra-large brick fired in a Panguitch kiln. The home's lumber and shingles also came from a local sawmill. Two blocks north you'll find the town's first jail, 45 S. Main, built in 1890 under the supervision of a probate judge. The tiny, one-room structure was constructed of 2 x 4s.

The building on the corner of 1st North and Main is a classic bit of architecture called the **Garfield Exchange**. It has housed just about every kind of business you can think of, from general merchandise to furniture, groceries and now a gift shop.

Prominent on Center (none of this region's main thoroughfares, like Center, Main and Tabernacle, go by the name "street") is the **Panguitch Social Hall Corporation**, 35 E. Center, which was first built in 1908 but burned shortly thereafter. On the same spot, using some original materials, another social hall was built. Now it houses the Panguitch Playhouse. Next door is a library that was built in 1908 thanks to a generous donation from Andrew Carnegie.

Finally, the city's **Daughters of the Utah Pioneer Museum**, Center and 1st East, is a lovely, brick monolith on the site of the old bishop's storehouse. Back in the mid-19th century, members of the Mormon Church paid their tithes with cattle and produce that were kept on this lot. Now, visitors trace the region's history here.

If you want to spend the night, cheap, clean

INSIDERS' TIP

Hoover Dam conducts special "Hard Hat" tours that take visitors beyond the standard tour. They are given daily and cost $25.

and very basic describes the motel rooms in Panguitch. But the nicer lodging is in Bryce Canyon.

The only one of the original trio of National Park Service properties that hasn't been devastated by fire, the **Bryce Canyon Lodge**, (801) 586-7686, is listed on the National Register of Historic Places. The three types of rooms — suites, cabins and doubles — fit most budgets and tastes. Splurging on a suite is a treat. These rooms ooze romance, from the white-wicker decor to Cleopatra chairs to the makeup mirror. Quaint log cabins have gas fireplaces, porches and dressing areas. Regu-

Photo: Las Vegas News Bureau

Hoover Dam, only 20 minutes south of Las Vegas, is southern Nevada's top tourist attraction.

lar rooms are furnished in Southwestern style. Open only from spring until late fall, the lodge tends to book well in advance.

Grand Canyon

No matter how many spectacular landscapes you've seen in your lifetime, none can quite compare with the Grand Canyon. And it always comes as a surprise whether you approach the North Rim or the South Rim. The landscape gives no hint that the canyon is there until suddenly you find yourself looking into the chasm 10 miles wide from rim to rim and a mile down to the Colorado River, winding silver through the canyon's inner depths.

The Grand Canyon is 277 miles long, extending from the western boundary of the Navajo Reservation to the vicinity of Lake Mead and Las Vegas. Only the highest section of each rim of the Grand Canyon is accessible by motor vehicle. Most of Grand Canyon National Park, both above and below the rim, is designated wilderness area that can only be explored on foot or by river raft.

The North Rim and the South Rim of the Grand Canyon are essentially separate destinations, more than 200 miles apart by road. This section covers the developed areas on both rims.

The Grand Canyon's **North Rim** is about 280 miles from Las Vegas, at the end of Arizona Highway 67, which forks off Utah Highway 89 at the resort village of Jacob Lake. From Las Vegas drive east on I-15 to the Utah 9 Exit north of St. George, Utah, about 130 miles. Continue east on Utah 9 through the towns of Hurricane and Springdale, then turn south on Utah 89 at the Mount Carmel junction.

To reach the canyon's **South Rim**, drive southeast on U.S. 95 through Boulder City to Kingman, Arizona, about 90 miles, then east on Interstate 40 to Williams. Exit and drive north on Ariz. 64 and Ariz. 180 to Grand Canyon Village, about 260 miles from Las Vegas.

More than 5 million years ago, the Colorado River began carving out this canyon that offers a panoramic look at the geologic history of the Southwest. Sweeping away sandstones and sediments, limestones and fossils, the river made its way through Paleozoic and Precambrian formations. By the time mankind arrived, the canyon extended nearly all the way down to schist, a basement formation.

The North Rim of the Grand Canyon receives only about one-tenth of the number of visitors as the South Rim. Snowbound during the winter, the North Rim is only open from mid-May through October, while the South Rim is open year-round.

The North Rim does not have the long, heavily traveled scenic drives that the South Rim has. The main road into the park deadends at the lodge and other tourist facilities at **Bright Angel Point**. The only other paved road is **Cape Royal Scenic Drive**, a 23-mile trip through stately ponderosa pine forest that takes you to several of the national park's most beautiful viewpoints — **Point Imperial**, **Vista Encantadora**, **Walhalla Overlook** and **Cape Royal**. Another road, unpaved and only passable in a high-clearance vehicle, runs 17 miles to Point Sublime. Other viewpoints on the North Rim are reached by hiking trails.

Adventuresome motorists can visit a separate area along the North Rim, **Toroweap Point**, by leaving Ariz. 89A at Fredonia, about 75 miles north of the North Rim entrance. Fill up the gas tank in Fredonia because you won't see another gas station for nearly 200 miles. Next, proceed west for 15 miles on Ariz. 389 to **Pipe Springs National Monument**, (602) 643-7105. Take time to see the monument. The remote, fortress-like old Mormon ranching outpost, once had the only telegraph station in the Arizona Territory north of the Grand Canyon. The ranch buildings and equipment are well-preserved, and the duck pond provides a cool oasis.

Backtrack 6 miles and turn south on an unpaved road. It goes 67 miles to the most remote point that can be reached by motor

INSIDERS' TIP

Built in 1932, the Boulder Theatre in Boulder City often hosted live performers, such as Hollywood greats Will Rogers and Boris Karloff.

vehicle on the Grand Canyon rim. The road is wide and well-maintained, easily passible by passenger car, but very isolated. You won't find a telephone or any other sign of habitation anywhere along the way. Have fun experiencing this wide-open countryside that's as empty as all of Arizona used to be long ago.

A small, primitive campground sits at **Toroweap Point**, but there's no water, and you'll probably have the place all to yourself. The elevation is 2,000 feet lower than at the main North Rim visitor area, so instead of pine forest the vegetation around Toroweap Point is desert scrub. Being closer to the river, still some 3,000 feet below, you can watch the flotilla of river rafts drifting past and even eavesdrop on passengers' conversations.

The **South Rim** of the Grand Canyon is the busy part of the park. From **Grand Canyon Village**, the large concession complex where the hotels, restaurants and stores are on the rim near the south entrance, two paved rim drives run in opposite directions.

The **West Rim Drive**, which follows the canyon rim for 8 miles west of Grand Canyon Village, is closed to private vehicles during the summer months. Visitors see it by free park shuttle bus or by bicycle. The road clings to the rim of the canyon as it takes you to a series of overlooks, each more spectacular than the last. **Pima Point**, in particular, offers what is probably the best of all Grand Canyon views. The drive ends at a place called **Hermit's Rest**, a former tourist camp where there are a snack bar and a hikers' trailhead.

The **Grand Canyon Visitor Center**, (602) 638-7888, is about 1 mile east of Grand Canyon Village. The most interesting exhibit in the visitor center is the display in the outdoor central plaza of boats that have been used to explore the Grand Canyon by river. A burned fragment is all that remains of one of the original wooden boats used by Major Powell in 1869. Other wooden boats are of more recent vintage. There is also one of the original inflatable river rafts used by the woman who in 1955 invented whitewater rafting as we know it today.

The **East Rim Drive** goes 25 miles east to the national park's east entrance, which is the entrance you will use if you are driving in from the North Rim. The **Yavapai Museum**, (602) 638-7890, about a half-mile east of the visitor center, offers detailed information on the canyon's geology, showing the ages and compositions of the many colorful layers of rock that make up its walls. You'll also find explanations of how and why the Colorado River could have formed the canyon by slicing its way through the highest plateau in the area instead of simply meandering around it.

As you proceed along East Rim Drive toward the east entrance, other overlooks — **Lipan Point**, **Zuni Point**, **Grandview Point**, **Yaki Point** — will beckon, each with a different perspective on the canyon's immensity.

There's another interesting museum along East Rim Drive. The **Tusayan Museum**, (602) 638-2305, 23 miles east of Grand Canyon Village near the park's east entrance, has exhibits on the Hopi people and their Anasazi ancestors who used to live along the rim of the Grand Canyon. In the Hopi belief system, the canyon is said to be the *sipapu*, the hole through which the earth's first people climbed from the mountaintop of their previous world into our present one.

The last point of interest you come to before leaving the park on East Rim Drive is the **Desert View Watchtower**, built in the 1930s as a replica of an ancient Hopi watchtower. It offers the last panoramic view of the Grand Canyon.

Real Estate

Welcome to America's hottest real estate market. In this city that attracts 5,000 new residents a month, more than 19,799 homes were sold in 1996, and the 1997 total was projected to top 20,000. And the supply is just barely keeping up with the demand.

Unlike other metropolitan areas, which have a balanced inventory of newer and older housing, upward of 60 percent of Las Vegas' real estate sales involve brand-new homes. On top of this, roughly 9,000 apartments are being built annually — and occupancy rates exceed 90 percent. Averaging 25 building permits per 1,000 residents, the city leads the entire nation in construction activity.

The net effect of all this has been a steady rise in housing costs. Once a bargain, Las Vegas' median home price now tops $120,000, which is comparable to regional and national figures. The rent for an average one-bedroom apartment is nearly $600. Gimme shelter!

Though the pace is dizzying, and the prices are creeping ever upward, don't despair. Averages can be misleading, and bargains exist if you look hard enough. Fact is, the Las Vegas housing market offers more variety than ever. From spanking new condominiums selling in the mid-$50,000s to multimillion-dollar custom estates, southern Nevada has something for every homebody.

Fierce competition among builders has kept new and resale home prices from skyrocketing out of sight. With 20 construction companies each selling more than 200 houses annually, buyers reap the benefits of economies of scale. The aggressive cost-cutting consciousness in the new-home market has also dampened appreciation among resales.

Indeed, astute buyers are finding that older homes may be the best value. Already equipped with window coverings, mature landscaping and perhaps a pool, some 5- and 10-year-old properties in Las Vegas can be purchased for only fractionally more than the price of an unimproved new dwelling.

The rising price of land is the No. 1 factor that's driving up new-home pricetags. Once dirt cheap, the value of Las Vegas real estate has been heading up, up, up. Builders are compensating by building smaller units on shrinking plots of land. The median size of a new home is a modest 1,566 square feet. That figure factors in condominiums, which now account for nearly 12 percent of the housing market.

Using concrete block walls to separate properties — and to encircle neighborhoods — builders are packing seven or eight dwellings onto a single acre. In new subdivisions, it is unusual to find a lot larger than 90 feet by 100 feet. If you want more, you'll be asked to pay extra in the form of a "lot premium."

As a trade-off for this claustrophobia, some developers have established common grounds for parks and lushly landscaped greenbelts along streets to give a feel of openness. Called master-planned communities, such developments are increasingly popular.

Master-planned communities are usually defined by their CC&Rs, the commonly used acronym for covenants, codes and restrictions. These neighborhood codes voluminously detail what is and isn't allowed. Most specify standards for landscaping, yard maintenance and color schemes. Some even dictate how long you can leave your garage door open. The codes are enforced by property managers hired by homeowner associations or developers. Master plans strive to deliver a total living experience, including retail shopping, recreational facilities and even office parks.

Though they may seem onerous and exacting, CC&Rs aim to enhance property values. By going beyond city and county codes, these neighborhood regulations escalate the fight against blight and neglect. It seems to be a popular selling point, as a growing percentage of new neighborhoods carry CC&Rs.

Two of the largest master-planned communities in the country are here: the 15,000-home Green Valley in Henderson and the 60,000-home Summerlin in the northwest. Like homeowners in other master plans scattered around the valley, these residents pay monthly association dues ranging from $25 to $125 a month. Additionally, Summerlin and Green Valley residents are assessed an annual charge to finance their community's capital expenditures for parks, roads and other amenities. Called Special Improvement Districts or Local Improvement Districts, these programs levy a household fee, usually based on the size of the homeowner's property. A typical lot might be assessed up to $10,000, paid over a 10- or 20-year period. That's over and above the usual property taxes.

Developers are usually forthcoming in divulging any applicable CC&Rs. So, too, are most real estate agents. But it behooves the savvy home shopper to always inquire about the existence of such codes and financial obligations. For homeowners who bridle at conformity and extra assessments, Las Vegas offers plenty of eclectic neighborhoods. Housing tracts —large and small, newer and older — await your perusal.

To help you get your bearings, we have divided the region into seven geographic areas. Because incorporated Las Vegas neighborhoods and unincorporated Clark County neighborhoods are virtually indistinguishable in terms of services and ambiance, this chapter does not arbitrarily separate the two. Instead, we use the broader directional groupings commonly favored by local residents. The cities of North Las Vegas, Henderson and Boulder City, however, do have unique identities and merit their own sections.

This chapter concentrates on larger-scale developments and the characteristics that define the area. It is not intended to be an exhaustive compendium of the builders and housing tracts in southern Nevada. With hundreds of locally based contractors and new housing additions springing up each month, such information would be unwieldy, not to mention outdated by press time. Current news about builders and communities can be obtained in the Sunday real estate section of the *Las Vegas Review-Journal and Sun* (online at www.lvrjsun.com) and from a variety of free home-shopping guides available at all major grocery stores.

Descriptions of the valleywide rental market and real estate companies appear at the end of the chapter.

Neighborhoods and Developments

Downtown

Some of the oldest homes in the valley can be found here. Like downtown districts in most cities, Las Vegas' central neighborhoods are a mix of the dilapidated and the exquisite. Three bedroom homes can be purchased for as little as $45,000, but these are usually in poor condition and mired in crime-ridden areas.

The areas directly adjoining the downtown core are among the most dangerous sections of the valley. The so-called "Naked City" around the Stratosphere Tower has a particularly poor reputation. Police have made a practice of stopping cab drivers and other motorists rolling through the area in an effort to crack down on drug deals and prostitution.

INSIDERS' TIP

Seventy-nine percent of the homes purchased in Clark County sold for less than $150,000 in 1996. Just 7.5 percent cost $250,000 or more.

The Finest Apartments in Las Vegas are as Close as Your Telephone!

Apartments for Every Budget & Lifestyle
Over 20 Communities to Choose From

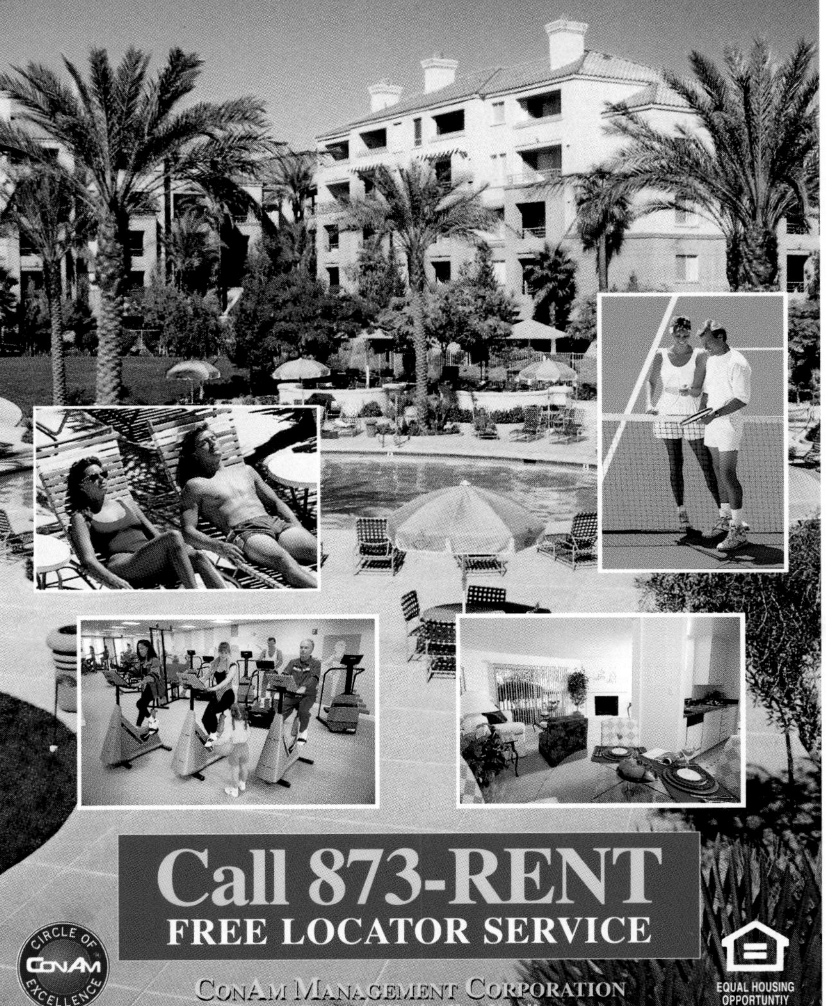

One enclave, however, has managed to keep urban blight at bay. The quiet, tree-lined residential streets just southeast of the intersection of Charleston and Las Vegas boulevards feature well-maintained homes from the 1940s and 1950s. Residents are a mixture of long-established Las Vegas families and young professionals such as lawyers and accountants. Lots are roomy, and prices range from $80,000 for cute bungalows to more than $300,000 for more sprawling ranch-style lots (no horses allowed, though!).

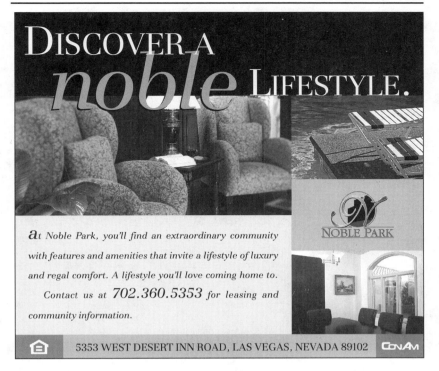

Just west of Interstate 15, along Alta and Rancho drives, more posh homes can be found. Popular spots for doctors (Valley Hospital Medical Center and University Medical Center are nearby), these established neighborhoods are only a five-minute drive to downtown.

Two of the most exclusive neighborhoods are **Rancho Circle** and **Rancho Bel Air**, both of which are gated and guarded by a 24-hour security staff. Among Rancho Circle's most famous residents is Phyllis McGuire of the McGuire Sisters singing trio. Home prices range from the mid-200,000s for a modest 1950s bungalow to more than $1 million for large estates.

Northwest

The fastest-growing section of the city, the northwest spreads north of Charleston Boulevard and west to the hills. The giant Summerlin master-planned development sprawls over the largest single chunk of territory, but the northwest defies easy description.

Low-income sections are generally clustered on the older, eastern edges. Toward the north, long-established ranch estates, complete with barns, are set cheek-by-jowl with encroaching tract homes. Like much of the Las Vegas Valley, the northwest has the look of a checkerboard, with tightly-packed neighborhoods punctuating larger expanses of uninhabited desert.

But those raw pieces of land are disappearing quickly. Commercial centers are following the steady march of new development. New roads are being built, and existing roads, including the U.S. 95 Expressway, are being widened. Housing tracts are now being built more than 20 miles northwest of downtown.

Desert Shores, a planned community of man-made lakes, has 3,500 homes at Summerlin's northeastern border. **Painted Desert**, a golf course community of 1,600 homes, is 10 miles to the north along U.S. 95. Both have all but finished building, but an army of new developers forges ahead. Among their projects are the 2,700-home **Elkhorn Springs** and the 1,700-home **Iron Mountain Ranch** in the far northwest. The homes run the gamut from $60,000 condominiums to $300,000 semicustom houses.

Sun City Summerlin also has wrapped up construction. Restricted to homeowners 55 years old and older (no children are allowed to live here) this retirement community features duplexes and freestanding homes. All built since the late 1980s, the residential decor is stucco-and-tile Southwestern. Nearly all homes are single story. Prices, which started in the low $100,000s, have risen steadily, with the community showing some of the best appreciation rates in the valley. The developer, the Del Webb Corp., has launched a slightly smaller retirement community in Henderson.

Summerlin, whose master developer is the Howard Hughes Corp., continues to push west into the foothills and south into the unincorporated county. At buildout, more than 185,000 residents will call Summerlin home. Organized into "villages" of roughly 2,000 homes apiece, Summerlin's dwellings range from apartments to multimillion-dollar mansions. Condominiums start in the low $100,000s, and most tract homes sell for between $150,000 and $300,000. Being Las Vegas, six hotel-casinos, reminiscent of Scottsdale, Arizona resorts, will be added to the mix as the development unfolds.

The 22,500-acre Summerlin community has built parks that are free and open to the public, not just the homeowners. The Summerlin Community Association keeps the venues hopping by sponsoring periodic concerts and art fairs. The latest large-scale project is construction of an Olympic-size pool complex adjacent to a newly constructed high school and branch of the community college. Ultimately, the Summerlin Trail — a scenic paved path for walkers, joggers and bicyclists — will connect all villages and extend more than 50 miles in length.

Tournament Hills, the posh custom-home development bordering the private Tournament Players Club golf course, is particularly impressive for its unsurpassed array of architectural styles. Tudor, Southwestern, French Provincial and a wide variety of ultramodern motifs are set alongside each other. Smaller than most villages, Tournament Hills has fewer than 300 custom lots. The homes run $800,000 and up. Like most upscale neighborhoods, it is gated and guarded by a security staff, so you'll need an invitation or a Realtor to get in.

West Valley

South of Charleston Boulevard and west to the hills, the west valley is generally county territory. Home to Spring Valley, the region's first attempt at a master-planned type of community, this area features some of the most exclusive addresses in Clark County.

On its eastern fringe, the **Scotch 80s** are south of Charleston Boulevard and east of Rancho Drive. The origin of its name is as enigmatic as the neighborhood itself. Once on the outskirts of town, it is now surrounded by apartments, modest homes and noisy thoroughfares. Its entrances have been blocked, and access can only be gained via a guarded

INSIDERS' TIP

As of 1996, there were 274,809 children younger than 18 in Clark County. While that's 25 percent of the population, and represents a 7.4 percent increase from the previous year, 70 percent of the county's households have no minor children at all. North Las Vegas has the highest percentage of households with children younger than 18, at 46 percent.

gate. It has been a longtime home to some of Las Vegas' elite, including, at one time, Mirage Resorts Chairman Steve Wynn and his family. Prices tend to be in the high six figures, but there are some smaller homes that can be found at less than $200,000. Those may be aging fixer-uppers, however.

West of Rainbow Boulevard, between Flamingo Road and Charleston Boulevard, are areas generically known as **Sections 7 and 10**. There are no strict neighborhood codes here, so the custom architecture ranges from southwestern to Tudor. Larger lots and wide open spaces define these sections. Some three-bedroom homes run less than $200,000, while larger estates top $1 million.

More typically, though, the west valley is turning toward master plans and planned communities. Launched by **Spring Valley**, a 4,000-home tract started in the late 1970s, a steady stream of such communities has followed. Spring Valley is still a desirable location, 6 miles due west of the southern Strip. But it's a mixed bag, with some of its 1970s homes beginning to show their age. Built in the days before tile roofs were common, these modest tract homes are past their peak of appreciation and can be purchased for less than $100,000.

The Lakes, built in the mid-1980s at what was then the end of Sahara Avenue, embraces more than 4,000 homes in, you guessed it, an aquatic setting of man-made lakes. Prices range from the low $100,000s to more than $1 million. Lots tend to be small, and the homes have a uniform tile-and-stucco look in neutral tones. At the northern entrance is a giant Citibank credit card processing center and a collection of medical offices.

Across Sahara Avenue, **Canyon Gate**, a more pricey enclave, features a private golf course, its own lakes and 550 homes that begin around $250,000. It's impressive entry features large waterfalls and, of course, a large security station and gate.

To the west is **Peccole Ranch**, a grassy enclave of 3,600 homes priced from the mid-$100,000s to more than $500,000. Southwestern motifs prevail here, with lots of young trees and grassy play areas. Unlike The Lakes and Canyon Gate, which are virtually built out, Peccole (pronounced pe-KO-lee) continues to expand. Incorporating a series of community parks and stunning views of Red Rock Canyon 10 miles to the west, Peccole Ranch will ultimately be adjoined by Summerlin's southern extension. One striking community on Peccole Ranch's northern edge is **Queensridge**. The gated community features Old European architecture, a stunning contrast to the prevailing Southwestern themes of this valley. An elaborate bronze statue of 17-foot-tall galloping horses marks the entry. Home prices begin in the $250,000 range.

South of Tropicana Avenue are **Spanish Trail**, **Spanish Hills** and **Rhodes Ranch**. Spanish Trail, built in the mid-'80s, is designed around a private golf course. Like Canyon Gate, its homes run $300,000 and up. Greg Maddux, the Cy Young Award-winning pitcher and Las Vegas native, owns two homes in Spanish Trail. The Sultan of Brunei purchased nearly 20 acres on the community's western edge to build a massive compound for his family and entourage. Spanish Hills, directly to the west, is still under construction, with $200,000 homes mixed in among million-dollar estates. Custom lots start at $120,000 and have some of the best east-facing views of the city. To the south, Rhodes Ranch is breaking ground on 1,000 acres, which will accommodate 4,000 tract houses starting in the mid-$100,000s, a golf course and recreational facilities. Both are projects of Rhodes Development, a locally owned company.

East Valley

The east valley is the west valley's older sibling. Much of Las Vegas' early growth headed east from The Strip. The first large apartment complexes were spawned here, and the first single-family homes were built just beyond them.

East valley neighborhoods, which sprang up in the late 1970s, range from modest dwellings to rural estates. One notable area runs along Tomiyasu Lane, bordering the giant Sunset Park (it's generically referred to as Tomiyasu). Entertainer Wayne Newton and boxer Mike Tyson are two celebrities who call this area home. This neighborhood, with its deep setbacks and individual gates, affords the kind of privacy rarely found elsewhere around town.

By contrast, the rest of the east valley is a generally unremarkable collection of 1970s vintage homes. Most areas are built out, and tract houses sell for $100,000 and up. A few upscale homes lay behind security gates. And some tract neighborhoods are quaint refuges lined by big shady trees and generous landscaping that has flourished over time.

But sections along Boulder Highway, as it extends from downtown, have not aged particularly well. High crime and low-minded graffiti mar the commercialized areas. High-density apartments have a rundown look after just 10 or 15 years. Some say that the proliferation of casinos along what is called the Boulder Strip has contributed to the decay.

Meantime, a couple of newer neighborhoods have sprung up on opposite ends of east valley. **Silverado**, featuring 2,000 homes set on 1,000 acres, is being developed in a southwestern pocket off Maryland Parkway, about 6 miles south of UNLV. It is being developed by American West Homes, along with other builders including Astoria, Watt, Pageantry and Woodside Homes. Residences from three to six bedrooms start in the high $100,000s. In the eastern foothills, the **Orchards** will have 2,500 homes squeezed onto 465 acres. Since it is not a master-planned community, this Lewis Homes development has no parks or common grounds of its own. It is, however, near a large county park. Prices at both projects begin in the low $100,000s.

North Las Vegas

Directly north of downtown, this city is home to blue-collar families and a high percentage of low-income residents. Its southern sections have large African-American and Latino populations. And while the city is refurbishing some of its main thoroughfares in this older area, the residential sections tend to be a hodgepodge of small and sometimes seedy dwellings.

INSIDERS' TIP

Clark County has 150 mobile home parks and more than 30,000 mobile homes. Also called manufactured homes, their prices range from $30,000 to $60,000. An information clearinghouse for buyers is the Mobile Home Finder, at 454-1050.

The northern section of the city is an entirely different story. This burgeoning area, between U.S. 95 and Interstate 15, is the fastest growing sector of the entire valley. Modest tract homes, most fewer than 2,000 square feet, are packed into walled-off subdivisions. They sell fast because prices here are, on average, 10 to 20 percent less than comparable homes elsewhere. However, due to past financial difficulties, North Las Vegas' property taxes are the highest in the valley. The commute south into the valley is no picnic either. And the city's crime rate consistently ranks as the worst in southern Nevada — though much of that crime is concentrated in the older sections.

The largest development is called **Eldorado**. Stretching across the city's northern plateau, this Pardee Homes community opened in 1990. It encompasses 1,080 acres and 8,500 homes ranging in price from the low $100,000s to $250,000. The only large-scale master-planned community in North Las Vegas, it features generous common grounds and wide boulevards.

Overall, North Las Vegans probably feel more growing pains than most southern Nevada communities. Parks, police, athletic fields and libraries are in chronically short supply here. Many major streets are still works in progress. And neighborhood shopping centers have been virtually nonexistent until recently.

Henderson

Once an industrial city, Henderson has taken on something of a split personality. Like North Las Vegas, it's a tale of the old and the new. Fifteen miles southeast of downtown Las Vegas, the oldest sections of Henderson have changed little since the city's incorporation in 1944. With names like Titanium and Magnesium streets, these working-class neighborhoods are lined with humble bungalows. Built with concrete blocks, they have stood the test of time. The downtown center, running along Water Street, retains a 1950s flavor of small shops — some are quaint, and some are barely holding on. Housing prices also seem to be a throwback to an earlier era, with older two-bedroom homes selling for $60,000 or so.

Just to the west, and seemingly light years away, is **Green Valley**. Begun in 1974, this master-planned community developed by the American Nevada Corp. extends over 8,400 acres. So far, 15,000 homes have been built. Another 6,000 homes are under construction in a southern addition called **Green Valley Ranch**. Prices run from $75,000 condominiums to million-dollar golf course estates. Green Valley, while inside Henderson's city limits, is for all practical purposes a freestanding community. Its residents, while varied, tend to be newcomers and move-up buyers.

Golf Course Communities

Ah, home on the range.

Golf course living is alive and growing in Las Vegas. Dozens of link-side communities have sprung up in recent years. And as southern Nevada continues to expand, more newcomers are seeking their place along the fairways and greens.

The economics aren't for the fainthearted. Lot premiums for property facing golf courses can run from a few thousand dollars up to $500,000. Most lots are less than a quarter-acre, and golf privileges are almost invariably extra, with memberships ranging from $3,000 to $30,000.

Nonetheless, builders and homebuyers are coming. At Seven Hills, in the southern end of the valley, nine builders are constructing 3,600 houses in the $100,000-to-$300,000 range. In northwest community of Summerlin, custom homes are sprouting like weeds, albeit expensive ones, along two Tournament Players Club courses. Semi-customs in Country Club Hills start around $500,000, and lot premiums run in the low $100,000s. Tournament Hills features custom estates and pricetags into the millions.

Lake Las Vegas, a master-planned community being built along the shores of a man-made lake in Henderson, is even more exclusive. The south shore features a Jack Nicklaus-designed private course dotted with 380 custom homes that start at $1 million. On the north shore, four public courses are planned, along with a Hyatt resort encircled by smaller homes and condominiums.

Photo: Jim Decker/Review-Journal

Dozens of link-side communities have sprung up in Las Vegas in recent years.

To entice and entertain homeowners, some of the newer communities have added important amenities. Seven Hills integrates parks and trails throughout the neighborhoods while providing some of the best panoramic views in the region. Rhodes Ranch — a 1,000-acre, 4,000-home development weaving in and around a new golf course in the southwest section of the valley — features a full-scale recreation center anchored by an Olympic-size swimming pool. The concept is similar to the Sun City retirement communities at Summerlin and MacDonald Ranch in Henderson, except that Rhodes Ranch does

— continued on next page

not impose Sun City's rule that homeowners must be 55 or older. Queensridge, an upscale blend of new custom and tract homes along the Badlands Golf Course on Las Vegas' far west side, will soon be accompanied by a giant regional shopping mall.

Many Realtors believe that golf course properties can be good investments — if you honor the old location-location-location adage.

"Spanish Trail (in the southwest) has a very strong market in resales, particularly at $1 million and above," said one broker, noting that its maturity and its exclusively 27-hole private course help to keep prices firm.

Other experts suggest that shrewd shoppers should zero in on developments still under construction because the builder will usually continue to keep prices down until close-out. Either way, local real estate observers figure that golf course properties will almost always accrue in value faster than other residential areas.

A local appraiser specializing in golf properties sees Las Vegas as an emerging leader in golf course communities: "We have the climate to allow year-round play," he said. "We're becoming a retirement community, and golf is a big thing with those folks."

Country Club Hills, at the TPC, confirms those hunches. When the tract opened in 1993, homes were selling in the $200,000s. Now that the 171-unit development is built out, those same models are fetching $400,000.

Its schools, while part of the countywide school district, tend to be a cut above the rest. It has its own commercial centers and, recently, casinos.

In general, Henderson and Green Valley residents have been supportive of taxpayer bond issues for public works projects and, thus, the city has a higher per-capita share of parks and recreation facilities. The American Nevada Corp. does its part by sponsoring family-oriented park activities and art shows.

Due to Green Valley's explosive growth, Henderson is now the third-biggest city in Nevada behind Las Vegas and Reno. And from a transportation standpoint, this area has had problems. Residents frequently complain about the circuitous maze of streets to U.S. 95, the nearest freeway. That's changing, though, with the construction of the southeastern beltway (U.S. 215) that will connect the community with the southern end of The Strip and Interstate 15. Overhead, however, residents still must endure the constant parade of jets flying into McCarran International Airport. Green Valley's hillside neighbor, **Whitney Ranch**, is particularly susceptible to that daily dull roar of jet engines as it lies directly under the busiest flight path.

Other notable communities within Henderson are **Sun City MacDonald Ranch**, **Seven Hills** and **Lake Las Vegas**. Sun City MacDonald Ranch, an age-restricted community in the southern foothills, is modeled after its Summerlin counterpart. Still under construction, it will have 6,500 homes and a full complement of golf and recreational facilities. Prices are just slightly less than Sun City Summerlin (see our Northwest section of this chapter), and the age minimum for homeowners has been lowered to 50 here.

Seven Hills, a new mix of tract and custom homes, is just west of Green Valley Ranch. Seven Hills is selling now and will continue to build out for at least five years. Its 3,600 homes will be set in a hilly, parklike enclave that will feature some of the best views of the valley. Its landscaping, utilizing mainly natural desert flora, is a distinctive departure from many de-

INSIDERS' TIP

The biggest home builders in Clark County in 1996 were Lewis Homes, Del Webb Corp., American West Homes, Pardee Homes, Rhodes Homes, Pacific Homes and Pulte Home Corp. Lewis alone sold 1,500 homes, and the seven companies' combined sales accounted for 30 percent of the new-home market.

velopments. Instead of the omnipresent bermuda and fescue lawns, Seven Hills features tall deer grass, native trees and flowering plants. Prices for the tract homes start in the lower $100,000s. Custom-lot prices begin at $60,000 for a quarter-acre. A golf course was under construction as this book went to press.

Lake Las Vegas is east toward Lake Mead. Spreading along the 10-mile shoreline of a 320-acre man-made lake, this upscale community features custom estates, golf and resort living on 2,245 acres. The south shore is home to 350 custom estates and a private Jack Nicklaus-designed golf course. Lake Las Vegas homes average more than $1 million, with some topping $2 million. The north shore, still in the planning stages, will feature a Hyatt resort and a Marriott, more than 1,000 homes and, of course, more golf. Most north shore dwellings will be townhouses or tract homes starting in the low $150,000s. Because of Lake Las Vegas' relatively remote location among winding roads and hillsides, the commute to the Las Vegas Strip or downtown can take nearly an hour.

Boulder City

If you're looking for something away from the crowds and the casinos, Boulder City is your place. This self-proclaimed "clean, green" community lies 30 miles southeast of downtown Las Vegas and overlooks Lake Mead. Originally established as a federally run community for the workers building Hoover Dam in the 1930s, Boulder City remains the most unconventional of Nevada cities. Gambling is illegal, and not a single slot machine can be found here. And growth controls are so strict that the population has barely budged over 14,000.

Much of the housing stock is 30 years old or older. And, unlike some Las Vegas Valley neighborhoods that take on a tattered look after just a few years, Boulder City residents take pride in longevity. The sense of tradition is exemplified in the community's robust schedule of citywide festivals. (For a rundown, see our Annual Events chapter.) That pride translates into generally strong residential resale values.

A few new housing tracts have cropped up in recent years, and homes can be purchased in the mid-$100,000s. But the city's growth controls have virtually prohibited the kind of large cluster developments so common in Las Vegas. Most of the building activity in Boulder City is oriented toward custom homes set on single lots.

About the Industry

With residential housing permits valued at $1.6 billion each year, building is big business in Clark County. The **Southern Nevada Homebuilders Association**, 3685 Pecos McLeod Street, 794-0117, is the local consortium that embraces the building trades — from the biggest contractors to mom-and-pop plumbers.

For newcomers trying to pick and choose among the scores of builders in the valley, the SNHA recommends its affiliated *Homebuyers Guide*. This free monthly publication, which can be found at supermarkets and convenience stores everywhere, highlights new developments on an easy-to-use map. It also contains price ranges and telephone numbers. The Saturday and Sunday editions of the *Las Vegas Review-Journal and Sun* carry similar information.

But as the old saying goes: Buyer beware. No publication rates the quality of homebuilders' workmanship. Consumers need to do their homework. In Las Vegas, it's not uncommon for shoppers to tour scores of model homes in dozens of developments as the best way to narrow their search. By closely inspecting the models and questioning the sales staff, prospective buyers can usually get a good feel for the company's quality and culture.

Home seekers should ask what kind of warranty coverage is offered. They should inquire about upgrades and incentives. And they ought to tour some of the builder's already established neighborhoods to see how those communities have held their value.

Buyers of existing or custom houses should be equally diligent and vigilant. Realtors, while not essential in purchases at new-home tracts that have full-service sales staffs, are most helpful in resale transactions. The

Greater Las Vegas Association of Realtors, 1750 E. Sahara Avenue, 732-8177, registers Realtors and ensures that proper disclosures are made about properties. When a Realtor is acting as a buyer's agent, he or she has expertise to protect your interest.

The **Nevada Division of Real Estate,** 2501 E. Sahara Avenue, 486-4033, regulates the industry, issuing Realtor licenses and adjudicating disputes between Realtors and their clients.

Another resource is the state **Contractors Board**, 4220 S. Maryland Parkway, Suite 800. This agency licenses contractors and investigates construction-related disputes. The board can tell you if a builder is licensed or if a company has any complaints filed against it. The Contractors Board's Las Vegas number is 486-1100. With this boom town's insatiable appetite for builders, some unlicensed contractors slip under the radar screen. So it's a particularly good idea for custom-home shoppers to check any builder's status with the Contractors Board.

But there is a loophole here. Small-scale custom home builders don't have to be licensed if they own the land and call themselves "owner builders." Ironically, non-licensed outfits are beyond the purview of the Contractors Board precisely because they are not licensed. Aggrieved buyers have found themselves in this Catch-22 and mired in protracted civil litigation trying to recover damages for faulty workmanship. Authorities say it's best to insist on licensed credentials up front.

Apartments

Roughly one-third of Clark County's population resides in apartments. With more than 100,000 units in the area, apartments can be found in every corner of the valley. Most, however, are clustered along major freeways and thoroughfares.

The residential housing stock in the central north-south corridor bracketing The Strip — from Maryland Parkway on the east to Decatur Boulevard on the west — is predominantly apartments. As urban development extends outward, many new apartment complexes can be found along U.S. 95 heading northwest and southeast. Monthly rents for a studio unit range from $400 in older sections of the city to $800 at gate-guarded luxury complexes. The citywide average for a two-bedroom, two-bath unit is $650.

Today, Las Vegas apartments are becoming more like condominiums, with personal washers and dryers, covered parking (a major plus in the summer) and exercise facilities. Automated gates and manicured grounds lend a look of exclusivity. Those amenities are factors that explain those rising rents. But Las Vegas' itinerant demographics, which include a higher-than-usual

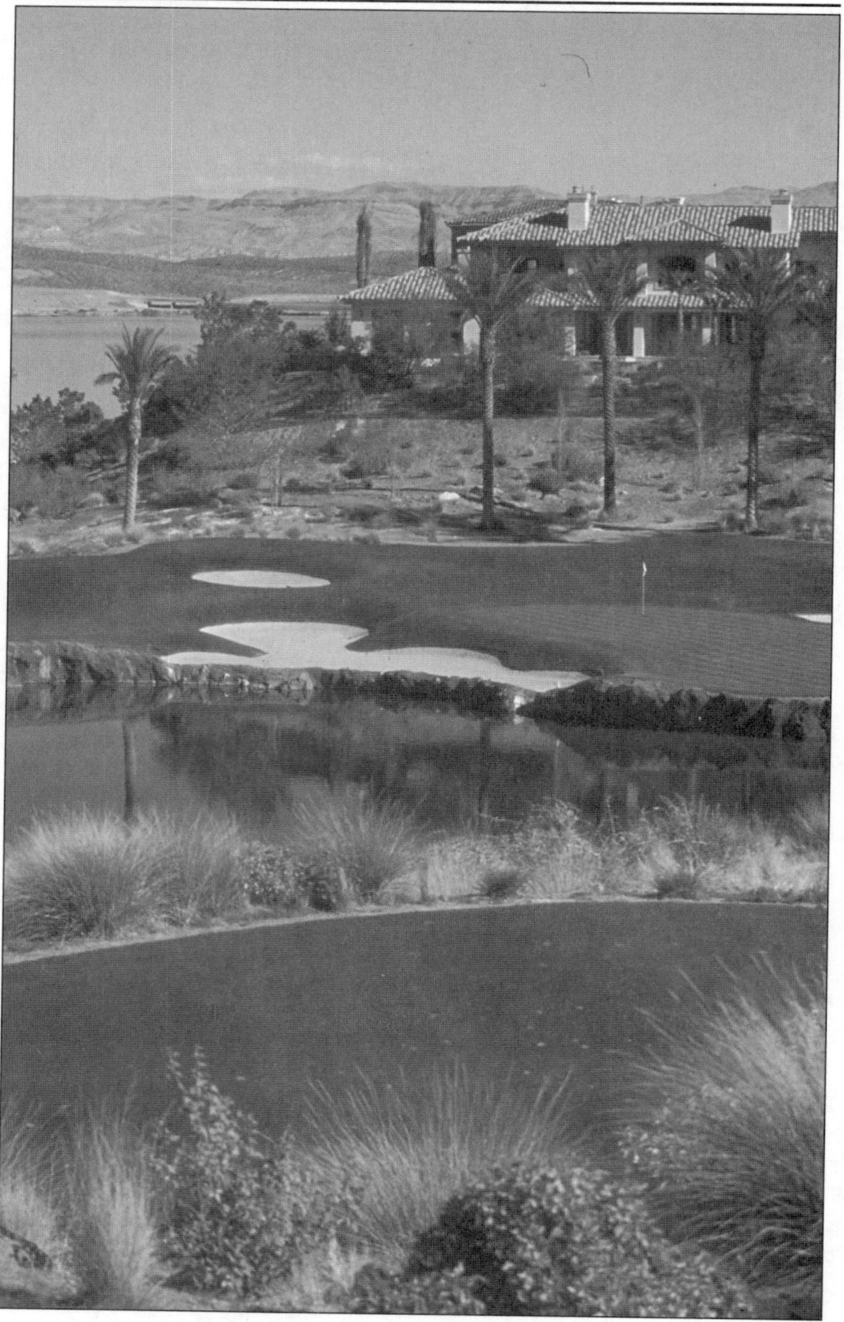

Photo: Jim Decker/Review-Journal

Lake Las Vegas, a lakefront community in Henderson, features million-dollar estates and a private golf course.

percentage of newcomers, drive costs upward too. The constant churn of residents fuels a busy rental market.

So how do you find what's right for you? It depends on what you're looking for.

Two companies — **Pacific Properties** and **Oasis Development** — operate large, modern complexes all over town. Many of the upscale units blur the distinction between rented apartments and purchased townhouses. Furnished and unfurnished flats come with fireplaces, ceiling fans, microwaves and vaulted ceilings.

Oasis is Las Vegas' No. 1 apartment company, with 48 complexes, 13,000 units and rental prices ranging from $390 to $1,300. Pacific Properties, which has 12 complexes with a total of more than 3,000 units, will even apply rent dollars toward a new-home purchase with its sister corporation, Pacific Homes. Oasis can be reached at 435-9800. Pacific's telephone number is 735-0191. Another major player in the local apartment scene is **Con Am Management Corp.**, 256-1797, which has 9,380 rental units at 30 properties, including the brand new Noble Park Apartments, 5353 W. Desert Inn Road. Rent rebates of up to $300 are given to Con Am tenants who refer friends or co-workers to the company's apartments. Con Am also has a relocation number, 873-RENT. Another company to try is **H & L Management**, 385-5611.

The wide variety in the market is typified in the densely populated area just east of The Strip. Off Flamingo Road, near Paradise Road, is the 680-unit **Meridian at Hughes Center**. This gate-guarded complex is inside one of Las Vegas' leading corporate office centers, and its two-bedroom suites rent for up to $1,400 a month.

Less than a mile to the south, the gigantic **Harbor Island** complex on Harmon Avenue rents 1,000 units for less than $600, all utilities paid. Some smaller complexes nearby will even undercut that price.

To help wade through the thicket of rental possibilities, a number of free apartment guides are available at local supermarkets and convenience stores. *For Rent* magazine is one of the thickest publications, publishing nearly

300 pages twice monthly. The magazine is organized geographically and spotlights special move-in deals and discounts. Other free, albeit slimmer, publications include the *Apartment Tour Guide* and the *Greater Las Vegas Apartment Guide*. The *Las Vegas Review-Journal and Sun* carry daily updated listings of rental properties, including houses and rooms to share.

The **Nevada Apartment Association** is a good source of information about tenant rights. Complaints can be filed on the association's hotline, 382-3256. Disputes between landlords and tenants also can be taken to the **Nevada Fair Housing Office**, 333 N. Rancho Drive, Suite 700, 388-6500.

FYI

Unless otherwise noted, the area code for all phone numbers listed in this chapter is 702.

Real Estate Companies

The **Greater Las Vegas Association of Realtors**, 732-8177, maintains a list of more than 4,000 registered Realtors in the valley. The list is available for free at the association's offices at 1750 East Sahara Avenue. Like the homebuilders association, however, the Realtors group does not make specific recommendations. The best advice is to shop around and, if possible, utilize referrals from friends and coworkers.

The following list highlights a cross-section of real estate brokerages in the valley. All have access to the local computerized Multiple Listing Service, which contains more than 5,000 homes for sale. Many of the firms are large franchises affiliated with major chains, which have national networks and relocation services. But we have also included some smaller companies that enjoy solid local reputations. In instances where a firm has multiple offices, the main addresses and phone numbers are listed.

Americana Better Homes and Gardens

3420 E. Tropicana Ave. • 796-7777, (800) 456-4885

With five offices around the valley, Americana has sold more properties in the last decade than any other local brokerage. The company's 1996 sales volume topped $1 billion, and last year it opened the state's largest realty office, a 19,000-square-foot complex on E. Tropicana Avenue. Home to 100 of Americana's 400 agents, the office contains private offices, spacious conference rooms and the latest high-tech computer links to affiliated franchises across the United States and Canada, a helpful tool to customers moving into and out of Nevada. A new program called "Value Link" provides local discounts to newcomers on a host of household products and services ranging from water softeners to gardening equipment.

Asian American Realty

4033 Spring Mountain Rd. • 222-0078

Seven agents, fluently speaking seven Asian dialects, specialize in helping Chinese and others from the Pacific Rim find homes in Las Vegas. In bridging the language gap, founder and owner Betty Chan personally sold more than $10 million in homes and real estate in 1996. Opened in 1993, Asian American Realty sells most of its properties in the $150,000 to $300,000 range. Many of its transactions are in the southwest section of the valley, an area roughly bounded on Charleston Boulevard on the north and Jones Boulevard on the east.

Bond Realty

213 E. Colorado Ave. • 388-0030

This small office, established in the 1950s, specializes in the purchase and sale of raw land. With a clientele that ranges from local residents to international investors, Bond scours southern Nevada for real estate values. Much of the company's business involves small parcels of 2½ to 5 acres. Says one broker: "In the '50s, you could buy 5 acres for $500. Today, that same piece may cost $300,000. We try to give small investors a chance to be a player in the market."

Century 21 Money World

4310 E. Tropicana Ave. • 435-8300, (800) 4HOUSES

The world's largest network of real estate agents has 18 independently owned and operated offices in the Las Vegas Valley. With 100,000 agents across the globe, Century 21 uses computer technology to link operations and facilitate relocations. The company maintains its own computerized list of home listings nationwide. Money World, with two outlets, is the longest established Century 21 brokerage in the city.

Coldwell Banker Premier Realty

3690 E. Tropicana Ave. • 458-7070, (800) 758-7071

Relocation is a specialty of this national franchise, which has 180 local Realtors. On a personal level, this brokerage will compile information packets for prospective out-of-state buyers, with data on schools, neighborhoods, shopping and recreation. The material is customized to the family's interests and needs. Coldwell Banker also links up with local companies to furnish "area orientations" to incoming job applicants. Services include hotel reservations and airport pickups. Unlike many Las Vegas firms, Coldwell Banker will also show property in outlying communities such as Pahrump and Mesquite. The firm annually handles $280 million in residential transactions.

Creative Realty

1405 W. Sunset Rd. • 547-1800

If you're looking for a brand-new home, this 17-agent office may be a good place to begin. Creative Realty, which is headquartered in Las Vegas, has the design plans for new-home tracts throughout the valley. The company's agents also have access to many developments even after their model home centers close for the day. Half of Creative's sales involve new homes, a higher-than-average figure for Realtors.

Fortune Properties

1601 S. Rainbow Blvd., Ste. 140 • 255-2800

This brokerage, founded in 1992, has 35 agents and transacts $20 million in property sales annually. Working with newcomers and locals alike, Fortune offers customized relocation information to out-of-towners. One specialized niche is Fortune's work with small business owners who are looking to move their operations here or are seeking to expand their existing trade. The company helps such firms find small commercial and retail space.

Howard Hughes Properties

1480 Town Center Dr. • 255-2500

Want to build a home? This company, specializing in Summerlin, has custom lots available. Inside gated communities and not carried on the Greater Las Vegas Association of Realtors' Multiple Listing Service, these exclusive lots range from $80,000 to $300,000. To help newcomers winnow the large field of residential construction companies, Hughes provides a Featured Builders List of eight local contractors. Hughes also has a small inventory of newly constructed luxury homes erected by these builders. These Summerlin estate homes are priced from $500,000 to $1.5 million.

Liberty Realty

4055 S. Spencer St., Ste. 130 • 734-2525

One of the largest independent realty companies in the valley, Liberty has agents working in just about every facet of residential property. One particular specialty is the Las Vegas Country Club and Regency Towers, upscale communities just east of The Strip. The 28-story Regency Towers feature 218 condominium dwellings overlooking the exclusive private club, and Liberty brokers account for a majority of the towers' sales. The Liberty brokers frequently work with tourists who, on the spur of the moment, want to check out local real estate offerings.

Nevada First Business Brokers

4850 W. Flamingo Rd., Ste. 13 • 368-2500

The largest business broker in Nevada, this company buys and sells everything from pizza joints and taverns to motels and manufacturing plants. Investment property, including undeveloped acreage and apartment complexes, also is in this firm's portfolio. With statewide reach, it even lists bordellos in the rural counties where prostitution is legal. Nevada First Business Brokers employs 25 licensed real estate agents who conduct appraisals and provide confidential market analyses. Its clients include entrepreneurs, investors and professional buyers.

Properties Plus

2001 E. Flamingo Rd., Ste. 115 • 732-7587, (800) 867-7587

The biggest nonfranchised real estate company in Nevada, Properties Plus has expanded to 400 agents since its founding in 1991. Locally owned and operated, the company has four offices covering the four corners of the valley. A new department called the Nevada Relocation Plus Team assists out-of-town home buyers, and a variable-rate sales program gives homeowners a choice of three different commission rates. Properties Plus sells an average of $250 million in real estate annually, with 80 percent of it in the residential market.

Prudential Southwest Realty

2950 S. Rancho Dr., Ste. 100 • 251-1010, (800) 827-5523

2001 S. Rainbow Blvd. • 243-3500

Formerly Jack Matthews Realty, this brokerage has offices around town, including outlets at the Meadows mall at Valley View Boulevard and U.S. 95 and at the Galleria mall, 1300 Sunset Road in Henderson. With 225 agents, Prudential operates a large relocation division as well as a commercial property division. The company, which sells $280 million in residential property annually, also offers "value range marketing," which establishes a high and low asking price, instead of a fixed figure.

Realty Executives

1903 S. Jones Blvd., Ste. 100 • 873-4500, (800) 533-6166

Opened in 1990, this company has grown rapidly to embrace 210 agents and three offices. Its Realtors are among the most experienced and active in the valley, generating a whopping $610 million in annual sales. Realty Executives ranks as the 99th biggest local broker in the nation. All agents are trained in relocation services. Realty Executives also maintains a property management division, which oversees residential and commercial properties.

Re/Max Sunset

2700 Sunset Rd. • 736-1333

Home shoppers in the Southeast valley can find a small but energetic office of 12 veteran agents here on the western edge of Green Valley. Some of the Realtors specialize in Las Vegas' burgeoning retirement market, including military retirees. As such, they are always on the lookout for single-story homes coveted by senior citizens. With deep roots in the valley, these agents enjoy assisting newcomers with information about ways to get involved in the community, volunteer opportunities and part-time employment prospects. The agency also does a bustling business in the move-up market, sometimes helping its original customers trade up to newer and bigger homes.

Spanish Trail Realty

6767 W. Tropicana Ave., Ste. 100 • 362-9797, (800) 331-6274

Upscale buyers are the target audience of this brokerage that specializes in private residential properties. The average sales price of homes sold through Spanish Trail Realty tops $800,000. The firm's office is quietly luxurious, with plenty of private space for Realtors and clients to confer. With just five agents, Spanish Trail does not rely on high volume but instead concentrates on concierge-style service to its relocating customers, with the staff even taking newcomers shopping at the valley's leading department stores.

Home Guides

Las Vegas is one of the most robust real

INSIDERS' TIP

To check the latest and best lending rates, look for the "Las Vegas Mortgage Review" in Sunday's *Las Vegas Review-Journal and Sun*. It lists more than 30 leading lenders in the valley, itemizing rates and points for 30-year and 15-year fixed and variable mortgages.

estate markets in the country, and real estate guides do a veritable booming business here. Every grocery and convenience store has racks of these free publications that advertise residential property of every size, shape and price. For renters and buyers alike, the following are some of the best. If you can't find one of these titles at the neighborhood store, just call the phone numbers listed below and they'll send you one.

Apartments for Rent

7330 Smoke Ranch Rd., Ste. A
• 255-3700

The heftiest and most widely distributed apartment guide in the area, this one routinely runs 300 pages or more. Published every other week, *Apartments for Rent* can be picked up free at grocery and convenience stores throughout the valley. The magazine is divided into geographic zones and contains a detailed checklist of features and prices for easy browsing. Each issue also carries a large number of discounted specials for prospective renters. The publication was founded in 1986.

Homebuyers Guide

1455 E. Tropicana Ave., Ste. 400
• 891-8420, (800) 723-0301

Sorting out the plethora of new communities in Las Vegas is no easy task. This guide unclutters things a bit by focusing exclusively on new neighborhoods. Published every other month, the *Homebuyers Guide* indexes communities by geographic zones and highlights selected builders with color pictures and locator maps. The magazine also operates a 24-hour 800-line that features recorded messages about the communities. If you leave a message at the number above, a sales representative will call you back.

Homes & Living

2500 Chandler Ave. Ste. 1 • 891-0095

The valley's thickest new home guide highlights emerging tracts around town, from starter homes to upscale estates. Feature stories and color pictures appear throughout this guide, along with helpful driving maps. The back of the book contains floor plans and de-

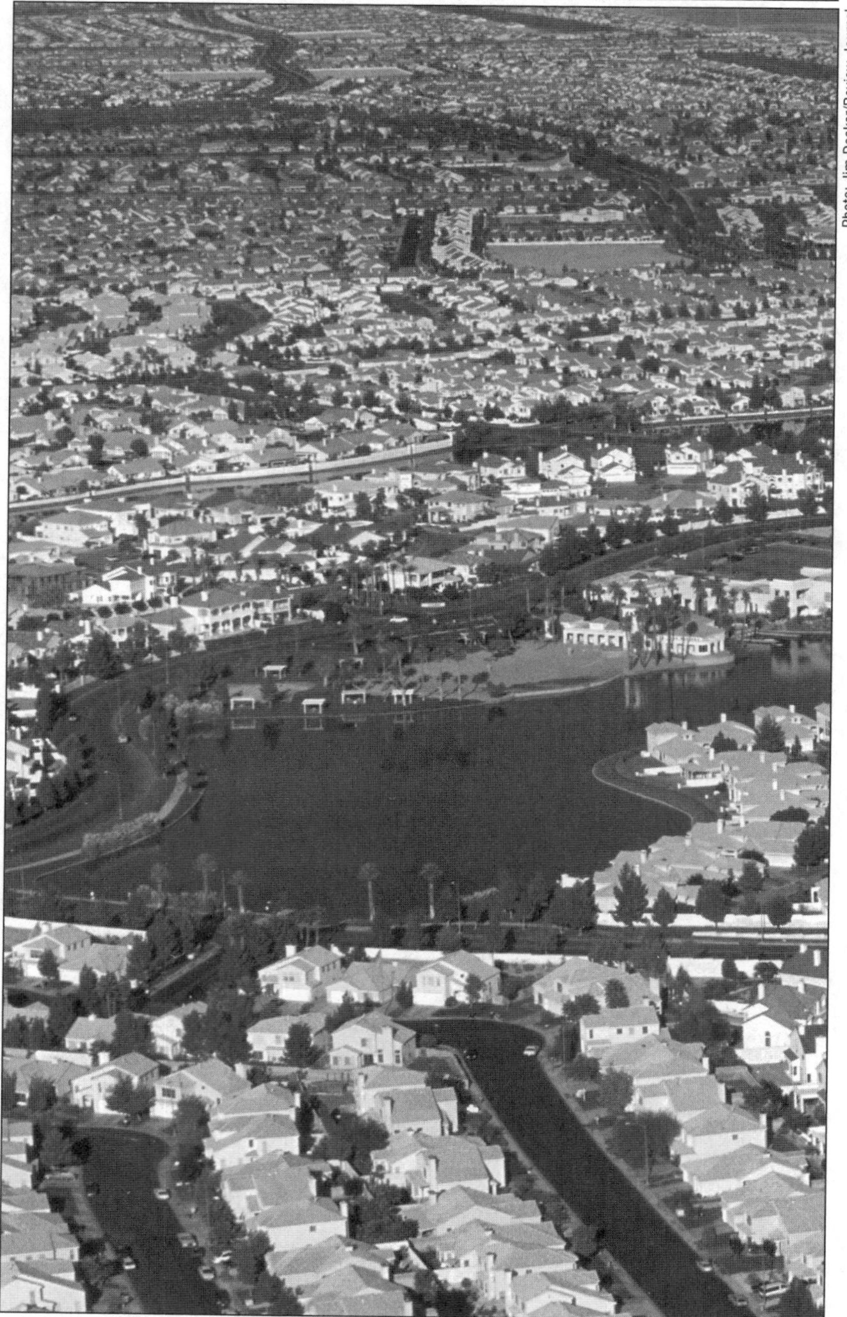

Photo: Jim Decker/Review-Journal

Desert Shores, in northwest Las Vegas, features three man-made lakes suitable for fishing and paddle boating.

tailed lists of standard and optional features in more than two dozen tract-home communities. Published since 1993, *Homes & Living* is distributed monthly to grocery stores throughout the valley.

Showcase of Homes

3139 S. Eastern Ave. • 731-4000

Houses, houses and more houses! This 200-page monthly publication contains pictures and listings of homes for sale across the valley. Cross-indexed by Realtor and realty company, this compendium circulates 30,000 copies to grocery and convenience stores. In business since 1992, *Showcase of Homes* is owned by Harmon Publishing Co., which also produces three sister publications, *Today's Homes*, *Homes of Southern Nevada* and the *Century 21 Real Estate Guide*.

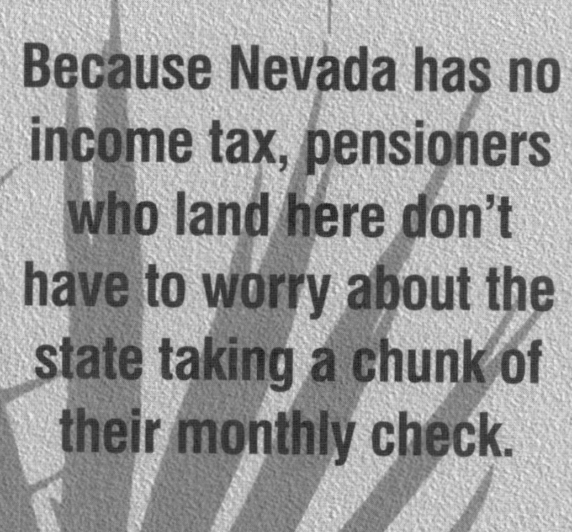
Because Nevada has no
income tax, pensioners
who land here don't
have to worry about the
state taking a chunk of
their monthly check.

Retirement

The Las Vegas Valley is fast becoming a mecca for retirees. With year-round sunny weather and a casual Southwestern lifestyle, it's little wonder that one in five newcomers to southern Nevada is retired, making seniors the fastest-growing population group.

A favorable tax climate is also attracting senior citizens. Because Nevada has no income tax, pensioners who land here don't have to worry about the state taking a chunk of their monthly check. All the more to play bingo with!

Retirees in Las Vegas are an eclectic lot. While 17 percent of their households earn less than $15,000 a year, 42 percent earn $35,000 or more. Thirty-three percent of the retirees have been in the region five years or less — slightly more than the 29 percent who have lived here for 20 years or more.

On balance, most retirees love Las Vegas. According to the 1996 Las Vegas Perspective Survey, 40 percent of the senior citizens were "very satisfied" with living in southern Nevada, and another 38 percent were "somewhat satisfied."

With the gray wave, Las Vegas has steadily added services, activities and housing options designed for active senior citizens. Local agencies have also bolstered programs that provide a safety net for those who need it. And age definitely has its privileges. Many casino restaurants offer low-cost food specials, and the three major utilities companies — Nevada Power, Southwest Gas and the Las Vegas Water District — waive deposit fees for residents 62 and older.

Since almost everyone in Las Vegas is from somewhere else, seniors find southern Nevada to be an invigorating experience with new friends, new vistas and new pursuits. To find out what's happening, two publications are especially useful. *The Sunday Las Vegas Review-Journal and Sun* carries a weekly list of senior-oriented activities in its "Living" section. The monthly *Senior Press*, a free periodical found at most grocery and convenience stores, contains a similar compendium as well as news stories and features of interest to retirees.

This chapter is dedicated to senior citizens. It is broken into four sections: activities, centers, transportation and housing. While our focus is on active seniors, we also include resources for those who may need a helping hand. Because of the multitude of senior centers, we have organized them by region for easier access.

Due to our emphasis on active and independent lifestyles, the housing section contains no listings of nursing homes. Residents seeking such information are advised to call Senior Placement Services, 650-0799, a nonprofit agency that maintains a referral list of reputable homes, or the Clark County Nursing Home Placement Office, 455-3565.

The residential communities listed in this chapter generally require a minimum age of 55 and are accessible to wheelchairs and walkers. At additional charges, some communities also provide assisted living programs that offer cafeteria-style meals and housekeeping

INSIDERS' TIP

Many casinos provide free round-trip shuttle service and meal discounts for seniors. Among them: the Rio, the Gold Coast, Binion's Horseshoe, Santa Fe, Texas, Fiesta, Showboat and Sam's Town. Call the casino for pickup times. The Four Queens even has a Club 55, which hosts social activities for residents 55 and older.

services. All require residents to be ambulatory.

What's Going On? Services, Activities and Clubs

From senior Olympians to senior companions, Las Vegas offers a wide variety of programs that energize and support retirees. The programs listed here are free unless noted otherwise. For additional club activities, be sure to check out the senior centers listed in the next section.

American Association of Retired Persons

340 N. 11th St. • 386-8661

Opened in mid-1997, this AARP center provides information on just about everything from consumer issues to volunteer opportunities. An all-volunteers staff maintains an extensive referral list of local agencies, and they'll even help prepare tax returns. All the services are free, whether you are one of the 95,000 local AARP members or not. The center, located within the Howard Cannon Senior Center (see our write-up in the next section), is open 9 AM to 4 PM.

FYI

Unless otherwise noted, the area code for all phone numbers listed in this chapter is 702.

Community Home-based Initiatives Program

340 N. 11th St. • 486-3545, (800) 992-0900 ext. 4210

Seniors in need of help around the house can get assistance from this program known as CHIPs. Providing nonmedical services to residents 65 and older, CHIPs assigns caregivers to assist with baths and showers, run errands and perform light household chores such as laundry and cleaning. The assistants, who are licensed and bonded, are provided free of charge to residents whose income is less than $968 a month. Seniors making up to $1,450 a month can still qualify for the program but must pay a sliding-scale fee.

EXCELL

University of Nevada, Las Vegas, 4505 S. Maryland Pkwy. • 895-4469

The Center for Lifelong Learning (EXCELL), located on the UNLV campus, is a learning and teaching society made up of about 200 Las Vegas senior citizens. The members develop their own courses, which tend to revolve around topics such as poetry, history and music appreciation. These not-for-credit workshops run during regular UNLV semesters. Each session requires a $35 membership fee.

55 Alive

Cannon Center, 340 N. 11th St. • 254-3140

Drivers 55 and better can brush up on the motoring skills at any of 15 locations around southern Nevada. Sponsored by the American Association of Retired Persons and conducted by volunteer driving instructors — who also are seniors — 55 Alive helps older drivers handle adverse road conditions. But there's a lot more than just rules of the road in this eight-hour class. Instructors can help participants save on auto insurance and better understand the effects of medication on driving acuity. The fee for the class and instructional materials is $8. In addition, the Cannon Center location conducts Department of Motor Vehicles license renewals each month. The line is a lot shorter than any you'll find at the DMV offices.

Homemaker Home Health Aide Service

1600 Pinto Ln. • 455-4430

This county program contracts with private agencies to provide homemaker services, including general housekeeping, grocery shopping, laundry, bathing and meal planning and preparation. Residents 55 and older are eligible if they meet income guidelines, which are available at the office. The office will also make referrals to nursing programs if medical assistance is required. The home aide program is a popular one, so most applicants end up on a two- or three-month waiting list.

Lend a Hand

400 Utah St., Boulder City • 294-2363

Operated by and exclusively for the residents of Boulder City, this nonprofit agency brings companionship and assistance to seniors in their homes. Volunteers, many of them seniors themselves, provide household help and transportation to residents age 60 and older. Hours are flexible, as are the hourly rates, which are a suggested contribution not to exceed $5 an hour. To help foster independence at home, Lend a Hand's Geriatric Care Management program will coordinate its efforts with out-of-state relatives who want to make sure their elders are being looked after. However, no medicine or medical help is available through this program.

Meals on Wheels

Catholic Charities, 808 S. Main St. • 385-5284

Residents older than 60 can enjoy nutritious lunches for a suggested donation of $1.65 at any of 15 sites around the valley. Sponsored by Catholic Charities, the Meals on Wheels program serves lunches only, between the hours of 11 AM and 1:30 PM. The program runs Monday through Friday. Home delivery of meals is also available to homebound seniors. Henderson residents can call 565-7980.

Nevada Senior Games

P.O. Box 27947, Las Vegas, NV 89126 • 294-2954

Athletes 48 and older compete in 18 sports ranging from archery and bocce ball to tennis and the triathlon. Every two years, local qualifiers move on to the national finals, called the National Senior Sports Classic. Competition categories are segmented by age groups. More than 100 southern Nevadans joined 10,000 competitors in the national games in Tucson, Arizona, in 1997. Participants pay a $25 to $40 charge, which covers entry fees and a newsletter.

Respite Care Referral Service

Cannon Center, 340 N. 11th St. • 382-0721

This affordable program serves families who have a homebound member older than age 60. The program pre-screens workers' references and establishes a schedule and compensation agreement. In-home assistance, which gives other family members a regular respite from healthcare obligations, runs $6.50 an hour, plus 25¢ a mile for transportation. A onetime fee of $35 is assessed to perform the screening.

www.insiders.com
See this and many other
Insiders' Guide® destinations
online — in their entirety.
Visit us today!

Retired Senior Volunteer Program (RSVP)

Cannon Center, 340 N. 11th St. • 382-0721
27 E. Texas St., Henderson • 565-0669
1001 Arizona St., Boulder City • 293-0332

You can lend a hand to any one of hundreds of community groups in the valley through this program. Participants work as clerical assistants, help handicapped children, serve as museum guides and perform a variety of other worthwhile tasks. Seniors can also help homebound retirees through household visits and supportive telephone calls.

Senior Citizen's Health Program

Clark County Health District, 625 Shadow Ln. • 383-1354
Satellite office, 129 W. Lake Mead Dr., Henderson • 564-3232

A free health-screening program is available to residents 60 and older at the Clark County Health District. The exam, available on a walk-in basis, includes medical history, blood pressure, height and weight, urine test, hematocrit, vision screening, tonometry, audiometric screening, pap smear for women and blood pressure screening. The program is also available at the health district's satellite office in Henderson.

Senior Citizens Law Project

340 N. 11th St. • 229-6596

Residents 60 and older can get free legal help here. This busy office of three attorneys and two paralegals provides expert advice on Medicare, Medicaid, Social Security and nursing home issues. Tenant rights and consumer disputes are also dealt with here, though the project's attorneys do not take cases to court. When litigation is needed, the office will make referrals. There are no income restrictions to use the law office, except for will writing. To qualify for this most popular service, a senior's estate cannot exceed $50,000 (excluding home). Appointments are required, but the law project's staff will also answer some questions right over the phone. The program is funded by the city and through clients' donations.

Senior Community Service Employment Program

330 W. Washington Ave. • 648-3356

Low-income residents 55 and older can find part-time jobs through this free program. Banks are among the local businesses that are actively recruiting and hiring seniors for teller positions. Other hot trades include clerical staffing, customer service representatives and the Metropolitan Police Department, which hires school crossing guards. In addition to employment leads, this program assists with resumes.

Senior Companion

Catholic Charities, 808 S. Main St. • 382-0721

If you're older than 60 and like to drive, this program helps you help others. Senior Companion provides assistance and friendship to homebound elderly residents. Primary duties include transportation to medical appointments and shopping. Participants receive a monthly stipend of $200, plus a mileage reimbursement, for 20 hours of service weekly. To qualify, applicants must have a monthly income of less than $810 and reliable transportation.

Mall Walking

Call it cardiovascular commerce. Each morning, hundreds of seniors descend on the area's four major shopping malls to walk for their health.

While indoor activity may seem strange in a city that enjoys nearly 300 sunny days a year, there's a perfectly good explanation — and plenty of incentives. First, Las Vegas' sunny skies come with broiling temperatures from May through September. The winter months are frigid, and spring and fall days are often blustery. So air-conditioned (or heated) malls make sense. And they provide a level of safety not always found on city streets.

What's more, the malls have partnered with health providers and even aerobics instructors to offer some useful and inexpensive services. While most of the programs are open to all age groups, senior citizens have been the most involved.

The idea is to get the blood circulating before the stores open and the shoppers arrive. Striding along the cavernous corridors, seniors enjoy the chance to window shop at their own pace while, perhaps, shedding a few pounds. Dedicated walkers have even formed clubs, which provide fellowship, friendship and a few perks along the way.

Here's a rundown on what's happening where:

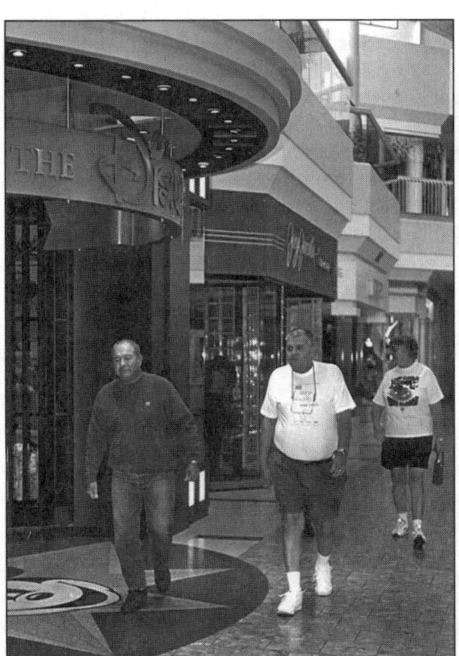

Photo: Jim Decker/Review-Journal

Before the malls open, why not do a little window shopping while exercising in crowd-free, air-conditioned comfort?

- Boulevard Mall, 3528 S. Maryland Parkway, 732-8949. The Boulevard Mall Walking Club struts its stuff from 7 to 10 AM on weekdays. Though you can walk for free, a onetime $10 membership provides free blood pressure checks on Tuesdays and Thursdays, a T-shirt and merchant discounts. A complimentary continental breakfast with an entertaining speaker is hosted quarterly.
- Meadows Mall, 4300 Meadows Lane, 878-3331. The Hip and Healthy program begins at 7 AM every day — and it's all free. Aerobics classes and blood-pressure checks are conducted from 8 AM to 9 AM on Tuesdays and Thursdays. The aerobics class, of the low-impact variety, is led by staff from the YMCA.
- Galleria at Sunset, 1300 Sunset Road, Henderson, 434-2409. Walkers can hoof it from 7 AM to 9 PM Monday through Saturday and from 10 AM to 6 PM on Sundays. Free blood pressure screenings are held from 8 to 10 AM every Monday.

— continued on next page

Optional membership in the SunStriders Walking Club costs $5 annually and entitles card holders to free aerobics classes, lectures, a T-shirt and store discounts.

• Fashion Show, Spring Mountain Road and Las Vegas Boulevard S., 735-7275. The Movers and Shakers Walking Club is free, and you can walk from 8 AM to 10 PM on weekdays. Sponsored by Humana Health Care Plans, the group produces a newsletter and hosts fitness lectures.

Senior Friends

3101 S. Maryland Pkwy., Ste. 314 • 735-5510
2809 Green Valley Pkwy. • 434-6500
8524 Del Webb Blvd. • 255-5404

These clubs promote health, wellness and active living for adults 50 years and older. With 10,000 members in the Las Vegas valley, Senior Friends conducts classes and seminars year-round. Topics are eclectic, with such titles as "Understanding Wall Street," "The History of Las Vegas" and "How to Keep Your Skin Safe from the Summer Sun." For a $15 annual fee, members receive discounts from area merchants, monthly newsletters and free copying and notary services.

Silver Sage

Community College of Southern Nevada, 3200 E. Cheyenne Ave. • 651-4000

Based on the campus on the Community College of Southern Nevada, this program offers classes specifically designed for seniors. Subjects include tai chi, metaphysics, computers, cooking and Spanish. Tuition for these noncredit courses runs about $1 an hour. Also, in what has to be one of the best deals around, CCSN waives tuition in its academic classes for residents 62 and older.

UNLV Senior Adult Theatre

4505 S. Maryland Pkwy. • 895-1517

Actors wanted! Each year, UNLV's Department of Theatre Arts invites senior citizens to become part of its nationally acclaimed program, which emphasizes acting and creating oral history plays. Residents 62 and older can earn up to six free credits if they are among the 100 selected each fall. No prior theater experience is necessary, with students ranging from retired homemakers and cab drivers to doctors and lawyers.

Where To Go: Senior Centers

If you're looking to meet and interact with fellow senior citizens, the following list is a good place to start. Operated by city, county and nonprofit agencies, these centers are excellent clearinghouses of information for all seniors. For newcomers, they're great places to make new friends and to indulge in long-time hobbies. Many provide regular programs such as bingo, movies, field trips, exercise classes — and even inexpensive meals. Some have specialized day-care and nursing assistance for local residents with health problems. All centers are open Monday through Friday unless stated otherwise. Most of the classes are free or ask only for a modest donation to defray costs. The centers' programs are generally open to anyone 55 and older, though some may lower the minimum age to 50.

Downtown

Arturo Cambeiro Center

330 N. 13th St. • 385-0909

Operated by the Nevada Association of Latin Americans, this bilingual center offers citizenship classes, conversational English courses, crafts, exercise, folkloric dance, table games and even ukulele lessons. Lunches are available for $1.25 beginning at 11:30 AM. The center's hours are 9 AM to 4 PM.

Howard W. Cannon Center

340 N. 11th St. • 366-1522

The most comprehensive center in the region, this facility houses representatives of the Community Health Centers of Southern Nevada, Catholic Community Services, the Clark County Public Guardian, the Nevada Division of Aging and the Las Vegas Senior Citizens Law Project.

These groups provide services and referrals free of charge. Vision screenings are performed on alternate Thursdays, and seniors can get minor repairs and adjustments to their eyeglasses on the second Thursday of each month. The Department of Motor Vehicles provides license renewal service on the first Monday of the month, and Citizens Area Transit sells monthly passes and tokens to the center. The center's hours are 9 AM to 4 PM.

Doolittle Center

1901 N. J St. • 229-6125

A community garden project sprouts on the grounds of this center just northwest of downtown. Seniors are invited to grow flowers, vegetables and fruits here. For those who prefer indoor endeavors, the center offers line-dancing classes, bingo, table tennis, card games and sewing classes. An outdoor pool is reserved for adult swimming on Monday, Wednesday and Friday mornings. The center operates from 9 AM to 3 PM.

EOB Center

330 W. Washington Ave. • 647-2536

This center, operated by the nonprofit Economic Opportunity Board of Clark County, offers low-cost lunches, educational programs and a thrift shop. It is particularly helpful to handicapped seniors, providing a free shuttle program that provides door-to-door service. A foster grandparents program offers seniors the opportunity to help a child who is mentally

INSIDERS' TIP

When pricing retirement communities, be sure you know your needs. Rent for regular independent-living apartments, with recreational amenities, begins in the low $600s. Meal and maid service provided by assisted-living communities run the monthly tab to $1,200 and up.

Important Phone Numbers and Hotlines

The following agencies and associations can provide useful information on health and related services available to the senior-citizen population. For programs not listed here, try Help of Southern Nevada, 369-HELP, a referral agency for social services.

Alzheimer's Disease Association, 248-2770
American Cancer Society, (800) ACS-2345
American Diabetes Association, 369-9995
American Heart Association, 367-1366
American Lung Association, (800) LUNGUSA
Arthritis Foundation, 367-1626
Clark County Health District, 383-1354
Eldercare Helpline, (800) 677-1116
Las Vegas Stroke Club, 233-0447
Medicare Information, 486-4602
Nevada Association for the Handicapped, 870-7050
Nevada Division of Aging Services, 486-3545
Parkinson's Disease Support Group, 564-5416
Senior Citizens Protective Services, 455-4291
Southern Nevada Sightless, 642-6000
Self-Help for the Hard of Hearing, 229-6454

and emotionally disabled, neglected or abused. A small stipend is available for those who can lend a hand. The center's hours are 8 AM to 4:30 PM.

Hollyhock Center

380 N. Maryland Pkwy. • 382-0093

Also operated by EOB, the Hollyhock Center provides supervised day-care programs for impaired individuals. Activities include healthcare, recreation and family support groups. Hollyhock staffers are specially trained to work with Alzheimer's sufferers. Free transportation is available through EOB's network of shuttle buses. Hours are 7:30 AM to 5:30 PM.

Katherine Center

580 E. St. Louis Ave. • 732-2054

Want a free haircut? Interested in learning French? These are among the activities at this center, located inside Reformation Lutheran Church. Seniors at this active center take frequent field trips around the region and enjoy live music on Fridays. Reduced-price lunches are served at 11:30 AM, though reservations are required one day in advance. Katherine Center is open 9 AM to 12:30 PM.

Las Vegas Senior Center

451 E. Bonanza Rd. • 229-6454

One of the few centers open on Saturday, this facility has a large gymnasium and a full medley of 70 classes meeting each week. The eclectic curriculum ranges from a Clogging and Humanities Discussion Group to Shirt Design and Painting. Pinochle, bridge and, of course, bingo are among the games that people play here. If you like dancing, there's just about everything from hula to ballroom. And if current affairs are your bag, check out the TV News Club that meets to critique the news and the newsmakers every evening. Registration is just $1 for most programs. The Las Vegas chapter of Self Help for the Hard of Hearing meets on Saturday. Senior Tripsters, a nonprofit group, convenes on the second Thursday of each month to plan local and extended tours. The center is open from 9 AM to 10 PM Monday through Saturday.

East Valley

Friendship Center

830 E. Lake Mead Dr., Henderson • 565-8836

Functionally impaired seniors receive personal attention and supervision at this Salvation Army-run daytime center. Open 6 AM to 6 PM, the center hosts recreational and social events, along with a variety of therapeutic programs. Participants must be ambulatory, and free transportation is available.

Henderson Center

27 E. Texas Ave., Henderson • 565-6990

Active seniors will find a lot to do here. Daily recreational activities include arts and crafts, billiards, bingo, woodcarving and even a senior orchestra. The Retired Seniors Volunteers Program (RSVP) recruits and places seniors in jobs throughout the community. And a number of agencies — including the Department of Motor Vehicles, Citizens Area Transit, Clark County Social Services and the Veterans Administration — make regular visits to provide information and services. Additional health and social programs are provided by the American Legion Auxiliary, Deaf Seniors of Southern Nevada and local eye clinics. Lunches are served daily at 11:30 AM for a suggested donation of $1.25. A Saturday brunch is also laid out for the same price from 9 to 11 AM.

Parkdale Center

3200 Ferndale St. • 455-7517

What's your game? Pinochle and Scrabble competitions are held weekly at this center. Potluck lunches are served every fourth Thursday of the month, and monthly trips are taken around southern Nevada. Participants stay informed with a regular newsletter that contains a calendar of events. Hours are 7:30 AM to 5 PM daily and 10 AM to 2 PM Saturday.

Whitney Center

5700 Missouri Ave. • 455-7576

A $1.75 lunch (reservation required a day before) is served daily at 11:30 AM. Center activities include bingo, card games, ceramic classes, guest speakers, line dancing and oil painting classes. Regular field trips are scheduled, with transportation provided. The center hosts four parties each year with live entertainment and dancing. Whitney's hours are 9 AM to 4 PM, except for Tuesdays, when the center's pinochle club keeps the lamps lit until 9 PM.

West Valley

Derfelt Center

3333 W. Washington Ave. • 229-6601

Fitness is the watchword here. TOPS (Take Off Pounds Sensibly) meets on Thursday mornings and features guest speakers, support groups, literature and regular weigh-ins. Fitness classes, tap lessons and yoga also are offered for nominal costs of $1 to $3 per course. This center is set in Lorenzi Park, a lushly landscaped city facility that includes a lake and the Nevada History Museum. Hours are 8 AM to 4 PM.

Lied Center

901 N. Jones Blvd. • 648-3425

Frail and disabled seniors receive special attention at this EOB-operated facility. Individualized care, medication supervision, stroke exercise classes and other therapies are among the services offered. Families can learn about caring for their relatives through counseling and support groups. Nutritious meals are served at the center, which is open from 7 AM to 10 PM Monday through Friday. Unique to the area, the Lied Center is also open on Sundays from 7 AM to 5:30 PM.

Northwest Community Center

6841 W. Lone Mountain Rd. • 229-4924

Senior Fun Times, an active social group that conducts low-cost daytrips and hosts parties, calls this place home. Also based here is the Senior Action Club, which recruits volunteers to serve as goodwill ambassadors in neighborhood parks. As park ambassadors, seniors greet visitors, distribute informational literature about cultural activities and report any vandalism or needed repairs. Other vol-

INSIDERS' TIP

The average cost of nursing home care in Las Vegas is $4,228 a month.

unteer opportunities are available through the center's Senior Outreach Office. Aerobics, line dancing and fitness classes are conducted for a modest charge of $1 to $3. Hours are 7 AM to 3 PM.

How To Get There: Transportation

Don't have a car? Need help getting around town? A number of agencies have wheels for you. The Senior Ride Program is a subsidized service that uses Clark County taxicabs. Half-off discount coupons may be purchased by any resident 60 years and older and can be used 24 hours a day, seven days a week. The coupons are sold at the Cannon Center, 340 N. 11th Street, 486-6535. Once registered for the program, participants can renew their coupon allotment by mail.

Citizens Area Transit's Paratransit Service offers small, specially equipped buses to shuttle handicapped riders, including those in wheelchairs. It provides round-trip service throughout the valley for just $1 each way. The service is a shared, curb-to-curb ride with reservations taken in advance. Hours of operation vary by location. The paratransit service operates out of 301 E. Clark Street, Suite 300, and information can be obtained at 228-4800.

The Economic Opportunity Board runs a valleywide shuttle service for residents 55 and older (no wheelchair accommodations). One-way trips cost $3, and roundtrips are $5. Reservations must be made at least 24 hours in advance. EOB's transit office is at 2228 Comstock Drive. Check for hours of operation by calling 646-2062.

Where To Live: Housing

East Valley

Camlu Retirement Apartments

4255 Spencer St. • 732-0652

Located 2 miles east of The Strip, Camlu rents studio and one-bedroom apartments. The emphasis here is on the extras, with three daily meals, weekly maid and linen service, a shuttle bus and planned recreational activities. Camlu has a two-tier pricing structure at its 73 units — a lower rate for fully independent dwellers and a higher rate for those who need assisted living services such as medication supervision, help with bathing and catered meals. The units have no kitchens but come equipped with a wet bar. Lounges, a library, a game room and an exercise area are on the common grounds.

Carefree Senior Living

3210 Sandhill Rd. • 641-4700

Just built in the summer of 1997, this modern Spanish-style complex incorporates the latest conveniences for adult living. Three three-story clustered complexes each have elevators. All showers are of the walk-in variety, which seniors find more convenient than stepping into bathtubs. Twelve of the 180 apartments are designed to accommodate residents with disabilities, and one building is designated as nonsmoking. Selected units allow pets. All units have full kitchens and hookups for washers and dryers. The largest flats, at 695 square feet, come with private patio decks. Common areas include a clubhouse, entertainment center, a small pool, library and group kitchen. An on-site van shuttles residents to stores and on regularly scheduled field trips.

Concorde

2465 E. Twain Ave. • 732-0020

With 115 furnished studio apartments, this apartment community accommodates active adults as well as those who need some help getting through their days. Three meals are served daily, and a 24-hour staff is available to attend to medical needs. Laundry is done weekly by the housekeeping staff, though residents can do their own at the free washers and dryers on site. Kitchenettes also are available in some units. Transportation is provided for errands, and an activities director leads daily exercise programs in the recreation room.

Sun City MacDonald Ranch

2000 Horizon Ridge Pkwy., Henderson • 269-4300, (800) 564-5660

In the midst of building 2,500 homes in the

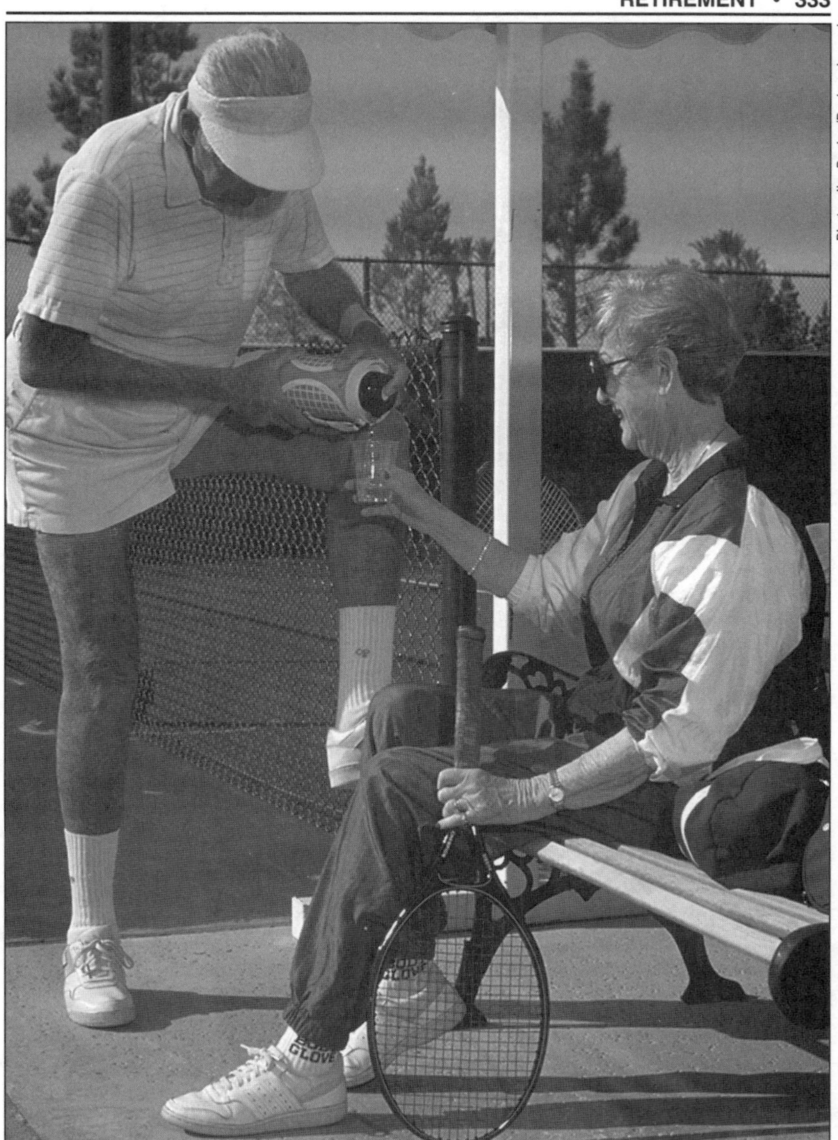

Photo: Jim Decker/Review-Journal

Attracted by sunny weather and no state income tax, senior citizens are finding the good life in southern Nevada. Tennis, anyone?

hills south of Henderson, MacDonald Ranch is smaller and slightly less expensive than its sister across the valley in Summerlin. While comparably designed and equipped, homes here run an average of $20,000 less, with the largest dwelling spanning 2,027 square feet. And the minimum age requirement is lower too — 50 instead of 55. MacDonald Ranch has one 18-hole golf course and a 36,000-square-foot recreation center with a heated outdoor pool. As with all Sun City communities, residents enjoy a full schedule of activities, from bocce ball to tennis to hiking clubs. And if you want to have some fun with that Social Security check, MacDonald Ranch, like Sun City Summerlin, is a favorite stop for free shuttle buses that provide round-trip service to casinos around the valley.

Villa Monterey

1270 Burnham Ave. • 474-7700

With a pool, spa and fitness center, Villa Monterey provides a country club atmosphere for active adults. The modern Mediterranean-style two-story complex, built in 1993, contains 320 units ranging from "junior one bedrooms" to 800-square-foot two-bedroom suites. All come with a full kitchen (no microwaves, though) and an oversized storage closet. The community is gated for security, and the parking spaces are covered. If needed, Villa Monterey staffers will, for a fee, run errands and help with household chores. But the emphasis here is on independent lifestyles. Grocery shopping is just two blocks away.

West Valley

Carefree Senior Living

1600 S. Valley View Blvd. • 259-6687

One of the largest adult-oriented apartment communities in the valley, this 344-unit complex is also one of the most affordable. A "junior one-bedroom,'' whose monthly lease runs in the low $500s, has a full kitchen and enough square footage for a single dweller to live comfortably. Two years older than its sister community on the east side of town, this facility also has shuttle service and plenty of recreational activities. There is a pool and a well-equipped fitness room with exercise machines and weights. Free luncheons are served on Fridays, and bingo is a weekend favorite. There are no elevators in this two-story complex. Garages are available for an additional charge.

Country Club at the Meadows

300 Promenade Blvd. • 258-1121

This 303-unit community is virtually identical to the Country Club at Valley View (see next listing), 2 miles to the south. The layout, amenities and vintage of the two facilities are the same. There are, however, two noteworthy differences. The Meadows location has a security staffer guarding its gate 24 hours a day. It also is a couple of blocks away from major thoroughfares, giving it a more sedate ambiance. While it's a longer walk to the bus stop, residents here value their peace and quiet. For these privileges, the Meadows' tenants pay a little more for comparably sized units.

Country Club at Valley View

1400 S. Valley View Blvd. • 878-6266

If you're looking for activity, this place has it. A large pool, ideal for lap swimming, is open 24 hours a day. Dances, bingo, shuffleboard, aerobics and happy hours with wine are scheduled regularly at the large community center room. Also on site is a beauty salon and fitness center. The 312 apartments in this two-story complex span up to 848 square feet and include full kitchens. Washers and dryers are available in some of the units. The complex is gated for security and has a shuttle bus available for errands.

Montclif

4175 S. Decatur Blvd. • 220-7200

With full kitchens and apartment layouts of up to 976 square feet, Montclif offers independent living in modern Southwestern decor. Large closets and in-room washers and dryers are included in each of the 220 units. Recreational amenities at this gate-guarded community are an indoor and outdoor spa, a heated pool, putting green and fitness center. The recreation room includes exercise equipment and billiards. Covered parking and picnic areas round out the grounds. And bring Fido along because small pets are welcome.

INSIDERS' TIP

If you like to get involved in politics, you might check out the Clark County chapter of the National Council of Senior Citizens. For meeting information, call 645-1048.

Sun City Summerlin

10351 Sun City Blvd. • 363-5454, (800) 987-9875

If you're in the market for a home in a retirement community, Sun City is a great place to look. Sun City Summerlin, the first Sun City project in the area, is wrapping up construction at its 8,500-home tract along the northwestern foothills. The Del Webb Corp., which developed the Sun City concept, is nationally renowned for building communities that cater to active adults, and its Las Vegas location is no exception. The Summerlin community has three golf courses and four large recreation centers that include spacious swimming pools (indoor and outdoor), spas and workout rooms. The homes are all single-story layouts, ranging from duplexes of less than 1,000 square feet to larger freestanding homes around 2,500 square feet. All feature neutral-toned stucco and Spanish tile roofs. The yards are small and, unlike other neighborhoods around town, there are no concrete block walls separating the homes. This allows grounds crews to cut the grass and perform yard work throughout Sun City. The preferred mode of transportation in the community is the golf cart. While Sun City requires homeowners to be at least 55, spouses need not be. Children, however, are forbidden to reside here.

With 194,000 students in 1997, CCSD is the 10th-biggest public school system in the country. And it's adding roughly 12,000 students a year.

Education

Education is big business in Clark County. The giant Clark County School District, with more than 18,000 teachers, administrators and staff, is one of the largest employers in the valley. Southern Nevada's community college and university are large and getting larger.

But the numbers distort the reality, which is that education is not especially high on the community's overall priority list. Nevada is tied for last (with Alaska) among states sending high school graduates to college. Just 36 percent of local high school grads enroll in community colleges or universities, far below the national average of 54 percent. The local and statewide dropout rates perennially rank at or near the bottom.

Southern Nevada's booming economy, in an ironic way, is partly to blame. With so many jobs being created, young adults have relatively easy access to steady employment. Since many of those jobs are in the service industry or the construction business, diplomas and degrees are not a prerequisite for success.

While the Clark County School District continues to grow along with the population, expending a $1 billion annual budget, the region has disproportionately few private schools. In the last 10 years, a few new nonsectarian schools have begun to pop up. But with their generally small facilities, enrollment has been limited. Meantime, parochial schools, a staple in Las Vegas' Catholic community, have not kept up with the valley's growth and, therefore, tend to cater almost exclusively to their respective parishes.

A handful of families have gone the home-schooling route, which is growing in popularity around the country. More than 1,500 local pupils are home-schooled. Home-schooling in Clark County must be approved by the Clark County School District. Materials and curriculum guides are available through the district by calling 799-8642.

For adults in need of a high school diploma or General Education Degree (GED), the school district operates an adult education program. Day and night classes are offered around the valley. The program includes a career development center staffed by counselors and support personnel. In 1996-97, enrollment exceeded 7,000. For information, call 799-8650.

This chapter provides an overview of the educational offerings throughout the valley — from public to private, from kindergarten to Ph.Ds. Also included is a section on trade schools. Day-care providers are listed separately in our Child Care chapter.

So let's go to school.

Public Schools

Clark County School District

2832 E. Flamingo Rd. • 799-5011

The Clark County School District has the distinction of being one of the nation's largest and fastest-growing educational systems. With 194,000 students in 1997, CCSD is the 10th-biggest system in the country. And it's adding roughly 12,000 students a year. Since 1989, the district's enrollment has ballooned by more than 70 percent.

Such rapid expansion has created growing pains. As its name implies, the district encompasses all 7,910 square miles of Clark County, bumping against the borders of California, Utah and Arizona. But most of its 194 campuses are concentrated in the Las Vegas Valley. In the last 10 years, more than $1.3 billion has been spent in a school-building frenzy — and yet classrooms remain overcrowded.

One-third of CCSD schools are on year-round schedules, designed to maximize campus capacity. Periodically, some acutely overenrolled campuses are put on double sessions, in which pupils are divided into two groups and attend classes from 6 AM to noon or from noon to 6 PM. The district tries to minimize the amount of time that schools are on double sessions since students lose about 40 minutes of instructional time each day they are on such shortened schedules.

As a largely urban school system, CCSD suffers from many of the same educational woes afflicting big-city districts everywhere. Its standardized test scores are flat or falling. Where Las Vegas students routinely scored above national averages in the 1980s, local results sometimes fall below the country's norms. CCSD has the nation's highest dropout rate, fluctuating between 10 and 12 percent.

FYI

Unless otherwise noted, the area code for all phone numbers listed in this chapter is 702.

Still, there are a number of bright spots. Class sizes have been reduced in grades 1 and 2, where the state-mandated student-to-teacher ratio is set at 16-to-1. Educators feel that these smaller classes — roughly half the average size — help young pupils adjust to the school environment. Efforts are being made to extend the program into 3rd grade.

CCSD maintains a strong performing arts program districtwide. Roughly one-third of CCSD's middle school and high school students are in performing arts classes and activities, compared with about 15 percent nationally. And the district is in the midst of installing $20 million worth of computer equipment at 128 campuses — one of the largest technology connections in the country.

More than 6,000 students are enrolled at 10 magnet schools around the valley. These campuses offer specialized academic programs at all grade levels. Concentrated curricula include math and science, programs for international students, tourism, aerospace, health professions and advanced technologies. Admission is generally conducted by lottery and a review of test scores. But preference points are issued based on ethnicity, as the magnets also serve as a desegregation tool. Information on magnet schools can be obtained by calling the Magnet Schools Project Office at 799-5479. The district also has two vocational schools.

For high-achieving students, elementary and middle schools have a Gifted and Talented Education (GATE) program with accelerated studies. Each high school has Advanced Placement courses and an Honors Program that offers a rigorous college-prep curriculum. Overall, Clark County's students fare well on college entrance exams. The district average on the combined SAT is 1019, or six points above the national average. The ACT average is 21.1, compared with a U.S. average of 20.9.

To give juniors and seniors a leg up on their post-secondary pursuits, CCSD has joined with the Community College of Southern Nevada to create the Community College High School. Students in this program, which is conducted at selected high school and community college campuses, earn dual credits toward their high school diploma and as much as a full year of community college credits by the time they complete 12th grade.

Nevada law requires school attendance between ages 7 and 17. Kindergarten is part of the regular school program but is not mandatory. A child must be 5 years old on or before September 30 to attend kindergarten and must be 6 years old by that date to enter first grade.

To find out which school your residence is zoned for, contact the Attendance Zones Office at 799-7573. Enrollment is done at individual campuses. Families with special education needs can contact the Special Education Office at 799-7446.

To get enrolled in the Clark County School District, newly arrived families need to provide two forms of proof of address. These include

INSIDERS' TIP

The Classroom on Wheels program provides free bilingual preschool education to children ages 3 to 5. Operated on black-and-white spotted school buses, COW specializes in instructing low-income and at-risk children. Information can be obtained by calling the COW office at 870-7201.

a utility bill, a rent receipt or a residential lease or sales contract. (A driver's license, telephone bill or cable bill will not be accepted.) Also, parents must furnish proof of the child's identity. Acceptable documents include an original birth certificate, a passport or a baptismal certificate. Up-to-date immunization records will be requested at the time of enrollment. New pupils must have four DPT shots, three polio doses and two MMR shots.

The following information is helpful for placement in appropriate classes: the most recent report card, the most recent achievement test scores and information about any disabilities or special health or educational needs.

Bus service is provided to all students who live more than 2 miles from their schools. Route and schedule information is available by calling the neighborhood school.

Private Schools

Nearly two dozen private schools operate in Clark County. There are a handful of large academies, but most are smaller, more intimate centers. Some have just two or three rooms. Annual tuitions are as modest as a few hundred dollars or as much as $9,500. Most have a religious affiliation.

The following list is a representative sampling of some of the leading private schools in southern Nevada. Each is licensed by the Nevada Department of Education, which establishes courses of study, textbooks, graduation requirements and testing standards. Note that the grade configuration varies from school to school. Some facilities are geared only to children in the lower elementary grades, while others offer a full kindergarten-to-12th grade curriculum.

Faith Lutheran Junior-Senior High School
1251 Robin St. • 648-7047

Instructing in grades 6 through 12, Faith Lutheran is a Christian-oriented campus that accepts students of all denominations. Only 20 percent of its 490 students come from Lutheran families, but religion is an integral component, with a class on religion required annually. Uniforms are also mandatory. Curriculum is college prep, with college-placement exams given in English, Spanish and biology. The school is competitive in athletics, fielding teams in most sports. Faith's athletes perform in the classroom as well, consistently winning statewide academic honors for maintaining top grade-point averages. By 1999, this school, founded in 1979, expects to move to a new and larger campus in Summerlin. The new facility, set on 33 acres, will feature an amphitheater, student activities center and 116,000 square feet of floor space. With waiting lists in all grades, families are encouraged to contact the school by February of the upcoming school year. Placement exams are given each spring.

First Presbyterian Academy

1515 W. Charleston Blvd. • 382-3611

With the motto of "academic excellence in a Christian environment," this academy has 190 students in kindergarten through 8th grade. Religious education and weekly chapel services are held at this school that is affiliated with the city's First Presbyterian Church. As for academics, the academy features what it calls an "enhanced" curriculum that offers Spanish at all grade levels and a solid math and science coursework. A number of its graduating 8th graders go on to Clark County's High School Math and Science magnet.

Bishop Gorman High School

1801 S. Maryland Pkwy. • 732-1945

This 1,100-student campus is the only Catholic high school in Las Vegas. Founded in 1954, it is also the oldest parochial school in the area. Gov. Bob Miller is among its most famous grads. The college-prep curriculum is an offshoot of Jesuit-style instruction called Viatorian, emphasizing small classes and strict discipline. Honors programs are offered for accelerated students, with juniors and seniors earning college credits upon passage of an advanced-placement exam. A campus ministry program involves students in community services and an "Interfaith Hospitality Network" that works with the homeless in Las Vegas. Admission to Bishop Gorman is competitive, based on middle-school grades, activities and attendance. Enrollment is roughly 85 percent Catholic, though no preference is given to students from Catholic elementary and middle schools. Approximately 95 percent of each Gorman graduating class goes on to college.

Hebrew Academy

9700 Hillpointe Rd. • 255-4500

Despite its title, this is a nondenominational academy. It is, however, a school of choice among Jewish families in Las Vegas. Opened in 1990, the school has 330 students and has expanded to embrace all grades, K through 12. Secondary students study a college-prep curriculum and virtually all go on to attend college. Religious studies, with an emphasis on Judaism and Jewish culture, are included in the course offerings.

Hillpointe Country Day School

9001 Hillpointe Rd. • 242-3230

Opened in fall 1997, this nonparochial campus in Summerlin has classes in grades K through 5. With a modern new campus, this school's small class sizes are hallmarks. The program that places a heavy emphasis on science and the arts. Entrance exams are required for pupils in grades 3 through 5. Enrollment is capped at 300.

Las Vegas Day School

3198 S. Jones Blvd. • 362-1180

It's called a day school, but students here spend a lot of time studying at night too. Offering an "accelerated" K through 8 curriculum, this nonparochial school has a competitive entrance exam and rigorous course requirements. Its teaching philosophy is grounded in the fundamentals of reading, writing and arithmetic. Founded in 1962, the school has 500 students. A pre-kindergarten program also is available.

The Meadows School

8601 Scholar Ln. • 254-1610

Arguably the most exclusive private school in the valley, and certainly the most expensive, The Meadows offers instruction from kindergarten through 12th grade. Set on 40 acres in Summerlin, this nonsectarian school emphasizes college prep curriculum. Opened in 1984, the school has grown to 660 students but has kept class sizes at a maximum of a 20-to-1 student-teacher ratio. Admission is competitive in all grades, based on scores from a standardized entrance exam. Many of Las Vegas' leading business executives and government leaders send their children here. In addition to highly regarded humanities and science programs, The Meadows also fields athletic teams. Uniforms are worn by all students.

Montessori Academy

6000 W. Oakey Blvd. • 870-5117

This school educates kindergartners through 6th-graders in the Montessori method. Founded in 1968, the academy has 200 students. Pupils in the first two grades share a classroom, allowing first-graders to do more advanced work if they are able. The philosophy of the school is to "let children learn at their own pace." Admission is open and noncompetitive.

Our Lady of Las Vegas

3036 Alta Dr. • 878-6841

Just a few miles west of downtown on the grounds of Our Lady of Las Vegas Catholic Church, this school educates 350 students in grades pre-kindergarten through 8. Like most Catholic campuses in Las Vegas, this one has a lengthy waiting list. Parishoners' children get first priority for admission, but each student is tested for academic readiness. Founded in 1959, the school offers a strong religious component, with students engaging in prayer at least three times daily. All students are Catholic.

St. Christopher's School

1840 N. Bruce St., North Las Vegas • 657-8008

This school provides a classic Catholic education in grades K through 8. Serving the North Las Vegas community since 1965, St. Christopher's is open to all students. But with a constant waiting list, parish families are the first to get in. Unlike some schools, St. Christopher's will place pupils' name on the waiting list without a charge or deposit. The 300-student campus has an 18-station computer lab and computers in each classroom.

St. Viator's Academy

4246 S. Eastern Ave. • 732-4477

Founded in 1970, this school is the largest of the Catholic elementary and middle schools with an enrollment of 700. St. Viator's makes extensive use of computers in every classroom, with terminals even included in kindergarten classes. In additional, two well-equipped computer labs are on the pre-kindergarten through 8th-grade campus. The school placed first in the small-school division of the statewide Math Counts mathematics competition and consistently performs well in regional science fairs, spelling bees and geography bees. Though this campus also has a long waiting list and gives preference to members of its parish, St. Viator's has admitted non-Catholics.

Trinity Christian School

950 E. St. Louis Ave. • 734-0562

Affiliated with the Trinity Life Center, an Assemblies of God church, Trinity Christian School has 500 students from kindergarten through 12th grade. Teachers instruct with a Christian philosophy, and the coursework is fully accredited. Dress and behavioral codes are strictly enforced. High school students receive a college-prep curriculum, and all 1996-97 graduates went to college. The school, founded in 1976, has an honors program and an interscholastic sports program.

Warren Walker School

2150 Windmill Pkwy., Henderson • 896-0780

The only nonparochial private school in

INSIDERS' TIP

The Clark County School District operates a Homework Hotline during the school year from 3:30 to 5:30 PM Monday through Friday. Volunteer instructors are available to help students with their studies. Some questions are answered on cable channel 4 from 4 to 5 PM. The hotline number is 799-5111.

Henderson, Warren Walker offers K through 8 instruction. Parents appreciate the small class sizes and after-school programs at this 25,000-square-foot school that opened in 1992. Enrollment is currently 320, and that number will increase after the school completes construction on a separate middle school campus for grades 6, 7 and 8. An entrance exam is given to all applicants to determine ability and placement.

Colleges and Universities

When it comes to post-secondary education in Las Vegas, the public choices are simple. The Community College of Southern Nevada is the two-year college. The University of Nevada, Las Vegas is the four-year institution.

Privately speaking, there are a few more options. Las Vegas College, the University of Phoenix and Webster University offer fully accredited degree programs in a variety of disciplines, though they're mainly focused in the business world.

Specialized vocational and trade colleges are listed in the next section.

Public Education

Community College of Southern Nevada

3200 E. Cheyenne Ave., North Las Vegas • 651-4000

The largest and fastest-growing college campus in the state, CCSN's enrollment now exceeds 30,000. The college offers associate arts degrees in 17 fields. Its culinary and dental hygiene programs are rated among the best in the nation.

Other heavily enrolled subjects are nursing, health sciences, automotive technology, air conditioning, criminal justice and information technologies.

A massive computer lab, with 700 terminals and full Internet access, is a hot spot for students at the main campus on Cheyenne Avenue. A comparable facility is at the CCSN branch campus at 6375 W. Charleston Boulevard, 877-1133. A slightly smaller lab is at the branch at 700 College Drive in Henderson, 564-7484. The computers have network access to library resources and the state's university system mainframes.

The college works closely with local businesses to provide training and skill development programs. In a novel twist, CCSN guarantees employers that workers will succeed in mastering the agreed-upon job training. If the worker fails the company's performance test, the school will waive all tuition charges.

The typical CCSN student is a 30-year-old woman with a young child (or two). The college conducts more than half of its classes in the evening to accommodate working students. And to make things easier for parents, the Cheyenne campus offers child-care services on site.

Applicants for admission generally must be high school graduates or GED holders. However, exceptions will be made under certain circumstances. High school students may be accepted with a recommendation from their principal. Others may qualify under the school's open-door admissions policy. Additional information on admission can be obtained by calling 651-4060. Community education programs, which are offered on a no-credit basis, have no admission requirements.

University of Nevada, Las Vegas

4505 S. Maryland Pkwy. • 895-3011, (800) 334-UNLV

Founded as a southern branch of the University of Nevada, Reno in 1951, UNLV has, in many ways, surpassed its older sibling. From 12 students in single room at Las Vegas High School, UNLV has grown into a 335-acre campus with enrollment topping 20,000.

UNLV offers more than 130 undergraduate, master's and doctoral degree programs. Its 1,100 faculty members instruct in disciplines

INSIDERS' TIP

Two public high schools — Green Valley in Henderson and Moapa Valley in rural Logandale — rated spots on *Redbook Magazine*'s list of "America's Best High Schools."

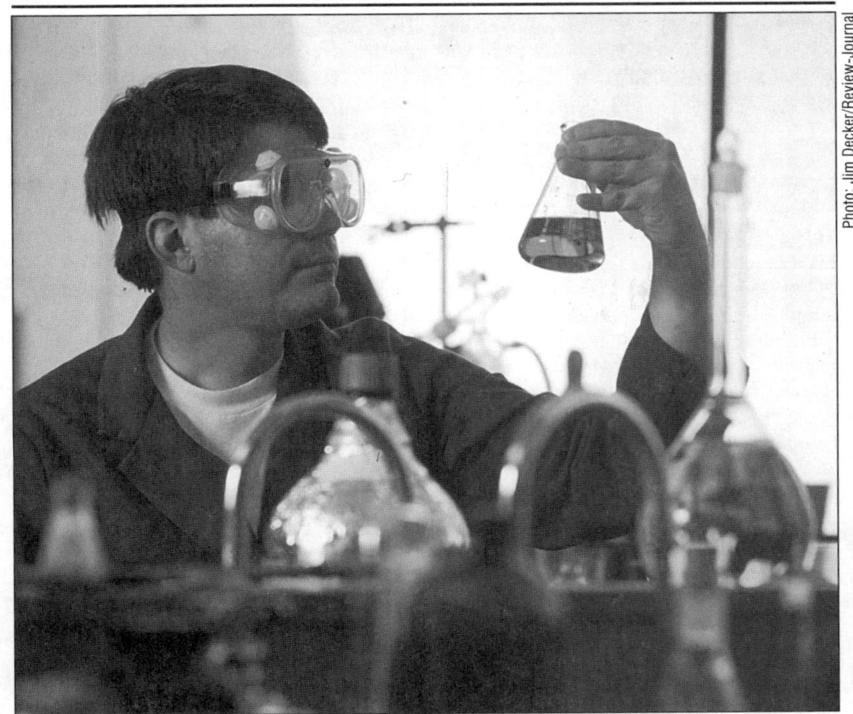

Photo: Jim Decker/Review-Journal

The Community College of Southern Nevada offers associate arts degrees in 17 fields, including biological sciences.

ranging from business and economics to human performance and development. The school has a large College of Education, which graduates more than 600 teachers each year.

One of the most noteworthy colleges on campus is the William F. Harrah College of Hotel Administration. Consistently ranked among the top three in the nation (along with Cornell and Purdue), the school offers first-hand, state-of-art exposure to students who learn all aspects of the hospitality and gaming industry at some of the world's largest hotels, less than 2 miles from campus.

While the University of Nevada, Reno houses the state's medical school, most of the practical work, including residencies and internships, are done at Las Vegas' University Medical Center. By the year 2000, UNLV will be home to Nevada's first law school. Currently under construction is a 300,000-square-foot research library, the biggest in the state.

Athletics, more than anything else, have put UNLV on the map. The Runnin' Rebels basketball team won the NCAA national championship in 1990. The golf team is among the best in the country. The school's tennis and baseball squads are also top NCAA performers. And UNLV even has a rough, tough rodeo team.

Admission to the Hotel Administration school is highly competitive. So, too, is the graduate program in business. But, generally, UNLV's entry requirements are not particularly strict. Applicants must have graduated from high school (or have a GED) and have attained at least a 2.5 grade point average (2.0 for Nevada residents). ACT or SAT test results must be submitted to the admissions office, but no minimum score is required.

Noncredit classes in the continuing education division also are conducted on campus. Each semester, more than 200 classes are offered in subjects that include real estate, computers, architecture and construction management. Information on these courses is available at 895-3394.

Private Education

Las Vegas College

3320 E. Flamingo Rd. • 434-0486

Formerly called Phillips Junior College, this school continues to offer associate arts degrees in business, accounting and computer science. Specialized certification programs also are awarded for paralegals, court reporters and administrative assistants. Acquired by Corinthian Colleges, a national chain of private two-year schools, Las Vegas College focuses on personalized education. Student-to-instructor ratios are a cozy 10-to-1. Extensive hands-on training is done in the school's high-powered Pentium computer lab. Students are guided into internships and benefit from the school's job-placement service. Current enrollment is 315. Applicants must have a high school diploma (or GED) and attain a minimum score on the school's entrance exam.

Nova University

2320 Paseo del Prado, Ste. 307 • 365-6682

This highly specialized school grants only one kind of degree: a master's in education. Headquartered in Florida, this private, nonprofit school conducts classes on Saturdays. Applicants must hold a bachelor's degree from an accredited college or university. Nova's students come from a variety of disciplines, but many are local teachers looking to hone their pedagogical skills and reach a higher rung on their schools' pay scale that a master's degree confers. Students progress at their own pace, though they must complete their studies within four years. Thirty faculty members instruct between 400 and 600 students annually.

University of Phoenix

2975 S. Rainbow Blvd. • 876-5004
333 N. Rancho, Ste. 300 • 638-7279
4475 England Ave. • 652-5527
4 Sunset Way, Henderson • 433-7008

A total of 1,000 undergraduate and graduate students are enrolled in the University of Phoenix's four area centers. The schools offer degrees in business, information systems, organizational management and education. Also available is a teacher certification program. Most classes are conducted at night, since the average student is a 35-year-old who has been in the workplace for 12 to 15 years. The average classroom, with 14 students, is equipped with computers, VCRs and overhead projectors for presentations. Applicants must be at least 23 years old and have a high school diploma (or GED). Undergraduates must have work experience. Graduate school applicants must have maintained at least a 2.5 grade point average in their undergraduate studies.

Webster University

3430 E. Flamingo Rd., Ste. 350 • 435-6660

Offering an exclusively postgraduate curriculum, Webster University grants master's degrees in business administration, computer resources, information management and human resources. Night classes are taught in four-hour blocks, with a heavy emphasis on presentation graphics and research. A computer lab with full Internet access is on site. Student-to-instructor ratios are extremely low, with 60 students and 24 adjunct professors. Applicants must have an undergraduate degree from an accredited college or university. All students are on probationary status during their first four classes, meaning that they must maintain at least a B- average.

Trade Schools

If you're looking to launch a new career, Las Vegas has the economy — and the schools — for you.

INSIDERS' TIP

Parochial schools are invariably crowded, with long waiting lists. Parishioners of affiliated churches receive priority on admissions and discounted tuition.

It wouldn't be surprising if Las Vegas has more card-dealing and bartending schools than any other city in the world. This is, after all, the gambling mecca of the globe. And its taverns operate 24 hours a day, seven days a week.

Dozens of casino gaming schools offer daytime and nighttime programs to teach table skills. Though neither the state nor its gaming establishments require any formal training of card and table dealers, local trade schools can help newcomers get their foot in the casino door. A certificate of completion from a reputable school elevates an applicant's chances. And the better schools, which cultivate good relations with local casinos, can provide effective job-placement services.

Prospective bartenders are required to hold a Techniques of Alcohol Management certificate. This verifies that the holder has been trained in the legal nuances of selling spirits, screening minors and handling over-imbibing customers. Such certification can be obtained through local bartender and cocktail-server schools. But TAM training does not involve the practice of actually mixing and serving drinks. Though not required, certificates of completion from local schools can be helpful in landing employment.

There are a number of allied trades for which the Las Vegas resort industry has strong demand. Among them: slot machine mechanics, security guards and hotel front-desk staff. Numerous schools specializing in these professions can be found in the Yellow Pages, listed under "Schools — Business and Vocational." Note: It's always a good idea to compare these private schools' credentials and costs with comparable programs available at the community college.

Other leading occupational fields in high demand here are computer programming, real estate, medical assistance and modeling. Scores of schools specialize in these fields.

One trade school that merits mention by name is Embry-Riddle Aeronautical University. A branch of the world's oldest, largest and most prestigious university specializing in aviation and aerospace, Embry-Riddle is at Nellis Air Force Base. It offers associate's, bachelor's and master's degrees in aviation business administration, professional aeronautics and management of technical operations. Major airlines hire more alumni from ERAU than from any other program. The Las Vegas branch is at 4475 England Avenue, Suite 217. The phone number is 643-0762.

Information about accreditation of occupational programs can be obtained through the state's Commission on Post-Secondary Education, which licenses and regulates private schools. The commission's Las Vegas office is at 1820 E. Sahara Avenue, Suite 111. The phone number is 486-7330.

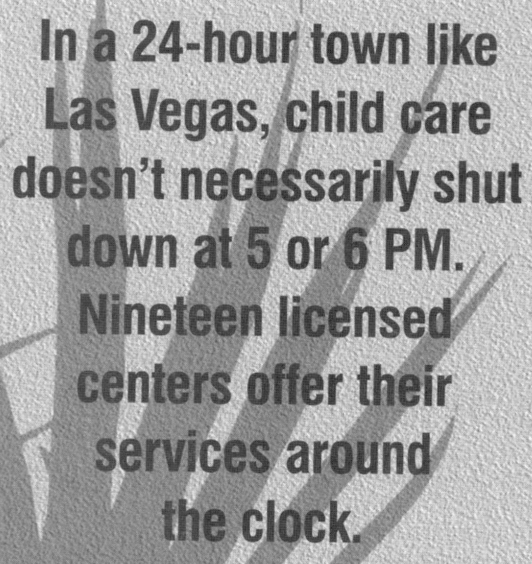

In a 24-hour town like Las Vegas, child care doesn't necessarily shut down at 5 or 6 PM. Nineteen licensed centers offer their services around the clock.

Child Care

Southern Nevada has more than 500 licensed child-care providers with roughly 21,000 spots for children. Most of the major national chain operations are here — and it seems like a new branch pops up every day.

In a 24-hour town like Las Vegas, child care doesn't necessarily shut down at 5 or 6 PM either. Nineteen licensed centers offer their services around the clock, some on a drop-in basis.

For visitor and newcomer alike, the word "licensed" can be important. Though the Yellow Pages and newspaper classifieds carry advertisements for a host of preschools, not all are licensed. Size doesn't necessarily separate the grain from the chaff; quality can be found at private homes as well as at big franchised centers.

So what's a mom or dad to do?

Resources

Child-care businesses are licensed and regulated by the cities, county and state. This jurisdictional split can be somewhat confusing because the different governmental entities do not share their information and referrals. Depending on where you are — and where you want your child to be — you will want to contact the appropriate agency for a list of licensed providers. They are:

- Clark County Social Services Licensing Board (unincorporated areas), 1600 Pinto Lane, 455-3894
- Las Vegas Licensing Board, 400 E. Stewart Avenue, 229-6922
- North Las Vegas Business License Department, 2266 Civic Center Drive, North Las Vegas, 633-1000
- State Licensing Board, 620 Belrose Street, Suite C, 486-5099 Note: This office licenses child-care operations in Henderson and Boulder City. It also licenses North Las Vegas centers caring for more than four youngsters.

Licensed centers are required to undergo staff-training sessions covering safety issues, CPR and techniques to recognize child abuse. Owners are instructed on insurance, contracts and facilities management. All staffers must be issued a sheriff's department child-care card and health card, which authorizes them to work in the county. Directors must have a child development certificate. Each employee receives six hours of training a year.

Staff-to-child ratios are established by the agencies. The ratios start at 1-to-4 for infants and go up from there. A typical center of 80 children may, however, have just six staffers since supervision rates are appreciably lower for older youngsters.

Each of the licensing agencies can tell you about any complaints lodged against centers in their area. They also have information about any special programs and hours that may be offered. They do not, however, track tuition rates. All information is free to the public.

Consumer assistance is also available from private nonprofit groups. The Clark County Child Care Association, 734-0504, one such organization, is a clearinghouse for child-care matters. The association provides helpful telephone referrals to the public and sponsors training workshops for child-care employees.

The majority of child-care centers and preschools in the valley are run out of private homes. Regulators limit such mom-and-pop outfits to six children. But that doesn't mean they're not busy. Many, in fact, offer 24-hour service, and a few will even accept drop-in customers if space is available.

Home Sweet Home, 896-1132, is a privately run, nonprofit group that serves as a specialized referral service for in-home centers. Callers can obtain free referrals for places near their home or work as well as get information on homes geared to children with special physical or emotional needs. Drop-ins are accommodated on a space-available basis.

For space reasons, this chapter eschews listing specific centers (except for those at hotels). One community facility is notable, however. The UNLV Preschool is the only center in Las Vegas to receive accreditation from the National Association for the Education of Young Children. The certification designates the center as meeting stringent standards for curriculum, employee training and staffing ratios (generally one staffer for every five children). Only 5 percent of the child-care centers around the country receive the NAEYC seal of approval. The 170-child facility, on campus at 4505 S. Maryland Parkway, is open to the public from 7:30 AM to 7 PM and accepts children ages 2½ to 6 on a first-come, first-served basis. For information call 895-3779.

FYI

Unless otherwise noted, the area code for all phone numbers listed in this chapter is 702.

Nannies and Babysitters

Kids Care Connection, 871-5555, provides nanny placement and a babysitting registry. This service, which acts as an employment agency, performs rigorous background checks on all of its workers. Staffers have CPR certification, along with health cards and child-care cards from the sheriff's department. Such screening and training is helpful, because the local governmental agencies do not regulate or refer nannies and babysitters.

Nannies' hours can range from just a couple of hours a day to live-in arrangements, with weekly rates starting around $250. About 10 percent of the nannies employed through this service live at their employers' residence. Kids Care Connection is affiliated with the International Nanny Association.

The babysitting registry provides 24-hour service. Clients can call Kids Care Connection at any hour of the day or night — an especially helpful feature for tourists in need of short-term care on short notice. Some sitters specialize in watching after sick or handicapped children. Rates generally run about $8 an hour.

Vacation Babysitting, 655-9084, has experienced sitters on call to provide childcare in hotel rooms throughout the city. They charge $38 for a four-hour minimum stay.

Mothers just looking to get out of the house for a couple of hours of adult camaraderie can take their toddlers (newborns to age 6) with them to Central Christian Church. The church-sponsored Moms of Preschoolers (MOPS) conducts a 2½-hour program every other week. Here, the children are can romp around in a supervised center while the moms retreat to enjoy a carry-in breakfast and guest speakers. Topics range from household finance to child psychology, and the presentations are followed by a group discussion and a craft-making period. MOPS is open to the public at a rate of $50 for eight programs, and there are discounts for moms who assist with child care. Central Christian Church is at 3375 S. Mojave Road. For information on MOPS in Las Vegas, call 735-4004 ext. 232.

Latchkey and After-School Programs

The child-care conundrum doesn't end when children go off to school. Working parents still need to find care for their youngsters before and after school.

One potential solution can be found at local day-care centers that provide shuttle service to and from schools. Most of the larger companies operate a fleet of vans to do just that. To ease the transportation task, more centers are being built adjacent to schools.

The public schools also are extending their hours to provide child care. A Safekey program operates at 125 elementary schools around the valley and enrolls about 9,000 children. Students can participate in before-school and after-school programs that run from 7 AM to 6 PM. Fees can be paid on a daily or weekly basis, with five-day rates running around $25 for after-school and $18 for before-school.

The Safekey program is coordinated by local parks and recreation departments and features athletic programs, guest speakers and other activities. School personnel also lend a helping hand with homework until mom and dad arrive.

With one-third of the Clark County School District's elementary campuses on year-round schedules, Safekey also offers track break programs. These daylong sessions keep kids active during the three-week mini-vacations scat-

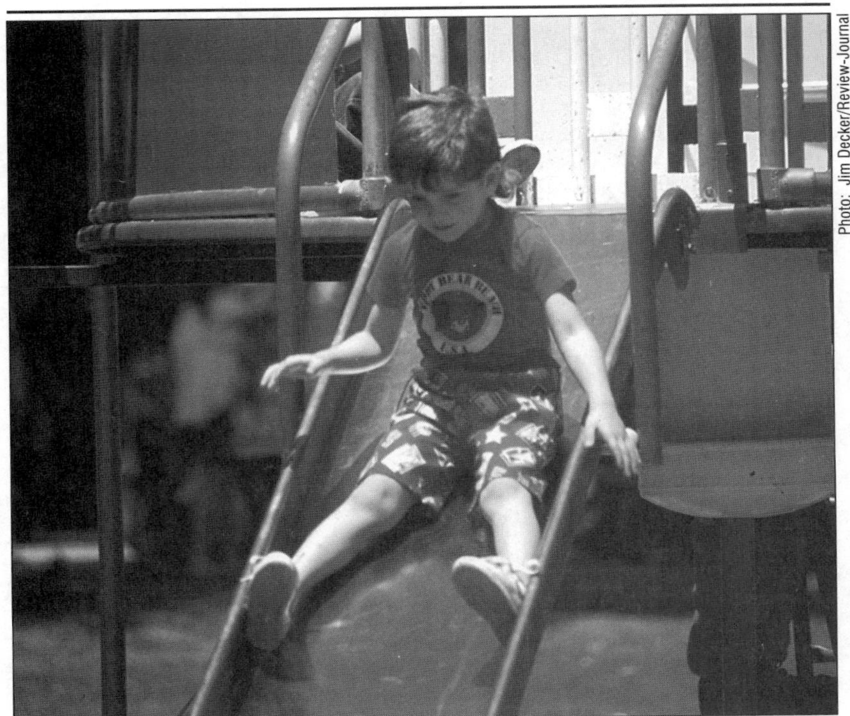

Photo: Jim Decker/Review-Journal

Day-care centers frequently plan field trips to area parks for recreation and picnics. There are more than 500 licensed child-care providers in the valley.

tered throughout the school year. Like the after-school program, the track break offerings are conducted on campus and include sports, crafts and movies. They also feature the occasional field trip. Safekey's information lines are 229-6729 and 733-0794.

Most private schools have pre-kindergarten programs, with many offering child-care programs after school. Enrollment in the pre-kindergarten programs may give your young child a leg up when it comes time to enroll in 1st grade classes, many of which have long waiting lists.

Another after-school program of note is operated by the Boys and Girls Clubs around the valley. Games, crafts and study groups are among the offerings. And shuttle service is provided at selected schools. Track break programs also are offered. To locate the club nearest your child's school, and to find out about transportation and tuition fees, contact the Boys and Girls Club's main office at 367-2582.

The YMCA, 877-9622, offers track break programs from 9 AM to 4 PM daily. Students or their families must be Y members (annual children's rate is $20). There is no after-school program, though members can use the facilities throughout the school year.

If you are a student with young children, the Boys and Girls Club can also help in this area. This nonprofit organization operates child-care centers on the Cheyenne Avenue and Charleston Boulevard campuses of the Community College of Southern Nevada. Open from 3 PM to 11 PM, this allows afternoon and evening students to bring their youngsters to school with them. The program is geared toward school-aged children, and counselors are on hand to assist with homework assignments before the games begin. Participants must be at least 6 years old. For information on fees call 367-2582.

Hotel Child-care Programs

Though Las Vegas markets itself as a family-friendly destination, don't expect every hotel to have child-care programs. In fact, only a handful of resorts provide such services.

If you are looking for in-room babysitters, the concierge desk is a good place to start. Most hotels keep a short list of providers who will come to your room. In addition, most hotels usually can recommend nearby child-care centers that accept drop-ins (also see our Nannies and Babysitters section in this chapter).

In any event, tourists should note that late nights at hotel arcades are NOT considered a suitable form of child care. In 1997, the Clark County Commission tightened local curfew laws along The Strip. Unsupervised children younger than 18 are barred from hotel arcade and game rooms from 10 PM to 5 AM on weekdays and from midnight to 5 AM on weekends and holidays. Unattended minors are not allowed on the streets after 10 PM Sunday through Thursday or after midnight on Fridays and Saturdays. Any child who violates the curfew rules, or any parent or guardian of the child, could be fined up to $300.

Here's a rundown on the ones that do. Note: Unless stated otherwise, hourly rates apply. Fees usually run around $5 an hour, though they will vary depending on the time and day.

Boulder Station

4111 Boulder Hwy. • 432-7777, (800) 683-7777

This hotel-casino on the east side of town features a Kids Quest child-care center. Open from 9 AM to midnight, this indoor playground has lots of room for children to gambol while the adults gamble. The center accepts infants as young as 6 months and as old as 12 years. A separate room houses the toddlers. This facility and its sister center at Sunset Station are the only hotel-casino programs that don't require children to be potty trained.

Gold Coast

4000 W. Flamingo Rd. • 367-7111

Just minutes west of The Strip, this hotel-casino houses a center that's open from 8:30 AM to midnight. The facility is free to the children of hotel guests and visitors, with a three-hour daily limit. The center features movies, toys, crafts and a listening center where children can enjoy music and stories. Children must be ages 2 to 8.

MGM Grand

3805 Las Vegas Blvd. S. • 891-3200

It figures that the largest hotel in Las Vegas would put on a big production for kids. The King Looey Activity Center accepts children ages 3 to 12. The preschool facility for ages 3 through 6 features a playhouse, tumbling mats, puppets and other entertainment. Older children have a well-appointed game room offering Foosball, Ping Pong and mini pool tables. Other diversions include a supervised visit to the adjacent MGM Grand Theme Park. Both groups can enjoy an arts and crafts room as well as a lounge area equipped with a large-screen TV showing the latest in children's films. Only the children of registered hotel guests are admitted.

Sam's Town

5111 Boulder Hwy. • 456-7777

Just down the road from Boulder Station, this casino provides three free hours of daily child care. Children must be 3 to 8 years old. The center's staffers get involved with the kids, making crafts and organizing games. A TV and VCR are available for on-screen entertainment. Hours are 9 AM to midnight Mon-

INSIDERS' TIP

When interviewing prospective child-care centers or homes, ask to see their license. It should be displayed and current.

day through Thursday, 4 PM to midnight Friday and Sunday and 5 PM to midnight on Saturday.

Silver Nugget

2140 Las Vegas Blvd. N., North Las Vegas • 399-1111

Children can stay and play for up to three hours for free at this casino just north of downtown. Loaded with toys and equipped with a TV and VCR, the facility is open to children ages 2 to 12. A separate nap room is available for youngsters tuckered out by all the excitement. The center is open from 3 to 11:30 PM.

Showboat

2800 Fremont St. • 385-9123

Just east of downtown, this hotel-casino's child-care center is open to youngsters ages 2 to 7. Equipped with toys, blocks and a TV-VCR, the center is open from 9 AM to 11:45 PM.

Sunset Station

1301 W. Sunset Rd., Henderson • 547-7777

Like its stable mate up the road, this hotel-casino's child-care center is operated by Kids Quest. With high ceilings and lots of gymnastic equipment, this facility is open from 9 AM to midnight. Children ages 6 months to 12 years are accepted. Also like Boulder Station, there are movie theaters next door — affording youngsters yet another source of entertainment.

Support Groups

With its high divorce rate and plethora of single parents, the Las Vegas area offers some very useful support groups.

For young mothers, Columbia Hospital Sunrise hosts a Baby and Me program. Open to mothers and their children up to 18 months old, Baby and Me provides instruction on such things as feeding and diapering during weekly 90-minute classes. The program is free and open to the public. Enrollment information can be obtained by calling 731-8703.

The La Leche League also runs free programs geared specifically to breast-feeding moms. Weekly meetings are held around the valley, where moms can exchange information about child care and other family issues. For information on the league's activities and schedules, call 658-7843 or 875-4084.

Parents Anonymous, 368-1533, hosts free parenting support groups throughout the year. The sessions provide problem-solving tips, along with educational information about parenting and family life. These support groups also serve as networking links to identify daycare services. A similar program called the Parenting Project is sponsored by the Clark County Department of Social Services, 455-5295.

Parents Without Partners, 366-0002, has an active local chapter with more than 250 members. This group focuses on activities that appeal to both children and adults. Camping trips, drive-in movies and birthday parties are scheduled regularly throughout the year. Parents take turns supervising children so that adults have time to interact. This group is also a valuable source for learning about child-care facilities. Members are required to take an orientation class before joining.

For low-income families, two ongoing programs can help. The Economic Opportunity Board provides financial assistance for child care. The nonprofit agency, at 820 Shadow Lane, Suite 401, maintains a list of participating providers around the valley. Approximately 3,000 families receive discounted rates, based on their income level. For information and eligibility requirements, call EOB at 387-0985.

The Nevada Association of Latin Americans operates its own bilingual day-care center for children ages 2 to 6. Fees are based according to a family's ability to pay. The NALA center is at 323 N. Maryland Parkway, and its number is 382-6252.

INSIDERS' TIP

Citicorp Nevada is the only local company with an on-site child-care center for the children of its employees. Launched in 1991, the facility at 8725 W. Sahara Avenue cares for 160 youngsters.

A widening range of medical treatment is available here, meaning that Las Vegans no longer have to leave town to get topnotch care in most fields.

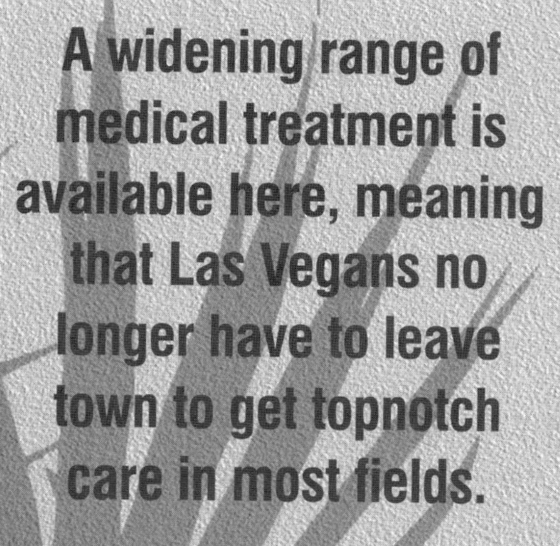

Healthcare

As a growing city, Las Vegas is rapidly adding hospital beds, walk-in clinics and a variety of specialized healthcare. It's a good thing, too, because Nevada exhibits some unhealthy lifestyles. The state's aggregate health index (measuring such habits as smoking, drinking and drug use) rates near the bottom — 45th of the 50 states. The state ranks highest in the nation for suicide rates, alcohol consumption and smokers (30.5 percent). It is 11th in the nation in per-capita AIDS cases.

Many of the statistics are skewed by Las Vegas' huge tourist population. Smoky casinos ply players with free drinks and fattening buffets while encouraging a 24-hour lifestyle. Recognizing the risks, one casino, Sam's Town on Boulder Highway, has purchased a hospital-style "crash cart," complete with defibrillator, to respond quickly to patrons who may suffer a heart attack. The hotel-casino has trained staff to operate the equipment and stabilize patients while waiting for paramedics. Other resorts are considering similar upgrades for their in-house medical operations.

Whether or not they indulge in gambling and its attendant vices, local residents feel the effects of high-risk behavior. Health insurance rates are on the high side in Las Vegas, and the county's public hospital, University Medical Center, is often overcrowded and perennially in debt.

Fortunately, new hospitals are springing up and adding facilities. The local hospital bed count now exceeds 2,600. And a widening range of medical treatment is available here, meaning that Las Vegans no longer have to leave town to get topnotch care in most fields. However, southern Nevada still lacks the medical staff and facilities to conduct heart, lung and liver transplants. For those procedures, patients must travel to Los Angeles or Phoenix, 300 miles away.

This chapter details the scope of healthcare in Las Vegas, from neonatal care to hospice services. Included are listings of useful emergency and referral services. Also noteworthy is the section on some of the region's emerging medical specialties, such as corrective eye surgery and plastic surgery.

We'll start with the area's major hospitals, listed in alphabetical order. All have 24-hour emergency rooms. As in our other chapters, all facilities are in Las Vegas unless otherwise designated.

Hospitals

Boulder City Hospital

901 Adams Blvd., Boulder City • 293-4111

This 67-bed facility recently underwent remodeling, expanding an intensive care unit. The 58,000-square-foot nonprofit hospital offers a full lab, radiology services, respiratory and physical therapy, and obstetric care. The community hospital, with a staff of 170, performs orthopedic surgery, plastic surgery, laparoscopy, and glaucoma and cataract surgery. Roughly half the beds are utilized by the hospital's long-term and convalescent care facility. The hospital also offers a home healthcare program, which assigns nurses to attend to house-bound patients. Physicians staff a weekend clinic to treat minor illnesses.

Columbia Sunrise Hospital and Medical Center

3186 S. Maryland Pkwy. • 731-8000

The largest hospital in Nevada with 688 beds, this complex includes Sunrise Children's Hospital, which specializes in treating pediatric cancer patients. It is rated one of the premier children's healthcare facilities in the Southwest and has a 145-bed unit that includes a pediatric open-heart surgery suite.

As a leading trauma facility, Sunrise has a 72-bed adult critical care unit. Kidney transplants are performed at the renal transplant center. More than 600 open-heart surgeries are performed annually. Sunrise also has the only bone-marrow transplant unit in southern Nevada. Other special programs include a separate Women's Pavilion, a 55-bed unit that houses labor, delivery, nursery, gynecology and fetal assessment. The hospital provides a full range of neonatal and obstetric services. Also on site are day surgery and a sleep-disorder center.

The for-profit hospital — owned by Columbia-HCA, the nation's largest hospital chain — opened in 1958 and has expanded to 510,000 square feet and 24 surgical suites. Its staff of 2,500 now sees an average of 489 patients a day.

FYI

Unless otherwise noted, the area code for all phone numbers listed in this chapter is 702.

Columbia Sunrise Mountain View Hospital

3100 N. Tenaya Way • 255-5000

Constructed in 1996 in the city's burgeoning northwest area, this still-growing hospital has 120 beds and some of the region's most modern diagnostic equipment, including computerized tomography scanners and magnetic resonance imagers. An urgent care center is next door in the emergency room. In its next phase of construction, the hospital will expand its current 220,000 square feet to reach a total of 400 patient rooms. The hospital also is owned by Columbia-HCA.

Desert Springs Hospital

2075 E. Flamingo Rd. • 733-8800

This 225-bed facility on the city's near-east side specializes in cardiology. It offers Nevada's only Coronary Heart Disease Reversal Program, which utilizes research showing that heart disease can be prevented, slowed and, in some cases, reversed through changes in diet and lifestyle. The Desert Springs Nutrition Clinic, affiliated with the hospital, is nearby at 4225 S. Eastern Avenue, 369-7961. The for-profit hospital, opened in 1971, spans 256,000 square feet and has nine surgical suites with a staff of 1,100. Also on site is the Diabetes Treatment Center, the only diabetic patient education program in Nevada recognized by the American Diabetes Association in accordance with the National Standards for Diabetes Patient Education Programs. Another special department is the Maternity Center, which features labor, delivery, recovery and postpartum suites. The center offers a six-week childbirth class, siblings class, refresher childbirth class and an ongoing breastfeeding support group.

For tourists and residents alike, Desert Springs also operates Call for Health, 733-6875. With telephone lines open from 8 AM to 5 PM Monday through Friday, this nurse-run service matches a physician to the caller's specific medical needs and assists in making appointments. Additionally, the nurses can provide information on a wide range of medical topics.

Lake Mead Hospital Medical Center

1409 E. Lake Mead Blvd., North Las Vegas • 649-7711

Opened in 1960, this 185,000-square-foot facility includes a Women's Plaza, with four labor and delivery suites, 20 postpartum beds and a surgical suite for Cesarean deliveries. The hospital offers a full range of neonatal, obstetric and pediatric services. Postpartum moms are offered a second day free if they would otherwise be unable to stay due to

INSIDERS' TIP

Free AIDS tests are available at the Clark County Health District. For hours and locations of the nearest clinic, call 385-1291. The American Cancer Society offers a referral service for smokers who are trying to kick the habit. The number is 798-6857. From the first Monday in May until the last Thursday in August, the ACS also offers free skin-cancer screenings. Call their number for times and locations.

insurance constraints. As a community service, the hospital sponsors free birthing classes that include infant CPR and sibling classes.

Lake Mead Hospital is one of 60 hospitals nationwide to offer transfusion-free medicine and surgery. The technique requires no blood transfusions and can be used in a variety of procedures, including open-heart and bypass surgery. The for-profit facility has 198 beds and 622 staffers and is the main hospital for the city of North Las Vegas.

St. Rose Dominican Hospital
102 E. Lake Mead Dr., Henderson • 564-2622

Serving the southeast valley, St. Rose is the region's only religiously affiliated healthcare provider. The facility, which opened in 1947, owes its continued success to the Adrian Dominican Sisters, who paid one dollar and assumed the debt of the facility in 1953. They promised to stay 25 years — and they're still there.

Today the main campus features 147 beds in a 220,000-square-foot complex that employs 650 staffers. It has four surgical suites, including a 10-bed coronary care unit. Cardiology and obstetrics are among the leading specialties. The hospital plans to add a satellite medical center in neighboring Green Valley some time in 1998.

Summerlin Medical Center
655 Town Center Dr. • 233-7000

Opened in 1997 in the city's western foothills, this medical center has 149 beds and 265,000 square feet of space. Unique to southern Nevada, Summerlin Medical Center has all private rooms and baths, with one bed to a suite. Next door is an 111,000-square-foot medical office building, which includes an outpatient diagnostic and surgical center, a mammography suite and an urgent care center.

Like the Mountain View hospital, just 7 miles to the north, Summerlin Medical Center is affiliated with a larger established medical center closer to downtown. In this case, the parent campus is Valley Hospital. A helicopter pad allows the medical center to use Valley Hospital's Flight for Life air ambulance.

University Medical Center
1800 W. Charleston Blvd. • 383-2000

With 600,000 square feet, this sprawling three-block hospital is the public health facility for Clark County. Opened in 1931 with 20 beds, it has steadily grown to include 560 beds and seven surgical suites. In addition to fulfilling its public health mission and serving as the state's designated trauma center for southern Nevada, UMC has become a specialist in oncology and cardiology. It also houses Nevada's only Burn Care Center. Plans to implement a heart, liver and lung transplant program are being considered.

UMC is affiliated with the University of Nevada School of Medicine, which operates a residency program in internal medicine, obstetrics, gynecology and general surgery. An average of 357 patients are seen daily, the second-highest volume behind Columbia Sunrise. UMC has 15 surgical suites and 2,500 staffers.

Valley Hospital Medical Center
620 Shadow Ln. • 388-4000

Just two blocks away from UMC, this for-profit hospital is best known for its Flight for Life helicopter that airlifts patients from far-flung venues. Injured rock climbers in Red Rock Canyon and victims of boating accidents at Lake Mead have been flown to Valley Hospital, with minutes meaning a matter of life or death. Flight for Life even goes beyond Clark County's borders to serve rural counties and neighboring areas of California, Arizona and Utah.

The hospital, built in 1971, has added a state-of-the-art neonatal nursery and cardiology department and continues to specialize in oncology treatment. It also has a FastER program, an expansion of its emergency room services. Valley has 400,000 square feet, 417 beds and 15 surgical suites staffed by 1,300 employees.

Specialized Facilities

Charter Hospital of Las Vegas
7000 W. Spring Mountain Rd. • 876-4357

Treating mentally ill and chemically dependent patients, this 82-bed private facility focuses its care on drug and alcohol abusers and compulsive gamblers. The hospital has a locked inpatient facility with an admissions office that's open 24 hours. Teams of registered nurses and therapists also will go into crisis situations, such as crime scenes and hospital emergency rooms, to counsel victims. Such assessments, whether done in-house or in the field, are performed free. Adult psychiatric patients account for half the inpatient population. The hospital has a separate wing for adolescents, who compose nearly 20 percent of the patients. Length of stay averages around eight days.

Day treatment programs also are offered. Patients spend eight hours per day, Monday through Friday, in intensive treatment and can return home to their families in the evening. Charter has outpatient branches at 2080 E. Flamingo Road, 794-0004, and 6877 W. Charleston Boulevard, 254-8348.

JHC Health Center

1001 Shadow Ln. • 388-3688, (888) 527-3422

Occupational safety and healthcare are JHC's specialties. From employment screening to postoperative pain control, this publicly run outpatient facility is a medical bridge between employers and employees. In addition to handling workers' compensation claims for the usual array of strains and sprains, the center's staff of nurses and doctors provides neuro-rehabilitation, speech therapy and other specialized services. The 100,000-square-foot facility, staffed by 40 healthcare professionals, has traditionally been the final stop for injured workers on their way back to the job. In recent years JHC has become more proactive at the front end, administering pre-employment physicals and drug tests. By putting prospective hires through a battery of simulations using actual equipment, the center helps employers determine the ability of applicants to perform the necessary job functions.

Las Vegas Mental Health Center

6161 W. Charleston Blvd. • 486-6000

Operated by the state of Nevada, this 76-bed facility provides inpatient care to the mentally ill. A crisis unit is staffed 24 hours a day by psychiatrists who assess prospective patients. Referrals also are made. A medication clinic and outpatient counseling are available on site. Inpatients participate in a range of programs, including psychosocial rehabilitation, activity therapy and off-campus work duty.

Montevista Hospital

5900 W. Rochelle Ave. • 364-1111

This 80-bed private facility offers 24-hour care for patients suffering from drug and alcohol abuse, depression, stress, phobias and eating disorders. An affiliate of the Behavioral Health Care chain, which has 42 facilities nationwide, Montevista offers a full range of inpatient and outpatient psychiatric services for adults and adolescents. It also has a unique residential program for children ages 5 to 12 and a geropsychiatric division for people 65 and older. Free assessments are conducted at the hospital or by appointment. Montevista, with a staff of 200, also sponsors periodic workshops and seminars on substance abuse and psychological disorders.

Nathan Adelson Hospice

4141 S. Swenson St. • 733-0320

This community-sponsored facility serves the terminally ill and their families. Designed to comfort patients in their final days, Nathan Adelson attends to physical, emotional and spiritual needs. Patients are encouraged to stay as active as possible, and the center conducts numerous programs on site for patients and loved ones.

INSIDERS' TIP

Clark County has 1,480 licensed physicians and 360 dentists and oral surgeons. Doctors are licensed through the state Board of Medical Examiners, 486-6244, while dentists are licensed with the state Board of Dental Examiners, 255-4211. These offices can tell you if a healthcare provider is a member in good standing.

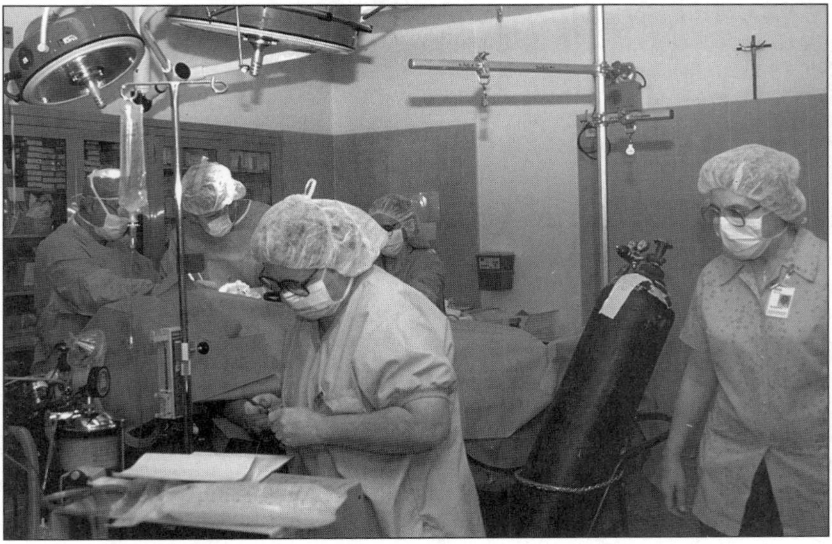

Photo: Jim Decker/Review-Journal

Surgical specialties are expanding as Las Vegas grows. Local residents no longer have to leave town for many major operations.

Most of the care is provided in the patient's home, with inpatient care available for short-term stays. Enrollment is based on need, with charges based on income. Medicare payments are accepted. The facility is open 24 hours every day.

Inn-House Doctor

300 Fremont St. • 259-1616

Yes, some Las Vegas doctors still make house calls — or more specifically, room calls. Catering to guests of local hotels and motels, Inn-House Doctor will dispatch a physician to any room in the city within 30 minutes. This 24-hour medical "valet" service is linked with Valley Hospital and will transport patients there as needed. The doctors refer to their program as VIP treatment and handle outpatient treatment and prescriptions as well as inpatient admissions.

Rehabilitation Hospital

1250 Valley View Blvd. • 877-8898

An acute care facility for recovering patients, Rehabilitation Hospital treats serious postoperative cases. The facility has 63 beds for inpatients and a clinic for outpatients. A brain-injury unit and short-term care facility are among the specialized programs offered by this private center opened in 1993. The average inpatient stay is 16 days at this hospital, which has 100 medically licensed staffers.

Shearing Eye Institute

2575 S. Lindell Rd. • 362-3937

State-of-the-art cataract surgery is performed at this outpatient facility, the first in Nevada to do no-shot, no-stitch operations under topical anesthetic. Founded in 1970, the institute has been honored for its pioneering work in ophthalmology. It specializes in laser-guided corneal and refractive surgery to correct nearsightedness, in addition to treating glaucoma. Founder Steven Shearing is listed in "The Best Doctors in America," a roster compiled by a national poll of physicians. The institute conducts free screenings for cataracts and glaucoma by appointment.

Southwest Institute

341 N. Buffalo Dr. • 242-4616

Cosmetic surgery, often called plastic surgery, is a major business in Las Vegas, where residents strive to retain their youthful looks. This outpatient facility specializes in body contouring —which includes breast enlargements and reductions, liposuction, tummy tucks and face-lifts — and reconstructive surgery for sun-damaged skin. For additional related services, see the referral list in this chapter.

THC Hospital

5100 W. Sahara Ave. • 871-1418

Bridging the gap between traditional hospitals and convalescent centers, THC is a long-term acute care facility. Usually used as a referral center, THC treats patients who may be discharged from acute care hospitals but are not ready for rehabilitation or nursing facilities. This privately run, 52-bed hospital specializes in the treatment of "medically complex" patients. These include patients recuperating from serious wound complications or major surgery. Special beds are designed for patients with infectious wounds and for those undergoing cancer treatments. A pulmonary program cares for patients who have difficulties breathing and are dependent on ventilators or airway maintenance devices. Recovering patients are assisted in weaning themselves off ventilators. The average length of stay is 35 to 45 days. Though THC has no emergency room or surgical suites, it maintains many of the same departments found in conventional hospitals, including cardiology, internal medicine and radiology.

Walk-in Clinics

Urgent care clinics are found throughout the Las Vegas Valley. The following is a list of private urgent care clinics with extended or 24-hour schedules. These facilities, also open on weekends, do not require appointments and are equipped to handle nonsurgical emergencies and illnesses. You will want to check with your insurance company to determine if coverage applies. Some clinics have additional locations with shorter hours of operation. The phone numbers listed here may used as references for those other locations.

Note: If you are a local resident in need of nonemergency care, the **Clark County Health District**'s main offices at 625 Shadow Lane and at 129 W. Lake Mead Drive in Henderson offer a variety of walk-in services, including well-baby check-ups. The main office number is 385-1291. The Henderson clinic can be reached at 564-3232. Provided free or at a nominal charge are sexually transmitted disease tests and immunizations. Tests and shots are given during regular office hours, Monday through Friday from 8 AM to 4 PM. A $10 fee is charged but is waived if the patient cannot pay. The health district also

Emergency Numbers

Police, fire and ambulance	**911**
Addiction Treatment Center	**383-1347**
Adult Children of Alcoholics	**369-2262**
Aid for AIDS	**382-2326, (800) 342-AIDS**
Al-anon Family Groups	**642-7438**
Alcoholics Anonymous	**598-1888**
American Red Cross	**384-1225**
Child Abuse and Neglect Hotline	**399-0081**
Child and Adult Sexual Assault Center	**366-1640**
Community Action Against Rape	**385-2153**
Domestic Crisis Shelter	**646-4981**
Gamblers Anonymous	**385-7732**
Homemaker Home Health Aide	**455-4430**
Lupus Foundation	**369-0474**
Mental Health Crisis Unit	**486-8020**
Narcotics Anonymous	**369-3362**
Planned Parenthood	**(800) 322-1020**
Poison Center (Columbia Sunrise)	**732-4989**
Senior Citizens Protective Center	**455-4291**
Suicide Prevention Center	**731-2990**
Youth Crisis Hotline	**(800) 448-4663**

operates 34 satellite clinics, including a first-aid clinic at McCarran International Airport.

Fremont Medical Centers, 520 E. Fremont Street, 382-5200; 4415 W. Flamingo Road, 382-5200; 595 W. Lake Mead Drive, Henderson, 566-5500

Galleria Urgent Care, 600 Whitney Road, Henderson, 454-8898

Green Valley Urgent Care, 6301 Mountain Vista Street, Henderson, 451-3636

Hogan Clinics 4241 S. Nellis Boulevard, 898-1405; 4 Sunset Way, Henderson, 434-1111

Industrial Medical Group, 3673 Polaris Avenue, 871-1721; 151 W. Brooks Avenue, North Las Vegas, 399-6545

Inn-House Doctor (on-call service), 300 E. Fremont Street, 259-1616

Las Vegas Medical Center, 150 E. Harmon Avenue, 796-1104

Nevada Medical Center Urgent Care, 5701 W. Charleston Boulevard #100, 877-9500

Pueblo Medical Center, 8551 W. Lake Mead Boulevard, 256-8474

Southwest Medical Associates, 888 S. Rancho Drive, 877-8600

UMC Quick Care Centers, 1800 W. Charleston Boulevard, 383-2074; 2760 Lake Sahara Drive 254-4900; 4333 N. Rancho Drive, 658-4507; 61 N. Nellis Boulevard, 644-8701; 1769 Russell Road, 261-3600

Referral Services

The following names and numbers can put you in touch with healthcare specialists and professionals. Note that most hospitals also maintain referral lists for physicians.

American Society of Plastic Surgeons, (800) 635-0635

Clark County Dental Society, 255-7873

Clark County Medical Society, 739-9989

Nevada State Chiropractic Association, (702) 324-2299

Alternative Healthcare

If conventional medicine doesn't work for what ails you, Las Vegas has hundreds of licensed practitioners specializing in a wide array of healing arts.

Chiropractors can be found throughout the valley, with more than 200 certified by the state. Chiropractic is the manual adjustment of joints, particularly the spine, to treat disease. In addition to the typical neck and back adjustments, some offices provide laser pain therapy, some specialize in sports injury treatment and others have stress management programs. The state's Board of Chiropractic Examiners, based in Reno, licenses all chiropractors and will furnish a list of certified practitioners. The office phone number is 688-1919.

In 1973, Nevada became the first state to license acupuncture as medical treatment. A Chinese medical technique, acupuncture is used primarily for the relief of pain but also for curing disease and improving general health. It consists of inserting hair-thin needles into muscles. More than a dozen Asian acupuncturists work in the valley. Some specialize in electric or laser acupuncture and purport to treat ailments ranging from arthritis and gout to prostate problems and baldness. Their credentials can be checked through the state's Board of Oriental Medicine at 432-8248.

Another state-sanctioned form of healthcare is homeopathy. Based on the principle that "likes are cured by likes," homeopathy teaches that drugs that cause disease symptoms in healthy individuals can also be used to cure illnesses that produce the same symptoms in sick individuals. Homeopathy uses substances to stimulate the body's natural defenses and recuperative powers. A physician referral list can be obtained through the state Board of Homeopathy at 258-5487.

Still other alternative providers believe that inner consciousness is the key to health. Holistic clinics use hypnosis, biofeedback and nutrition therapy and other practices to treat patients. Some chiropractors use touch-oriented therapies to promote greater relaxation, to improve body alignment and functioning or to enhance sensory awareness. Likewise, acupuncturists provide "acupressure" massage. Other practitioners employ herbal medicines or vitamin therapy. "Psychic healing" is practiced by some to "clean the body's aura" to loosen muscles and relieve soreness. Such "relaxation therapy" is not recognized by any local or state agency, and no referral sources are available.

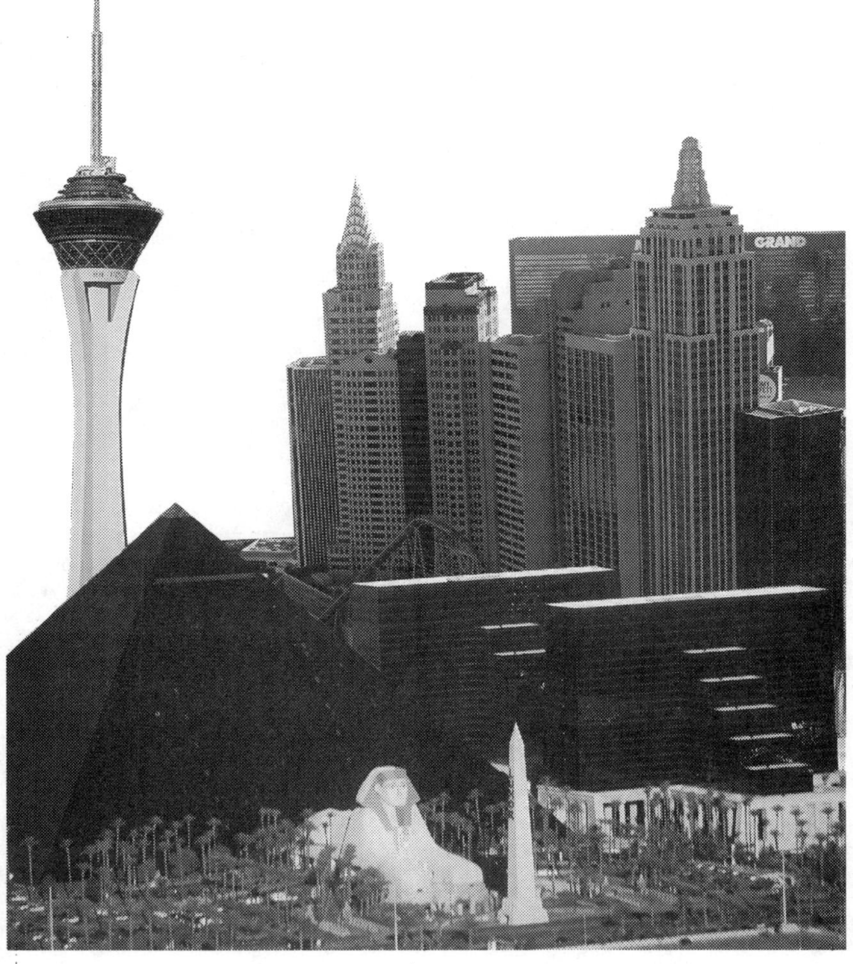
GRAND

Media

Las Vegas is a gawky teenager in the media market. As a city founded in this century, its relatively young media are still expanding and maturing. And it's all happening with great rapidity. Ranked so low that it was almost off the proverbial radar screen just a few years ago, the Las Vegas media market has burst into the nation's top 100. As of summer 1997, it was the country's 61st largest media market — a figure that's been climbing as fast as a Megabucks jackpot.

Radio speaks volumes about the growth. Once home to just a handful of small homespun AM stations, the Las Vegas market now has more than 30 radio outlets, giving the city one of the highest stations-per-capita rates in the United States. You'll find most of the nation's syndicated talkers somewhere on the local dial.

Though Las Vegas is not ringed by suburbs and satellite communities, which boost metropolitan populations of some smaller cities elsewhere, this desert valley's population of 1.1 million puts Las Vegas on the national media map. As such, advertising rates have increased and a wider variety of programming can be heard and seen over the airwaves.

Outside publications have taken note too. The latest editions of the *Los Angeles Times* are flown into town and sell for just 50¢ at newsstands around town. *The New York Times* and *USA Today* offer home delivery.

Meantime, homegrown media are thriving and evolving here. In addition to the mainstream press, free and alternative periodicals can be found in copious quantities at stores and in newsracks. Specialty publications range from church periodicals to some of the heftiest home and apartment guides you'll ever see (check our Real Estate chapter for home guide listings). Indeed, there's enough bulk here to roll your own Presto Logs in the winter. So read on.

Newspapers

Las Vegas' two daily newspapers share a rough-and-tumble tradition that continues to this day. In head-to-head competition since 1950, the *Las Vegas Review-Journal* and the *Las Vegas Sun* provide Las Vegans with an increasingly rare luxury — a morning and afternoon paper.

Though the *Review-Journal*, known in the local shorthand as the *R-J*, is the far bigger publication, the rivalry has continued under the auspices of a federally approved joint operating agreement. The JOA, as it's called in the newspaper business, consolidated the two papers' business operations in 1990. Under the agreement, the *R-J* sells the advertising, runs the press and handles the delivery of both newspapers. By merging these business functions, the papers consolidated their costs, and the *Sun*, which had been failing financially, lives on.

Despite the JOA, the editorial staffs of the *R-J* and *Sun* remain fiercely and aggressively independent of each other. Reporters strive to scoop their competition, and the editors periodically fire editorial potshots over each other's news coverage.

Bare-knuckled competition notwithstanding, the *R-J/Sun* arrangement can still be a bit confusing. The papers publish joint morning editions on Saturdays, Sundays and major holidays, with virtually all the content provided by the *R-J*. And while much of the two newspapers' advertising is identical in the weekday editions, the thicker *R-J* has more ads from retail giants like Macy's and Nieman Marcus.

Ultimately, the reader's choice comes down to personal preferences. The JOA's unofficial motto puts it best: Different papers, different views. Read on for more.

This section is divided into daily and weekly segments — both containing publications of general interest. Specialty periodicals can be found in the subsequent section titled "Magazines and Other Print Media." Unless stated otherwise, the publications are purchased through subscriptions or at newsstands.

Dailies

Las Vegas Review-Journal
1111 W. Bonanza Rd. • 383-0211

In its early days, the dusty little town of Las Vegas had three newspapers. The first, the *Las Vegas Age*, began publishing in 1906—a year after the city was incorporated. Rising and falling with the ebb and flow of the local economy, the *Age* was variously a weekly, a semi-weekly or a daily. The *Review* and the *Journal* each came on the scene in subsequent years and prospered with the town. By 1947, the three papers merged under the *Review-Journal* nameplate. Arkansas newspaper mogul Don Reynolds bought a controlling interest in the paper in 1949, and it has become the flagship of the Donrey Media Group.

FYI

Unless otherwise noted, the area code for all phone numbers listed in this chapter is 702.

Over the years, the *R-J* reflected the region's pioneer heritage. Its morning edition was called the "Trailblazer," and the afternoon edition was the "49er," with the former depicting a frontiersman and the latter bearing the caricature of a miner.

The *R-J* is unabashedly conservative in its outlook. Its editorial philosophy is live-and-let-live, which generally plays well among Nevadans who fashion themselves as fiercely individualistic and suspicious of government. The newspaper aggressively pursues its role as the public's watchdog, fighting for open meetings and fiscal accountability by local and state officials.

On its news pages, the *R-J* carries a balanced diet of local, state, national and international news. Its Friday "Neon" section is a veritable bible for weekend entertainment and dining news. And the paper has some of the best-known and widely respected writers in the state, including popular columnist and author John L. Smith.

Over the years, the *R-J* has become a media powerhouse. The largest newspaper in Nevada, the *R-J* is distributed from Laughlin, 120 miles south of Las Vegas, to Tonopah, 200 miles north. As the controlling partner in the joint operating agreement with the *Sun*, the *R-J* continues to grow along with southern Nevada. It sells 162,000 copies daily and 225,000 on Sunday.

The *R-J* is big in other ways. Its daily editions routinely run 100 pages or more. The Sunday paper weighs in at more than 500 pages, including a robust real estate section. In late 1997, the *Review-Journal* launched a new community Internet site, lasvegas.com, to provide news and community information to Las Vegas visitors, residents or relocators.

In addition, the *R-J* produces weekly "View" publications that provide zoned neighborhood news. These tabloid supplements are inserted into the newspapers. They also are delivered to the doors of nonsubscribers free of charge.

Las Vegas Sun
800 S. Valley View Blvd. • 385-3111

Founded during a strike by *R-J* press operators in 1950, the *Sun* takes a more liberal view of the world. Owned by the Greenspun family, the *Sun* switched from morning to afternoon publication when the joint operating agreement was signed in 1990.

In its heyday in the 1970s, the Sun's circulation approached 70,000, nearly matching the *Review-Journal's*. At that time, both papers were publishing AM and PM editions, complete with color headlines to pump up street sales. One memorable *Sun* banner screamed: "Killer Rats Invade New York."

In spite of such promotional efforts, or because of it, advertisers began to gravitate to the *R-J*, and the *Sun* began to hemorrhage. By the time founder Hank Greenspun died and the *Sun* converted to afternoon-only delivery under the JOA, its circulation had fallen sharply. Today it sells about 40,000 copies Monday through Friday.

Carrying on its community-oriented tradition, the *Sun* concentrates on local news, devoting relatively token amounts of space to national and international stories. Its editorial position tends to be middle-of-the-road, endorsing slightly more Democrats than Republicans.

The Greenspun family also owns the region's cable franchise, Prime Cable, and an in-room hotel movie service called the Hospitality Network. The Greenspuns also publish *ShowBiz* entertainment magazine and *Las Vegas Life* magazine.

Weeklies

Boulder City News
1227 Arizona St., Boulder City • 293-2302

This weekly community paper publishes each Thursday. Founded in 1937, the *News* reflects the quiet and wholesome community it serves. Unlike other publications that are full of murder and mayhem, this newspaper's page one is likely to feature to a citywide picnic and a photo of a 100-year-old resident. The community calendar and name-dropping features are must reading for locals. Circulation is 5,700.

CityLife
3335 Wynn Rd. • 871-6780

The alternative weekly for the Las Vegas valley, *CityLife* is a tabloid that takes on the establishment. Progressive, feisty and hip, *CityLife* is aimed at younger readers. Stories regularly tweak the dailies, skewer the politicians and take aim at corporate moguls — a true sentinel of Generation X. News and views blend seamlessly in the reportage, with a recent cover story on traffic titled "Highway to Hell." Music and movie coverage are especially strong, as is the events calendar. This free publication, which circulates about 51,000 copies on Thursdays, can be found at just about any convenience store or grocery store and in big maroon street racks all over town.

Henderson Home News
2 Commerce Ctr., Henderson • 435-7700

Published on Tuesdays and Thursdays, the *Home News* has been Henderson's community voice since 1951. With a circulation of 11,500 in Nevada's third-biggest city, the *Home News* gives blanket coverage to local meetings and events. It even has its own TV guide on Thursday. Twice monthly, nonsubscribers receive *Green Valley Plus*, a 15,000-circulation paper that culls top stories from the *Home News*. The *Home News* is a sister publication of the *Boulder City News*.

Las Vegas Business Press
3335 Wynn Rd. • 871-6780

This publication is found on the desks of most CEOs around town. Published each Monday, the *Business Press* features lengthy Q-and-As with business leaders and entrepreneurs as well as breaking news. Weekly updates are reported in more than a dozen departments, ranging from real estate and retail to technology and, of course, gaming. And say you want to know the 10 biggest (fill in the blank) companies in town. The *Business Press*' weekly list ranks everything from casinos to travel agencies. A Carson City correspondent provides Statehouse news, and a restaurant critic furnishes gastronomic advice for power lunches. The Las Vegas Chamber of Commerce inserts its regular newsletter into this publication. The *Business Press*, circulation 8,500, is owned by Wick Communications, an Arizona-based chain that also publishes *CityLife*.

Latitude Newspapers

2949 E. Desert Inn Rd. • 650-9050

These free community publications are home-delivered by zone. The *North by Northwest* newspaper is published on the first Wednesday of each month. *South by Southwest* is published every Friday. And *This Week in Summerlin* appears each Wednesday. Localized events, calendars and meeting notices are mixed in with human interest stories and features. A section on bingo — a popular pastime for local retirees — is loaded with casino advertisements and promotions.

Magazines and Other Print Media

Beehive

1916 S. Maryland Pkwy. • 732-1812

The community news publication of the Church of Jesus Christ of Latter-day Saints, the *Beehive* circulates 19,000 copies 10 times a year. This tabloid prints official church news from the Salt Lake City headquarters as well as features and profiles of local Mormon activities. Weddings, Eagle Scout promotions and new business announcements by church members have been staples of the *Beehive* since its founding in 1975. Mail subscriptions are available, or copies may be found at grocery stores and LDS book shops around town.

Bullseye

Nellis Air Force Base HQ AWSC/PA, 4370 N. Washington Blvd. • 652-5814

Written by and for the staff of Nellis Air Force Base, the *Bullseye* provides news about one of America's leading air-training complexes. This free publication is distributed on the base each Friday. It is full of schedules, events and profiles of Nellis personnel and squadrons. It also carries news about the Air Force worldwide. Because this is a military-oriented publication, the Bullseye is not circulated off base.

Casino Journal

3100 W. Sahara Ave. • 736-8886

A leading trade publication for the gaming industry, this monthly magazine reports on gaming and wagering news around the country. Coverage includes news and commentary on legal affairs, politics, marketing, technology and personnel in the casino business. Its large 12-inch by 17-inch format accommodates generous display of photographs and industry advertisements. Founded in 1989 as a spin-off of its Atlantic City-based forerunner, *Casino Journal* has a circulation of 30,000 and is available via subscription.

Casino Player

3100 W. Sahara Ave. • 736-8886

A sister periodical to *Casino Journal*, *Casino Player* is the nation's largest consumer gaming publication. Selling nearly 200,000 copies monthly, *Casino Player* provides game strategies written by professional gamblers and industry experts. A "Vegas Tips" insert focuses on Las Vegas gambling and dining venues. The magazine, launched in 1988, distributes four regionally zoned editions that can

INSIDERS' TIP

If you want to take in one of those pay-per-view specials, your cable-ready TV won't be enough. You'll need to have a converter box from Prime Cable. The boxes can be rented for $2.56 a month, or prorated for onetime use.

be purchased by subscription and at selected bookstores nationwide. It is also placed in rooms at selected hotel-casinos.

Dirt Alert

1555 E. Flamingo Rd. • 796-5440

No, this isn't some muckraking tabloid. It is, however, the most comprehensive source for inside information on the entertainment industry. Local performers — from dancers to ventriloquists — use *Dirt Alert* as an employment guide. If there's a stage or show job opening, chances are it's listed here. And the work isn't just local; Disney, the Ice Capades, cruise lines and Broadway shows also post positions. The publication features columns by agents and actors from around the country, focusing on markets from Biloxi to Branson. Founded in 1988, this twice-monthly publication can be received via the mail or picked up at local bookstores and costume shops.

El Mundo

845 N. Eastern Ave. • 649-8553

The Spanish newspaper of Las Vegas, *El Mundo* distributes 23,000 free copies every Saturday. Founded in 1980, *El Mundo*, which means "the world," carries local news as well as national, international and sports reports from the Associated Press and other wire services. Running up to 100 pages a week, this tabloid is chock-full of advertising. You can pick it up at most 7-Elevens and Lucky supermarkets.

Gaming Today

4577 Industrial Rd. • 798-1151

If you want to know what's happening inside the casinos, this is a good guide. A blend of industry news and sports betting tips, *Gaming Today* can be picked up free at virtually any hotel-casino on The Strip and at McCarrran International Airport. This weekly publication, in business since 1976, breaks some big stories and provides a steady diet of wagering data for players at the race and sports books. While focusing mainly on Las Vegas, *Gaming Today* also publishes regular reports on the business of gaming across the country, with particular emphasis on Reno-Lake Tahoe and Atlantic City. It has a circulation of 62,000 in Las Vegas and other casino cities nationwide.

Jewish Reporter

3909 S. Maryland Pkwy., Ste. 405 • 732-0556

One of two Jewish newspapers in town, this twice-monthly publication is produced by the local Jewish Federation. Its community news, which includes activities at area synagogues, is accompanied by consumer-oriented features, including health, personal finance, travel and kosher recipes. An arts and entertainment guide that features community organizations is especially helpful to locals. Founded in 1976, the *Jewish Reporter*'s free circulation is 11,000, and copies are available via free mail subscription and at selected newsstands around town.

Las Vegas Bugle

3131 Industrial Rd. • 369-6260

Local gay and lesbian news is the stock and trade of this monthly publication. A large cadre of local freelance writers provides news and features on Las Vegas' gay community. One of the most widely read departments is titled "Auntee Social," a not-so-serious notebook of local happenings. Cover stories for the 80-page magazine explore such issues as gay youth and corporate benefits for same-sex partnerships. The *Bugle*, launched in 1985, has a circulation of 15,000. Free copies can be found at gay and lesbian bars and at Borders bookstores.

Las Vegas Employment News

4040 Pioneer Ave. • 247-4151

Looking for a job? This biweekly tabloid carries classified and display help-wanted advertisements from local companies. Also included are features on labor-related issues and personal finance. With a free circulation of 40,000, the locally owned *Employment News* can be found at most convenience stores as well as at Lucky and Vons grocery stores.

Las Vegas Israelite

P.O. Box 14096, Las Vegas 89114 • 876-1255

Top stories in this publication range from the Mideast peace talks to the Las Vegas Hadassah's gala fund-raiser. Replete with local columnists and social announcements, this is a community newspaper with an eye on Israel. Often called "the Jewish paper of record," the *Israelite* has been published twice monthly since 1964. It has a circulation of 43,000, a combination of free copies available at local grocery stores and paid mail subscriptions.

Las Vegas Kidz

9208 Sienna Vista St. • 233-8388

A magazine for families, *Kidz* is a playful and helpful guide. Its monthly issues revolve around a theme, such as fitness, education, health and family fun. Written and edited for local residents since 1989, this magazine reflects the "normal" lifestyles of Las Vegas — away from The Strip and the gambling halls. It can be picked up at Lucky grocery stores, libraries and schools. Mail subscriptions also are available to this 40,000-circulation publication.

Las Vegas Life

820 S. Valley View Blvd. • 259-4180

A new city magazine, *Las Vegas Life* began monthly publication in late 1997. Owned by the *Las Vegas Sun*, this periodical is heavily pictorial, with lots of locally oriented feature stories. Staples include a local personality profile called "One in a Million," and a fast-paced news and notes column called "The Buzz." *Las Vegas Life* took over the publications formerly produced by the local public radio and television stations, incorporating their program listings. The initial circulation is 30,000, with copies available via mail subscription or at area bookstores.

Las Vegas Magazine

3131 Meade Ave., Ste. C • 257-2206

This rival city magazine, founded in 1993, publishes eclectic feature-length stories about Las Vegas lifestyles and trends. It also goes further afield to report on topics ranging from the latest JFK conspiracy theories to the netherworld dealings of the CIA. *Las Vegas Magazine*, with a quarterly circulation of 91,000, is available through mail subscriptions and at local book shops.

Las Vegas Residents' Magazine

3025 Las Vegas Blvd. S., Ste. 208 • 792-4057

Part city magazine and part consumer guide, *Residents' Magazine* publishes light features and entertainment reviews. Its most noteworthy department is its calendar of events, which may be the most comprehensive arts guide in the valley. This new monthly also contains regular how-to columns on interior design, auto care and health and fitness. It is available via mail subscription and is sold at 7-Elevens, Lucky's and Albertson's stores.

Las Vegas Reviewer

4616 W. Sahara Ave., Ste. 347 • (800) 606-8733

Marketing itself as an "unbiased critique of the hotel casinos of southern Nevada," this bimonthly newsletter presents detailed reviews of local gaming resorts. It also provides consumer tips to visitors and a calendar of upcoming events, including slot tournaments, conventions and sporting events. A comprehensive dining guide is published twice annually. The *Reviewer* is available by mail subscription only.

Las Vegas Senior Press

3335 Wynn Rd. • 871-6780

One of three senior-oriented publications in southern Nevada, the *Senior Press* is a sister publication of the *Business Press* and *CityLife*. Using the news-gathering resources of these newspapers and a stable of freelance writers, the *Senior Press* focuses on human interest stories and political issues of interest to active retirees. A comprehensive list of senior services and organizations fills the back of this monthly publication.

Las Vegas Sentinel Voice

900 E. Charleston Blvd. • 380-8100

Las Vegas' African-American newspaper since 1958, the *Sentinel Voice* is published every Thursday. By far the best local source for news and events in the black community, the tabloid paper also carries stories on minority issues from the national scene. Editorials are hard-hitting and don't hesitate to challenge the local political establishment. This free newspaper's press run is 7,000, and copies are available at most libraries, at selected convenience stores and at all Borders book shops.

Las Vegas Sporting News

1174 S. Highland Dr. • 387-6866

Want the latest lines for the upcoming football weekend? Need inside information on any sport? This free weekly, with a national circulation of 40,000, is a sports bettors' bible. It won't win any awards for photography or graphic design, but this tabloid is loaded with handicaps, predictions and analyses. For the gaming-oriented tourist, it also contains "news and notes" columns highlighting new hotel and casino developments here and at other major gaming venues such as Atlantic City. The *Sporting News* can be picked up at most casino sports books.

Las Vegas Style

3201 W. Sahara Ave. • 871-6040

With a sharp eye on the local entertainment scene, this slick monthly magazine features exclusive interviews and reviews from The Strip and around town. Since its founding in 1992, *Las Vegas Style* (30,000 of which are distributed nationally) has grown to a circulation of 110,000. In addition to guiding visitors through the showrooms and lounges, this magazine contains loads of information about restaurants and other local attractions. The gaming industry is also covered in-depth. *Las Vegas Style* is available at bookstores and is distributed on a complimentary basis at many hotel rooms along The Strip.

Nevada Magazine

1800 U.S. Hwy. 50 E., Ste. 200, Carson City • 687-5416

Though it's not published in Las Vegas, this bimonthly magazine can't help but devote a substantial percentage of its content to the Silver State's biggest city. It's worth a look on that basis. Yet there's more. *Nevada Magazine* is the best overall publication to learn about the state's history, lifestyle and entertainment offerings. In-depth features and voluminous listings are published for each of the state's five regions, making it a helpful planner if you're planning to roam far beyond the Las Vegas valley. *Nevada Magazine*, published by the state since 1940, is available by mail subscription and at selected newsstands.

Nevada Legal News

516 4th St. • 382-2747

More than just legal notices, this publication is a daily compendium of vital statistics about Las Vegas. Building permits, bankruptcies and every court filing is summarized in the *Legal News*. On page one, a feature titled "80 Seconds Around the World" distills the day's news from Reuters wire service. With a readership of 2,500 Monday through Friday, the *Legal News* has been locally owned and operated since 1960.

Nevada Senior World

2340 Paseo Del Prado, Ste. 304 • 367-6709

The largest senior-oriented publication in southern Nevada, the *Senior World* is delivered free to more than 75,000 homes monthly. News-you-can use features include health tips, a travel guide, a calendar of events and a personal finance section. Edited and published in Arizona, *Senior World* is zoned for northern, western and southeastern Las Vegas. While there is some local news in this publication, much of its content comes from nationally syndicated sources and wire services.

Nevada Woman

2685 S. Rainbow Blvd. • 258-4322

Successful women grace the pages of this 80-page magazine, published six times a year. From high-tech entrepreneurs to the wardrobe mistress for Siegfried and Roy, *Nevada Woman* profiles the state's female movers and shakers as well as some of its most interesting characters. A "Nevada Woman in Training"

INSIDERS' TIP

Subscription rates to Las Vegas' daily newspapers are a relative bargain. The *Las Vegas Review-Journal*'s home delivery rate is roughly half the newsstand price, and the *Sun*'s is even less. Seven-day delivery of the *Review-Journal* runs $3.50, while the *Sun* costs $2.

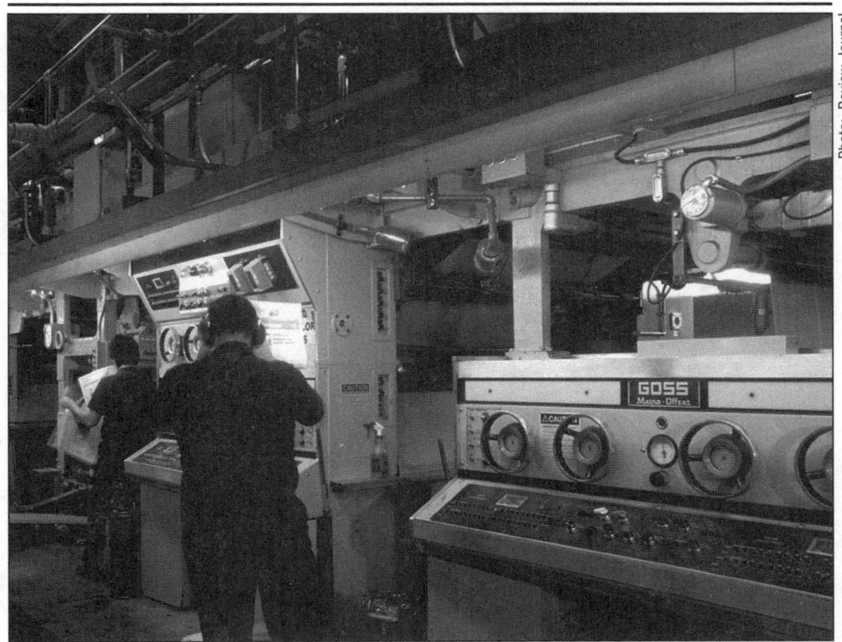

Roll 'em! The full-color presses at the *Las Vegas Review-Journal* print 200,000 newspapers daily.

feature spotlights up-and-coming teens, while a "He Says" column gives male writers a chance to sound off. Founded in 1995, the magazine is available at bookstores and newsstands and by mail subscription.

Q Tribe

4001 S. Decatur Blvd., Ste. 37-129 • 871-6981

Advertised as "the Las Vegas gay, lesbian and bisexual newsmagazine," *Q Tribe* carries nationally oriented features of interest to the gay community. Local coverage consists mainly of short announcements and an events calendar, along with a listing of gay clubs. Syndicated columns bear such hip titles as "Deep Inside Hollywood" by Miss Paige Turner and "Queer Science." The new free monthly tabloid can be found at local libraries and at gay establishments.

Scope

800 S. Valley View Blvd. • 256-6388

If beatniks were still around, they would be charter subscribers to this alternative publication that hits the streets every two weeks. Aimed at young hipsters, Scope is a melange of literary arts and pop culture. It regularly covers the local music scene and occasionally delves into local political issues, with a bent that is both libertine and libertarian. Extensive listings of nightclubs and restaurants fill the back of the book, along with capsule movie reviews. Scope is free, with 40,000 copies distributed at java joints, libraries and bookstores.

Senior Spectrum

P.O. Box 40095, Reno • 248-1240 (local number)

This 40,000-circulation monthly carries senior news about Las Vegas, but its publishing headquarters is in Reno. Like its two sister publications in northern Nevada, the *Senior Spectrum*'s pages are filled with local columnists writing about retirement, entertainment and area personalities. The free tabloid, published since 1986, is delivered door-to-door in selected areas of the city. Copies can also be picked up at Vons, Sav-On and Price-Rite stores.

ShowBiz

820 S. Valley View Blvd. • 385-3111

As its name suggests, this weekly magazine lives in the world of Las Vegas entertainment. Packed with show reviews and personality profiles, *ShowBiz* is strictly a tourist-driven publication, available only in hotel and motel rooms. However, visitors planning a trip here can call the magazine's office and receive a free copy by mail. *ShowBiz* prints about 130,000 copies a week, and its 150-page issues are full of discounts and coupons for shows and restaurants.

Vegas Golfer

2450 E. Chandler Ave., Ste. 4 • 736-3550

Looking for a challenging course? Want to know about upcoming golf events? Or just want to tune up your swing? *Vegas Golfer* is a good link to the local links. With strong local features and photography, this magazine is an enjoyable and useful read for those who want to get up to speed on the region's golf scene. Advertisements include discounts at courses throughout the area that will save you a little green too. *Vegas Golfer* can be picked up at most golf stores and pro shops and is available via mail subscription.

What's On

4425 S. Industrial Rd. • 891-8811, (800) 494-2876

Anointing itself as the "Las Vegas Survival Guide," this free magazine is a blend of show reviews and entertainment listings. Virtually every local attraction advertises in this 160-page bimonthly publication that can be found at most hotels and many stores. And many of the ads come with coupons or other discount offers. As befitting a well-rounded guide with a circulation of 150,000, *What's On* also includes maps as well as handy updated guides to dining, museums, shopping and buffets.

Radio

In keeping with its status as a sports-betting mecca, Las Vegas is jam-packed with five sports-talk stations. Even some of the news-talk stations get in on the action, broadcasting selected sporting events. The sports format continues to add stations each year, giving listeners a chance to hear any number of games and plenty of peanut-gallery commentary year-round.

Though Las Vegas does not have a true 24-hour news station, the news-talk format provides an earful at five other spots on the dial. As with the sports programming, the talk shows are a mix of local hosts and syndicated schmoozers.

Following is a listing of Las Vegas stations, categorized by format.

Adult Contemporary

KMXB 94.1 FM
KMZQ 100.5 FM
KSNE 106.5 FM

Alternative Rock

KEDG 103.5 FM
KXTE 107.5 FM (Howard Stern)

Christian

KILA 90.5 FM
KKVV 1060 AM

Country

KFMS 102 FM/1410 AM
KWNR 95.5 FM

Jazz

KUNV 91.5 FM (UNLV)

News-Talk

KDWN 720 AM (plus L.A. Dodgers baseball)

INSIDERS' TIP

Liven up your 300-mile drive between Las Vegas and Los Angeles by tuning in one of the very few clear signals on this desert stretch of Interstate 15 south of the California-Nevada border. The "Highway Stations," 98.1 FM and 99.1 FM, air contemporary country music and news about road conditions.

KXNT 840 AM (Rush Limbaugh, Paul Harvey, UNLV sports, NFL)

KNUU 960 AM (AP, CBS)

KNPR 89.5 FM (Classical music during day)

KVBC 105.1 FM (Don Imus, CNN)

Home Shopping

KSHP 1400 AM (plus L.A. Kings hockey and University of Washington, Washington State football)

Oldies

KBGO 93.1FM

KJUL 104.3 FM (musicals)

KQOL 105.5 FM

Rock

KKLZ 96.3 FM (classic)

KOMP 92.3 FM

KXPT 97.1 FM

Spanish

KDOL 1280 AM

KLSQ 870 AM

Sports

KBAD 920 AM (UCLA sports)

KENO 1460 AM (USC sports, NFL)

KFSN 1140 AM (Notre Dame football, Phoenix Diamondbacks, Suns, Coyotes)

KLAV 1230 AM (Nebraska football)

KRLV 1340 AM

(See additional sports listed under news-talk.)

Top-40

KLUC 98.5 FM

Urban Contemporary

KCEP 88.1 FM (soul and rap)

Television

Las Vegas' television market has come a long way since 1953, when KLAS cranked out the area's first TV signal. Fast-forwarding into the future, 10 over-the-air channels now broadcast in the valley. All seven major networks — ABC, CBS, NBC, PBS, Fox, UPN and WB — are represented here, and a handful of independents liven the mix with specialty programming.

There is one valleywide cable provider, Prime Cable, 121 S. Martin Luther King Boulevard, 383-4000. It carries more than 40 channels in its basic programming package, including the Disney Channel, which, in many other cities, is only available to premium-rate subscribers. WANTV provides an antenna-based service that pulls in 30 basic channels. WANTV, 566-9268, is at 975 American Pacific Drive in Henderson.

As Las Vegas has grown, its TV stations have added hours to their newscasts. Each of the three network affiliates airs four or more hours of local news on weekdays. Each has helicopters and a phalanx of vans and minicams to cover the valley. Meantime, two Spanish-language stations have popped up, serving the rapidly expanding Latino community.

If there is a gaping hole in the local program schedule it's public access television. Unlike comparably sized markets elsewhere, Las Vegas does not yet have a channel where the general public, including nonprofit agencies, can post community announcements and produce homegrown programs.

The *Sunday Review-Journal and Sun* publishes a comprehensive "TV Review" for the week. It lists all the stations, including their cable channel designations, and includes movie capsules and a special section on sports programming. Monday through Friday, the afternoon *Las Vegas Sun* carries the best 'round-the-clock daily listings.

Here, for your viewing pleasure, is a rundown on the local TV scene. The channels listed are the same for antennae and cable unless otherwise noted.

KTNV-ABC

3355 S. Valley View Blvd. • 876-1313

Las Vegas' ABC affiliate, Channel 13 has some of the city's best news reporters. The investigative team of Glen Meek and Angela Rodriguez consistently breaks big stories. And the station's 11 PM news show is the fastest-paced in town, providing 11 rapid-fire minutes of commercial-free reports at the top of the hour. KTNV's sports staff, led by Ron Futtrell, also scores a number of exclusive stories. After Monday Night Football, Futtrell hosts *Monday Night Quarterback*, a local show that focuses on area athletes.

KLAS-CBS

3228 Channel 8 Dr. • 792-8888

The area's first TV station, Channel 8 is a widely respected news source. Its main anchors, Gary Waddell and Paula Francis, are veteran newscasters who also reach out into the community to host a variety of public forums on topical issues. Another veteran, George Knapp, has some of the best sources in town and uses them to regularly scoop the competition. His on-air commentaries afflict the comfortable and comfort the afflicted. On Saturday mornings, local students ages 12 to 17 host a youth-oriented news and feature show, *KLAS Kidz*.

KVBC-NBC

1500 Foremaster Ln. • 642-3333

No. 1 in the local news ratings, Channel 3 is helped by NBC's perennially strong primetime lineup and its own savvy syndicate purchases (*Jeopardy* and *Wheel of Fortune* follow the 6 PM news). KVBC also boasts a three-hour morning blitz of *Regis & Kathie Lee*, *Montel Williams* (who has a home in Las Vegas) and *Leeza*. One of the station's most noted personalities is Nate Tannenbaum. The hyperactive, bowtie-clad weatherman keeps busy on the set and seems to be all over town. He even finds time to host radio programs on sister station KVBC-FM and the public radio station, KNPR-FM.

KLVX-PBS

4210 Channel 10 Dr. • 799-1010

Operated by the Clark County School District, Channel 10 has extended its air time to 24 hours a day. It carries a rich selection of PBS programming, including many cultural and educational shows. One of the more popular local segments is *Nevada Week in Review*. This Friday night program brings journalists and politicians together to discuss current events and issues. During the school year, students from area high schools match wits on a Saturday evening trivia tiff called *Varsity Quiz*.

KVVU-Fox

25 TV5 Dr., Henderson • 435-5555

With one of the most powerful signals in the valley, Channel 5 is home to *The Simpsons*, the *X Files* and NFL football. KVVU does not yet have a local news show, though station officials say one is in the works. For now, syndicated reruns, talk shows and movies fill much of the air time. A Sunday morning program, *New Homes Las Vegas*, highlights the newest residential communities around the valley.

KUPN-UPN

920 S. Commerce St. • 382-2121

Channel 21 (cable Channel 2) is the home of UNLV sports. The station follows the Rebel football and basketball teams on the road, airing live coverage of all the away games. KUPN, as you might have guessed, was also one of the first stations to sign on with the UPN network (home of *Star Trek: Voyager*). Non-network hours are filled with some of the more widely syndicated reruns, including *Roseanne*, *Seinfeld*, *Cheers* and *Baywatch*.

KFBT-WB

3820 S. Jones Blvd. • 873-0033

Though it's an affiliate of the Warner Brothers network, Channel 33 (cable Channel 6) is best known for reruns and movies. Because the WB network has struggled to fill in a primetime lineup, KFBT relies heavily on syndicated material and infomercials.

KBLR-Spanish

5000 W. Oakey Blvd. • 258-0039

Channel 39 (cable Channel 9) provides the only local Spanish-language TV programming in Las Vegas. A local news segment airs between 6 and 7 PM each day. A weekly show,

INSIDERS' TIP

The Las Vegas market changes so quickly that the telephone company produces two phone books annually. Out-of-towners can order one by calling Sprint Telephone Co. at (800) 877-7077. Have your credit card handy; the cost for shipping and handling is $7.25.

Punto de Visita, hosts area Latino leaders and community activities. There are even locally produced Spanish-language videos on two other weekly programs: *Revista Musical* and *Ritmo en la Calle*. KBLR is an affiliate of the Telemundo network.

KINC-Spanish 22

500 Pilot Rd. • 434-0015

This affiliate of the Spanish-speaking Univision network can be found on Channel 15 (air and cable). It carries no local programming.

KTV-Independent

2675 E. Flamingo Rd. • 431-6363

A station dedicated to the disabled and the chronically ill, Channel 63 (cable Channel 42) offers programming for "health, wellness and ability." Most shows emanate from the health-oriented Kaleidoscope Network, including sports programming that runs the gamut from skydiving to Special Olympics. Eight hours of paid programming airs Monday through Thursday evenings, produced by local healthcare practitioners.

Clark County Community Television/UNLV-TV

4505 S. Maryland Pkwy. • 895-3876

Channel 4 on the cable dial, this station is a hybrid of government news, university programming and CSPAN II. Once primarily an operation of UNLV, this channel has broadened its reach to include community affairs shows produced by Clark County government agencies. Offerings range from call-in segments with public officials to informational pieces profiling the inner workings of county departments. Likewise, university programs feature campus activities and teaching projects. When local programming signs off, CSPAN II, the official channel of the U.S. Senate, picks up. Channel 4 can only be accessed via Prime Cable.

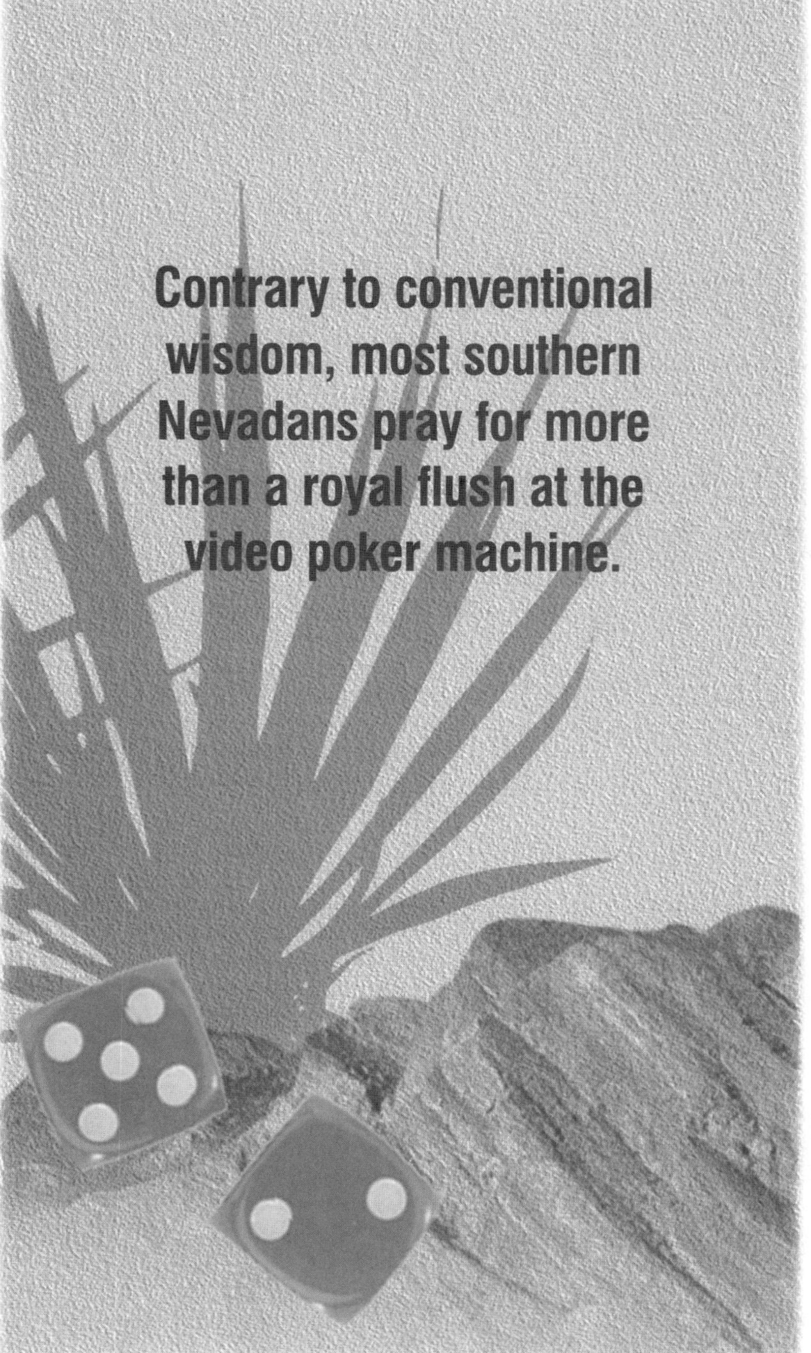
Contrary to conventional wisdom, most southern Nevadans pray for more than a royal flush at the video poker machine.

Worship

Las Vegas, according to pop culture books and movies, is the capital of nonstop hedonism and sacrilege. Not so, say the city's boosters, who like to brag that Las Vegas has more houses or worship per capita than any other city in America.

The gospel truth lies somewhere in between.

While Las Vegas specializes in sensuous entertainment, games of chance and free-flowing liquor, that's only one side of this so-called Sin City. It's a tourist-driven image that distorts the larger reality.

Contrary to conventional wisdom, most southern Nevadans pray for more than a royal flush at the video poker machine. To seek spiritual solace and guidance is to be human, and those needs are universal here as they are anywhere else. In fact, the pervasiveness of gambling in Las Vegas may even inspire a stronger longing for penance.

With more than 300 churches, temples and synagogues, Clark County has a wide variety of religious options. But that figure, while impressive, doesn't support the claims that this is the most "churched" community in the nation. Though exact figures are hard to confirm, the best estimates put Las Vegas' church-to-resident ratio at 1-to-2,447, according to U.S. Census statistics and the Glenmary Research Center of Atlanta. That puts the city behind such places as Tulsa, Tampa, Memphis, Austin, Tucson and San Diego. Even the gambling towns of Reno and Atlantic City have more churches per person.

In terms of religious affiliation, Nevada ranks last among all states. Just 32 percent of the Silver State's residents belong to a religious congregation. Surveys have shown that one-third of Las Vegans never attend church.

OK, so Las Vegans aren't No. 1 in church statistics. That doesn't mean the city is a den of atheists and agnostics. Indeed, it is home to a Mormon temple. It has substantial and growing Catholic and Jewish communities. It has 81 Baptist churches. Overall, the valley offers a smorgasbord of spiritual experience, from Sikhs to Scientologists.

This chapter highlights some of the religious groups and programs found in the valley. Space does not permit a complete listing of all places of worship. That information can be found in the phone book's Yellow Pages, under the headings of "Churches" and "Synagogues." For a compendium of local services, check the Saturday edition of the *Las Vegas Review Journal and Sun* and the Wednesday *View* supplement in those papers. Additional information can be accessed online at www.lvrj.com. Just click on the Community Link icon and point your mouse to Religious Centers.

Mormon Beginnings

When it comes to worship, the Church of Jesus Christ of Latter-day Saints molded Las Vegas' pioneer days. Mormons dispatched by church president BrighamYoung were the first white settlers in 1855. They scratched the desert as farmers and miners, but neither venture was particularly successful. They tried to convert the few Native Americans who migrated through the region, but that effort also bore little fruit.

After just two years, the discouraged Mor-

INSIDERS' TIP

For information on local Mormon Church activities, get a free copy of *The Guide* magazine. The publication can be picked up at any Cumorah Credit Union office.

mons returned to Utah. But that discouragement didn't last long. Church members established themselves permanently when Las Vegas slowly began to take root and grow in subsequent years.

Situated between the church's home base in Salt Lake City and burgeoning Southern California, Las Vegas' Mormon community has swelled over time. It is significant that the city's oldest building is the Mormon Fort, and that one of its most distinguishable landmarks is the ultramodern Mormon Temple.

From the start, many of the region's political and business leaders have been Mormons. The Clark County School District has long been a leading employer of church members, from teachers to the superintendent. With 85,000 members, Mormons have made their mark on the community. Among them are Perry Thomas, a leading developer and banker; Richard Bunker, director of the casino consortium called the Nevada Resort Association; and a host of politicians including U.S. Sen. Harry Reid, County Commissioner Bruce Woodbury and assistant State Senate Majority Leader Ray Rawson.

FYI

Unless otherwise noted, the area code for all phone numbers listed in this chapter is 702.

Resource Organizations

But Las Vegas is hardly a one-religion theocracy. Its ecumenical spirit is embodied by the **Southern Nevada National Conference,** 913 E. Charleston Boulevard, 387-6225, which embraces all faiths. Formed nationally in 1927 and locally in 1958, the National Conference (formerly called the National Conference of Christians and Jews) promotes religious, racial and ethnic inclusiveness. Regular Interfaith Forums are conducted, bringing together congregations from all over the city. The meetings are free and open to the public. By moving the sessions around town, participants have the opportunity to experience different houses of worship. The group also hosts an annual Prayer Breakfast, which attracts 1,000 attendees.

Each summer, the National Conference's local branch offers weekend youth retreats at Mount Charleston, 40 miles north of town. Called Camp Anytown, this program attracts high school students representing a kaleidoscope of religious, racial and ethnic groups and teaches them how to respect and appreciate their differences.

The National Conference is a rich source of information on religious activities, with two dozen local spiritual leaders on its Interfaith Council.

Though not strictly religious, another umbrella organization that promotes interfaith cooperation is the **Anti Defamation League**. The local chapter, at 1050 E. Flamingo Road, 862-8600, is new and just developing a list of programs. Ecumenical workshops, social service projects and guest speakers from across the country are on the ADL's agenda.

Where Las Vegas Prays

Virtually every conventional denomination — and some unconventional ones — can be found around the valley. Catholics and Protestants each account for an estimated 30 percent of the churchgoing population in Clark County. Mormons represent roughly 9 percent, and another 5 percent are of the Jewish faith.

In Las Vegas, you're never far from a Mormon, or LDS, sanctuary. The church has nearly 50 houses of worship in the area. The churches are distinctive because they use a single long, narrow spire as their identifying icon. The buildings, most of which have been built in the last 20 years, share a modern design with brownish-red roofs and stucco walls. The grounds are usually manicured expanses of grass landscaping.

INSIDERS' TIP

Teens Against Prejudice is a club started by graduates of the National Conference's Camp Anytown program. The group performs monthly skits at local schools to demonstrate the harmful effects of prejudice and stereotyping.

Photo: Jim Decker/Review-Journal

With more than 300 churches, temples and synagogues, Clark County has a variety of religious options.

It is common for two or more congregations — called wards — to share a building, so Mormon churches are busy places from dawn until dusk on Sundays. Las Vegas Mormons are also strongly involved in the local Boy Scout organization, and the churches are the home bases for many troops. That ensures the buildings are used during the week too. Information on LDS services and programs is available at 435-8545.

While the LDS churches are open to all interested visitors, the Mormon Temple is not. One of just 50 worldwide, the temple is accessible only to invited members of the church. With its slate-gray spires and steeply angled rooflines, the temple, built in 1989, is architecturally striking. Located at 827 Temple View Drive at the foot of Sunrise Mountain on the city's east side, it is illuminated at night and can be seen throughout the valley.

Interestingly, the temple does not operate on Sunday. That's when Mormons worship at their neighborhood church. But on the other six days of the week, sacred religious ceremonies are conducted inside by members and church officials. Private weddings of devout church members are performed here.

Though temple rituals are closely guarded

secrets, one commonly known rite is baptism of the dead, in which deceased ancestors are inducted into the Mormon faith. The church-going descendants, always LDS members in good standing, usually serve as surrogates or proxies in the baptismal ceremonies. To exercise its belief that souls can be rescued posthumously through such baptisms, the Salt Lake City-based Mormon church maintains the world's most extensive genealogical database. Records are free and open the general public locally at the church's Family History Center at 509 S. Ninth Street, 382-9695.

Jewish congregations also have been growing steadily with Las Vegas' population. Half of the city's 14 congregations have been started since 1990. But Temple Beth Sholom, founded in the 1940s, is the valley's oldest synagogue. It offers a wide range of programs to its members and the community, including preschool and day care for children.

Like many religious groups in Las Vegas, Temple Beth Sholom is also on the move. As the city's residents spread outward, churches are migrating with them. Temple Beth Sholom expects to build another synagogue in the newly developing Summerlin South community, 15 miles west of its current home.

Of the denominations that maintain their own buildings, the mainline Protestant churches are well-endowed in bricks and mortar. Lutherans have 19 churches, Methodists have 14 and the Episcopalians have 10. Pentecostal, Apostolic and Assembly of God have another 40 churches combined. To locate a house of worship near you, three Protestant churches have resource numbers: Lutheran, 897-7762; Episcopal, 737-9190; and Methodist, 369-7055.

One church riding the crest of the valley's growth is the Central Christian Church. This independent church, founded in 1962, has expanded to 3,600 members today and is building a 148,000-square-foot worship center in Henderson. On 60 acres at 1000 Mark Avenue, just off U.S. Highway 95, the cathedral will seat 3,100 — making it the largest in southern Nevada when it's completed in late 1998. Included in the complex will be a smaller chapel, seating 400, dozens of classrooms, a bookstore and even a food court.

Other churches that cannot afford to build their own sanctuaries lease space in public schools or community centers. This marriage of church and state is exemplified at one local elementary school, which houses a Jewish congregation on Saturdays and a Baptist church service on Sunday.

With 32 houses of worship, the Catholic Church is well-represented across the valley. The city's oldest continuously operating church is St. Joan of Arc, founded in 1908 downtown. St. Joseph Husband of Mary is the latest addition, dedicated in 1995 on the western edge of the valley.

While tending to its spreading flock, the Catholic Church has also been attuned to meeting the needs of Strip tourists. The Guardian Angel Cathedral, a half-mile east of The Strip between Desert Inn Road and Convention Center Drive, celebrates three Masses on Saturday and five on Sunday, along with two daily Masses. Fittingly, in a city widely considered to be a den of iniquity, confessions are heard before each Mass.

The church is not shy about Las Vegas' omnipresent gambling and entertainment industry. The sanctuary's elaborate and unique stained-glasswork depicts a harlequin hovering over a hotel and a pair of rolling dice at the foot of a cross. Services, however, are conventional.

In addition to the standard currency, tour-

INSIDERS' TIP

Two Las Vegas radio stations carry Christian programming: KILA 90.5 FM features contemporary music, and KKVV 1060 AM broadcasts local and syndicated talk shows.

ists often will drop casino chips into the collection plate, and each week a priest redeems the tokens at a Strip gambling hall. Arguably the busiest church in town, the Guardian Angel's 4 PM Mass is usually standing-room-only. When Danny Thomas was a regular headliner here, the Guardian Angel was his place of worship, and his charitable donations helped to furnish the church, whose beautiful floors are paved with marble.

At the south end of The Strip is the Shrine of the Most Holy Redeemer. Just south of Tropicana Avenue, across the street from the Excalibur Hotel, this church, the largest in the city, was erected in the early 1990s to relieve the crush of parishioners at Guardian Angel.

A unique ecclesiastical feature on The Strip is the Church at the Riviera. Pastor Charlie Brolin conducts nondenominational Sunday services at the hotel-casino, 2901 Las Vegas Boulevard South. Believed to be the only minister employed by any casino anywhere, Brolin preaches in a relaxed, informal style. If space is not available in one of the hotel's meeting rooms, Brolin's flock will recess to a 200-seat showroom occupied nightly by the "Crazy Girls," the hotel's bare-breasted dance troupe.

Brolin, an ordained Southern Baptist minister, will also venture outside the hotel to make hospital visits to ailing guests and is on-call 24 hours a day for tourists in need of solace and advice.

Speaking of Strip entertainment, the Church of Scientology operates a "Celebrity Center." The Scientology movement, which was founded in the late 1950s by L. Ron Hubbard, combines elements of holistic medicine, Eastern religion and Freudian psychology. The church is prominent among Hollywood movie stars and counts John Travolta, Priscilla Presley, Tom Cruise, Kirstie Alley and musician Chic Corea among its members. Likewise, the Las Vegas Celebrity Center has attracted local dancers, artists, musicians and entertainers, some of whom regularly perform after Sunday services. The center offers daily courses to the public for fees starting at $10.

In a similar vein, a separate group, the University Church Institute, offers what it terms "spiritual science." Adherents believe that psychology and physics can be applied to religious teachings for greater self-awareness.

A vibrant voice in the gay and lesbian community is the Metropolitan Community Church, which meets at the Unitarian Universalist Church at 3616 E. Lake Mead Boulevard. Services are nondenominational and open to all.

The African-American community in West Las Vegas near downtown is home to more than a dozen churches, primarily the African Methodist Episcopal (AME) and Baptist denominations. Islamic prayer and studies are centered at the Masjid As-Sabur mosque. Hindus, Sikhs and Jains meet weekly at local homes. The National Conference has information on these meetings.

Las Vegas has two Buddhist temples, and selected Christian congregations conduct services in Chinese, Korean and Japanese. The churches run the gamut from Southern Baptist to Presbyterian. Spanish also is spoken at a growing number of churches, including the Church of Christ and the Church of God. Such services are listed in the Yellow Pages by denomination.

Index

Symbols

A

B

D

E

F

M

P

Q

R

S

W

X

Y

Z

Index of Advertisers

Insiders' Publishing Inc. • P.O. Box 2057 • Manteo, NC 27954
Phone (919) 473-6100 • Fax (919) 473-5869 • INTERNET address: *http://www.insiders.com*